102 032 898 3

ONE WEEK

This book is due for return on or before the last date shown below.

D1422646

ROUTLEDGE HANDBOOK OF SPORT, GENDER AND SEXUALITY

The *Routledge Handbook of Sport, Gender and Sexuality* brings together important new work from 68 leading international scholars that, collectively, demonstrates the intrinsic interconnectedness of sport, gender and sexuality. It introduces what is, in essence, a sophisticated sub-area of sport sociology, covering the field comprehensively, as well as signalling ideas for future research and analysis. Wide-ranging across different historical periods, different sports, and different local and global contexts, the book incorporates personal, ideological and political narratives; varied conceptual, methodological and theoretical approaches; and examples of complexities and nuanced ways of understanding the gendered and sexualized dynamics of sport. It examines structural and cultural forms of gender segregation, homophobia, heteronormativity and transphobia, as well as the ideological struggles and changes that have led to nuanced ways of thinking about the sport, gender and sexuality nexus. This is a landmark work of reference that will be a key resource for students and researchers working in sport studies, gender studies, sexuality studies or sociology.

Jennifer Hargreaves is retired as a full-time university professor. She is now a freelance writer/consultant/guest speaker. An early pioneer of sport sociology specializing in gender issues and the politics of the body, she has published prolifically with translations into different languages; given addresses all over the world; and worked as a guest professor in Germany, Hong Kong and Japan. Professor Hargreaves was awarded the North American Society for the Sociology of Sport (NASSS) best book of the year award for *Sporting Females: Critical Issues in the History and Sociology of Sport* (1994), the NASSS Distinguished Service Award (2008), and the North American Society for Sports History (NASSH) Max and Reet Howell Award (2006), following the publication of *Heroines of Sport: the Politics of Difference and Identity*. In 2011 Jennifer delivered The Sir Derek Birley Memorial Lecture for the British Society for Sport History (BSSH).

Eric Anderson is a sociologist and a professor of sport, masculinities and sexualities at the University of Winchester, UK. His research shows an increasingly positive relationship between gay athletes and sport, as well as a growing movement of heterosexual masculinities becoming softer and more inclusive. Professor Anderson has published twelve books, including *Sport, Theory and Social Problems; Inclusive Masculinity* and *Sport; Masculinities and Sexualities;* and *21st Century Jocks: Teamsport Athletes and Modern Heterosexuality*.

ROUTLEDGE HANDBOOK OF SPORT, GENDER AND SEXUALITY

Edited by
Jennifer Hargreaves and Eric Anderson

Routledge
Taylor & Francis Group

LONDON AND NEW YORK

First published 2014
by Routledge
2 Park Square, Milton Park, Abingdon, Oxon OX14 4RN

and by Routledge
711 Third Avenue, New York, NY 10017

Routledge is an imprint of the Taylor & Francis Group, an informa business

British Library Cataloguing in Publication Data
A catalogue record for this book is available from the British Library
Library of Congress Cataloging-in-Publication Data
Routledge handbook of sport, gender and sexuality / edited by Jennifer Hargreaves, Eric Anderson.
pages cm.—(Routledge international handbooks)
ISBN 978-0-415-52253-3 (hardback)—ISBN 978-0-203-12137-5 (ebk) 1. Sports—Sociological aspects.
2. Sports—Psychological aspects. 3. Athletes—Sexual behavior. 4. Sports for women. 5. Sex role.
6. Gay athletes. 7. Lesbian athletes. I. Hargreaves, Jennifer, 1937– II. Anderson, Eric.
GV706.5.R88 2014
306.4'83—dc23
2013029100

ISBN: 978-0-415-52253-3 (hbk)
ISBN: 978-0-203-12137-5 (ebk)

Typeset in Bembo
by Swales & Willis Ltd, Exeter, Devon

Printed and bound in Great Britain by
TJ International Ltd, Padstow, Cornwall

CONTENTS

Contents

Contents

CONTRIBUTORS

Natalie G. Adams is Director, New College, and Professor, Social and Cultural Studies in Education, at the University of Alabama (USA). She is co-author of *Cheerleader! An American Icon* (Palgrave Press 2003) and co-editor of *Geographies of Girlhood: Identities In Between* (Lawrence Erlbaum and Associates 2005), both with Pam Bettis. She is also co-author of *Learning to Teach: A Critical Approach to Field Experiences* (Lawrence Erlbaum and Associates 2005).

L. Anima Adjepong is a graduate student in the Sociology Department at the University of Texas, Austin. Her research interests are at the intersection of gender, race, and sexuality. She is currently studying how sport is a contested site for the (re)production of racialized and gendered identities.

Dean Allen is currently based in Cape Town, South Africa. He is a lecturer in Sports Management at Cape Peninsula University of Technology (CPUT) and a senior research associate of Stellenbosch University. Having worked at universities in the UK, Ireland and Australia, he has published widely on the history and politics of sport and society throughout the British Empire, most notably South Africa. His particular interests are colonialism, imperialism and the identity of sporting groups and nations. Dr Allen was the recipient of CPUT's 'Researcher of the Year' award for 2012 and his book *Empire, War and Cricket in South Africa* will be published in 2014 by Print Matters (Cape Town).

Terry L. Allison has undergraduate degrees in economics and political science from the University of California, Berkeley, and graduate degrees, including a PhD in literature, from the University of California, San Diego. Allison has published and presented in comparative literature, English, gender and sexuality studies, library science, popular culture, and sports. He swam for and coached a LGBT master's swim and served on the boards of the Federation of Gay Games as well as International Gay and Lesbian Aquatics.

Eric Anderson is a Professor of Sport, Masculinities and Sexualities at the University of Winchester, UK. He is recognized as an academician of the British Academy of Social Sciences, and a fellow of the International Association of Sex Researchers. His research on sport, masculinities and sexualities shows an increasingly positive relationship between gay male athletes and sport, as well as a growing movement of young heterosexual men's masculinity becoming softer and more inclusive. Professor Anderson also researches matters related to men's monogamy and the positive function of relationship cheating, men's improving recognition of bisexuality, and the increased acceptance of young heterosexual men kissing. He has written twelve books and is regularly featured in old and new media.

Tansin Benn is a visiting professor at Plymouth University. Over a long career in teaching and research in the fields of physical education and sport, Professor Benn has become a leading scholar in socio-cultural studies, focusing on increasing opportunities for Muslim girls and women in physical education and sport.

Pamela Bettis is a faculty member in the Cultural Studies and Social Thought in Education doctoral program at Washington State University (USA) where she tries to understand the dynamics of gender and schooling. Although she was not selected for the cheerleading squad, she still became a friend and collaborator with her co-author Natalie Adams, who was selected for her school cheerleading squad.

Kasia Boddy is lecturer in American Literature at the University of Cambridge. She has written extensively on American and British literary and cultural history, and her publications include *Boxing: A Cultural History* (Reaktion 2008) and several articles on the wider cultural resonances of boxing and other sports.

Hans Bonde is Professor and section leader of Sport, Politics and Welfare at the University of Copenhagen. He is author of, among others, *Gymnastics and Politics* (Museum Tusculanum Press 2006); *Niels Bukh: A Visual Documentation* (Museum Tusculanum Press 2007); *Football with the Foe* (University Press of Southern Denmark 2008); and *The Politics of the Male Body in Global Sport: The Danish Involvement* (Routledge 2010).

James Brighton is with the Department of Sports Science, Tourism, and Leisure at Canterbury Christ Church University. His research interests revolve around how people experience embodiment in sport with particular emphasis on disability, cyborg theory, and how people may modify their bodies in the pursuit of bodily perfectionism.

Rachael Bullingham is a PhD student at the University of Winchester. Her research interests include the portrayal of women in the media and homophobia within women's sport. In addition to her studies, Rachael has taught at the University of Gloucestershire on both undergraduate and postgraduate courses and she also teaches physical education at a large secondary comprehensive school.

Ben Carrington teaches Sociology at the University of Texas, Austin and is a Carnegie Research Fellow at Leeds Metropolitan University in the UK.

Helen J. Carroll is the Director of the National Center for Lesbian Rights' Sports Project, which aims to ensure that lesbian, gay, bisexual, and transgender players, coaches, and administrators receive fair and equal treatment – free from discrimination. She joined NCLR in 2001 after spending 30 years as an athlete, national championship basketball coach, and NCAA collegiate athletic director. Carroll now devotes all of her efforts to helping the sports world recognize that the inclusion of people who are lesbian, gay, bisexual, and/or transgender or intersex, diversifies and strengthens the sport experience. Carroll is co-author, with Dr. Pat Griffin, of *On the Team: Equal Opportunity for Transgender Student Athletes* (2010) and the National Collegiate Athletic Association guide, *NCAA Inclusion of Transgender Student Athletes* (2011). She has been a featured speaker with Nike, ESPN's 'Outside the Lines', the *New York Times* and many others, and is featured in Dr. Pat Griffin's book, *Strong Women, Deep Closets* (Human Kinetics 1998) as well as *The Outsports Revolution: Truth and Myth in the World of Gay Sports* by Jim Buzinski and Cyd Ziegler Jr (Alyson Publications 2007).

Jayne Caudwell works at the University of Brighton. She teaches socio-cultural approaches to sport and leisure and her research engages with qualitative research methodologies, gender theories and theories of sexualities. She is editor of *Sport, Sexualities and Queer/Theory* (Routledge 2006), *Women's Football in the UK: Continuing with Gender Analyses* (Routledge 2012) and co-editor of *Sexualities, Spaces and Leisure Studies* (Routledge 2012).

Elizabeth Cavalier is an Assistant Professor of Sociology at Georgia Gwinnett College in Lawrenceville, Georgia. She studies the intersections of sexuality, gender, and sport, as well as the social dynamics of physical activity among youth and young adults.

Simon Creak holds a PhD in history (Australian National University, 2010) and is Associate Professor at Kyoto University, where he is affiliated with the Hakubi Center for Advanced Research and Center for Southeast Asian Studies. His first monograph, *Body Work: Sport, Physical Culture and the Making of Modern Laos* (forthcoming from University of Hawaii Press), uses sport to illuminate the history of that country in its extraordinary transitions from colonialism through socialism to the modern development state. He is currently researching his second monograph, a history of nationalism, cultural diplomacy and regionalism in the Southeast Asian Games (1959–2015).

George B. Cunningham PhD (Ohio State University) is a Professor and Associate Dean for Academic Affairs in the College of Education and Human Development at Texas A&M University. He holds the Marilyn Kent Byrne Chair for Student Success and is the director of the Laboratory for Diversity in Sport. Author of over 150 articles and book chapters, he studies diversity, group processes, and employee attitudes. Cunningham is author of the award-winning book, *Diversity in Sport Organizations* (Holcomb Hathaway 2011).

Symeon Dagkas is a Reader at the University of East London. His research interests lie in intersectional issues in youth sport and physical activity through the examination of multiple layers of disadvantage including socioeconomic factors, ethnicity and race, gender and religion. His is the editor of the book *Inclusion and Exclusion through Youth Sport* (Routledge 2012).

Jinxia Dong is the founding director of the Peking University Research Centre for Gender, Sports and Society, and received her PhD from the University of Strathclyde (UK) in 2001. She has authored hundreds of articles in both Chinese and English on sport, the Olympics, culture and gender. She has been invited to universities and international conferences in Germany, Britain, Greece, Denmark, Canada, the USA, Japan, Korea, India, Hong Kong and Taiwan to lecture or present papers. She won the International Max & Reet Howell Award of the North American Society of Sports History in 2007.

Scarlett Drury is a Lecturer in the Social Sciences of Sport and Leisure at Leeds Metropolitan University. She is based in the School of Sport, which is part of the Carnegie Faculty. Her PhD research focused on the dynamics of homophobia and heteronormativity in gay sports spaces.

Kenneth R. Dutton is a retired university professor and administrator who has written several books on weight training and on cultural history, including *The Perfectible Body: The Western Ideal of Physical Development* (Cassell 1995).

Caroline Fusco is an Associate Professor in the Faculty of Kinesiology and Physical Education at the University of Toronto. She received a BA and Education degree from the University of Ulster, an MSc from the University of Manitoba and her PhD from the University of Toronto. Her research draws on critical cultural geographies, poststructuralist feminist theories and qualitative methodologies to study the social landscapes of play and pleasure in children's lives, biopedagogies and youth subjectivities, and the hyper-consumption of animal bodies in sporting spectacles.

Michele R. Gregory is Associate Professor of Sociology at York College of the City University of New York, where she coordinates the Sociology program and is acting coordinator of Black Studies. Her published and current research is in the area of gender, sexuality, race and ethnicity in organizations. She also works on sport, masculinities, and management.

Pat Griffin is Professor Emerita in Social Justice Education at the University of Massachusetts Amherst. She is author of *Strong Women, Deep Closets: Lesbians and Homophobia in Sport* (Human Kinetics 1998) and co-editor of *Teaching for Diversity and Social Justice* (Routledge 2007). She is the co-author of *Champions of Respect: Inclusion of LGBTQ Student-Athletes and Staff in NCAA Programs* (2012) and *On the Team: Equal Opportunities for Transgender Student-Athletes* (2010). She is the founding director of Changing the Game: The Gay Lesbian Straight Education Network Sports Project and consults with the NCAA and individual college and university athletic programs on LGBT issues in women's and men's sports

Jennifer Hargreaves is retired as a full-time university professor. She is now a freelance writer/ consultant/guest speaker. She was an early pioneer of sport sociology specializing in gender issues and the politics of the body. Jennifer has published prolifically with translations into different languages; has given addresses all over the world; and has worked as a guest professor in Germany, Hong Kong and Japan. She was awarded the North American Society for the Sociology of Sport (NASSS) best book of the year award (1994), the NASSS Distinguished Service Award (2008), and the North American Society for Sports History (NASSH) Max and Reet Howell Award (2006). In 2011 Jennifer delivered the Sir Derek Birley Memorial Lecture for the British Society for Sport History (BSSH).

Mike Hartill is a sociologist in the Department of Sport and Physical Activity at Edge Hill University. He conducts and publishes research on child maltreatment in sport. In particular, he conducts research on sexual violence against children in sport and the implementation of safeguarding in sport policy. He sat on the English Child Protection in Sport Research and Evidence Advisory Group since 2003 and works with a number of national and international sports organizations in the field of child protection and safeguarding.

Vanessa Heggie is a University Fellow in the History of Medicine at the University of Birmingham. She has researched and published on a range of topics in nineteenth and twentieth century history of medicine and life sciences. Her first book, *A History of British Sports Medicine* was published by Manchester University Press in 2011.

Leslie Heywood is Professor of English at SUNY-Binghamton. She is the author of nine books, including *Built to Win: The Female Athlete as Cultural Icon* (University of Minnesota Press 2003), *Bodymakers: A Cultural Anatomy of Women's Bodybuilding* (Rutgers University Press 1998), and *The Women's Movement Today: An Encyclopedia of Third Wave Feminism* (Greenwood Reference Works 2005).

Jeffrey Hill is Emeritus Professor of Historical and Cultural Studies at De Montfort University, Leicester, UK, where until 2007 he was Director of the International Centre for Sport History and Culture. He has written on various aspects of the representation of sport, most recently in relation to public history (Hill, Moore and Wood (eds) 2012) *Sport, History and Heritage: Studies in Public Representation*. Woodbridge. UK: The Boydell Press). He is currently working on the relationship between leisure, voluntary associations and politics in interwar Britain.

Keiko Ikeda is Professor Faculty of Education at Yamaguchi University. She was Visiting Research Fellow at the University of Warwick (1997–1998) and De Montfort University (2010), and is the author of *Pre-Victorian Sport: Pierce Egan's 'Sporting World'* (Fumaido Publishing 1996) and other books and articles on British and Japanese sport history in the nineteenth and twentieth centuries.

Kay Inckle is with the School of Social Science and Social Work at Plymouth University. Her research interests include body politics and practices, gender, sexuality, 'dis'ability and critical approaches to mental health/illness in academic, practitioner and activist contexts. Books include: *Writing on the Body? Thinking Through Gendered Embodiment and Marked Flesh* (Cambridge Scholars Publishing 2007), and *Flesh Wounds? New Ways of Understanding Self-Injury* (PCCS Books 2010).

Edward (Ted) M. Kian is the Endowed Welch-Bridgewater Chair of Sports Media at Oklahoma State. Previously he was the founding coordinator of the graduate program in Sport Leadership and Coaching at the University of Central Florida. A former professional sportswriter, Dr. Kian's scholarly research focuses on sport media. Specifically, he examines portrayals of gender and LGBT in print media articles, new media, attitudes and experiences of sport media members, and marketing of sport to LGBT consumers.

Kelly Knez is a qualitative researcher at Aspetar – Qatar Orthopaedic and Sports Medicine Hospital, and holds an adjunct position with the School of Human Movement Studies at the University of Queensland. She is interested in the intersection of religion and culture with meanings of health and physical activity.

Jorge Knijnik is with the School of Education at the University of Western Sydney, Australia. He is the author of *Girls and Boys in PE: Gender and Embodiment in the 21st Century* (SP/Fontoura, 2010); *Gender and Sport: Masculinities and Femininities* (Rio Apicuri, 2010) and *Gender and Equestrian Sport-riding Around the World* (edited with M. Adelman, Springer forthcoming).

Håkan Larsson is Professor of Sport Pedagogy at the Swedish School of Sport and Health Sciences in Stockholm, Sweden. In 2001, he published a PhD thesis on the construction of gender in competitive sport, and since then he has continued working with gender issues both in sport and physical education. At present, he leads a research group of about fifteen researchers in sport pedagogy.

Woojun Lee is a doctoral student in the Department of Health and Kinesiology at Texas A&M University. His research is in the area of diversity, with a focus on cross-cultural comparisons. In addition to publishing in a variety of outlets, he has presented at national and international conferences.

Katharina Lindner is a lecturer in Film and Media Studies at the University of Stirling, UK. Her research interests are interdisciplinary and include gender and queer theory, feminist film and cultural criticism, question of identity, subjectivity and embodiment, film phenomenology, as well as media and sport. She has published work on athleticism and cinema, dance in film, sport and (post)feminism, as well as on bodily performance and embodiment and/in film. Her current research engages specifically with queer critiques of traditional (film) phenomenology and explores questions of embodiment, sensuousness and affect in relation to a variety of film bodies.

Adam Love is an Assistant Professor of Sport Studies in the Department of Kinesiology and a member of the Gender Studies faculty at Mississippi State University. He conducts research on the production and reproduction of gender ideology in the context of sport and physical activity.

Jordan J.K. Matthews is a Sociology of Sport PhD research student in the Sport Development and Management department at the University of Chichester. His thesis is provisionally titled 'A critical analysis of the development, outcomes, and definition of the Women and Sport Movement'. He has completed research for the International Working Group on Women and Sport (IWG) by analysing IWG Progress Reports and is also Clerk of the Anita White Foundation.

Mark McCormack is a Lecturer in Sociology at Durham University. His research examines the influence of decreasing homophobia on the gender and sexual identities of male youth. He has published widely in international journals, and his book *The Declining Significance of Homophobia* (2012) was published by the Oxford University Press.

Ian McDonald is a sociologist and documentary filmmaker based at the School of Arts and Cultures at Newcastle University, UK. He has published widely on sport and is currently writing a monograph on sport documentaries. He recently completed his award-winning debut feature documentary, *Algorithms*, about young blind chess players from India.

Mary G. McDonald is Professor and the Homer C. Rice Chair in Sport and Society in the School of History, Technology and Society at the Georgia Institute of Technology (USA). McDonald's research focuses on the intersections of gender, race, class and sexuality within sport and popular culture. A recent interest includes extending this focus into issues of health and sustainability.

Rory Magrath is a PhD student at the University of Winchester. His research interests include gender, sexuality, violence and racism within football fandom. In addition to his studies, Rory teaches at Southampton Solent University and the University of Winchester.

E. Nicole Melton PhD (Texas A&M University) is an Assistant Professor of Sport Management at Texas Tech University. Her research is in the area of LGBT inclusion and ally behavior. She has published a number of articles and book chapters in a variety of outlets, including the *Sociology of Sport Journal* and *Journal of Sport Management*.

Christopher Merrett used to be an inter-provincial umpire and secretary of non-racial (South African Council on Sport) cricket in Pietermaritzburg in the 1980s. He worked for thirty years as a librarian at the universities of London, Cape Town and Natal; and then as campus administrator at the University of KwaZulu-Natal. He has a PhD in History from UCT and writes on issues relating to the history and politics of South African sport; and on human rights issues, especially freedom of expression and information. He now works in the editorial department of *The Witness*, Pietermaritzburg's daily newspaper.

Kathi Miner PhD (University of Michigan) is an Assistant Professor at Texas A&M University, holding a joint appointment in Psychology and Women's and Gender Studies. Her research is in the area of diversity and incivility, and she has published in a variety of outlets, including the *Journal of Applied Psychology*. Miner has received external funding from the National Science Foundation.

Payoshni Mitra is an independent researcher and actvist who has written and advocated on issues related to gender discrimination in sport in India and is involved in creating a Standard Operative Procedure for better management of female athletes with intersex conditions at the Department of Sports, Ministry of Youth Affairs and Sports, Government of India. She is a SYLFF Fellow from Jadavpur University, India. She is also a University Blue in Badminton and a coach.

David Nylund MSW, PhD is a Professor of Social Work at California State University, Sacramento. He serves as the Clinical Director of The Gender Health Center, a counselling agency serving the needs of the transgender and queer communities. He is the author of *Beer, Babes, and Balls: Sports Talk Radio and Masculinity* (SUNY Press 2007).

Scott Ogawa lives in Chicago and is a PhD candidate in Economics at Northwestern University in Evanston, IL. Scott's primary work focuses on the economics of education and behaviour, though he has always had an interest in academic research of sport.

Carol Osborne is Senior Lecturer in Sport, Leisure and Culture at Leeds Metropolitan University. She completed her PhD in the Department of History, Lancaster University in 2005. She is co-editor (with Fiona Skillen) of *Women in Sport History* (Routledge, 2012).

Andrew C. Pickett is a doctoral student in the Department of Health and Kinesiology at Texas A&M University. He studies diversity, with a focus on LGBT issues in sport.

Elizabeth C.J. Pike is the Head of Sport Development and Management, a Reader in the Sociology of Sport and Exercise, and the Chair of the Anita White Foundation at the University of Chichester. Her recent publications include a co-authored book (with Jay Coakley) entitled *Sports in Society: Issues and Controversies* (Open University Press/McGraw Hill 2009), and a co-edited book (with Simon Beames) examining *Outdoor Adventure and Social Theory* (Routledge 2013). She is currently a member of the Executive Board of the International Sociology of

Sport Association, and serves as the President of this association and of the Sociology of Sport Research Committee of the International Sociological Association.

Martin Polley is Senior Lecturer in Sport at the University of Southampton. He is the author of *Moving the Goalposts: a History of Sport and Society Since 1945* (Routledge, 1998), *Sports History: A Practical Guide* (Palgrave, 2007), and *The British Olympics: Britain's Olympic Heritage, 1612–2012* (English Heritage, 2011). He has written articles and book chapters on many aspects of sports history, including politics, professionalism, national identity, and the Olympic Games, and he is an editor of the journal *Sport in History*. He is a regular broadcaster on sporting issues, and has contributed to news and documentary programmes on television and radio stations in the UK, Canada, Australia and Japan.

Stacey Pope is a Lecturer in Sport at Durham University. She is especially interested in issues of gender and sport. Her research has incorporated the sociology of football and rugby union; comparative research in sports fandom and issues of gender, place and social class; the meaning and importance of sport for women; and the formative experiences of females across different generations. She has published widely on the topic of female sports fandom and her work has appeared in journals such as *International Review for the Sociology of Sport*, *Journal of Sport and Social Issues*, *Leisure Studies* and *Sport, Education and Society*.

Richard Pringle is Associate Professor of socio-cultural studies of sport and physical education at the University of Auckland. He is the co-author (with Pirkko Markula) of *Foucault, Sport and Exercise: Power, Knowledge and Transforming the Self* (Routledge 2006), co-editor (with Murray Phillips) of *Examining Sport Histories: Power, Paradigms and Reflexivity* (FIT publishers 2013), and serves on the editorial boards of the *Sociology of Sport Journal*, *Asia-Pacific Journal of Health, Sport and Physical Education* and *Annals of Leisure Research*. His research has appeared in numerous journals associated with the sociology of sport, sport history, leisure and physical education.

Aarti Ratna is a Senior Lecturer at Leeds Metropolitan University. Her research centres on the connections between 'race' and gender in the context of sport and leisure. She has published in a number of journals including *Sociological Research Online*; *Young*; *Leisure/Losir*; *International Review for the Sociology of Sport* and *Soccer and Society*.

David Rowe is Professor of Cultural Research, Institute for Culture and Society, University of Western Sydney, Australia, where he was Director of its predecessor unit, the Centre for Cultural Research (2006–2009). Professor Rowe's books include *Sport, Culture and the Media: The Unruly Trinity* (second edition, Open University Press, 2004); *Global Media Sport: Flows, Forms and Futures* (Bloomsbury Academic, 2011); *Sport Beyond Television: The Internet, Digital Media and the Rise of Networked Media Sport* (authored with Brett Hutchins, Routledge, 2012); *Digital Media Sport: Technology, Power and Culture in the Network Society* (edited with Brett Hutchins, Routledge, 2013), and *Sport, Public Broadcasting, and Cultural Citizenship: Signal Lost?* (edited with Jay Scherer, Routledge, 2013). His work has been translated into several languages, including Chinese, French, Turkish, Spanish, Italian and Arabic.

Georgina Roy is a PhD student at the University of Brighton, funded by an ESRC studentship in sociology. The topic of her research is the feminist significance of the women's surfing 'boom' and the gendered experiences of female surfers, in Britain. In addition to women's surfing, her research interests include sport, gender and sexuality, as well as feminist theory more broadly.

Katia Rubio has a bachelor in Journalism from Casper Libero School (1983), a degree in Psychology from the Catholic University of São Paulo (1995), an MA in Physical Education from the University of São Paulo (1998) and a PhD in Education from the University of São Paulo (2001). She is an associate professor at the University of São Paulo and visiting professor at the Institute Seat of Wisdom. Her experience is in psychology with an emphasis on sport psychology, acting on the following themes: sports psychology, social psychology of sport, Olympism, sports psychology in Brazil and applied sport psychology.

Fiona Skillen is a Lecturer in Sport and Events Management at Glasgow Caledonian University. She completed her PhD in the Department of Economic and Social History at the University of Glasgow in 2008. Her monograph, *Women, Sport and Modernity in Interwar Britain* is forthcoming in 2013 (Peter Lang).

Maureen M. Smith is a Professor in the Department of Kinesiology and Health Science at California State University, Sacramento. She teaches in the areas of sport history and sport sociology. Her research interests are varied; she has published on topics ranging from big wave surfing, sport and popular culture, as well as sport statues and other material culture. Smith is the past president of the North American Society of Sport History.

Andrew C. Sparkes is with the Research Institute for Sport, Physical Activity and Leisure at Leeds Metropolitan University. His research interests revolve around the ways that people experience different forms of embodiment over time in a variety of contexts. He seeks to develop interpretative forms of understanding via the use of life history, ethnography, narrative approaches and a range of representational genres.

Caroline Symons is a Senior Lecturer in the College of Sport and Exercise Science and Institute of Sport, Exercise and Active Living at Victoria University, Australia. She has received numerous research and community awards for her work on the history of the international LGBT sport movement and the furthering of LGBT rights in sport within Australia.

Claudio Tamburrini is a Senior Researcher at the Centre for Healthcare Ethics, Stockholm University. Tamburrini is an active researcher in European contexts, where he was part of the EU-financed projects 'Enhance' and 'Tiss.EU'. His has written several books and articles in the areas of penal philosophy, sport ethics and medical ethics. He is the author of *Crime and Punishment?* (Almkvist & Wiksell International, Stockholm, 1992) and *The Hand of God? – Essays in the Philosophy of Sports* (Acta Universitatis Gotheburgensis, 2000). He has also co-edited *Values in Sport: Elitism, Nationalism, Gender Equality and the Scientific Manufacture of Winners* (E & FN Spon, 2000), *Genetic Technology and Sport: Ethical Questions* (Routledge, 2005), *The Ethics of Sports Medicine* (Routledge, 2009) and, more recently, *Recidivist Punishments: The Philosopher's View* (Rowman & Littlefield, 2011).

Patricia Vertinsky is a Distinguished University Scholar and Professor of Kinesiology at the University of British Columbia in Vancouver, Canada. She is a social and cultural historian working across the fields of women's and gender history, sport history and sociology, popular culture, modern dance and the history of health and medicine.

Nikki Wedgwood PhD is a lecturer in the Faculty of Health Sciences at the University of Sydney. A sociologist with a particular interest in life history research, her past research includes a study of the gendered embodiment of male and female Australian Rules footballers as well as research into the role of sports participation in the lives of young people with physical impairments. Her current research explores how young people with disabilities meet the developmental challenges of adolescence and emerging adulthood.

Jean Williams is Senior Research Fellow in the International Centre for Sports History and Culture, De Montfort University Leicester. Jean has recently published *A Contemporary History of Women's Sport* (Routledge, 2013) and *Globalising Women's Football: Europe, Migration and Professionalisation 1971–2011* (Peter Lang, 2013). She is currently working on *Send Her Victorious: A History of British Women Olympians 1900–2012* (Manchester University Press, 2014).

Alison M. Wrynn is a Professor in the Department of Kinesiology at California State University, Long Beach (CSULB). She has produced three comprehensive reports (with co-author Maureen Smith) for the Women's Sports Foundation on gender, leadership and participation in the Olympic and Paralympic Movements. She is a former International Olympic Committee, Olympic Studies Centre, Postgraduate Research Grant recipient, the current editor of the *Journal of Sport History* and a Fellow (#514) in the National Academy of Kinesiology.

ACKNOWLEDGEMENTS

We have a huge debt to pay to our 68 colleagues who are contributors to this *Handbook*. We worked with them over a period of two years during the production process. From the start, they unanimously shared with us great enthusiasm for the project and worked uncomplainingly when we asked for changes and additional drafts. It was especially difficult and time-consuming for those who were struggling to write in a second or even third language. Their contributions, when put together, constitute an accessibly- and dynamically-written, as well as wide-ranging and original, research and study resource which we believe will stand the test of time.

Very many thanks also go to Simon Whitmore, our commissioning editor, for his unwavering confidence and support in our partnership as co-editors of the *Handbook*.

Jennifer Hargreaves and Eric Anderson

Introduction

1

SPORT, GENDER AND SEXUALITY

Surveying the field

Jennifer Hargreaves and Eric Anderson

Introducing the Handbook

When Senior Commissioning Editor, Simon Whitmore, invited us to edit this *Routledge Handbook of Sport, Gender and Sexuality* for the Sport and Leisure list, we grasped the opportunity to produce—in a single publication—a notable resource for academics, and an informative and interesting book for sport professionals and general readers. The result is a handbook that is wide-ranging across different historical periods, different sports, and different local and global contexts. It incorporates personal, ideological and political narratives; varied conceptual, methodological and theoretical approaches; and examples of complexities and nuanced ways of understanding the gendered and sexualized dynamics of sport.

To accomplish our task, we sought chapters from established scholars who have made important contributions to the field of sport, gender and sexuality, as well as from emerging scholars who are breaking new ground. We also looked outside the field of sports studies to those from other disciplines and to some outside academe. We wanted to reflect the growing interest in sports studies in countries outside the West, but found difficulty securing enough contributions to give a truly global feel to the *Handbook*. The lack of literature in the developing world in the specific field of sport, gender and sexuality, and the problem of writing in English for non-English speakers, were major barriers. However, we have allocated one section of the *Handbook* to countries from across the world, and there are contributions about non-Western countries in other sections as well. The chapters are original, written specifically for this *Handbook*. The outcome is an eclectic range of contributions and topics.

Featuring the sport, gender and sexuality nexus

From the mid-nineteenth century, when modern sport in the West took an organized form, right up until the present day, it has been a distinctly gendered activity. So, it is to be expected that using gender as a conceptual and organizing principle for a handbook about sport provides essential knowledge about sport's fundamental character. However, because sport has been dominated by men, the focus on gender is very often equated with the story of "women in sport" and their struggles over many years for equality with men.

In this *Handbook*, we have included several contributions about women's sport based on rich empirical data. But we recognize that gender is a very complex and changing social category of analysis both in relation to the "opposite" sex and within one's sexual category. Thus, it is insufficient only to show evidence of male and female differences and women's accomplishments. Crucial to gender's complexity is its close relationship to sexuality, both in terms of cultural practices and sport specifically; so that we cannot discuss one without the other.

In Western societies a gendered dichotomy between males and females—known as the gender binary—has been socially constructed in accordance with commonsense interpretations of biological sex differences. We are influenced in all aspects of our lives by the gender—masculine or feminine—to which we are socially ascribed at birth. Because of the strength of the association between the male and masculinity and the female and femininity, even though "gender" (a cultural category) and "sex" (a biological category) are not synonymous, in commonsense discourse they are used interchangeably. Together, they have produced dominant ideas of males and females, masculinity and femininity; ideas that were cemented into sport during its early history and subsequent spread from the West to other countries throughout the world.

But gender is not innately connected to one's physical anatomy, but, more accurately, to the interconnections between sex and gender, and to one's sense of biological self and personal identity (both of which may vary from what is socially ascribed). The different chapters of this *Handbook* thus recognize the complexities of both sex and gender in different sports and varied social contexts. This is the same with sexuality; it may vary widely from the heterosexual–homosexual binary commonly ascribed.

Taking account of all fifty-two chapters, it is clear that there is huge gender and sexual diversity in sport; a diversity which reflects the personal preferences of sportsmen and women and breaks down commonly-understood norms of gender and sexuality. It is clear, too, that patterns of male and female participation, concepts of self as male or female, and biological or assigned sex, alongside sexuality, have changed historically in ways relating to scientific, cultural, social and political ideas and practices. This *Handbook* incorporates numerous ways in which the gendered character of sport is inseparable from sexuality and how gender and sexual identities have influenced, or been influenced by experiences in sport.

Consider, for example, that sports are closely aligned to the *moving physical* body, to its musculature, strength, speed, skill, agility and artistry. Unsurprisingly, because sports clothing is typically sparse, and/or clings to the body, the "actual" body can be seen or imagined. In the associated practices of changing and showering, the body is stripped naked for fellow athletes, trainers and friends to see. It is not unexpected that the capacity for human beings to enjoy the sensuous nature of the moving body and to have erotic feelings is commonplace in sport. For example, increasingly, and explicitly in the case of athletes in soft-porn poses photographed for publicity calendars, the bodies of sportswomen and increasingly sportsmen are openly sexualized (Coad, 2008). The aim is to build on the public acclaim of successful athletes in order to infuse desire, even arousal, leading to the successful commercialization of the sexy sporting body. The experiences of sexuality in sport have meaning because they are linked to those in society at large. We are bombarded by images and discourses of sexuality and by cultural ideas of beauty and fitness which become part of taken-for-granted, everyday life.

We want to emphasize that the socially constructed sporting body is readily experienced as sensuous, eroticized and sexualized, by both performers and spectators. But we want to emphasize, too, that for most people the immediate focus of sports participation or viewing is not sexuality—it is the love of the game, the hope of staying healthy, or to win medals. But for many who love sport, its sexualized culture has presented barriers to participation.

Until relatively recently, the complex characteristics of sport, gender and sexuality were always framed according to heterosexual norms, putting pressure on many young males and females with different sexual orientations to compare their own body-types and identities with those of mediated images of young, beautiful and desirable (by implication heterosexual) bodies, not infrequently leading to a hatred of having their own bodies on view and even to a loathing of sport in general. Through history, fear of homophobia has encouraged most players with non-normative sexual orientations to hide their differences, to pass as straight. Homosexuality has been systematically vilified in sport, with consistent attempts to negate homoeroticism in sex-segregated sports by framing same-sex desire as taboo (Pronger, 1990). In recent years, however, notably in the West, a rapidly growing recognition of sexual diversity and greater tolerance of homosexuality has led to a relative lessening of homophobia (Anderson, 2009) and bisexual phobia (Ripley, Anderson, McCormack and Pitts, 2011) in sport. But in many countries outside the West, homosexuality remains illegal and frequently sanctioned by criminal prosecution, including the death penalty. In these cultures, gay and lesbian sportsmen and women stay deeply closeted, fearful of exposure for their safety. Troubles and struggles have been amplified for those who are transgendered or intersexed athletes. It is only just now that the West is beginning to recognize that sexual diversity is more than just homosexuality, it is also biological diversity.

Many chapters of the *Handbook* highlight the multiplicity and complexity of both gendered and sexual orientations in sport. Although simplified notions of gender and sexuality (male–female and gay–straight) were dominant in early social accounts of sport, their complexities should be fundamental to the practice and analysis of all sports and physical cultures in future research.

Gender and sexuality in sport scholarship and practice

It is because the formation of modern sport occurred in the West, and it was in universities in particular in Canada, the UK, and the USA that pioneering research was carried out and publications and courses in sport studies occurred, and that the generalizations we make about sport in this chapter, unless otherwise identified, concern Western contexts.

A wealth of popular writing about sport has been in evidence for many years (going back to the beginning of the nineteenth century). There were sports reports, histories, autobiographies, biographies, films, and novels. Together, they amount to a long tradition of celebrating men's sports and men's lives in sports, especially those that arguably reflect the essence of sport's hypermasculinity: cricket, rugby, soccer, American football, ice hockey, baseball, boxing, and horse racing. But with very few exceptions, there was a failure to systematically record the history of women's participation in sport.

The huge imbalance between the public's recognition of men's and women's sports incorporates, in the first place, a long-established commonsense ideology that males, by their very natures, are more suited to take part in energetic and aggressive forms of physical activity than are females. Secondly, it reflects the power of men to dominate sport participation, mediation, management, and finance.

Unsurprisingly, when sport history and sociology became newly-accepted academic disciplines in the 1970s, the gender imbalance was repeated, and though increasingly residual, is still in place today. In sport history texts accounts of men's sports, written by men, have overwhelmingly predominated, and in sports sociology, men's participation was the main focus of analysis. Women tended to be relegated to a separate chapter of their own, and not integrated into the general theoretical arguments. Citing several sports academics from North America and Western Europe who constitute the early social theorists of sport—all of whom are men—

John Hargreaves (1982) has argued that the main thrust of their approach—either explicitly or implicitly—was functionalist (pp. 34–35). He maintained that they viewed sport as a means of helping in the formation of "stable identities or personalities" and thus supportive of existing social arrangements. Social divisions such as class, gender and sexual orientation were in general treated as descriptive categories of difference and not as relations of power.

It was also in the 1970s that the first wave of female sports academics addressed the marginalization of women in sport and in the academy. Ann Hall, an early pioneer of sport feminism explains:

> Despite the growth of the sociology of sport in the 1970s, it was clear that girls and women were not represented in the studies and literature. By 1976 there were 13 texts and anthologies (all from the United States) with a sociology of sport focus. Of those, only three had a separate chapter or section devoted to females, and of some 200 separate articles in the anthologies, fewer than one tenth were written or co-written by women. The material on females in these texts and anthologies represented less than 3 percent of the total content. This made me angry.
>
> *(1996: 6)*

Hall and other "angry" female colleagues in the field responded by positioning women as the subjects of research, articles and books. Their early work was important for putting women "on the map" with detailed accounts of male domination and gender inequalities. Over the following years, the concern for a more critical and insightful analysis was fuelled by developments in sport sociology and theoretical trends in mainstream sociology and cultural studies, as well as radical advances in feminist analysis (Lorber, 1998).

In the USA, sport feminist intellectuals were also lobbying for social and legal reforms in order to achieve equality of opportunity between the sexes. In 1972, Title 1X of the Education Amendments Act was passed. It was intended to remove advantages on the basis of sex in programmes receiving federal funding. The effect was an immediate and dramatic increase in resources and participation rates for school-age girls and undergraduate students. But later, following the integration of men's and women's sport departments and programmes, the men secured most of the senior coaching, leadership and decision-making positions, reaffirming their dominance (Hargreaves, 1994). Soon after, in 1975, the UK Sex Discrimination Act, and then the work of the UK Sports Council, made arguments for gender equality more powerful, leading to improvements in opportunities for females in both the public and private sectors of sport.

Legislation in most Western countries has resulted in improved opportunities and, significantly, has made women more aware of sporting possibilities. Increasing numbers of women were prepared to struggle for cultural and legal equality in sport. Those theorizing about sport and those working in practical sport (often the same people) were becoming more demanding and more sophisticated in their arguments and strategies. Their efforts were influenced by advances in women's rights and the growth of a Western feminist movement. In effect, cross-fertilization between theory and practice was born.

The 1980s and 1990s women's movement

By the 1980s, there was growing interest in theoretical ideas that took account of social relations of power. In 1982, *Sport, Culture and Ideology* was published, edited by Jennifer Hargreaves and based on an interdisciplinary conference of the same name. An important theoretical rationale for the conference was the emergent and fast-growing field of cultural studies, and in particular, Gramsci's concept of hegemony, which was used to explain the contradictory features of connections between culture (sport), ideology, and economic and political aspects of the totality. The book was a critique of the empiricist, atheoretical tradition of historical and comparative studies of sport, a compilation of "facts" characteristically taking primacy over interpretation. Described as "a watershed text" for sport scholarship in the social sciences, it provided a more complex way of understanding sexual divisions and male dominance in sport.

Two chapters were specifically about women. First, "Women and leisure" (Griffin et al.: 88–116) was written by a group of four committed feminists who described patriarchy as "a situation of dominance of men over women . . . based on at least two major facets: control over women's sexuality and fertility, and the sexual division of labour". They stressed "the importance of race, gender and class as fundamentally structured in relations of power" and went on to highlight the importance of "the ways in which these relations interweave" and "are constructed and expressed through dimensions of age, physical ability, and so on" (p. 89). Sensitive to the "specific view of women", they explored the social conditions that, characteristically for women more than men, militate against time and autonomy for leisure (sport). Second, "Women in sport in ideology" (1982: 117–135), was a revised version of a paper given by Paul Willis at the "Women and Sport" conference at Birmingham University in 1974. Willis argued that because biological beliefs about gender differences in sport appear as "natural", we take them for granted. "The natural", he explained, "is one of the grounds of ideology because of its apparent autonomy from 'biased' interpretation". He suggested that:

> . . . a team of high-ability women will be better, even in so-called masculine qualities, than a low-ability men's team. And yet, the meanest local 5th division, male works' team gets more respect in popular consciousness, than a women's national team.
>
> *(p. 117)*

Willis went on to argue that a female athlete's sexuality is commonly given precedence over her sporting ability, hence she would be "symbolically vapourised and reconstituted as an object, a butt for smutty jokes and complacent elbow nudging" (p. 122). In order to understand the complex and contradictory features of gender and sexuality in sport, Willis proposed "analytic cultural criticism", an approach "concerned with meaning, and values, and social explanation, without attempting positivistic rigour" (p. 120). In common with feminism, it is an approach that leads to an understanding of the complexities of (gender and sexual) discrimination, that in turn can lead to political action and change.

The link between sports theory and practice was observable during the 1970s and 1980s with regard to the foundation of women-only sports organizations. The US Women's Sports Foundation (WSF) was founded in 1974; followed by the Canadian Association for the Advancement of Women and Sport (CAAWS) in 1981; and then the British WSF (now the Women's Sport and Fitness Foundation) in 1985. Many of the founders of these organizations were sport sociologists in university departments who believed that separatism gave women greater autonomy and hence was the best way towards equality with men.

These organizations were pre-dated by the International Organization of Physical Education for Girls and Women (IAPESGW, founded in 1949) whose members were physical education professionals critical of the creeping commercialization and corrupt practices of sport. It had an international membership with an almost exclusively Western, middle-class, elitist and white ethnic hegemonic stance. Many of its members were resistant to positioning physical education within the cultural and political contexts of its member countries and to recognizing the growing interconnectedness of developments in physical education and sport. But over the years other IAPESGW members were influenced by the women's movement and were looking for more radical solutions to the difficulties and inequalities faced by women in physical education and sport across the world. In essence, they wanted to co-ordinate intellectual and political approaches.

Their first initiative was the inauguration of the Women's International Sports Coalition (WISC, 1992), replaced by the Women Sport International (WSI, 1994). Active during the first international conference on women and sport, held in Brighton, England, WSI has shown that intellectual work can feed into practical initiatives, and vice versa.

An important outcome of the conference was a statement of principles: *The Brighton Declaration on Women and Sport* (Sports Council, 1994). Another strategy was to bring the gender gap and the needs of women to the attention of powerful men in sport from numerous countries across the world. The women's activism influenced the International Olympic Committee (IOC) and other international sports organizations to adopt the Brighton Declaration. At national level, countries throughout the West, in the Far East, the Middle East, South America and the African continent also signed the Declaration (Hargreaves, 2000, Chapter 7).

During the 1990s, and into the twenty-first century, the struggle for better opportunities for women in sport had spread to most parts of the world, incorporating women with different social, cultural, political and religious backgrounds. There was a notable growth of women's sports organizations at local, regional, national and international levels. Single-sex organizations placed women's experiences at the centre of decision-making, resisting male control and sexist attitudes and practices, in order to avoid assimilating women's sports to male structures (Birrell and Richter, 1987). However, women also worked to get the co-operation and backing of men in order to advance their cause.

Directions in 1990s sport studies

As women were actively campaigning for rights in sport, there were also radical developments in sport sociology. It became increasingly clear that women from different social backgrounds—relating, for example, to age, class, disability, race, and sexuality—were not equally represented in "women's rights" initiatives. Experiences of homophobia highlighted specific problems for lesbians in sport and academics pioneered a wealth of research and writing about them (e.g. Griffin, 1998). Men's responses to women's participation, and heterosexual women's responses to lesbian visibility in sport, were new initiatives. These were all reminders that gender and sexuality are not just categories of difference, but relations of power which do not come from heterosexual males alone.

For example, throughout the 1990s, heterosexual females participating in competitive team sports often found that their sexuality was called into question not only by men, but by other women as well (McDonagh and Pappano, 2007). Hargreaves (2000: 140) argued that, "The effects of hatred and fear directed against lesbians in sport is deeply divisive . . . heterosexual women fear being labelled as lesbians and lesbian women are driven to 'pass' as straight for fear of victimization." In attempts to reduce the stigmatized association of female athletic competency with lesbianism many women overtly and covertly promoted cultures of sport that were inhospitable to lesbians (Cox and Thompson, 2001; Krane, 2001). A less overt mechanism, used by straight women to distance themselves from what Griffin (1998: 59) calls "the lesbian bogeywoman", was by emphasizing their femininity and heterosexual identities (Felshin, 1974).

Straight athletes were wearing feminine clothing, jewellery and makeup, despite its impracticality (Krane, 2001). Griffin (1998) gives the example of a female basketball coach pacing the paraffin courtside lines wearing high heels and a miniskirt, suggesting that to hyper-feminize herself deflected suspicion about her sexuality (Cox and Thompson, 2001). This gendered phenomenon is described as an "apologetic" (Felshin, 1974), a tool for policing orthodox gender roles.

Most research on lesbian American sportswomen was carried out in the 1980s and 1990s, an era Anderson (2011a) describes as being not only high in homophobia, but also homohysteria, which he summarizes as a "homosexually-panicked [organizational or macro] culture in which suspicion [of homosexuality] permeates" (p. 87). A homohysteric environment has consequences for the experience of openly lesbian athletes. As heterosexual athletes symbolically distance themselves from lesbians, it generates further "othering" and hostility (Lenskyj, 2003). Lesbian athletes find themselves to be outsiders in different groups because of their gender, their choice to pursue sport, and their sexual orientation (Anderson and Bullingham, forthcoming).

Sykes (1998) has explained that the fear of lesbianization in women's sport facilitates the silencing of homosexuality in sport, permitting heterosexuality to remain unchallenged; and Hargreaves (1994: 194) showed that media portrayal of female athletes reinforces heterosexuality, with the use of "sexualized images" and statements about femininity and marital status.

Still, there is no monolithic athletic culture. In the 1990s Griffin (1998) described different sport environments for women, ranging from hostile, to conditionally tolerant, to open. More recent research on the attitudes of coaches has shown that prejudice against lesbians was lessening (Cunningham, 2007; Sartore and Cunningham, 2009).

Connecting sport feminisms to ideas and actions

The specific quest for equality of opportunity in sport has been the main thrust of feminist interventions. Linked to policies and programmes of positive discrimination in favour of women, this approach has been characterized as liberal sport feminism. In contrast, radical sport feminism emphasises the failure of equal opportunity initiatives, focusing attention on the centrality of sexuality to women's oppression in sport and the redistribution of power through separatism. But although well-documented leisure patterns of working-class women confirm the oppressive nature of capitalist class relations (Green et al., 1990), economic Marxism has not been popular with sport feminist researchers, some of whom have turned to cultural (or socialist) feminism (also deriving from Marxism) which "recognises that women are active agents struggling creatively for better opportunities in sport; that male domination and other forms of discrimination are incomplete; and that there is a dialectical relationship between agency (freedom) and determination (constraint)" (Hargreaves, 2004: 190).

An important feature of cultural feminism has been recognising the heterogeneity of women, taking into account the way in which gender intersects with class, race, sexuality and other systems of domination. Ann Hall (1996: 34–37) discusses whether "feminist cultural studies" provides an adequate way in which to analyse and understand "difference". For example, in the West, lesbians (often radical feminists) have been centrally involved in the sport feminist movement since the 1970s, focusing on the link between gender and sexuality, particular problems faced by lesbians (and gay men), the politics of sexuality, and the damaging character of compulsory heterosexuality and homophobia in sport (e.g. Cahn, 1994; Griffin, 1998).

But women from other categories of difference remain marginalized and are under-represented as activists or as the focus of research. Jennifer Hargreaves (2000) has worked with groups of women from different parts of the world using difference and identity as a conceptual and analytical tool—for example, Black women in South Africa; Muslim women in the Middle East; Aboriginal women from Australia and Canada; lesbian women and disabled women from different countries across the world, and women representing the global expansion of women's sport, many from the developing world. With some exceptions, publications have been written by outsiders (usually white academics) to the marginalized groups under scrutiny (Birrell, 1990; DePauw, 1997; Guthrie and Castelnuovo, 2001; Lovell, 1991; Paraschak, 1997; Ratna, 2011; Smith, 1992; Wearing, 1995).

Gender and sexual discrimination are much greater problems for women from second- and third-world countries, where male domination and powerful sexual taboos, often linked to neo-colonialism and politico-cultural, traditional and religious influences, are part of everyday life. For example, in some African and Middle Eastern countries exceptionally harsh oppressions hugely reduce or deny opportunities in sport for lesbian women and gay men (Hargreaves, 2000).

Taking account of power has been problematic in the development of sport feminisms. For example, the influence of postmodernism has led to a rejection of "grand narratives" relating to capitalist, patriarchal or racial relations of power and attention has shifted to the fracturing of experience resulting from *intersections* between categories of difference and the complexities of modern life. References are made to Foucault's discourses of pleasure and discipline, surveillance techniques, and the production of "docile bodies" (Chapman, 1997; Duncan, 1994; Markula, 1995; Rail, 1998; Sykes, 1996, 1998). Particularly significant has been Judith Butler's (1993) concept of "performativity", used to argue that gender and sexuality are not "naturally" ascribed, but changing social constructs, concretely expressed through public performance. Cheryl Cole (1998) argues that the worked-on body is a question of lifestyle at the centre of the postmodern impetus, relevant increasingly to men as well as to women. But with postmodern influence has come a notable loosening of the links between theory and praxis and the original emancipatory politics of sport feminism.

Queer theory is a further example of the influences of postmodernism, and of the politics of sexuality. It is a rejection of fixed identities and traditional categories of gender and sexuality, incorporating the "unapologetic" attitude of increasing numbers of mostly sportswomen and also some men. Broad (2001: 181) claims that the "unapologetic" in women's rugby is comprised of "transgressing gender, destabilizing the heterosexual/homosexual binary, and 'in your face' confrontations of stigma—all characteristics of queer resistance". She shifts away from viewing sexuality as a civil rights issue towards a critique of "normative" heterosexuality. By playing traditional men's games, like rugby and soccer, a new generation of sportswomen are redefining and celebrating their participation in sport "on their own terms"—not in the shadow of men or in comparison with them. Heywood and Dworkin (2003: 45) argue that:

> Athleticism can be an activist tool for third wave feminists and can have important social consequences. Today, women nationwide are participating in classes like kick-boxing, spinning, rock-climbing, and boxing, relegating to the dustbin mythologies of the "weaker" sex and assumptions of female incompetence. Any day you can walk into your local gym and see the women seating alongside the men and walking in the same proud way, owning their bodies like never before.

Female football is a good example. Today, there are 29 million women and girls playing the game worldwide. It is an increasingly popular spectator sport, too—in 1999, the Fédération Internationale de Football Association (FIFA) Women's Soccer World Cup Final was played in front of 90,185 spectators. FIFA has the intention to accelerate this trend. FIFA's "Live Your Goals" campaign "aims to encourage girls and young women to play football and to inspire, nurture and consolidate an enthusiasm for the women's game" (FIFA.com). In countries where women's football remains in a fledging state, FIFA offers member associations multifaceted support and has planned eleven programmes for the period 2012–2015 in four geographical areas across the world.

So while women are redefining their world of sport by participating in growing numbers in the most popular traditional male sport in the world, they are at the same time assimilated to a male-dominated system. For the success of development programmes there is a growing dependence on established infrastructures at local, national and international levels, and most notably on football's hugely rich male-owned-and-controlled international sports federation, FIFA. It has been well documented that male domination is entrenched in the ownership and management of sport organizations and hugely difficult for women to get into powerful decision-making positions (McKay, 1997), but with constant pressure and growing acquiescence to gender equality from male leaders of sports organizations—including the IOC—the growth of women's sport continues. Gender relations of power are simultaneously being reproduced and transformed.

Sport feminist activism and literature have emanated mostly from Western Europe, North America, Australia and New Zealand, and women from other parts of the world have been marginalized. But as the rise of female sports organizations and the FIFA soccer initiative both show, activism to promote women's sport is spreading outside the West; and although gradual, there is also a spread of sport scholarship across countries in every continent.

Those who come from very different backgrounds with very different opportunities make relations of power and human agency critical to our understanding of gender and sexuality in sport. As Sylvia Walby (2000: 189) points out, "Differences of social location, such as those of class, 'race', ethnicity, nation, religion, linguistic community, sexual orientation, age, generation and ablebodiedness, as well as those based on gender, are important and need to be included in feminist theory." In the 1990s, feminist theory was also utilized to understand the social organization of masculinities, and their relationship to patriarchy.

Adding an analysis of men

The 1990s also saw a broadening of the field of sport sociology and history, particularly through the pro-feminist study of men (Messner, 1992; Pronger, 1990). Connell was the most influential theorist of this time. Her 1987 book *Gender and Power* saw the formation of her theory of hegemonic masculinity, which was brought to fruition in her (1995) book, *Hegemonic Masculinity*.

Connell describes hegemonic masculinity as ". . . the configuration of gender practice which embodies the currently accepted answer to the problem of the legitimacy of patriarchy". Although recently critiqued in both sport studies and masculinity studies and not empirically supported in the sociological literature to explain patriarchy (Anderson, 2009; Demetriou, 2001; Grindstaff and West, 2011), the concept of hegemonic masculinity was used by Messner (1992) and others to argue that in team sports boys and men construct their identities and sculpt their bodies to align with hegemonic perspectives. Throughout the 1990s, research confirmed that in competitive team sports boys and men were encouraged to exhibit, value and reproduce conservative notions of masculinity, including misogyny, aggression, competitiveness, a willingness to sacrifice, obedience to authority, compulsory heterosexuality and—essential to the study of masculinities—men's homophobia (Kimmel, 1994).

It was the hyper-masculinisation of male athletes that was thought to help men to symbolically "prove" their right to dominate women (Burstyn, 1999), *and* to make sport extremely inhospitable to openly gay male athletes. As women increasingly involved themselves with the games boys and men played, sport could at least be marked as the exclusive domain of heterosexual men.

Following a moral panic at the turn of the twentieth century over the supposed softening of boys (Dunning, 1999), competitive sport provided a mechanism to re-recreate masculinity (Walvin, 1994). But Anderson (2005, 2009) has suggested that the value of competitive team sports was also bolstered during this time because male homosexuality was associated with men's softness/femininity. He says that in order to prove their sexuality, heterosexual men aligned their gendered identities with an extreme (orthodox) form of masculinity (particularly the case when Connell established her theory, the mid-1980s).

It is because of the entanglement of one's socially-perceived gender typicality or a-typicality with sexuality that Kimmel (1994) argued that men desiring to be thought of as heterosexual had to prove and reprove their heterosexuality. This was accomplished by the performance of hypermasculinity; so much so that masculinity became synonymous with homophobia. Hence, males who were successful competitive sportsmen sought immunity from being labelled as soft, weak, feminine and thus gay. In the mid-1980s as homosexuality became more visible, even among gender-typical men (Peterson, 2011), this association was pushed to extremes. As a result of both HIV and a religious right's backlash against sexual minorities, ever more extreme masculinity was required to distance oneself from being thought of as gay (Ibson, 2002). Homophobia thus became a central tool in heterosexualizing men in this highly homohysteric culture (Anderson 2009).

There is a lack of research concerning the relationship between sport, masculinities and homosexuality before the 1980s, with the notable exception of Garner and Smith (1977) and Donald Sabo's (Sabo and Runfola, 1980) work. This was for two reasons: the first was because gay athletes had not yet begun to emerge from their sporting closets. For example, when Pronger (1990) studied closeted Canadian gay athletes in the late 1980s, he was unable to find men who were out to their teammates. Whether participating in individual sports (e.g. tennis, swimming, and running) or team sports (e.g. football, basketball, and rugby), there were few openly gay athletes in the Western world. They remained closeted because they assumed that the high degree of homophobic discourse, even among teammates, indicated that they would have a troubled experience coming out (Woog, 1998).

The second reason was because there were few pro-feminist men studying sport with an interest in the lives of gay men. Messner and Sabo (1990) were exceptions. In 1992, Messner wrote that, "The extent of homophobia in the sportsworld is staggering . . . Boys (in sport) learn early that to be gay, to be suspected of being gay, or even to be unable to prove one's heterosexual status is not acceptable" (p. 34). These attitudes extended into recreational-level sporting leagues. Discussing the Netherlands, Gert Hekma (1998) wrote, "Gay men who are seen as queer and effeminate are granted no space whatsoever in what is generally considered to be a masculine preserve and a macho enterprise" (p. 2).

It was in this cultural zeitgeist that in 1993 co-editor, Eric Anderson, came out of the closet as America's first publicly-recognized openly-gay high school coach (Anderson, 2000). After he and his heterosexual athletes were subjected to years of abuse (including physical battery), he determined to better understand the relationship between men, sport and homosexuality. Earning his PhD in 2004, he showed that the relationship between men's sport and homophobia was changing—mostly in response to decreasing cultural homophobia within Western societies (Anderson, 2009).

Sport, gender, and sexuality in the new millennium

It appears that attitudes toward gay men today are increasingly less differentiated between athletes and non-athletes. Bush, Carr, and Anderson (2012) provide the first-ever quantitative survey of British university athletes' attitudes toward having a gay male teammate. They found that attitudinal dispositions of homophobia had decreased from minimal (upon entrance in 2006) to non-existent (upon exit in 2009), and Cashmore and Cleland (2012) found that 93 per cent of UK football supporters would accept an openly gay player on their team. Further research (Anderson, 2011b) shows significant progress for gay male athletes in recent years who are now widely accepted by their teammates, with whom they feel closer than before they came out.

These findings have important implications for heterosexual men as well (Anderson, 2012). Diminishing homophobia frees them to act in ways that were not long ago stigmatized as feminine, without threat to their heterosexual identity. It would appear that we have dropped out of cultural homohysteria and the policing by men of gendered behaviours in order to avoid suspicion of homosexuality. Without homophobia, there is nothing to enforce a hegemonic form of masculinity so that multiple and varied masculinities can flourish without hierarchy (McCormack, 2012). Recognizing the limitations of hegemonic masculinity, Eric Anderson (2011a) has conceptualized inclusive masculinity as a way of understanding the social organization of different masculinities in relation to varying levels of homophobia and homohysteria.

Inclusive masculinity is used to explain that as cultural homophobia continues to dissipate (particularly among university team sports) athletes are coming out in greater numbers than ever. This is clear if one clicks on Outsports.com, where hundreds of articles related to openly-gay athletes are available.

Elite and professional players

It remains the case, however, that there are very few openly gay professional sportsmen. Association football, the most popular world sport, provides a good case study. In 2011, it was claimed that "homophobia is rife in global football from the top to the bottom" (*Guardian* 29.9.2011, G2: 7–9). Justin Fashenu was the first English professional football player to come out in 1990. He subsequently faced constant prejudice and later committed suicide. At English Premier League level players have stayed firmly closeted—the presumption is that they fear being targeted by aggressive outbursts and hostile homophobic chanting which, together with racist chanting, are part of football fan culture. Following on from Fashenu's tragic death, Ged Grebby (Chief Executive of Show Racism the Red Card) has made a film in an attempt to tackle homophobic bullying in society and in football and to "empower people to recognize and reject homophobia". In the film he interviews the Professional Football Association chairman, and several straight professional players and managers past and present. Showing that football culture has progressed, he said, "This range of support is unprecedented in football . . ." (*Guardian* 29.09.2011: 11).

The years since the millennium have seen a trickle of professional sportsmen coming out, which is the start of a process of normalizing gay men in elite sport. Most have come out after retirement, but others have come out while still actively playing, including: Gareth Thomas (rugby), Anton Hysén (football), Steve Davies (cricket), and Orlando Cruz (boxing). Robbie Rogers (football) came out and today plays for LA Galaxy. More recently Jason Collins is recognized as the first player to come out in a top-four American team sport but he did so after the season's completion and, because of his poor performance record, was not picked again. Because of their celebrity status and media coverage these gay sportsmen are arguably making it easier for others to follow their path and to accelerate a possible trend in process.

The visibility of lesbian women in top sport started somewhat earlier. The hugely successful tennis player, Billie Jean King, was outed in the media in 1981, followed later the same year by another tennis player, Martina Navratilova. They both faced setbacks and prejudice as a result—King was asked to resign her presidency of the Women's Tennis Association because of her "sexual perversion" and what was described as "a lesbian witch hunt" followed (Festle, 1996: 238, 241). Both she and Navratilova lost huge amounts of money in sponsorship, advertising and endorsements (ibid.). But they both became activists for lesbian and gay rights—a pattern followed by other out lesbian elite sportswomen.

The situation today is that elite lesbian, gay, and bisexual (LGB) sportswomen are open about their sexuality in far greater numbers than are elite gay sportsmen. In a list of notable lesbian, gay, bisexual and transgender (LGBT) sportspeople (http://en.wikipedia.org/wiki/list_of_lesbian,_gay,_bisexual,_and_transgender_sportspeople, accessed 10.05.2013), there are over 100 women, mostly from Western Europe (including Scandinavia), North America, Australia and New Zealand, and also the Czech Republic, Puerto Rico, Slovenia and South Africa. They compete in numerous different sports, including many in football, golf and tennis, and fewer numbers in basketball, bodybuilding, boxing, cycling, field and ice hockey, handball, lacrosse, martial arts, powerboat racing, rowing, skiing, softball, speed skating, volleyball, and wrestling. From their biographies, a clear pattern emerges that many lesbian and bisexual sportswomen are activists, working together for LGBT rights through organizations and clubs. However, it is only very recently that problems specific to transgender athletes in sport are being addressed.

Many LGBT sportspeople turn to gay sports clubs and organizations and competitions—what has been called a "gay sports phenomenon" which creates space to be "insiders" rather than being "outsiders" in mainstream sport (Hargreaves, 2000: 153; Symons, 2010). Pronger makes it clear that, "Gay culture is a response to homosexual oppression" (1990: 219).

We have also seen a growing network of organizations supporting sexual and gender minorities in sport. For example, the Gay and Lesbian Athletic Foundation was organized in 2002 and has worked through the years to benefit its members. In common with the FA, US Major League Sporting Associations have announced plans for promoting sexual-orientation-equality in sport, including the National Collegiate Athletics Association. Straight male superstar athletes, like rugby player Ben Cohen and collegiate wrestler Hudson Taylor, have begun social movements as well. There are also a number of predominantly internet-based campaigns, of which the most long-standing has been Outsports.com, together with Facebook pages Athlete Alley, and Equality Coaching Alliance.

At the same time that advances are being made in the West, there remain huge barriers for LGBT men and women from other countries and cultures to be open about their sexuality, to participate in gay sport competitions or to join organizations and campaign for their rights. A stark and tragic event took place in South Africa, where Black lesbians routinely face hate crimes and "corrective rape". Knowing the risk, Eudy Simelane, who had played for the national women's football team between 1977 and 2008 and was an LGBT activist, was gang-raped, and fatally beaten and stabbed twenty-five times in the face, chest and legs (http://www.guardian.co.uk/world/2009/mar/12/eudy-simelane, accessed 8.10.2013). This example brings to our attention that while sexual difference in sport in the West is increasingly accepted, we know remarkably little about the enormous discrimination preventing its acceptance in much of the rest of the world.

Sport also provides an ideal context for other forms of abuse that lead to physical and sexual harassment and violation. When there are unequal relations of physical and sexual power that come from dependency and trust, as happens in coach/athlete relations, young athletes and particularly children are vulnerable. Celia Brackenridge (2000: 8) reminds us that:

> Sexual abuse and harassment are not new phenomena: both male and female athletes
> have suffered sexual degradation from their peers, coaches and others for decades,

through hazing and initiation rituals, domineering training regimes and thought control processes. Yet . . . the dome of silence has operated effectively to reinforce both personal and organizational denial.

Sexual abuse of athletes has been scandalous, shocking and widespread, but it is only in the last two decades that, as a result of the research work of committed feminists, it has been exposed as a problem endemic in sport (Brackenridge, 2001; Kirby, Greaves, and Hankivsky, 2000). The WSI Sexual Harassment Task Force has produced a *Brochure on Sexual Harassment and Abuse* (http://www.sportsbiz.bz/womensportinternational/taskforces/harassment_brochure.htm) which comprehensively covers the nature of the abuse culture and methods of prevention for the attention of sport personnel and institutions. Homophobia and sexual abuse are social problems which have been confronted head on by activists who want to eradicate them. The value of the link between theory and praxis is once again clear.

Reading the *Handbook*

In order to position the chapters into some sort of logical order, the *Handbook* is divided into eight parts. Inevitably there are overlaps and inter-relationships between different parts and chapters. The field of research is huge and it has been impossible to cover the topic comprehensively, but the *Handbook* provides a taste of the scope and complexities and possibilities for research in the field.

As we have discussed, the *Handbook* reflects the predominance of research from countries in Western Europe, North America, New Zealand, and Australia. It also reflects the ways in which the Western model of organized sport is practised in countries throughout the world and that we see similar structures of power based on gender and sexuality replicated in sport in disparate nation states. But we can also see in the *Handbook* examples of sports practices that are culturally-specific, co-existing with globalizing imperatives. We are aware of and sympathetic to many of the cultural and political criticisms of modern sport, especially those levelled at elite-level competitive sport and huge hyper-commercialized sporting competitions, but we only had time and space to include conventional, mainstream and institutionalized examples of sport, and did not take account of community initiatives or indigenous sports which, in many instances, encourage gender equality of opportunity and the breaking down of gender and sexual stereotyping.

The field of sport, gender and sexuality has been burgeoning with monographs and edited volumes for several decades. But we are confident that this *Handbook* is sufficiently comprehensive, inclusive, contemporary and interdisciplinary to add significantly to knowledge about the field and to signal the need for future research in particular areas. We anticipate that it will stand as a valuable learning, teaching and research resource. We are a committed and compassionate duo and our combined expertise is extensive and complementary. Jennifer Hargreaves is English while Eric Anderson is American (now working in England). Jennifer, who is now retired from full-time work and university affiliation, remains active as a freelance writer and consultant in the field.

She was one of the pioneers of the sociology of sport. Eric is a professor at the University of Winchester, at the cutting edge of developments. Both are experts in sport, gender and sexuality. Jennifer's work has focused on women in sport, the politics of the body, discrimination, difference and identity. Eric is known for his research on sport, masculinities, sexualities and homophobia. They both have notable international reputations in the field and have published widely, winning awards for their scholarship. Jennifer is heterosexual while Eric is gay; and there are twenty-five years between them in age.

We believe that the combination of different nationalities, sexualities, genders, and ages provided us with full potential for understanding the breadth of the subject of this *Handbook*. Each of us has inhabited an academic social network almost entirely unknown to the other so that together we have connections with most of the significant players in the field. We believe that our differences have served as a strength, which, together with two years of close collaboration, has resulted in what follows in the main body of the *Handbook*.

References

Anderson E (2000) *Trailblazing: The true story of America's first openly gay high school coach*. Hollywood, CA: Alyson Press.

Anderson E (2005) *In the Game: Gay athletes and the cult of masculinity*. Albany: NY, State University of New York Press.

Anderson E (2009) *Inclusive Masculinity the Changing Nature of Masculinities*. London: Routledge.

Anderson E (2011a) The rise and fall of Western homohysteria. *Journal of Feminist Scholarship* 1: 80–94.

Anderson E (2011b) Updating the outcome: Gay athletes, straight teams, and coming out in educationally based sport teams. *Gender and Society* 25: 250–268.

Anderson E (2012) Shifting masculinities in Anglo-American cultures. *Masculinities and Social Change* 1: 40–60.

Anderson E and Bullingham R (forthcoming) Openly lesbian team sport athletes in an era of decreasing homohysteria. *International Review for the Sociology of Sport*.

Birrell S (1990) Women of color: Critical autobiography, and sport. In Messner M and Sabo D (eds) *Sport, Men, and the Gender Order: Critical feminist perspectives*. Champaign, IL: Human Kinetics, pp. 185–199.

Birrell S and Richter D (1987) Is a diamond forever?: Feminist transformations of sport. *Women's International Forum* 10(4): 395–409.

Brackenridge CH (2000) Preface in Kirby S, Greaves L and Hankivsky (2000) *The Dome of Silence: Sexual harassment and abuse in sport*. London: Fernwood Publishing.

Brackenridge CH (2001) *Spoilsports: Understanding and preventing sexual exploitation in sport*. London: Routledge.

Broad, KL (2001) The gendered unapologetic: Queer resistance in women's sport. *Sociology of Sport Journal* 18(2): 181–204.

Burstyn V (1999) *The Rites of Men: Manhood, politics, and the culture of sport*. Toronto: University of Toronto Press.

Butler J (1993) *Bodies that Matter: On the discursive limits of "sex"*. New York: Routledge.

Cahn SK (1994) *Coming on Strong: Gender and sexuality in twentieth century women's sport*. London: Harvard University Press.

Cashmore E and Cleland J (2012) Fans, homophobia and masculinities in association football: Evidence of a more inclusive environment. *The British Journal of Sociology* 63(2): 370–387.

Chapman G (1997) Making weight: Lightweight rowing, technologies of power, and technologies of self. *Sociology of Sport Journal* 14(3): 205–223.

Coad D (2008) *The Metrosexual: Gender, sexuality, and sport* (Vol. 283). Albany, NY: State University of New York Press.

Cole C (1998) Addiction, exercise, and cyborgs: Technologies and deviant bodies. In Rail, G (ed.) *Sport and Postmodern Times*. Albany, NY: State University of New York Press, pp. 261–275.

Connell RW (1987) *Gender and Power: Society, the person and sexual politics*. Stanford, CA: Stanford University Press.

Connell R (1995) *Hegemonic Masculinity*. Berkley, CA: University of California Press.

Cox, B and Thompson S (2001) Facing the bogey: Women, football and sexuality. *Football Studies* 4(2): 7–24.

Cunningham GB (2007) *Diversity in Sport Organizations*. New York: Holcomb Hathaway Publishers.

Demetriou DZ (2001) Connell's concept of hegemonic masculinity: A critique. *Theory and Society* 30(3): 337–361.

DePauw K (1997) Sport and physical activity in the life cycle of girls and women with disabilities. *Women in Sport and Physical Activity Journal* 16(2): 225–235.

Duncan M (1994) The politics of women's body images and practices: Foucault, the panopticon, and *Shape* magazine. *Journal of Sport and Social Issues* 18(1): 48–65.

Dunning E (1999) *Sport Matters: Sociological studies of sport, violence and civilization.* London: Routledge.

Felshin J (1974) The triple option . . . for women in sport. *Quest* 21: 36–40.

Festle M (1996) *Playing Nice: Politics and apologies.* New York: Columbia University Press.

Garner B and Smith R (1977) "Are there really any gay male athletes?" An empirical study. *The Journal of Sex Research* 13(1): 22–34.

Green E, Hebron S and Woodward D (1990) *Women's Leisure, What Leisure?* London: Macmillan.

Griffin P (1998) *Strong Women, Deep Closets: Lesbians and homophobia in sport.* Champaign, IL: Human Kinetics.

Grindstaff L and West E (2011) Hegemonic masculinity on the sidelines of sport. *Sociology Compass* 5(10): 859–881.

Guthrie SR and Castelnuovo S (2001) Disability management among women with physical impairments: The contribution of physical activity. *Sociology of Sport Journal*, 18(1): 5–20.

Hall MA (1996) *Feminism and Sporting Bodies: Essays on theory and practice.* Springfield, IL: Human Kinetics.

Hargreaves JA (1982) *Sport, Culture and Ideology.* London: Routledge and Kegan Paul.

Hargreaves JA (1982) Sport, culture and ideology. In Hargreaves JA (ed.) *Sport, Culture and Ideology.* London: Routledge and Kegan Paul, pp. 30–61.

Hargreaves JA (1994) *Sporting Females: Critical issues in the history and sociology of women's sport.* London: Routledge.

Hargreaves JA (2000) *Heroines of Sport: The politics of difference and identity.* London: Routledge.

Hargreaves JA (2004) Querying sport feminisms: Personal or political? In Giulianotti R (ed.) *Sport and Modern Social Theorists.* London: Palgrave, pp. 187–206.

Hekma G (1998) "As long as they don't make an issue of it . . .": Gay men and lesbians in organised sports in the Netherlands. *Journal of Homosexuality* 35: 1–23.

Heywood L and Dworkin S (2003) *Built to Win: The female athlete as cultural icon.* Minneapolis, MN: University of Minnesota Press.

Ibson J (2002) *Picturing Men: A century of male relationships in everyday life.* Washington, DC: Smithsonian Books.

Kimmel M (1994) Homophobia as masculinity: Fear, shame and silence in the construction of gender identity. In Brod H and Kaufman M (eds) *Theorizing Masculinities.* Thousand Oaks, CA: Sage, pp. 223–242.

Kirby S, Greaves L and Hankivsky O (2000) *The Dome of Silence: Sexual harassment and abuse in sport.* London: Fernwood Publishing.

Krane V (2001) We can be athletic and feminine, but do we want to? Challenging hegemonic femininity in women's sport. *Quest* 53(1): 115–133.

Lenskyj H (2003) *Out on the Field: Gender, sport and sexualities.* Toronto: Women's Press.

Lorber J (1998) *Gender Inequalities: Feminist theories and politics.* Los Angeles, CA: Roxbury.

Lovell T (1991) Sport, racism and young women. In Jarvie G (ed.) *Sport, Racism and Ethnicity.* Brighton: Falmer Press, pp. 58–74.

Markula P (1995) Firm but shapely, fit but sexy, strong but thin: The postmodern aerobicizing female bodies. *Sociology of Sport Journal* 12(4): 424–453.

McCormack M (2012) *The Declining Significance of Homophobia: How teenage boys are redefining masculinity and heterosexuality.* New York: Oxford University Press.

McDonagh E and Pappano L (2007) *Playing with the Boys: Why separate is not equal in sports.* New York: Oxford University Press.

McKay J (1997) *Managing Gender: Affirmative action and organizational power in Australian, Canadian, and New Zealand sport.* Albany, NY: State University of New York Press.

Messner M (1992) *Power at Play: Sports and the problem of masculinity.* Boston, MA: Beacon Press.

Messner M and Sabo D (eds) (1990) *Sport, Men and the Gender Order: Critical feminist perspectives.* Champaign, IL: Human Kinetics.

Paraschak V (1997) Variations in race relations: Sporting events for native peoples in Canada. *Sociology of Sport Journal* 14 (1): 1–21.

Peterson G (2011) Clubbing Masculinities: Gender shifts in gay men's dance floor choreographies. *Journal of Homosexuality* 58(5): 608–625.

Pronger B (1990) *The Arena of Masculinity: Sports, homosexuality, and the meaning of sex.* New York: St Martin's Press.

Rail G (ed) (1998) *Sport and Postmodern Times.* New York: State University of New York Press.

Ratna A (2011) "Who wants to make aloo gobi when you can bend it like Beckham?" British Asian females and their racialised experiences of gender and identity in women's football. *Soccer and Society* 12(3): 381–400.

Ripley M, Anderson E, McCormack M, Adams A and Pitts R (2011) The decreasing significance of stigma in the lives of bisexual men. *Journal of Bisexuality* 11(2–3): 195–206.

Sabo D and Runfola R (eds) (1980) *Jock: Sports and male identity*. Englewood Cliffs, NJ: Prentice-Hall.

Sartore ML and Cunningham GB (2009) Gender, sexual prejudice and sport participation: Implications for sexual minorities. *Sex Roles* 60(1–2): 100–113.

Smith Y (1992) Women of color in society and sport. *Quest* 44: 228–250.

Sports Council (1994) *The Brighton Declaration on Women and Sport*. London: Sports Council.

Sykes H (1996) "Contr(i)(u)cting lesbian identities in physical education: Femininity and post-structural approaches to researching sexuality. *Quest*, 48: 459–469.

Sykes H (1998) Turning the closets inside/out: Towards a queer-feminist theory in women's physical education. *Sociology of Sport Journal* 15(2): 154–173.

Symons C (2010) *The Gay Games. A history*. London: Routledge.

Walby S (2000) Beyond the politics of location the power of argument in a global era. *Feminist Theory* 1(2): 189–206.

Walvin J (1994) *The People's Game: The history of football revisited*. Edinburgh: Mainstream.

Wearing B (1995) Leisure and resistance in an ageing society. *Leisure Studies* 14: 263–279.

Willis P (1982) Women in sport in ideology. In Hargreaves JA (ed.) *Sport, Culture and Ideology*. London: Routledge and Kegan Paul, pp. 117–135.

Woog D (1998) *Jocks: True stories of America's gay male athletes*. Los Angeles, CA: *Women's Studies International Forum*, Special Issue on "The Gendering of Sport, Leisure, and Physical Education", Vol.10. No. 4, 1987. For example, see articles by S Birrell and DM Richter; L Bryson; K Fasting; H Lenskyj; N Theberge.

PART I

Historical perspectives

Links between past and present

2

"GAMES FOR THE BOYS"

Sport, empire and the creation of the masculine ideal

Dean Allen

Introduction

Within Britain and Her colonies, male-dominated sports came to symbolise the essence of patriarchal, Victorian society. Team games like rugby and cricket were part of the distinctly masculinised modern sport phenomenon that originated in the boys' public schools of Victorian Britain and infiltrated societies across the world. In these schools sport was rapidly transformed from simple, localised games into highly organised activities which became powerful and symbolic representations of all that was deemed by the ruling classes to be worthy in the Anglo-Saxon male.

The mid-nineteenth century was a time of complacency, chauvinism and opulent pride. Queen Victoria had expanded her Empire to all corners of the globe and sport came to symbolise the civilising mission of the British male abroad. Sport had the added advantage of providing a healthy distraction from the enforced domination by Britain of her colonial subjects. The Empire was seen to improve the lives of those it colonised and, as Brantlinger (1988: 11) notes, sporting pursuits became a relaxing couch for conscience. In reality though, "athletic proselytism was a statement of masculine cultural superiority as much as a gesture of general benevolent altruism" (Mangan 1992: 6) and throughout the British Empire sport replicated the model at "home".

This chapter examines the foundation of sporting masculinity – how "games for the boys" were created and then maintained in the Victorian public schools in Britain and abroad. Mangan and Walvin (1987: 2) examine the "cult of manliness" in the spread of sport throughout the British Empire. "Between approximately 1850 and 1940," they argue, "the cult of manliness became a widely pervasive and inescapable feature of middle-class existence in Britain and America: in literature, education and politics, the vocabulary of the ethic was forcefully promulgated."

The qualities embraced by "manliness" were also strongly associated with military service: "Physical courage, chivalric ideals, virtuous fortitude with additional connotations of military and patriotic virtue" (Mangan and Walvin 1987: 1). In agreement, McDevitt (2004: 11) investigates the "connection between the playing field and the battlefield" that characterised sporting endeavour throughout the Empire: "By the late Victorian and Edwardian age, a dominant vision of athletic masculinity in the British Empire," he suggests, "was characterised by the ideals of sportsmanship, strength and endurance" (2004: 9) and Winks (1999: 658) also recognises the importance of studies of manliness and sport in imperial history. Both Mangan and McDevitt highlight how women were not considered part of this Victorian sporting revolution.

The expansion of the Empire, described as "a scramble for remaining territory in Africa", "a Darwinian atmosphere of survival of the fittest" (Louis 1999: 2) underpins the masculinised construction of sport during the 1880s onwards. A vibrant and jingoistic identity became associated with the Empire around the time of the Anglo-Boer War in South Africa and provides the specific context for this chapter in its analysis of sport's link to Empire, war and masculinity. Indeed, the development of male-dominated sport in South Africa took place against a backdrop of an assured "Britannic nationalism" that, in the words of Darwin (1999: 72) "rested upon an aggressive sense of cultural superiority as the representatives of a global civilization then at the height of its prestige". It was a confidence that had been instilled within the public schools of Empire.

The role of the public schools

Sandiford (1998a: 11) explains that, in Victorian times, the modern sport phenomenon was nurtured by key institutions and agencies which regarded male sport as a major cultural virtue. Its moral, social and masculine attributes were extolled and many believed that behind England's success as a true world power was the national passion for men's sport:

> Much less than any other nation do the English need to be taught the art of preserving health. They are admitted to be the strongest of races – proof enough that they are the healthiest . . . Racing, riding, rowing, skating, curling, and among field sports cricket, with the like of hygienic agencies, must, and do in great measure, quicken Englishmen, and make them to a great extent what they physically and morally are.
>
> *(Box 1877: 72–73)*

In mid-Victorian times the elite boys' public schools became the main seats of training for England's next generation of the ruling classes. The aristocracy and the landed gentry had become firmly convinced of the inherent social value of sport, and along with the upper-middle classes, who had emerged from the industrial revolution, there was a move to ensure that sport's "school of moral training" would continue for successive generations of young men. Commenting on public school sport during the 1850s, *The Times* stressed the importance of securing "a race of young Englishmen who in days to come . . . shall retain the grasp of England upon the world" (cited in Podmore 1937: 60).

Team games at the boys' public schools, such as Eton, Harrow and Winchester had become important features of Britain's imperial agenda and played a key role in producing the future "custodians of empire". In 1864 the Clarendon Commission commended the public schools for "their love of healthy sports and exercise" which helped young men "to govern others and to control themselves" (cited in Holt 1989: 76). This attitude still prevailed when Theodore Cook was writing in 1927. The purpose of a public school education, he explained, "is the formation of an elite, not for its own sake, not for its own glory, but for the advancement and benefit of society at large". This leadership would come from "men whose character and hearts have flourished in the sunshine of the fair play they are always ready to extend to others", for it is a "fundamental fact of nature that some people are born to govern and others to work" (Cook 1927: 2).

The public school system compounded the class divisions already prevalent in Victorian society. "The class which mattered most, both to the national and international spread of the games and to the emerging and rapidly enlarging Empire was," according to Perkin (1992: 212), "the class educated at the public schools." Britain's realm was expanding and there was a perceived need for men of "calibre" to govern throughout Her Empire. The public seats of learning with their sports pitches and venerated codes of practice had become the training grounds where the next generation of male imperial administrators were moulded.

In 1883, Gurdon (1883: 31) reflected on the importance of investing in a sporting education at Britain's public schools:

> A very slight reflection will convince us that our Public Schools are the nursery grounds of our cricketers, and that if we neglect to supply our plants with the requirements necessary for their growth and full development, we shall turn out in the end but a sorry stunted crop. Let us pay them every attention in their tender years.

He was, however, preaching to the converted. By this stage, team sports had replaced scholarship, and in many cases, the pulpit, as the primary device used by the guardians of Britain's public schools to write a cultural code upon their charges. Mangan (1988, 2000) has demonstrated how the sports field became a place where boys throughout the Empire were taught the virtues of loyalty, obedience, discipline and conformity which were held to be the characteristic virtues of idealised "gentlemen". Such "virtues", it was hoped, would serve Britain capably throughout Her Empire.

As Taylor (2002: 78) has shown, public school athleticism shaped the ideal of manhood and character, differentiating gentlemen from the "masses" and creating the amateur–professional distinction that dominated British and colonial sport for over a century. "This high-minded moral guidance was routed in notions of self-discipline and virtue and was indicative of the puritanical strain in nineteenth-century British *bourgeois* philosophy." It found voice in *Athletic News* in 1876:

> Moralists may well give this subject a portion of their consideration. Excellence in athletics is only possible to those who cultivate habits of temperance, and it is the critical period between youth and manhood that habits and inclinations are formed which may influence a person's entire subsequent career. The young athlete is less likely to stray from the right path than those who have no such motive to control them, and hence a great social problem would be in a fair way to be solved.
>
> *(Cited in Taylor 2002: 78)*

The "right path" was to serve one's country and, inevitably for many, this meant a career in the military. At the time of the Anglo-Boer War (1899–1902), many speakers and preachers were visiting the boys' schools to press home the imperial message. One such orator was cricketing enthusiast E.W. Hornung, author of the best-selling Raffles tales and brother-in-law of Sir Arthur Conan Doyle. At Uppingham, Hornung's old school, a cadet corps was thriving. In February 1900, C.H. Jones, the commanding officer, left for active service in the Boer War, and his adventures in South Africa were reported in the school magazine in vivid detail: "We hear that Mr. Jones has killed five Boers single-handed. We congratulate him heartily on the exploit and hope that he will dispose of many more" (cited in Tozer 1992: 18).

At the time of the war in South Africa, approximately half the school were in the corps, and by 1905 over a thousand cadets had passed Uppingham's "Recruit Drill and Fire Exercise". To

Edward Selwyn, headmaster, the corps was "one of the glories of the school". To the visiting Lord Roberts – Commander in Chief in the Boer War – who came to open the school's South African War Memorial – a gymnasium – Uppingham's lead in military matters was an example to set before all public schools (Tozer 1992).

Bound by social pressures, Victorian women's involvement in "traditional" male sports was limited. Although Georgian women had been active in the game of cricket, for example, a pronounced and protracted slump occurred in the female game from the 1830s until the 1880s (Sandiford 1994: 44–49). While female participation in sports such as tennis and hockey were being encouraged, the "manliness" associated with cricket contrasted sharply with the Victorian notions of feminine weakness and passivity. This was fortified within the schools and universities and, up to 1914, none of the colleges at Oxford had ever produced a female cricket team (McCrone 1988: 4).

As McCrone (1988: 144) points out, medical opinion at the time was divided regarding women's sport. The male-dominated Theory of Constitutional Overstrain, supposedly "scientifically" based, proposed that women had a fixed degree of energy which, following puberty, should be conserved for the functions of procreation and child-rearing – essential to the "health of the nation" (Hargreaves 1994, see Chapter 3). Nevertheless, by the end of the nineteenth century, students at girls' public schools (notably St Leonards, Roedean and Wycombe Abbey), Colleges of Physical Education (e.g. Dartford, Bedford and Anstey), and university colleges (e.g. Cambridge and Oxford) played sport enthusiastically. However, they did so in gendered spheres, away from the general public in order to avoid fierce and demeaning opposition (ibid., see Chapter 4). For example, in 1899 W.G. Grace[1] felt compelled to add his considerable weight to the argument and wrote of the "Lady Cricketers" who had dared to tour the country and play exhibition matches during that season:

> They claimed that they did play, and not burlesque, the game, but interest in their doings did not survive long. Cricket is not a game for women, and although the fair sex occasionally join in a picnic game, they are not constitutionally adapted for the sport. If the Lady Cricketers expected to popularise the game among women they failed dismally. At all events, they had their day and ceased to be.
>
> (Grace 1899: 219)

Richard Daft, another famous Victorian cricketer, was also pessimistic about ladies' cricket in his weekly column in *Athletic News* and "there is no doubt," says Sandiford (1994: 46), "that Daft and Grace spoke for the majority of Victorian male chauvinists".[2]

Hargreaves argues that the breakthrough of girls and young women into glaringly chauvinist male games was essentially symbolic. As soon as play was over, previously prescribed "feminine-appropriate" roles and behaviours were assumed. There was general concern for female propriety and assurances that women did not seek to emulate men or encroach on their preserves. She argues that, "The ambivalence of, and irony in, the way women accommodated to their roles in sport is unwittingly, but perfectly, encapsulated in the compliment paid to a headmistress about the behaviour of her cricket team: 'Your girls play like gentlemen and behave like ladies.'" (Hargreaves 1994: 68; citing Dove 1891: 407)

A man's game: sport in South Africa

An unequal gender order in sport was being firmly established in the British context, and in South Africa's male-driven society, the gap between men's and women's opportunities was even greater. Roedean School, opened in Johannesburg in 1903, was a replica of Roedean School in England which had opened earlier in 1885. All British colonies readily adopted Britain's model of gender inequality, and opposition and restrictions emanating from men have forced women to struggle for greater equality in sport throughout the twentieth century until today (Hargreaves 1994). Brink (1990: 273) explains how "one of the means by which men in male-dominated societies control women is by giving them a well-defined but circumscribed position within society, to which some status, honour and respectability are attached".

English-speaking South Africans understood this gender-based hierarchy but Afrikaner nationalists took it to a higher level as they strove for cultural independence, portraying men as the active agents of Afrikaner history, and women as ideological figureheads. In his seminal study of Afrikaner civil religion, Moodie (1975: 17) wrote that "civil faith reserved a special place of pride for the figure of the Afrikaner woman". For Moodie, man remained "the instrumental agent who worked out God's will in Afrikaner history", yet in the struggle against British Imperial oppression, it was the woman who "provided a deep well of moral fortitude which complemented and even surpassed her husband's more practical exploits" (ibid.).

According to Allison (1993: 4), in its capacity "to give meaning to life, to create and interconnect senses of achievement and identity", sport has a "complex and important interaction with nationality and the phenomenon of nationalism". In the case of South Africa, the British used sport in the creation of a common Empire, whereas Afrikaner males used sport, and rugby in particular, in their pursuit of separate identity and recognition. A specific role was allocated to women by men in Afrikaner society and was used as an integral part of emergent Afrikaner identity. Sustained through male-controlled politics, together with rugby, the ideology of the *Volksmoeder* or "Mother of the Nation" was a concept of "ideal womanhood" which became a central feature of Afrikaner nation-building (Allen 2001).

One of the key cultural facets of Afrikaner nationalism was the sport of rugby (Booth 1998; Grundlingh et al. 1995; Nauright 1997), used by the male Afrikaans population to beat their English counterparts "at their own game" (Allen 2003). Throughout its history in South Africa, rugby has been imbued with masculine values and ideals and its cultural centrality has reinforced male hegemony within British colonial and Afrikaner societies. Rugby has been explored by Nauright and Chandler (1996) as a crucial vehicle for "making men" throughout the Empire. Nowhere has this been more applicable than in South Africa, where "rugby is *the* crucial cultural form that entrenched the social order . . . with white males at the top, distinguished from women and other races who did not (apparently) share the same passion or derive the same cultural lessons from the game" (Nauright 1996: 241).

During times of conflict, rugby, like cricket, has been linked with masculine honour and a sense of duty to "one's country" (Collins 2009). Nationalist pride has been called upon as the boundaries between sport and confrontation are readily dissolved to suit war-mongering propaganda. Nicholson typifies the sentiment offered to South African "rugby men" who had fought and died on the side of Britain in the Great War:

> Those great-hearted and gallant men who played a bigger game in a greater cause, and in doing so laid down their young lives. On the bloody battle fields of Empire . . . virile and valiant, they gladly answered the Mother Country's call in her hour of need, and rugby men in legions went forth to humanity's aid.
>
> *(Nicholson 1933: 35)*

In preparations for war South African rugby influenced and reinforced dominant relations of gender. The "maleness" of the sport, Grundlingh (1996: 200) notes, "was one of the aspects of

[British] imperial rugby culture which Afrikaners adopted and even reinforced without further thought". From a very young age, white boys in South Africa were socialised into a rugby-playing world in which the very culture of the sport, imbued with its strong sense of tradition, encouraged conformity to male-defined values (ibid.).

Excluded from the intimacies of male rugby culture, South African women, however, had only a peripheral role to play. In the 1930s and 1940s women enthusiastically attended rugby matches at Stellenbosch in support of the men, a trend which has continued to this day. However, as Grundlingh (1996: 199) later discloses, women were welcomed into the fold not through the promotion of equal opportunity, but rather "because it served the interest of men and the sport in general". Thompson (1988: 207) in particular decries the "endless list of chores traditionally done by women for the benefit of men and boys who play rugby". South African rugby supremo, Danie Craven, revealingly said that a woman "should be soft, soft by nature, soft by word of mouth. If they are not soft, they simply do not have influence over a man" (cited by Grundlingh 1996: 200). It was "games for the boys" and South Africa in this respect was no different from other rugby-playing societies.

The men's club: sport in the colonies

Sport had become an imperial bond of cultural encounters between the controlling British and subordinate groups in the colonies. Middle-class colonials were steering their sons towards sports like cricket and rugby in the hope of furnishing them with the same strength of character and upstanding morals that were being preached back in Britain. As early as 1862, a writer in *Temple Bar* laid claims to cricket being "a healthy and manly sport; [which] trains and disciplines the noblest faculties of the body, and tends to make Englishmen what they are – the masters of the world" (cited in Rayvern Allen 1987: 19).

In South Africa and the West Indies, schools such as Bishops in Cape Town and Harrison College in Barbados became training grounds for white boys to learn about the virtues of masculine sport. The sons of the indigenous elite were, on occasion, also allowed entry to public school education. However, the majority of the local indigenous populations, having also taken to sport, administered and developed their own games in the face of colonial arrogance and exclusion. "That they did so at all," suggests Sandiford, "speaks volumes for the awesome power of cultural imperialism which, historically, has proved as capable of inspiring mimicry as enforcing obedience" (1998b: 3–4).

A "sporting education" within the Empire could also be used selectively for political and administrative purposes. Many "British-style" public schools were founded across the Empire with the aim of inculcating "a healthy tone and manly habits" among future leaders (Mangan 1998: 133). For example, by the establishment of "an Eton in India", a privileged Indian boy, selected to exercise authority, would be "brought up [under British supervision] as a gentleman should be" (Colonial Agent Captain F.K.M. Walter, cited in Mangan 1998: 125). In the Caribbean, cricket became a means of moral instruction, rising above other team games to inculcate the desired virtues of patience, effort and discipline. The belief that sport was an allegory of life, and that life, like the body politic, was a matter of balancing individual rights and public duties was successfully conveyed to the children of the Empire's elite. But organised games perpetuated a patriarchal hierarchical system within a multi-racial Empire in which, as Perkin (1992: 213) points outs, "a tiny white minority maintained its ascendancy over a multitude of 'the lesser breeds without the law'".

Conclusions – the masculine ethos

Mangan and Walvin (1987: 3) talk of how "a neo-Spartan ideal of masculinity was diffused throughout the English-speaking world with the unreflecting and ethnocentric confidence of an imperial race". In a process of "parallel evolution, emulation and adaption [sic]", the concept of manliness and sport was readily transferred by men who had been taught this mantra in public schools throughout Britain and the Empire.

This chapter has shown how, from the mid-nineteenth century, "codes for a new type of ideal 'Imperial' manliness were emerging as a norm for British manhood" which was "disseminated through public schools, the Boy Scout movement, and an expanding market for adventure fiction featuring fantasies of the soldier, the hunter, and the pioneer on the colonial frontier represented as an exclusively masculine world" (O'Hanlon 1999: 392). Alongside the military, sport's benefactors and educators revelled in their role as the patriarchal colonials, creating wealth and opportunity for fellow males within the exotic landscape of Britain's expanding Empire. Here, on the "colonial frontier", men could ride and hunt and indulge in the manly pastime of sport. In *Scouting for Boys*, Robert Baden-Powell, fresh from his exploits in the South African War, deified these "frontiersmen of all parts of our Empire . . . [They are] real men in every sense of the word . . . They are accustomed to take their lives in their hands, and to fling them down without hesitation if they can help their country by doing so" (cited in MacKenzie 1987: 176–177). Frontiersmen were muscular, strong, aggressive and brave – similar characteristics to those of competitive sportsmen, incorporating the masculine mystique that had been created within the public schools.

The sports of cricket and rugby are particularly significant. McDevitt (2004: 51) describes cricket as "the great inculcator of English masculinity and school of manhood". Many of those who fought and died in South Africa at the dawn of the twentieth century were indeed schooled in an appreciation of rugby, cricket, Christianity and patriotic duty. In her examination of Victorian sport and the formation of "manly character", Park (1987: 33) recognises how, on the playing fields of Britain's public schools, "young men learned lessons which they would need to succeed in life and lead their country to a position of world eminence" – a point which is reiterated in an early history of the influential Marylebone Cricket Club: "On our school playing fields, our village greens and our impromptu pitches . . . it is the initiation of our youth into manliness" (*The Times* 1937: 1)

These "lessons of masculinity" were passed down from generation to generation. As Park (1987: 33) explains, this was all part of a Victorian parent's moral training:

> The role of the middle-class family in teaching its boys the ideals of the Masculine Achiever and the Christian Gentlemen is readily evident from private documents. Indeed, one of the main topics in nineteenth-century correspondence between parents and sons was ideals of manhood. The teaching of the two ideals differed in one especially important way: women stressed the Christian Gentleman, while men tended to emphasise the Masculine Achiever.

Mrozek (1987: 220–221) argues that, "the Victorian age lent special approval to courage and valour among 'the qualities eminently becoming a man'". It was all part of the creation of the masculine ideal. "Within imperial sport racism, sexism and imperialism were as valid a Trinity as athleticism, militarism and imperialism," Mangan (1992: 6) has claimed that, "to a considerable extent imperial sport was a favoured means of creating, maintaining and ensuring the survival of dominant male elites." Indeed, throughout South Africa and the British Empire at large, "the ideal of being a 'good sport' and showing 'good form' was instilled through games for boys and came to be seen as required for all phases of life from warfare to gambling to cricket to parliamentary politics" (McDevitt 2004: 102). This chapter has shown how, in a climate of military action, capitalist expansion and cultural imperialism, the genders were systematically separated and sport became intrinsic to exclusively masculine social networks during this period. As McDevitt (2004: 102) suggests, "this sporting ethos, which grew out of the games revolution, was founded on the creation, stabilisation, and maintenance of hierarchical relations of power". Within Victorian society sport was strictly "for the boys" and in many respects this is the foundation upon which sport's gender inequalities of today are still constructed.

Notes

1 William Gilbert ("W.G.") Grace (1848–1915): Famous English cricketer considered one of the greatest players of his generation and instrumental in the development of the game during the Victorian era. See D. Frith, *The Golden Age of Cricket 1890–1914*, 1978.
2 In 1879, when Britain was at war with the Zulus in South Africa, Richard Daft captained an English cricket side visiting Canada and America. In 1893 in *Kings of Cricket*, he proclaimed the manly virtues of cricket as the *"national game"*.

References

Allen D (2001) Volksmoeder: Mother of a Rugby Playing Nation. *South African Journal for Research in Sport, PE and Recreation* 23(2): 1–6.
Allen D (2003) Beating Them at Their Own Game: Rugby, the Anglo-Boer War and Afrikaner Nationalism, 1899–1948. *The International Journal for the History of Sport* 20(3): 37–57.
Allison L (1993) The Changing Context of Sporting Life. In: Allison L (ed) *The Changing Politics of Sport*. Manchester: Manchester University Press, pp. 1–14.
Booth D (1998) *The Race Game: Sport and Politics in South Africa*. London: Frank Cass.
Box C (1877) *The English Game of Cricket*. London: The Field Office.
Brantlinger P (1988) *Rule of Darkness: British Literature and Imperialism, 1830–1914*. Ithaca, NY: Cornell University Press.
Brink E (1990) Man-made Women: Gender, Class and the Ideology of the Volksmoeder. In: Walker C (ed) *Women and Gender in Southern Africa*. Cape Town: J. Currey, pp. 273–312.
Collins T (2009) *A Social History of English Rugby Union: Sport and the Making of the Middle Classes*. Abingdon: Routledge.
Cook T (1927) *Character and Sportsmanship*. London: Williams & Norgate.
Daft R (1893) *Kings of Cricket*. Bristol: J.W. Arrowsmith.
Darwin J (1999) A Third British Empire? The Dominion Idea in Imperial Politics. In: Brown JM and Louis WR (eds) *The Oxford History of the British Empire. Volume IV: The Twentieth Century*. Oxford: Oxford University Press, pp. 64–87.
Dove JF (1891) Cultivation of the Body. In: Beale D, Soulsby LHM and Dove JF (eds) *Work and Play in Girls' Schools*, London: Longman, pp. 396–423.
Frith D (1978) *The Golden Age of Cricket 1890–1914*. Guildford: Lutterworth Press.
Grace WG (1899) *Cricketing Reminiscences and Personal Recollections*. London: James Bowden.
Grundlingh A (1996) Playing for Power? Rugby, Afrikaner Nationalism and Masculinity South Africa, c.1900–70. In: Nauright J and Chandler TJL (eds) *Making Men: Rugby and Masculine Identity*. London: Frank Cass, pp. 181–204.
Grundlingh A, Odendaal A and Spies SB (1995) *Beyond the Tryline: Rugby and South African Society*. Johannesburg: Ravan Press.
Gurdon C (1883) Public school cricket. In: Lillywhite J (ed) *James Lillywhite's Cricketer's Companion for 1883*. London: James Lillywhite, pp. 30–38.
Hargreaves J (1994) *Sporting Females: Critical Issues in the History and Sociology of Women's Sports*. London: Routledge.
Holt R (1989) *Sport and the British*. Oxford: Oxford University Press.

Louis WR (1999) Introduction. In: Brown JM and Louis WR (eds) *The Oxford History of the British Empire. Volume IV: The Twentieth Century*. Oxford: Oxford University Press, pp. 1–46.

MacKenzie JM (1987) The Imperial Pioneer and Hunter and the British Masculine Stereotype in Late Victorian and Edwardian Times. In: Mangan JA and Walvin I (eds) *Manliness and Morality. Middle-Class Masculinity in Britain and America 1800–1940*. Manchester: Manchester University Press, pp. 176–198.

Mangan JA (1988) Imperialism, history and education. In: Mangan JA (ed) *Benefits Bestowed? Education and British Imperialism*. Manchester: Manchester University Press, pp. 1–22.

Mangan JA (1992) Britain's Chief Spiritual Export: Imperial Sport as Moral Metaphor, Political Symbol and Cultural Bond. In: Mangan JA (ed) *The Cultural Bond: Sport, Empire, Society*. London: Frank Cass, pp. 1–10.

Mangan JA (1998) *The Games Ethic and Imperialism: Aspects of the Diffusion of an Ideal*. London: Frank Cass.

Mangan JA (2000) *Athleticism in the Victorian and Edwardian Public School: The Emergence and Consolidation of an Educational Ideology*. London: Frank Cass.

Mangan JA and Walvin J (1987) Introduction. In: Mangan JA and Walvin I (eds) *Manliness and Morality. Middle-Class Masculinity in Britain and America 1800–1940*. Manchester: Manchester University Press, pp. 1–6.

McCrone KE (1988) *Playing the Game: Sport and the Physical Emancipation of Women, 1870–1914*. London: Routledge.

McDevitt PF (2004) *May the Best Man Win. Sport, Masculinity, and Nationalism in Great Britain and the Empire, 1880–1935*. Basingstoke: Palgrave Macmillan.

Moodie TD (1975) *The Rise of Afrikanerdom*. Berkeley, CA: University of California Press.

Mrozek DJ (1987) The Habit of Victory: The American Military and the Cult of Manliness. In: Mangan JA and Walvin I (eds) *Manliness and Morality. Middle-Class Masculinity in Britain and America 1800–1940*. Manchester: Manchester University Press, pp. 220–241.

Nauright J (1996) Sustaining Masculine Hegemony: Rugby and the Nostalgia of Masculinity. In: Nauright J and Chandler TJL (eds) *Making Men: Rugby and Masculine Identity*. London: Frank Cass, pp. 227–244.

Nauright J (1997) *Sport, Cultures and Identities in South Africa*. London: Leicester University Press.

Nauright J and Chandler TJL (eds) (1996) *Making Men: Rugby and Masculine Identity*. London: Frank Cass.

Nicholson CFS (1933) South African Rugby Football Board. In: Difford ID (ed.) *The History of South African Rugby Football (1875–1932)* Cape Town: Speciality Press, pp. 27–39.

O'Hanlon R (1999) Gender in the British Empire. In: Brown JM and Louis WR (eds) *The Oxford History of the British Empire. Volume IV: The Twentieth Century* Oxford: Oxford University Press, pp. 379–397.

Park RJ (1987) Biological Thought, Athletics and the Formation of a "Man of Character": 1830–1900. In: Mangan JA and Walvin I (eds) *Manliness and Morality. Middle-Class Masculinity in Britain and America 1800–1940*. Manchester: Manchester University Press, pp. 7–34.

Perkin H (1992) Teaching the Nations How to Play: Sport and Society in the British Empire and Commonwealth. In: Mangan JA (ed) *The Cultural Bond: Sport, Empire, Society*. London: Frank Cass, pp. 211–219.

Podmore A (1937) Public Schools Matches. In: *The Times, The M.C.C. 1787–1937*. London: The Times Publishing Co., pp. 58–63.

Rayvern Allen D (ed.) (1987) *Cricket's Silver Lining, 1864–1914*. London: Guild Publishing.

Sandiford KAP (1994) *Cricket and the Victorians*. Aldershot: Scolar Press.

Sandiford KAP (1998a) England. In: Stoddart B and Sandiford KAP (eds) *The Imperial Game*. Sandiford, Manchester: Manchester University Press, pp. 9–33.

Sandiford KAP (1998b) Introduction. In: Stoddart B and Sandiford KAP (eds) *The Imperial Game*. Sandiford, Manchester: Manchester University Press, pp. 1–8.

Taylor H (2002) Play Up, But Don't Play the Game: English Amateur Athletic Elitism, 1863–1910. *The Sports Historian* 22: 75–97.

Tozer MA (1992) Sacred Trinity – Cricket, School, Empire: E.W. Hornung and His Young Guard. In: Mangan JA (ed) *The Cultural Bond: Sport, Empire, Society*. London: Frank Cass, pp. 11–26.

Thompson S (1988) Challenging the Hegemony: New Zealand Women's Opposition to Rugby and the Reproduction of a Capitalist Patriarchy. *International Review for the Sociology of Sport* 23(3): 205–212.

The Times (1937) *The M.C.C. 1787–1937*. London: The Times Publishing Co.

Winks RW (1999) Future of Imperial History. In: Winks RW (ed) *The Oxford History of the British Empire. Volume V: Historiography*. Oxford: Oxford University Press, pp. 653–658.

3

SPORT, GENDER AND SEXUALITY AT THE 1908 LONDON OLYMPIC GAMES

Martin Polley

At the 2012 Olympic Games in London, a small revolution in gendered sport seems to have taken place. For the first time, women were allowed to compete in every sport on the programme. Boxing was perhaps the most symbolic event. The arrival of women in the ring intimated that the old Olympic model of what a sportswoman should be like was being laid to rest, while the admission of women into such a masculine preserve was a tacit recognition that the lines distinguishing male from female sport were becoming blurred. This suggests a breakdown in the culture of separate sporting spheres that had dominated the Olympic Games for so long.

This breakdown is perhaps not quite as radical as it initially appears. Even with all sports open to women, the ratio of male to female competitors at 2012 was still not 50:50. Only eventing allows men and women to compete in mixed teams with no distinctions, unlike, for example, mixed doubles in tennis, played to three sets rather than five. When men and women compete together in the Olympics' only mixed aesthetic sport, the winter sport of ice dancing, they assume heteronormative roles, with the man as the leader and the woman as the led. Women have fewer disciplines open to them than men in athletics, cycling, and swimming, and men are barred from rhythmic gymnastics and synchronised swimming. The masculine Olympic motto of *Citius, Altius, Fortius* ('Faster, Higher, Stronger') still dominates. Meanwhile, the International Olympic Committee (IOC) is yet to have a female president. The intrusive sex test for female athletes, created in the 1960s, has now gone, but the IOC is still grappling with transgenderism and hyperandrogenism.

This snapshot suggests that we are in a period of change, a time in which the IOC is becoming more flexible, more aware of nuances, and more open to debate on issues that, for much of Olympic history, have not been negotiable; but some of the old ways are still entrenched.

The keynote for this conservative tradition comes from the founder of the IOC, Pierre de Coubertin. In July 1912, Coubertin wrote an article on women and the Olympic Games for his journal, *Revue Olympique*. Here, he made his clearest statement on the subject of Olympic gender roles:

> In our view, this feminine semi-Olympiad is impractical, uninteresting, ungainly, and, I do not hesitate to add, improper. It is not in keeping with my concept of the Olympic Games, in which I believe that we have tried, and must continue to try, to put the

following expression into practice: the solemn and periodic exaltation of male athleticism, based on internationalism, by means of fairness, in an artistic setting, with the applause of women as a reward.

(*Coubertin, 1912, p.713*)

He maintained his 'wariness of feminism' (Coubertin, 1928, p.189), and as late as 1935, he repeated his ideal that women's roles at the Olympic Games 'should be above all to crown the victors' (Coubertin, 1935, p.583). His view was based in part on his objection to the spectacle: 'If some women want to play football or box, let them,' he wrote soon after the 1928 Olympics, 'provided that the event takes place without spectators, because the spectators who flock to such competitions are not there to watch a sport' (Coubertin, 1928, p.189). Whatever the basis of his views, they remained entrenched, and did much to shape the IOC's gender politics in the long term. As Hargreaves (1994, p.209) observed, 'From the start, the modern Olympics was a context for institiutionalized sexism, severely hindering women's participation. They were a powerful conservatizing force.'

With this in mind, this chapter explores the politics of gender and sexuality at the Games of the 4th Olympiad, held in London in 1908. By taking a case study approach to these Games, which were held in the IOC's early years when Coubertin's influence was great, we can explore the proximity between rhetoric and reality.

I have chosen the 1908 Olympics for three reasons. First, these are widely seen as the first recognisably modern Olympic Games, after the experiments of Athens (1896), Paris (1900), St Louis (1904), and the Intercalated Athens Olympics, held in 1906 to mark the tenth anniversary of the first Olympics. The British Olympic Council (BOC), which organised the 1908 Games for the British Olympic Association (BOA), compiled the first comprehensive set of regulations for all sports, including definitions of amateurism and professionalism, and all events were notionally contested by national teams under the control of national committees. Second, the 1908 Olympics included women in various ways. There were more female competitors in more sports than ever before, and some women, notably Queen Alexandra and Lady Desborough, had high profiles in Olympic ceremonies. Yet all this was done within a setting in which male sport was the norm, with male competitors hugely outnumbering female.

These Olympics become even more attractive as a case study when we consider the debates that were going on in Britain at the time. 1908 was one of the high points of the Women's Social and Political Union's (WSPU's) campaign, and some newspapers printed Olympic stories alongside Suffragette stories. For example, the *Daily Express* carried a picture of the German Olympic skating pair Anna Hübler and Heinrich Burger immediately under an illustrated spread on the WSPU's demonstration in the House of Commons. The waltzing skaters form a fascinating juxtaposition to the pictures of Helen Fox being escorted to court by two policemen (30 October 1908, p.7). There was a growing acceptance of women in education and medicine, and new kinds of women were being captured in the public imagination by advertisers, artists and novelists. H G Wells' heroine Ann Veronica, who appeared in the eponymous novel in 1909, captured this mood with her desire to break away from convention: 'The world, she discovered . . . had no particular place for her at all, nothing for her to do, except a functionless existence varied by calls, tennis, selected novels, walks, and dusting in her father's house' (Wells, 1909, p.6). For men, too, times were changing. Heterosexuality remained the unspoken norm, and homosexual acts were punishable by imprisonment – although this in itself was some kind of an improvement on the death penalty for sodomy, which was removed from the statute books only in 1861. When influential author and dramatist, Oscar Wilde, was jailed for two years' hard labour for gross indecency in 1895, the judge, Mr Justice Wills, summed up the establishment view of what being a man should entail. He compared Wilde's 'extensive corruption of the most hideous kind among young men' with the standards of 'decency and morality' that 'every man of honour' should feel (Quoted in White, 1999, p.59). However, while this was the orthodox view, the Edwardian period saw a growing debate about homosexuality. Edward Carpenter, political activist and poet, exemplifies this best. His influential *The Intermediate Sex*, published in the Olympic year, aimed at promoting 'knowledge and enlightened understanding of the subject' amongst 'medical men, teachers, parents, magistrates, judges, and the like' (2007, p.5).

It is these contextual factors that make the 1908 Olympics so fascinating, as it is within this setting that any critique of Olympic conservatism, chauvinism, and heteronormativity has to take place.

At Athens in 1896, approximately 245 all-male competitors took part in nine sports (Mallon and Widlund, 1998). However, Lennartz (1994) has shown how two Greek women ran the Marathon route in the weeks around the Olympics as they were denied official entries. The Paris Olympics of 1900 formally included women's events. Working with the notoriously unreliable records from these games, Mallon concludes that ten women competed in golf, seven in lawn tennis, three in croquet, and one each in the equestrian events and yachting, a total of 22 women. This first group of female Olympians comprised under 2% of the total entry alongside 1,235 men (Mallon, 1998, pp.26–27). At St Louis in 1904, there were fewer women, and they made up a smaller percentage of the total: six women, all of them American archers, compared to 624 men (Mallon, 1999a). Things were even more imbalanced at Athens in 1906: from a total of 847 competitors, only six were women – one Frenchwoman and five Greek women, all competing in the lawn tennis (Mallon, 1999b).

The numbers reflected the notion that sport was a male sphere. The sports themselves reinforced this. Men had the sports that embodied masculinity, variously testing speed, strength, endurance, discipline, technical ability, and teamwork. With the exception of the one anonymous woman who might have competed in the yachting at Paris, and the French horsewoman Elvira Guerra at Paris, the pre-1908 Olympic women all competed in the classically genteel sports of the period: lawn tennis, golf, croquet, and archery.

It was in this context that the BOC started work in 1906 when the IOC accepted London's offer to host the 1908 Olympics. There were no IOC directives on which sports were to be open to either sex: the programming was based more on common sense and the hosts' interests. This is why it is important to remember the British context as well as the precedent from previous Olympics and Coubertin's masculine ideology. Hargreaves (1984, p.56) notes that 'the entry of women into the Olympics occurred almost as an accident, part of the laissez-faire arrangements of the early years when authority was handed to the organising committees of the respective host countries, and before the IOC had made its administrative and policy-making procedures watertight'. She is right: but the context is important. The debate over women's suffrage, the quiet discussions about male sexualities, the provision of team sports and gymnastics for females at private schools, polytechnics, and training colleges, the increasing presence of women in the workplace: these trends were all present in Britain at the time of the Olympic Games. This was the environment in which the planners conceived the most adventurous and experimental Olympic programme yet.

The BOC developed the programme in 1906 and 1907, and the IOC approved it at their meeting in The Hague in 1907 (Mallon and Buchanan, 2000, pp.6–8). The idea was to make it the biggest Olympic Games yet, and to include all that was best in British sporting culture. The programme also had an Edwardian flavour of mechanical innovation: and while aircraft flying and motor racing did not make it into the final version, motorboat racing did (Mallon and Buchanan, 2000, pp.6–8, 298–300). There is no evidence that the planners were leaving women out or bringing them in: but the programme that they settled on, while overwhelmingly male, also involved the highest number of women's sports to date, and included men in the dance-based sport of figure skating.

Using Mallon and Buchanan's (2000) version of the programme alongside Theodore Cook's *Official Report* (1908), there were 24 competitive sports for men: archery, athletics, boxing, cycling, diving, fencing, figure skating, football, gymnastics, hockey, jeu de paumme, lacrosse, lawn tennis, motorboating, polo, racquets, rowing, rugby union, shooting, swimming, tug-of-war, water polo, wrestling, and yachting. All of these were open to men, and all of them tested different characteristics that Edwardian society valued in the male, ranging from teamwork and endurance to courage and technical ability. Then promoters used gendered language for their descriptions of some sports: on gymnastics, for example, Cook argued that 'Young men who do not care to serve their country . . . might at least improve themselves, as citizens and fathers of citizens to be, by regular gymnastic exercise' (1908, p.196). Figure skating was the most clearly aesthetic sport in the programme, although its dance-based structure was a setting for heteronormative courting behaviour. In the vehicle-based sports of cycling, sailing, and motorboat racing, men from different income brackets could show off their ability to control equipment and work as technological sportsmen.

By contrast, the BOC provided only three competitive sports that were designated for women: archery, figure skating, and lawn tennis. In archery, there were separate-sex events, attracting 32 men and 25 women. This was the only women's competition to take place in the Great Stadium. The lawn tennis competition, held at Wimbledon, consisted of men's singles and doubles on both open and covered courts, and women's singles, also on both open and covered courts. There was no mixed doubles, as there had been at Athens in 1906, and no women's doubles. Overall, 50 men and 10 women took part. Figure skating was held at Prince's Skating Club in Knightsbridge in October. There were individual and special figure competitions for men, an individual event for women, and a pairs skating competition, the only event at the 1908 Olympics where men and women competed together. In all, 21 men and 7 women took to the ice.

As well as these events that were formally open to women, two other sports featured female competitors: sailing and motorboat racing. In both cases, the presence of women seems to have been accidental rather than planned. Two women were involved in the yachting, alongside 63 men. The first was Constance Edwina Cornwallis-West, Duchess of Westminster, who owned the boat *Sorais* which came third in the 8 metre class race at Ryde. The *Official Report* lists her only as the boat's owner (Cook, 1908, p.339), but contemporary press coverage suggests a more active role. *The Field* noted that she 'sailed on board' (1 August 1908, p.233), while the *Daily Mirror* of 29 July included a photograph of the Duchess on her boat under the headline 'Duchess of Westminster Takes Part in Olympic Yacht Race'. Less ambiguous as a competitor was Frances Rivett-Carnac, who crewed for her husband Charles on his 7 metre yacht, the aptly-named *Heroine*, which won the class in a walkover. The third woman on the water was Mrs John Marshall Gorman, whose own name is lost behind Edwardian marital convention. With her husband, she raced *Quicksilver* in the B-Class motorboat event. She was the only woman in this sport which attracted 13 men, a fact which *The Times* praised: '[*Quicksilver*] was steered by Mr. Gorham, and it is worthy of special remark as an example of feminine endurance that Mrs. Gorham was also on board' (*The Times*, 29 August 1908, p.4; Mallon and Buchanan, 2000, pp.200–204). These three women show some of the nuances at work in the 1908 Olympics: it was not only the genteel and aesthetic sports that were open to females. This was, of course, a class issue, as access to these sports depended upon disposable income and free time. These women were the Olympic counterparts of the upper- and middle-class women of this period who were mountaineering, skiing, and hunting.

Additionally, there were two demonstration events for women in diving and gymnastics. Both were competitive sports for men, so the experiment of adding a women's programme was a statement of possible Olympic expansion. The gymnastics events were staged in the Great Stadium, with team displays by women from Denmark, Norway, and Sweden as part of the opening ceremony, and an additional exhibition two days later involving the Danes again, along with teams from the Northern Polytechnic Institute and the Yorkshire Amateur Gymnastic Association (Mallon and Buchanan, 2000, p.300). The diving exhibition involved only two women, Valborg Florström of Finland and Ebba Giscio of Sweden, which compares unfavourably with the 39 men, but was still revolutionary. It was the first time that women had competed in any swimming-based sports at the Olympics (Mallon and Buchanan, 2000, p.298), an important development considering the sport's dress codes compared to the modest clothing worn by archers, tennis players, skaters, and sailors.

The programme was thus still male-dominated, but the number of sports in which women competed – five competitions plus two displays – was the biggest yet. The number of 45 women competing (40 of them British) was far higher than at any previous Games, but compares unfavourably to the 1,979 men. Women made up only 2.2% of the total: but when we note that the highest previous female presence was 21 at Paris, where women made up 1.9% of the field, the increase, though tiny, is visible.

How were the sportsmen and women received at the time? Newspaper reports for the men's sports used a gendered vocabulary full of military metaphors and an emphasis on strength, stamina, and courage. The *Daily Express* (14 July 1908, p.7) described the 'army of athletes' at the opening ceremony. The *Daily Mirror* printed a spectacular action photograph of the diving, and praised the men for their 'astonishing skill, grace and daring' (25 July 1908, p.9), while *The Field* emphasised 'power and precision' in its report on the skater Ulrich Salchow (31 October 1908, p.790). Occasionally, journalists' admiration for the men's bodies veered from moral appreciation into something more homoerotically-charged, as in The *Daily Mail*'s description of the Scandinavian men at the opening ceremony: 'They made walking a beautiful thing. Long and supple in limb and big-chested, the outline of their muscles quite traceable through their thin jerseys, they might have stood for the coming race' (14 July 1908, p.3). The over-riding theme, whether expressed in aesthetic and eugenic terms or in the less-nuanced language of power and strength, was that the male athletes were real men, displaying valued masculine traits.

The coverage of the women was similarly orthodox. This starts with naming conventions. Women were referred to by their titles, like 'Miss Newell' in the archery (*Daily Mirror*, 20 July 1908, p.1) and skaters 'Froken Montgomery' and 'Mrs Syers' (*The Field*, 31 October 1908, p.790). Beyond that, the narratives of the women's sports emphasised conventional femininity. *The Field*, for example, in the same report that stressed Salchow's power, had this to say about the female skaters: 'Mrs Syers . . . excelled in rhythm and time-keeping, and her dance steps, pirouettes, &c. were skated without a fault. Fräulein Rendschmidt's skating was distinguished by a most engaging gaiety. She seemed quite at home on the ice, and danced through her programme in the happiest possible manner' (31 October 1908, p.790).

This approach was clearest in the coverage of the Danish gymnasts, whose knee-length culottes meant that they revealed far more of their legs than any other female Olympians. All newspapers and magazines emphasised the gymnasts' appearance as well as their performance in ways that ranged from the admiring to the salacious. It was no coincidence that all of the illustrated newspapers printed photographs of the gymnasts: indeed, they made the front page of the *Daily Mirror* (14 July 1908, p.1). *The Sphere* carried a side/rear view of 16 of the women bending forwards, with the caption 'Gymnastic Display by Danish Women which Aroused great Enthusiasm' (18 July 1908, p.52), and the *Illustrated London News* published a full page montage with

11 action photographs of what it called the 'Danish Dianas' under the heading 'The Drill that Makes Woman Physically Perfect':

> At the Olympic Games the most beautiful exhibition of gymnastics was given by the team of Danish girl athletes, who among all the competitors in the Stadium were unsurpassed for splendid physical development and grace of movement. The prettiness of their 'ensemble' was increased by their charming costume, which was of cream colour with amber stockings.
>
> *(25 July 1908, p.137)*

The *Daily Mirror* also included a photograph, taken from below, of one of the gymnasts standing on one leg on the beam, along with a caption that verged on the voyeuristic: 'Though a man-made law prevents ladies from competing in the Olympic Games, the spectators are occasionally treated to feats of feminine agility' (17 July 1908, p.9).

It was not just the sporting stories that maintained gender stereotypes. Olympic-themed advertisements also reinforced the message. The *Daily Mirror* carried an advertisement for OXO beef stock on 14 July (p.6), endorsed by 68 male competitors under the heading 'Let the experience of Britain's healthiest sons teach you the value of OXO as a strengthener': Britain's daughters, healthy or otherwise, were not mentioned in this context of strength. The *Daily Mail*'s Olympic Supplement of 13 July carried a Sports & Games Association advertisement for boxing gloves, dumb bells, and Sandow's Famous Developer alongside a preview of the athletics headed 'The Best Men' (*Daily Mail*, Olympic Games Supplement, 13 July 1908). The advertisement for Dr Martin's Miracletts – 'No case is too obstinate for this wonderful medicine' – ran under the heading 'Olympic Records. How are they made?': 'Men who feel weak and languid are gazing with half-expressed envy on the magnificent specimens of manhood who are breaking records and carrying home the laurels of fame.' The ailments that this wonder tonic purported to cure included constipation and indigestion, as well as those enemies of Edwardian manliness, 'lassitude, weak nerves, [and] sleeplessness' (*Daily Mirror*, 27 July 1908, p.13). Products and services aimed at women were rare in advertisements near the Olympic stories, save for the sumptuously-dressed croquet player in a Gamage's spread in the *Daily Mail* on 13 July, and notices for Woodward's Gripe Water in the *Daily Express*'s coverage of the Queen at the Olympic prize-giving ceremony (27 July 1908, p.7).

These press samples suggest that the sports of 1908 worked within predominant paradigms of how men and women should behave. The assumptions were all about heteronormativity, and about men and women having separate roles, separate interests, and bodies that needed to be treated in different ways. Mixed sex sport was there simply to allow both sexes to display these truths, and there was certainly no awareness of Carpenter's 'intermediate sex'. Any explicit references to emotional and/or sexual relationships assumed heterosexuality. So, for example, married couples who competed together, like the Gorhams in the motorboat racing or Madge and Edgar Syers in the figure skating, were admired as a norm. When the Italian Marathon runner Dorando Pietri took to the London stage to talk about his experiences, the *Daily Mail* revelled in the story of how 'he received several letters from young ladies, demurely indicating that a proposal of marriage from him would receive favourable consideration' (28 July 1908, p.3). Less pleasantly, Buchanan reports on how Dr Herbert Moran, the captain of the victorious Australian rugby union team, thought the greatest achievement of his team's visit to England was not their Olympic medal, but that none of the players had contracted venereal disease (Buchanan, 1997, p.13).

Gender-specific patterns of representation were also evident in administrative and ceremonial settings. The BOC was all-male, under the leadership of Lord Desborough, and all of the decision-making was in the hands of aristocratic and upper-middle class men. This makes the relatively high profile given to women's sport more surprising: new ideas about women must have been pervasive to have persuaded such a conservative group of men to make these changes, which even included the designation of a Ladies Dressing Room in the Stadium (Cook, 1908, plan opposite p.13). However, while there were no women on the committees, they certainly had a presence in Olympic ceremonies. Queen Alexandra attended the opening ceremony with her husband, and presided over the prize-giving along with the Duchess of Rutland, the Duchess of Westminster, and Lady Desborough (Cook, 1908, p.370). The marathon started on the lawn at Windsor Castle, with the Princess of Wales giving the signal. Lady Desborough, the BOA's President's wife, gave prizes at Henley and attended Olympic banquets. Her biographer makes little of this, simply showing it as part of the round of a society wife (Davenport-Hines, 2008, pp.147–149). Royal and aristocratic women such as these perfectly fitted in with Coubertin's vision of the social character of the Olympics.

The Queen, the Princess of Wales, and Lady Desborough may have been the archetypes of the applauding female, but visual evidence shows that plenty of other women watched the Games. Attendances in the stadium were low on some days, and turnstile evidence tells us nothing about gender, but women were present in all parts of the ground, with clothes and hats showing their status. The crowd at Henley for the all-male rowing regatta was mixed-sex. Just as interesting is the high number of women in the crowds that lined the streets for the marathon.

Other female archetypes were also evident in the 1908 Olympics prizes. The certificates featured women dressed in ancient Greek clothing, as did the Diploma of Merit (Cook, 1908, opposite pp.18–19). The medals depicted St George killing the dragon in front of a half-naked princess on the reverse, and two women draped in ancient Greek costumes crowning a naked male athlete with laurels on the obverse (Cook, 1908, opposite p.30; Polley, 2011, p.113). These representations fitted in well with Coubertin's ideal of women doing nothing more in the Olympics than rewarding the men.

Overall, then, the politics of gender and sexuality at the 1908 Olympics were nuanced and ambiguous. The Games were overwhelmingly male, evident in the type of sports, the number of competitors, the composition of decision-making bodies, and the tone of the press coverage; and yet they involved more women, and more sports for women, than any previous Olympics had done. The male sports remained rooted in the IOC's Faster, Higher, Stronger culture, and yet they included fancy diving and figure skating; and while the sports for women were predictably genteel, three women competed in the more demanding yachting and motorboat racing. Theodore Cook, in the BOC's *Official Report*, reflected on these developments:

> The successful appearance of ladies in these competitions suggests the consideration that since one of the chief objects of the revived Olympic Games is the physical development and amelioration of the race, it appears illogical to adhere so far to classical tradition as to provide so few opportunities for the participation of a predominant partner in the process of race-production. More events . . . might be open to women, whether they are permitted to compete with men or not. . . . They have competed in skating, archery, and lawn tennis in the Olympic Games. Perhaps it may be worth considering whether in future Olympiads they may not also enter for swimming, diving, and gymnastics, three branches of physical exercise in which they gave most attractive displays during the Games in London. In rifle-shooting, and possibly in other sports, they may also have a fair chance of success in open competitions.
>
> *(Cook, 1908, p.295)*

The attitude may have come straight from the contemporary moral panic of the Physical Deterioration debate (Inter-Departmental Committee of Physical Deterioration, 1904), but this official BOA statement signals a clear shift in Olympic attitudes towards women. While Coubertin remained staunchly opposed to more women's sports, his ideas were fast becoming obsolete in an age of changing attitudes towards women's social, political, economic, and cultural positions. The fact that women's diving and swimming were introduced as medal events at the Stockholm Olympics in 1912 shows how quickly attitudes were changing. The 1908 Olympics thus gave women new opportunities, and set a path for future expansion. However, it is also important to stress that gender was just part of the structure of inequalities operating in these Olympics. While some men from working-class backgrounds competed in the boxing, cycling, athletics, and swimming, the only women able to access the offered sports were from middle and upper class backgrounds. The costs of these sports, and their social character, ensured that no working class women could hope to compete. Again, this changed when swimming was introduced at Stockholm in 1912. Indeed, Britain's first individual female swimming medalist, Jennie Fletcher, trained around her manual job in a Leicester factory. As with gender, class constraints gradually changed after London 1908. These Olympics thus stand as a fascinating case study in the politics of gender and sexuality in Olympic history. In 1908, we can see old attitudes and practices being contested by new ways of thinking. Coubertin's vision of 'male athleticism' and 'female applause' still had currency: but its days were numbered.

References

Newspapers

Daily Express; *Daily Mail*; *Daily Mirror*; *The Field*; *Illustrated London News*; *The Sphere*; *The Times*.

Bibliography

Buchanan, Ian (1997), 'Rugby Football at the Olympic Games', *Journal of Olympic History*, vol. 5, no. 1, pp. 12–14.

Carpenter, Edward (2007 edition), *The Intermediate Sex*. London: Echo Library.

Cook, Theodore (1908), *The Fourth Olympiad: being the Official Report, the Olympic Games of London celebrated in 1908*. London: British Olympic Council.

Coubertin, Pierre de (1912), 'The Women at the Olympic Games', in Coubertin, Pierre de, *Olympism: selected writings*. Lausanne: IOC, 2000, pp. 711–713.

Coubertin, Pierre de (1928), 'Educational Use of Athletic Activity', in Coubertin, Pierre de, *Olympism: selected writings*. Lausanne: IOC, 2000, pp. 184–194.

Coubertin, Pierre de (1935), 'The Philosophic Foundation of Modern Olympism', in Coubertin, Pierre de, *Olympism: selected writings*. Lausanne: IOC, 2000, pp. 580–583.

Davenport-Hines, Richard (2008), *Ettie: the intimate life and dauntless spirit of Lady Desborough*. London: Weidenfeld & Nicolson.

Hargreaves, Jennifer (1984), 'Women and the Olympic phenomenon', in Tomlinson, Alan and Whannel, Garry, eds, *Five Ring Circus: money, power and politics at the Olympic Games*. London: Pluto Press, pp. 53–70.

Hargreaves, Jennifer (1994), *Sporting Females: critical issues in the history and sociology of women's sport*. London: Routledge.

Inter-Departmental Committee on Physical Deterioration (1904), *Report of the Inter-Departmental Committee on Physical Deterioration*. London: HMSO.

Lennartz, Karl (1994), 'Two Women Ran the Marathon in 1896', *Citius, Altius, Fortius*, vol. 2, no. 1, pp. 19–20.

Mallon, Bill (1998), *The 1900 Olympic Games: results for all competitors in all events, with commentary*. Jefferson, NC: McFarland.

Mallon, Bill (1999a), *The 1904 Olympic Games: results for all competitors in all events, with commentary*. Jefferson, NC: McFarland.

Mallon, Bill (1999b), *The 1906 Olympic Games: results for all competitors in all events, with commentary*. Jefferson, NC: McFarland.

Mallon, Bill and Buchanan, Ian (2000), *The 1908 Olympic Games: results for all competitors in all events, with commentary*. Jefferson, NC: McFarland.

Mallon, Bill and Widlund, Ture (1998), *The 1896 Olympic Games: results for all competitors in all events, with commentary*. Jefferson, NC: McFarland.

Polley, Martin (2011), *The British Olympics: Britain's Olympic heritage 1612–2012*. London: English Heritage.

Wells, H.G. (1909), *Ann Veronica*. London: Unwin.

White, Chris, ed. (1999), *Nineteenth-Century Writings on Homosexuality: a source book*. London: Routledge.

4

THE DANCING BODY, SEXUALITY AND THE EMERGENCE OF THE 'NEW WOMAN'

Patricia Vertinsky

> The body is the site where culture marks its control, history marks its passage, and where dance enacts its compliant resistance.
>
> *(Karayanni, 2004, p. 109)*

In 1905, twenty year old Ida Rubinstein watched with admiration as Isadora Duncan danced on the St Petersburg stage. Duncan's radical, free flowing modern dancing with Grecian robes and classical music was taking Russia by storm and Rubinstein was nurturing the beginnings of her own career and life-long passion for theatre, gesture and the dance. In their famed performances, the history of sexuality and the story of 'the New Woman' merge. The concept of the late 19th century 'New Woman' reflected changing ideas about female sexuality and the desire to step outside traditional gender roles. As Michel Foucault has shown, the same era saw the emergence of different styles of sexual prohibitions and the articulated notion of homosexuality as pathology, even disease. Medicine and sexology played a decisive role in enabling the emergence of the concept of sexuality which came to be increasingly regarded as a personality trait and a mode of sensibility (Davidson, 2001, p. 64; see also Beccalossi, 2011).[1] Yet what looked like sexual anarchy in the context of fin de siècle anxieties, suggests Elaine Showalter (1992, p. 11), might also be viewed as the embryonic stirrings of a new order. With the emergence of modernism, images of the body, especially the female body, were being redefined and transformed while approaches to movement swung between the dichotomous kinaesthetics of industrial efficiency and artistic expressiveness (Veder, 2011).

In the leap from the nineteenth to the twentieth century, bodily practices were a potent barometer of cultural transition. The dancing body which had never been considered more than a distraction became a conspicuous participant in the social, cultural and political life of the West, especially in Europe.[2] Dance culture was informed by vigorous debates about gender, nature, artifice and human subjectivity. Furthermore, women drove this dance culture; men, initially, were largely spectators of it. It provides therefore a fertile ground for exploring the performance of gendered and sexualized identities, physical culture and the active female body in the early years of the twentieth century. It was a time when the meanings of femininity and masculinity were being redefined and modern dance was becoming a site of contention about

39

the nature of movement, performance and art. It also throws light upon the vexed history of the relationship between dance and sexuality which has languished on the margins of dance scholarship but which is now acknowledging the need to study the kinaesthetics of sexuality (Desmond, 2001). Dance, concludes Ann Daly (2002, p. xiii) 'gives us the world under glass, magnifying questions of identity, culture, expression and sexual politics'.

Performing both on and off the stages of high society in the early decades of the twentieth century, the celebrated dancers, Isadora Duncan and Ida Rubinstein had remarkable, though significantly different, impacts upon the international public, contributing to and challenging attitudes about women, art and dance movement aesthetics. Both rebelled against formalism and the conventional image of dance, becoming influential figures in the creation and presentation of new, alternative images of women.[3] Both led unconventional lives, travelled widely, enjoyed female as well as male lovers, and viewed their bodies as central to their pursuit of fame. Ida Rubinstein, a dominant figure in Paris's 'belle époque' of the early twentieth century, incarnated the decadent vision of the femme fatale, projecting Oriental tales of deviant and transgressive sexuality in her dance performances. Tall, thin and exotically beautiful, she represented an icon of sexual inversion as well as an object of fascination for male homosexual artists and the lesbian milieu. From this perspective, suggests Toni Bentley (2002, p. 154), 'she presented a startling modern image, an early metaphor for the athletic demanding woman ruling her fearful emasculated man'.

In those same years, modern dance's first and most famous advocate, American-born Isadora Duncan, insisted that she wanted to use the dancing body to re-conceptualize women's place in Western culture. Opposing the longstanding notion that women on stage were invariably eroticized, public figures, she opened the possibility for the modern female dancing body to carry other meanings and aspirations. Her stage performances were in many respects enactments of agency and feminist practice, presenting the female form as unconfined, deregulated and stripped down. Carried along in the cross currents of modernism's search for physical and spiritual renewal and the urge for self expression, she claimed that the dance was about 'becoming a self', rather than about 'displaying a body' (*New York Times*, cited in Daly, 2002, pp. 274–6).[4] She had her greatest success in Europe, especially in Paris, the epicentre of modernism, where *New York Times* dance critic John Martin (1965, p. 225) called her 'a peculiarly sensitive channel for an idea whose time had come'. We can begin to see that the dancing bodies and lifestyles of Isadora Duncan and Ida Rubinstein carried rather different messages about femininity and sexuality (as well as class and race), illustrating the complexity and range of meanings one can draw from histories of physical culture and embodied practices in modernity. As Jane Desmond points out (1993–1994, p. 36), 'movement is a primary not secondary social "text" – complex, polysemous, already always meaningful, yet continually changing . . . [It] serves as a marker for the production of gender, racial, ethnic, class and national identities [and] can also be read as a signal of sexual identity, age, and illness or health.'

Isadora Duncan crossed the Atlantic in 1899 and established her career as an expressive dancer and educator in a changing Europe long before her own country fully accepted her feminist ideas about dancing and the female body. It was Isadora, said Paul Magriel (1947) who, through her dancing, first brought to Europe and then to her own country, a new attitude. European audiences showed a greater willingness than puritanical America to give Isadora's innovative dancing a sympathetic hearing. 'Never shy of self promotion, she became the prototype of the uninhibited young American whose freshness and originality charmed jaded old Europe' (Gottlieb, 2001).[5] Making her home there for most of her adult life, she moved through the cities of Europe, especially between Paris, Berlin and St. Petersburg where, in addition to her stage performances, she established schools of dance. En route, she captivated audiences with barefoot dancing, indulged in free love, took up with political radicals and leading artists of the day, experienced more than her fair share of personal tragedies (including the accidental drowning of two of her children), and earned the nickname 'Isadorable Drunken' for her lifestyle excesses. It is quite certain, said the *New York Times* shortly after her untimely death in Nice in 1927, 'that no other American woman has so impressed the world outside of America – made such a mighty stir, commanded such a following at home and abroad, left behind her such a legend of personality and such a trail of effects' (Brock, 1928).

Far fewer details exist about the contours and influence of Ida Rubinstein's personal life and dancing career, though her impact was considerable at the time. Born in the Ukraine in 1883 and brought up in St Petersburg, Rubinstein was a Jewish heiress of enormous wealth who orchestrated a lengthy, flamboyant, extravagant and eccentric career as diva, dancer, choreographer and producer in Russia and France. When she died in 1960, having lived in France for most of her adult life and retired to a life of solitude in her later years, *Le Figaro* commented with surprise: 'Last month Ida Rubinstein died in Vence. Her death was ignored by the whole world.' Not a breath, said Vicki Woolf (2000, p. 1), 'about a woman who danced and entranced the courts of Europe, who danced with Nijinsky, who commissioned Ravel's *Bolero* and Debussy's *St Sebastian*, whose audience was threatened with excommunication from the Catholic Church.' She had died a virtual recluse and her jewels had disappeared with her housekeeper.

Though their lives, training and stage careers took different paths, both Rubinstein and Duncan were influenced by major shifts in attitudes toward physical movement that were affecting their milieu and the dance and physical culture world. In his studies of body culture, Henning Eichberg explains how modernism was not only characterized by a universal standardization and homogenization of sport and body culture, corresponding to the homogenizing effects of the industrial system seen in the rationalized, disciplined and mechanized body of Taylorized assembly line workers, physical education jumping jacks, and the modern military assembly. It simultaneously supported a counteracting, subversive tendency towards multiplicity and heterogeneity that broke through in social–historical situations of change and unrest such as in the early decades of the twentieth century. At such moments, he suggests, society tended to react against attempts to enclose physical culture spatially or to make it more technical by focusing upon relaxed, flexible and individualized forms of movement (Eichberg, 1997).[6] Among such new approaches to movement were the influential ideas of François Delsarte on gesture and those of Émile-Jaques Dalcroze on rhythm,[7] both Europeans who, in somewhat different ways, wanted to show how emotion and movement were intrinsically related (rather than customary and formal as in much of classical ballet). From Delsarte's perspective, movement could be at once expressive and operative. If one moved wisely, he said, gesture would be the true reflection of self, or the role portrayed (Schwartz, 1992). This kinaesthetic of streamlined gestures with well controlled rhythmic impulses was carried from Europe to America by Delsarte's student Steele MacKaye, reinterpreted more broadly as harmonic gymnastics and then reintroduced to Europe and beyond by a number of physical culturists, dancers and actors (see Ruyter, 1999). As outlined by Genevieve Stebbins, an important popularizer of the Delsarte system, especially among women, Delsarte's three important principles, sequence, opposition and correspondence, could be combined into a physical culture system which would promote beauty of form, graceful motion and artistic presentation. Stebbins was keen to convey the kinds of 'exotic expression' influenced by Western enthusiasms for Greek art and Oriental forms of dance from the 'mysterious East' (Stebbins, 1885). She encouraged statue posing, spiral curves and pantomime, called plastic dancing or 'plastique', as integral to this new expressive movement system. At the same time, through her approach to movement as an expressive medium, Stebbins had an important and perhaps under-appreciated impact upon much of what would be attributed to modern dancers such as Isadora Duncan. Stebbins' view that the female body was not a thing to be repressed strongly resonated with Duncan who scoffed at the way traditional ballet crippled dancers' bodies (and souls).

Duncan's idea of expressivity in movement owed much to the semiotic system of Delsarte, though she was reluctant to acknowledge the extent of his influence, claiming that nature was the true source of her creative ideas. Her particular genius was to establish herself as a solo dancer, choreographing her own dances, and sustaining the interest of an audience for an entire concert using a variety of instrumental or orchestral music. This fusion of music and movement based upon walking and skipping movements was central to her performance style and artistic appreciation. Her appearance in St Petersburg in 1905 with its impact on the petri-fied traditions of the Imperial Royal Ballet was, according to Serge Diaghilev, sensational and timely, corresponding as it did with tendencies already underway to discard obsolete traditions and old conventions (Souritz, 1995).[8] If she had never come to Russia, he said, probably there would be no Diaghilev ballet. She pointed the way and we followed. Her marvellous plastic sensibility, her expressive hands, bare feet and un-corseted body were all commented upon by observers (Steegmuller, 1974, p. 41). Vaslav Nijinsky was reputed to have claimed that 'Isadora opened the door of the cell to the prisoners', though in fact classes in expressive movement had been available for some time in Moscow and St Petersburg and Rubinstein had attended some (Homans, 2010, p. 294).

Growing up in the cultural centre of Russia amidst St Petersburg's high society Rubinstein had access to tutors of languages and the classics as well as teachers of arts, dancing, singing, and drama at the Mariinsky theatre. Ironically she excelled at almost everything except dancing which was to become her lifelong passion and the foundation of her career in the theatre. She developed a particular affinity for gesture and reportedly spent hours in front of the mirror to perfect her poses. It was a habit redolent of the decadent poetry of Charles Baudelaire which it is likely she had read (although it was banned in Russia at the time) and it presaged a lifelong dedication to beauty and an obsession with her own physical appearance and mimetic abilities (Baudelaire, 1868). Quite against her family's wishes, Rubinstein sought out a career on the stage at an early age by hiring well-known artist and stage designer Leon Bakst to assist in a performance of Sophocles' Greek play *Antigone* at St Petersburg's *New Theatre*. The performance left an impression on Diaghilev who was further enamoured of Rubinstein's stage presence when he saw her dance the role of *Salomé* in 1908 – a part that she had prepared for by reading Oscar Wilde's controversial play and taking dancing lessons from Mikhail Fokine, choreographer of the Russian ballet. Much to the annoyance of Anna Pavlova, the ballet's prima ballerina, Diaghilev invited Rubinstein to become the star of the first performance of his newly-formed *Ballets Russes* in Paris in 1909 in the role of Cleopatra. With the ballet's deluge of exaggerated 'Orientalism', Rubinstein's personification of Cleopatra's sexual daring and murderous femininity became the toast of Paris. Though her per-formance was described as essentially static, a series of poses and gestures strung together in a way that bridged ballet, modern dance and burlesque, it was widely admired as 'the art of beautiful postures'. 'The mystery is in the surface,' said theatrical auteur Robert Wilson. 'You see more when the body is not moving' (Daly, 1995, pp.191–4).

Rubinstein's success with Parisian audiences was of the sensational rather than critical order (Mayer, 1988, p. 33). If not a dancer, she was an excellent mime artist with a charismatic, mesmeric presence. While Duncan had displayed her curvaceous, lilting body, dancing for Auguste Rodin and his artist friends in his Parisian sculpture garden and making them weep at her creative abilities, Rubinstein's tall, slender figure and the beautiful and vibrant costumes Bakst designed for her stage appearances were instrumental in changing fashion and street attire (Mayer, 1988, p. 35). Unlike Duncan who rarely had the means to support her flamboyant lifestyle, Rubinstein had a seemingly inexhaustible supply of money allowing her do exactly as she pleased and perform as she wanted in contexts of her own making. Her wealth allowed her to be eccentrically extravagant, keeping exotic pets in her Paris homes, hunting wild game and traveling extensively to faraway places. She had motor cars, yachts and eventually an airplane at her disposable. Scrupulous in maintaining a thin, almost emaciated body, contemporaries reported that she lived on biscuits and champagne which she drank from Madonna leaves. She reputedly never wore the same gown twice, had the flowers in her house matched to her clothes when entertaining and travelled from place to place with many tons of luggage. She was, suggests Elaine Brody (1985, pp. 502–3), 'an intense, domineering woman with inimitable panache who created a sensation whenever and wherever she appeared in public, usually on the arm of a distinguished gentleman'.[9] In short she made herself an object of fascination, a trap for the gaze both on and off the stage.

Showalter (1992, p. 160) portrays Rubinstein as a kind of *fin de siècle* 'Cher', harbinger of the boundary-bending New Woman, but forever linked to the unnatural, artificial and perverse ideology of the Decadents.[10] Adored by fellow aesthetes and influential decadent poets, especially Count Robert de Montesquiou and Gabriele D'Annunzio, she was also an intimate of actress Sarah Bernhardt as well as wealthy American-born artist Romaine Brooks, a leading member of the lesbian milieu in Paris which included Natalie Barney and Gertrude Stein.[11] As a dancer she did not belong to the major successions of twentieth century dance though as a producer and participant she was very much part of the shifting frontiers of art and dance that were awakening in modernity, especially through the new and expressive approaches to movement and modern dance that were sweeping through Europe and North America as well as Russia. And while Rubinstein saw her body as her art, it did not serve her well as a dancer. On stage she was often accused of paying more attention to feeling her parts than learning about them, leading former lover Romaine Brooks to describe her unkindly as 'a great deal less than she seemed' (Woolf, 2002, p. 155). When Diaghilev stopped offering her desirable roles in the *Ballets Russes* she left and set up her own competing company in Paris, *Les Ballets Madame Rubinstein* (de Cossart, 1983). Frederick Ashton reflected later that 'like the *Hameau* built by Marie Antoinette, where the queen, dressed in silks and satins, played at being a milkmaid, Rubinstein's company allowed her to play at being a ballerina' (Ashton, quoted in Mayer, 1988, p. 36). With her enormous wealth she was able to hire those writers, designers, choreographers, and musicians who were among the most important and influential in their professions and who, together, created for her a series of mime dramas in which she played the roles of *St Sebastian*, *Salomé*, *La Pisanelle* and many others.

Neither Rubinstein nor Duncan aged well in the eyes of their public. Rubinstein's insistence on being the star of every production of *Les Ballets Madame Rubinstein* engendered bitterness in her company. 'It was an unprecedented display of ageing vanity and warped judgment' and, much to the annoyance of the younger dancers in the company, at age fifty Rubinstein was still appearing on points with sagging tutu (Bentley, 2002, p. 152). Her last appearance as a dancer took place in Paris after twenty-five years on the stage, after which she began to withdraw from public life, converting to Catholicism in 1936 and becoming one of the Dominican Order's tertiary sisters. Her final appearance on stage as Joan of Arc in her production of *Jeanne d'Arc au Bûcher* was particularly poignant.[12] Rubinstein always said that she lived her roles, and she was, perhaps, at her best in her portrayals of Joan of Arc and San Sebastian. Says Bentley (2002, p.162):

> Ida's triumph as Joan of Arc at the age of fifty four was absolution for her entire career
> . . . [She] had begun her search for identity in the pagan land inhabited by the 19th

century femmes fatales of Salomé and Cleopatra and finished her self definition with two androgynous saints, one male and one female. In an ironic gender twist, Sebastian the beautiful boy received the phallic arrows whereas Joan of Arc, a boyish girl, delivers them.

It was a trajectory that 'illustrated the very personal progression of Ida Rubinstein from a fatal woman to a phallic woman – the feminist of today with the glamour intact' (ibid.).

The pattern of Duncan's fifty years was woven on a different, more doubled loom – on the one frame the design and implementation of her dancing practices, on the other the snarls and knots of the fabric of her private life and personal politics (Macdougall, 1960, p. 7). Most of Duncan's biographers contrast the sprightly, youthful barefoot dancing years in the salons and conservatories of European capitals surrounded by adoring audiences and avant-garde artists with the later, post-war majestic ponderousness of her ageing body moving in sympathy with revolutionaries of different stripes while striving to cope with the growing financial demands of her schools, itinerant lifestyle and unruly lovers. It became increasingly obvious that Duncan's body, and hence her dancing, was showing the physical decay of an increasingly undisciplined life, the tragedy of losing her children, and excessive drinking. 'If you didn't see her when she was twenty,' said ballet critic André Levinson, 'you didn't see her at all' (Levinson, undated, 1921 or 1923).

When the Russian revolution presented an opportunity to set up a dance school in Russia, Duncan took on the mantle of a communist with ease, even getting married to Serge Esenin, the young 'poet of the Russian revolution'. Given his reputation for drunkenness and hooliganism, and her antipathy to the confines of marriage, their partnership was predictably disastrous. On their travels in Europe and America, Esenin became ever more manic, draining Duncan's creative energy and resources before committing suicide in 1925. By that time, she had already angered audiences and forfeited her American citizenship because of her impolitic public statements about her Bolshevik leanings. As her American tour disintegrated and her dancing became increasingly erratic, she was accused in Boston of 'looking pink, talking red and acting scarlet' (Kurth, 2001, p. 402). A year later, her dancing career stalled, she was dead, strangled with her own scarf in a bizarre car accident in the south of France.

Despite her efforts to reject movement conventions, Duncan's movement aesthetic was distinctly feminine, for she celebrated the female body as a site of natural free expression, choreographed mostly for girls and women.[13] Nor was she a feminist in any organized or political way, pursuing radical individualism and ownership of one's body without being interested in women's suffrage (Offen, 2000, p. 184). While she rejected marriage as oppressive, she ardently promoted voluntary motherhood and had three children with different lovers. She paid a price for her views and free love practices; the estrangement of family members; bouts of neurasthenia; and anxiety over the tension between her desire to be both artist and lover – along with its financial and emotional ramifications. Yet Duncan's expressive and curvaceous leap onto the twentieth-century stage, her body unconfined and un-corseted, opens a space for us to rethink the hierarchy of modern movement culture.[14] Through modern dance she achieved international prominence as a symbolic embodiment of freedom which vividly reflected the complexities of feminist politics and shifting movement cultures during the early decades of the twentieth century.

Rubinstein's legacy is more complex. Preoccupied with her art and her body she showed little concern for the disintegrating Tsarist society in which she had grown up, or her family from whom she was estranged. She may have cast off her Jewish identity by converting to Catholicism but the stereotype of the Jewess clung, coding her dark beauty and sexuality as exuding

Oriental appeal, at once exotic, erotic and dangerous – *la belle juive* as femme fatale (Gilman, 1993, p. 195). Sexually ambiguous, she had concurrent short-lived love affairs with women and men, as well as a discreet and long lasting liaison with Walter Guinness with whom she travelled extensively on exotic trips until his death during WW2, and who reputedly poured a third of his immense beer fortune into her many lavish productions. With the luxury of her own as well as his extreme wealth she became a symbol of extravagance and conspicuous consumption, but she also became an important and influential patroness of the arts and influencer of the Parisian couture industry, presiding as commissioning angel for many creative artists of her day.

The issue of sexuality in dance is a sensitive one (Hanna, 2010), though dance, like sports and modelling, encourages us to look at bodies for pleasure and to link them with sexual desire. The sexual gaze upon dance was, as Foucault reminded us, a force of control and surveillance, though for both Isadora Duncan and Ida Rubinstein we could argue that sexuality was a significant source of power. As we have seen, they both used sexuality in dance to advance themselves and their agendas, asserting agency as well as feeling empowered by the performance itself. Through the *Ballets Russes* and her own ballet company, Rubinstein especially explored unorthodox sexualities and subversive gender attachments. Both, however, subscribed to a conception of art as 'a culture of feeling' making dance in all its manifestations a particularly rich arena for future study around sexuality, gender and the moving body.

Notes

1 Arnold Davidson sheds light on the conditions that enabled the emergence of the concept of sexuality in the nineteenth century – an anatomical model of reasoning was replaced by a psychological style of reasoning which conceptualized new symptoms related to drives, inner states and consciousness – hence to the idea that knowing a person's sexuality was a way of knowing that person.

2 The revival of the Olympic Games in 1896 reflected the unparalleled interest in physical culture and fascination with the classical Greek ideal of the body that consumed the Western world at this time.

3 The Romantic tradition of ballet with formal codification of movement and artificial manipulations was seen as outdated and unnatural.

4 Her autobiography – reissued thirteen times and translated into numerous languages – was said to be a fearless confession, a rite of initiation of aspiring female dancers. It spoke of a quest for life without compromise as both a woman and an artist, and recorded through her eyes the corresponding 'tableau vivant' of Europe's political, cultural and aesthetic history. See Daly, 2002, pp. 274–6.

5 Smith-Rosenberg (1985, pp. 177–8) includes Isadora in the second generation of 'New Women' in America: these women placed more emphasis on self-fulfillment and the flamboyant presentation of self, moving into creative and artistic fields and rejecting bourgeois sexual conventions.

6 Artists revolted against the restrictive academic formalism of nineteenth century thinking and sought a 'mystic-spiritual' construction of life and embodiment.

7 Popularly known as *Eurhythmics* and sometimes called rhythmic gymnastics.

8 For a brief history of the ballet where male dancers had become essentially hydraulic lifts for the poses of lighter-than-air ballerinas, see Brandstetter, 2005.

9 Those most remarked upon were the British heir to an enormous beer fortune, Walter Guinness; the Parisian dilettante, Count Robert de Montesquiou; and Italian poet and playwright, Gabriele D'Annunzio.

10 Wollen (1985, pp. 22, 29) explains further how the true significance of the Decadence lay in its sexual politics, its refusal of the natural, its retextualization of the body in terms that had previously been considered perverse. It included a fascination with androgyny, the return of the decorative and ornamental, and the insistence of female desire.

11 The counterpart to the male homosexual world that Diaghilev dominated. She had a brief affair with D'Annunzio as well as a longer one with artist Romaine Brooks.

12 Joan of Arc had been canonized in 1920.

13 Rather than a spontaneous, effortless act, she claimed every effort was worked out beforehand. She developed an innovative performance form, the solo dance choreographed to romantic music followed

by curtain-call speeches explaining and defending her choreography, theories of education and political positions. See Preston, 2005.
14 For further discussion see Eichberg, 1997, pp. 111–64.

References

Baudelaire, C (1868) *The flowers of evil*. Selected and edited by Marthiel and Jackson Mathews. Revised ed. 1989. New York: New Directions Publishing Corporation.

Beccalossi C (2011) Female same sex desires: Conceptualizing a disease in competing medical fields in nineteenth century Europe. *Journal of the History of Medicine and Allied Sciences* 67 (1): 7–35.

Bentley T (2002) *Sisters of Salome*. Lincoln and London: University of Nebraska Press.

Brandstetter G (2005) The code of Terpsichore, the dance theory of Carlo Blasis: Mechanics as the matrix of grace. *Topoi: An International Review of Philosophy* 24 (1): 67–79.

Brock H I (1928) Isadora Duncan found her rhythms in nature. *New York Times*, 16 Dec.

Brody E (1985) The legacy of Ida Rubinstein: Mata Hari of the Ballets Russes. *The Journal of Musicology* 4 (4): 491–506.

Daly A (2002) *Critical gestures: Writings on dance and culture*. Middletown, CT: Wesleyan University Press.

Daly A (1995) *Done into dance: Isadora Duncan in America*. Bloomington, IN: Indiana University Press.

Davidson AI (2001) *The emergence of sexuality: Historical epistemology and the formation of concepts*. Cambridge, MA: Harvard University Press.

de Cossart M (1983) Ida Rubinstein and Diaghilev: A one-sided rivalry. *Dance Research: The Journal of the Society for Dance Research* 1 (2): 3–20.

Desmond J ed. (2001) *Dancing desires. Choreographing sexualities on and off the stage*. Madison, WI: University of Wisconsin Press.

Desmond J (1993–1994) Embodying difference. Issues in dance and cultural studies. *Cultural Critique* 26: 33–63.

Eichberg H (1997) *Body cultures: Essays on sport, space and identity*. J. Bale and C. Philo, eds. London and New York: Routledge.

Gilman S L (1993) Salomé, syphilis, Sarah Bernhardt and the 'modern Jewess'. *The German Quarterly* 66 (2): 195–211.

Gottlieb R (2001) Free spirit. *The New York Times* Book Review. Available at: http://www.nytimes.com/2001/12/30/books/free-spirit.html?ref=isadoraduncan (Accessed 9 February, 2012).

Hanna J L (2010). Dance and sexuality: Many moves. *Journal of Sex Research* 47 (2–3): 212–41.

Homans J (2010) *Apollo's angels. A history of ballet*. New York: Random House.

Karayanni S S (2004) *Dancing fear and desire. Race, sexuality and imperial politics in Middle Eastern dance*. Waterloo, ON: Wilfred Laurier University Press.

Kurth P (2001) *Isadora: A sensational life*. Boston, MA: Little, Brown and Company.

Levinson A (undated, 1921 or 1923) Comoedia-Illustré. In: *Dance collection*, New York Public Library for the Performing Arts.

Macdougall AR (1960) *Isadora Duncan. A revolutionary in art and love*. New York: Thomas Nelson and Sons.

Magriel P (1947) *Isadora Duncan*. New York: Henry Holt and Company.

Martin J (1965) Republication of the original edn. First published in 1939. *Introduction to the dance*. Brooklyn: Dance Horizons.

Mayer C M (1988) Ida Rubinstein: A twentieth century Cleopatra. *Dance Research Journal* 20 (2): 33–51.

Offen K (2000) *European feminisms, 1700–1950: A political history*. Stanford, CA: Stanford University Press.

Preston C J (2005) The motor in the soul: Isadora Duncan and modernist performance. *Modernism/Modernity* 12 (2): 273–89.

Ruyter N L C (1999) *The cultivation of body and mind in nineteenth century American Delsartism*. Greenwood Press, Westport, CT: London.

Schwartz H (1992) Torque: The new kinaesthetic of the twentieth century. In: J. Crary and S. Kwinter, eds. *Incorporations*. New York: Zone Books 6.

Showalter E (1992) *Sexual anarchy: Gender and culture at the fin de siècle*. London: Virago Press.

Smith-Rosenberg C (1985) *Disorderly conduct: Visions of gender in Victorian America*. New York: Alfred A. Knopf.

Souritz E (1995) Isadora Duncan's influence on dance in Russia. *Dance Chronicle* 18 (2): 281–291.

Stebbins G (1885) *Delsarte system of expression*, 6th ed., New York: Edgar S. Werner Publishing and Supply Company, revised and enlarged, 1902.

Steegmuller F. ed (1974) *Your Isadora. The love story of Isadora Duncan and Gordon Craig.* New York: Random House and New York Public Library.

Veder R (2011) The expressive efficiencies of American Delsarte and Mensendieck body culture. *Modernism/modernity* 17 (4): 819–38.

Wollen P (1987) Fashion/orientalism/the body. *New formations* 1: 5–33.

Woolf V (2000) *Dancing in the vortex. The story of Ida Rubinstein.* Amsterdam: Harwood Academic Publishers.

5

WOMEN AND SPORT IN INTERWAR BRITAIN

Carol Osborne and Fiona Skillen

Introduction

The years between the end of the First World War and the beginning of the Second World War in Britain can be understood as a period of contradictions. In spite of rising unemployment and tense industrial relations, there was also unprecedented growth in leisure-related consumption, underpinned by the rise of new technologies and social and political changes following the First World War. Howkins and Lowerson (1979) discerned a significant increase in leisure-related activities, including sports participation and spectatorship during the first decade after the war. Subsequent research demonstrates increasing female participation, a group which had previously experienced limited access for reasons attributed to both social class and gender. One explanation for this is that the expansion of employment amongst women during the interwar years enabled greater numbers to access a variety of leisure pursuits. Historiography indicates that those most likely to have experienced new interests were young, unmarried women with more spare time and income compared to married women (see Todd, 2005). Given the phenomenal appeal of the cinema and dancing during these years, the latter observed by Graves and Hodge (1940) as 'the chief contemporary pastime', it is perhaps unsurprising that these activities have become focal case studies within leisure research. Yet, Huggins and Williams (2006) assertion that by the 1930s female participation in sport was annually depicted as occurring in over twenty different activities within newsreels, indicates that more extensive examination of the inroads women had made into sport and physical recreation is long overdue.

Physical education

All aspects of sport and physical exercise were evolving during the interwar period. In particular the development of physical education within schools took on new significance, in part because some policy makers and educationalists viewed it as a productive and cost-effective way of enabling the cultivation of healthy, strong children. The implementation of a new syllabus in 1919 in England and Wales and its subsequent adoption in Scotland highlights the government's desire to create a coherent education system, one that cultivated both a healthy mind and body. There was also growing recognition that the curriculum could be used more broadly to promote 'character training' or 'training for citizenship', although there was some dispute as to what precisely the purpose of such training should be (Skillen, 2009).

These ideas were not new. Organised, competitive games such as rugby and cricket had increasingly been used since the 1860s at boys' boarding schools to instill various qualities, for example, courage, team spirit, independence, strength and confidence. Arguably, the claim that these qualities could be inculcated through regular participation in team games, as well as the insistence that they contributed to the development of a 'manly' character, had impeded replication of a comparable sporting curriculum at girls' schools. Rather, in the interests of maintaining a gender distinction, middle-class girls found themselves constrained in their modes of play and the contact sports played by boys were simply not considered an option for girls (McCrone, 1988).

By building upon existing notions about the 'natural' roles and duties of each sex, an explicit gender division in sport was maintained. Physical education complemented other aspects of the curriculum; for girls this meant undertaking domestic sciences, such as cookery, childcare and health education, all of which aimed to provide skills for their assumed future roles as wives and mothers. Unlike for their male counterparts, vigorous sport was not considered to be necessary for girls. Instead, gymnastics, introduced into the curriculum in the late Victorian period, remained central to girls' physical education, but the 1927 Board of Education *Memorandum on Physical Education in Secondary Schools* explained that it

> must not, however, be allowed to be regarded merely as a form of relaxation . . . the kind of discipline aimed at is not the rigid unthinking discipline associated with the word "drill" but is the self-discipline which comes from learning to control the body and to work in harmonious concert with others.
>
> *(p.5)*

However, a shift in attitudes was also evident: the *Memorandum* reflected the increasing interest in games for girls amongst policy reformers via recognition of their positive 'social' effects. It was recommended that: 'In girls' schools it is desirable, and now usual, for at least one period per week in school hours to be given to training in games. Without this a large number of girls may be excluded from the open air activity' (p.3). This more progressive outlook can be traced through the successive subject-specific curricula of the period where activities such as rounders, netball, relay races and hockey were promoted. Nevertheless, attempts were made to ensure that the introduction of such activities was conducive to public opinion. Notions of female respectability continued to loom large, so emphasis was placed upon the fact that these games would be pursued within single-sex groups, under the supervision of fully qualified female staff and that girls' games would be less strenuous and demanding than those played by boys. Once debates relating to *whether* girls needed to receive physical training and exercise had subsided, they were quickly replaced with discussions about *which* activities, venues, clothing and rules were both appropriate and suitable for young sportswomen.

Treagus (2005) has argued that the use of team games were of key importance to educationalists wishing to teach young girls, albeit unobtrusively, about their expected future roles in society. For example, netball taught girls about being a 'team player', subjugating their own needs or a personal desire for glory for the good of their team. As was the case for boys' participation in sport, an apparently easy justification presented itself for the way in which team games could prepare girls for their future roles as wives and mothers and the implied values this would promote. The development of the formal physical education curriculum was part of a wider movement, one focused initially on the ways in which exercise could be used to promote health and prevent illness; however, as the period progressed there was even stronger recognition of the potential to use a range of activities for character training. On the one hand, this represented an important departure from earlier more restrictive attitudes to female involvement in sport, whereby school became a legitimate space where girls were *actively encouraged* to swim, play rounders, cricket, basketball, dance, and in some cases run and jump. On the other hand, external factors still restricted opportunities for some. These ranged from values which simply did not hold with female participation in robust games, to the varying financial positions of different educational authorities which influenced provision of suitable facilities in state schools necessary for those sports advocated by the new curriculum (Skillen, 2009).

Changes in attitudes towards girls' physical education cannot, however, be taken as an easy predictor of participation in adulthood when, for many women, regardless of social class, domestic responsibilities associated with home making and childcare came to the fore. Whilst this situation suggests – and certainly underpinned – a continued division of labour which facilitated male participation in sport, recent research reveals there were a number of ways women could access sport and physical recreation during the period. In doing so, they simultaneously challenged and accommodated to social expectations in the process.

Increased participation: club and municipal opportunities

Drawing on oral history interviews, club, association, council and work-based records, Skillen (2013) has identified a broad picture of women's sports participation during the interwar years. Substantial increases in both levels of active participation and levels of provision across several sports, including hockey, golf and tennis, demonstrate that women were beginning to consolidate their presence in activities where previously they had been impeded by cultural practices as expressed through attitudes to feminine propriety and dress codes (Hargreaves, 1985). For example, between 1919 and 1939 the number of clubs, schools and colleges affiliated to the All England Women's Hockey Association grew from 89 to 2,100. Scotland followed suit, with a growth from 11 affiliated clubs and schools in 1900 to 186 in 1939. Golf was also experiencing increased popularity amongst female players. The number of clubs or ladies sections affiliated to the Ladies Golf Union increased from 479 in 1914 to 1417 in 1939. Women's lawn tennis was untypical for the time in that it did not have a separate organisational body; however, the number of clubs affiliating to the Lawn Tennis Association (LTA) indicates growth in both female and male participation at local club level. In 1926 there were 1830 clubs affiliated to the LTA and by 1938 this had increased to 2874 (Skillen, 2013).

It is difficult not to conclude that the widespread take-up of tennis was partly influenced by increased levels of public visibility. In Britain Wimbledon not only provided a stage for the best international players, but was a lens through which gender dynamics were literally played out, on account of its emerging female stars. Hargreaves (1994) has noted that by the 1920s tennis was viewed as a less masculine game; a condition which perhaps enabled female players to exploit their existing niche within the game. Notably, the on-court battles and sustained successes of champions Suzanne Lenglen from France and Helen Wills from the United States were renowned for their demonstrations of athletic prowess and steely mental stamina respectively – characteristics barely witnessed before by spectators in the context of women's play. Year-on-year extensive press coverage generated public excitement, thereby providing a more convincing view of female vigour in sport. Wagg (2011) suggests that through such reportage Lenglen became the world's first female sport celebrity. The step-change in modes of dress and play which she and others subsequently exhibited provided reassurance that athleticism and femininity did not need to be mutually exclusive and rendered tennis an eminently suitable *and* physically challenging sport for girls and women.

Public provision in the form of tennis courts, pitches, courses and swimming pools were increasing throughout the period, although due to lack of consistently kept records it is difficult to identify the nature of usage with accuracy. However, through oral testimony and press sources Skillen (2013) has established that such facilities were popular for both informal participation and competitions. Public swimming provides an informative example in terms of altered attitudes because it evolved from being an activity pursued on a 'single' sex basis for reasons of propriety, to one where 'open' (mixed male and female) bathing became commonplace. Enjoyed across all social classes, the numbers swimming at local pools grew throughout the period, no doubt aided by the expansion of provision. In Scotland one journal noted in 1929 that 'swimming as a recreation is becoming more and more popular' with an estimated '381,213 females and 950,093 males swimming in the Glasgow area alone' (*Glasgow Herald*, 12 June). Similarly, in Edinburgh, during 1932–1933, 942,892 people were reported as using public pools, with 191,708 men, 114,152 women and 6378 children admitted to the Portobello district pool alone during that year.

The above statistics are not to suggest that these were the only activities women pursued during the period, or that they were necessarily the most significant in challenging perceptions of who would play which sports in society, and how. The range was more diverse and, as the following examples show, the workplace was particularly important in facilitating that diversity, even fostering sporting cultures which arguably held the promise of being women's own.

Workplace sport

As Roberts (1984) demonstrated in research about women in Preston, Barrow and Lancaster, the manufacturing industries of north-west England supported a vibrant and well-accepted culture of female waged employment. Oliver's (1997) subsequent research about interwar leisure in the region identified how the Bolton textile mills gave rise to a thriving rounders league, the game played exclusively by single and married working-class women. Fixtures regularly drew large crowds comprised of men, women and children to watch skilful players incentivised by rewards for the highest scores and best catches. Albeit played on a much smaller scale than men's football, rounders spawned its own local female stars, although neither they, nor their sport can be asserted as having achieved equal status with the stars and sports of men.

Women's football provides an interesting contrast to rounders during the same period because its emergence was underpinned by the specific conditions brought about by the First World War, rather than any sense that participation in sport might be beneficial for female workers. In this case, female substitution in the workplace literally played out in sport. Single and married women in munitions factories formed the backbone of a vibrant female football culture which, from 1917 to 1921, increasingly attracted the attention of the press, not least due to the thousands of spectators attending the charity fixtures. North-west England is again identified as the cradle of this activity, the representative team of the movement being Preston-based Dick, Kerr's Ladies under the management Alf Frankland (Williams, 2003).

The liberation implied by women's wartime work and the associated incursion into football beyond 1918 was entirely underpinned by the conscription of men for the war effort. Whilst women may have benefitted from relatively well-paid employment and the respect they achieved as footballers, the fragility of their achievements became clear when in 1921 the Football Association (FA) imposed a ban on women's teams playing on FA-affiliated grounds. Without executive positions within the FA itself and lacking an organised national body through which to forcefully oppose the ban, women had little alternative but to accept it. The critical blow was the transfer of matches from bespoke pitches to municipal recreational grounds; the latter neither encouraged nor accommodated enough spectators to sustain the success women had managed to achieve in the game in previous years.

It is generally argued that the 1921 FA ban was orchestrated to protect the status and privileges associated with the men's game. Instrumental within this was appeal to essentialist arguments which questioned women's suitability to play football at all, in spite of huge public enthusiasm which teams like Dick, Kerr's had secured. This example therefore provides a salutary reminder that in spite of the inroads women made into sport during the interwar years they could never fully transcend the conventional notion of women's place in sport: namely, as secondary to that of men.

More generally, throughout the period workplace sport varied greatly from company to company, some providing halls and playing fields specifically for their staff, while others only hired local facilities as and when they were needed, on a 'pay-and-play' basis. The latter scenario could not easily establish and increase membership as a means of forming a group or club so as to encourage regular participation (Skillen, 2013). Work-related sport participation was therefore generally very different from that of the voluntary private club which also typically offered the benefit of space for social functions – but this came at a cost.

Sport and social class: ability to pay or ability to play?

Whilst the number of private and public sports facilities grew on an unprecedented scale during the interwar years, the nature of these provisions was defined by geographical location. Urban areas benefitted from more growth than rural areas, with municipal and workplace facilities appearing in more densely populated towns and cities. Outlying suburban areas especially lent themselves to the eminently 'clubbable' sports of tennis and golf which required space in the form of courts or links. Typically supported by middle-class participation, the privatised nature of the tennis or golf club – many of which could claim pedigrees back to the nineteenth century – assured social exclusivity for members and in the case of golf gender exclusivity too. This was not only on account of location (which in itself defined the membership demographic) but because membership was conditional upon recommendation, as well as ability to pay joining fees and annual subscriptions. Such conditions variously applied across a raft of clubs, ranging through well-established sports like bowls and tennis to cricket which maintained sex distinction in spite of thriving female participation.

The social tone was underpinned by a clubhouse mentality which turned upon being a regular player and participation in a range of associated non-sporting events. Whether in the single-sex club world of golf, or the open club world of tennis, sociability and funds for maintenance and improvement of facilities came by way of tea parties, seasonal dinner dances, and games nights where both 'guests' (invariably spouses) and players could mingle. Hill (2002) has noted that complex social and political dynamics underpinned 'the club principle'. Nevertheless, the private sports club can be broadly understood as representing a safe haven for members, a place where those of equal social standing could meet and consolidate their status through sport.

Whilst municipal and workplace facilities can be understood as providing alternative forms of access to sport for those who could not afford to join a private club, in practice this was compromised by the variable nature of provision from locality to locality. Gender roles predicated on sex difference were also significant in mediating access to sporting opportunities. Contemporary researcher Margery Spring-Rice (1939) found the predicament of working-class housewives particularly acute: trapped by responsibility for domestic chores, childcare and thrift, she asserted they had little or 'no leisure at all'. Even those who were better placed in terms of free time and a little disposable income, found their leisure choices curtailed due to family and household responsibilities. For these women research suggests swimming was a popular option because it was cheap, accessible and could be undertaken more easily with children. So whilst the press, newsreels and radio provided more avenues to see and hear about sport during the interwar years, Davies (1992) and Todd (2005) both observe that after men it was still young, single women who were most likely to benefit from the interwar leisure 'boom', whatever their social class.

For women without 'ties' or those of adventurous spirit, free time, disposable income and a relaxation in public attitudes to freedom of movement were the necessary conditions to strike out independently. Thus it was in the 1920s that top-flight female climbers, drawn from the British, American and French middle classes, proudly recorded their first 'manless', guideless climbs in the Western Alps. In Britain, this development came on the back of the foundation of the Pinnacle Club (1921), explicitly formed to foster independent climbing for women. The founders were not only tired of too often relinquishing responsibility for their climbing to otherwise supportive male partners, but also conducting business in the 'open' Fell and Rock Climbing Club in the thrall of those same men (Osborne, 2005). This example highlights the general lack of executive power women generally had within the few open sports clubs they were permitted to join. Other outdoor pursuits, such as hiking, also enabled a less risky escape from urban environments to the countryside and in the company of the opposite sex. By the 1930s it was considered a fashionable thing to do, evidenced by the mass appeal it gained across all social classes (Holt, 1987). In hiking, as in other sports, sartorial norms were challenged, characterised by what Graves and Hodge (1940) described as 'unisex' dress: berets, open-necked shirts and 'potato' or khaki coloured shorts. Such 'get up' was criticized for lack of modesty and inelegance, but by this time practicality took precedence when it came to female participation in sport, whether this be the shortening of tennis dresses, or the wearing of 'slacks' for golf. However, other critical debates proved more resilient.

Public discourses

Whilst male participation in sport, whether as spectators or players, was uncontested, women's increasing engagement did not pass without comment. Despite the sanctioning of team games at school, female participation in football and the unashamed physicality of tennis 'stars', the interwar years saw a continuation of some debates which harked back to the anti-participation discourses of the Victorian and Edwardian periods. For example, during the 1920s contributors to the *British Medical Journal* discussed the potential physical 'damage' the playing games could do to young female bodies. Concern extended to adult women and the threats female reproductive capacity was placed under in the face of too much physical exertion. Acknowledging that women had been quick to recognize how sports could improve fitness, in 1922 *The Times* asserted that 'Rough games are "mentally" unsuitable to women – and are not, in spite of statements to the contrary, being very much played by them.' Over a decade later *The Times* (1935) was still questioning the legitimacy of female participation, asking: 'Has the devotion of women to sport unfitted them relatively for the task of motherhood?' However, appeasement had already arrived in 1930 via the formation of the Women's League of Health and Beauty. Women from all over the country rallied to founder Mary Bagot Stack's mantra of regular 'keep fit' to cultivate inner strength (for what was still considered women's primary function: childbearing) and outer beauty (Matthews, 1990).

It is open to question as to whether the movement can be understood as diversionary or detrimental in its impact upon perceptions of women's relationship to sport. Arguably, it situated motherhood firmly at the core of discourse about participation in physical activity and, with hindsight, the collective value of the League's mass displays stood in marked contrast to the features of the highly competitive and increasingly commercialised male-dominated team sports of the time. The League's *raison d'être* was shored up by medical research which advocated the benefits of *moderate* exercise for females. Yet, the same medical knowledge also laid to rest the misconception that female anatomy and physical stamina limited the ability to play certain sports without modified rules. For example, until the early interwar years received wisdom said that women's shoulder structures differed from those of men. It was therefore a foregone conclusion that they could not effectively achieve positive 'over-arm' techniques, thus restricting their proficiency in games like cricket and tennis. Increased visibility of women's games and reporting of them in the press helped to undermine such myths. Of a Women's Cricket Association game at the Oval in 1937 a correspondent for *The Times* wrote that the 'ladies' played

> a game of technical efficiency, liveliness and enthusiasm, . . . In every respect, in bowling, batting, and fielding alike, there was a lesson to be learned by men who relatively potter about at their game . . . I had been falsely told that ladies could not throw. I hope those who had formed that idea were present on Saturday.

Similarly in golf where women continued to meet with significant resistance when it came to accessing club membership and therefore facilities, they demonstrated ability to hold their own on the links. A contemporary champion observed that

> . . . lady golfers have obtained a more secure position than ever they occupied before the war. The change is distinctly perceptible . . . the feeling is steadily gaining ground that women are capable of playing the same kind of golf as the men – naturally on a different level of power – but still a game of the same character and played in much the same way.
>
> *(Wethered and Wethered, 1922: 10)*

Sport and modernity

Zweiniger-Bargielowska (2011: 107) has suggested that, 'The emergence of a strong, fit modern woman challenged established ideas of feminine weakness and the rise of female sport and physical culture contributed towards liberating the female body.' No better was that liberation expressed than through the take up of motor racing and aviation by a few intrepid women. What these sports allowed more than others, was a reprieve *from* the gendered discourse of physical prowess to the efficiency of equipment as a principle of engagement. Motorised sports did not depend alone upon physical power, but rather all-round stamina, technological acumen and a willingness to embrace life to the full in the pursuit of adventure and excitement – whatever the risks entailed. The likes of driver Kay Petre and pilot Amy Johnson were challenged on account of their sex for making unusual sporting choices, but they were also elevated to star status, celebrated for their pluck and their pioneering endeavours. Off the track and out of the cockpit they colluded with their projection as glamorous 'speed queens'. As Burman (2000: 304) notes: 'For their own publicity purposes (including the need to attract audiences and sponsorship and to publicise their business ventures), they deployed with considerable skill all the turns and stratagems of film stars in front of the lens.' Thus they fully embodied a range of attributes consistent with the spirit of modernity.

Representations of the strong, fit, modern woman took many forms, inviting the female audience to wear new types of clothing, perceive their bodies in new ways and pursue more athletic and physically demanding activities than ever before. The growth of distinct sports fashions and the dedicated advertisement of these acknowledged the existence of a critical mass of sportswomen. The inclusion of adverts on the fashion pages of mainstream women's magazines indicates how physical recreation was embedded within broader understandings of interwar leisure and lifestyle. Images of sportswomen used to promote non-sporting goods increased, emphasising the centrality of physical culture to modern living and an acceptance of the sportswoman as a central motif within it (Skillen, 2013).

The female body became symbolic of interwar modernity; the way it was dressed, its hair styled and even its shape expressed conformity to associated ideals. Sport provided a way to train and tone the body into the idealised 'boyish' shape, although Lenskyj (1986) argues that this same fashion infantalized women, rather than rendering them 'mannish' and threatening to the gender order. As the period progressed, sport also became a marker of sociability, whether at the club, in the workplace or the more limited environments of public provision.

Conclusion

Physical culture as expressed through sport and physical recreation became a vehicle through which to identify oneself as 'modern' during the interwar years. However, factors such as social class, stage in the lifecycle and discourses concerning the suitability for females of some sports rather than others mediated the degree to which each woman could immerse herself within that modern ideal although those who apparently did so were a minority. Nevertheless, the interwar period can still be considered as generally radical for women's sport in many ways; schools began to provide a more varied and challenging physical education curriculum for girls, but perhaps more significantly opportunities opened up beyond school in adulthood: through voluntary, club-based sport for those middle-class women with leisure time on their hands; through municipal facilities which provided affordable, albeit more limited options for working-class women; and through workplace provisions which spawned the remarkable, even if short-lived, rise of women's football. There were also the mavericks: women whose sporting achievements and appearance embodied the very essence of modernity with which the interwar years have become equated. Through their innovative play and sporting choices they challenged the established gender divide in sport and brought publicity to women's participation in the process. Yet, as exceptions rather than the rule, these talented women posed no threat to the male-dominated world of sport. Like their working-class counterparts they could neither penetrate nor significantly influence the associated organisational structures. Furthermore, whilst sporting females could thrive as members of their own dedicated sport organisations – all of which expanded during the period – there is little to suggest that this translated into tangible influences within wider social, economic and political spheres.

References

Board of Education (1927) *Memorandum on Physical Education in Secondary Schools*. London: HMSO.

Burman, B (2000) Racing Bodies: dress and pioneer women aviators and racing drivers. *Women's History Review* 9 (2): 299–326.

Davies, A (1992) *Leisure, Gender and Poverty: working-class culture in Salford and Manchester 1900–1939*. Buckingham: Open University Press.

Graves, R and Hodge, A (1940) *The Long Weekend: a social history of Great Britain 1918–1939*. (1991 ed.) London: Cardinal.

Hargreaves, J. (1985) 'Playing like Gentlemen while Behaving like Ladies': contradictory features of the formative years of women's sport. *British Journal of Sports History* 2 (1): 40–52.

Hargreaves J. (1994) *Sporting Females: critical issues in the history and sociology of women's sport.* London: Routledge.

Hill, J (2002) *Sport, Leisure and Culture in Twentieth-Century Britain.* Houndmills: Palgrave.

Holt, A (1987) Hikers and Ramblers: surviving a thirties fashion. *International Journal of the History of Sport* 4 (1): 57–67.

Howkins, A and Lowerson, J (1979) *Trends in Leisure, 1919–1930.* London: The Sports Council and Social Science Research Council.

Huggins, M and Williams, J (2006) *Sport and the English, 1918–1939.* London: Routledge.

Lenskyj, H (1986) *Out of Bounds: women, sport and sexuality.* Toronto: The Women's Press.

Matthews, JJ (1990) They Had Such a Lot of Fun: the Women's League of Health and Beauty between the wars. *History Workshop Journal* 30: 23–54.

McCrone, K (1988) *Sport and the Physical Emancipation of English Women 1870–1914.* London: Routledge.

Oliver, L (1997) 'No Hard-Brimmed Hats or Hat-Pins Please'. Bolton women cotton-workers and the game of rounders, 1911–39. *Oral History* Spring: 40–5.

Osborne, CA (2005) Gender and the Organisation of British Climbing, c.1857–1955. PhD Thesis, University of Lancaster, UK.

Roberts, E (1984) *A Woman's Place: an oral history of working class women 1890–1940.* Oxford: Blackwell.

Skillen, F (2009) 'A Sound System of Physical Training': the development of girls' sports education in interwar Scotland. *History of Education* 38 (3): 403–18.

Skillen, F (2013) *Women, Sport and Modernity in Interwar Britain.* London: Peter Lang.

Spring-Rice, M (1939) *Working Class Wives: their health and conditions.* London: Pelican Books.

Todd, S (2005) Young Women, Work and Leisure in Interwar England. *The Journal of Historical Studies* 48 (3): 789–809.

Treagus, M (2005) Playing Like Ladies: basketball, netball and feminine restraint. *The International Journal of the History of Sport* 22 (1): 88–105.

Wagg, S (2011) 'Her Dainty Strength': Suzanne Lenglen, Wimbledon and the coming of female sport celebrity. In Wagg, S (ed.) *Myths and Milestones in the History of Sport.* Houndmills: Palgrave Macmillan, pp.122–40.

Wethered, J and Wethered, R (1922) *Golf from Two Sides.* London: Longman, Green and Co.

Williams, J (2003) *A Game For Rough Girls? A history of women's football in Britain.* London: Routledge.

Zweiniger-Bargielowska, I (2011) *Managing the Body: beauty, health and fitness in Britain, 1880–1939.* Oxford: Oxford University Press.

6

HISTORY OF GENDER AND GENDER EQUALITY IN THE OLYMPICS AND PARALYMPICS

Maureen M. Smith and Alison M. Wrynn

Introduction

To the contemporary spectator, the Olympic Games appear to be a sport setting where female athletes share virtually equal competitive space with males. Events are contested in the same arenas and sports grounds, women receive the same medals, and they appear equally devastated when they lose. Media coverage of female athletes is rich and detailed during the Games—designed, perhaps, to reinforce this notion of equity.

However, as one looks deeper into the Olympic Games, it is evident that gender inequity persists. Women have only recently approached having an equal number of competitive slots as men in the Summer Olympic Games, but there is a greater gender discrepancy in both the Winter Games and in the Paralympic Games. This chapter examines participation opportunities for women in the most recent summer and winter Olympic and Paralympic Games. It provides a brief analysis of women's historical participation in the Games and examines continuing challenges facing women participants and leaders in the Olympic Movement. It makes clear that male hegemony in the sports world continues to impact on women's opportunities as athletes and leaders in the Olympics and Paralympics, and that on-going male-dominated attitudes about women and their abilities still limit women's chances to compete in all events that are offered for men.

Historical struggles for inclusion and equity

In 1894, Frenchman Pierre de Coubertin founded the International Olympic Committee (IOC). It was his intent to provide for young men from around the world an outlet to exhibit their athletic talents. In particular he was concerned that French boys and men were not as interested in participating in vigorous sports as their British and American contemporaries. De Coubertin's vision was deeply imbued with nineteenth-century upper-class notions about appropriate events and competitions for elite male athletes. He was also influenced by the ancient Pan Hellenic athletic festivals. De Coubertin wanted to re-create an Olympic event exclusively in celebration of male athleticism, so women were barred from the first Summer Games in Athens in 1896. However, four years later, women were permitted to take part in 'unofficial' competitions, without official recognition or rewards. Women's events were very slowly added to future Olympic programmes, initially in upper-class sports such as golf, fencing, equestrian team events and tennis. As a result of struggle and compromise after the First World War the women's programme expanded to include other sports. Women were included in the inaugural Winter Olympic Games in Chamonix in 1924, again, also in a very limited manner (Wallechinsky, 2004).

Increasing the numbers of women in the Olympic programmes was slow. The main reason for their hindrance came from 'scientific' explanations of harm caused by athletic competition (Hargreaves, 1994, see Chapter 9). However, following the Second World War, when the Soviet Bloc nations entered the Games (Riordan, 1977), there was an accompanying expansion of the Summer Olympic programme for women. Soviet dominance in gymnastics and basketball encouraged other countries to take sport for women more seriously and the addition of team sports, in particular, boosted the numbers of female Olympians. Women did not surpass 20% of the Summer Olympic participants until the 1976 Games in Montreal.

In the final three decades of the twentieth century a number of events were added for women. Women were finally allowed to run the marathon distance in 1984, but it took until the Centennial Games in 1996 in Atlanta, USA, for women to be allowed to compete in football and a highly popular sport for women, softball—a sport which was subsequently cut from the Olympic programme after the 2008 Games.

In the twenty-first century, as women have pushed to be included in all facets of the Olympic programme, including wrestling, boxing and ski jumping, inequities remain. There are fewer weight classes in freestyle wrestling and boxing and there are still events women do not participate in, including the 50km race walk, shooting events, and some canoe/kayak events, as well as Greco Roman wrestling. Even when the number of events in a sport is equal for men and women, men outnumber women in those events. For example, in the sport of cycling, when the 2012 Olympic programme was modified to include five events for both male and female cyclists, male cyclists continued to outnumber female cyclists, 318 to 180.

Female participation in the Winter Olympic Games has increased even more slowly. The percentage of women did not exceed 30% until the 1994 Games in Lillehammer. Women were excluded from ski jumping and the Nordic combined events during the 2010 Games, although—after lengthy negotiations by individuals committed to gender equality—ski jumping will be on the programme for women in 2014 in Sochi, Russia (Thomas, 2011). However, women will still be excluded from the ski jumping team event, the larger hill jump, and the sport of Nordic Combined.

The 2012 Summer Olympic Games

The 2012 London Olympic Games accounted for a number of significant firsts for female athletes. Women accounted for just under 45% of Olympic participants, and for the first time competed in boxing. Three Arab countries included female athletes in their delegations for the first time as well: Brunei, Qatar and Saudi Arabia. Also, despite finishing 30 seconds behind her competitors in the 800m run, Sarah Attar was greeted at the finish line with a standing ovation for being the first Saudi Arabian woman to compete in an Olympic athletics competition. However, three countries also failed to include any female competitors: Barbados, Nauru and the Federation of Saint Kitts and Nevis. And for the first time in the organization and administration of the Games, Lord Sebastian Coe, Chair of the London Organizing Committee for the Olympic Games (LOCOG) had gender equity as a guiding principle in the organization and operation of both the Olympic and Paralympic Games (International Olympic Committee, 2012).

The 2012 Games were in some ways a celebration of women in the West. American women accounted for 56% of the United States' medal total, while Great Britain's women tallied ten gold medals, a number that would have placed them seventh in the medal standings. But this merely reflects the lack of women competitors overall from many National Olympic Committees (NOCs): the delegations of only 22 countries were comprised of at least 50% females.

Despite growing trends towards achieving gender equity at the Olympic Games, structural barriers remain in place that will keep women from achieving 50% participation in the Games overall. These structural barriers come from sports that allow for more male participants; sports that allow for more men's teams; and events offered to men only (Smith & Wrynn, forthcoming). These structural barriers remain firmly entrenched as a result of paternalist attitudes of the IOC preventing any significant movement towards eradicating gender inequalities for female athletes.

The 2010 Winter Olympic Games

At the most recent 2010 Winter Olympic Games in Vancouver, Canada, women made up only 40% of the participants and were only provided with the opportunity to compete in 41 of 86 total events. Male athletes received more competitive slots in Alpine skiing, luge, bobsleigh and ice hockey. Just as in the Summer Games, where women are forced to compete at shorter distances in a number of events compared to their male counterparts, this also occurred in winter sports. The Vancouver Games included 19 countries that did not send any female athletes (only two nations did not include men in their delegations). The Winter Games are a much smaller undertaking and geographical limitations restrict many countries from sending teams to these Games. Accordingly, compared to the Summer Games, far less attention has been paid to the exclusion of women (Smith and Wrynn, 2010).

One significant advance for women in the Winter Olympic Games came in 2011, when the IOC relented and have now included women's ski jumping in the 2014 Olympic programme in Sochi (Thomas, 2011). The inclusion of women's ski jumping came after much debate. IOC members were opposed to the event based on outdated ideas concerning the threat of damage to women's reproductive organs supposedly caused by the physical trauma inflicted on the body by ski jumping, despite women's participation in the sport for over one hundred years (Vertinsky, Jette, and Hofmann, 2009).

The Paralympic Games

If the Olympics have been slow to achieve gender equity in terms of the number of female participants, as well as the number of sport and event offerings, progress at the Paralympic Games has been even more exceptionally long and drawn out. The Paralympic Games were first held at the same time as the Summer Games only in 1960 in Rome, and the Winter Paralympics were first held in 1976 (DePauw & Gavron, 2005). The Rome Paralympics drew 44 women and 91 men (along with three athletes identified in mixed events, but not by gender). In the years since those initial Paralympic Summer Games, the rate of progress for female athletes has occurred in small increments. In the recently concluded 2012 London Games, women comprised less than 40% (1523 of 4302) of the Paralympic athletes. Smaller, less developed nations typically bring very small delegations to the Paralympics or do not even have a National Paralympic Committee (NPC) (there are only 175 NPCs, 164 of which competed in London, compared to 205 NOCs). Wealthier nations are able to provide more services to people with disabilities and generally have a larger number of athletes competing in the Paralympics.

In both the Summer and Winter Paralympic Games, male athletes are provided with more competitive (and potential medal-winning) classifications than their female counterparts. Women are also not given the opportunity to compete in football 5-a-side and football 7-a-side, or in some athletic events (for example, high jump, triple jump, and 4x400m relay). Sports specified as mixed typically include very few women. For example, in Wheelchair Rugby, 2 women joined 88 men in the competition. Only two sports (equestrian and rowing) had more female athletes than male athletes. However, some progress is being made in other sports, with female athletes making up over 40% of the participants in goalball, powerlifting, sitting volleyball, swimming, and wheelchair basketball in 2012.

The Winter Paralympic Games are slightly worse than the Summer Games in terms of the numbers of male and female participants. There are fewer sports and participation opportunities, but also shorter distances for female athletes. At the 2010 Winter Paralympic Games in Vancouver, females accounted for only 24% of the athletes. The sport of sledge hockey offered 117 participation opportunities for men, but although the International Paralympic Committee (IPC) announced that women could be added to the 2010 rosters, no women were included in this new 'mixed' sport (ctvolympics.ca, 2009). One mixed sport that has a better record of including female competitors is wheelchair curling. At the 2010 Winter Games, 15 women competed with 35 men in the mixed event. Female Paralympians compete in shorter distances in cross country skiing and the biathlon.

A variety of reasons have been suggested to explain differences in male and female participation in the Paralympic Games (Brittain, 2004, 2010; DePauw, 2001). One on-going contention is that more males than females have spinal cord injuries, and more men are injured in war, thus there is a larger population of men than of women to draw from (Shackelford, Farley, and Vines, 1998). However, the Paralympic Games include athletes with a variety of other disabilities that do not have such discrepancies between males and females. Female Paralympians also face stereotypes that focus on their perceived fragility, more than is the case for males, as well as facing challenges about appearing feminine while being athletic (Gilbert and Schantz, 2008).

Equity in events and participation opportunities

In spite of advances, gender equity remains a significant issue in both the Olympic and Paralympic Games; this is not just about equality of those participating either. There remain substantial barriers to women's representation behind the scenes as well: including low numbers of women in leadership positions in governing bodies, national federations, the IOC and the IPC (Smith and Wrynn, 2009, 2010, forthcoming; Zurn, Lopiano, and Snyder, 2006). It is in the governing body of the sport that decisions continue to be made that favour men. It is mathematically impossible for women to comprise 50% of all the athletes given the structurally based gender inequalities the IOC has created. Female athletes need to be afforded an equal number of competitive slots in sports where they are presently restricted.

Inequality also persists in terms of performance effort. To be equal, women should be allowed to race the same distances as male athletes. This would require changes to the Olympic and Paralympic programmes that might necessitate an expansion overall (Brennan, 2010). In the Paralympics this would include an extension of classifications within certain events.

With upcoming changes to the Olympic programme, including the addition of new sports, such as golf and rugby, several questions arise. What sports, and which athletes, would be prepared to see their numbers drop to allow for these new sports? If the Games cannot grow larger, which has been the mantra of the current IOC president, Jacques Rogge, how will more women be added to the programme? For example, when the sport of softball was cut, it eliminated over 100 women Olympians, with only 36 new women coming into the sport of boxing. The IOC has historically been willing to expand the number of Olympic participants through the wild card programme, which allows athletes from smaller NOCs to compete in swimming and athletics, despite not achieving the Olympic standard. However, the IOC is not willing to expand the Olympic programme to achieve gender equity through offering the same number of competitive slots in sports and events. It remains to be seen if the IOC will remove competitive slots for male athletes to keep the Games at their current size. It would be unfortunate if competitive opportunities were taken away from men, but if there is no other way to expand women's opportunities, this would be the only option. In a recent meeting of the IOC's Executive Board, the 15-member group voted to eliminate wrestling from the Olympic programme beginning in 2020, while agreeing to keep modern pentathlon. Wrestling will have one more opportunity to argue for its inclusion; however, if the IOC is successful in removing the ancient sport, it will mean a reduction of 344 total athletes, 268 men in Freestyle wrestling and Greco Roman wrestling, and 76 women in Freestyle wrestling. Such a reduction of male athletes actually helps the percentage of female athletes in terms of achieving equity. Unfortunately, it comes at the cost of male athletes and without any actual increase in the numbers of female athletes (Irving, 2013; Longman, 2013; Whiteside, 2013).

The issue of size is less about finances than about traditional attitudes concerned with keeping the length of the Games manageable, as well about the illusion of limiting competitors to the world's elite athletes (despite the inclusion of wild card athletes, who fail to meet the minimum qualification standards, but are included to ensure the participation of the highest number of NOCs). To reach gender equity in the Paralympic Games is a more basic challenge at present, since those Games have yet to achieve 40% female participation. New strategies must be implemented to help boost the participation opportunities for female athletes with disabilities at all levels, with the aim of enhancing their numbers at the highest level of competition (International Olympic Committee, 2002).

Muslim women in the Olympics

Muslim countries that have historically sent no female athletes as part of their delegations have made improvements over the last several Olympiads, providing models for other Islamic and Arab countries to emulate (Benn, Pfister, and Jawad, 2010). Issues related to modesty, women competing in the presence of men, rules by sport governing bodies specific to uniforms that prevent Muslim women from wearing head scarves, and differing interpretations of Islamic beliefs make the participation of Muslim women varied by NOC (Benn et al., 2010; Khaleeli, 2012; Walseth and Fasting, 2003). At the London 2012 Games, Saudi Arabia's Wojdan Shahrkhani, competing in the +78kg weight class in judo, initially was not allowed to compete in a head scarf for safety concerns. Eventually, following lengthy negotiations, the ruling was overturned, allowing Shahrkhani to participate wearing a modified head covering. In addition to the need to be included, women from some Muslim nations also need access to training opportunities in their home countries.

As noted earlier, three Muslim nations sent women to the Olympic Games for the first time in 2012. This came as a result of extensive pressure on the NOCs of Brunei, Qatar and Saudi Arabia, and illustrates the power the IOC is able to exert over NOCs. Financial incentives, in the form of additional Olympic Solidarity funding, could be provided to countries that demonstrate improvement in gender equity in participation and leadership. Less developed countries need to be encouraged and supported in their training of Paralympic athletes as these countries are underrepresented in the Paralympic Games.

Women in leadership

The IOC has been very slow to include women in their leadership structures. The first two female members of the IOC were added in the early 1980s, Pirjo Haggman of Finland and Venezuela's Flor Isava-Fonseca. The first IOC World Conference on Women and Sport was held in 1996. At this initial meeting the need to bring women into the leadership structure was discussed and an initial 10% threshold for including women in leadership structures in the Olympic Movement was established. In addition, a Women and Sport Working Group was created within the IOC (it was not accorded the status of official Commission until 2004). Beginning with their Brighton Declaration, in 1994, WomenSports International, working in conjunction with the United Nations, contended that girls and women needed access to sport throughout the world and that sport participation led to a greater sense of empowerment for young women.

In 2000 the IOC established a 20% threshold for female involvement in all leadership structures across the Olympic Movement—including the IOC, the International Federations and NOCs. This threshold was to be reached by 2005; and even in 2012 the IOC had still not quite reached its own 20% threshold. There are now three women included on the 15 member Executive Committee of the IOC for the first time in history.

The 5th IOC World Conference on Women and Sport was held in 2012 in Los Angeles, California. Once again, one of the primary topics of discussion was the need to include more women in the leadership structures of elite sports. Best practices were examined, including by the International Triathlon Union which has 35% female representation on its Executive Board and was led by a woman, Marisol Casado. There is only one other female president of a summer sport International Federation (IF), HRH Princess Haya Bint Al Hussein of the Fédération Equestrian Internationale. The other 26 federation presidents are men. This is still a better situation than the seven Winter Sport IFs which as of the 2010 Games had no female presidents.

Realizing a need to find a way to include more women in the leadership structure of the Olympic Movement, the IOC commissioned a report on the status of women in leadership positions in the Olympics. This report, released in 2010, determined that it was not enough for change to occur at the top of the structures—which is what the IOC 20% threshold was attempting to accomplish—but that modifications needed to happen within the entire organization in order for women to be prepared to lead organizations from the top (Henry and Robinson, 2010). Within the Paralympic Movement a higher standard of 30% for the inclusion of women in leadership structures has been set. Although the IPC and its affiliated structures have not quite reached that number (most hover in the mid-20% range) they are higher than most traditional Olympic leadership structures.

Unless the IOC mandates women's place in the leadership hierarchy—and then holds groups accountable when they do not meet the standard—or sets a goal of 50% instead of 20% for true gender equity, the movement towards parity will be thwarted. The IOC has finally pressured all participating NOCs to include female athletes in their delegations, which marks a significant achievement in the fight for gender equity in the Olympic Games.

Sexual and gender minorities

The IOC, in 2004, established a policy on transsexual athletes, which allows transgender athletes to compete if they meet three conditions: gender reassignment surgery, legal recognition of their gender reassignment, and at least two years of hormone therapy (Sykes, 2006). Other sporting organizations have modelled their policies on transgender athlete participation on the IOC policy. Born female but identifying as male, Keelin Godsey, an American hammer thrower, sought to qualify in the women's hammer throw, and had he qualified would have been the first openly identified transsexual athlete in the Olympic Games. After failing to qualify, Godsey indicated he would begin the medical phase of his transition, thus ending any chance of competing in the women's event (Borden, 2012).

Despite the fact that mandatory gender testing has ended, there will be continued concerns over athletes who do not fit neatly into a gender binary. Caster Semenya of South Africa, who competed in the 800m in Athletics at London, is the most recent example of this contentious issue. Semenya won silver in 2012, over two years after the International Association of Athletics Federation (IAAF) required her to submit to a gender test (at the time, Semenya believed she was being drug tested) at the African Juniors Championships in 2009. Results of the gender test have never been released, but Semenya competed in the women's 800m run in London (Buzuvis, 2011; Ellison, 2012; Levy, 2009; Nyong'o, 2010; Schultz, 2011). Currently, the IOC continues to deal with gender verification on a case-by-case basis. The inclusion of gender minorities in sport, as well as gender testing, is addressed at length elsewhere in the handbook.

The issue of lesbians (and gay men) in Olympic and Paralympic sport has not been addressed by the IOC. Representatives from the Federation of Gay Games commented that there was a complete lack of discussion on lesbian issues at the 5th IOC World Conference on Women and Sport, held in 2012. This was despite the fact that homophobia is evident in the Olympic Movement. The most obvious example was in 2011 when the head coach of the Nigerian women's football team claimed to have 'driven' all the lesbians off her team (Ziegler, 2012). Recent statements by the head of USA boxing also indicate a serious lack of sensitivity to issues surrounding homophobia in the Olympic Movement (Kiue, 2012).

Conclusions

This (2013) is the final year of Jacques Rogge's term as President of the IOC. His legacy, as it relates to gender, specifically women's participation in the Olympic Games, is still undetermined. The Games have seen an expansion in the number of participation slots for women during his tenure; however, his attitudes about women have not been positive. Rogge pushed for the elimination of women's softball and has talked about women's ice hockey not being competitive enough. He also resisted the inclusion of ski jumping for women (Associated Press, 2010; Brennan, 2009).

At this point in Olympic Games history, much progress has been made. The Games are a mega-event that de Coubertin would have a difficult time recognizing, notwithstanding his dismay at the inclusion of women in so many sports in such great numbers. As the Games move forward in the twenty-first century, if female Olympians continue to have consistent and sustained successes, opportunities should continue to grow. This will not happen without vigilance on the part of advocates for women in the Olympic and Paralympic movements. However, the story of women's progress in the Olympic Games and Paralympic Games is one of progress without full equity.

References

Associated Press (2010) Disparity could erase women's hockey. *ESPN Winter Olympics*, 26 February, available at http://sports.espn.go.com/olympics/winter/2010/icehockey/news/story?id=4947679
Benn T, Pfister G and Jawad H (2010) *Muslim Women and Sport*. London: Routledge.

Borden S (2012) Transgender Athlete Fails to Qualify. *New York Times*, 21 June, available at http://london2012.blogs.nytimes.com/2012/06/21/transgender-athlete-fails-to-qualify/

Brennan C (2009) Under Rogge, Women's Sports are Getting Short Shrift in the Olympics. *USA Today*, 22 April, available at http://usatoday30.usatoday.com/sports/columnist/brennan/2009-04-22-olympics_N.htm

Brennan C (2010) Jacques Rogge's IOC No Advocate for Women Athletes. *USA Today*, 25 February, available at http://www.usatoday.com/sports/columnist/brennan/2010-02-24-IOC-women_N.htm?POE=click-refer

Brittain I (2004) Perceptions of disability and their impact upon involvement in sport for people with disabilities at all levels. *Journal of Sport & Social Issues 28*: 429–452.

Brittain I (2010) *The Paralympic Games Explained*. London: Routledge.

Buzuvis E (2011) Caster Semenya and the Myth of a Level Playing Field. *The Modern American*, 6, 6.

ctvolympics.ca (2009) Sledge Hockey Teams Can Add Women For 2010 Games. *TSN*, 3 April, available at http://www.tsn.ca/olympics/story/?id=273618

DePauw KP (2001) The Paralympic Movement: Past, present, and future. *Journal of the International Council for Health, Physical Education, Recreation, Sport & Dance 37*(2): 42–47.

DePauw KP and Gavron SJ (2005) *Disability Sport*, 2nd ed. Champaign, IL: Human Kinetics.

Ellison J (2012) Caster Semenya and the IOC's Gender Bender. *The Daily Beast*, 26 July, available at http://www.thedailybeast.com/articles/2012/07/26/caster-semenya-and-the-ioc-s-olympics-gender-bender.html

Gilbert K and Schantz OJ (eds) (2008) *The Paralympic Games: Empowerment or side show?* Maidenhead: Meyer & Meyer.

Hargreaves J (1994) *Sporting Females: Critical issues in the history and sociology of women's sports*. London: Routledge.

Henry IP and Robinson L (2010) *Gender Equality and Leadership in Olympic Bodies: Women, leadership and the Olympic Movement, 2010*. Lausanne: International Olympic Committee.

International Olympic Committee (2012) 5th IOC Conference on Women and Sport Calls for More Women in Leadership Roles. Available at http://www.olympic.org/losangeles2012

International Olympic Committee (2002) Comparative Evolution of Women's Participation in the Olympic Games. Available at http://multimedia.olympic.org/pdf/en_report_206.pdf; updated as Women's Participation, http://multimedia.olympic.org/pdf/en_report_993.pdf

Irving J (2013) How Wrestling Lost the Olympics. *New York Times*, 15 February, available at http://www.nytimes.com/2013/02/16/opinion/how-wrestling-lost-the-olympics.html?_r=0

Khaleeli H (2012) Sports Hijabs Help Muslim Women to Olympic Success. *The Guardian*. 23 July, available at http://www.guardian.co.uk/sport/the-womens-blog-with-jane-martinson/2012/jul/23/sports-hijabs-muslim-women-olympics

Kiue D (2012) USA Boxing's Hal Adonis: 'Most Female Boxers are Lesbians Who Were Molested as Little Girls.' *KOCO Sports*, 27 October, available at http://kocosports.com/2012/10/27/boxing/usa-boxings-hal-adonis-most-female-boxers-are-lesbians-who-were-molested-as-little-girls/

Levy A (2009) Either/or: Sports, sex, and the case of Caster Semenya. *New Yorker*, November: 46–59.

Longman J (2013) Olympic Fixture Since 708 B.C. Will Be Dropped. *New York Times*, 12 February, available at http://www.nytimes.com/2013/02/13/sports/olympics-may-drop-wrestling-in-2020.html?pagewanted=all

Nyong'o T (2010) The Unforgivable Transgression of Being Caster Semenya. *Women & Performance: A Journal of Feminist Theory 20*(1): 95–100.

Riordan J (1977) *Sport in Soviet Society: Development of sport and physical education in Russia and the USSR*. Cambridge: Cambridge University Press.

Schultz J (2011) Caster Semenya and the Question of 'Too': Sex testing in elite women's sport and the issue of advantage. *Quest*, 63(2): 228–243.

Shackelford M, Farley T and Vines CL (1998) A comparison of women and men with spinal cord injury. *Spinal Cord 36*: 337–339.

Smith MM and Wrynn AM (forthcoming) Women in the 2012 Olympic and Paralympic Games: An analysis of participation and leadership opportunities. *A Women's Sports Foundation Research Report*. New York: Women's Sports Foundation.

Smith MM and Wrynn AM (2010) Women in the 2002, 2006 and 2010 Winter Olympic and Paralympic Games: An analysis of participation and leadership opportunities. *A Women's Sports Foundation Research Report*. New York: Women's Sports Foundation.

Smith MM and Wrynn AM (2009) Women in the 2000, 2004 and 2008 Olympic and Paralympic Games: An analysis of participation and leadership opportunities. *A Women's Sports Foundation Research Report.* New York: Women's Sports Foundation.

Sykes H (2006) Transexual and transgender policies in sport. *Women in Sport and Physical Activity Journal* 15(1): 3–13.

Thomas K (2011) After Long Fight for Inclusion, Women's Ski Jumping Gains Olympic Status. *New York Times*, 6 April, available at http://www.nytimes.com/2011/04/07/sports/skiing/07skijumping.html?_r=0

Vertinsky P, Jette S and Hofmann A (2009) 'Skierinas' in the Olympics: Gender politics at the local, national and international level over the challenge of women's ski jumping. *Olympika XVIII*: 25–56.

Wallechinsky D (2004) *The Complete Book of the Olympics: Athens 2004 edition.* Wilmington, DE: Sport Media Publications.

Walseth K and Fasting K (2003) Islam's View on Physical Activity and Sport. *International Review for the Sociology of Sport* 38(1): 45–60.

Whiteside K (2013) Olympic Wrestling Faces Uphill Battle for Reinstatement. *USA Today*, 13 February, available at http://m.usatoday.com/article/news/1915305

Ziegler C (2012) Olympics' Women in Sport Conference Virtually Ignores Lesbian Issues. *Outsports.com*, 5 March, available at http://outsports.com/jocktalkblog/2012/03/05/olympics-women-in-sport-conference-virtually-ignores-lesbian-issues/

Zurn L, Lopiano D and Snyder M (2006) Women in the 2006 Olympic and Paralympic Winter Games: An analysis of participation, leadership and media coverage. East Meadow, NY: Women's Sports Foundation.

7

THE GENDERED GOVERNANCE OF ASSOCIATION FOOTBALL

Jean Williams

There now remain a few subjects upon which the FA have taken a definite stand from the beginning and remained unwavering in their attitude towards them. Amongst these may be counted Women's Football, Greyhound Racing, Betting and Rough Play [sic].

(Green 1953: 533)

Introduction

Geoffrey Green is regarded as an innovator of serious popular writing about Association Football, having produced articles in *The Times* during the 1930s. His seminal history of the Football Association (FA) was written ninety years after the governing body was formed by 'gentlemen and scholars' in 1863 (Mason 1980: 10). Green consigned women football players as a rather irritating problem but not 'a subject ever to bring about a crisis within the Association' (Green 1953: 533). Another writer who sought to distill the essence of the game for the informed enthusiast, Brian Glanville (1973), was no more of a fan of women playing football than Green. In this, they reflected the orthodoxy of the time.

Both men supported the FA ban against female players issued in 1921 that lasted almost fifty years. This was their resolution:

Complaints have been made as to football being played by women, the Council feel impelled to express their strong opinion that the game of football is quite unsuitable for females and ought not to be encouraged.

Complaints have also been made as to the conditions under which some of these matches have been arranged and played, and the appropriation of the receipts to other than Charitable objects. The Council are further of the opinion that an excessive proportion of receipts are absorbed in expenses and an inadequate percentage devoted to Charitable objects. For these reasons the Council request the clubs belonging to the Association to refuse the use of their grounds for such matches.

(The Football Association 1921: 3)

The FA Council reissued this ruling repeatedly during the life of the ban, most noticeably in 1946 (The Football Association 1946: 7). The tone of exclusion still defines the participation of women and girls to some extent today, although much has changed in the last sixty years.

England's (men's) Football World Cup victory of 1966 has been constantly presented as a historical moment in the Association game, especially in Britain. The Final tournament was relatively small, limited to sixteen teams, although the commercial marketing was innovative. This enabled consumers of all kinds to follow England in new ways: a smiling, furry 'World Cup Willie' was the first England mascot, for example, and the 'King of Skiffle' Lonnie Donegan's (1965) unofficial anthem of the same name reminded punters: 'He's tough as a lion and never will give up, That's why he is the favourite for the Cup' (1965). Copyrighted images of World Cup Willie appeared on the record cover by permission of the FA.

One of the myths frequently told about 1966 is that it inspired a whole generation of women to begin playing football (Lopez 1997: 42–43; Owen 2005: 13–15). However, another possible interpretation is that football was more successful in selling its many wares to female fans than in encouraging female players – an issue beyond the scope of this chapter. The Women's Football Association (WFA) was created in 1969, but although for some important England international players and coaches, such as Lopez and Owen, 1966 did seem to be some sort of catalyst, the general situation was considerably more complex (Williams 2003, 2007). There is emerging evidence of a continuity of interest in women playing football worldwide from the first recorded games in the 1880s.

In 2011, the 'Lino-gate' controversy in England involved two television presenters, Richard Keys and Andy Gray, who made disparaging remarks about the assistant referee of a men's game, Sian Massey, insinuating that she did not understand the offside rule (Taylor 2011). However, although sacked from Sky Television, Keys and Grey were then reportedly employed on six figure salaries by the radio programme, TalkSport (Plunkett 2011). This event reflects the enduring demeaning of women by men and misogynist customs, even although the highly skilled participation of women in football over the last century is now well-established in academic circles and cultural industries (Pielichaty 2009; Yates and Vasili, 2011; Dhami 2011).

But the suicide in 1998 of Justin Fashanu – the first professional footballer to come out as gay – was a harsh reminder that discrimination resulting from homophobia was also rife. Since then, greater acceptance of difference, and anti-discrimination activity in sport in relation to gender and sexuality, have increased. For example, in 2009 the Welsh rugby international with over 100 caps, Gareth Thomas, came out to widespread admiration, and cricket was equally supportive of Steve Davies in 2011. Then, although in 2012 the FA launched an anti-homophobia campaign, it was criticised by John Amaechi as a cosmetic attempt to repair the damage of a wider organizational culture populated by 'eighteenth-century dinosaurs' (BBC 2012). Football's understanding of gender and sex discrimination appears to be less progressive than in some other sport cultures. For example, male chauvinism in football, like that encouraged by the BBC's *Radio 5 Live* chat show, continues to thrive, tending to drown out the quietly supportive volunteer culture and huge developments in women's football. As a consequence, prominent female England international players, coaches and administrators remain guarded about their sexuality and private lives (Smith 2012).

These are depressing aspects of the sports' present reality in Britain, but in other countries gender discrimination and homophobia can be extreme, dangerous and even a threat to life. For example, in 2009, Eudy Simelane, former star of South Africa's acclaimed Banyana Banyana national female football squad and an equal rights campaigner, was 'correctively' gang-raped and killed for being a lesbian (Kelly 2011). In Britain, the lack of transparency and opportunity at elite levels of administration and play are 'polite' forms of exclusion compared with cruel intimidation, violence and murder. As Jayne Caudwell's (2002) work on gender, sexuality and race reminds us, categorising women by their commonality can divert attention from differences between them. While Simelane was killed in South Africa because of her sexuality, some lesbian players in Britain have found empowerment in, and through, football.

The debate about gender and sex discrimination is also considered here in a wider context of the gendered performance of football as a profession. In Italy, in 1999, a star football player, Carolina Morace, accepted an appointment to third division (men's) Italian side Viterbese. She resigned after two matches to become coach to the women's national team. In 2003 Italian side Perugia made an offer to German World Cup winner Birgit Prinz; the club had previously tried to sign Sweden's Hannah Ljungberg which would have made her the first female player in Series A. In 2004 Maribel Dominguez reportedly signed for Mexican men's side Celaya. But 'mixed' football teams of male and female players remain one of the most controversial and contested issues at all levels of the game and women-only professional football remains the norm.

The language we use to describe female participation is problematic. 'Football' usually means the game as played by men and boys: 'women's football' is, observers insist, a different variant. 'The women's game' and other descriptors therefore express gender differences in ways that are both symbolic and embodied (Kunz 2010: 44–45). For example, you might see a male referee in a women's game but are much less likely to see a female referee in a men's match and as in the case of the Lino-gate incident, the myth that women are incapable of understanding football's intricacies continues to be recycled by the media.

There is also a fundamental problem relating to the exclusion of women from football's managerial elite, although there has been a shift towards more women representatives. The Union of European Football Association (UEFA) was formed in Switzerland in 1954 with thirty member associations and today fifty-three countries are affiliated (Turner and Idorn 2004: 140–141). UEFA has grown from an administrative body with three people working full-time in 1960 to an organization of over 340 employees functioning across multiple languages and cultures. It first had a European women's competition in 1984. Karen Espelund, a respected Norwegian player and administrator who headed the UEFA women's committee, was 'co-opted' on to the seventeen-person executive board in 2011. Then, in 2012, Lydia Nsekera, President of the Burundi Football Association; a member of the FIFA Committee for Women's Football and the FIFA Organising Committee for the Olympic Football Tournaments, became the first woman to be co-opted on to the FIFA Executive Committee. Women have led both national associations and territorial bodies – for example, Josephine King was General Secretary of the Oceania Football Confederation (OFC). Nsekera became the first elected women to join FIFA's twenty-five-strong Executive Committee, though two additional elected female posts supplemented her appointment.

In this chapter, I consider the history of organized women's football going back to 1881, including the high profile of female players between 1917 and 1921, and some recent twenty-first century developments in professionalizing football for women. A particular focus is the gendered governance of football and its effect on the orthodoxy of 'recent' interest among women players.

A brief overview of women's football from 1881 to 1951

The first example of international women's football was probably an unofficial game played under some FA rules in 1881, between teams calling themselves Scotland and England. The English Hopewell sisters, Mabel, Maude and Minnie, deserve their place in football's hall of fame as pioneers. Nevertheless the Scottish players were far superior, winning by three goals to nil. The British Ladies' Football Club, formed in London in 1895, combined the talents of middle-class Nettie Honeyball as player–secretary with the non-playing president, Lady Florence Dixie. Honeyball, Mrs Graham and 'Tommy' briefly became stars until 1897. There is emerging evidence of female football during the next twenty years when it received transnational impetus from the gymnasium movement in France and the changing nature of women's work in Britain to become unprecedentedly popular (Williams 2007).

Between 1917 and 1921, 'Munitionettes' football involved women playing matches in front of crowds of up 55,000 in aid of charity (Brennan 2007). The most famous team, Dick, Kerr's Ladies had began to play seriously in October 1917, based at the Strand Road tram building and light railway works, originally founded by W. B. Dick and John Kerr of Kilmarnock (Newsham 1998). However, the team would play more in peacetime than during hostilities. There were other work-based women's teams such as Horrockses' Ladies, of the mill owned by the family known as the Cotton Kings of Preston, and Atalanta, an affiliation of professional women, such as teachers and nurses. The Lancashire United Transport Company based in Atherton had a female team as early as 1915 and the women of the Preston Army Pay Corps soon after. Lyons tearooms had several women's football squads. Football was an example of 'rational recreation', providing social and community benefits. It is difficult to know whether players received payment in addition to expenses, but Lily Parr, one of the most famous Dick, Kerr players' was said to have received 'broken-time' payments of ten shillings a game in her career (Williams 2003: 25). There were up to 150 such teams and some evidence of regional league structures.

French female football teams were also founded by 1916: the Fédération des Societies Feminines Sportives de France (FSFSF) was established and organized a national championship for teams from Marseille, Rheims, Paris and Toulouse. Alice Joséphine Marie Million, a young rower from Nantes in France, became an important figure for international women's sport (Drevon 2005: 5). Married (Alice Milliat), then widowed, she worked as a translator and became President of the Femina women's sports club in 1915. En Avant and Académia also supported a range of physical activities including football and rugby (barette). A French national track and field athletics meeting in 1917 showcased some of the leading all-round sportswomen like javelin and shot put enthusiast Violette Gourard Morris. 'La Morris', as she became celebrated, was an imposing athlete who also boxed, swam, played football and drove cars professionally (Bouzanquet 2009: 24–25).

International games became more widespread. England played an Irish eleven in Belfast over Christmas 1917 (Brennan 2007: 37). However, some teams who called themselves England, Ireland or Scotland did so in order to sharpen local loyalties and should perhaps be considered works' teams. Visits between Femina and English teams, including Dick, Kerr's, were sustained from 1920 until well after World War Two. They illustrate a form of practical feminism of working-class women, combined with the political activism of the middle classes and civic boosterism. The games raised money for charities, and local communities respected the women players. However, in spite of crowds of up to 53,000 at Everton in 1920, the supposed misuse of money raised for charity, as outlined in the introduction, resulted in the FA ban of women's football in 1921.

Women's football also developed in Germany and Austria after the First World War and there is some evidence of a game in Russia. The United States and Canada had college-based soccer programmes for women since the early 1920s, at least, and there is some evidence of female college players in Hong Kong. When the Fédération Française de Football (FFF) was founded in 1919 it refused to accept ladies' teams as members but did not institute a ban on their play. Jules Rimet, who became president of both the FFF and FIFA, assisted in two female Paris-based matches attended by 10,000 spectators in 1920 (Dietschy 2010: 503). European associations had a rather haphazard approach to formal and informal prohibition (Williams 2007: 24). In 1919 Austrian Weekly *Allgemeine Sport-Zeitung*, based in Vienna, reported matches; in 1920 a Frankfurt women's football team turned to rowing after public ridicule; and by 1925 there were debates in *Sport und Sonne* about the essentially masculine nature of football – an article headline claimed, 'Das Fussbalspiel ist Männerspiel' ('Football is a Man's Game' – Hoffmann and Nendza 2006: 14).

The German Football Association (Deutscher Fußball-Bund (DFB)) regularly discouraged women from playing and banned men's teams from forming women's squads. Opportunities and attitudes to women's sports were, nevertheless, changing – for example, the elegant 'sport girl' exemplified by the willowy tennis player in whites and the 'new woman' of boxing and athletics in the Weimar Republic graced the covers of *Sport und Sonne* in the 1930s (Jensen 2011: 25). Pioneers of women's football, like nineteen-year-old Lotte Specht, were represented in the Frankfurt weekly press looking very much like they had just played a hard match. However, only around forty women played for DFC Frankfurt in 1930 while 850,000 female participants took part in the nationalistic gymnastics' Turnen movement. Emerging evidence shows a history of female football as a European-wide activity, albeit on a relatively small scale (Hoffmann and Nendza 2006: 24).

Although women's football was becoming more widespread, representatives of the female game were not part of the expansion of FIFA at a crucial early period in world governance. By 1924 all the continental European countries had joined FIFA (though the English FA was to leave on more than one occasion until after World War Two). By 1928, football became more global when the Southern hemisphere appeared on the cover of the FIFA handbook for the first time. In an effort to establish FIFA's independence from the International Olympic Committee (IOC) and because of the success of the football tournaments at the 1924 and 1928 Games (both won by Uruguay), the first World Cup was held in that country in 1930.

However, the 1930 tournament has been described as localized rather than a world event, with Belgium, France, Romania and Yugoslavia the only four European countries present (Taylor 2007: 7–30). Uruguay won and the competition produced impressive financial returns. The World Cup hosted by Italy four years later took on a political dimension, due to Mussolini's presence, and the home team won in an intensely nationalistic atmosphere. The remaining inter-war competition took place in France in 1938 (won again by Italy). Lack of South American participation and European turmoil meant that the title of World Cup was somewhat misleading and it was to be the last tournament for twelve years. At its resumption in Brazil in 1950, World Cup competition was thereafter to be an important means of stimulating football's worldwide development and commercial profile (Glanville, 1980).

Women's football and changing global governance 1951–2012

In 1951, six European states formed the European Coal and Steel Community (ECSC), via the Treaty of Paris. This began a process of economic integration which now involves thirty states in a complex arrangement of political, social and cultural ties in the European Union (EU). Increased European connectivity coincided in 1951 with an event that seemed entirely unrelated. T. Cranshaw of the Nicaraguan football association wrote to the secretary of FIFA, concerned that he had seen women's football in Costa Rica and knew of almost 20,000 female players in the United States (Eisenberg et al., 2004: 187). FIFA responded that it had no control over women's football and could not rule or guide on this issue. The Manchester Corinthians – an amateur team – had formed in 1949 and had already played against British and French opponents (Williams 2003: 54). Manchester Corinthians were holders of the 1951 Festival of Britain trophy, one of many unofficial 'national' tournaments for women's teams from the United Kingdom at the time.

In West Germany, Ingrid Heike and Ildiko Vaszil founded a club in 1955, in spite of a ruling that women were not recognised by the DFB that year (Hoffmann and Nendza 2006: 32). The club joined a network, centred on Duisburg, to form a West German Women's Football Association. With backing from Essen businessman Willi Ruppert as the Chair, it became the German Ladies' Football Association. An international game against the Netherlands took place in 1956. Recorded for the weekly newsreel, *Die Wochenschau*, Germany won 2-1. An inter-club competition, titled the European championship, was hosted under the auspices of an International Ladies' Football Association in 1957 (Eisenberg et al. 2004: 187). Teams from England, Austria, Luxembourg, the Netherlands and West Germany took part. Manchester Corinthians won the tournament, led by their thirty-three year old captain, Doris Ashley. The high profile tournament was an important moment in the continuing internationalisation of women's football

Interest by business and commercial sponsors pre-dated the creation of an official FIFA World Cup by twenty years. By 17 May 1968 nine Italian women's football teams had announced formation of the Federazione Italiana Calcio Femminile (FICF) in Viareggio (Ambrosiana, Cagliari, Fiorentina, Genova, Lazio, Napoli, Milano, Piacenza and Roma) with Real Torino joining a year later (*The Times* 18 May 1968: 8). In November 1969, another organization, the Fédération Internationale Européenne de Football Féminine (FIEFF) ran a 'world cup' tournament with the support of drinks company Martini and Rossi. In the four-team tournament in Turin, Italy, Denmark, England and France were provided with kit, equipment, all-expenses-paid travel and accommodation. This was another milestone in the global awareness of the women's game. A third Italian professional women's league, the Federazione Femminile Italiana Gioco Calcio (FFIGC), was established in Rome in 1970 with fourteen teams. The resulting women's world championship there in 1970 and another in Mexico in 1971 meant that businessmen independent of the governing bodies had begun to explore the commercial potential of female football at the elite level. This prompted FIFA to accept responsibility for all football activities or see the women's game go its own way. The ban on women's football was lifted piecemeal by national associations in the 1970s; in England in 1971 in Brazil in 1975 (The Football Association 1969).

This new attitude to female players coincided with the 1972 Equal Rights Amendment of the American constitution. In the same year Title IX of the Education Amendments to the Civil Rights Act of 1964 began to realign federal-funded education programmes to achieve gender equity in the United States. The broad application of this legislation later led to the 1979 Title IX Athletics Policy Interpretation. The correlation between the introduction of Title IX and an increase in both female sport and physical education is compelling. By the early 1990s women who had come through college soccer programmes and been selected for the Women's National Team, were becoming aspirational role models for other young women. The first FIFA Women's World Championship was held in PR China in 1991 and the country also hosted the 2007 Women's World Cup (WWC). The United States has held two WWC competitions – in 1999 and 2003; Sweden hosted the WWC in 1995; and in 1996, the USA showcased women's Olympic football. Thereafter, Australia, Greece and China were hosts of Olympic women's football. FIFA awarded the finals of the WWC to Germany in 2011, breaking attendance records for a female-only tournament on the continent. The final also created a new record of over 7,100 Twitter social networking messages a second: more than world events like the British Royal Wedding, the death of Osama Bin Laden or the Japanese Tsunami the same year (Fanning 2011). During the 2012 Olympic Games in London, over 660,000 people attended women's matches. However, it is well to remember that national associations routinely under-fund their women's national teams. The 'Iron Roses' of PR China were noticeably absent from the 2011 WWC finals for the first time ever, for example.

By 1991, first Michelle Akers, then Mia Hamm, became international soccer stars. By the time of the 1999 World Cup, Hamm, the US national team's number 9 player, shared the limelight with Michael Jordan in the so-called 'consciousness industries' of commercial sporting products. Their media spin-offs promoted Hamm as the second most important Nike-sponsored athlete (Hamm 1999; Hamm and Thompson 2004). Hamm's story was of a child born with misshapen legs, but able to achieve world fame due to dedication and off-field modesty. The 1999 World Cup Final was a record-breaking event with 93,000 spectators and worldwide TV coverage. The twenty women of the US squad became sufficiently well known to found the Women's United Soccer Association (WUSA), a professional league in what has been called the most competitive sports market in the world. Perhaps uniquely, Mia, Julie, Joy, Kristine, Brandi, Michelle (along with Briana, Tiffeny and Carla) rose to levels of fame with the US public making surnames unnecessary.

Conclusion

The supposed 'newness' factor of women's interest in football is an invented tradition aimed to preserve an exclusively manly image and organizational culture of football's past which I have only briefly outlined. Since 1996, the crowded playing calendar of women's matches has included Olympic tournaments and confederation, regional and national competitions. There are now also two FIFA youth trophies; the U-20 and U-17 WWC tournaments, held in Germany and Trinidad and Tobago respectively in 2010. Gender remains a significant organizing principle. For example, the Olympic competition was more important for women who represented the female Great Britain team in 2012 than for the men who were allowed only four players aged over twenty-three in the squad. Issues to do with the sponsorship and the commercialization of women's football have become increasingly significant, but exploitation of women's links with popular culture has been slow. For example, Katie Taylor, a former member of Ireland's Women's National Team and the 2005 Irish Youth Footballer of the Year, competed in the 2012 London Olympics in boxing having held world championship belts in the under 60K category. Her commercial endorsements included a Lucozade promotion with members of a pop group. It is sometimes easier to earn a media profile as an individual athlete, even in a very new Olympic discipline like boxing, than as part of a team which relies on selection and the politics of team games ruled by diverse national associations.

The rise in the number and variety of international fixtures for women players is football's most conspicuous move toward equity in the last twenty years. The FA in England took full control of women's football as late as 1993; Scotland did not fully affiliate the Scottish Women's Football Association until 1998. Dramatic changes seemed to follow incorporation. In 2002 football overtook netball as the most popular participation sport in England, and there are now over 150,000 FA-affiliated female players. In both Scotland and England, we are constantly told that it is 'The Fastest Growing Team Sport' for females.

My recent book on female migration, *Globalising Women Football: Migration and Professionalisation 1971–2011*, has identified some trends relating to professional player career paths in football's global gendered labour market (Williams 2013). There is a gradual but widening public recognition of women who pioneered professional and semi-professional roles in football, in part due to the increasingly practice of electing key individuals to respective Halls of Fame. At the National Football Museum, Preston, England female inductees Debbie Bampton; Pauline Cope; Gillian Coultard; Sue Lopez; Lily Parr; Hope Powell; Brenda Sempare; Marieanne

Spacey; Karen Walker; and Joan Whalley are celebrated (National Football Museum 2011). At the Scottish Football Museum (2011) Rose Reilly was inducted in 2007. She remains the sole woman to be recognized in this way. Others, like Welsh international Karen Jones, have been awarded honours – in this case the Member of the Order of the British Empire (MBE) for services to football as an administrator and volunteer.

With an estimated 26 million female players globally, of which 6 million are based in Europe, the evolution of football as a sport and as an industry over the last sixty years has been dramatic (FIFA 2006). However, there are reasons to be cautious in the optimism that surrounds the growth of the women's game. The same survey claims only a total of 21 million *registered* European players, male and female, compared with an educated guess of 62 million unregistered participants. It is not uncommon to include those who intend to participate in the next year, as well as those who actually do play, for example. Globally today, even by FIFA's own enthusiastic figures, women make up ten per cent of the total number of football players *at best*.

When we look at elite players able to earn a living from the game, the gender disparity is amplified: of say 60,000 professional players registered in Europe, very few are women. This is striking because the idea of amateurism has, to a large degree, defined what it is to be a professional: under FIFA rules, if a player earns more for playing football than the expenses that are incurred, they must have a written contract and are thereby considered a professional. While those who do not meet these criteria are considered amateurs, the word professional encompasses essentially casual participants supplementing their main income through football, to the multi-millionaire male players of Europe's big five leagues in England, France, Germany, Italy and Spain. So, the following 'big' question remains: how many women are involved in professionalism in world football? I await the first female President of FIFA with some anticipation. I hope that she will be an admirable woman who will appoint her colleagues on the basis of competence rather than gender and gradually replace the 'little men in grey suits' who currently run the world game. I am equally impatient to hear the multiple stories of the world's female players. Even more, I look forward to a time when gender is only one of many differences celebrated in and through the world game, to better reflect global diversity.

References

BBC (2012) 'John Amaechi says "reactive" FA responsible for homophobia'. Alistair Magowan, BBC Sport 20 February 2012, http://www.bbc.co.uk/sport/0/football/17086342 (accessed 20 February 2012).

Bouzanquet, Jean-François (2009) *Fast Ladies: Female Racing Drivers 1888–1970*. Dorchester: Veloce.

Brennan, Patrick (2007) *The Munitionettes: A History of Women's Football in North East England During the Great War*. Donmouth: Donmouth Publishing.

Caudwell, Jayne (2002) 'Women's experiences of sexuality within football contexts: A particular and located footballing epistemology'. *Football Studies* Vol. 5 No. 1 pp. 24–45.

Dhami, Nrinder (2011) *Katy's Real Life: The Beautiful Game Series*. London: Orchard.

Dietschy, Paul (2010) *Histoire du Football*. Paris: Librairie Académique Perrin.

Donegan, Lonnie (1965) *World Cup Willy*. London: Pye Records, December.

Drevon, André (2005) *Alice Milliat: La Pasionaria du Sport Feminine*. Paris: Vuibert.

Eisenberg, Christiane, Pierre Lanfranchi, Tony Mason and Alfred Wahl (2004) *100 Years of Football: The FIFA Centennial Book*. London: Weidenfeld and Nicholson.

Fanning, Evan (2011) 'Women's World Cup final between USA and Japan sets Twitter record'. *The Guardian* 18 July 2011, http://www.guardian.co.uk/football/2011/jul/18/womens-world-cup-twitter-record (accessed 28 September 2011).

FIFA (2006) 'FIFA big count 2006: 270 million people active in football'. *FIFA.COM* http://www.fifa.com/aboutfifa/media (accessed November 2010).

Glanville, Brian (1973) 'Goals and gals don't really mix'. *The Sunday Times* 24 June.

Glanville, Brian (1980) *The Story of the World Cup*. London and Boston: Faber and Faber Ltd.

Green, Geoffrey (1953) *A History of the Football Association*. London: Naldrett.

Hamm, Mia (1999) *Go For the Goal: A Champion's Guide to Winning in Soccer and Life*. New York: Harper.

Hamm, Mia with Carol Thompson (2004) *Winners Never Quit!* New York: Byron Press Visual Publications.

Hoffmann, Eduard and Jürgen Nendza (2006) *Verlacht, Verboten und Gefeiert: Zur Geschichte des Frauenfußballs in Deutschland*. Weilerwist: Landpresse.

Jensen, Erik (2011) *Body by Weimar: Athletes Gender and German Modernity*. Oxford: Oxford University Press.

Kelly, Annie (2011) 'Raped and killed for being a lesbian: South Africa ignores "corrective" attacks'. *The Guardian* 12 March 2009, http://www.guardian.co.uk/world/2009/mar/12/eudy-simelane (accessed 28 September 2011).

Kunz, Matthias (2010) 'The female figure: Vital statistics from the women's game'. *FIFA World* Zurich: FIFA March.

Lopez, Sue (1997) *Women on the Ball: A Guide to Women's Football*. London: Scarlet.

Mason, Tony (1980) *Association Football and English Society 1863–1915*. Brighton: Harvester.

Newsham, G. (1998) *In A League of their Own*. London: Scarlet.

Owen, Wendy (2005) *Kicking Against Tradition: A Career in Women's Football*. London: Tempus.

Pielichaty, Helena (2009) *Do Goalkeepers Wear Tiaras Too?* London: Walker.

Plunkett, John (2011) 'Richard Keys and Andy Gray join TalkSport'. *The Guardian* 8 February 2011, http://www/guardian.co.uk (accessed 22 March 2011).

Scottish Football Museum (2011) 'Rose Reilly'. http://www.scottishfootballmuseum.org.uk/hall-of-fame/ (accessed 26 March 2013).

Smith Kelly (2012) *Footballer: My Story*. London: Bantam.

Taylor, Louise (2011) 'Sky Sports: the perfect TV set for the boors who will be boors'. *The Guardian* 27 January 2011, http://www.guardian.co.uk accessed (22 March 2011).

Taylor, Matthew (2007) *The Association Game: A History of British Football*. Harlow: Pearson Longman.

The Football Association (1921) *Minutes of the FA Consultative Committee*. 5 December.

The Football Association (1946) *Minutes of the FA Council*. 16 December.

The Football Association (1969) *Minutes of the FA Council*. Item 37, 1 December.

Turner, Graham and John Idorn (2004) *UEFA: 50 Years*. Nyon: UEFA.

Williams, J. (2003) *A Game for Rough Girls: A History of Women's Football in England*. Oxon: Routledge.

Williams, J. (2007) *A Beautiful Game: International Perspectives on Women's Football*. London: Berg.

Williams J. (2013) *Globalising Women's Football: Migration and Professionalisation 1971–2011*. Bern: Peter Lang.

Yates, Colin and Phil Vasili (2011) 'Moving the Goalposts: History of Women's Football in Britain Exhibition (1881–2011)'. *The Peoples History Museum in Manchester* 15 March 2011, http://www.football-fineart.com (accessed 12 April 2011).

8

A POST-COLONIAL CRITIQUE OF THE INTERNATIONAL 'MOVEMENTS' FOR WOMEN AND SEXUALITY IN SPORT

Elizabeth C.J. Pike and Jordan J.K. Matthews

Introduction

The existence of a variety of international organisations, networks, and individuals working to break down barriers for women in sport has been collectively recognised as 'a social movement which reputedly represents a global community of women from different countries and social and cultural groups throughout the world' (Hargreaves, 2000, p. 215). The shared mission of these groups is to break down participation barriers and enhance sporting opportunities for marginalised groups, particularly with respect to gender and sexuality issues. This chapter will draw on post-colonial feminist theory in order to critically evaluate the argument that policies have been dominated by Western ideologies, and to question whether there has ever even been a coherent 'movement' for gender and sexuality issues in sport. With no concrete framework of analysis, post-colonial feminism allows researchers to move away from macro-sociological theories and homogenisations in order to analyse 'marginal' or 'peripheral' groups of women (Mills, 1998).

The International Association of Physical Education and Sport for Girls and Women (IAPESGW) was formed in 1949 and is widely acknowledged as the first of many groups advocating the participation and involvement of women in sport and physical activity. Since then, several regional, national and international associations have formed with complementary agendas, but also with some important differences that bring into question the existence of a coherent 'movement' for women and sport.

For example, WomenSport International (WSI) was established in 1994 after initial debates that emanated from the 1993 North American Society for Sociology of Sport (NASSS) Conference in Ottawa, Canada. There was discussion of 'limited financial resources and some member discontent with IAPESGW's apparent lack of addressing important issues' (Kluka, 2008, p. 89). WSI's intention is to 'serve as an international umbrella organisation that can bring about positive change for girls and women in these important areas of their lives' (WSI, 2011), and uses evidence-based research to inform its direction. Also in 1994, the first formally recognised World Conference on Women and Sport was held in Brighton, UK, resulting in the *Brighton*

Declaration on Women and Sport, the establishment of the International Working Group (IWG) on Women and Sport and the *1994–1998 International Strategy on Women and Sport*. The *Declaration* has been described as a 'tool' (Houlihan and White, 2002, p. 65) and a 'valuable prop' (Hargreaves, 1999, p. 466) for understanding the issues confronted by women in sport. The Brighton Conference has been argued to have formed a new collective for the international women's sport movement and, since 1994, has facilitated activism across much of the world with subsequent quadrennial conferences held in Namibia, Canada, Japan and Australia (IWG, 2012).

In addition to the international organisations, there are regional associations such as European Women and Sport (EWS), the Sport Association of Arab Women (SAAW) and the African Women in Sport Association (AWISA). Established in 1993, EWS was the first European group dedicated to women and sport. Further regional groups emerged in other parts of the world due to the activism and support that emanated from the Brighton Conference. SAAW (for Arab women) was formed at the International Women and Sport Conference in Egypt, in 1995, and formally launched by the Council of Arab Ministers of Youth and Sport in 1996. The 1995 conference, according to White (1998, p. 45), 'without doubt gave momentum to Arab women's sport and provided a forum for exchange of ideas and the development of best practice that will benefit all Arab women'. AWISA (for African women) was officially launched in 1998 just before the 2nd IWG World Conference on Women and Sport in Windhoek, Namibia, after a committee of African women had informally met four years beforehand during the Brighton Conference (UK Sports Council, 1998).

At a national level, some of the more recognised groups are the Canadian Association for the Advancement of Women in Sport (CAAWS), established in 1981 and heavily involved with the post-2002 IWG World Conference on Women and Sport work in Montreal. The U.S. Women's Sport Foundation (WSF) was formed in 1974, and the United Kingdom WSF followed a decade later (it has since changed its name to the United Kingdom Women's Sport and Fitness Foundation (WSFF)). Each organisation continues to pressure and lobby relevant governmental, non-governmental and wider sporting groups in their country, in order to improve opportunities for women in sport.

While these organisations are ostensibly representative, and at the forefront of Women's and sexuality issues around the globe, membership of the various organisations has consisted predominantly of White, Western women and 'neo-colonial elites' – women from predominantly non-Western nations with a 'Western consciousness and strong links to state apparatuses and the Western "sports establishment"' (Hargreaves, 2000, p. 216). Hargreaves (2000) questions how representative neo-colonial elites are of non-Western people and groups.

Method and theoretical framework

This chapter forms part of a wider study that critically analyses the international women's sport organisations and activities, drawing on data collected by a mixed-methods approach. A documentary analysis was undertaken of meanings and relationships (Denscombe, 2004) evident in policies, committee meeting minutes, conference proceedings and published reports located in the Anita White Foundation International Women and Sport Archive based at the University of Chichester, UK. Themes from the documentary analysis informed a basic structure of questions that were asked of current and former personnel from IWG, WSI, EWS and WSFF personnel.

It is worthy of note that this chapter draws on the work of two researchers: both White Westerners, one male (Matthews) and one female (Pike). We were careful to adopt research processes and analysis informed by feminist ideology 'in relation to feminism's central tenets, thus allowing women's voices to be heard, exploitation being reduced by giving as well as receiving during fieldwork and women not to be treated as objects to be controlled' (Bryman and Teevan, 2005, p. 161).

Advocates of post-colonial feminist theory criticise Western feminists who argue as if women, and especially women from the non-Western developing world, are a homogenous group (Lewis and Mills, 2003; Mohanty, 1995; Spivak, 1999). However, the terminology and dichotomies used when dealing with complex groups has led to criticisms of imprecise and inadequate language (Mohanty, 2004) and to realisations that they perform a basic purpose of highlighting the power inequalities between groups (Connell, 2007). Examples that over-simplify and create supposedly homogenous groupings include North/South, West/non-West or subaltern, First World/Third World, developed/under-developed, coloniser/colonised and core or centre/periphery. However, despite the complexities, there are limited new terms and concepts being forged to advance the debate. Thus, for ease of use in the forthcoming argument, 'West' and 'non-West' will be applied to groups, but detailed description will be applied to avoid general homogenisations as much as possible.

The International Association of Physical Education and Sport for Girls and Women (IAPESGW) and developments prior to the *Brighton Declaration*

IAPESGW was the first recognised international group advocating physical activity and sport for women. It consisted of White, Western, middle-class women advocating a certain, yet limited, degree of power for women in sporting contexts (Hall and Pfister, 1999). However, the group can be seen as exclusionary toward non-White, non-Western, non-middle-class women. Overarching this situation was a 'double colonisation' (Ashcroft et al., 1995) whereby many of the women involved were less powerful than males due to the patriarchal context of Western society when IAPESGW was formed in 1949.

IAPESGW is considered to have been 'a pre-cursor to the women and sport movement' (White, 2011). The organisation initially focused solely on physical education but then expanded to include wider sport, all the time being a volunteer association. IAPESGW has held quad-rennial international congresses since 1949. However, Hargreaves (2000, p. 219) states that although 'IAPESGW undoubtedly sustained an important service for its members, it system-atically privileged Western physical education discourse and constructions as universal'. The organisation was conservative in focus throughout the first 40 years of operation and was rela-tively unwilling to address the issues raised by the growing Western women's liberation move-ment (Hall and Pfister, 1999).

By the start of the 1990s the growing awareness of issues facing women and sport and the conservative agenda of IAPESGW had clashed. Even though national groups such as CAAWS (Canada), the WSF and the WSFF had since been formed, IAPESGW was still at the time the only women and sport organisation with an international reach. Many women who were advo-cating change and the raising of awareness of issues facing women and sport were themselves members of the IAPESGW and they became increasingly critical of the organisation and its constraints on activism. At the 12th IAPESGW Congress in Melbourne, Australia, 1993, Celia Brackenridge delivered a keynote presentation that challenged the association to work with some of the Western women's liberation movement objectives, including gender equality and an end to discrimination against lesbians (Brackenridge, 1993). She argued:

If we, women in sport, cannot subscribe to these basic objectives as women then we cannot claim to be feminists, cannot claim to be part of the women's movement and cannot claim to be working for women's rights in sport and physical education. We may be IN SPORT but we are not FOR WOMEN.

(Brackenridge, 1993, p. 5, emphasis in original)

Archived documents show support for her keynote. In a letter from Margaret Talbot, Brackenridge is told, 'I hope your paper will kick-start some of the more reactionary members into realisation that a cosy IAPESGW can't survive' (Talbot, 1993). Furthermore, when interviewed, Brackenridge explains she was attempting to highlight 'harder issues' – such as the female athlete triad, sexual abuse and the impact of sexuality – to an organisation that 'had never paid any attention to these issues' (Brackenridge, 2011; see also Brackenridge, 2001, 2004; Brackenridge and Fasting, 2003; Fasting et al., 2004).

In addition to being a member of IAPESGW, Brackenridge was a founding member of the WSFF and worked closely with Anita White, who became Chair of the Foundation in 1988. After much campaigning, White managed to secure a meeting with the GB Sports Council. Brackenridge defined this as a key moment for women, arguing that 'you can scream and shout all you like from outside the establishment but all you do is get a sore throat. Sooner or later you have to work with the agencies of power in order to change them' (Brackenridge, 2011). She adds that White became 'our Trojan horse' by going on to secure a key position as Head of Development at the GB Sports Council. In 1993 the first policy on women and sport was finally agreed, having at first been rejected by the GB Sports Council. The document had to be written in a way that would accommodate the values of the policy- and decision-makers. Brackenridge argued that: 'While it was wishy-washy liberal and very deficient when looked upon now, it was the first step . . . you have to go through the liberal steps to achieve radical ends' (Brackenridge, 2011). The policy was also the first to incorporate sexuality issues, although in 'a very low-key way' (Brackenridge, 2011). White had also presented an overview of issues and barriers to the 2nd International Olympic Committee (IOC) Congress on Sport Sciences (White, 1991). In addition, more women and sport groups were being formed. EWS had been established, and Brackenridge had helped create the Women in Sport Coalition, which was the immediate pre-cursor to WSI. During the latter stages of the 1990s, many of the women's sport organisations began to move away from liberal agendas and to challenge issues of gender and sexuality in a more radical way.

Organisational responses to the 'harder issues'

The advocacy for awareness of 'harder issues' affecting women in sport generally emerged in the early 1990s. The newer groups differed from IAPESGW by tackling the 'harder issues' and at the Brighton Conference there were a number of workshops and seminars on issues affecting women in sport, including a 'Challenging Homophobia' seminar where delegates 'from a broad range of cultural backgrounds and different sexual orientations' welcomed homophobia as an issue otherwise surrounded by 'a silence so loud it screams' (Sport2, 1994, p. 13). These issues were being raised due to the culmination of discussions that had occurred in national women and sport groups meetings and conferences over time, and by the increasing influence of sport academics who were involved in women and sport groups.

By the time of the 2nd IWG World Conference on Women and Sport in Windhoek, Namibia, in 1998, sexuality was a focus of the final plenary session and led to the inclusion of sexuality in the conference report, the *Windhoek Call for Action*. White (2011) stated that there was some resistance from Arab delegates and nations to the inclusion of sexuality on the agenda, but that 'there was more support for its inclusion, than there was against'. The experience of resistance illustrates why sexuality remains such a 'hard issue', an issue we will return to shortly.

The 3rd IWG on Women and Sport World Conference in Canada led to the publication of *Seeing the Invisible, Speaking about the Unspoken: A Position Paper on Homophobia in Sport*. This was published by CAAWS as 'a first step in the process of addressing the issue of homophobia in sport' (IWG, 2006, p. 14). The CAAWS position paper highlights how homophobia can take many forms, that by addressing homophobia there may be a benefit to all regardless of sexual orientation, and that future steps to be taken were informed by adherence to a Call for Action. The paper highlights the specific 'Addressing Homophobia in Sport' initiative that is linked into Canada's broader stance on homophobia and equality rights (CAAWS, 2011).

In Australia, the Sports Commission (ASC) produced *Guidelines to Address Homophobia and Sexuality Discrimination in Sport* as part of its harassment-free strategy in 2000 (ASC, 2000). Furthermore, a media information package was compiled to further raise awareness and understanding (IWG, 2002, p. 39). Elsewhere, between the 3rd and 4th IWG Women and Sport World Conferences, the WSF (IWG, 2006, p. 63):

> Assembled a coalition of organisations to address the issue of eliminating homophobia in sport and also produced, 'It Takes A Team' – a kit and national training programme for school leaders to assist them in addressing homophobia in sport in order to remove this barrier to girls' sports participation.

WSI often uses research as a basis for its evidence. As early as 1994 it had created task forces to confront issues such as sexual harassment and gender verification. In 2004, gender and sexuality formed part of a WSI position statement which addressed homophobia, sexual ridicule and denigration, uncertainties over sexual identity, and 'challenges that female athletes pose to traditional notions of femininity' (WSI, 2004). A year later, in addition to the launch of new initiatives and committees to aid the group structurally, WSI created further task forces on homophobia and women's health (IWG 2006, p. 35) and also enhanced its collaborations with the IOC and United Nations International Children's Emergency Fund (UNICEF) regarding sexual harassment and abuse in sport.

Although it is encouraging that some leading women and sport groups are addressing sexuality as an issue within women's sport, there is generally very little mention of same-sex Games and non-Western programmes and events specifically relating to sexuality and/or homophobia in the IWG Women and Sport worldwide progress reports (IWG, 2006, 2010). The 'recognition of diversity' section of the *Windhoek Call for Action*, which included sexuality, was 'disappointingly thin, reflecting the few responses received on this action point' (IWG, 2002, p. 124). White (2011) reflected that the *Windhoek Call for Action* showed a more radical direction for activities than the *Brighton Declaration*, and this may be assumed to have taken more time to impact than the relatively more liberal (yet still radical for its time) *Brighton Declaration*.

Powerful partnerships

By the time of the 3rd IWG World Conference on Women and Sport in Montreal, Canada, in 2002, there had been sustained efforts to develop women and sport networks in Asia and South America in addition to those in Europe, Africa, the Arab States and the long-established CAAWS and WSF (Cameron, 2000). The more recent direction of the various women and sport organisations and agendas has been increasingly influenced by the lobbying of powerful sporting and non-sporting organisations.

The increase in activism and networks formed during the World Conferences facilitated the process of evidence-based lobbying and research to be considered by powerful organisations. As Brackenridge (2011) stated:

> We made successful inroads into the big organisations like the American College of Sports Medicine – which is one of the biggest sport science bodies – and eventually, heavens, we were invited to go to the IOC and write a consensus statement on sexual harassment and abuse! I would never have dreamt in a million, million years that they would have invited me to go and do work for them. UNICEF, we [WSI] have done work for UNICEF!

One year after the Brighton Conference, the IOC established its own Working Group on women and sport. In 1996, at the 105th IOC Session in Atlanta, USA, the Working Group 'presented a paper that was ratified by the executive board' (UK Sports Council, 1998, p. 16). Included within the paper were four specific actions relating to a figure of 10% of decision-making and leadership roles in groups affiliated to the IOC to be held by women, a strict enforcement of the issue from 2001, and an amendment included in the Olympic Charter.

From an analysis of the IWG reports produced since the Brighton Conference (IWG, 1999b; IWG, 2002; IWG, 2006; IWG, 2010; UK Sports Council, 1998), the impact of the IOC is clear. Although the targets have not been achieved in many sports organisations, federations and committees, since 1996 there has been a dramatic increase in Women and Sport Commissions, Committees and Associations being formed globally. In addition, the power of the IOC has allowed for international, regional and national conferences, seminars, symposiums and workshops on women's sport to take place, including the quadrennial IOC World Conference on Women and Sport. The consensus agreements at these conferences have provided the foundation for policy action, including the production of guidelines for the female athlete triad by the IOC Medical Commission (IWG, 2006). In addition, work with the United Nations (UN) and United Nations Educational, Scientific and Cultural Organization (UNESCO) has been undertaken by women's sport, physical activity and recreational groups. This includes the IWG and WSI publications and links with the UN Division for the Advancement of Women (IWG, 2010) and lobbying from IAPESGW in response to the 'world crisis facing school PE' to the Ministers and Senior Officials Responsible for Physical Education and Sport third international conference (IWG, 2002, p. 36).

Global and local tensions

There are also clear regional differences in activities related to gender and sexuality in sport. Throughout the 1990s and 2000s regional and national women and sport groups were being formed in Africa, Asia and Eastern Europe, although at a more embryonic stage of development than their Western counterparts. In some cases (as with the early issues experienced by IAPESGW, WSI [and previously the Women in Sport Coalition], EWS and the WSFF), establishing a network of contacts and securing finances took precedence over the 'harder issues'. This was repeated with AWISA who reported to 'now having basic office equipment and furniture in place, a fax/telephone line, a postal box, and are in the process of installing Internet service' (IWG, 1999a). Furthermore, in these early stages, AWISA was facing opposition as many women and sport groups do; 'being viewed in some cases as a threat to some of the male-dominated sports structures' (IWG, 1999a). As Pfister (2011) proposed, there are complexities in traversing between human rights and culturally-specific traditions and ideologies, which raises the question of whether sport is the right vehicle for crossing this divide. The IWG progress reports highlight this need to be culturally specific and aware of local contexts (IWG, 2002; IWG, 2006; UK Sports Council, 1998). Brackenridge (2011) was particularly critical of neo-colonial agendas among some women and sport organisations (see also Chowdhry, 1995; Marchand, 1995):

> It's the modern-day equivalent of muscular Christianity that took out the bible under one arm and the football under the other to the poor little Black babies in the Congo. Maybe we are just trying to peddle a model of Westernised sport like taking netball. Why? There are indigenous sports in all countries, why don't we foster those? Why do we have to McDonaldise sport and globalise in our own image?

However, the tensions between addressing global issues while remaining sensitive to local cultural and religious ideologies remains a significant challenge. What is clear is that the initial basis for the international women and sport movement is a Western produced and formulated document. Further work needs to be done to analyse women and sport policies around the world to see how issues of gender, sexuality and sexual abuse are incorporated, and what may be improved. This not only applies to non-Western groups but also Western groups. CAAWS (IWG, 2010, p. 42) states as recently as 2010 that:

> lesbians and gays in sport are virtually invisible, their existence seldom acknowledged and in the rare situations where an athlete or coach does 'come out', reactions are typically negative and such individuals receive little or no support from their sport leaders or sport governing bodies.

Conclusion

IAPESGW was the first established group advocating more opportunities for women's physical education and sport, but it has been criticised for failing to address 'harder' issues, such as sexual abuse, the female athlete triad and sexuality. Crucially however, it has managed to survive as a group and pursue the advancement of women's physical education, sport and physical activity for over 60 years. The early 1990s saw a tectonic shift in the way women in sport issues were discussed and dealt with. Not only were the 'core' women's sport issues now being further debated (such as participation and equal rights), but due to the advocacy of certain groups and individuals, 'harder issues' that had previously been ignored and/or silenced were coming to the fore, such as sexuality and sexual harassment. More coordinated activities were having a greater impact, influence and success in partnerships with key dominant groups, such as the IOC with sport, UNICEF with charities, and the UN and many governmental groups with politics. This helped to cement women in sport issues into policy consensus and, crucially, policy action.

How this is done is fundamental. For example, there is evidence of tension between different groups, and evidence that the neo-elite groups do not always represent girls and women from different communities in the ways that they would necessarily choose. As a result, while much has been achieved, there remains a caveat – it should be recognised that successes to date have been restricted, have varied hugely between contexts, and much more needs to be done to enable girls and women across the world to have widespread opportunities and autonomy in sport and physical education. However, we question whether there ever has been, or even needs to be, a coherent 'movement' for women and sport. Indeed, women and sport is still an emerging issue in some countries whose cultural and social ideologies may not permit radical proposals for women in sport even to be considered – itself a radical and sensitive topic.

References

ASC (2000) Harassment-free sport: Guidelines to address homophobia and sexuality discrimination in sport. Report, ASC, Belconnen.

Ashcroft B, Griffiths G and Tiffin H (eds) (1995) *The Post-Colonial Studies Reader.* London: Routledge.

Brackenridge C (1993) *'Don't Just Do Something – Stand there': Problematising community action for women in sport. Keynote paper to the 12th IAPESGW Congress, Melbourne Australia, 6th August 1993.* Available at the Anita White Foundation International Women and Sport Archive. WS/I/1/001/3. University of Chichester.

Brackenridge C (2001) *Spoilsports: Understanding and Preventing Sexual Exploitation in Sport.* London: Routledge.

Brackenridge C (2004) Women and children first? Child abuse and child protection in sport. *Sport in Society* 7(3): 322–337.

Brackenridge C (2011) Personal Communication. 15 September 2011.

Brackenridge C and Fasting K (eds) (2003) *Sexual Harassment and Abuse in Sport: International Research and Policy Perspective.* London: Whiting and Birch.

Bryman A and Teevan JJ (2005) *Social Research Methods.* Oxford: Oxford University Press.

CAAWS (2011) Publications and resources: Seeing the invisible, speaking about the unspoken. Available at: http://www.caaws.ca/e/resources/publications (accessed 18 November 2011).

Cameron T (2000) *Memo – International Working Group on Women and Sport Action Plan 2000–2001. From Trice Cameron (Secretariat) to all members.* Available at the Anita White Foundation International Women and Sport Archive. WS/I/1/007/2/6. University of Chichester.

Chowdhry G (1995) Engendering development? Women in development (WID) in international development regimes. In: Marchand MH and Parpart JL (eds) *Feminism, Postmodernism, Development.* London: Routledge, pp. 26–41.

Connell R (2007) *Southern Theory.* Cambridge: Polity.

Denscombe M (2004) *The Good Research Guide: For Small-scale Social Research Projects.* Maidenhead: Open University Press.

Fasting K, Brackenridge C and Sundgot-Borgen J (2004) Prevalence of sexual harassment among Norwegian female elite athletes in relation to sport type. *International Review for the Sociology of Sport* 39(4): 373–386.

Hall MA and Pfister G (1999) *Honoring the Legacy: Fifty Years of the International Association of Physical Education and Sport for Girls and Women.* Smith College, MA: IAPESGW.

Hargreaves J (1999) The 'women's international sports movement': Local-global strategies and empowerment. *Women's Studies International Forum* 22(5): 461–471.

Hargreaves J (2000) *Heroines of Sport: The Politics of Difference and Identity.* London: Routledge.

Houlihan B and White A (2002) *The Politics of Sports Development: Development of Sport or Development Through Sport?* London: Routledge.

IWG (1999a) *IWG Annual Meeting Papers – AWISA Report.* Available at the Anita White Foundation International Women and Sport Archive. WS/I/7/5/1999. University of Chichester.

IWG (1999b) *IWG Annual Meeting Papers – IOC Report.* Available at the Anita White Foundation International Women and Sport Archive. WS/I/7/5/1999. University of Chichester.

IWG (2002) From Windhoek to Montreal: Women and Sport Progress Report 1998–2002. Report, IWG Secretariat, Montreal.

IWG (2006) From Montreal to Kumamoto women and sport progress report 2002–2006. Available at: http://www.iwg-gti.org/conference-legacies/kumamoto-2006 (accessed 21 September 2011).

IWG (2010) From Kumamoto to Sydney women and sport progress report 2006–2010. Available at: http://www.iwg-gti.org/conference-legacies/sydney-2010 (accessed 21 September 2011).

IWG (2012) Past conferences and legacies. Available at: http://www.iwg-gti.org/conference-legacies (accessed 5 January 2012).

Kluka DA (2008) The Brighton Declaration on Women and Sport: A management audit of process quality. PhD Thesis. University of Pretoria, South Africa.

Lewis R and Mills S (eds) (2003) *Feminist Post-colonial Theory: A Reader*. Edinburgh: Edinburgh University Press.

Marchand MH (1995) Latin American women speak on development: Are we listening yet? In: Marchand MH and Parpart JL (eds) *Feminism, Postmodernism, Development*. London: Routledge, pp. 56–72.

Mills S (1998) Post-colonial feminist theory. In: Jackson S and Jones J (eds) *Contemporary Feminist Theories*. Edinburgh: Edinburgh University Press, pp. 98–112.

Mohanty CT (1995) Under western eyes: Feminist scholarship and colonial discourses. In: Ashcroft B, Griffiths G and Tiffin H (eds) *The Post-colonial Studies Reader*. London: Routledge, pp. 259–263.

Mohanty CT (2004) *Feminism without Borders: Decolonising Theory, Practicing Solidarity*. London: Duke University Press.

Pfister G (2011) Personal Communication. 28 August 2011.

Spivak GC (1999) *A Critique of Post-colonial Reason: Toward a History of the Vanishing Present*. London: Harvard University Press.

Sport2 (1994) Women, sport and the challenge of change. *The GB Sports Council*, May/June.

Talbot M (1993) *Letter from Talbot M. to Brackenridge C.H.* Available at the Anita White Foundation International Women and Sport Archive. WS/I/1/001/3. University of Chichester.

UK Sports Council (1998) Women and sport: From Brighton to Windhoek, facing the challenge. Report, London: UK Sports Council.

White A (1991) *'Women in Top Level Sport'. Paper presented to the second IOC Congress on Sport Sciences, Barcelona, 26–31 October 1991*. Available at the Anita White Foundation International Women and Sport Archive. WS/I/001/4/2. University of Chichester.

White A (1998) *'From Brighton to Windhoek – Success stories 1994–1998'*. Available at the Anita White Foundation International Women and Sport Archive. WS/I/1/007/2/1. Bognor Regis. University of Chichester.

White A (2011) Personal Communication. 6 May 2011.

WSI (2004) Position statement. Available at: http://www.sportsbiz.bz/womensportinternational/taskforces/wsi_position_statement (accessed 21 November 2011).

WSI (2011) About WSI. Available at: http://www.sportsbiz.bz/womensportinternational/about/index.html (accessed 21 November 2011).

PART II

Views from countries across the world

9

THE "LONG MARCH" OF WOMEN AND SPORT IN MAINLAND CHINA

Revolution, resistance and resilience

Jinxia Dong

Introduction

At the 2008 and 2012 Olympic Games, China placed second overall in the medal count, behind the USA, and it is well acknowledged that Chinese women have made the greatest contribution to China's meteoric rise in international sport. In fact, at the last seven Summer Olympics since 1988, Chinese women won more gold medals than their male counterparts. Their extraordinary performances have sparked considerable global interest as journalists from around the world have lavished stories on Chinese elite women athletes. In spite of an increased academic curiosity of Chinese women and sport, however, there remains a paucity of analytical literature, especially about elite women's sport, and a dearth of high-quality monographs in particular (c.f. Dong Jinxia, 2012). Very few indeed are written in English.[1]

The situation outlined above raises questions: What factors have contributed to the success of Chinese female athletes? How has the national identity of China been constructed through the pursuit of sporting victories? What part have Chinese sportswomen played in boosting China's new image in the world? What is the relationship between national identity, sport and gender in China? To answer these interlocking questions, it is necessary to scrutinize the political, economic, social, cultural and aesthetic relationships between globalization, market economy, traditional gender norms, and modern sporting culture for women in China.

Chinese women and sport prior to 1949

There has been a long history of Chinese women engaging in sport and physical activities. This is reflected in the paintings of women from the Kingdom of Yue (between 475 and 221 BC) playing swords or Emperor Ming and his beloved Concubine Yang playing polo during the Tang Dynasty (AD 618–907). However, after the Tang Dynasty, women's sport gradually declined. It was not until the 1840s, when China was forced to open its door to the West, and the idea of women's liberation was introduced into the country, that women's sport began to re-emerge. Missionary girls' schools played an important part in promoting the anti-foot-binding campaign and introducing modern sport to Chinese females by including gymnastics, athletics, swimming, basketball, volleyball and table tennis into the school curricula.

By the first decade of the twentieth century, gymnastics, running and games requiring physical prowess became major activities in women's physical education. Female students participated in the "First South Yangtze River United Athletic Meet" held in Nanking in 1907. Just a few years later, the 1911 Revolution overthrew the thousand-year monarchic system and replaced it with the Republic of China. Since then, Chinese society has undergone rapid change, including the further development of women's physical education

The May 4th Movement[2] which erupted in 1919, with a cry for democracy, science and equality, had an enormous impact on Chinese culture and ideology. The emancipation of women became a part of the widespread intellectual rebellion against the historic Confucian code and all its associated constraints (Yunming, 1994). In the meantime, Western ideas and customs were promoted and then accepted by an increasing number of people. Thus, modern sport including women's sport blossomed (Jianlin, 2004). Women from Guangdong province in the south of China played volleyball at the Eighth Provincial Games of the Old China in 1921, only four years after their male counterparts' debut. It was also in 1921 that Chinese women participated in the fifth Far-East Athletic Meet (Shanghai) and played volleyball and tennis. Women debuted at the National Games in 1922. Accordingly, the number of sports for women and the number of female participants increased over time.

Arguably, from the outset of the revolution there was nothing in the way of a gap between China and the West in terms of access to organized elite sport for women. This progress came to a near-cessation, however, as a result of the chaos of civil wars (1927–1937 and 1945–1949) and the Anti-Japanese War (1937–1945) and Chinese women were unable to engage seriously in sport or to participate in the Olympic Games.

Equality, women and sport in the People's Republic of China

In 1949 the People's Republic of China (PRC) was founded. China changed from a semi-feudal and semi-colonial country to an independent socialist state. The Marriage Law[3] decree in 1950 constituted a milestone in protecting women's rights within their family. In the same year, the Land Law for the first time established women's rights to own and inherit property. Women's equal status was clearly stated in the first Constitution of New China, promulgated in 1954. Education was now widely available to them. Chinese women "suddenly" obtained equal rights with men both in law, family and education and women were encouraged to enter previously male-dominated fields. "Women now developed and tested their abilities and potential outside the home. Their actions led to a slow redefinition of women's social position and ensured their increasing independence" (Dong, 2003). Thus, the political and cultural transformations laid down stepping stones for women to get involved in sport, including elite sport.

Elite sport was regarded as a possible career for both men and women from the early 1950s. Based on the principle of equality, women in the PRC were provided with equal coaching, equipment and facilities, as well as wages and rewards. This is in sharp contrast to many countries in the West, where women did not have the same kind of equality in sport until two decades or more or later (Brownell, 1995). Women's sport – both mass and elite – developed at an unparalleled pace during the Great Leap Forward (GLF) in the late 1950s. Rapid and ambitious targets were pursued in every project throughout the country (Tingyu, 1994) and sport became an essential part of the Great Leap Forward national development plan. "Sports weeks" and "sports months" were organized. Rapid expansion happened in all sports institutions: sports schools, national and provincial teams, and institutes of physical education. By the early 1960s Chinese women had (in terms of world rankings) outperformed their male counterparts in athletics, basketball, volleyball, speed skating and shooting (Gaotang, 1984). However, as intensive training was often emphasized disregarding scientific principles, sometimes even in disregard of common-sense knowledge, frequent sports injuries occurred, which consequently shortened the athletic careers of a number of athletes (Dong, 2003).

Another political movement, the Cultural Revolution (1966–1976), constitutes a unique, regrettable episode in the political history of Communist China. It had a huge impact on Chinese women and sport. Under the slogan, "women hold up half the sky", women, like men, threw themselves enthusiastically into the movement and demonstrated astonishing ambition, capability and courage. After the Cultural Revolution was unveiled, athletic training was replaced by denunciation meetings, street marches and other revolutionary activities. International activities were virtually abandoned. The chaotic years of the "revolution" brought China to the brink of economic collapse, which had an impact on sport. Sports investment fell annually from 89.964 million yuan in 1966 to 27.39 million yuan in 1968. As a result, elite sports teams shrank; the number of elite athletes and coaches dropped from 11,292 and 2,062 in 1965 to 6,288 and 1,530 in 1970, respectively (PRC's Sports Committee, 1979). But then, in the early 1970s sports teams resumed normal training and sports talents were recruited. This provided an asylum for some young people to evade the fighting and to avoid being sent to the countryside when the large-scale Rustication Campaign[4] (*shang shan xia xiang*) was underway from 1968 to 1980 (Dong, 2003).

The year 1979 was a turning point for Chinese society and sport as "Economic reform and opening up to the outside" (*jingji gaige yu duiwai kaifang*) was launched. This led to decades of impressive economic progress and a wealthier and more influential China. It was also in 1979 that China reoccupied its seat on the International Olympic Committee (IOC). Chinese athletes, women in particular, became involved continually and comprehensively in international competitions. Since then, they have achieved astonishing results and continue to play the major part in ensuring Chinese success in international competitions today.

Global competition, national identity and women's sport

Eager to redress over a century of humiliation (1840–1945) imposed by foreign powers, the Chinese wished to create a new global identity – one characterized by prestige, esteem and respect – even before the communist regime came to power in 1949. How to construct the national identity was an issue that intrigued the Party and the state. Given that international sport is grounded in the nation-state system, sport is undoubtedly an effective platform for the assertion of national identity. Just two years after the Chinese Communist Party (CCP) took power in 1949, some national and military sports teams were created, and the National and Provincial Sports Commissions were established between 1952 and 1954. Between 1953 and 1958, local provinces across the country organized their own specialized (now called elite) sports teams which were exclusively sponsored by the state. By the mid-1950s a centralized sports administration system had been established and China's sport became institutionalized, specialized and bureaucratized. From 1954 to 1957 female athletes created, on average, twenty-five new national records each year.

After China's place in the Asian Sports Federation was restored in September, 1973, the New China sent 269 athletes to the Seventh Asian Games in India, where China ranked second in total points (Shiquan, 1997). In 1979, China resumed its seat in the IOC from which it had withdrawn in 1958 due to insisting on the "One China" stance.[5] Benefiting from the open-door policy and renewal of Chinese membership of the IOC, Chinese athletes set out to establish themselves on the world stage. By the end of the 1970s, women had won world championships in many sports, such as gymnastics, fencing, judo, shooting, diving, table tennis and badminton. These early victories greatly inspired the Chinese people. The slogan "go beyond Asia and join the advanced world ranks" (*zhouchu yazhou, chongxiang shijie*), put forward by the Chinese Diving Team in 1980, became their overt ambition. Twenty-six Chinese men and women made their debut at the XIII Olympic Winter Games at Lake Placid in 1980, but they did not show up at the Moscow Summer Games in the same year, joining the US-led Western nations' boycott of the Games in protest against the Soviet invasion of Afghanistan. In 1981, the Chinese Women's Volleyball Team started its journey to five consecutive world titles, which led to the emergence of "Spirit of the Women's Volleyball Team" (*nv pai jing sheng*) and spurred millions of Chinese people to strive for the modernization of their country. Undoubtedly, Chinese sportswomen were a source of national exhilaration, pride and bonding. Women's accomplishments strengthened cohesion of the Chinese nation, dressed it with new pride, and demonstrated a new, confident face of China to the world.

China won several Olympic gold medals at the Los Angeles Games in 1984, further fuelling Chinese ambition to become a world sporting power. Consequently an "Olympic Strategy" was soon advocated. The national Olympic-oriented policy led to re-organization of provincial and municipal sports teams throughout the country. Non-Olympic sports teams were substantially reduced. By 1995, athletes in non-Olympic sports comprised only 7.34 per cent of the athletes in total. In addition, team sports that demanded more investment than individual sports and that had no prospect for medals were terminated in most provinces and municipalities. This strategy greatly favoured women who had convinced the Chinese government of their part in building an applauded national identity through their prominent performances. As a result, many women's sports obtained special treatment. First, the percentage of female athletes at provincial and national levels had increased over time. In 2006, some 48.3 per cent of the 1,746 national team athletes were women. Chinese women had actually been represented in larger numbers than men since 1992, for example, 132 women and 118 men in 1992 and 225 and 171 in 2012, respectively.

Second, specific support at all levels and in all aspects was given to promising women athletes who were considered more likely than the men to excel in international competitions.[6] The adoption of "male sparring partners" (*nan pei nv lian*) is a reflection of this. Third, more women's sports such as judo, race walking, sailing, weight-lifting, soccer and wrestling were introduced at provincial and national levels and entered the national competition programmes in the 1980s. Actually, Chinese national competitions for race walking, judo, weight-lifting, Taekwondo, wrestling and sailing started earlier than the world championships or Olympic competitions in these sports. This might explain why Chinese women achieved good results in these sports in the 1980s and 1990s. Today there are over 1,000 elite female athletes for each of the following sports: shooting, track and field, wrestling, weight-lifting, rowing, Taekwondo, swimming and table tennis.

To secure Olympic success, in the early 1990s the National Sports Commission (NSC) adjusted its policies on the National Games: the timing of the National Games was changed from the year before the Olympics to the year after. To further stimulate local enthusiasm for the Olympics, Olympic results started to be incorporated into the scoring system of the National Games in 1993 (Guojia tiwei, 1993). Only Olympic sports (plus martial arts – traditional Chinese sports) were incorporated into the National Games after 1997.

Influenced by the international trend of "sport for all", improved living standards and increased leisure time, growing numbers of people wanted to take part in sports as recreation. Consequently, in early 1995 the NSC enacted the "National Fitness Programme" representing a milestone in the history of mass sport in China. To implement the programme, many activities including surveys of mass sport, fitness training, and testing and monitoring were organized throughout the nation (Haoran, 1998). The growing emphasis on mass sport, however, did not mean the downgrading of elite sport. In 1994 the "Olympic Honour-winning Plan" was drafted and came into effect in 1995. To ensure Chinese accomplishment in 2008, the "Plan to Win Glory in the 2008 Olympics" was drafted in 2002, followed by the "Project to Implement the Plan to Win Glory in the 2008 Olympics" which was designed by individual sports management centres. To maximize eventual Olympic performances in 2008, membership of the national teams expanded from 1316 to 3222.[7]

In summary, the Olympic victory of Chinese female athletes has been regarded as the embodiment of national strength, an instrument for building a positive national image, self-esteem and self-confidence to resume the historic role of "the pre-eminent power in East Asia", and "to bring to an end the overlong century of humiliation and subordination to the West and Japan" (Huntington, 1996: 229). National identity building and gender have thus been intimately intertwined in China.

Economic reform, commercialization and women's sport

The inauguration of economic reform initiated radical changes in society in general, and in the sports community in particular. The "responsibility system of production" (*sheng chan ze ren zhi*) and concomitant material incentives and bonuses were re-introduced. Sport was in the vanguard of the movement to overturn the egalitarian "big pot" (*da guo fan*) practice. From the early 1980s onwards material incentives, together with social prizes, were steadily used as an important means to motivate athletes. It is noticeable that state bonuses for winning athletes and coaches had increased over time. In 1981 when the Women's Volleyball Team won the World Cup championship, it was awarded 2700 yuan as a bonus. In 2003, the team again won the world championship and obtained 2 million yuan (US$241,633) as a bonus. This increase is the most pronounced in the winning bonuses for Olympic success. For example, an Olympic gold medallist in 1984 got 8,000 yuan (US$3,484). By 2008, this figure rocketed to 350,000 (US$50,725) yuan, increasing over forty-three times within twenty-four years. The winning bonus was twelve times the per capita groos domestic product (GDP) in 1984 and nineteen times in 2008. The winning bonus continued to rise in 2012. It reached 500,000 yuan (US$79,000). The massive political and financial rewards under the new system made elite sport a magnet to many young people. Rewards, victory and success became major aims in elite sports circles.

In conjunction with these vigorous economic and general reforms, sport underwent an extensive institutional change, namely a transformation from being an exclusively centrally-sponsored and centrally-controlled system to a multi-level, multi-channel system. Corporations and private individuals were invited to sponsor sports. In 1986 universities were also encouraged to run elite sports teams. After 1988, twelve sports (20 per cent of the total) were chosen to experiment with the "enterprization" (*shi ti hua*) of sports associations – transformation from government agencies to "public organizations" that take the interest of the public as their main concern.

Since the early 1990s, the Chinese sports community had embarked upon a transition to a market economy.[8] With the introduction of enterprise and private sponsorship, commercialization became pervasive after the mid-1990s. Athletic performance was the sole criterion determining the allocation of resources and the consequent strata of athletes in the sports community and in society at large. Sporting success led to huge political, social and financial rewards. Some were promoted to high-level coaching and administrative positions after they retired from training.[9] The former table tennis star Deng Yaping is one of them. She was first a member of the IOC athlete commission and the National Olympic Committee of China; then deputy director of the Beijing Olympic Village; and is now general manager of People Search Network, Ltd.

Women's success in international sport, together with the consequent financial and social benefits, have helped raise sportswomen in the public's esteem and promoted women's social status both in the sports community and society at large. Celebrated female athletes have established positive profiles in the Chinese media and have been frequently applauded by the media as national heroines. *Chinese Girls*, which featured the famous volleyball players, was adapted from a book into a TV documentary programme in the 1980s. Three world-famous female Chinese divers, Gao Min,[10] Fu Mingxia[11] and Guo Jingjing,[12] had been high-profile figures in media from the 1980s to the 2000s. Achievement in sport seems to provide opportunity for upward social mobility.

However, only the successful, confident *and* "nice-looking" sportswomen are likely to attract commercial companies. The above mentioned Guo Jingjing obtained endorsements from Coca Cola and Nike after Athens 2004, where she had won two gold medals. At the time she endorsed nine products with an income of 9.5 million yuan. Her successful reign at the Beijing Games with two gold medals under her belt consolidated her status as the highest profile woman in the media, before Li Na won a tennis grand slam in 2011. The less successful and less pretty girls are not so fortunate. Zhou Chunlan, the national weightlifting champion in 1988, ended up as a masseuse in a bath house, with a daily income of less than 5 yuan.

Since the Olympic Strategy was announced, a winning-oriented sports policy has dominated the sports community, from athletes to coaches, from researchers to administrators. One unintended by-product of this winning-oriented sports policy is drug abuse that was epidemic in the 1990s. The worldwide exposure of drug scandals by Chinese athletes in the 1994 Asian Games and the 1998 World Swimming Championships dealt a heavy blow to China's image. Under mounting international pressure China started to crack down on drug abuse in the sports community from 1999. The tightening domestic and international doping controls displayed their effect on such sports as athletics and swimming.

In summary, in the context of economic reform, the emergence of a professional league system, private sponsored clubs, swelling winning bonuses, as well as widening differences between successful and less successful athletes, the complexity of the sports community in China today has markedly increased.

Gender, culture and women's sport

Significant cultural changes have been taking place in China since the 1980s. Now Chinese women are seriously involved in previously "men-only" sports such as football, weightlifting and even boxing. Their presence in these traditional "male" sports was unquestionably a challenge to traditional gender stereotypes that consider women as weaker and inferior to men.

In China, the family remains central to women's existence, and the idea that family responsibilities are still primary tasks for women remains dominant. Unsurprisingly, the tradition of marriage and family often conflicts with women's pursuit of a career, specifically in sport. Consequently, until the mid-1990s, elite female athletes had to make a choice between a family and an athletic career. However, from the mid-1990s onwards an increasing number of women chose for themselves to delay their marriage *and* to resume training after having children. There appeared a number of female Olympic athletes who were married women and mothers, such as the thirty-three-year-old Olympic wrestler, Xian Dongmei,[13] the two-time badminton Olympic Champion Zhang Ning, the tennis player Li Na, and several members of the women's hockey, volleyball and football teams. Clearly, that these married women could continue their athletic careers after marriage must be inseparable from their husbands' support.

In modern China, quite a few husbands are more than content to play a supporting role to their wives whose victories in international competitions can even win respect and status for themselves and their families. Li Na has offered a vivid picture of her husband's support. He is a former tennis player and became the women's national team coach in 2007 so that he could accompany Li Na everywhere for competitions. His tolerance, comforting, instruction, massage, care and love have helped her enormously and her performance has improved significantly. She was a finalist in the Australian Open in January 2011 and won the French Open in June. She also became the first Asian woman to win a tennis Grand Slam. "Without exaggeration, it can be claimed that gender relations in the family, which directly affect women's commitment to elite and other sport, have been gradually changing from male dominance to male and female partnership" (Dong, 2003). This reflects the changing values associated with a woman's career and her family. The prolonged playing careers of increasing numbers of elite married sportswomen illustrates that the belief that love and marriage are something of distraction from sports commitment has been fading. Cultural changes have been taking place.

Influenced by Confucianism that regards female morality, obedience and hierarchy[14] as a source of order and harmony, women are often expected to be more obedient than their male counterparts in China. Nevertheless, female athletes have become notably more assertive and individualistic in the past decades. Since the 1980s, quite a few female sports stars, such as He Zhili,[15] Ma Family Army, Chen Lu and Peng Shuai, have overtly challenged conventional authoritarian management by expressing dissatisfaction and criticizing unfair or unsatisfactory aspects of the national system. The rhythmic gymnast Ding Ning, for example, attacked the biased judges at the National Games. In 2006, the long-distance runner Sun Yingjie[16] with three other teammates[17] sued their coach Wang Dexian for withholding their bonuses and salaries for years (Zhang, Ying and Wang, 2006). This event attracted maximum media attention and led to skeletons tumbling out of the sports community closet.[18] More than this, some female athletes even went beyond just verbal complaints. Wang Meng,[19] the four-time winter Olympic gold medallist of speed skating between 2006 and 2010, set an example. In 2011, she physically attacked the team manager, Wang Chunlu, which resulted in her withdrawal from the national team (Ying, 2011). The incident dominated headline news for months and evoked intense public debates about athlete education and management of sports teams. All this reflects both the complications generated by recent sports reform and the more independent, individualistic and self-assertive sportswomen in twenty-first-century China. Confrontation is essentially the product of a new self-assurance on the part of women athletes who now are even more conscious of their rights, their powers and their opportunities.

Nevertheless, while change is in the air, traditional forces can be resilient. For example, in spite of the once-impressive performances of the Chinese women's soccer team in the 1980s and the early 1990s, the team's performance has declined continuously between their world runner-up performance in 1997 and their failure to qualify for the Sixth World Cup in 2011 and the London Olympics in 2012. The reasons lie in the shortage of promising players and lack of appeal to the business world which is associated with, and has reinforced the re-emergence of, traditional female stereotypes. The Confucian ideal of a woman is as compliant, humble, yielding and respectful, but soccer requires competitiveness and aggression. Thus, a woman playing soccer is widely considered as vulgar, crude and "unfeminine". Tradition dies hard. Thus, "the conflicting professional and cultural demands can be difficult for women to reconcile on soccer fields" (Dong, 2002).

Conclusion

Embedded in a long history, the link between women and sport has developed in an organized and institutional way in the decades of New China. Based on the communist party's philosophies of gender equality, expansion of education for girls and centralized sports administration, women's sport has developed fast in the past decades, especially since 1979. Elite women performers have been favoured by their potential for and success in creating a vibrant national image for Chinese people and the rest of the world. They have benefited greatly from the medal-oriented policy. National identity building and gender have been intimately intertwined.

However, in spite of significant changes in the position of women in China in the past century, there has been a fundamental consistency in attitudes towards them based on Confucian precepts. It is evident that gender politics, contemporary commercialism and resuscitated traditionalism have made the lives of elite athletes both complex and contradictory.

Notes

1 Dong Jinxia's (2003) *Women, Sport and Society in Modern China: Holding Up More Than Half the Sky;* Fan Hong's (1997) *Footbinding, Feminism and Freedom – The Liberation of Women's Bodies in Modern China.*
2 Some 3,000 Beijing University students marched to Tiananmen Square, demanding that China's warlord government refuse to hand over German concessions to Japan after the end of World War I.
3 The Marriage Law banned outlawing compulsory betrothal, the marriage of children, infanticide, bigamy and concubinage. It consisted of eight sections and twenty-seven articles. To publicize and implement the Marriage Law a mass campaign was staged throughout the country. Women activists were sent to factories and the countryside to publicize and prompt the implementation of the Marriage Law. Books, pamphlets, drama and arts were used to popularize the law. By way of example, the women's magazine Xin zhongguo funv [The New Chinese Women], first published in July 1949, devoted a column to the topic of the Marriage Law in each issue throughout the year 1950–51.
4 Millions of high school students went voluntarily, or were forced to go, to the countryside and military construction camps in remote border areas, such as Helongjian, Inner Mongolia, Yunnan and Shanxi provinces, to be re-educated by peasants.
5 Both mainland China and Taiwan wanted to represent China in the IOC and other international sports organizations. But according to the IOC's own political criteria for membership, a national Olympic committee could only represent the territory and people controlled by its sponsoring regime, it is obvious that Taiwan under the power of nationalist party (Kuomintang) could no longer represent "China" in Olympic competitions as it no longer controlled most of China. In spite of the antagonism between Taiwan and the PRC, they were agreed upon one thing: there was only one China and Taiwan was part of it.
6 This belief is based on three reasons: first, many sports have been introduced to women recently; second, women's inequality is pervasive in the world, which leads to less investment in women's sport in many other countries; and third, Chinese women have the historical heritage of hard work and obedience.
7 Data from the State Sports Administration, unpublished.
8 The state, in a break with past practices, agreed to allocate each association or centre the same fixed budget package as previous years without reference to inflation. Five years later, the association had to finance itself.
9 Sun Jinfang, the former volleyball player, is now the director of the National Tennis Association; Lang Ping was the head coach of the Chinese Women's Volleyball Team between 1995 and 1999. She is now the head coach of the American Women's Volleyball Team; Tang Jiuhong, the seven-time world badminton champion in the 1990s, was promoted to Deputy Director of the Hunan Provincial Sports Administration in 2004.

10 Gao Min won all the competitions that she participated in between 1986 and 1992, including the 1988 and 1992 Olympic Games. She was regarded as a "diving queen".

11 She won four Olympic gold medals at the Olympic Games between 1992 and 2000. She was named World Best Woman Platform Diver by US magazine *Swimming World*. She went to the Tsinghua University to study after retiring from international competition and then married the former Finance Minister of Hong Kong Special Administration Region, Liang Jinsong, in 2002.

12 Guo Jingjing won two gold medals in both 2004 and 2008 Olympic Games and many more world titles in her competitive career.

13 Xian dongmei zuo keshi lu: san yuan yin rang wang zhe gui lai, shan heng lei lei de guan jun [Record of guest Xian Dongmei: three reasons made the winner, a champion with numerous injuries, return], http://2008.sina.com.cn, August 15, 2008.

14 He saw it as the prime need of mankind to resolve the problem of human conflict and create conditions of peaceful co-existence and harmony with the universe.

15 She openly challenged the practice of "Conceding" (*ranqiu*) to teammates in international competitions in 1987.

16 Sun, the champion of 5000m and 10,000m races at the 2002 Asian Games, was found to be drug positive at the National Games in 2005. Though she was banned for two years, she continued training and competed in national events in 2008 and 2009, but did not qualify for the 2008 Games. She married in 2009 and soon after ended her athletic career.

17 They were Ai Dongmei, Guo Ping and Li Juan.

18 It was claimed that coach Wang once beat Sun badly. The toes of the athletes who sued the coach in court had become disfigured due to overtraining. And, even worse, they were unemployed and had very difficult lives at the time when they filed the suit.

19 First in 2007, she publically criticized the teaching method of the head coach Li Yan who was invited back from America, and did not greet the coach at the Asian Winter Games. This disqualified her for the World short-track Championships and World Team Championships in 2008. However, this punishment did not stop her from wrong-doing. In 2009 she cursed a male teammate and even challenged referees at the National Games. Due to her extraordinary sports capabilities she was allowed to re-join the national team and then competed at the 2010 Winter Olympic Games where she won three gold medals. Such sporting success brought her enormous fame, status and arrogance.

References

In Chinese

Dong Jinxia (2012) 2006–10 woguo nuxing tiyu yanjiu zongshu [Literature review of women's sports studies between 2006 and 2010 in China]. To be published by Chinese Women's Association.

Gu Shiquan (1997) *Zhongguo tiyu shi* [*Chinese sports history*], Beijing tiyu daxue chuban she [Beijing Sports University Press].

Guojia tiwei [National Sports Committee] (ed.) (1993) *Zhongguo tiyu nianjian*, 49–91 jinghua ben (xia ce) [*China's sports yearbooks*, 49–91 hard cover (second volume)], Beijing: Renmin tiyu chuban she.

Jiao Yunming (1994) Lun jingdai zhongguo de funv jiefang shixiang [About women's emancipation in modern China] – Beijing daxue funv wenti di san jie guoji yantao hui lunwen ji [Collection of papers of the Third International Women Seminar in Beijing University].

Liao Jianlin (2004) Shehui bianqian yu jindai tiyu de fazhan – dui jiu zhongguo di san jie quanguo yundong hui de lishi kaocha [Social changes and the development of modern sport – historic examination to the third national games in Old China]. *Qiu suo* [*Seeker*] (4): 233–235.

Lu Tingyu (1994) *Zhonghua renming gongheguo lishi ji shi: quzhe fazhang* [*Historical record of the PRC: Zig and Zag Developments*] (1958 -1965). Beijing: Hongqi chuban she [Hongqi Press].

Rong Gaotang (1984) *Dandai zhongguo tiyu* [*Contemporary China's sport*]. Beijing: zhongguo shehui kexue chuban she [China Social Science Press].

Tian Ying (2011) Wang Meng bu ji gexing zhezhu jinpai guangmang, tiaoxin caipan dama nan duiyuan [Wang Meng uninhibited personality shadowed the glory of gold medals, provoking referees and scolding male teammates], *Xin Jing Bao* [*New Beijing Daily*]. July 28.

Xia Haoran (1998) Zhongguo shehui tiyu xiangzhuang diaocha jieguo gongbu [Promulgation of the survey results of the social sport in China], *Guangming Ribao* [*Guangming Daily*]. 8 August.

Zhang Ying and Wang Wei (2006) Xiri malasong guanjun, yishuang canjia du yusheng [The past marathon champions, a pair of damaged feet to lead their remaining lives], *Fazhi wanbao* [*Legal Evening Daily*]. Sept. 10.

Zhonghua renmin gonghe guo tiyu yundong weiyuan hui [PRC's Sports Committee] (1979) Quanguo tiyu shiye tongji zhiliao huibian 1949–1978 [Collection of statistical information of national sport (1949–1978)], Beijing: Renmin tiyu chuban she [People's Sports Press].

In English

Brownell Susan (1995) *Training the Body for China – Sports in the Moral Order of the People's Republic*. Chicago, IL and London: The University of Chicago Press.

Dong Jinxia (2002) Ascending then Descending? Women's Soccer in modern China. *Soccer and Society* vol. 3 (2): 1–18

Dong Jinxia (2003) *Women, Sport and Society in Modern China: Holding Up More Than Half the Sky*. London: Cass.

Fan Hong (1997) *Footbinding, Feminism and Freedom – The Liberation of Women's Bodies in Modern China*. London: Cass.

Huntington Samuel P. (1996) *The Clash of Civilisations and the Remaking of the World Order*. New York: Simon & Schuster.

10

FROM *RYŌSAI-KENBO* TO *NADESHIKO*

Women and sports in Japan

Keiko Ikeda

The concept of *ryōsai-kembo* and inauguration of girls' secondary education

For a long time participation in sports was considered unseemly for women in Japan. Change came after Japanese modern education was initiated by the Education Order of 1872. Secondary education for women was created with the Imperial Rescript on Education that was issued in 1899. Particularly relevant, however, was that the initial stage of secondary education for women in the late nineteenth century was influenced by educational principles based on the ideal of womanhood, *ryōsai-kembo*. This ideal was linked with the ideology of imperial nation-building through separating affairs of the home from other social disciplines understood as "women's territory" (Koyama 1999, pp.20–27; Muta 2000, pp.36–40).

The concept of *ryōsai-kembo* emerged after the conclusion of the Sino-Japanese War (1894–1895). It literally meant a "good wife (*ryōsai*) and wise mother (*kembo*)" and became a common principle during the earlier stages of Japanese modern education, especially for elite women. This theory fostered a belief that the future society of the Japanese Empire should have healthy and wise mothers. This became an essential educational principle for women. It was an "invented tradition" as discussed by the British Historians Eric Hobsbawm and Terence Ranger (Hobsbawm 1983, p.1), a new social code articulated under early Japanese Imperialism in the late eighteenth and early nineteenth centuries. Thus the girls' secondary education system was firmly established and linked with the context of a nationalistic policy around the time of the Sino-Japanese War. However, in the process, *ryōsai-kembo* became the first principle for initiating a girls' secondary education system with a curriculum that included more active participation in physical activities. It eventually included track and field athletics, gymnastics, dance, indoor baseball, croquet, lawn tennis, table tennis, marching game, volleyball, basketball and swimming. Organized competitive sports in the Taisho era (1912–1926) followed and flourished in the 1920s. The games and exercise taught at schools were more radical than the image of the ideal of *ryōsai-kembo* (Ikeda 2010, pp.539–541).

Some historians point out that the idea of *ryōsai-kembo* was a blend of Eastern Confucian ideas about traditionally-restrained women and the Western idea of the Victorian Woman, the "angel in the house", an ideology imported from the United Kingdom (Fukaya 1990, p.11; Koyama

1991, pp.1–9; Inose 1992, pp.95–105). There was a strong British cultural influence, especially following the 1902 Japanese-Anglo Alliance against Russia. When Elizabeth Phillips Hughes, the first Principal of the Cambridge Training College for Women (C.T.C., now Hughes Hall in Cambridge University) visited Japan to undertake educational research in 1901–1902, she praised the Japanese way of progress that mixed the best of Western values with traditional Japanese culture (Hughes 1902c, pp.1–10; Bottrall 1985, pp.33–34). Her influence on Japanese education was obvious. She visited higher education schools and institutes located in local areas such as Nagoya, Kanazawa, Kyoto, Kobe, Tottori, Chiba, Fukushima, Sendai, Hokkaido, Matsumoto, Wakayama, Himeji, Okayama, Hiroshima, Yamaguchi, Fukuoka, Kumamoto, Kagoshima, Nagasaki, Saga and Kokura, as well as universities and educational societies in Tokyo, covering the whole of Japan (Ōno 1989, pp.326–339). Some of her lectures were translated and published in Japanese educational journals as articles entitled "Exercise for Women" (Hughes 1901a, pp.1–8; Hughes 1901b, pp.1–6), "Modern British Ladies" (Hughes 1902a, pp.10–17; Hughes 1902b, pp.24–29), "On the Methods of Gymnastics"(Hughes 1902c, pp.1–10) and "The Ethical Ideal of the English Public School Boy" (Hughes 1902d, pp.324–327; Hughes 1902e, pp.406–409). She politely spoke to Japanese audiences about the significance of women's role in a new age through outdoor games (climbing, rowing), organized games (tennis, hockey and basketball) and gymnastics (Swedish exercises) which encouraged women's proper characters, self-restraint, cooperation and healthy bodies. She also mentioned women's scientific role as a wise mother who was responsible for the discipline of nursery children: "It is more important for women to administrate politics at home than for the country." In the same article, she concluded that her idea would bring something influential not only to ladies in Western countries such as the USA, but in Eastern counties, specifically Japan (Hughes 1902b, pp.24–29). Thus British influence became effective as an imported ideal for women.

Two Higher Women's Normal Schools (Colleges of Education) in Tokyo and Nara, the top educational establishments for daughters of the elites of Japanese society before World War II, also developed elite women's physical education through the teaching by Japanese women educationalists who had studied abroad. For example, Miss Akuri (Aguri) Inokuchi (1870–1931) was sent to the United States by the Japanese Ministry of Education. She studied at Smith College under the guidance of Miss Senda Berenson, and returned to Japan to become a professor at Tokyo Women's Higher Normal School (later Ochanomizu Women's University in Tokyo). Here she introduced the Swedish system of exercise which had been adopted as women's gymnastics at Smith College, on the east coast of America, and she introduced bloomers (the term used in American colleges as the uniform for gymnastics) as sportswear for students in Japan. Her reports were collected as a book entitled, *Theory and Practice of Physical Education*, published by the Japanese Investigation Committee for Gymnastics and Games in 1905 (Inokuchi 1906, pp.103–126; Koshimizu 1981, pp.103–126; Shindō 1986, pp.115–123;.Ikeda 2010, p.541). One of Inokuchi's students became a professor at another Higher Women's Normal School in Nara (later Nara Women's University). At both institutions, girls wore bloomers introduced by Inokuchi or tunics brought to Japan via England, by Tokuyo Nikaidō who had studied at Martina Bergman-Österberg's Physical Training College in London 1913. The course she followed included Swedish gymnastics and Western-style sports and activities like tennis, dance, baseball, the discus and the javelin (Nikaidō et al. 1963, p.65; Nishimura 1981, pp.165–168; Ikeda 2010, p.541). But the influences from America and England that resulted in Japanese girls and women learning modern sports were mixed with a traditional liberal education such as a classic study of Japanese poetry, playing the Japanese harp, sewing, handicraft, housework and cooking. Some graduates commented that their experience of school sports was like a dream, a time and space separated from their real life at home (Yoshida 2000, pp.129–136; Ikeda 2010, pp.543–544). Conventional sexual divisions in Japanese colleges were similar to those at Madame Österberg's college, reflecting Victorian familism and an educational training for a future life as a wife and mother. The idealization of the role of the woman in the family was a central feature of the version of feminism associated with the women's physical education profession (Hargreaves 1994, pp.77–78) in both England and Japan.

"Liberal education", organization and competition during the Taisho era

In 1911, just before the start of the Taisho period (1912–1926), a leader of the Women's Liberation Movement, Raichō Hiratsuka, set up the famous journal of Japanese feminism, *Seitō* ("Blue-Stocking") referring to the Blue-Stocking Society for Literature established in mid-eighteenth-century London. The name "Blue-Stocking" was used as an impact factor in order to promote the first Japanese feminist movement and the society substantially brought the image of "new women" to greater public prominence and had a significant influence on both women's and men's thoughts on marriage (Ikeda 2010, pp. 540–541). Hiratsuka graduated from Nihhon-joshi-daiggakō (now Japan Women's University). A founder of Nihhon-joshi-daiggakō, Jinzō Naruse (1858–1919) had an epoch-making scheme that particularly encouraged the Delsarte system (an expressionistic form of gymnastics invented by Francois Delsarte of France, 1811–1871) and other physical activities for women (Naruse 1896, p.213; Ikeda 2010, p.540). A feminist leader, Hiratsuka, and many of the other members of "Blue-Stocking" were graduates of Nihon-joshi-daigakkō. They enjoyed playing lawn tennis and basketball (Baba 2011, p.79). Naruse had experience of studying in the USA and, in the year of the foundation of the university, invited a British lady, Miss Elizabeth Phillips Hughes, to teach there for three months. Although Hiratsuka's feminism movement did not directly influence further developments in women's physical education, it stimulated the atmosphere of liberal education for women in society in general and encouraged greater freedom for women in different areas of life – a new "spirit of the age".

Tadashi Hjōdō, Japan's first female pilot, was an early high-profile example of a modern woman. She had been granted a pilot's license aged 23 in 1922. The news that a woman could be a pilot was partly attributable to "the Taisho democracy movement", and the ideas of "liberal education" adopted in this period and previously in the late Meiji era. Educationalists, for example, had attempted to adopt concepts such as "respecting individuality", "the principle of voluntarism", "autonomy" and "self-directed learning". After that, the fascist and totalitarian ideology came to dominate Japanese education and attempted to convert it into a new understanding of "liberal education" that fitted fascist ideology (*Kainan Shinbun* 1919; *Tokyo Nichinichi Shinbun* 1921; *Kainan Shinbun* 1922; *Tokyo Asahi Shinbun* 1922a; *Tokyo Asahi Shinbun* 1922b; Pfister 1989, p.4; Irie 1993, p.131; Ikeda 2010, pp.544–545).

In parallel, it was on 27 May 1922 that the first Women's Federal Athletic Meeting was held at the Tokyo Women's Higher Normal School. This athletic meeting was the first opportunity for women to participate in a well-organized national athletic competition in Japan (which was supported by Tokyo YMCA). In 1924, two years after this meeting, the first meeting of the Women's Olympic Games of Japan (in Osaka) and the Meijijingu Athletic Meeting were held. Track and field, basketball, volleyball and tennis were the women's sports in the latter meeting, which continued until 1943 (the fourteenth meeting). However, formal participants were confined to the students of upper secondary schools (Ikeda 2001, p.606).

Two years later, in 1926, the Japan Association of Physical Education for Women was formed, followed by the Japan Women's Sport Federation (JWSF). By 1930, this Federation was coordinated as a sub-organization of the Federation Sportive Feminine Internationale (FSFI) (Raita 1999, p.123). Also in 1926, Kinue Hitomi (1907–1931) participated in the International Ladies Games (the second Women's Olympic Games) held in Goteberg, Sweden. She was the only Japanese woman to do so and the first Japanese woman to succeed in international sports competition. Remarkably, she won gold medals in the long jump (5.5 m) and the standing long jump (2.49 m), as well as silver medals in the discus (33.62 m) and the 100-yard dash (12.0 sec). She also wrote two books, *The Traces of Spikes* (Hitomi, 1929) and *Reach the Goal* (Hitomi, 1931). However, this Japanese woman's impressive international participation and glories did not lead to increased sport participation for Japanese women in general. *Ryōsai-kembo* remained the dominant educational ideology and social ideal for girls.

Maternal feminism and restoration of the *budō* tradition leading towards war

The Sino-Japanese war of 1894–1895 and the Russo-Japanese war of 1904–1905 had led to a nationalization of educational ideologies that formed the core of the Japanese education system: one such ideal was *ryōsai-kembo*. Some traditional forms of Japanese physical culture were also resurrected just before World War II since Western society was increasingly perceived as an enemy. For example, the traditional Japanese martial arts, *budō*, were introduced into primary and secondary schools: *judō* and *kendō* (Japanese fencing) were for boys while *naginata* (Japanese pike) and *kyudō* (traditional archery) were compulsory events for girls. Although *budō* had already been taught in most schools prior to this revival, it became formally regulated in this period. Its purpose was to consolidate martial esprit rather than to actually use these skills on the battlefield. *Budō* was adopted for women's physical education in the 1930s and continued during the war. Because women were not subject to military conscription, an alternative disciplined training of both the mind and the body was the objective (Irie 1986, pp.146–147; Ikeda 2010, p.545). The Ladies' Society of National Defence of the Japanese Empire, for example, was formed for this purpose in 1932, following the Manchurian Incident. The feminist leader, Hiratsuka, even advocated an Imperialist course. In their hope to become part of an honourable nation, some women feminist leaders supported the nationalists. In the 1930s, even feminism fell under the influence of fascism, and became known as maternal feminism (Ueno 1998, pp.31–34, 38–49).

In this imperial course, a key figure was Toyo Fujimura, a female physical educationalist who had studied in Germany and introduced the virtues of German ladies to Japanese women. She argued that "in order to foster the nation with a vigorous and plucky character, firstly, we have to educate women since they have to become mothers and teachers in the near future". In *Women's Physical Education*, a journal issued by Toyo Fujimura between 1937 and 1941, words and phrases such as "the decisions of Japanese ladies and girls", "the consciousness of the home front", and "to welcome *Hitlerjugend* (Hitler Youth)" added to the wider fascist discourse. She also wrote about woman's preparation for childbirth, especially posture for lumbar-region abdominal training. This was commonly recommended in physical education in fascist Japan and comprised an analogy of maternal feminism conceived through Fujimura's experience in Germany (Kaminuma 1967, pp.81–82; Ikeda 2006, p.95). The swimmer Hideko Maehata succeeded Hitomi as Japan's leading female sportswoman, winning silver medals in the 200 m breaststroke in the Olympics in Los Angeles in 1932 and Berlin in 1936. Newspaper, radio and TV reported her win so fanatically that she temporarily became a media star. After Maehata's brilliance, sports were quickly taken over by the world of national defence (Ikeda 2001, p.606).

The influence of fascism was extended after the 1940s through the printed media. Advertisements from a book published in 1940 consistently indicated the need for a nationalistic cause for girls' physical education. Another advertisement for *budō* for Elementary School education, inserted in a magazine entitled *Physical Education and Athletic Sports*, highlighted the book's "explication of the true ethos of *budō*, the pivot of the national spirit" (Dainihon-taiiku-gakkai 1940). An article in the same magazine clearly suggested the purpose of *budō* as "the best teaching material for contributing to moulding people for the Japanese Empire", idealising nationhood, the fascist woman and "maternal feminism" (Sato, 1940).

When the war in the Pacific broke out on 8 December 1941, the Japanese educational institution decided to establish an organization for maintaining the spirit of solidarity and bonding the country. Both martial arts and Western sports activities were organized within a simulated army or sport-corps called *hokokutai* or *hōkoku-dan*. It was the duty of all staff and students to demonstrate their allegiance to the Japanese Empire (Ikeda 2010, p.547). When physical education for women emphasized women's role through maternal feminism and the importance of a strong mind for the nation during World War II, traditional *budō* for women was resurrected and some aspects of Western competitive sports for women were replaced by martial arts for a time.

Following a 1940 instruction from the Ministry of Education, *hōkoku-dan* and *hōkoku-tai* were formed in almost every school and was fully implemented in August 1941. Although girl students were not conscripted, girl students in the *hōkoku-dan* were imbued with the spirit of the home front. Games were taken over by a militaristic sports organization. The organization of *hōkoku-dan* at Japan Women's University comprised six sections: general affairs, culture, life, training, labour service and national defence drill, which had divisions for air drill, first aid, nursing and distribution of food (Japan Women's University, 1981, p.106). The case of Tokyo Women's Higher Normal School shows that the section for training in *hōkoku-kai* included the divisions of *kyūdo*, *naginata*, swimming, skiing, athletics, tennis, table tennis, basketball, volleyball, touring and *tairen* (a mass game of militaristic physical training and gymnastics). As a result, physical activities such as *hōkoku-dan* became more predominant than other sporting activities (Ochanomizu Women's University, 1984, pp.201–202). Another state women's university in Nara also formed both *hōkoku-dan* and *hōkoku-tai* in 1941. There were seven sections for the division for training: *naginata*, *kyudo*, touring, tennis, table tennis, athletics and dance. Later in the same year, it was changed to include nine sections: track and field, swimming, *naginata*, *kyūdo*, ball games, music exercise, cycling, agriculture and touring (Nara Women's University, 1970, pp.103–104). At a seaside school, a seaside drill was introduced in 1944 (Hōfu High School, 1989, p.63). Western-style physical education, dancing and competitive sports for women all lost popularity. After the war, the denial of the wartime system of education became the starting point of a new era (Ikeda 2010, p.547).

Post-war period

After World War II, Japanese civil law was revised according to the new Constitution of Japan. A more democratic basis included equal status for women with men. World War II had damaged the Japanese people both economically and psychologically. But the end of World War II opened up new opportunities. People's consciousness of women's sports rose to a new level. Great athletes, such as Hitomi, had already shown an individualistic approach to sports. Hiro Miura (1898–1992) had made efforts to improve the standards of women's physical educators and instructors in the Taisho era. She sought to improve women's health and strength through modern dance and the new aesthetic gymnastics influenced by Isadora Duncan (1878–1927), Rudolph Laban (1879–1958), Emile Jaques-Dalcroze (1865–1950), Rudolf Bode (1881–1970), Elizabeth Marguerite de Varel Mensendieck (1864–1957) and Mary Wigman (1886–1973). Miura's ideas and practice continued even in war time (1936–1941) and she gave lectures to school teachers after 1945 (Kunieda 1981, p.203–221; Yamamoto 2001, *passim*).

After the war the proportion of women in the workforce slowly increased from 36.9 percent to 39.4 percent from 1950 to 1995 (Management and Coordination Agency of Government 1996). In this period the number of female athletes, sports instructors and sports educators began to increase. And after the Tokyo Olympic Games in 1964, many competitive sports became popular for both men and women. Moreover, they diversified and flourished: female rugby players, bodybuilders, yachtswomen, boxers, karate women, ice-hockey players have all become common since 1970. After the first Tokyo International Women's Marathon had been held in 1979 women's marathons became the most popular sports event for Japanese women. Runners like Akemi Masuda and Yuko Arimori became national celebrities. A Japanese women's mountaineering team climbed Mt. Everest for the first time in 1975. In 1977 another famous sportswoman, a professional golfer, Hisako Higuchi, won the U.S. Open, the first Japanese woman to do so.

The Olympic Games saw growing numbers of Japanese women participating and winning medals. The all-Japan team of women volleyball players won a gold medal in 1964 (Tokyo). In 1992 at Barcelona, Kyoko Iwasaki won a gold medal in the 200m breaststroke at the age of fourteen, the youngest gold medallist ever. In winter sports, Seiko Hashimoto was chosen as the representative of all Japanese Olympic competitors in 1994, the first time a woman had been so honoured. The Nagano Winter Olympic Games also produced many young women who won medals in 1998. Tae Satoya won a gold medal in the freestyle mogul, the first Japanese woman to do so in the Winter Olympics (Ikeda 2001, p.607).

Changes in perspectives of gender and developments towards equality with men also took place through the inauguration and work of organizations at national and international levels, for example, the Japan Association of Physical Education for Women (JAPEW); the Japanese Association for Women in Sport (JWS) and the International Working Group on Women and Sport (IWG) (Hargreaves 2000, ch.7). Academic research has also reinforced the aim for women's equality in sports through specialized academic congresses. In 2001, the First Asian Conference on Women and Sports was held in Osaka offering nine workshops: "networking in Asia", "the leadership of women in sport", the "female body, exercise physiology and sports medicine", "adapted sports for women with disabilities", "history of women in sports in Asian countries", "issues in elite sport", "women and PE", "sports for middle-aged women" and "gender equity in sports". Leading scholars from Philippines, Nepal, Sri Lanka, Hong Kong, Mongolia, Cambodia, South Korea, Singapore, Malaysia, Thailand, Syrian Arab Republic and Indonesia were invited. In 2001, the "Osaka Five-Year Plan: Asian Action Plan for Gender Equity in Sport": "Clauses for women's participation and health promotion in each domestic law with regard to the promotion of gender equity in society" was unanimously adopted (Itani et al. 2001, pp.284–311; Raita 2001, pp.2–58), reaffirming the principles of the Brighton Declaration (at the first World Conference on Women and Sport in 1994) and the Windhoek Call for Action (at the second World Conference on Women and Sport in 1998). Then in 2002, a preparatory committee for the Japan Society for Sport and Gender Studies (JSSGS) was set up, followed by the first congress of the study of Sport and Gender Studies held at the Dawn Centre, an institution dedicated to the promotion of independence and equal opportunity for men and women. Academics from physical education and sports studies initiated the event, and altogether sixty-one academics from a wide variety of the fields such as history, sociology, pedagogy, psychology, anthropology and literature also attended. Three years later, the JSSGS was officially inaugurated (Yamaguchi 2012, p.23). JSSGS publishes an annual journal, the *Journal of Sport and Gender Studies*. The tenth issue, published in May 2012 celebrates the achievements of the society over the previous decade (Mizuno 2012, pp.2–3; Yamaguchi 2012, pp.23–28).

Symbolically, on 19 July 2011, *The Japan Times* published an article entitled "Japan celebrates Women's World Cup win: "*Nadeshiko*' lifts the nation with surprise victory over Americans". It explained the meaning of *Nadeshiko*. It said that "the team, whose *Nadeshiko* nickname comes from a pink frilled carnation symbolizing grace and beauty, is sure to be given a heroes' welcome when it returns after capturing the imagination of the Japanese public" (*The Japan Times* 2011). *Nadeshiko* is the abbreviation of *Yamato-nadeshiko*. The term *Yamato* means "Ancient Japan" and has been often used for nationalistic purposes. *Nadeshiko* is a nationalistic representation similar to "Samurai Japan" for men's sports. The 1920s women athletes who participated in the Olympic Games were called *Yamato Nadeshiko* and so were the winners of the 2011 Football World Cup.

In modern Japan, most kinds of sports are played recreationally by both men and women. However, the media retain the legacy of "Samurai Japan" for men's sports and *Yamato Nadeshiko* for women's sports, a cultural metaphor and an interesting manifestation of the longevity of gender-biased idioms and images. However, new generations are more active in their sports than former generations, and traditional gender divisions are being constantly undermined and re-invented. The old and the new still co-exist in many ways, but the World Cup triumph has surely opened up a new world of women's professional football and symbolizes new possibilities for women and new relations of gender in all areas of sport and life.

References

Baba, Tetsuo (2011) Nihon-joshi-daigakkō-de-mananda "Atarasii-Onna' tachi-to Taiiku Supōtsu ["New women" educated at Nihon-joshi-daigakkō and PE& Sports]. In: The Society of "New Women" (ed.) *"Seitō' to Sekai no "Atarashii-Onna' tachi* [*"Blue Stocking" and "New Women" in the World*]. Tokyo: Kanrin Shobō.

Bottrall, Margaret (1985) *Hugh's Hall 1885–1985*. Cambridge: Rutherford Publications.

Dainihon-taiiku-gakkai (ed.) (1940) *Taiiku-to-kyōgi* [*Physical Education and Athletic Sports*] 19–9: on the page of advertisements.

Fukaya, Masahi (1990) *Ryōsai-kembo-shugi-no-kyō-iku* [*Education based on the principle of Ryōsai-kembo*]. Nagoya: Reimei Shobo Co., Ltd.

Hargreaves, Jennifer (1994) *Sporting Females: Critical Issues in the History and Sociology of Women's Sports*. London: Routledge.

Hargreaves, Jennifer (2000) *Heroines of Sport: The Politics of Difference and Identity*. London: Routledge.

Hitomi, Kinue (1929) *Supaiku-no-Ato* [*The Trace of Spikes*] reprinted in *Hitomi Kinue: Honoo-no-Sprinter* (1997). Tokyo: Nihon Tosho Center.

Hitomi, Kinue (1931) *Gōru-ni-hairu* [*Reach the Goal*] reprinted in *Hitomi Kinue: Honoo-no-Sprinter* (1997). Tokyo: Nihon Tosho Center.

Hobsbawm, Eric (1983) Introduction: Inventing Traditions. In: Eric Hobsbawm, Terence Ranger (eds.), *The Invention of Tradition*. Cambridge: Cambridge University Press.

Hōfu High School (ed.) (1989) *Bōkō-hyaku-jū-nen-no-ayumi* [*A Hundred-and-ten-years History of Hōfu high school*]. Hōfu: Hōfu high school, Yamaguchi Prefecture, Japan.

Hughes, E. P. (1901a) Exercise of Women I. *Onna* [*Women*] 1–10: 1–8.

Hughes, E. P. (1901b) Exercise of Women II. *Onna* [*Women*] 1–11: 1–6.

Hughes, E. P. (1902a) Modern British Ladies I. *Onna* [*Women*] 2–2: 10–17.

Hughes, E. P. (1902b) Modern British Ladies II. *Onna* [*Women*] 2–3: 24–29.

Hughes, E. P. (1902c) A translation of her lecture, Taisōhō-ni-tsuite [On the Methods of Gymnastics] at the meeting for Nihon Taiiku-kai [Society of Japanese Physical Education] organized on 24 May 1902 in Tokyo: in *Taiiku* [*Physical Education*] 103: 1–10. Tokyo: Dōbunkan, 25 June.

Hughes, E. P. (1902d) The Ethical Ideal of the English Public School Boy. *Kokushi* [*Persons who dedicated themselves to Nation*] 41: 324–327.

Hughes, E. P. (1902e) A Japanese translation of "The Ethical Ideal of the English Public School Boy". *Kokushi* [*Persons who dedicated themselves to Nation*] 42: 406–409.

Ikeda, Keiko (2001) Japan. In: K. Christensen, A., Guttmann, G. Pfister (eds.), *International Encyclopedia of Women & Sports*. Berkshire Reference Works and Macmillan Reference, Massachusetts, U.S.A., pp.604–607.

Ikeda, Keiko (2006) The Body and Grass-roots Fascism during World War II: "the topos" of the Emperor in a personal-body-mechanism in Japan. *International Journal of Eastern Sports & Physical Education* 4–1: 91–103.

Ikeda, Keiko (2010) "*Ryōsai-kembo*", "Liberal Education" and Maternal Feminism under Fascism: Women and Sports in Modern Japan. *The International Journal of the History of Sport* 27–3: 537–552.

Inokuchi, Akuiri (1906) *Taiiku-no-riron-oyobi-jissai* [*Theory and Practice of Physical Education*]. Tokyo: Kokkō.

Inose, Kumie (1992) *Kodomotachi-no Daieiteikoku* [*The Children and the British Empire: The British Interpretation of "Hooligan" at the Turn of the Century*]. Tokyo: Chuokoron-shinsha inc.

Irie, Katsumi (1986) *Nihon-fashizumu-kano-taiiku-shisō* [*The Thought of Physical Education under Japanese Fascism*]. Tokyo: Fumaido Publishing Co.

Irie, Katsumi (1993) *Taisho-Jiyū-tatiiku-no-kenkyū* [*The Study of Liberal Physical Education in the Taisho Period*]. Tokyo: Fumaido Publishing Co.

Itani, Keiko, Tahara, Junko and Raita, Kyoko (eds.) (2001) *Josei-supōtsu-hakusho* [*A White Paper on Women's Sports*]. Tokyo: Taishukan Publishing Co.

Japan Women's University ed. (1981) *Zusetsu Nihon-joshidaigaku-no-ayumi* [*An Illustrated History of 80 years of the Japan Women's University*]. Tokyo: Japan Women's University.

Kainan Shinbun [local newspaper in Ehime prefecture] (1919) 7 December.

Kainan Shinbun (1922) 1 April.

Kaminuma, Hachiro (1967) *Kindai-Nihon-Joshi-Taiikushi-Josetsu* [*The Exordial book of the History of Modern Japanese Girls' Physical Education*]. Tokyo: Fumaido Publishing Co.

Koshimizu, Harumi (1981) Inokuchi Akuri [Akuri Inokuchi]. In: Josei-taiikushi-kenkyūkai (ed.) *Kindai Nihon Joshi Taiikushi* [*Modern Japanese History of Girls' Physical Education*]. Tokyo: Nihon Taiikusha, pp.103–126 (ch.6).

Koyama, Shizuko (1991) *Ryōsai-kembo-to-iu-kihan* [*The Standard of Ryōsai-kembo*]. Tokyo: Keisō-shobō.

Koyama, Shizuko (1999) *Katei-no-Seisei to Josei-no-Kokuminka* [*Generating of the Concept of Home and Nationalization of Women*]. Tokyo: Keiso Shobo.

Kunieda, Takako (1981) Dansu-ni-yoru-Jidō-Chusinshugi-no-Jissen [Children-centrism through Dance Education]. In: Josei-taiikushi-kenkyūkai (ed.) *Kindai Nihon Joshi Taiikushi* [*Modern Japanese History of Girls' Physical Education*]. Tokyo: Sports and Physical Education Publishing Co., pp.197–221 (ch.10).

Management and Coordination Agency of Government (1996) *Josei-no-Genjo-to- Shisaku 1995* [*The Report of Present Situations and Problems on Issues of Women in 1995*]. Tokyo: Okurashō-insatsu-kyoku [Printing Office of the Ministry of Finance].

Mizuno, Eri (2012) Nisen-Jūichi-nen wo Furikaette [Looking Back to the Year 2011]. *Journal of Sport and Gender Studies* 10: 2–3.

Muta, K. (2000) Ryōsai-kembo-shisō-no-omoteura [Two Sides of the Thought on *Ryōsai-kembo*: Modern Japanese Domestic Culture and Feminism]. In: T. Aoki, S. Kawamoto, K. Tsutsui, T. Mikuriya & T. Yamaori (eds.), *Onna-no-bunka* [*Women's Culture*]. Tokyo: Iwanami Shoten Publishiers, pp.23–46.

Nara Women's University (ed.) (1970) *Nara-joshi-daigaku-rokujū-nenshi* [*Sixty-years History of Nara Women's University*]. Nara: Nara Women's University.

Naruse, Jinzō (1896) *Joshi-Taiiku* [*Girls' Education*]. Tokyo: Nihontosho Center Co., reprinted in 1983 (orig. pub. 1896).

Nikaidō, Seiju, Tokura, Haru and Nikaidō, Shinju (1963) *Nikaidō-Tokuyo-den* [*A Biographical Story of Tokuyo Nikaidō*]. Tokyo: Fumaido Publishing Co. (orig. pub.1957).

Nishimura, Ayako (1981) Nikaidō Tokuyo [Tokuyo Nikaidō]. In: Josei-taiikushi-kenkyūkai (ed.) *Kindai-Nihon-Joshi- Taiikushi* [*Modern Japanese History of Girls' Physical Education*]. Tokyo: Nihon Taiikusha, pp.151–176 (ch.8).

Ochanomizu Women's University (ed.) (1984) *Ochanomizu-joshi-daigaku-hyaku-nenshi* [*A Hundred-year History of Ochanomizu Women's University*]. Tokyo: Publishing Committee for a Hundred-year History of Ochanomizu Women's University.

Ōno, Nobutane (1989) E. P. Hughes in Japan (1901–1902). *The Annual collection of Essays and Studies, Faculty of Letters, Gakushuin University* 36: 323–346.

Pfister, Gertrud (1989) Daughters of the Air: On the Role of Women in the History of Aviation. In: S. Shimizu (ed.) *ICOSH Seminar 1986 Report: Civilization in Sport history*, translated from German by J. W.

Gabriel. Kobe: Committee of ICOSH seminar (orig. pub. Fliegen-Ihr Leben. Die ersten Pilotinnen, Orlanda Frauenverlag, Berlin: Orlanda Frauenverlag, 1989).

Raita, Kyoko (1999) The Movement for the Promotion of Competitive Women's Sport in Japan 1924–35. *The International Journal of the History of Sport* 16–3: 120–134.

Raita, Kyoko (ed.) (2001) *Abstracts of the First Asian Conference on Women and Sports*, the conference held at Osaka International House, Osaka, Japan, pp.1–58.

Sato, Ukichi (1940) Kokumingakkō-taiikuka-budō (zoku) [The *Budō* in the Curricula for Physical Education for National Elementary Schools, the sequel]. *Taiiku-to-kyōgi* [*Physical Education and Athletic Sports*] 19–9: 3–6.

Shindō, Kozō (1986) *Inokuchi Akuri joshi-den* [*A Biographical Story of Akuri Inokuchi*]. Akita: Onkokan.

The Japan Times (2011) Japan celebrates Women's World Cup win: "*Nadeshiko* lifts the nation with surprise victory over Americans. 19 July.

Tokyo Asahi Shinbun [newspaper] (1922a) 7 August.

Tokyo Asahi Shinbun (1922b) 1 September.

Tokyo Nichinichi Shinbun [newspaper] (1921) 30 November.

Ueno, Chizuko (1998) *Nashonarizumu-to-jenda* [*Engendering Nationalism*]. Tokyo: Seidosya.

Yamaguchi, Rieko (2012) Nihon Spōtsu to Jenda Gakkai: Jūnen no Sōkatsu to Kadai [The Japan Society of Sport and Gender Studies: the Summary of the Last Decade and the Agenda towards the Future]. *Journal of Sport and Gender Studies* 10: 23–28.

Yamamoto, Tokuro (2001) Miura-Hiro-no-senkanki-taiiku-eno-omoide [Hiro Miura's Memory of Physical Education during the War]. A presentation paper at the Spring Seminar for the Historical Research Section of Japan Society of Physical Education, Health and Sport Sciences, at Hitotsubashi University, 12 May 2001.

Yoshida, Aya (2000) Kōtō-jogakkō-to-joshi-gakusei [Girls' Upper Secondary Schools and Girl Students: Westernized Modernity and Modern Japan]. In: T. Aoki, S. Kawamoto, K. Tsutsui, T. Mikuriya and T. Yamaori (eds.), *Onna-no-bunka* [*Women's Culture*]. Tokyo: Iwanami Shoten Publishers.

11

SUMO AND MASCULINE GIGANTISM

Hans Bonde

Contemporary sumo is an immensely popular sport in Japan, though less popular than certain imported Western sports, notably baseball and soccer. Also, to foreigners, especially from the 1990s onwards, Japanese sumo has become popular as part of the image of Japan, as a TV sport, and as an integral part of tourism in Japan (Masao 1998).

Sumo can be dated back to the early times of imperial Japan. From the eighth century sumo was performed at the imperial court. Its main purpose seems to have been to confirm the authority of the emperor, who wanted to become a Chinese-inspired ruler with an unquestionable authority and a centralized government system. Sumo wrestlers were commanded to be sent from every corner of the imperial territory whereby confirming the borders of the empire and the loyalty of the imperial vassals to the emperor (Guttmann and Thompson, 2001: 16ff). The large, strong, well-fed sumo bodies became symbols of imperial wealth and stability celebrated in annual court ceremonies at the imperial palace area.

From its historic beginnings, sumo was rooted in Japanese samurai warrior society. It was originally never intended to be a female preoccupation; a patriarchal trait that has persisted in modern sumo and which makes it highly interesting as a study subject of male bonding. The martial aspects of the sport not only stem from a specifically masculinised form of physical confrontation but also from different rituals such as a 'dance with the bow' where prescribed choreographic movements are undertaken by a low-ranking sumo wrestler.

Furthermore, sumo is also deeply connected to the Japanese nature religion Shinto. Still today, in the so-called Crow Sumo Ceremony, young boys compete in sumo as part of the religious festival of Shinto shrines (Nelson, 2000) such as the Kamigamo-Jinja Shinto Shrine in Kyoto.[1] In the twenty-first century sumo increasingly became a mass spectator sport that could link modern Japanese culture with past traditions.

The basic rules of modern Japanese sumo are simple. Two contestants in a circular arena (*Dohyō*) made of a mixture of sand and clay try to defeat one another by means of two basic methods. Either the opponent is forced to touch the ground with a body part, other than the soles of his feet, or he is pushed outside the ring. This means that the weight of each contestant really matters, because in a small ring it is possible to simply push the opponent out of the ring. However, a great variety of techniques gives the smaller man a chance to outperform the bigger man by turning his body and occasionally throwing his opponent to the ground or out of the ring.

Today's sumo is an amalgamation of tradition and modernity. For example, video decisions are made by the referees if the outcome of the game is difficult to measure. Sumo is well adjusted to the modern media world, since the small arena is easily overlooked by the cameras so that there is sophisticated surveillance of the competitors. The extremely short time from the clash of the colossal bodies to the end of the bout as a rule offers a dramatic climax and, if in doubt, the winner is confirmed by video replay.

From a gender perspective, it is noticeable that sumo as arranged by the traditional Japan Sumo Association (*Kyokai*) is an all-male activity and that female tournaments cannot be arranged within the confines of the Association. All coaches and owners of a training stable (*heya*) are male. At present, throughout the whole of Japan, around 54 sumo stables include around 700 wrestlers. The members of the *Kyokai* are all former wrestlers and have exclusive rights to lead sumo stables to which all professional sumo wrestlers have been associated.

For expert connoisseurs of the game the actual corporeal 'clash of the giants', when the bodies of opponents meet in the middle of the ring, might not be the most exciting moment. The two sumo wrestlers (*rikishi*) are not allowed to attack before both touch the ground with their fists. This gives the opponents a possibility to 'psyche' their adversaries by simulating an attack that constitutes a tension-building initial phase.

Sumo is deeply imbedded in the traditional religion of Japan – *Shinto*. The sumo referee is dressed as a Shinto priest, and above the ring is raised a roof similar to that of a Shinto shrine, most noticeably experienced in the sumo 'mekka' of the giant hall, *Kokugikan*, in Tokyo. Sumo is highly ritualized. As part of the building up to the actual physical clash, the two contestants throw salt into the ring in order to cleanse it from evil spirits. This act of purification also has important gender implications, since a woman in the ring is seen to evoke the evil spirits.

The exclusion of women from the ring is taken so seriously that the female prefectural governor of Osaka since 2005 has been repeatedly forced to send a male counterpart to replace her when the traditional governor's prize is presented in the arena to the winner of the Osaka Tournament (AbcNEWS, 2007).

As a patriarchal institution professional Japanese sumo shows many traditional characteristics typical of other male competitive organizations summarized by 1) meritocracy, 2) hierarchy, and 3) stoicism. Sumo is fundamentally organized according to meritocratic principles that regulate the sumo wrestlers' place in the sport hierarchy. In a tournament, sumo wrestlers are promoted or downgraded, according to their performances in the prior tournament. Professional Japanese sumo consists of six divisions, and at the absolute top of the system are the ranks of the titleholders (*Sanyaku*) with the grand masters (*Yokozuna*) as its pinnacle. Very few attain the rank of honour of a yokozuna, which means that periodically there is only one or two in this top category. Like superstars, they attract maximum media attention (Thompson, 1998).

There are enormous differences in payment between the different divisions and only the wrestlers in the top divisions (*sekitori*) receive payment, since the wrestlers in the lower divisions are categorized as apprentices. In addition, it is only in the top prestige bouts that different companies donate economic support in exchange for advertisements executed by men parading in the ring with the company names before the start of the match. This highlights the fact that Japanese sports did not traditionally avoid commercialisation in the same manner as the Western split between amateurism and professionalism.

However, the meritocratic system is not complete unless a yokozuna exhibits a well-mannered and specifically 'Japanese' moral conduct (*hinkaku*: dignity) epitomized in the words: 'The yokozuna is sumo's representative man' (Thompson, 1998: 181). Furthermore, a yokozuna has to continuously perform at a top level and ideally win all tournaments in order to retain his title, and if he can't live up to these high expectations, he is expected to retire from active competition.

A foreign yokozuna is expected to act as if he is Japanese, speak Japanese, marry a Japanese wife, and behave according to Japanese customs. Therefore, traditionally it was very difficult for a foreigner to attain the rank of yokozuna. Very strict rules of behaviour, imposed on both Japanese sumo wrestlers and on foreign sumo wrestlers, are intrinsic to the production of a unique expression of masculinity. Yokozunas are expected to display perfect moral behaviour, as well as power and skill in the ring. In 2007 the Mongolian Asashoryu became the first yokozuna ever to be suspended from competition after having participated in a charity soccer match in his native country, during an alleged period of recovery from a sumo-related injury.

In 1972, the Hawaiian Jesse Kuhaulua, using the Japanese wrestler name Takamiyama (Daigorô), became the first foreigner to win the 'Emperors' Cup' but was never appointed yokozuna (Takamiyama et al., 1973). However, the first foreigner to break the glass ceiling by becoming a yokozuna was his apprentice, the Hawaiian born giant, Akebono, who did so in 1993 (Maeda, 2007: 11ff).

The inherent problem in the yokozuna system is the tension between adherence and achievement which means that many yokozunas are forced to leave the world of competition sumo at a very young age because they cannot live up to the moral requirements and/or the demand for continuous victories.

A great deal of stoicism is also demanded of sumo wrestlers, probably as a relic from samurai days when a warrior was expected to keep calm and avoid displaying emotions publicly as a response to either victory or defeat, expressed in the old samurai slogan requiring constant alertness: 'After victory, tighten your helmet cords!' Consequently, sumo wrestlers are expected to restrain their feelings of joy or resentment during and after the game. Furthermore, the sumo wrestlers are not expected to complain about the referee's decisions but must calmly accept his sovereign judgements.

This tradition for stoic demeanour is an integrated part of a greater value system of traditional Japanese sport and masculinity based on the principle of *Wa* which means 'harmony' (Whiting, 2009). All participants in the sumo world are expected to support the system and keep problems within the sumo movement as a strictly internal 'family' business.

These attitudes are still held in high regard by the older generations of Japanese to whom sumo has its widest appeal, whereas younger generations often feel more attracted to Japanese soccer which cultivates emotional and individual expressiveness in line with the international profile of this game.

To a Westerner sumo presents a strange mixture of martial traditions and male aesthetics. Sumo wrestlers attract huge crowds of female spectators both in Japan and abroad who not least are fascinated by the aesthetics of the game, and who idolise the wrestlers and follow their careers avidly. The long *hair* of the sumo wrestlers is prepared by hairdressers who have specialized in the use of special oil that helps to keep the top knot in place. The sumo wrestlers' hair is a symbol of his strength. As a consequence, a high-ranking wrestler's retirement ceremonies climax with the cutting of his top knot symbolizing that he is now stripped of this old samurai style of hair in order to enter the realm of the civilian world. The retirement ceremonies are witnessed by maybe thousands of his devoted fans.

During the opening ceremony of a sumo tournament, the highest ranking sumo wrestlers wear a *keshō-mawashi*, an ornate, embroidered silk 'apron' which typically symbolizes their strength in the form of a dragon or a mountain. Very rarely does a top wrestler lose his belt (loincloth) which is made of silk. If this does happen during a bout, it is seen as highly embarrassing and would immediately lead to disqualification.

Not only the body itself is aestheticized but, in addition, the many ceremonies during the 15-day sumo tournament rest upon the ability of the high ranking sumo wrestlers to perform short choreographic dance-like movements with dignity and poise. In particular the opening ceremony of the yokozuna resembles scenes from a male fertility cult with smooth and pronounced forwardly-oriented movements of the hips. During this act, the yokozuna is wearing a rope around his waist that weighs about 15 kg. Five zigzag paper strips that symbolize lightning hang from the front of the 'belt'. They are doubtlessly inspired by the lightning symbols that signal that you are entering a Shinto sanctuary.

Maybe the most peculiar characteristic of sumo is the overt celebration of the fat male body due to the fact that there are no weight categories in sumo. Often the more slim, agile and fit wrestler manages to defeat his bigger and fatter opponent which in general is highly popular with the audience. Whereas Western male sporting aesthetics are characterized by admiration of the slim, tight, well-defined muscular body, sumo offers more space for the celebration of the heavy, fat, strong body. In contrast to the Western athletic-looking aesthetic, over-size and weighty sumo wrestlers are adored by many Japanese women and become popular sex symbols. Perhaps the sufferings of the Japanese people during the Second World War postponed the development of more slim Westernized body ideals. Fat continued to be a symbol of health and wealth in the troubled Japanese culture for many decades following the Second World War. And, although increasingly residual, is still idealised today.

However, sumo also negotiates different ideals of masculinity. For the Japanese, the smaller man's victory over the giant is always popular, mirroring the achievements of the relatively small Japanese group of islands in competition against much bigger and more densely-populated states. The golden time of Japanese sumo surely took place in the early 1990s when the two strong and elegant Japanese brothers Takanohana and Wakanohana dominated sumo to such an extent that both of them became yokozunas. However, to the dismay of the Japanese fans, soon after, the hugely fat sumo wrestlers from Hawaii took over, which meant that greater body mass now mattered more than speed and technique. Today, Mongolian top wrestlers dominate Japanese professional sumo with their ability to combine traditional sumo with techniques from Mongolian wrestling (Hays, 2009a).

Furthermore, sumo exhibits a significant display of nationalism especially in the form of restrictions against the influx of foreign sumo wrestlers. This tendency is actually limiting the range of the ideal of meritocracy by favouring Japanese-born citizens. Today, a policy of 'one foreigner per stable' has been adopted. The reason is to make sure that Japanese-born citizens get the chance to win tournaments and hopefully even reach the level of yokozuna.

Sumo is a public celebration of masculinity that links a specifically Japanese sport to national pride. However, in general the direct symbolism of the nation is restricted to the raising of the Japanese national flag on the final day of the tournament. In the great sumo hall of Kokugikan in Tokyo, the occasional presence of the emperor and the imperial family in the imperial box naturally adds flavour to the national sentiments.

In recent years, the sumo world has been shocked by a number of scandals such as drug abuse. For example, in 2008 two Russian wrestlers were dismissed for smoking marihuana. The involvement by the Japanese mafia (the *yakuza*) in collaboration with sumo players in match fixing in baseball also has occurred (Capria, 2010). Furthermore, the misconduct of former yokozunas sometimes makes it to the headlines as did for instance Akebono's 'career', when he participated in the rather dubious form of martial arts, K1, in Seoul 2005. Akebono did not exhibit any talent whatsoever but his enormous body prevented many opponents from getting close enough to knock him out (Panek, 2006).

The worst case for sumo's already declining image has been revelations about the cruelties of the authoritarian and violent stable master–apprentice system which in its extreme form led to the death of a 17-year-old sumo wrestler in 2007. It turned out that he was beaten to death by the more senior sumo wrestlers and the stable master himself who were outraged by the young man's desire to leave the stable (Hays, 2009b).

In addition, during recent years meritocratic principles have been threatened by the revelation of a form of match fixing, i.e. that sumo wrestlers 'swap' victories in individual bouts, not least to help a colleague to avoid demotion from a division or even for pure material gain by means of secret payments (Hays, 2009b).

In 2008, as a response to the many scandals, the Ministry of Education appointed three external advisors who in reality were appointed to govern the sumo association. One of these officials actually functioned as the head of the sumo association during the suspension period of the former leader, Musashigawa. Furthermore, match fixing led to the suspension of sumo from television coverage at the Nagoya Tournament in 2010 (Hays, 2009b).

All in all, sumo offers an amalgamation of tradition and modernity which gives the strong, fat, male, Japanese sumo body a global appeal through televised sport. In this way, sumo expresses a form of *Glocalization* (Robertson, 1995) that combines the local Japanese perspective with global televised sport – in other words, the particular simultaneously with universal tendencies. In the case of sumo, the exoticism of the sport including the grotesqueness of the grandiose male body actually forms the main focus of attraction in the international desire for sumo entertainment.

However, nowadays traditional Japanese sumo is being challenged by international so-called 'amateur sumo' performed in many countries and ultimately aiming at participation at the Olympic Games. In this process of modernization, women have also been included as practitioners of the sport (Gilbert, 2010).

In summary, the long tradition of martial arts in Japanese history and the combination of upper class and warrior codes of behaviour in the times of samurai society is still echoed in modern society in the continued rather bourgeois taste for sumo especially in the older generations.

In many ways, sumo with its persistent patriarchal traits can be considered an anomaly in the modern globalized sports world. However, this is exactly what makes sumo scholarship interesting since it offers the possibility to study male bonding in its more 'pure' and original forms, as well as contemporary changes and practices.

Note

1 For a video of this ceremony, see: http://www.youtube.com/watch?v=zeSoYgTokuk

References

AbcNEWS (2007) 'Unclean' women banned by sumo association. *AbcNEWS*, Tokyo 6 March. Available at: http://abcnews.go.com/International/story?id=81421&page=1 (accessed 6 March 2013).

Capria A (2010) Sumo body-slammed by scandal. Available at: http://www.playthegame.org/news/detailed/sumo-body-slammed-by-scandal-4865.html (accessed 6 March 2013).

Gilbert HL (2010) Wrestling with globalisation: Amateur sumo as a nascent global sport. PhD Thesis, University of Auckland, NZ.

Guttmann A and Thompson L (2001) *Japanese Sports: A History*. Honolulu: University of Hawai'i Press.

Hays J (2009a) Hakuho, Harumafuji and other Mongolian sumo wrestlers. Available at: http://factsand-details.com/japan.php?itemid=751 (accessed 6 March 2013).

Hays J (2009b) Sumo scandals: Marijuana smoking, hairdresser incident and death of 17-year-old wrestler. Available at: http://factsanddetails.com/japan.php?itemid=755&catid=18 (accessed 6 March 2013).

Maeda M (2007) *Wild Men, Bad Boys, and Model Citizens: The Integration Foreigners in Sumo Wrestling*. Master Thesis, Faculty of the Graduate School, University of Southern California, US.

Masao Y (1998) Sumo in the popular culture of contemporary Japan. In: DP Martinez (ed) *The Worlds of Japanese Popular Culture: Gender, Shifting Boundaries and Global Cultures*. New York: Cambridge University Press, pp.19–29.

Nelson JK (2000) *Enduring Identities: The Guise of Shinto in Contemporary Japan*. Honolulu: University of Hawai'i Press.

Panek M (2006) *Gaijin Yokozuna: A Biography of Chad Rowan*. Honolulu: University of Hawai'i Press.

Robertson R (1995) Glocalization: Time-space and homogeneity-heterogeneity. In: M Featherstone, S Lash and R Robertson (eds) *Global Modernities*. London: Sage Publications, pp.25–44.

Takamiyama D (Kuhaulua J), Wheeler J and Givens DT (1973) *Takamiyama: The World of Sumo*. Tokyo: Kodansha International.

Thompson LA (1998) The Invention of the Yokozuna and the championship system, or, Futahaguro's revenge. In: S Vlastos (ed) *Mirror of Modernity: Invented Traditions of Modern Japan*. Berkeley and Los Angeles: University of California Press, pp.174–187.

Whiting R (2009) *You Gotta Have Wa*. New York: Vintage Books.

12

RITUALS OF THE MASCULINE STATE

Sports festivals, gender and power
in Laos and Southeast Asia

Simon Creak

Introduction

In December 2005 the seventh National Games opened in the city of Savannakhet in Laos, a small land-locked country in mainland Southeast Asia, ruled since 1975 by a Leninist one-party state. Based on the familiar Olympic format, the opening ceremony's local features made it meaningful for the Lao audience. One of these was a giant billboard of revolutionary leader Kaysone Phomvihane (1920–1992), a native of Savannakhet, beaming benevolently at the party leaders seated opposite and the common folks below. Reflecting on-going efforts by the Lao People's Revolutionary Party to create a leadership cult around Kaysone, the entire event was transformed into what might better be called the Kaysone Games.[1] A second local touch was a trio of women attired colourfully in the traditional dress of *lao lum* (lowland Lao), *lao thoeng* (Lao of the mountain slopes) and *lao sung* (Lao of the mountain tops), mirroring Laos's officially obsolete but still popular trinomial ethnic classification system. Striking a vivid contrast with the resplendent white of the uniformed military marching band, behind which they amiably sauntered, the three women led the athlete's procession carrying a banner pronouncing: 'Rejoice the VIIth National Games, Savannakhet, 13–21 December 2005'.

The striking aesthetics and semiotics of the opening ceremony highlight the fusing of gender and nation in sporting events like these. The three women highlighted the representation of female bodies as mannequins of national culture, tradition and, in the multi-ethnic states of Asia, ethnic essentialism, rendering them passive, ornamental and static. In contrast, the martial aesthetics of the military band and the image of 'Uncle Kaysone', founder of the revolutionary armed forces and father of the nation, reinforced the message that men make history. Such stereotypes are ubiquitous in postcolonial narratives: 'the female body in particular, with its softness and openings, has often been used to symbolise the endangered or dangerous social body', in dialectical contrast to 'hegemonic constructions of the state as masculine' (Ong and Peletz, 1995: 7). Whereas women's bodies stand as metaphors of the nation, men's are rendered as synonyms or metonyms of it; they *are* the nation (Radcliffe, 1999). Although similar gender representations can be found throughout Laos, their ubiquity in the National Games highlights the multifaceted ways in which sports and especially sports festivals materialise linkages between gender, the body and power in Laos and elsewhere in Southeast Asia.

Gender and power in Laos and Southeast Asia

Scholars of Southeast Asia have long emphasised the region's relative gender complementarity. In Laos and its Theravada Buddhist neighbours – Cambodia, Myanmar (Burma) and Thailand – this position flows from traditional arrangements of bilateral kinship, matrilocality and inheritance by the youngest daughter (Van Esterik, 2000: 14). It is also widely recognised, however, that 'women's "relatively high status" in Southeast Asia glosses autonomy in the home and economic control of resources', including a prominent role in commerce (Van Esterik, 2000: 28). By contrast, men and masculine institutions – notably the region's military forces – have maintained an overwhelming grip on national political power. Despite this recognition, the lack of attention to men and heteronormative masculinities has led scholars to critique the conflation of *gender* with *women* (Ong and Peletz, 1995: 7). Even while recognising that certain types of *men* possess the cultural sources of formal and informal political power, earlier studies of Southeast Asian political culture generally failed to appreciate the gendered, and specifically masculine, features of power (e.g. Anderson, 1990). Overlooking 'the man question', in Clark's (2010) felicitous phrase, 'misses a major, perhaps *the* major, way in which gender shapes politics – through men and their interests, their notions of manliness, and masculine micro and macro cultures' (Nagel, 1998: 243).

Although scholars have in recent years started to pay serious attention to men and masculinities in Southeast Asia, many have failed to address the most direct links between gender and power. For instance, a recent volume edited by Ford and Lyons (2012), sets out to critique RW Connell's (1995) defining formulation of hegemonic masculinity, particularly 'globalizing masculinities', by examining the region's marginalised masculinities. As a result of this focus, only one chapter (Jacobsen, 2012) examines the theme of leadership and masculinity, an area of Southeast Asian political culture that might challenge Connell's tendency towards universalising. Despite a chapter on minority Malay national servicemen in Singapore (Lyons and Ford, 2012), the book also overlooks how masculinity is allied to mainstream political power in the military and security services, an astonishing lacuna given such institutions' fundamental part in the region's postcolonial politics. Most significantly, the book altogether ignores sport and physical culture, which, in Southeast Asia in common with countries across the world, is a major site where hegemonic masculinity is formed and reproduced (Creak, 2010a; Pattana, 2005). The volume editors echo familiar concerns that hegemonic masculinity is too often conflated with dominant men, but by skimming over (or ignoring) regional leadership, military institutions and sports, they overlook not only the dominant men, but also modes of masculinity that are critical in the maintenance of male political power.

In modern Southeast Asia, male cultures of leadership and militarism bind masculinity and autocratic power. Across the region we can observe a 'personal style of leadership that one is inclined to label fascist [but which] is better understood in other terms' (Reynolds, 2012: 271). Always male, leaders of this kind often possess a military background and epitomise the 'strongman'. Ascetic qualities are often a feature of this mode of leadership; despite apparent contradictions, both military and monastic training embody discipline. At the same time, assumptions of non-attachment in Buddhist societies conceal the reality that Southeast Asian Buddhism is replete with images of the body, which offer 'security and promote the value of abundance' (McDaniel, 2011: 176). The Lao and Thai word for abundance (*udom sombun*) appears ubiquitously in discussions of sport and health, illustrating how physical culture constituted 'a kind of "muscular Buddhism" that drew on the character- and state-building logic of European muscular Christianity, but was also enmeshed in the ideas and practices of Buddhism' (Creak, 2011a: 19). The importance of the body in masculinity is reflected in the popularity among men of protective rituals and amulets, believed to bestow physical invulnerability and good fortune (McDaniel, 2011; Reynolds, 2011), and the ubiquity of sex, as leaders have often benefited from reputations as womanisers (Jacobsen, 2012).

These qualities of masculine leadership can be observed in the *nakleng*, the Thai rural tough who was equally feared and admired as he exercised authority, within and outside the law (Keyes, 1986; Reynolds, 2011). Such modes of leadership are related to traditions glossed as the 'big man', 'man of (Buddhist) merit' and 'man of prowess', which are replicated across Southeast Asian societies (Wolters, 1999). From villages to national capitals, big men and little big men jostle for power and its spoils. Gaining and retaining this kind of power traditionally depended on performance: of benevolence, charisma and strength and ruthlessness, all of which enhanced a leader's *barami*, his charisma and innate authority (Reynolds, 2012). Far from disappearing, modes of performance related to leadership and masculinity have been enhanced with modern technologies of power and communication.

In the post-war era of decolonisation, national games and similar regional sports festivals emerged as a key genre of state performance that bound the muscular body to masculine leadership. Of course, political leaders everywhere perceive benefits in associating themselves with athletes and sporting events. But the persistence of themes from colonial-era sport, particularly the military aesthetics of the sports festival, highlights qualitative links between sport, masculinity and political power that abound in the postcolonial societies of Southeast Asia. Such festivals are archetypically postcolonial, not only temporally and in the sense that they have derived from local and colonial traditions, but also because they express the cultural and political struggles that have occurred since decolonisation (Ong and Peletz, 1995). As a product of colonialism, royalist nationalism and revolutionary socialism, modern Laos provides fertile ground on which to explore these themes.

Colonial antecedents

Laos was created as a colonial territory in French Indochina in 1893 from a number of Lao kingdoms previously under Siamese (Thai) suzerainty. Although linkages between gender, physical culture and political power predate colonial times (Creak, 2010a: ch.1), early colonial physical culture linked the male body to power in novel ways, by seeking to ameliorate 'deficiencies' of the native body. Mirroring colonial stereotypes that contrasted the 'lazy Lao' with the 'dynamic and industrious Vietnamese' (Ivarsson, 2008: 104), such corporeal representations helped to facilitate colonialism (Larcher-Goscha, 2003: 20). In institutional terms, the first physical culture programmes in Laos were organised by Indochina's Central Committee of Physical Education and Military Preparation, establishing military links that would persist for decades (Creak, 2010a). Together with the emergence of male-only sporting clubs in the Mekong valley and the fact that few girls completed school, where physical education was taught, these military roots ensured that early colonial physical culture was overwhelmingly for men.

Links between masculinity, physical culture and colonialism intensified during the so-called Vichy National Revolution (1940–1944), when the Vichy regime in French Indochina 'cloned' the ultra-conservative metropolitan programme of fostering cultural identities, promoting physical culture and reinforcing 'traditional' gender roles (Jennings, 2001). As in the empire more generally, the Indochinese National Revolution tied sport and physical culture to gender, race and civilisation, seeking to use sports and physical education to 'transfigure' the Indochinese 'race'. In 1942, the governor general, Admiral Jean Decoux, boasted that 'a new type of man is being born, or should I say, the true type of Indochinese man is being reborn, after centuries of indifference to physical development' (Jennings, 2001: 188).

In line with Vichy's paradoxical policy of promoting parallel local, federal and imperial identities, the Lao version of the revolution, the Lao Nhay or 'Great Laos' movement, attempted to foster a proto-national Lao identity in the face of Siamese irredentism (Ivarsson, 2008). The federal sport and physical training programme – including the establishment of youth cadre schools and high-profile *grandes manifestations sportives* (great sporting events) – was replicated on a smaller scale in Laos, where healthy bodies were linked instrumentally and metaphorically to the renovation of the Lao *petite patrie* (small homeland) within the Indochinese federation and French empire (Creak, 2010a: 88).

According to the overt essentialism of Vichy gender ideology – construed as 'modern' in Laos – these linkages took place through the masculine body. The physically adept male body was equated with the emergence of the proto-national Lao identity, whether it was pictured toned, shirtless and muscular on the pages of *Sport et Jeunesse de l'Indochine*, or sketched in the Lao youth uniform, sporting the Lao letter 'L' for Laos, on the pages of the *Lao Nhay* newspaper. By contrast, women's physical culture was modified to protect the reproductive anatomy, and rhythmic gymnastics, said to be 'uniquely adapted to the particular physiology and destiny of the woman', replaced the French method (Creak, 2010a: 73). Basketball was also acceptable for women; in a celebrated case, a young princess founded a basketball team in the royal capital of Luang Prabang. But, more generally women had a different role to play in the movement. Defining them as 'people who do housework and manage the household', the intellectual Pierre Somchin Nginn urged women to join Lao Nhay women's groups to learn the 'modern system of housework' (Creak, 2010a: 87).

The colonial and postcolonial sports festival

The gendered politics of Vichy-era physical culture was summed up in the 'great sports day' (*grande journée sportive*), which linked power and the body in unprecedented displays of military masculinity. Based on Olympic precedents and military themes, sport and youth groups would march into a stadium and assemble behind flag masts, before being reviewed by military dignitaries. Then would follow a flag-raising ceremony, the sportsman's oath, acclamation of names (of imperial, federal and local leaders), and gymnastics displays and sports competitions (Creak, 2010a: 92–93). The resplendent human movement of the *grande journée* brought to life Vichy-era patriotism and ideology. The marching and arrangement of sporting groups momentarily transformed the stadium into a proto-national space, representing the symbolic unity of Laos, while the acclamation of names showed that the *petite patrie* existed only within, and thanks to, the federal Indochinese and French imperial spaces. The sports events embodied the subject-forming characteristics of diligence, discipline, hierarchy and self-reliance.

Although debates continue over whether Vichy France (and its colonies) was fascist, the aesthetics of the *grande journée* certainly had much in common with those of Vichy's fascist contemporaries: disciplined and uniformed bodies in formation under the gaze of military leaders; the official 'Olympic salute', identical in appearance to the Nazi salute; and the toned, shirtless bodies of young men. We do not know with certainty if women marched or not, but they do not appear in pictures. Even if they did participate, the scripted militarism and male oversight of sports days, together with the men's sporting events that followed, gave them an element of 'aggressive masculinity' that is a core element of fascist style (McDonald, 2008: 57). Such masculine physical cultures and aesthetics emerged around the same time elsewhere in the region, often due to Japanese influence. In the late 1930s Thailand's first military dictator, Field Marshal Phibul Songkran, was impressed by Japanese militarism and *bushido*, Japan's traditional warrior ethic, while Indonesia's independence fighters were shaped by contacts with the Japanese during the Second World War.

As Laos moved towards independence after 1945, associations between physical culture and masculinity were enthusiastically appropriated in the name of the independent nation of Laos. The Kingdom of Laos was formed with limited autonomy in 1946, before acquiring additional powers in 1949–1950 and 1953–1954, when colonialism officially ended. As the military expanded exponentially, both in size and influence, military modes of masculinity were grafted onto existing sources of male power, which in some cases were also militaristic. Military masculinity was developed in the body, through physical training and in the uniform, and by means of character-training in attributes such as diligence, courage, strength, proficiency, discipline, spirit, and especially friendship, or what Thai historian Nidhi Eoseewong (2012) calls 'deep bonding' with other soldiers, always male. Military masculinity was also institutionalised in the national police, scouts and the National School for Youth and Physical Education Cadres, based on Vichy-era predecessors. Symbolising parallels with monastic masculinity, the school was based in the cloister of the That Luang, a sacred pagoda and symbol of the nation (Creak, 2010a).

Despite its official designation as a nation, royalist Laos remained weak and dependent on external support in these years. With the communist Pathet Lao fighting alongside Vietnamese communists for a different national future, the royal government could not boast a monopoly over the legitimate use of lethal force, let alone control of national territory. As one of the few expressions of nationhood available to the new state, state performances of military masculinity gave symbolic substance to the emergent nation. This was captured in militarised sports and youth events such as one held in 1950 to mark the transfer of powers from France to Laos. Such events encapsulated the military and masculine cultures of the new Lao state, demonstrating the extent to which the disciplined male body became a motif of independent Laos.

Masculine power and performance in postcolonial sports festivals

In Laos and elsewhere in Southeast Asia, decolonisation saw the establishment of national and international sports festivals. In transforming the region's existing cultures of political pomp and performance, these events drew on colonial-era antecedents, the format of the Olympics and Asian Games, and modern technologies of communication (Creak, 2010c). As these influences were refashioned to serve the ideologies and concerns of the postcolonial moment – nation building, modernisation, anti-communism, anti-imperialism, and region formation – sports festivals emerged as a powerful and fashionable stage on which charismatic Southeast Asian autocrats could perform the masculine rituals of modern statesmanship.

The common feature of these festivals was their link to autocratic modes of masculinity and leadership. The South East Asia Peninsular (SEAP) Games, which brought together Burma, Cambodia, Laos, Malaya, Singapore, South Vietnam and Thailand, were founded in 1959 by the Olympic Committee of Thailand (OCT), headed at the time by Lieutenant-General Praphat Charusatien, a protégé of the charismatic and ruthless anti-communist, Field Marshall Sarit Thanarat. For his part, Sarit epitomised the pro-American military strongman of the Cold War era, espousing military virtues of discipline, unity and strong leadership, granting himself untrammelled powers, and committing violence with impunity. More subtly, he restored royal rituals that allowed him to benefit from the *barami* (Buddhist charisma) of King Bhumibol, and surrounded himself with beautiful women, enhancing his *barami* more directly (Baker and

Pasuk, 2005). Capturing the mutually beneficial embrace between an ascendant military and resurgent monarchy, the inaugural 1959 SEAP Games in Bangkok were overseen by Sarit and opened by the king.

In parallel to the SEAP Games, the National Games of Indonesia (PON) and the Games of the New Emerging Forces (GANEFO) were founded (respectively in 1948 and 1963) by Indonesia's charismatic independence leader and self-styled moderniser extraordinaire, President Sukarno. While never a military man, Sukarno rose to prominence under the Japanese occupation and was said to admire Hitler for his oratory, air of superiority and strong leadership (Anderson, 1990). If in the PON he performed the role of national unifier and moderniser, GANEFO allowed him to flaunt his growing power and rising international profile on the world stage (Brown, 2008; Pauker, 1965). The second GANEFO in 1966 was held in Phnom Penh under Prince Sihanouk, another charismatic leader of formidable political skills, who loomed similarly over Cambodian political life in the postcolonial era.

Founded in 1961, the Lao National Games were similarly associated with a single autocratic leader, General Phoumi Nosavan. An anti-communist strongman in the mould of Sarit, to whom he was related by marriage, and epitomising 'a particular cultural ideal of the tough *phu nyai*' (big man), Phoumi emulated Sarit's rise on the back of American patronage and ruthless self-interest in the context of the Cold War (Evans, 2002: 115). At a time when Laos was rife with disunity, the National Games gave Phoumi a stage on which to display his self-styled image as national unifier and moderniser, no matter how inaccurate the claim, as the stadium was momentarily transformed into the nation in miniature. Though he was certainly not the most charismatic leader of the times, Phoumi perhaps saw the games as a way to match the prestige of his rivals, and the event collapsed with his exit from the political scene in 1965 (Creak, 2010c).

Susan Brownell has noted how the Chinese national games 'dramatize and reinforce a world-order . . . with the state portrayed as the keeper of that order' (Brownell, 1995: 122). In postcolonial Southeast Asia such events reflected, and reinforced, masculine modes of autocracy under particular leaders rather than a monolithic state. Anderson (1990, Ch.1) argues that in Javanese political culture autocracy is nothing to shy away from; what matters is whether an autocrat is worthy of his power. In a circular fashion, worthiness can be demonstrated by performance of that power. Echoing Geertz's polemical study of political pomp as an end in itself, power is performance and performance is power (Geertz, 1980). Scholars have rightly criticised Anderson's notion of power as essentialist and ahistorical, stressing that we must identify the specific social, political and historical contexts that produce or reproduce it (Eklof, 2007). These are often more recent than they might seem. Combining militaristic pomp, cosmopolitan rituals of Olympism, and modern media and communications technologies from public address systems to photography and television, postcolonial sports festivals provide an especially striking example of how modern history has shaped political cultures of autocracy in Laos and Southeast Asia more generally.

Most critically, sports festivals highlight the gendered features of such performance and power, specifically that masculine power is masculine performance and masculine performance is masculine power. Like appearing with actresses and beauty queens, overseeing sports festivals enhanced the sign of an autocrat's masculinity and his *barami*. As in the case of Phoumi, an amateur boxer in his youth, the games could enhance the self-image of the leader as physically adept and even a sportsman. But, more importantly, by overseeing sports events leaders could absorb and display the power of the masculine performance and the bodies before him. In postcolonial Indonesia, stresses Anderson, local modes of power could be absorbed from potent cultural sources including power-full words, power-full experiences and power-full collectivities (Anderson, 1990: 26). To

117

this repertoire we must add power absorbed from power-full bodies, which Anderson overlooks as a means of concentrating, displaying and associating oneself with the masculine power represented by the hard, defined and even aggressive athletic body.

Given the spectrum of political positions they buttressed, it would be mistaken to label Southeast Asia's postcolonial sporting games as fascist. But like fascist physical culture, they were characterised by an authoritarian style and aesthetics that was muscular and masculine, in spite of and because of participation by female athletes. This was not because militaristic aesthetics are essentially masculine, but because of the historical and cultural factors that make this appear so (Hargreaves, 1994). These aesthetics reflected the extreme violence and aggressive masculinity of postcolonial Southeast Asia, as exemplified by the hot and cold wars that defined the times, state violence and impunity to sanction, and atrocities in Indonesia (1965–1966) and Cambodia (1975–1979). While women certainly took part in sports games, making them a symbolic part of whichever body politic was assembled, their presence could not diminish the era's dominant atmosphere of masculine militarism, confirmed by the unconcealed womanising of leaders of the masculine state – Sarit, Sukarno, Sihanouk and Phoumi alike. The similar benefits for each leader's masculine image of being associated with women and sports added heterosexuality to the potent mix of masculinity, militarism and the sporting body, the amalgam of which enhanced symbolic masculine power.

In Laos these patterns changed after 1975, when the Lao People's Revolutionary Party seized power and proclaimed the Lao People's Democratic Republic. As part of its sweeping 'revolution in culture and ideology', the party-state sought to build a 'new socialist person' defined by physical and moral attributes and, more broadly, constructed a cosmology of socialist transformation couched in physical metaphor and idiom (Creak, 2010b). Although the new regime's policy of promoting gender equality was easily criticised – the so-called 'three goods' urged women to be a 'good wife, good mother, good citizen' – it paid increased attention to women's sports, including them in national celebrations such as National Day and International Women's Day. Table tennis player Souphavanh Phiathep was awarded a military honour and later feted as a heroine for her 'great victory' at the Three Continents Championships in Mexico City in 1976. The new socialist Lao National Games, conducted from 1985, included large numbers of both women and men, whose similar modes of movement and dress in mass callisthenics displays resembling those in China and other communist countries flattened distinctions between them (Creak, 2010a). In addition, while the national leadership remained male, authoritarian and militarised, the party structure reduced the emphasis on individual leaders. These changes reflected broader social realities as the militarist state became more inclusive of women, including them in the armed forces and militia training.

High socialism lasted little more than a decade in Laos. With economic reforms introduced in 1986, the collapse of communism in Europe a few years later hastened the return of pre-1975 cultural features of nationalism (Evans, 1998). As rhetoric of the new socialist person faded away, the idea of 'renewing' people remained in the reformulated concept of 'culture in the new era' (Pholsena, 2006). Cultural displays became an increasingly important and sophisticated part of the National Games, especially from the 1990s as, despite obvious budgetary differences, new expressions of national culture reflected the influence of global mega-event norms. As indicated in the opening vignette of this chapter, these included highly-stylised and stereotyped images of gender and ethnicity.

The cultural performances of the 2009 Southeast Asian (SEA) Games, the first time Laos hosted this successor of the SEAP Games, encapsulated the return to earlier gender norms, constituting a grand demonstration of official culture, in which dancing women represented grace and combative men strength and dynamism. Although militarism is less pervasive today in both sport and society, militarist features in the 2009 games included military marching bands and military units marching with flags. Performances continued to buttress the image of the party above individual leaders, though in recent years they have increasingly celebrated heroic figures ('national ancestors') in official historiography. Whether these are revolutionary leaders like Kaysone (as mentioned above) or kings of a different era, these figures are all men, again reinforcing the links between masculine performance and the masculine nation and state (Creak, 2011b).

Conclusion

The aggressive militarism of the sports festivals of the 1950s and 1960s may have faded in more recent years, but on-going symbolic links between the militarised, masculine body and the militarised, masculine state demonstrate a persistent alliance between masculine physical culture and autocratic rule in Laos and Southeast Asia. Although the role of such festivals in buttressing authoritarian state power has attracted much attention in sports studies and other fields, there has been a tendency to focus on extremist regimes, such as those of fascist Europe or the communist bloc. By contrast, the widespread presence of such themes in Southeast Asia, which took root under colonialism and blossomed under postcolonial regimes of all political shades, illustrates how 'ordinary' these associations have become. It is precisely this ordinariness that allows official public displays of masculine strength and power to normalise and thus reinforce, again and again, the masculine culture of authoritarian state power.

Note

1   In Laos, people are referred to by their first names. For the Kaysone cult, see Evans (1998).

References

Anderson B (1990) *Language and Power: Exploring Political Cultures in Indonesia*. Ithaca: Cornell University Press.
Baker C and Pasuk Phongpaichit (2005) *A History of Thailand*. Cambridge: Cambridge University Press.
Brown C (2008) Sport, modernity and nation building: The Indonesian National Games of 1951 and 1953. *Bijdragen tot de Taal-, Land- en Volkenkunde (BKI)* 164: 431–449.
Brownell S (1995) *Training the Body for China: Sports in the Moral Order of the People's Republic*. Chicago: University of Chicago Press.
Clark M (2010) *Maskulinitas: Culture, Gender and Politics in Indonesia*. Caulfield (Victoria): Monash University Press.
Connell RW (1995) *Masculinities*. Berkeley: University of California Press.
Creak S (2010a) 'Body work': A history of sport and physical culture in colonial and postcolonial Laos. PhD Thesis, Australian National University, Australia. Revised version to be published as: Creak, S (2014) Body Work: *Sport, Physical Culture and the Making of Modern Laos*. Honolulu: University of Hawaii Press.
Creak S (2010b) Cold War rhetoric and the body: Physical cultures in early socialist Laos. In: Day T and Liem M (eds) *Cultures at War: The Cold War and Cultural Expression in Southeast Asia*. Ithaca: Cornell Southeast Asia Program Publications, pp.103–130.
Creak S (2010c) Sport and the theatrics of power in a postcolonial state: The National Games of 1960s Laos. *Asian Studies Review* 34(2): 191–210.
Creak S (2011a) Muscular Buddhism for modernizing Laos. *Journal of Lao Studies* 2(2): 1–22.
Creak S (2011b) Sport as politics and history: The 25th SEA Games in Laos. *Anthropology Today* 27(1): 14–19.
Eklof, S (2007) *Power and Political Culture in Suharto's Indonesia: The Indonesian Democratic Party and Decline of the New Order (1986–98)*. Copenhagen: NIAS Press.

Evans, G (1998) *The Politics of Ritual and Remembrance: Laos since 1975*. Chiang Mai: Silkworm Books.

Evans, G (2002) *A Short History of Laos: The Land in Between*. Crows Nest (NSW): Allen and Unwin.

Ford M and Lyons L (2012) Introduction. In: Ford M and Lyons L (eds) *Men and Masculinities in Southeast Asia*. London and New York: Routledge, pp.1–19.

Geertz C (1980) *Negara: The Theatre State in Nineteenth-Century Bali*. Princeton: Princeton University Press.

Hargreaves J (1994) *Sporting Females: Critical Issues in the History and Sociology of Women's Sports*. London and New York: Routledge.

Ivarsson S (2008) *Creating Laos: The Making of a Lao Space between Indochina and Siam, 1860–1945*. Copenhagen: NIAS Press.

Jacobsen T (2012) Being *broh*: The good, the bad and the successful man in Cambodia. In: Ford M and Lyons L (eds) *Men and Masculinities in Southeast Asia*. London and New York: Routledge, pp.86–102.

Jennings, E (2001) *Vichy in the Tropics: Pétain's National Revolution in Madagascar, Guadeloupe, and Indochina, 1940–1944*. Stanford: Stanford University Press.

Keyes C (1986) Ambiguous gender: Male initiation in a northern Thai Buddhist society. In: Bynum CW, Harrell S and Richman P (eds) *Gender and Religion: On the Complexity of Symbols*. Boston: Beacon Press, pp.66–96.

Larcher-Goscha A (2003) Sport, colonialisme et identités nationales: Premières approches du 'corps à corps colonial' en Indochine (1918–1945). In: Bancel N and Fates DY (eds) *De l'Indochine à l'Algérie: La Jeunesse en Mouvements des Deux Côtés du Miroir Colonial*. Paris: Éditions la Découverte, pp.15–31.

Lyons L and Ford M (2012) Defending the Nation: Malay men's Experience of National Service in Singapore. In: Ford M and Lyons L (eds) *Men and Masculinities in Southeast Asia*. London and New York: Routledge, pp.139–158.

McDaniel JT (2011) *The Lovelorn Ghost and the Magical Monk: Practicing Buddhism in Modern Thailand*. New York: Columbia University Press.

McDonald, I (2008) Political somatics: Fascism, physical culture, and the sporting body. In: Hargreaves J and Vertinsky PA (eds) *Physical Culture, Power, and the Body*. Milton Park, Oxon, and New York: Routledge, pp.52–73.

Nagel J (1998) Masculinity and nationalism: Gender and sexuality in the making of nations. *Ethnic and Racial Studies* 21(2): 242–269.

Nidhi Eoseewong (2012) The culture of the army. In: Montesano MJ, Pavin Chachavalpongpun and Aekapol Chongvilaivan (eds) *Bangkok May 2010: Perspectives in a Divided Thailand*. Singapore: ISEAS Publishing, pp.10–14.

Ong A and Peletz MG (1995) Introduction. In: Ong A and Peletz MG (eds) *Bewitching Women, Pious Men: Gender and Body Politics in Southeast Asia*. Berkeley: University of California Press.

Pattana Kitiarsa (2005) 'Lives of hunting dogs': Muai Thai and the politics of Thai masculinities. *South East Asia Research* 13(1): 57–90.

Pauker ET (1965) Ganefo I: Sports and politics in Djakarta. *Asian Survey* 5(4): 171–185.

Pholsena V (2006) *Post-War Laos: The Politics of Culture, History and Identity*. Singapore: ISEAS Publishing.

Radcliffe S (1999) Embodying national identities: *Mestizo* men and white women in ecuadorian racial-national imaginaries. *Transactions of the Institute of British Geographers* 24(2): 213–225.

Reynolds CJ (2011) Rural male leadership, religion and the environment in Thailand's mid-South, 1920s–1960s. *Journal of Southeast Asian Studies* 42(1): 39–57.

Reynolds CJ (2012) The social bases of autocratic rule in Thailand. In: Montesano MJ, Pavin Chachavalpongpun and Aekapol Chongvilaivan (eds) *Bangkok, May 2010*. Singapore: ISEAS Publishing, pp.267–273.

Van Esterik P (2000) *Materializing Thailand*. Oxford and New York: Berg.

Wolters OW (1999) *History, Culture, and Region in Southeast Asian Perspectives*, revised edition. Ithaca: Cornell Southeast Asia Program Publications.

13

GENDERED BARRIERS TO BRAZILIAN FEMALE FOOTBALL

Twentieth-century legacies[1]

Jorge Knijnik

Introduction

The 2011 Women's Football World Cup, hosted by Germany, was seen by the Brazilian team as an opportunity to win the gold medal, consequently improving the situation for women's football in Brazil. The captain, Aline Pellegrino, told the international press that her team was looking for better conditions for female footballers in Brazil: 'We want the right to play football with dignity and minimal conditions in our country. We don't need the millionaire wages of the men's football, but we need respect', she declared (UOL, 2011). Hence, the team's hope had been to win a major title in order to realise better conditions for female football in Brazil.

Their expectations of a good result in the tournament were justified: the Brazilian team had won silver medals in all major competitions in the previous few years; they were run-ner-up at both the Athens and the Beijing Olympic Games, as well as at the 2007 Women's World Cup hosted by China. Marta, the star of the team, had also been elected five times by FIFA as the world's best female player. However, despite high expectations for the 2011 Women's Football World Cup, the Brazilian women's football team lost to the United States in the quarter-finals. With that unexpected and premature defeat, the future of the players, and of female football in Brazil, was once again uncertain. The players knew that they would be returning to Brazil with no guarantees of their careers; the same lack of support and the same prejudices would remain.

In her recent paper on feminism and football studies, Caudwell (2011: 341) discusses many issues that can help to 'maintain the momentum of the feminist project in football'. She high-lights that in the UK the social and legal changes pushed by the liberal feminist agenda have 'helped young women and girls take up sports, such as football' (Caudwell, 2011: 332). Never-theless, she makes clear that behind the histories of female participation in football, it is possible to see 'harassment, discrimination and abuse' (Caudwell, 2011: 330). Caudwell therefore argues that 'sexism and misogyny are very sharp and chilling reminders that gendered social relations remain significant influencing forces in society and in football contexts' (Caudwell, 2011: 331).

Caudwell's points are critical to understanding today's female participation in football in South America – particularly in Brazil.

Facing a history of legal prohibitions, gender and sexuality discrimination and all types of barriers to playing the sport, women footballers have entered the twenty-first century burdened with a heavy inheritance: football, the major symbol of Brazilian culture, is still seen as a male space across the country (Knijnik, 2011). Brazilian women have felt excluded from what Bellos (2002) describes as the 'Brazilian way of life', football, the cultural expression that makes Brazilians proud of themselves (Natali, 2007).

Therefore, and borrowing Caudwell's points and feminist agenda, to further football studies in South America, in this chapter I ask: what is the 20th century legacy for women's football in Brazil? How do the 'sexism and misogyny' noted by Caudwell for the UK context operate in Brazilian football today? Do the female Brazilian players see themselves as challenging gender barriers and the normative heterosexuality imposed on them or do they conform to the dominant norms in order to survive on the football field?

In the following section, I give a historical account of what I call the *gendered 20th century legacy of Brazilian football.* I explain the policies, historical facts and social context that have contributed to this legacy. Then, following an explanation of my research route into the world of female football, I carry out a discourse analysis of in-depth interviews (Minichiello et al., 1995) with high-level female football players to reflect on their concepts of femininity(ies), on the use of their female bodies, and on sexuality. In this analysis, I use a theoretical framework of the 'technologies of sexiness' provided by Radner (2008), as well as some of the gender issues raised by Caudwell (2011: 339) in her 'effort to make complex our approach to critical analyses of football cultures'. Finally, I offer some possible scenarios for both further research and for the development of female football in Brazil.

Rotten roots: a brief history of Brazilian sports laws affecting women

For many decades 'women's sport has been trivialized and marginalized by a sexist culture' (Anderson, 2010: 131). Though referring to the USA, this quotation finds an extraordinary echo in Brazilian sports history. During the first four decades of the last century, an increasing number of experts – medical doctors, educators, physiologists and lawyers – engaged in public and tense debates about the female body, its possibilities and limitations. With a misogynistic agenda grounded in unscientific facts – such as the 'inappropriateness and ungracefulness' of the female body for physical contact sports like martial arts or football, which were considered to be in opposition to the 'natural feminine soul' (Ballaryni, 1940: 36) – these were male voices undertaking a public campaign to spread their chauvinistic ideas about women in sports. As a consequence of their efforts, in 1941 the National Sports Council agreed on legislation which disallowed women to practise sports considered improper for the 'female's body nature' (Goellner, 2005: 147). At that time, girls and women in Brazil were limited or outlawed from participating in sports such martial arts, pentathlon, decathlon, indoor and outdoor football (Mourão and Morel, 2005).

As a direct effect of the 1941 legislation, many good female teams were forced to close their doors (Rigo, 2005) and female football practically stopped across the country. It took 38 years for the law to be dismissed and Brazilian women to be allowed to openly play football in parks, schools and stadia. Only in 1979 was the law abolished by sports legislators, and, four years later, female football was officially acknowledged as a sport by the National Sports Council (Rigo, 2005). By 1983, several female teams were being organized in the main states of the country (Votre and Mourão, 2003).

However, if the law had changed, mentalities had not. Homophobia, considered by Anderson (2010: 132) to be the 'most common type of sexual harassment' in sport settings was strongly present in all game contexts. Women who wanted to enter this male fortress were discriminated against as 'non-feminine' and lesbian, and stereotyped as mannish women. As Votre and Mourão (2003: 265) write, 'whenever there is talk of women's football, the erotic dimension again takes precedent over the technical'.[2]

The result was that, after the 'boom' during the 1980s, female football in Brazil was gradually cut down by the same old prejudices. First, the big clubs and then the small ones started to close their space to female players. By the end of the twentieth century, female football in Brazil was struggling to survive even as an amateur activity. The better players went to play abroad, most to the US league, and those who stayed in Brazil were obliged to take any sort of work in order to survive (Knijnik, 2013). Female football had once again been dumped in Brazil.

At the beginning of the twenty-first century, female football in Brazil was in a tattered state, with no places to play and no support of any type for the players. Then, in 2001, one of the most important and richest Brazilian sports bodies, the Sao Paulo Football Federation (FPF), decided to promote a new female championship. Initially, this looked to be a positive move as it was fed by the legacy which continues to undermine women's football in Brazil. The powerful (male) FPF managers had advertised a 'new era' for female football, in which they would combine technique with aesthetics (Knijnik and Horton, 2013). Accordingly, they organized a tournament in which all players were expected to comply with a 'normative femininity' (Caudwell, 2011). While the 'rules' of normative femininity are sometimes blurred, this time the managers were clear: they advertised for beautiful young girls, no older than 23, preferably blonde and with long hair – no shaved heads or short haircuts were allowed.

Following this desire, during the trials, when the FPF managers were choosing players for the teams, they selected white-skinned players even over more talented darker athletes. In common with FIFA's president, they considered 'femininity' to be 'foremost' (Caudwell, 2011: 335) in female football. Their attempt to exclude any external signs of homosexuality was clear; they were looking to produce a female football competition in which the dominant version of femininity was 'white-heterosexual' (Caudwell, 2011: 338). In this exclusion, they also omitted athletes who had played at the Sydney Olympics, many of whom were black, had shaved heads, or were older than 23.

The FPF championship, entitled the *Paulistana* (meaning a woman born in Sao Paulo), received reasonable TV coverage, with some matches broadcast live by a free channel on Saturday mornings. The *Paulistana* was strongly criticized for its violations of the basic human rights of the players (Knijnik and Horton, 2013). Dr. Rosinha, a federal representative and member of the Worker's Party, made a formal denunciation against the FPF to the public prosecutor. In his representation, Dr. Rosinha was denouncing the discriminatory acts that happened in the *Paulistana*; he said that 'if male professional football is corrupted and full of irregularities, [. . .] to the female football we must add *machismo* and racism as new ingredients' (Brazilian Parliament Press, 2001). As it was under attack from several directions, the *Paulistana* has never been repeated.

Female football in Brazil remained in the doldrums for the next three years. At the beginning of 2004, and after the male team's defeat in the qualifiers for the Athens Olympics, the Brazilian Football Federation organized a female national team, calling in the best players who had been playing overseas. This team drew the country's attention, as it did very well at the Athens Olympics, ending up with the silver medal.[3]

It was only after the success in Athens that in the second half of 2004, a female football championship was again organized in Brazil. On this occasion, however, the organizer was not the FPF. The idea and the action came from the Sports Department of the State Government of Sao Paulo, at that time led by Lars Grael. As a former Olympic athlete, Grael was aware of the lack of support that many athletes received in Brazil. He was also conscious that female footballers were struggling to find locations to play. Recognizing the quantity of skilled female players with the desire but lacking the resources, he put the employees in his department to work on a solution. The result was the creation of a major female football championship, organized and implemented in less than two months. Despite this rush, the championship was a success, with more than 50 teams and nearly 1,000 thousand players from several small cities throughout Sao Paulo registering for the event.

My research

I had been following the female football situation in the country for some time and had undertaken interviews with the women who had played in the *Paulistana*. I saw this new championship in 2004 as an opportunity to extend my research in the world of female footballers. Thus, as soon as the competition started, I went to a stadium where four teams were to play a three-day round[4] and began to seek interviews. Thus, the interviews I present in this chapter were carried out in the context of this championship, the first major female football event in Brazil after years of oblivion. All names have been anonymized.

My research became easier as, on my very first day while I was waiting for the matches to start, I noticed an old student of mine, Daniela. She was looking for her team when I called her name. With a big smile, she replied: 'I can't believe you remember me, teacher!' I did remember her: a left-handed and concentrated goalkeeper, who had never missed sports practice at school. She was also dark-skinned, and from a lower socio-economic background. Daniela quickly told me her story of the last few years.

She had had a young child with a man, probably a drug trafficker, who had been killed by the police. She worked as a driver of illegal public transport while playing football. She introduced me to all her teammates and to her coach, who happened to be the only female coach of the four teams which were playing that round. The coach allowed me not only to talk to her athletes, but also invited me to stay with them during the three days of that round.

Throughout our conversations it became clear that, despite claiming their rights as players and therefore being able to challenge the various gender hurdles that daily confront them, many interviewees were still dominated by what I call twentieth-century gendered ideologies and legacies. This is to say that they rely on assumptions about the female body, female sexuality and the 'technology of sexiness' (Radner, 2008). Many players still believe that they suffer prejudice as footballers only because their bodies do not conform to a notion of normative femininity and heterosexuality. It also became clear that the players do not yet have any strong politically-motivated organization to fight on their behalf and so they continue to rely on men's goodwill for the chance to play football.

Am I a woman or a footballer? Gender identities amongst footballers

Sometimes it seems that the words 'woman' and 'football' cannot cohere in Brazilian society. When asked about their identities as women footballers, a group of the interviewees said they regard themselves as 'different' women because they play football. But they want to be 'ordinary' women. As Iara told me: 'On the field I'm one person, off it I'm a woman just like every woman, I follow all the rules to be a woman.' And what type of rules are they? 'Football is a very cool sport. I can play it and nothing prevents me from being a woman, from taking care of my appearance.'

As these interviewees indicate, women perceived that when they play a masculine sport they must be attractive. As they play this 'masculine' sport, they must feel the compulsion to display their 'femininity' in ways they know are acceptable to others. They should appear as 'feminine' as they can; a femininity that is emerging in all female football cultures. Caudwell writes (2011: 337): '*footie chick* femininity is delicately laced with a new type of sexiness and suggests a heterosexualizing of women's football culture'. Caudwell explains that Footie Chic is also a new fashion sportswear brand aiming to produce girls and women who can display the *right* femininity both on and off the field – far from the *butch women* that have previously been associated with female football. Caudwell's views are supported by some of my interviewees: Celia is clear about conceptions of normality when she talks about herself as a woman who plays football: 'I think that in football some people lost their femininity. I didn't, I see myself as a real woman, unlike certain people . . .'

The 'certain people' Celia is talking about are the players who do not conform to the ideal of a marketable femininity, those who do not represent the ideal of a consuming body (Radner, 2008). Their bodies are the opposite of what, from the last century to the *Paulistana*, Brazilian football managers have idealized as the body (and the woman) they are looking for: the docile and saleable body. As indicated by Radner (2008: 98), 'for a woman to be desirable (and thus to identify herself as a "real woman") she must be adept at manipulating and presenting herself according to the strict codes of consumer culture'. In other words, some of the players identified themselves as ordinary and real women, as if they were manipulated and adherent to the managers' 'rules' of being a woman.

However, rather than defining themselves as women, others thought of themselves foremost as footballers. When asked the same question about being a woman who plays football, they went straight to their passion. Paula showed her football fever in a transparent way: 'I love playing football. I have played it since I was a young child. I never had any support. I have always fought for the thing I love most: playing football.' Vanda adds, 'It's a way of life. I live for it. I think of it. I wake up, I go to football practice and I sleep dreaming of football.'

There were others who express this sentiment. When they reflect on their identities, their first concern is not their bodies or their femininities; rather, they express that their souls are linked to football. There is a blurring of gender since, in common with most Brazilians, football is their way of life, described by Bellos (2002: 10) as 'a single sport that unifies the fifth largest country in the world'. These players live this passion with all their strength; football is their primary identity and they will carry this identity and fight for it as far as they can. Lucia defines this feeling: 'I fight so much; I think you are what you wish to be. I want to be an excellent player, so I have to believe. And to fight I need to follow my dream.'

For some in this second group, this attitude seems to be linked to their individual aims and feelings; their thoughts are not on the bigger picture of football in a *machista* society.

However, there is another group of passionate footballers which is highly conscious of the way football operates in Brazilian society, and the way it is used to perpetuate an unequal gender order. They are aware of 'prejudice' and 'discrimination', as well as of their rights to play. Tais commented:

> It's a challenge for us to play football being a woman, in a country where there is still strong prejudice against women who play football. But is also good to play this sport as we can show that women can also play football, we can break down these barriers even if the women's football space is still very small.

Tais is not talking about her own individual identity; she talks about a collective – women who are fighting against gender barriers and prejudices. And she claims football as a legitimate space for this battle.

Adding to this discourse, Bia said that,

> It's in my blood, but it's very tough for a woman to play football, as they say this is a men's thing; but we persist, as I believe that women must have the freedom to do whatever they want, whatever they like.

Again, Bia speaks for a collective, the right and the freedom for women to play and to do what they want to do. These players reflect on the ways the gendered biases act to build barriers for women who want to play football in Brazil. Their words show that they no longer think of their own femininity, but are becoming conscious of the power of the discourses where 'dominant femininity is produced and reproduced' (Caudwell, 2011: 336). They are becoming aware of the sexist and manipulative discourses that mix gender and sexuality, using sport to control female bodies. They also call for football to be acknowledged as a valid social space for the struggle for gender equality. As Ana says 'football is for everybody'.

'You shouldn't be playing football, you're such a princess!'
Prejudice, sexuality and the players' bodies

Another discussion concerned the ways in which the players are regarded as women and footballers by their families, and communities. The players provided a unified response to these questions: *prejudice*. Most interviewees denounced the prejudices that society holds towards them, prejudices manifested in the ways women's bodies are seen or spoken about.

As prejudice is common in the players' talk, I would like in this section to call attention to three different types of comments. Each reflects one facet of the above mentioned football feminist agenda (Caudwell, 2011). Sara said:

> My friends always tell me that 'you shouldn't be playing football. You're such a princess.' This is true. I always wear short skirts. My make-up is always well done. I'm very feminine. My friends' prejudices towards women playing football is because the other players look like men, their bodies are very tight and rigid, they think I don't fit in that world.

Sara herself denounces her friends but, ironically, manifests the same prejudices as them. She tries to look 'feminine' to somehow avoid being misinterpreted as one of 'them'; that is, players who do not appear as feminine as she sees herself. She allows her body to do the work of producing a '"desiring woman" for whom sexual subjection is compulsory' (Radner, 2008: 98). Radner explains Sara's paradox by pointing out that this production of a 'docile body' seems to the body's owner to be a manifestation of her own will rather than a pervasive cultural constraint on 'appearing desirable according to the codes of consumer culture'. This is what Radner (2008: 98) refers to as the 'technology of sexiness'.

The second type of talk is more ambiguous, but also discriminatory. Here people are not explicit about their fears about women who play football. Deise's talk clearly illustrates this: 'In my family my uncles always pushed my mum: "Football? Your daughter could do ballet, or play volleyball, but football? This is not a girl's thing."' This type of thinking does not openly state the underlying fears, namely that participating in such a 'male' sport as football will turn the girl into a man, or worse, into a masculinised woman. This ideology clearly transforms a cultural phenomenon – the sport – into a 'natural' thing, biologically determined to be performed only by one sex, and draws on spurious biological arguments to explain 'cultural inequalities and dis-

126

crimination' (Hargreaves and Vertinsky, 2007: 4). It reiterates the early twentieth-century views when women were forbidden to play 'masculine' sports in Brazil as they were considered to be detrimental to a supposed 'essential' 'feminine' nature.

Finally there is the open talk about homosexuality. Carla says that:

> Everybody is prejudiced about lesbians. Because in female football there are many lesbians, they think that, if you are in this environment, you are one as well. But that's not truth! There are many who aren't! But women's football can't make progress because of the prejudice against lesbians. [. . .] So, if you have short hair, many teams won't accept you.

Again, but this time in an overt way, the body is the boundary that sets what is acceptable (sexual) behaviour and what is not. This time, short hair is perceived as an external sign of being a lesbian. But this creates a huge problem for female football, so containing the 'signs of female masculinity' (Caudwell, 2011: 336) is the bigger purpose of the teams. The prejudice is against the players who are homosexual, but if they stay in the closet, or better, if they can display the acceptable body of a real (heterosexual) woman – long hair is a mark of this, as it was in the *Paulistana* – they will not be excluded from the game. And not only will lesbians be accepted if they demonstrate the right behaviour and the right bodies, but as per Carla's thoughts, no players will be discriminated against and women's football will finally progress; the players' bodies are the final frontier. As has been the case since last century, the female body is the centre of this drama: being included means accepting a compulsory heterosexuality. It means also being subjected to the codes of the body's consumer culture (Radner, 2008).

Perspectives

With so many prejudices, what might be the next step in the advancement of female football in Brazil? One point is clear: Brazilian female football has always depended upon the goodwill of men: sometimes in good hands at other times in bad. But Brazilian feminists have rarely seen sport as a site to advance the overall fight for a fairer society on gender terms.

This battle must be addressed. Brazil will be the stage of the 2014 FIFA World Cup and the 2016 Olympic Games. Public and private money have already begun to flow to all levels and types of sports. There is support available. Every day the whole society is becoming more 'sporty' (Tavares, 2011). Women must stand up for their space and rights; as the captain of the women's national football team said, female footballers don't need to become millionaires, but they need respect. The feminist movement should regard these sport events as real opportunities to advance the struggle for equity for girls and women in the world of Brazilian football and in Brazilian society more generally.

Notes

1 The author would like to acknowledge Dr. Constance Ellwood for her support in the English editing of this chapter as well as all the players and coaches who have opened their hearts to me throughout our meetings.
2 The authors here are emphasizing that in the media and everyday conversation, the central topic of talk about female football is always the players' sexualities: their bodies and their similarities to 'men'. Omitted from this talk are the topics of the game itself: the matches, the great moments of the games, the goals, the winners and the losers.
3 For a complete account of the history of the silver-medal winning team see Knijnik, 2011.

4   The teams played across the state of Sao Paulo, in several cities, always in three-day rounds, starting on Friday afternoons and finishing on Sunday afternoons. It was a very tough 'game marathon', under very hard conditions, such as the hot midday sun that made the temperature on the fields sometimes reach 60° C. But it was seen as the only way to promote female football, and the players grabbed this opportunity.

References

Anderson E (2010) *Sport, Theory and Social Problems: A Critical Introduction*. London: Routledge.

Ballaryni H (1940). Por que a mulher não deve praticar o futebol [Why woman should not play football]. *Revista Educação Physica*, Rio de Janeiro, 49: 34–41.

Bellos A (2002) *Futebol: The Brazilian way of life*. London: Bloomsbury.

Brazilian Parliament Press (2001) *Deputado denuncia racismo no futebol feminino* [Federal Representative denounces racism on female football]. Available at http://www2.camara.gov.br/agencia/noticias/12505.html (accessed 14 February 2012).

Caudwell J (2011) Gender, feminism and football studies. *Soccer and Society*, 12: 330–344.

Goellner S (2005) Mulheres e futebol no Brasil: entre sombras e visibilidades [Women and football in Brazil: Between shadows and visibilities]. *Brazilian Journal of Physical Education and Sport*, 19(2): 141–151.

Hargreaves J and Vertinsky P (2007) *Introduction*. In: Hargreaves J and Vertinsky P (eds) *Physical Culture, Power, and the Body*. Oxon: Routledge, pp. 1–24.

Knijnik J (2011) From the cradle to Athens: The silver-coated story of a warrior in Brazilian soccer. *Sporting Traditions*, 28(1): 63–83.

Knijnik J (2013) Visions of gender justice: 'Untested feasibility' on the football fields of Brazil. *Journal of Sport & Social Issues*, 37 (1): 8–30.

Knijnik J and Horton P (2013) 'Only beautiful women need apply': Human rights and gender in Brazilian football. *Creative Approaches to Research*, 6 (2) (forthcoming).

Minichiello V, Aroni R, Timewell E and Alexander L (1995) *In-depth Interviewing*. Melbourne: Longman.

Mourão L and Morel M (2005) As narrativas sobre o futebol feminino: o discurso da midia impressa em campo [The narratives on female football: The discourse of the printed media on the field]. *Brazilian Journal of Sports Science*, 26(2): 73–86.

Natali M (2007) The realm of the possible: Remembering Brazilian Futebol. *Soccer & Society*, 8(2/3): 267–282.

Radner H (2008) Compulsory sexuality and the desiring woman. *Sexualities*, 11, (1–2): 94–100.

Rigo L C (2005) Memórias de corpos esportivizados: a natação feminina e o futebol infame [Memories of sporting bodies: Female swimming and the infamous football]. *Revista Movimento*, 11 (2): 131–146.

Tavares O (2011). Megaeventos esportivos. *Revista Movimento*, 17 (3): 11–35.

UOL (2011). *Esporte Uol*. Available at http://esporte.uol.com.br/futebol/campeonatos/mundial-feminino/ (accessed 14 July 2011).

Votre S and Mourão L (2003) Women's football in Brazil: Progress and problems. *Soccer and Society*, 4(2/3): 254–267.

14

THE PARTICIPATION OF WOMEN IN BRAZILIAN OLYMPIC SPORT

Katia Rubio

Introduction

When narrating the trajectory of Brazilian women in sport, we see close connections between women's accomplishments in sports and in other cultural spheres. Women were excluded from sport at first, encountered discrimination for many years, and most recently became indispensable participants.

Specifically in relation to the Olympic Games during the twentieth century, female athletes in Brazil witnessed significant transformations moving from rules banning their participation in some sports to the winning of medals in a widening range of international competitions. Although Brazil participated for the first time in the Olympic Games in 1920, it was an all-male team and it was only in 1932 that the first Brazilian woman gained the right to represent her country in Los Angeles. Maria Lenk was both the first Brazilian woman and the first Latin American woman to compete in the Olympic Games. Although the right to participate was granted in 1932, inadequate access to training facilities delayed trips to the winners' podium for 74 years, when women in Brazil's national volleyball, beach volley and basketball teams won their first Olympic medals in the 1996 Games in Atlanta.

Understanding gender relations in Brazilian sport: the role of cordiality

Brazil's history is marked by Portuguese colonization and European coexistence with Brazilian natives (Indians), and with black Africans captured to work as slaves on the plantations and in mining ventures. This social and economic landscape underwent deep changes during the nineteenth century, when abolitionist campaigns led to the liberation of slaves and triggered new migratory flows intended to create a supply of unforced labour and the "whitening" of the population, which had become very mixed by this time. European and Asian migrants came to Brazil bringing with them their cultural heritage, which was gradually mingled with existing cultural practices (Holanda, 2006).

In his noteworthy book, *Raízes do Brasil*, originally published in 1936, Holanda (2006) provides a key theory for understanding Brazilian society. He explains how the mixture of Portuguese colonization, mainly anchored in a rural mode of production, the patriarchy embedded in Portuguese culture and the presence of Africans who participated in society as slaves cannot be understated when deciphering Brazil and its people in the twentieth and twenty-first centuries. He considers the repercussions of this mixture and outlines a framework to explain how the country and its inhabitants could overcome the feeling of relative "backwardness" from the beginning of the Republic through the processes of industrialization, urbanization, and the rise of free labour during the nineteenth century.

This country that Brazilians today see as modern and free is grounded in socio-historical constructions that marked various social movements during the twentieth century. For example, one of Holanda's main observations about Brazilian culture is the extent to which cordiality pervades social relations. Represented by kindness in manners, hospitality and generosity, and taken as a virtue by foreigners, cordiality is for Holanda a dominant trait of Brazilian character—based on ancestral patterns of human coexistence and formed in the rural and patriarchal milieu of Brazil's history.

The use of cordiality in confronting social conflicts has long been a central and unique feature of social and political organization in a country that has gained its political independence and established a republican form of state without armed conflict. This removal of the military option, and open conflict in the process of confronting and solving problems, has given rise to a similar strategy for dealing with, minimizing, and even negating public and private tensions in nearly all spheres of life. Understanding the dynamics and pervasiveness of this taken-for-granted strategic process is a prerequisite for understanding the history and current existence of the feminist movement in Brazil.

Brazilian feminism

Feminism in Brazil became organized from around the end of the nineteenth century, but expressed itself in a unique form when compared to feminist movements in North America and Europe. In a social and cultural context characterized by conservative and patriarchal rural structures and a political Left which holds conservative views related to gender, women in Brazil developed their own approach to bringing about progressive changes. Their approach has been marked by the use of oppositional, yet cordial strategies, instead of using open confrontation with those in positions of power. It is in this social and cultural landscape that various forms of feminism have been developed and female athletes have achieved changes in parallel with those achieved in other spheres of social life (Tralci Filho & Araujo, 2011).

According to Tralci Filho and Araujo (2011), the goals of the feminist movement in Brazil presented a serious challenge to the established order. There have been a wide range of organized efforts by Brazilian feminists to improve the lives of girls and women and to have family rights, resulting in government recognition and policy-making. However, some of the progress made has been rolled back by conservative governments, by the military, and also by leftist political movements that have seen feminism as a threat to their own goals and organizations.

According to Pinto (2003), there are three moments, or waves, of the feminist movement in Brazil. The first encompasses the period between the end of the nineteenth century and the achievement of women's suffrage in 1932. The second wave of feminism encompasses the period of the military dictatorship from the 1970s through re-democratization at the close of the 1980s. The third wave occurred from the latter stages of re-democratization through to the present (2012). Of note, these three waves represent historic landmarks that identify the emergent forms of Brazilian feminism that were closely aligned with social movements focused on achieving civil rights and equal political representation.

For the purpose of this chapter, it is clear that Brazilian feminism has had a major impact on the organization of sport and the provision of participation opportunities for girls and women.

The participation of women in sport in Brazil

The exclusion of women from the Olympic Games of 1896 was rationalized by allegations of everything from female physical and mental frailty to females being incapable of dealing with competition (Müller, 2000). Although some sportswomen in North America and Europe rejected these allegations and, without the official consent of the International Olympic Committee (IOC), participated in the Games of 1900 and 1904 (Hargreaves, 1994, p. 210), it took another 32 years for the first Brazilian woman, Maria Lenk, to gain the right to compete in the Olympic Games. This change coincided with the first wave of Brazilian feminism.

According to a study done by Mathias and Rubio (2010), there are records showing that beginning in the nineteenth century there were some women who resisted prohibitions against female participation in sport by exercising in public places, albeit these cases were relatively rare. The official public responses to these women reflected the values of a phallocentric society, as they were described as prostitutes, mad or criminals. However, despite continued opposition, women struggled to increase their participation in physical activities during the early twentieth century.

Although sports activities for women were restricted in public spaces, those from wealthy families had access to private clubs where they did engage in competitive physical activities. However, the full development of a female sport culture required the participation of immigrants and their descendants from European countries where involvement in physical activities was being promoted for educational and health reasons (Mathias and Rubio, 2010; Hargreaves, 1994).

Through the early years of the twentieth century, the dissemination of physical activities for Brazilian girls and women—increasingly present in clubs and schools—was closely linked to a larger gendered system of corporal control that was grounded in a combination of hygienic, eugenic, medical, moral and disciplinary concerns. For example, there was a sharp distinction between the practices recommended for women and men, so that participation patterns clearly reinforced the corporal and behavioral characteristics that were popularly associated with each gender. For example, young men were expected to consume sports news, participate in events organized in stadiums, support a soccer team, concern themselves with being in good physical shape, and, especially, to practise sports. In contrast, the traditional discourse about physical activities for women assumed that the female physical constitution was limited in its capacity for vigorous exercise and, in particular, not suited to those sports that were aggressive in character and required muscularity, power and strength. However, as the century progressed, there was a gradual transformation of attitudes to women's sports and exercise with an emerging emphasis on the creation of the "new woman" who could successfully meet the challenges of modernity. Female frailty and indolence became devalued, and idleness and laziness were associated with the evil of the soul. The vitality of the female body came increasingly to signify an ability to stand up to the harshness of everyday life (Engel, 1997).

The social transformation in attitudes to the female body was leading to a greater acceptance of women's participation in physical activities, in part facilitated by the dedication of some intellectuals who developed the idea that the physical and moral attributes of female gymnasts contributed to the general aggrandizement of the nation. For example, Goellner (2003) and Schpun (1999) each point to the importance of Fernando de Azevedo and his publications during the 1920s. De Azevedo's work led to the creation of a pedagogic doctrine through which girls' physical education in Brazil was linked with the social prestige of European gymnastic methods, or more specifically, with the hygienist and eugenic presuppositions on which the European methods were based.

De Azevedo identified swimming as ideal for women, because he argued that it brought a soft harmony to the body and inspired graceful movements (Devide, 2003). Additionally, he believed that swimming required an intuitive bodily rhythm, which was related to the female's perception, and the inconstancy of the liquid environment was compatible with the woman's soul, and therefore attracted them more than it attracted men. Even though competitive swimming for women had only recently become popular, there were faint-hearted attempts to publicize the participation of female swimmers during the 1920s.

Given this history it is easy to see why it was not until 1932 that Maria Lenk was the first and only Brazilian woman to participate in the Olympic Games in Los Angeles, and why it was not until 1936 that the Brazilian Olympic delegation included five female athletes—four swimmers (Sieglind Lenk (Maria's sister), Piedade Coutinho, Scylla Venâncio and Helena de Moraes Salles) and one fencer (Hilda Puttkammer). Also important to note is that these athletes competed in individual sports because team sport participation was still not seen as being compatible with the temperament of women. This pattern continued to exist for several decades into the twentieth century.

Additionally, most athletes in the 1930s trained in private sport associations and clubs founded and frequented by immigrants or descendants of immigrants, who had come from countries where sport participation, including the participation of women, was much more common than it was in Brazil. For example, Maria Lenk and her sister Sieglind were daughters of German parents, and received in early childhood their first swimming lessons from their father Paul Lenk (Lenk, 1982). This was typical in that swimming was an individual rather than a team sport and training occurred in private clubs with support and supervision provided by parents. In contrast to the situation in many European countries, the development in Brazil of competitive sport for women—in particular team games—lagged behind

Swimming and fencing, the two sports in which female athletes participated in Brazilian national teams, were among the sports that physicians and physical educators during that period recommended for women, because they were believed to be compatible with the female "soul" and physical "structure" (Devide, 2003). In retrospect, it is remarkable how medical and educational discourses served to affirm conservative values and delay women's participation in other sports.

After the 1930s, concerns about physical education for girls and women were no longer a matter for physicians and educators alone. Representatives of the Catholic Church joined the national conversation and admonished educators for encouraging young ladies to "exhibit themselves half-naked" and to "train them for fights in stadiums rather than for the sacred duties of maternity". The clerics clearly believed that the appropriate role of physical education was to enable young ladies to become "healthy in their bodies and saintly in their souls" (Betti, 1991).

At the same time before World War II when clerics were making this case, a few sport leaders such as Silvio Guimarães, the second secretary of the *Liga Carioca de Atletismo* (an association whose headquarters were in Rio de Janeiro, then the federal capital), expressed concern about Brazil's failure to support female athletes (Guimarães, cited in Araujo, 2011, p. 142[1]). In making this observation, Guimarães declared that, "It is impressive the indifference, up to now, regarding female athletics. Is our [society] unaware of the noticeable role women are showing in athletic games in the international scenery?" (Guimarães, cited in Araujo, 2011, p. 142). He referred directly to France, Italy, the USA, and Czechoslovakia, and said that, "Female competitions in these countries are perhaps much more important today than our male competitions!"

According to Araujo (2011), examples such as this suggest the existence of international pressure, although indirect, to support the participation of Brazilian girls and women in competitive sports if the nation was to be in step with the international trend. Despite this pressure, it was not until the 1948 Olympic Games in London that Brazilian women first participated in athletics (track and field).

If the 1930s and 1940s marked the establishment and acceleration of sport participation among women in Brazil, and created the expectation that participation would continue to expand, the 1950s and 1960s marked the stagnation of this process, as can be seen in Figure 14.1. In the 1952 Olympic Games in Melbourne, the Brazilian delegation included six fewer women than were in the delegation at the 1948 games in London, when 11 women participated. Also noteworthy is that up to that time, Brazilian women had participated just in swimming and athletics, and there was no Olympic participation in team sports, even though basketball and volleyball were already practised in some clubs and universities. Through the early 1950s, Brazil's national Olympic programme continued to ignore team sports for women.

The scenarios that followed were even more sombre in terms of progress for women in sports. In the three Olympic Games between 1956 and 1964, each of the Brazilian delegations included only one woman: Mary Dalva Proença participated in acrobatic diving in Melbourne (1956), Wanda dos Santos ran the 80 meter hurdles in Rome (1960), and Aída dos Santos participated in the high jump in Tokyo (1964).

These data point to a policy of exclusion that was reinforced by Resolution n° 7 of the National Sports Council in 1965, which prohibited the participation of girls and women in the practice of fights of any kind, soccer, indoor soccer, beach soccer, water polo, polo, rugby,

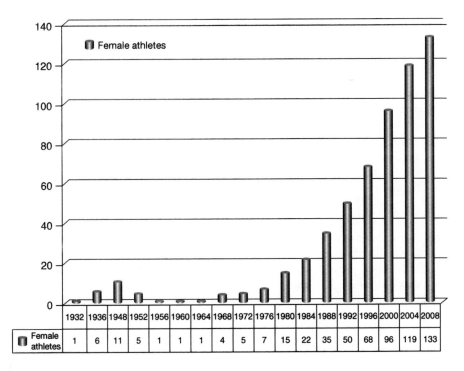

Figure 14.1 Participation of Brazilian female athletes in the Summer Olympic Games, 1932–2008

weightlifting and baseball (Castellani Filho, 2007). This law was revoked in 1979, but for 15 years it determined the sphere of female sport in the country, be it in schools, clubs or public spaces. Under this discriminatory law, four female Brazilian judo players participated in the South American Championship in Uruguay, in 1979, under the names of men, a fact that triggered the repeal of the Council's policy.

In 1985, a commission was created for the Reformulation of the National Sports. The Commission proposed changes in the legal structure of Brazilian sport, and this inspired a passage of the Brazilian Constitution, Article 217, making sport participation for every Brazilian citizen a constitutional right (Tubino, 1996). This change in the Federal Constitution ushered in a new era for women's sports.

Brazilian women in the twenty-first century

The 1980s were marked by the emergence of new political expectations combined with deep social and economic changes. At the same time that the incumbent military dictatorship was losing its legitimacy, labour unions were expanding and growing stronger, the family structure was altered with a new divorce law approved in 1977, and emerging but previously dormant ideas about the role of women came together to produce actions that transformed the patriarchal structure of society (Mesquita and Nascimento, 2011).

Ironically, the boycotts of the Moscow Games in 1980 and the Los Angeles Games in 1984 benefited Brazilian women who participated in Olympic sports other than swimming and athletics (Rubio, 2004). The chronic technical gap between Brazilian female athletes and their European and North American counterparts had previously limited participation by Brazilian women in sports that demanded qualification through achievements recorded in international competitions. But as a result of the 1980 boycott by the United States and its allies, the qualification standards were altered so that Brazilian women could compete in gymnastics, archery and, for the first time, in a team sport (volleyball). In Los Angeles, Brazilian women debuted in tennis, shooting, synchronized swimming, and rhythmic gymnastics. From then onwards, the disparity between men and women representing Brazil has steadily decreased.

According to data from the IOC, the Brazilian delegation in Moscow (1980) consisted of 109 athletes, 94 men and 15 (13.8%) women. In Los Angeles (1984), the number of athletes increased to 151—129 males and 22 (14.5%) women. Although the percentages of female athletes were low, the absolute numbers represented previously unimaginable progressive change. In turn, this inspired the next generations of girls to develop Olympic dreams of their own. As a result, females athletes constituted 26% of the Brazilian delegation at the 1992 games in Barcelona—51 women out of 197 athletes.

But it was not until the Atlanta games in 1996 that Brazilian women first won medals. A 64-year waiting period had passed before this happened. This success has meant that women have become indispensable in Brazil's quest for a good place in the medal table, which is defined by some politicians and sport directors as a symbol of the overall strength of the nation as well as the success of Brazil's sport policy (Rubio, 2007). In 1996, Brazil's female Olympians secured bronze medals in volleyball, a silver medal in beach volleyball and a silver medal in women's basketball (with that team being world champions in the same year), indicating the emerging importance that women's sports have in the country's sports culture.

In Beijing in 2008, the Brazilian delegation of 277 athletes included 133 women (48%) many of whom engaged in noteworthy performances. Of the three gold medals won by Brazilian athletes, women claimed two of them: in volleyball and with Maurren Maggi in the long jump. Women also won a silver medal in soccer, and bronze medals in judo, tae kwon do, and sailing.

With these results, it was possible to make the argument that women had become proportionally more productive than men, as illustrated in Figure 14.2.

The athletic accomplishments of Brazilian women are irrefutable and mark significant progress in access to sport participation for girls and women. However, corresponding changes in the leadership and management of sport have not occurred, and the representation of women in these positions remains at the same levels that they were at the beginning of the twentieth century.

Women in leadership and sports management positions

Although the data clearly show that the participation of women in competitive sports is increasing, the positions of power in sports, such as coaches, technical assistants and directors remain firmly in men's hands.

An analysis of the Brazilian delegation that participated in the Beijing Olympics shows that for the three main team sports—basketball, handball, and soccer—all were controlled by male coaches (Fetter and Silva, 2011). Also, of 17 professionals in technical positions for the men's and women's volleyball teams, only two were women. The social recognition and prominence given to the coaches of national teams is especially significant in Brazil, and the powerful influence of coaches on regional and school teams across nearly all sports is undeniable. But despite

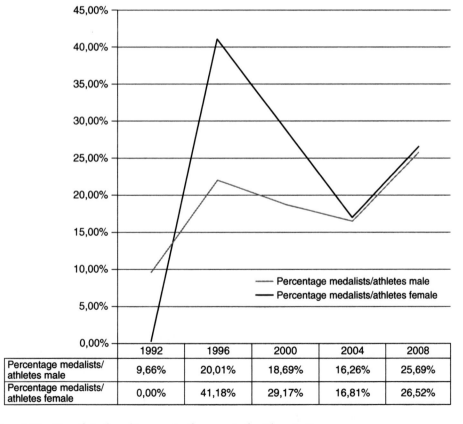

	1992	1996	2000	2004	2008
Percentage medalists/ athletes male	9,66%	20,01%	18,69%	16,26%	25,69%
Percentage medalists/ athletes female	0,00%	41,18%	29,17%	16,81%	26,52%

Figure 14.2 Growth in the achievements of women in the Olympic Games

the increasing participation of women athletes in the Brazilian delegation, the number of women in leadership positions in these delegations is disproportionately and disappointingly low.

Fasting and Pfister's (2000) study of women on several national soccer teams showed that athletes view female coaches as having a higher level of empathy, as well as a higher communicative capacity and willingness to cooperate than male coaches have. Similar research also shows that even though men have dominated coaching in the past, an increasing number of women now have competitive experiences beginning early in their lives and they have acquired the knowledge and qualifications to become competent coaches. Therefore, there is no reason why there cannot be a new generation of female coaches who can serve as models for all girls and women in sports. Twenty-five years ago, Annelies Knoppers (1987), referring to Western Europe, observed that the low number of female coaches was attributable to the scarcity of models for this role plus a process of stereotyping that identified coaching/training as a male function. These factors, she concluded, discouraged female athletes from aspiring to perform these roles. It was a similar situation in Brazil and other Latin American countries.

Mourão and Votre (2003) reported that hundreds of men were coaches in sport clubs in Rio de Janeiro, whereas only 34 women were in coaching positions, and nearly all of them coached youth squads. They also noted that a female coach rarely accompanied her athletes as they moved up to higher and more elite levels of competition. Even today, only three national teams are headed by women: Rosicléia Cardoso Campos in judo; Andrea Curi, Maura Lucia Xavier, and Roberta Perilier in synchronized swimming; and Camila Ferezin in rhythmic gymnastics. Both rhythmic gymnastics and synchronized swimming are sports currently perceived as being essentially for women, and men have no experience in them.

The predominance of men in positions of power in sport organizations is also a historically-pervasive phenomenon which has diverse causes and lasting effects. The growth and professionalization of sport in Brazil has not meant that there has been a corresponding increase in the participation of women in decision-making positions. However, it must also be noted that women have not aggressively sought these positions because they require resources and attributes that many women have not claimed for themselves (Mourão & Votre, 2003). In the past, this was clearly due to an internalized sense of inferiority and a lack of support based on a history of secondary status in Brazilian society (Tawil & Costello, 1983). But even though women now participate in physical activities and sports in greater numbers, this change has occurred through conciliation and not direct confrontations (Mourão, 1998). In this way, increased sport participation by women was not marked by the intention of changing the female condition, the social order in the entire society, or even the hierarchy of gender that characterized Brazilian society. Therefore, the inclusion of women in positions of power in sports continues to present a major challenge, and to persuade people to willingly accept women as coaches of national teams is not a simple task.

Although Article 5 in the revised Brazilian constitution of 1988 states that "everyone is equal before the law, without distinction of any nature, ensuring to Brazilians and foreigners residing in the Country the inviolability of the right to life, to freedom, equality, safeness and property in the following terms" (Constitution, 1988), it is easy to document that certain roles, functions, and professions remain the domain of men and exclude women in practice if not by law. For example, current data on women in the management of Brazilian sport shows that only 7.7% of all leadership positions in clubs, federations and confederations are held by women—a proportion that does not even begin to reach the goal set by the IOC. In 1996 the IOC asked its members to increase female participation in management committees to 20% by 2002 (Pfister, 2003).

The low representation of women in the management of Brazilian sport is due less to gender prejudice (although sexism does exist and is influential) than to a notable effort to preserve traditional patterns of prestige and privilege in these institutions and the practices that support them. In other words, Brazilian women remain excluded not so much because they are women, but because of a corrupt system sustained by the unquestioned and uncritical acceptance of cordiality as a taken-for-granted attribute of social relations.

Final considerations

The trajectory of women in Brazilian Olympic sport is most accurately viewed as being grounded in a long, gradual, and generally progressive process. Through this process women today are crucial in the country's sporting profile and future plans. After almost two decades—between 1980 and 2000—of living in the shadow of male teams and receiving far fewer rewards than those bestowed on male athletes, there is an emerging recognition of the need for gender equality in some sports. This has not yet been extended to soccer, widely defined as a national male asset, with women perceived as invaders, even though they have already won more Olympic titles than the Brazilian men and have never failed to qualify for any of the Olympic Games since women's soccer was first included in the programme in 1996.

The major challenge now faced is to gain equal representation in all leadership roles, including those in coaching and organizational directorships—positions at present held by men who show no willingness to relinquish their power.

As we approach the Olympic Games of Rio de Janeiro in 2016, it is expected that there will be progress made in moving towards gender equality in positions of power. This will be accomplished through a system of quotas requiring gender equity combined with training programmes for women who aspire to hold leadership roles in Brazilian sports. The ultimate goal is to reach a point where we can finally say that women have reached the top of the podium.

Note

1   Guimarães, S. (1934, julho). O desporto feminino. Revista de Educação Física (Rio de Janeiro), (12). Recuperado em 02 de dezembro de 2008, de http://www.revistadeeducacaofisica.com.br/artigos/1934/16_odesporto.pdf

References

Araujo, S. E. C., 2011. As mulheres e o esporte olímpico brasileiro entre as décadas de 1930 a 1960 – as políticas públicas do esporte e da educação física. In: K. Rubio (ed.) *As mulheres e o esporte olímpico brasileiro*. São Paulo: Casa do Psicólogo.

Betti, M., 1991. *Educação Física e Sociedade*. São Paulo: Movimento.

Castellani Filho, L., 2007. *Educação Física no Brasil: A história que não se conta*. Campinas: Papirus.

Constitution, 1988. Constituição da República Federativa do Brasil de 1988, available at http://www.planalto.gov.br/ccivil_03/constituicao/constitui%C3%A7ao.htm. Last access: 19/12/2011.

Devide, F. P., 2003. História das Mulheres na natação feminina Brasileira no século XX: das adequações às resistências sociais. *Motus Corporis*, Rio de Janeiro, 10 (1), pp. 125–44.

Engel, M., 1997. Psiquiatria e Feminilidade. In: M. D. Priore (ed.) *Historia das Mulheres no Brasil*. São Paulo: Editora Contexto.

Fasting, K. & Pfister, G., 2000. Female and male coaches in the eye of soccer players. *European Physical Education Review*, 6 (1), pp. 91–110.

Fetter, J. C. S. S. & Silva, E. M., 2011. A atleta, o técnico. O atleta, a técnica. In: K. Rubio (ed.) *As mulheres e o esporte olímpico brasileiro*. São Paulo: Casa do Psicólogo, pp.183–200.

Goellner, S.V., 2003. *Bela, maternal e feminina: imagens da mulher na Revista Educação Physica*. Ijui: Editora Unijui.

Hargreaves, J., 1994. *Sporting Females: critical issues in the history and sociology of women's sports*. London and New York: Routledge.

Holanda, S. B., 2006. *Raízes do Brasil*. São Paulo: Companhia das Letras.

Knoppers, A., 1987. Gender and the coaching profession, *Quest*, 39, pp. 23–35.

Lenk, M., 1982. *Braçadas e abraços*. Boa Vista: Grupo Atlântica.

Mathias, M. B. & Rubio, K., 2010. A mulher e as práticas corporais na cidade de São Paulo dos anos 1920. *Revista Portuguesa de Ciências do Desporto*, 9, pp. 195–202.

Mesquita, A. M. & Nascimento, I. S., 2011. A participação da mulher brasileira no esporte a partir dos anos 1980: o que de fato mudou? In: K. Rubio (ed.) As mulheres e o esporte olímpico brasileiro. São Paulo: Casa do Psicólogo, pp.167–81.

Mourão, L., 1998. *Representação social da mulher brasileira na atividade físico-desportiva: da segregação a democratização*. PhD. Universidade Gama Filho.

Mourão, L. & Votre, S., 2003. Brazilian women and girls in physical activities and sport. In: I Hartmann and G. Pfister (eds). *Sport and Women: social issues in international perspective*. London: Routledge, pp. 179–91.

Müller, N. (ed.), 2000. *Olympism Selected Writings. Pierre de Coubertin 1863–1937*. Lausanne: International Olympic Committee.

Pfister, G., 2003. Líderes femininas em organizações esportivas. Tendências mundiais. *Movimento*, 9, (2), pp. 11–35, maio/agosto.

Pinto, C. R. J., 2003. *Uma história do feminismo no Brasil*. São Paulo: Fundação Perseu Abramo.

Rubio, K., 2004. *Heróis Olímpicos Brasileiros*. São Paulo: Zouk.

Rubio, K., 2007. *Medalhistas Olímpicos brasileiros: memórias, histórias e imaginário*. São Paulo: Casa do Psicólogo.

Schpun, M. R., 1999. *Beleza em jogo: cultura física e comportamento em São Paulo nos anos 20*. São Paulo: Boitempo.

Tawil, L. & Costello, C., 1983. The perceived competence of women in traditional and nontraditional fields as a function of sex-role orientation and age. *Sex Roles*, 9 (12), pp. 1197–1203.

Tralci Filho, M. A. & Araujo, S. E. C., 2011. As possíveis relações entre os feminismos e as práticas esportivas. In: K. Rubio (ed.) *As mulheres e o esporte olímpico brasileiro*. São Paulo: Casa do Psicólogo.

Tubino, M. J. G., 1996 *O esporte no Brasil, do período colonial aos nossos dias*. São Paulo: Ibrasa.

15

PERPETUAL OUTSIDERS

Women in athletics and road running in South Africa

Christopher Merrett

Two central and inter-related themes of the history of South African sport are identity and the consequent existence of insiders and outsiders. Until the late 1970s it was either common practice or official policy, underpinned to varying degrees by law and bureaucratic force, to ensure that the insiders were white. Those that were classified under apartheid as Coloured, Indian and African were outsiders. So, too, were all women. The history of South African track and field athletics and road running was dominated by white men, drivers of a chauvinistic nationalism (Merrett, 2004: 233). Ira Emery (1956: 25–6), a long-serving sports administrator, expressed pride that South Africa 'with relatively only a handful of men interested in long-distance running . . . could produce . . . wondermen . . . [with] . . . that innate gift of untiring stamina . . . the heritage of Young South Africa'. This confirms Morrell's view (1997: 173–4) that 'Sport is pre-eminently an arena of display where masculinity is performed publicly.' And much of this was based on sheer physicality, discounting skill (Morrell, 2001a: 23). From early in the colonial period, sport in white communities in South Africa was predominantly a symbol and celebration of racial superiority and masculinity (Grundlingh, 1996; see also Chapter 2 in this *Handbook*).

The stamp of white male sport is well illustrated by the Comrades (ultra) Marathon, established to perpetuate the fraternity of the First World War battlefields. Comradeship, it was argued, could be replicated by a feat of endurance equal to that shown at the front by relatively unfit men engaged in forced marches. The route of the Comrades Marathon runs through the province of KwaZulu-Natal for approximately 89 kilometres (56 miles), along the hilly roads between the cities of Durban and Pietermaritzburg. It is the oldest ultramarathon race, run for the first time on 24 May 1921 (Merrett, 2007: 242).

Although during the inter-war years (1919–39) privileged women from western countries and their colonies were taking part in vigorous outdoor sports, such as climbing and skiing, there were still powerful medical arguments opposing energetic exercise for women on the grounds that it was damaging to their health (Hargreaves, 1994: 118–20). The dominant image of femininity did not fit with the ideals of masculine endurance and wartime courage that underpinned the Comrades Marathon and from the start women were banned from participating. However, as early as 1923 a white woman, Frances Hayward, ran the race unofficially, strongly supported by the press and the public despite popular myths about possible adverse health effects. Hayward's entry form and fee were initially accepted, but the South African Athletics Association subsequently disqualified her. Conservative administrators excluded official women entrants until 1975 and given the overall white male control of the socio-political context and popular symbolism of male sporting superiority, fear of loss of hegemony (Cahn, 1994: 53–4) is a plausible explanation. Ironically, of the 34 male competitors in the 1923 Comrades Marathon, 18 males failed to complete the race whereas Hayward, running unofficially, finished in the dark in the respectable time of 11 hours and 35 minutes. The men's winning time was 8 hours and 59 minutes. Reactions to Hayward's success were mixed. Support from the crowd was so enthusiastic that mounted police had to clear her way into Lord's ground in Durban and the *Natal Advertiser* (Durban) referred to 'another signal of women's emancipation from the thraldom of good-natured disdain in which mere man has held her' (25 May 1923). But other press reports were patronizing, mentioning her as plucky, and the *Natal Witness* (Pietermaritzburg) felt that the race was too far for anyone's health (23 May 1923). Hayward lived until 1975, dying at the age of 85.

For the next eight years women had a marginal, supporting role, although at the finish of the Comrades Marathon in 1926, in Alexandra Park in Pietermaritzburg, a one mile event specifically for women was arranged. But women faced another 50 years before they could become official ultramarathon competitors. 'How long must women wait?' asked the *Natal Witness* (23 May 1927). Four years later Geraldine Watson ran the first of three consecutive unofficial Comrades Marathons. In 1931 she finished last, but press reports spoke of her bravery and she received a warm public reception. The following year she took nearly 12 hours. But in 1933 she came 42nd out of 85 runners in the excellent time of 9 hours and 31 minutes. She claimed plausibly that many of the men behind her would not have finished if it had not been for her presence. Nevertheless, she was the last female entrant for over 30 years, except for four walkers (two finishers) in 1935. By breaking unofficially into the Comrades Marathon, Watson was bringing the struggle of women to participate in an endurance event to the public's attention and particularly to the attention of the international community of female athletes. Her struggle was replicated by other women who wanted to participate in international long-distance events. For example, it was not until 1984 that women won a long battle to run in an Olympic marathon (Hargreaves 1994: 217).

Apart from a woman on horseback in 1950 there were no further female participants in the Comrades Marathon until 1966. Over the next ten years a number of unofficial female entrants made an appearance. One was the famous endurance runner Mavis Hutchinson who had previously established records at 100 miles and for a 24-hour race (Merrett, 2007: 253). Women's struggles did not go unnoticed and they continued to have the support of the spectators and the press. In 1972, for example, 'some of the loudest cheers of the day went to the women' (Alexander, 1985: 229). There was a clear contradiction between the desires and abilities of women athletes to take part and the attitudes of the all-white male officials who were trying to control events and keep the race as their own. Women were finally admitted officially in 1975, but not before there was some high-profile administrative bungling. In 1973 official runner 901 was a 19-year-old woman Iva Mayall, admitted by mistake. The next year Aleth Kleynhans was also accepted in the belief that she was a man, but at the finish she was disqualified on the bizarre grounds that she did not fulfill the qualifying requirement of a 'European male' and her time and position were withheld. Also disqualified was a 14-year-old girl who had finished for the second year in a row. Since 1921, the Comrades Marathon had been an explicit athletic celebration of white masculinity which over the years was threatened by female interventions. However, male hegemony was never complete and by 1975 was sufficiently weakened to have become ineffectual.

The Comrades Marathon reflects the inter-relatedness of gender relations of power and racial relations of power. 'Women, blacks and Indians felt like goats and pigs in those days because at the end we weren't allowed to cross the finish line, but were herded into a small corral,' reported leading woman runner Lettie van Zyl who wore her name on her vest instead of an official number (La Trobe, 1984: 8–9). The *Daily News* editorial of 30 May 1974 brought attention to the outmoded attitudes of the managers, steeped as they were in gendered and racialised power and privilege when it stated that Comrades 'means White males . . . in the nineteen-seventies this is an absurd anachronism . . . The Comrades are misnamed if they persist in holding out against women's lib or just plain human lib.' The following year two white women were permitted to run, but although van Zyl was the first woman home in 8 hours 50 minutes she was not officially recognized and had to give up her medal in favour of Elizabeth Cavanagh. Instead van Zyl received a blazer, and had to wait until the following year to be recognized as the winner.

Similar racial and authoritarian trends were evident in less high-profile long distance events. The Cape Town to Simonstown walk of 50 miles, which predates the Comrades by nearly 20 years, provided a 22½ mile version for (white) juniors, veterans – and women (Mirwis, 1965: 38). In the Two Oceans Marathon run round the Cape Peninsula, the first white woman runner, Theresa Stadler (Spartan Harriers), was accepted in 1974 although she came in well outside the cut-off time (Cameron-Dow, 1997: 39–40). Black male runners had to wait another year, and the first black woman runner, Mandy Molope (Rand Athletic Club), appeared in 1982 (Cameron-Dow, 1997: 89). The acceptance of outsiders in originally all-white male long distance athletic events followed a similar pattern reflecting the levels of power held by different social and ethnic groups – white women were accepted first, then black men, then coloured and black women.

Disregarding the discrepancy between the participation of white women and black women, South Africa was not far out of kilter with the rest of the world regarding women's participation in distance running. The hostility of officials to women runners was shown by lack of recognition of Millie Simpson's 1964 marathon world record in New Zealand and the assault by an official on Kathy Switzer in the 1967 Boston Marathon (Jutel, 2003: 18, 20). Indeed, Switzer was not the only long-distance female runner to be physically attacked on the road in the United States in the 1960s (Rhodes, 1978: 245), something of which there is no record in South Africa. However, in apartheid South Africa, there were distinctly different opportunities and forms of oppression for white and black female athletes. Affluent white women had good athletic facilities, clubs, coaching and competitions. Until the anti-apartheid sports boycott, white women could compete internationally. Most black women had impoverished facilities and opportunities and were banned from running abroad. However, running required relatively few resources and there were black athletic competitions. Notable were those run by South African Council on Sport (SACOS) whose SACOSSPORT festivals were known as the Olympics of the Oppressed (Hargreaves, 2000: 16–25).

The culture of long-distance running in South Africa remained predominately white and male in a country that was highly militarised and developed into a police state from the early 1960s. For black females the situation was particularly challenging given that their male counterparts ran the risk of stone throwing while training in white areas. Runners from Springs Striders, a white men's running club, were accused of intimidating women, but disdain was more common: a trophy known as the Dinner Gong was awarded to the winning women's team in the Comrades Marathon and raised widespread objections for its disparaging implications. Nevertheless, the 1980s were a decade in which long distance running flourished (Hauman, 1982). After a ten kilometre run at Cape Town on 26 September 1981, the black female runners Blanche Moila and Celia Tumo entered the all-time list in positions 8 and 28. In 1983 Moila (classified Coloured and born in 1956) was the best woman at 16 and 21 kilometres and by 1984 she had won national colours after second place in the cross-country championships. Moila figured strongly in long distance running from five kilometres to the marathon and won four national titles between 1982 and 1985 continuing to achieve placings well into the 1990s. Her best ranking in the marathon was third (Hauman, 2000: 52). Other black women to emerge at marathon level in 1985 were Nellie Mogatle and Lizbeth Ntozini with wins at Vereeniging and King William's Town respectively. Another runner making her mark was Laura Xaba at 10 kilometres and in the half marathon. In 1988 the name of Evelina Tshabalala entered the list of top distance runners and remained there for many years.

By 1990, the initial year of South Africa's political transition when the liberation movements were unbanned, men's long distance running was already being challenged by black runners. Amongst the women the situation was changing, but at a notably slower pace than for men. At 3,000 metres, two black women runners featured in the top 50; three at 10 kilometres; six at 15 kilometres; seven in the half marathon; and three in the marathon. This situation fluctuated over the next few years without disturbing the fact that black women constituted a decided minority amongst long-distance runners with their main consistent strength at 10 and 15 kilometres and in the half marathon.

The history of organized athletics in South Africa goes back to the early nineteenth century either under the influence of the British Army or as part of Afrikaner *boeresport* associated with *Nagmaal* (quarterly Holy Communion). But most of what has been recorded refers to white women, both before and during the years of apartheid. Women do not make an appearance until after 1900, competing in short sprints and longer races known as cake walks (Coghlan, 1986: 444–5). They emerged in track and field competition in the 1920s, but were treated in such a casual way by South African administrators that they were often forced to compete in, or even for, Britain. Their full debut in the South African senior championships had to wait until 1929 (Leach and Wilkins, 1992: 25). Marjorie Clark was a world-class all-rounder in the late 1920s and early 1930s in the short sprint, high hurdles and long and high jumps (Eales, 1974). In 1928 she won the 100 yard hurdles and high jump at the English championships and then came sixth in the Olympic high jump although she had attained the winning height of 5' 3" in England (Beinart, 1961). She was subsequently the first woman member of a South African athletic team at the 1932 Los Angeles Olympics where she won bronze in the 80 metres hurdles; going on to take gold in both the 80 metres hurdles and high jump at the 1934 Empire Games in London. That was followed by the Fourth World Women's Games at which all the South Africans, Clark included, fared poorly.

In 1935, Barbara Burke ran 100 yards in a world record 11.0 seconds (and the 220 yards in 24.8 seconds just 0.2 seconds outside the world best). But as had happened with Clark's 5' 2¼" high jump in 1927, no formal application was made for recognition. The authorities were also slow to adopt international standards: the women's 100 yards hurdles became the 80 metres hurdles in 1929, but South Africa made the change only in 1935. This also deprived Clark of a shared world record in the 80 metres in 1930 because her performances went unrecognized (De Swardt, 2000: 43). As late as March 1941, Esther van Heerden (later Brand) jumped 5' 5⅜" to equal Dorothy Odam's (later Tyler, Great Britain) world record, but the South African authorities wrongly believed the record was an inch higher. Extraordinarily, the records were officially corrected only in 1962 (Beinart, 1967: 47).

Burke was nominated for the Berlin Olympic Games in 1936 but was told she could not compete because a single female athlete did not justify the cost of a chaperone. Born in London, she ran for Great Britain instead, although she had lived in South Africa since the age of eight months, having won both sprints and the sprint hurdles in the national championships. In Berlin she won a silver medal in the sprint relay. Two years later, in the Sydney Empire Games, she competed for South Africa and won gold in the 80 metres hurdles (Emery, 1956: 121). Another South African woman forced overseas was Bernice Steyl who went to England and won the national shot put title (Beinart, 1962: 35–6). At the turn of the twenty-first century Clark and Burke were awarded belated recognition and named amongst South Africa's ten leading women athletes of all time (De Swardt, 2000: 42–3).

However, from the 1950s women's athletics in South Africa flourished, possibly to some extent as a result of socio-economic changes following the war. There were successes in a full range of running, jumping and throwing events in national competitions, at the 1952 Helsinki Olympic Games, and at the Commonwealth Games of 1954 and 1958. Two world records and an Olympic Games record were set, and gold and silver medals won. White women's athletics was clearly making strides.

In 1965 the South African Women's Athletics Association was established at Potchefstroom and on 9 April 1966 Johanna Cornelissen claimed top world ranking in the 100 yards. In June and July 1968 a South African athletics team toured Europe, although the athletes (in common with those from other countries) often found themselves running non-specialist distances because their events were not on the programme.

The high-profile names involved in the early 1950s indicate that South African women's athletics was still dominated by English speakers, but from mid-decade it was popularly believed to have become a symbol of Afrikaner nationalism and by extension apartheid ideology. This assumption is borne out by an analysis of surnames of top women performers: every year between 1962 and 1967 Afrikaans names constituted at least two thirds and in two years exceeded 70% (Nel, 1969: 45). This is, of course, a crude measure: women with English surnames could be first language Afrikaans speakers, and vice versa. Regardless of name, an individual could be *tweetalig* (truly bilingual), although the surname test can be regarded as indicative. Young athletes emerged in numbers from small *platteland* (rural) towns that were predominantly Afrikaans speaking. For example, the obscure Orange Free State town of Boshof produced Magdel Myburgh, a sprinter, and Wilna Fraser, a shot putter, who were competing at senior level while still at school in the late 1950s (Le Roux, 2002: 27). In the 1969–70 season Claudie van Straaten equalled the world 100 metres record for her age group just before South Africa was suspended by the International Amateur Athletic Federation in August 1970. The reaction to this was to start a series of unofficial athletics meetings in defiance of global governance that required modifications to apartheid sports policy (multinationalism) by invoking the concept of the open international – meetings to which foreign athletes were invited to South Africa to compete following the sports boycott. At the meeting at Green Point, a neighbourhood of Cape Town, on 26–27 November 1971, South Africa's women won 7 of 11 events.

Another, perhaps more accurate, way of assessing the dominance of Afrikaans-speaking women in track and field events is to look at the annual university championships. In 1970 there were 12 events and thus 36 placings. Only two of the latter went to an athlete from an English-medium university, the rest belonging to the universities of Pretoria, Stellenbosch, Potchefstroom and Orange Free State. The universities of the Witwatersrand, Rhodes and Cape Town came fifth to seventh in the points table. In the 1971 version held in Durban, the situation was virtually unchanged with one win and two other placings from athletes from the universities of the Witwatersrand and Rhodes. By 1980 there were 42 placings (14 events) on offer at a meeting sponsored by the Maize Board, a parastatal organisation, but none of the English-medium universities took part (University of Port Elizabeth, a dual-medium institution, did however participate). Amongst the men, only University of Cape Town of the English-medium universities took part.

During the 1970s South Africa's geographical isolation was made worse by the political sports boycott. There was a general lament about youthful promise, early peaking and premature retirement. Beinart (1975: 8–11) felt that talent was insufficiently nursed and blamed a culture of young prodigies at national junior championships, but promising starts were not followed through (Le Roux, 2002: 27). For example, Denise van Wyk and Pauline Craven (long jump) peaked at 19 in 1970, whereas Mary Rand (Great Britain) and Heide Rosendahl (West Germany) reached their best in their mid-20s and won Olympic gold. The all-time listings were overwhelmingly (90%) populated by Afrikaans names, but Rosina Sedibane (born in 1958) appeared as the first black woman (800 and 1,500 metres) in 1977. Yet after 1979 she disappeared from the records and into obscurity. Nevertheless, in 1981 and 1982 six South African women appeared in the world top 30, with Charmaine Gale third in the high jump. In 1984 Zola Budd emerged as an outstanding talent by setting an unrecognized world record in the 5,000 metres at the extraordinary age of 17, but her subsequent career as a British Olympic runner on the strength of her father's ancestry illustrated the enormity of South Africa's isolation. The following year she achieved her world record in a 5,000 metres run for Britain. Castigated for evading the boycott, she was still regarded as South African as shown by the large number of township taxis that still bear her name (Vanderhaeghen, 2012). An equivalent talent, born at a more propitious time, was Elana Meyer who between February 1991 and July 1992 won 51 consecutive victories over various distances and ended with an Olympic medal (Hauman, 2002: 17).

Black male athletes developed from the facilities provided by elite schools on one hand, and the high-class facilities and coaching standards of mining houses, the steel industry, South African Railways and Harbours, and the police and army from the late 1940s on the other (Jokl, 1949: 448, 453–63). Black women did not feature until the 1980s and then in very small numbers. Athletics was an urban activity and the presence of African women and children in towns was discouraged by tight influx control regulation (Archer and Bouillon, 1982: 37). For example, at the South African Non-White Championships held on 1–2 May 1971 at Libanon, a gold-mining area, there were no women's events. The last such meet was held in 1976, again at Libanon, and women were still absent. The South African Amateur Athletics Union changed its constitution in 1977 to achieve fully open status (Le Roux, 1995), although this was regarded by the non-racial, anti-apartheid SACOS as a façade for reformed apartheid under continued white, paternalistic, establishment control. The government played its part by removing in 1979 those aspects of the Group Areas Act that underpinned urban segregation affecting sport. A ticket to a sports event was from then onwards a permit to visit areas otherwise strictly controlled, a fact that SACOS made part of its campaign to draw attention to the ongoing grip of apartheid in an era of supposed reform.

After the ending of apartheid, and with administrative unity finally achieved in South African athletics on 12 January 1992, the country was able to compete at the Barcelona Olympic Games. Elana Meyer (who was later to run the fastest debut marathon in 1994), won silver in the 10,000 metres, the country's first women's Olympic medal in over 40 years. By this time black women athletes were beginning to make a slight impression on the track, especially at shorter distances and in jumping events such as the triple jump. But whites remained totally dominant in throwing events, possibly because black schools had only rudimentary sports facilities and lacked expensive specialist equipment. In 1998 no black South African woman figured in the World lists, World junior top 20 or Commonwealth top ten. Indeed, only 9 out of 20 women's records had shown improvement since readmission to World sport in 1992. The reasons for this were ascribed to uncertainty arising from administrative restructuring, lack of development programmes and poor encouragement and incentives for promising young athletes (Russouw,

1998). That year, 7 of the 22 best performers at the 5,000 metres were black women, but they were barely visible in shorter track events and not at all in field events.

South Africa re-entered international competition on a tide of high expectations. In the case of women athletes the high jump had historically been the event at which South Africans excelled and they continued to do so (Le Roux, 2003: 14). Hope was initially justified in some sports, but not in athletics where the country's performance at the Stuttgart World Championships of 1993 was seen as a failure (van Wyk, 1994: 10–11). This extended to the Commonwealth Games of 1994 in Vancouver when, significantly, four of five medals won were women's and Elana Meyer excelled. The general verdict was that all athletes had been let down by poor selection (Zola Pieterse, formerly Budd, had been left out) and poor management (van Wyk, 1995). This was to become a familiar refrain, reviving memories of the shambolic state of women's athletics before the Second World War. There were no medals for female athletes from South Africa at the 1996 Atlanta Games.

It was not until 2002 that black sprinters emerged and the national sprint relay team was predominantly black. But black athletes continued to be absent from field events and walking. Amongst juniors there was equal representation of black and white competitors only at the 1,500 metres. Signs of change began to show from the middle of the decade with increasing parity between black and white runners, but jumpers, throwers and walkers were still overwhelmingly white.

Post-liberation governance of athletics managed by Athletics South Africa (ASA) was notoriously controversial under the disastrous and long-term presidency of Leonard Chuene. The most damning comment came from the coach Wilf Paish who departed from ASA prematurely in 1996 citing administrative chaos, the lack of a long-term strategy and a failure to serve the interests of athletes. The dominant issue, he complained, was politics which prevailed at the expense of proven expertise and potential, particularly at grassroots level. Athletics was run as a corrupt private fiefdom and the independent enquiry called for by Paish took over a decade to materialise. The casualties were many, but the most famous was middle-distance runner Caster Semenya whose eligibility as a female athlete was questioned after a meteoric rise to fame that culminated in a World championship 800 metre gold medal at Berlin in 2009. The detrimental effects of the inadequacies of sex testing are covered in other chapters of this *Handbook*, but that Semenya's case also exposed the devious and manipulative roles of powerful players including ASA administrators and politicians is beyond question (Merrett, 2009).

Pre-liberation sports administrators were on average more conservative than many athletes and some sections of the white public (Brickhill, 1976: 56). They operated in the background adhering strictly to law and government policy and observing what they argued was tradition and custom towards women and black South Africans. Morrell (2001b: 17, 55, 107) notes an 'intractable settler masculinity' founded on the team spirit generated by pervasive school sport that fed into later adult life where it shaped attitudes that dominated the ubiquitous club. They, together with lodges (particularly freemasonry), old boys' societies and ex-servicemen's shellholes (Memorable Order of the Tin Hat, or MOTHs) bound together men of varying class into a web of unity and conformity (Morrell, 2001b: 129).

Athletics has generally been seen as the most 'literal' and orthodox of all South African sports codes (Archer and Bouillon, 1982: 280) and during the apartheid years it was heavily influenced by the secretive think-tank, the Broederbond. Assumed authority was derived from a pervasive paternalism in South African life that was applied to women and blacks and sustained by those close to the centre of political power. The challenge to manhood was countered by a number of myths about women, particularly their frailty and the threat posed to reproductive powers by athletic exercise in the context of a colonial cult of motherhood (Morrell, 2001b: 229). Indeed, this was an international issue and after women ran the 880 yards at the Amsterdam Olympics of 1928 in what were deemed to be controversial circumstances (Derderian, 1994: 294) their longest race for many years was to be the 220 yards (Rhodes, 1978: 243). In terms of gender relations women were meant to be submissive and deferential, conforming to male expectations and the established order (Jutel, 2003: 34). During the 1920s and 1930s there was considerable support amongst white women for total segregation. This conservative outlook was not necessarily shared by the white public as a whole amongst whom there was ambivalence. But while they would turn out to applaud female athletes in an open display of support, there is no documentary evidence that they made any meaningful challenge to the colonial or apartheid status quo.

Conversely, in a liberated South Africa, administrators have turned out to be better known than most athletes, but for all the wrong reasons: financial corruption, managerial autocracy, political agendas and administrative incompetence. The reasons for this lie in expropriation of athletics yet again for purposes of nation-building, this time driven by the African National Congress, initially encouraged by the reformed National Party. Both the grassroots imperatives of the anti-apartheid sports movement and professional interests were sidelined to the detriment of women athletes yet again.

References

Alexander, M. 1985. *The Comrades Marathon Story* (Craighall: Delta, 3rd ed.).

Archer, R. and Bouillon, A. 1982. *The South African Game: Sport and Racism* (London: Zed).

Beinart, H.N. 1961. 'History of South African athletics' *South African Athletics Annual* 10: 23–8.

Beinart, H.N. 1962. 'History of South African athletics (1930–1960)' *South African Athletics Annual* 11: 32–40.

Beinart, H.N. 1967. 'South Africa and the world record list' *South African Athletics Annual* 15: 45–8.

Beinart, H.N. 1975. 'Why so much waste of junior talent?' *South African Athletics Annual* 23: 8–11.

Brickhill, J. 1976. *Race against Race: South Africa's Multi-National Sport Fraud* (London: IDAF).

Cahn, S.K. 1994. *Coming on Strong: Gender and Sexuality in Twentieth-Century Women's Sport* (New York: Free Press).

Cameron-Dow, J. 1997. *The Two Oceans Marathon Story* (Cape Town: Nelson, 2nd ed.).

Coghlan, D.V. 1986. *The Development of Athletics in South Africa* (Grahamstown: Rhodes University – PhD thesis).

De Swardt, A. 2000. 'A closer look at South Africa's best track athletes' *South African Athletics Annual* 48: 39–43.

Derderian, T. 1994. *Boston Marathon: the History of the World's Premier Running Event* (Champaign: Human Kinetics).

Eales, A. 1974. 'South Africa's greatest athletes' *South African Athletics Annual* 22: 19–23.

Emery, I. 1956. *Springboks of the Olympiad* (Johannesburg: APB).

Grundlingh, A. 1996. 'Playing for Power? Rugby, Afrikaner Nationalism and Masculinity in South Africa, c.1900–70'. Chapter 2 in *Making Men: Rugby and Masculine Identity*, edited by J. Nauright and T. J. L. Chandler (London: Frank Cass).

Hargreaves, J.A. 1994. *Sporting Females: Critical Issues in the History and Sociology of Women's Sports* (London: Routledge).

Hargreaves, J.A. 2000. *Heroines of Sport: the Politics of Difference and Identity* (London, Routledge), see Chapter 2, 'Race, Politics and Gender: Women's Struggles for Sport in South Africa', pp.14–46.

Hauman, R. 1982. 'Boom in SA road running' *South African Athletics Annual* 30: 89–94.

Hauman, R. 2000. 'Spotlight on South Africa's best road runners of the twentieth century' *South African Athletics Annual* 48: 47–52.

Hauman, R. 2002. 'Elana: a career without equal' *South African Athletics Annual* 50: 17–23.

Jokl, E. 1949. 'Physical education, sport and recreation' in *Handbook on Race Relations in South Africa*, edited by E. Hellmann and L. Abrahams (Cape Town: Oxford University Press).

Jutel, A. 2003. 'Thou dost run as in floatation: femininity, reassurance and the emergence of the women's marathon' *International Journal of the History of Sport* 20(3): 17–36.

La Trobe, C. 1984.'Women: the second sex no longer' *SA Runner* January: 8–9.

Le Roux, G. 1995. 'A century of South African athletics' *South African Athletics Annual* 43: 15–26.

Le Roux, G. 2002. 'Junior athletics: fifty glorious years' *South African Athletics Annual* 50: 27–30.

Le Roux, G. 2003. 'Esther Brand and Hestrie Cloete dominate South Africa's golden female event on world stage' *South African Athletics Annual* 51: 14–21.

Leach, G. and Wilkins, G. 1992. *Olympic Dream: the South African Connection* (London: Penguin).

Merrett, C. 2004. 'From the outside lane: issues of "race" in South African athletics in the twentieth century' *Patterns of Prejudice* 38(3): 233–51.

Merrett, C. 2007. 'Race, gender and political dissent in the Comrades Marathon, 1921–1981' *South African Historical Journal* 59: 242–60.

Merrett, C. 2009. 'So much for the Rainbow Nation' *The Witness* 10 November.

Mirwis, S. 1965. 'South Africa's greatest walking event' *South African Athletics Annual* 14: 38–9.

Morrell, R. 1997. 'Masculinity in South African history' *South African Historical Journal* 37: 167–77.

Morrell, R. 2001a. *Changing Men in Southern Africa* (Pietermaritzburg: University of Natal Press).

Morrell, R. 2001b. *From Boys to Gentlemen: Settler Masculinity in Colonial Natal, 1880–1920* (Pretoria: Unisa Press).

Nel, B. 1969. 'Ontleding van statistiek uit jaarboeke, 1962–1967' *South African Athletics Annual* 17: 45–6.

Rhodes, D. 1978. 'History of women's running' in *Complete Woman Runner* (Mountain View, California: World Publications): 241–55.

Russouw, J. 1998. 'The improvement in South African records since 1992' *South African Athletics Annual* 46: 21.

Van Wyk, J. 1994. 'Stemming the tide of rising expectations' *South African Athletics Annual* 42: 10–11.

Van Wyk, J. 1995. 'The thirty percenters in Victoria' *South African Athletics Annual* 43: 12–13.

Vanderhaeghen, Y. 2012. 'The flowering of Zola Budd' *The Witness* 13 January.

PART III

Diversity and division

16

MAPPING INTERSECTIONALITY AND WHITENESS

Troubling gender and sexuality in sport studies

Mary G. McDonald

Among the many contributions of critical theory is the notion that 'identity' is not simply a quality of personal or intergroup differences. Rather, critical theorizing across disciplinary boundaries suggests that identity is concurrently the product of historically specific social relations. Chicana feminist, Chela Sandoval (1991), is suspicious about any approach devoid of contextual and discursive understandings, suggesting instead that 'identity' serves as an ideological alibi for the promotion and the production of power. Class, race, gender and sexuality then, are important—not as individual descriptive characteristics—but as 'primary organizing principles of a society which locates and positions groups within that society's opportunity structures' (Baca Zinn and Thornton Dill, 1996: 323).[1]

Despite antecedents, historians often trace the development of explicit theorizing about the politics of identity to the social movements of the 1960s and 1970s including the post-imperial, black, Chicana, sexual liberation and feminist movements. Among the most incisive critiques within this legacy regarding the operation of power via (post)identity are arguments made by feminist theorists (King and McDonald, 2007). Given the breadth and depth of this theorizing, it would be impossible to fully map the contributions of feminism in all its iterations within and beyond sport scholarship. Instead, my intent with this chapter is more modest: I briefly discuss one theoretical manifestation—that of intersectionality, although, as detailed more fully below, the dialogic character of feminism means that numerous feminist frameworks have also embraced many of intersectionality's central tenets in diverse ways. Broadly speaking, to investigate intersectionality is to explore the ways in which interlocking forms of power produce difference or 'the relationships among multiple dimensions and modalities of social relationships and subject formations' (McCall 2005: 1772). McCall (2005: 1772) argues, intersectionality may be 'the most important theoretical contribution that women's studies, in conjunction with related fields, has made so far'.

While intersectional analysis has achieved ubiquity, its illuminative potential has not yet been exhausted (Levine-Rasky, 2011). A growing body of scholarship now offers a 'reconsideration of intersectionality theory as applied to the "other side" of power relations, that is to the intersections of whiteness and middle-classness rather than to the more traditional categories of racialization, gender, and working-classness' (Levine-Rasky, 2011: 239). This application reveals the complicated character of social relations, and encourages scholars to reconsider the ways in which current conceptualizations of gender and sexuality function in sport and critical sport scholarship.

As Douglas and Jamieson (2006: 120) suggest, a sizable portion of the critical sport scholarship 'that deals with race considers the experiences of African-American men, while analyses of gender and sexuality examine the experiences of white women'. This simplistic framing fails to account for the multiple ways in which power articulates and effects life chances within particular contexts. Furthermore, few analyses consciously investigate the power of whiteness as linked to sexuality within the gendered and classed realm of sport (Douglas and Jamieson, 2006). Scholarly orientations that presume rather than interrogate whiteness, fail to fully illuminate the interactive, contradictory ways in which power operates through sport and the body.

Given the unique status of this anthology in bringing together diverse theorizing and empirical studies related to gender and sexuality, the first purpose of this chapter is to explore the ways in which notions of gender and sexuality have been imagined and deployed within and beyond sport scholarship. I further suggest that intersectionality is a particularly useful framework for understanding the complicated character of whiteness. In sum, this chapter uses the lenses of intersectionality and whiteness, not to suggest their utility in all cases, but rather to join similar efforts (e.g. McDonald, 2006; Douglas and Jamieson, 2006; King, 2009) to productively trouble the ways sport scholars too often narrowly conceive of gender and sexuality in their analyses.

Challenging universal claims through intersectional analysis

Several authors have traced movements within feminist sport studies scholarship from the 1970s onward, noting the centrality of (post)identity and power within these analyses (Hall, 1988; Hargreaves, 1994; Birrell, 2000; Scraton & Flintoff, 2002; King & McDonald, 2007). These overviews suggest that initial feminist frameworks focused on how women's sporting experiences differed from men's. Many of these perspectives both explicitly and implicitly drew upon broader Marxist/socialist feminist conceptualizations of standpoint theory (c.f. Hartsock, 1983). This conceptualization—suggesting an epistemological shift to privilege the standpoint of women—frequently meant highlighting women's unique ways of knowing and presumed shared political interests as the grounds from which to both critique patriarchy and to change it. A feminist standpoint was additionally thought to counter androcentric bias thus allegedly illuminating 'not only how women are constructed as subordinate, but also how male sport structures operate to keep them that way' (Hall, 1985: 33).

Some sport scholars subsequently drew upon critiques by feminists of colour to question the presumption of a universal white woman and/or feminist subject thought to underlie standpoint epistemology and similar frameworks. These scholars also recognized the limitations of those material feminist analyses exclusively organized around class and gender as well as the lesbian, feminist critiques of sexism and heterosexism within sport. Drawing upon the writings of self-described 'Third World' feminists who repeatedly refused their positioning as 'other' in Western feminism, these critiques demonstrated the persistence of racism and ethnocentrism. Selected sport scholars continue to utilize black, Chicana, postcolonial and/or transnational feminism (among others) to question theories which mistakenly posit gender and/or sexuality as the primary marker(s) of oppression. Instead, they investigate intersectionality in recognizing that racism and classism are also salient interacting forces. This shift has been useful on multiple fronts, especially in making visible the complex articulations of power in the lives of women of colour.

Alongside and at times intersecting with intersectional analyses are poststructuralist and post-modern theories, which have also de-naturalized the presumed universality of the category of 'women', albeit for different reasons than the antiracist critiques offered by feminists of colour. Anti-foundational formulations, including those mounted by psychoanalytic, queer and post-colonial feminisms, continue to expose the modern assumptions upon which much North American and European feminist and sport studies scholarship rest (King and McDonald, 2007). These anti-foundational theorists question the modern presumption of a fully coherent, stable and agentic subject as well as the feminist politics indebted to this conceptualization. In this way anti-foundationalists argue against the trend championed in standpoint theories which unprob-lematically position and fix women's experiences as the central organizing point for feminist theory and praxis. Postmodernists argue that such a focus limits feminisms' analytic and political reach. Instead, anti-foundationalists seek to interrogate the knowledge claims made through the historical production of subjectivities as well as their interactive functioning(s) and discursive effects (King and McDonald, 2007).

Crenshaw (1989; 1991) first coined the term intersectionality in order to challenge the invisibil-ity of women of colour within legal doctrine, and within feminist and antiracist efforts. Crenshaw argued that too often the activities of feminists focused on structures affecting white women while antiracist struggles mostly centred on the issues facing men of colour. That is, within feminism, white middle-class women's positionality and experiences frequently were presumably universal and thus made to stand for all women despite the powerful processes of racialization, class forma-tions and nationalism. In a similar way the ideologies and social conditions effecting men of colour were often given greater focus without a sustained effort to understand complicated gender dynam-ics. These assumptions produced a lack of sufficient attention, for example, on the racial privilege afforded to white women and the gendered advantages enjoyed by men of colour. An additional result was that the multiple discourses influencing women of colour were rarely interrogated and challenged within legal standards, social service provisions and social justice movements.

An example which demonstrates the impact of structural intersectionality is found in domes-tic violence cases where race and class formations make women of colour's experiences of rape, violence and remediation 'qualitatively different from [those] of white women' (Crenshaw 1991: 1245). In many cases inequitable class and gender relations combine with 'racially discrim-inatory employment and housing practices' as well as 'disproportionately high unemployment' among people of colour making 'battered women of colour less able to depend on the support of friends and relatives for temporary shelter' (Crenshaw, 1991: 1246). Social service agencies, women's shelters and social justice movements which neglect these particularities in seeking to provide support and remediation also fail to understand the impact of interacting social forma-tions. Such failure helps to 'relegate the identity of women of colour to a location that resists telling' (Crenshaw 1991: 1242)

Significantly, Crenshaw's focus on intersectionality emerged amidst similar theorizing about interlocking forms of power generated via intellectual and political dialogue among women of colour. The product of a long historical trajectory (c.f. Brah and Phoenix, 2004) related visions include Collins' (1990) matrices of domination; Anzaldúa's (1987) mestiza and border-land's consciousness; Sandoval's (1991) 'third world' oppositional consciousness; Carby's (1987) reconstructing womanhood; Mohanty's (1988) critique of imperial feminism; and Baca Zinn and Thornton Dill's (1996) multiracial feminism, to mention but a few. Early applications of similar work applied an additive approach in theorizing, for example, the 'double jeopardy' or 'triple oppression' experienced by black women. Here disadvantage was thought to be cumula-tive and an effect of domination. Analyses subsequently sought to illuminate the diverse social formations that both produce difference and impact the lives of women of colour while also theorizing the complicated discursive workings of subordination and privilege more broadly (Baca Zinn and Thornton Dill, 1996; hooks, 1981).

Intersectionality continues to travel across a diverse array of epistemological realms as a theory, method and/or strategic intervention. This fluidity makes it difficult to map the nuances of each iteration. However, broadly speaking, some postmodern theorists see intersectionality as helpful in illuminating their 'project of deconstructing the binary oppositions and universalism inherent in the modernist paradigms of Western philosophy and science' (Davis, 2008: 71). Other theorists utilizing a variety of perspectives, including cultural studies, postcolonial, diasporic, poststructuralist and queer paradigms, are attracted to the ways intersectionality demonstrates that identities are not static as once thought, but fragmented, shifting and multiple (Davis, 2008). Brah and Phoenix (2004: 76) suggest some iterations signify 'the complex, irreducible, varied, and variable effects which ensue when multiple axes of differentiation – economic, political, cultural, psychic, subjective and experiential – intersect in historically specific contexts'. One contribution of these articulations is that most feminist research now assumes that 'subjectivites are always produced within intersecting matrixes of domination and subordination, inclusion and exclusion, and precisely how these forces coincide is contingent and, thus, unknowable in advance' (King and McDonald, 2007: 9).

One of the earliest sport pieces to tackle questions of intersectionality is Birrell's 'Women of color, critical autobiography, and sport'. Drawing upon black and Chicana feminism, Birrell (1990) reveals the general absence of writing about women of colour in sport scholarship, offering critical autobiography as a means to theorize the multiplicitous status of women of colour. Critiquing positivistic analyses of sport which conceived of race and gender as variables, Birrell instead argues for the usefulness of postmodern theories of identity and intersectionality to help reveal the tensions between experience, consciousness and sport. Smith (1992) also suggested the need to 'break the silence' regarding the 'outsider-within' (Collins, 1990)— or the raced, classed and gendered positionality of black, Latina, Native American, and Asian American women. Hargreaves (2000: 13) offered one of the first extended analyses to document the experiences of women typically positioned as 'outsiders within the mainstream of sport' in such diverse locales as South Africa, Australia, Canada and the Muslim Diaspora. In doing so, she also raised crucial theoretical 'questions about inclusion and exclusion, about power and privilege, and about local–global connections' (p. 13).

In the decades since these contributions were first made, sport scholars have increasingly provided analyses which use both social scientific and poststructuralist notions to interrogate the (inter)relations between gender, race, sexuality and class in a variety of locales. Still, Bruening's (2005) overview suggests that the experiences and discursive voices of women of colour, while growing, still remain under-represented in sport scholarship. The scholarship which has emerged since the initial call is impossible to sufficiently cite here but has drawn upon intersectional sensibilities to interrogate, for example, representations of the Women's National Basketball Association (WNBA) (Banet-Weiser, 1999); football in Britain (Scraton et al., 2005); as well as the politics of representation through celebrity athletes such as Austrian aboriginal track sensation Cathy Freeman (Bruce and Hallinan, 2001). Collectively, these and other investigations have demonstrated a central premise of poststructuralist intersectionality—that its effects are never given in advance but are instead always and everywhere in process, further influenced by temporal, spatial and (trans)national contexts. Nowhere is this notion more apparent then in the sporting lives of young Shia Muslim Canadian women, as Jiwani and Rail's (2010) discourse analysis reveals. The women they interviewed drew upon diverse understandings of physical activity experiences thus countering essentialistic, colonial legacies and gendered Islamaphobic understandings of both the young women's bodies and the hijab.

Collectively, this scholarship supports the contributions of initial intersectional critiques in revealing the heterogeneity that constitutes the socially-constructed category of 'women'.

> The scholarship on Black masculinity and sport (see for example, Carrington, 1998), marginal masculinities (Connell, 2002), and the representational politics of celebrity athletes like Michael Jordan (see for example Andrews, 2001; Andrews and Jackson 2001) likewise reveal a complex social order where all men do not share equally in power nor exert power over all women.
>
> *(Knoppers and McDonald, 2010: 319)*

This particular scholarship reveals the complicated discursive production of competing masculinities and femininities. It additionally reveals ways in which intersectional analyses 'move beyond the typical binary formulations endemic to Western thought: male/female; masculine/feminine; White/Black; and rich/poor' (Knoppers and McDonald, 2010: 319).

Much of the intersectionality sport scholarship continues to illuminate the complex working of power and the limitations of those feminists who continue to posit gender as the primary focus of analysis. Not only do such analyses presume universality, these frameworks which posit gender as primary also naturalize the workings of whiteness. Recent interventions have likewise demonstrated the ways in which sexuality is often insufficiently theorized. Despite important exceptions, in general sport scholars have too frequently 'focused on the experiences of a narrow stratum of North American and European lesbian and gay athletes whose sexual subjectivities are rendered in isolation from the processes of racialization and capital accumulation through which they are constituted' (King, 2008: 420).

This narrow scholarly focus is not just limited to sport studies. Self-described queers of colour have also challenged the singular focus on sexuality represented in much of queer theory and queer scholarship (McDonald, 2006). Among the notable exceptions to scholarship which reproduces a singular focus on sexuality within sport studies are the writings of Douglas (2012), Jamieson (2003) and King (2008). For example, Jamieson's (2003: 11) discussion of US college softball players reveals the diverse ways in which Latina players struggle 'with histories, acts of colonization, and the desire to engage with power through higher education and elite athletics'. Despite access to cultural capital as students and skilled athletes, at different times and locations several players are discursively placed as outsiders, thought to be linguistically and sexually exotic by teammates.

King's (2009) analysis of US basketball star Sheryl Swoopes in also instructive in revealing the complex relational character of media discourses and is among the few analyses of sport which theorize the relationship between whiteness and intersectionality. On the one hand, the narratives Swoopes' deploys in revealing a same-sex relationship with then partner Alisa Scott are remarkable for exhibiting desire against a backdrop of silence and invisibility which too often greets expressions of Black female sexuality. However, against these narratives the media 'redeployed a range of discourses about identity, sexual economy, and racialized sexuality' (King 2009: 273). These constructions performed powerful ideological work racializing the black community through commonsense discourses about homophobia while simultaneously representing an ideal subject of whiteness as the 'proper lesbian or gay subject, who is out, proud and fully invested in the economic individualism of consumer culture' (p. 286). This analysis is unique in sport scholarship for explicitly accounting for the ways whiteness colonizes gender and sexuality.

In sum, this brief review suggests that a growing body of intersectional scholarship illuminates the complicated workings of power especially in regard to discourses, knowledges and experiences related to 'minority' racialized subjects. Collectively, these writings reveal the limitations of theorizing gender and sexuality apart from racialization and class formations. However, before the promise of intersectionality can be more fully realized within sport studies scholarship, additional ways of thinking must be engaged. One path forward is to use the flexibility of the framework to incorporate an analysis of whiteness, a task which will be discussed more fully in the next section.

Against invisibility: troubling power in sport studies scholarship

Despite unmasking normative assumptions that unreflectively place white middle-class women's experiences as representative within feminism, the intersectional theorizing of women of colour has not been widely acknowledged within the body of scholarship on whiteness, which emerged in the 1990s. This lack of recognition is curious given the importance of the scholarship on whiteness, a project which cultural critic Toni Morrison suggests serves to shift 'the analytic gaze away from an exclusive preoccupation with the effects of racism on people of colour toward inquiry that targets the knowledge and subjects perpetuating racism' (McDonald, 2005: 246).

As Levine-Rasky (2011: 247–248) also makes clear, intersectional theory's focus on complexity makes it particularly well suited to engage with discussions of whiteness. One promising formulation posits that

> identity locations conventionally represented as gender, race, class, ethnicity, culture, religion, and so on, are shaped by material differences and are also lived subjectively and practised in relations with others. Moreover, they are co-produced through such interactions. The process is thoroughly relational.

In an earlier work (McDonald, 2002), I delineated such an understanding to also make clear that neither sexuality nor gender are primary to understanding the ideological importance of popular sporting representations. I did so by examining the public persona of the WNBA's Suzie McConnell-Serio. The two-time Olympic basketball gold medallist was celebrated in the US media as both an exceptional basketball player who exhibited superior sportsmanship, and as an outstanding wife and mother. The larger take-home point is that the marketers' emphasis on 'McConnell Serio's maternal commitments and moral strengths were co-produced through discourses of heterosexual femininity and bourgeois Whiteness to distance the league from both lesbian and Black bodies' among its fan base and playing force' (King, 2008: 425). This framing also serves to reinforce the contemporary conservative 'family values' climate where idealized images of white womanhood are projected as 'responsible, concerned and non-threatening' (McDonald, 2002: 385). The ideological effects of similar popular culture representations resemble late nineteenth-century dynamics around white middle-class womanhood in privileging 'a historically-specific vision of whiteness and heteronormativity' (McDonald, 2002: 385). These representations of McConnell-Serio now take on 'additional import in normalizing a particular version of white bourgeois heteronormativitiy amidst contemporary challenges brought by the feminist, civil rights and gay movements, and increased immigration by people of color' (p. 385).

Closer inspection of the politics of representation surrounding tennis playing sisters Venus and Serena Williams is also revealing in demonstrating contemporary articulations of power and resistance as Douglas (2012) demonstrates. The superstar African American sisters have long served to counter the dominant discourses of women's professional tennis as an exclusive space dedicated to the preservation of idealized norms of white middle-class heteronormativity. Winners of numerous grand slam and other prestigious tennis titles, their success and resolve is all the more impressive considering the context through which their achievements have been reached. Not only have they been framed within persistent controlling images (Collins, 1990) of black womanhood including tropes of sexual licentiousness and arrogance, but also as players selfishly more interested in their lives off the tennis court who lack sufficient dedication to their sport. These racialized gendered tropes, originally developed during slavery and reconstruction to justify white supremacy, are hailed in new iterations as a form of surveillance and as a means to both demonize the sisters' accomplishments while also policing white-created norms of appropriate behaviour. And yet, as Douglas suggests, the Williams' sisters have at times also resisted these symbolic and material framings politicizing their support from black communities and their own family as important sources of revolutionary strength and solidarity. This declaration of 'black love' as well as 'the sisters' expressions of (Black) pleasure and joy threaten the status quo, because self-actualization is one way to challenge sexism and White supremacy' (Douglas, 2012: 132). Additionally, this approach 'actively resists dominant ways of identifying the sisters as merely athletic labourers' and further demonstrates the need for constant struggle (Douglas, 2012: 140).

Concluding thoughts

A robust engagement with intersectional theory is important given that the 'cultural significance of sport lies in its power to represent and reproduce beliefs about gender, physicality, race, and sexuality' (Douglas and Jamieson, 2006: 134). A focus on the contributions of intersectionality suggests the ongoing need to rethink the ways in which gender and sexuality are often conceived within sport studies scholarship. Theories of intersectionality are instructive in demonstrating the need to join those scholars who have broadened conceptualizations beyond individualistic and singular axes of differentiation. This movement is important in challenging, for example, the racism, and classism which underpin such a singular focus on either gender and/or sexuality. Scholars should additionally take heed that the power of whiteness is rarely explicitly critiqued and continues to operate through contradictory positioning of universality and invisibility in sport studies scholarship related to gender and sexuality and beyond (Douglas and Jamieson, 2006). Further investigative mapping will likely reveal that whiteness exists 'as a process, not a "thing," as plural rather than singular in nature' (Frankenberg, 1997: 1).

The incorporation of whiteness into the framework of intersectionality is not without its own challenges and limitations, however. Indeed Winnubst (2006: 9) notes the dangers associated with similar practices which include 'playing into cultural discourses of white supremacy, to uncritically fixing white superiority, to reinscribing whiteness at the center of concern and focus' (Winnubst, 2006: 9). These results are made all the more likely given the ways in which whiteness colonizes other social relations while saturating the academy and contemporary analyses (King, 2005).

While this chapter has focused on the contributions of intersectionality as a theory, method and as a strategic lens, it should also be noted that this discussion is more than an academic issue. Indeed, feminists of colour have long been at the forefront in theorizing multiplicity and the concurrent need for coalition politics and praxis in working across culturally constructed differences and inequalities (Reagon, 1983). This recognition, coupled with an understanding of the historically powerful pull of both universality and invisibility suggests the constant need for reflection, broader dialogue and political action. It is my hope that this chapter contributes to this process in a small way by challenging the ways that gender and sexuality too frequently operate in sport studies scholarship in order to re-image fresh conceptualizations and coalitions in the ongoing movement toward justice.

Note

1   I acknowledge that gender, race, class and sexuality are not the only articulations of power to consider. Scholars have addressed formations of nationality, citizenship, ethnicity and disability to name but a few. I highlight gender, race, class and sexuality since these relations are most frequently cited in the feminist scholarship from which I am most familiar. As noted I also deploy this conception strategically to show the limitations of much of the sport scholarship on gender and sexuality, and as a means to decenter whiteness. Thanks to Parissa Safai for helping me to further develop and clarify this focus.

References

Andrews DL (2001) *Michael Jordan, Inc: Corporate, Sport, Media Culture and Late Modern America*. Albany: State University of New York.

Andrews DL and Jackson S (2001) *Sport Stars: The Cultural Politics of Sporting Celebrity*. London: Routledge.

Anzaldúa G (1987) *Borderlands/La Frontera: The New Mestiza*. San Francisco: Aunt Lute.

Baca Zinn M and Thornton Dill B (1996) Theorizing difference from multiracial feminism. *Feminist Studies* 22: 321–331.

Banet-Weiser S (1999) Hoop dreams: Professional basketball and the politics of race and gender. *Journal of Sport and Social Issues* 23: 403–420.

Birrell S (1990) Women of color, critical autobiography, and sport. In: Messner M and Sabo D (eds) *Sport, Men, and the Gender Order: Critical Feminist Perspectives*. Champaign: Human Kinetics, pp. 185–199.

Birrell S (2000) Feminist theories for sport. In: Coakley J and Dunning E (eds) *Handbook of Sports Studies*. London: Sage, pp. 61–76.

Brah A and Phoenix A (2004) Isn't I a women? Revisiting intersectionality. *Journal of International Women's Studies* 5: 75–86.

Bruce T and Hallinan C (2001) Cathy Freeman: The quest for Australian identity. In: Andrews DL and Jackson SJ (eds) *Sport Stars: The Cultural Politics of Sporting Celebrity*. New York: Routledge, pp. 257–270.

Bruening J (2005) Gender and racial analysis in sport: Are all the women white and the men black? *Quest* 57: 330–349.

Carby H (1987) *Reconstructing Womanhood: The Emergence of the Afro-American Woman Novelist*. New York: Oxford University.

Carrington B (1998) Sport, masculinity, and Black cultural resistance. *Journal of Sport and Social Issues* 22: 275–298.

Collins PH (1990) *Black Feminist Thought: Knowledge, Consciousness and the Politics of Empowerment*. Cambridge: Unwin Hyman.

Connell RW (2002) Masculinities and globalization. In: Wroth H, Paris A and Allen (eds) *The Life of Brian: Masculinities, Sexualities and Health in New Zealand*. Dunedin: University of Otago, pp. 7–42.

Crenshaw KW (1989) Demarginalizing the intersection of race and sex: A Black feminist critique of antidiscrimination doctrine, feminist theory and antiracist politics. *University of Chicago Legal Forum*: 139–167.

Crenshaw KW (1991) Mapping the margins: Intersectionality, identity politics, and violence against women of color. *Stanford Law Review* 6: 1241–1299.

Davis K (2008) Intersectionality as buzzword: A sociology of science perspective on what makes a feminist theory successful. *Feminist Theory* 90: 67–85.

Douglas DD (2012) Venus, Serena and the inconspicuous consumption of blackness: A commentary on surveillance, race talk and new racism(s). *Journal of Black Studies* 43: 127–145.

Douglas DD and Jamieson KM (2006) A farewell to remember: Interrogating the Nancy Lopez farewell tour. *Sociology of Sport Journal* 23: 117–141.

Frankenberg R (1997). (ed) *Displacing Whiteness: Essays in Social and Cultural Criticism*. Durham, NC: Duke University.

Hall MA (1985) Knowledge and gender: Epistemological questions in the social analysis of sport. *Sociology of Sport Journal* 2: 25–42.

Hall MA (1988) The discourse of gender and sport: From femininity to feminism. *Sociology of Sport Journal* 5: 330–340.

Hargreaves JA (1994) *Sporting Females: Critical Issues in the History and the Sociology of Women's Sport*. London: Routledge.

Hargreaves J.A (2000). *Heroines of Sport: The Politics of Difference and Identity*. London: Routledge.

Hartsock N (1983) The feminist standpoint: developing the grounds for a specifically feminist historical materialism. In: Harding S and Hintikka MB (eds) *Discovering Reality: Feminist Perspectives on Epistemology, Metaphysics, Methodology and Philosophy of Science*. Boston: D. Reidel, pp. 216–240.

hooks b (1981) *Ain't I a Woman: Black Women and Feminism*. Boston: South End.

Jamieson K (2003) Occupying a middle space: Toward a mestiza sport studies. *Sociology of Sport Journal* 20: 1–16.

Jiwani N and Rail G (2010) Islam, hijab and young Shia Muslim Canadian women's discursive constructions of physical activity. *Sociology of Sport Journal* 27: 251–267.

King CR (2005) Cautionary notes on whiteness and sport studies. *Sociology of Sport Journal*, [special issue. Whiteness and Sport] 22: 397–408.

King S (2008) What's queer about (queer) sport sociology now? A review essay. *Sociology of Sport Journal* 25: 419–442.

King S (2009) Homonormativity and the politics of race: Reading Sheryl Swoopes. *Journal of Lesbian Studies* 13: 272–290.

King S and McDonald, MG (2007) (Post)identity and sport: Introduction and overview. *Sociology of Sport Journal* 24: 1–19.

Knoppers A and McDonald MG (2010) Scholarship on gender and sport in *Sex Roles* and beyond. *Sex Roles* 63: 311–323.

Levine-Rasky C (2011) Intersectionality theory applied to whiteness and middle-classness. *Social Identities* 17: 239–253.

McCall, L (2005) The complexity of intersectionality. *Signs: Journal of Women in Culture and Society* 30: 1771–1800.

McDonald MG (2002) Queering whiteness: The peculiar case of the Women's National Basketball Association. *Sociological Perspectives* 45: 379–396

McDonald MG (2005) Mapping whiteness and sport: An introduction. *Sociology of Sport Journal* 22: 245–255.

McDonald MG (2006) Beyond the pale: The whiteness of sport studies and queer scholarship. In Caudwell J (ed) *Sport, Sexuality and Queer Theory*. London: Routledge, pp. 33–46.

Mohanty C (1988) Under Western eyes: Feminist scholarship and colonial discourse. *Feminist Review* 30: 61–88.

Reagon BJ (1983) Coalition politics: Turning the century. In Smith B (ed) *Home Girls: A Black Feminist Anthology*. New York: Kitchen Table, Women of Color Press, pp. 356–369.

Sandoval C (1991) US third world feminism: The theory and method of oppositional consciousness in the postmodern world. *Genders* 10: 1–24.

Scraton S and Flintoff A (2002) Sport feminism: The contribution of feminist thought to our understandings of gender and sport. In Scraton S and Flintoff A (eds) *Gender and Sport: A Reader*. New York and London: Routledge, pp. 30–46.

Scraton S, Caudwell J and Holland S (2005) 'Bend it like Patel': Centering, 'race,' ethnicity and gender in feminist analysis of women's football in England. *International Review for the Sociology of Sport* 40: 71–78.

Smith YR (1992) Women of color in society and sport. *Quest* 44: 228–250.

Winnubst S (2006) *Queering Freedom*. Bloomington: Indiana University.

17

BRITISH ASIAN FEMALE FOOTBALLERS

Intersections of identity

Aarti Ratna

Introduction

Within the sociology of sport, researchers have paid scant attention to intersectionality; the majority of research continues to focus on one dimension of 'gender' or 'race' (Scraton, 2001). Moreover, the gender and sexuality of ethnic minority athletes and/or the impact of 'race' upon the gendered and sexualised experiences of sportspeople are rarely acknowledged (see Anderson and McCormack, 2010a, 2010b; Caudwell, 2009; McDonald, 2002). McDonald (2006) also asserts that in much of the sport scholarship about gay and lesbian sexuality, 'white' is the normative frame of reference. This chapter therefore offers an important contribution to an otherwise neglected area of study.

In order to provide a critical analysis of intersectionality, I adopt the work of Butler and Bourdieu to analyse the experiences of British Asian[1] female footballers. I draw on a number of examples from my empirical research about British Asian female footballers, to elucidate the intersectionality of 'race', gender and sexuality. I argue that the idea of 'playing-up' and 'playing-down' markers of identity concomitantly is a useful way of understanding how intersectionality operates in practice. In this chapter, I argue that it is a method of doing intersectional research that reveals the intricacies of how British Asian women accommodate, negotiate and challenge the pre-dominant culture of women's football in order to facilitate their inclusion to, rather than their exclusion from, the sport.

British Asian women and sport

The popular film *Bend it like Beckham*, released in the summer of 2002, centres upon the life of a young, British Asian girl named Jasminder (Jess) who plays football. The film reached worldwide audiences, helping to raise the profile of both women's football and British Asian female footballers. Whilst as a form of entertainment the film achieved mass success, it is problematic as it also mocked and reproduced stereotypes about women's football and British Asian culture. For instance, the film represents Jess as a gender and cultural deviant. By playing football, she is challenging the long-standing myth that girls cannot and should not play football. Jess is also represented as a cultural deviant, going against the traditions of her South Asian heritage. South Asian traditions stipulate that girls should learn how to become good wives and mothers rather than play sport (Ratna, 2011). Despite such gendered and cultural dogmas, Jess eventually wins a scholarship to play football in America. Another aspect to the film is the sub-plot which focuses on sexuality. Although Jess is assumed to be the lesbian lover of Jules (her friend from her football team) by Jules' mother, the audience know this is not true and later in the film both girls' heterosexualities are affirmed through their mutual desire for Joe (the male coach). Further demarcating Jess' heterosexuality, she claims that 'Indian' people cannot be gay; alluding to the cultural and religious myth that being Indian and being gay are incompatible (Algeo, 2007; Gopinath, 2005). Thus, whilst homosexuality is mentioned in the film, it is quickly dismissed in preference for the celebration of hetero-sexual identities (Caudwell, 2009). Clearly, Jess' sporting experiences are not only shaped by her ethnic and gendered identities but also by her heterosexual identity (Scraton et al., 2005). There is clearly no challenge in the film to popular ethnic, gender and sexual stereotypes and little media or public debate about them either. Furthermore, and ironically, the few aca-demic studies that do tackle issues about British Asian women and sport are themselves often stereotypical in nature (see Ratna, 2011). This chapter aims to query commonsense ideas and to present an alternative perspective. In particular, I argue that sport sociologists should pay closer attention to multiple and intersectional identities.

At the time of *Bend it like Beckham*'s release, British Asianness was becoming an area of cultural fascination (Puwar, 2002). The British media had even dubbed 2001 as the 'Indian Summer' confirmed by the release of the Andrew Lloyd Webber's theatre production *Bombay Dreams*, and Channel Four's showing of a series of Bollywood films. Since this time, South Asian dance, culture, food and fashion are increasingly being celebrated at local festivals across different parts of England (Watson and Ratna, 2011). Yet, public and political discourses about British Asians also position them as an alien presence in British society (Alexander, 2000). Para-doxically, aspects of South Asian culture are celebrated yet also seen to reflect the segregation of South Asians from mainstream British society. Arguably, sport offers a lens through which to explore how British Asian women themselves understand, and respond to, popular assumptions about their cultures and identities.

Intersectionality and cultural space

Davis (2008) argues that intersectionality has been a 'buzzword' of feminist theory ever since its inception. As Crenshaw (1991) asserts, this is because an intersectional approach was crucial to addressing the experiences of ethnic minority women for two main reasons; firstly, because ethnic minority women's experiences and political struggles have been largely neglected by mainstream feminist movements; secondly, because anti-racism discourses have focused too heavily on the experiences of men, rendering invisible the experiences of women. Since this time, feminist researchers have used intersectionality to explore gender as a complex construc-tion inter-related to other social divisions such as sexuality, class, age, disability and so forth. As noted by Davis (2008), the use of intersectionality has become widespread within research across both sides of the Atlantic. Brah and Phoenix (2004) claim that the sociological appeal of intersectionality is that it explores the dynamic and contradictory operation of power across social difference. In a sports context, McDonald (2006) alerts readers to this complex operation of power with regard to ethnicity and sexuality: she argues that minority ethnic members of lesbian and gay communities do not simply advocate political and sexual solidarity; the impact of racism (and other forms of discrimination) affects their experiences of sport in both similar and different ways. Hence, as members of minority ethnic groups, they may experience forms of exclusion in ways taken for granted by 'white', lesbian and gay athletes.

Whilst researchers have stressed the importance of intersectionality, little is debated about how and why identities connect in the ways that they do, in the everyday lives of women (and men), and how we can understand these interconnections in practice. Valentine (2007) offers a useful framework, arguing that cultural spaces are given meaning by the social groups that predominantly occupy and hold positions of power in those spaces. The meaning associated with any cultural space is seen to be evolving: emerging, becoming dominant and residual as the power of hegemonic groups to define the space wanes or changes. Valentine (2007) argues that people view themselves differently according to the spaces they inhabit. In some spaces they are part of the hegemonic culture, they share similar identities to those in power, and hence feel accepted and valued. However, in other spaces, they do not represent the hegemonic group and feel marginalised from the dominant culture. Arguably, at certain times, individuals can play-up as well as play-down certain identities to best fit the dominant culture of a space, hence engineering their entry and acceptance. However, the choices individuals make about which identities to play-up or play-down, together and at once, are not necessarily free from constraint. As I will argue with regard to the theories of Butler and Bourdieu, the agency of individuals to perform identities is circumscribed by the intersectionality of narratives of 'race', gender and sexuality.

Theorising Butler and Bourdieu: 'playing' the game

The idea of playing-up and playing-down various identity positions has resonance with Butler's (1990) theory of performativity. She argues that identities are not a simple reflection of an innate self, but a parody that gives the illusion of a particular identity. Butler (1990) does not view performances as a regurgitation of behaviours that simply reproduce the binary categories of man and woman or heterosexual and homosexual, but that identities are performa*tive*. That is, in the performance of identities people disrupt the categories of gender and sexuality, for instance, creating and re-creating a proliferation of new ways of being that go beyond the set binaries. However, Black feminists have been particularly critical of Butler's theory as she over-privileges gender above other social categories including those of 'race' and ethnicity (Spelman, 1982). Butler (1997), using speech act theory, argues that 'race' is also performed by the way it is constituted in discourse, for example, in terms of the supposed binary between 'white' and 'black' groups. Discourses bring about what they name by citing racial norms, which are usually based on assumed racial differences between groups of people (Rottenberg, 2003). The historical context is important as, over time, western science and tradition has influenced the way we *see* racial groups. For example, the marking of superior 'white' races against those who are different, meaning inferior. Through speech acting, certain identities can be played-up whilst others can be played-down, illustrating how intersectional identities can operate together, at once. Hence, Rottenberg (2003) suggests that the appropriate performativity of 'race' can enable non-'white' people 'to pass' as 'white'.

Fraser (1999) argues that although the stylistic possibilities of doing and re-doing gender and 'race' are fluid, and centralise the agency of individuals within this process, individuals may not simply choose who they want to be in a particular social situation, as this ignores the continuing impact of dominant ideologies pertaining to gender and 'race'. For example, non-'white' people may act, behave and speak as if they are 'white', *because* they understand that being non-'white' carries social stigmas with which they do not want to be associated. Hence, exploring why some identity positions are played-up or played-down vis-à-vis other identity positions illustrates how intersectionality is performed in practice.

Bourdieu's (1990a; 1990b) term 'ontological complicity' is significant here as it further helps to explain belonging and the operation of intersectionality. When people – in terms of their class, gender, race, ethnicity, sexuality etc. – find themselves in a space in which their identities are hegemonic, they are like a 'fish to water' (see also Grenfell and James, 1998: 14). They simply need to be who they are to feel included and valued. Those who find that their identities are a mis-match to a certain cultural space, at a certain time, find that they must use various resources – which may be available to them or not – to consciously and/or subconsciously – negotiate their entry and acceptance (Puwar, 2004). This latter group are like a 'fish out of water', desperately trying to keep up with the habitual flow of a cultural space which is not instinctively 'theirs'. Arguably, linking back to the concept of performativity, they may choose to play-up or play-down their identity positions in particular ways to compensate for this habitus mis-match.

Although the application of Bourdieu's work is gaining popularity in studies about gender, sexuality and 'race', his over-deterministic stance renders individuals as passive dupes who have little control over their own lives (McNay, 1999; McLeod, 2005). However, his later work about habitus does more clearly centralise the role of individual agency and how habitus is constantly changing as individuals move through a greater number as well as greater array of social spaces during their lifespan, enabling them to learn and acquire knowledge about how to 'play' according to the hegemonic rules of any given cultural space. In this way, individuals are not perceived to be inevitably doomed by their prior class, 'racial', gender and sexual positions of identity. The work of Bourdieu and Butler can be used within a structure-agency framework, recognising that individuals can assert a degree of oppositional agency within determining social structures.

A note on the research

The research discussed in this chapter was conducted over an 18-month period between 2003 and 2005. It consisted of interviews and participant observations with 19 British Asian female football players (see Ratna 2007; 2011). The interviews were semi-structured and adopted a life history approach. The participants were invited to discuss their involvement in football, from their entry into the game to their current level of play. They were encouraged to talk about issues that affected their participation in the sport, including those relating to gender, sexuality, 'race' and ethnicity. They were also asked to comment on their relationships with other people: their family, friends and significant others. Participants' comments enabled me to gain a sense of 'who they were' in relation to other social groups, in the various spaces that they found themselves in, and during different phases of their football-playing careers. I also spent six months with a pre-dominantly British Asian Football Club (BAFC) attending training sessions and socialising with players on and off the field. This also gave me the opportunity to see how their identities intersected in practice, and how such intersections impacted upon their experiences of playing the game.

Fourteen of the nineteen British Asian girls and women had played or were playing for teams that competed at various levels of the Women's Football Pyramid, the elite organisation of women's football in England. I also interviewed five British Muslim girls and women in total who had represented the UK team at the 2001 and 2005 Muslim Women's World Games in Iran. The British Asian females that I interviewed played at elite levels and were different from each other in terms of the length of their playing careers, standard of play and their own playing aspirations. Furthermore, they held different religious beliefs and class backgrounds. The participants varied in age, ranging from 14 years old to 34 years old. As I did not ask the players to disclose their sexualities, their sexual preferences were not obvious in the way that their 'race' was signalled through their skin colour. However, some of the players explicitly and/or implicitly conferred their heterosexuality. It is important to mention this fact, as their performances of heterosexuality are likely to affect their views about the predominant culture of the game.

In this chapter I will refer to the research participants as 'players' of the game as some of them wanted to be seen as 'footballers' and not just in terms of their 'race' and ethnicity (see Ratna, 2007). Whilst the use of pseudonyms may be useful, the complexities associated with naming British Asian people in light of their different religious and cultural practices may cause offence if inaccurately and/or randomly applied. Therefore I felt it was not suitable to name the research participants.

The intersections of 'race' and gender

In the spaces of sport, becoming 'one of the girls' requires individuals to construct and manage their identities appropriately in order to negotiate their inclusion, and tackle forms of exclusion. Some of the British Asian players have been able to make the break to the top levels of play by aligning their beliefs about the game to those of the dominant group. For example, like the views of many players, coaches and administrators of women's football, some British Asian players have argued that racism does not exist within the game (Ratna, 2007). These British Asian players support women's football as a meritocracy, arguing that 'race' does not matter as sexism − rather than racism − is more likely to hinder their freedom to play the sport. They perpetuate the belief that as women's football is essentially fair: anyone with the right talent and determination is able to play at the highest levels of the sport, regardless of their 'racial' or ethnic background (Ratna, 2007). For example, Player 4, a girl of Sikh-Indian heritage who has always played for mainly 'white' teams, explains:

> That's what I mean about 'race' not being a problem kind of thing, as we're still proving we're girls. I mean that there's a lot of stereotypes like female footballers have to be butch or a lesbian to play women's football (laughs) . . . So 'race' doesn't really come into it.

A common perception amongst the participants of this study is that as women *they know* what it feels like to be discriminated against, and therefore they would not discriminate against any other group of women. Without disregarding the impact of sexism, or any other form of discrimination operating in women's sport, of course 'race' matters and racism does exist in women's football. Indeed, research about British Asian female footballers and their experiences of racism highlights that racisms are evident in the women's game but they are often ignored, reduced to the ignorant acts of individual players or trivialised as team banter (Ratna, 2007). Hence, behind the centralisation of gender in the testimonies of the British Asian players, racial identities were nevertheless inter-connected and in the background. To further unravel the intersections of gender and race, as will became evident in the discussion below, many of the players − both established and relative newcomers − were able to negotiate barriers to their exclusion and foster a sense of inclusion, despite their racial and ethnic differences, precisely because they understood the *heterosexual* norms and values associated with the women's game. They had gained enough knowledge about gender and sexuality, through their early socialisation in sport, to use it as a form of cultural capital as their careers progressed.

The intersections of gender and sexuality

British Asian women, like their 'white' female counterparts, understand the pre-dominantly heterosexual construction of women's sporting spaces. Their early involvement in the sport illustrates these tensions. For example, whilst many of them claim to have been tomboys during their childhood, they begin to show an understanding that as a 'girl' this identity is not acceptable as they reach adolescence (Paechter and Clark, 2007). Player 3 acknowledges that as a young girl playing a 'male' sport, she was not like the other girls at primary school. She suggests that:

> I was always seen as a tomboy from the start [by other girls] . . . it didn't actually surprise them that I wanted to play football . . . I never did what they were sort of doing . . . I never used to join in . . . I kinda found it boring . . . I just wanted to run around and be a bit more active . . .

At this age, Player 3 parodies an identity style that is most commonly associated with being a 'boy': that is, using their bodies in physically active ways (Young, 1990). But, as the players included in this research claimed, as they grew older their tomboyism waned. Bourdieu and Passeron (1977) further ague that as young girls grow older, gender behaviours at school are reinforced through subjects like physical education (PE), teaching girls and boys what they are allowed to do and what they not allowed to do with their bodies (cited in Skeggs, 2004). So at this early age, a young child learns wider structural regimes of gender practice that informs their social habitus (Gorely et al, 2003).

Later in Player 3's interview, whilst justifying her tomboy identity she also declared that she 'wasn't a lesbian y'know?' Another one of the players in this study also seemed keen to remove the lesbian tag associated with the game, suggesting that 'butch' women who used to play the game are not there anymore. The following quotation illustrates her viewpoint:

> There are a lot of stereotypes like female footballers have to be butch or lesbian to play women's football . . . But, like the new generation are coming in and they are more feminine than the older generation of female football players. The shorthaired butch kind of girl is not there anymore.
>
> *(Player 4)*

The strategic performance of Player 4 is interesting as she specifically uses language about a 'new generation' of players to articulate her heterosexual (and not homosexual) identity. It is clear that through this story she is showing that she understands the value of being seen to be both feminine and straight. Similarly, Player 3 suggests that the 'butch' image of women's football has disappeared and that players who 'look like men' are out of place. Significantly, through her performance, Player 3 reproduces a stereotypical binary of butch/femme identities. In contrast, in other studies women who play football adopt identities that do not necessarily fit this binary (Caudwell, 2003; 2006). However, it becomes apparent that through the complex intersections of identities relating to gender and sexualities, for some British Asian football players, the performance of feminine identities is clearly more advantageous to their acceptance in women's football than lesbian/butch identities. It is also the case that whilst their 'racial' identities in other circumstances may mark them out as visible 'others', by using a performative technique that infers their heterosexuality, they can negotiate this sense of outsider-ness. Thus, the appropriate intersectional play of British Asian players' gender and sexual identities can facilitate their acceptance within the spaces of women's football.

The intersections of gender and ethnicity

Some feminist critics have suggested that fashion and western ideals of beauty are practised in order to perform a feminine self (Hollows, 2000: 139 and 152). It is not surprising that British Asian female footballers, as citizens of a western country, understand and use these cultural practices to re-produce their own feminine identities. To elucidate upon the performance of femininity, I refer to an incident when I went to squad training with a particular group of British Asian football players. One Friday night in November 2003, we were waiting for the team football coach to arrive. At this time, I realised that I had lost my hair band and asked some of the girls standing next to me if they had a spare one so that I could tie up my hair for training. One of them handed me a hair band and at the same time suggested that 'the lads', the name she used to address a few of the girls who were waiting to the side of us, were unlikely to carry such things. The following extract from my field notes details what happened:

> Player 12 ('lad') starts to mock Player 15 ('girlie-girl') for wearing a hooded top tightly fixed around her face. Player 15 said that she had to wear her hood to protect her washed and straightened hair from kinking in the rain. She shrieks loudly, 'I've just straightened my hair!' In contrast, Player 12 pulls a woolly hat over her head and white football socks over her tracksuit bottoms. She declares, 'I look like a lad and I don't care!' We all laugh at her outburst . . . The 'girlie-girls' go on to tell the coach that they are going to a fashion show that night, organized by one of the girls' elder brothers, and they ask if they can leave training early to finish getting ready. They are keen to look their best and not get their hair messed up at football training . . . One hour later, the 'girlie-girls' leave the training ground. The rest of the team play a five-a-side game and as they leave, Player 12 ('lad') says 'Yep, you best go home and get fixed'.

This example suggests that female football players who do not reflect and perform feminised gendered images are to a certain extent, through team jokes and banter, positioned as different and distinct to the 'girlie-girls'. Another interesting aspect of this interaction relates to the fashion show mentioned by some of the 'girlie-girls'. By wearing clothes and make-up at a fashion show, which had been inspired by Bollywood film actresses, their South Asian identities could be used as a cultural resource to help them mark out their 'girlie-girl' image. As noted by Puwar (2002), during the 'Indian Summer', consumption of the exotic/orient was a cultural taste that had been given distinction. Hence, aspects of the British Asian players' ethnic identities were played-up in order to emphasize their 'girlie-girl' femininity, revealing the intersections of ethnicity and gender.

Concluding thoughts

Using the work of Butler and Bourdieu, I have argued that intersections of identity are consciously or sub-consciously *performed* by individuals. In this way, identities can be played-up and played-down simultaneously and at once. By performing identities in combination, in particular ways and at particular times, some British Asian females have been able to foster their inclusion in, and prevent their exclusion from, the spaces of women's football. They have done so precisely because they understand the hegemonic culture of the space as being 'white' and heterosexual. Thus they are able to use knowledge about gender and sexuality, garnered from their socialisation in physical education and sport, as a form of cultural power to pass and progress through the elite spaces of women's football. Additionally, within the spaces of women's football at BAFC, South Asian cultural resources were utilised to help the 'girlie-girls' distinguish themselves from 'the lads'.

Arguably, this type of intersectional analysis is useful as it reveals the ways in which complex inequalities in sport operate together, simultaneously, and in nuanced ways, subsequently revealing why they become so difficult to see, challenge and transform. In this chapter, this can be noted in two ways: firstly, by focusing on sexism, racism in the game is ignored. Secondly, by emphasising femininity, and rendering invisible lesbian players, homophobia is left unchallenged. Sadly, it becomes apparent that for British Asian players of women's football, dominant ideas about gender and sexuality are so deeply entrenched in the sport, that any transgressions from acceptable codes of femininity are limited. Indeed, many British Asian players are complicit in the normalisation of heterosexuality in the spaces of women's football. Many of the girls and women unwittingly perpetuate the mutual operation of racism, heteronormativity and homophobia. The consequences of their performances, (wrongly) support notions of sport being increasingly fair and socially inclusive.

It is hoped that the use of intersectional research discussed in this chapter has resulted in a better understanding of the manifestation and character of discriminatory practices in women's football, and in sport and society more generally.

Acknowledgements

I would like to thank Professor Jennifer Hargreaves, Professor Eric Andersen and Dr. Philippa Velija for providing feedback on earlier drafts of this chapter. I would especially like to thank Dr. Beccy Watson for her invaluable insights and support, which have been crucial to the development of this work.

Note

1   The term South Asian is used to describe people whose heritage and culture stem from the Indian subcontinent. However, the term British Asian is also used by many second and third generation South Asians, by fact of their citizenship, as a marker of their British identity.

References

Alexander, C. (2000) *The Asian Gang: Ethnicity, Identity and Masculinity*, Oxford: Berg.
Algeo, K. (2007) 'Teaching Cultural Geography with Bend it Like Beckham', *Journal of Geography*, 106(3): 133–143.
Anderson, E. and McCormack, M. (2010a) 'Intersectionality, Critical Race Theory, and American Sporting Oppression: Examining Black and Gay Male Athletes', *Journal of Homosexuality*, 57(8): 949–967.
Anderson, E. and McCormack, M. (2010b) 'Comparing the Black and Gay Male Athlete: Pattern in American Oppression', *The Journal of Men's Studies*, 18(2): 145–158.
Brah, A. and Phoenix, A. (2004) 'Ain't I a Woman? Revisiting Intersectionality', *Journal of International Women's Studies*, 5(3): 75–86.
Bourdieu, P. (1990a) *The Logic of Practise*, Cambridge: Polity Press.
Bourdieu, P. (1990b) 'La domination masculine', *Actes de la researche en sciences sociales*, 84(Sept.): 2–31.
Bourdieu, P. and Passeron, C. (1977) *Reproduction in Education, Society and Culture*, translated by R. Nice, London and Beverley Hills, CA: Sage.
Butler, J. (1990) *Gender Trouble: Feminism and the Subversion of Identity*. New York and London: Routledge.
Caudwell, J. (2009) '*Girlfight* and *Bend it Like Beckham*: Screening Women, Sport and Sexuality', *Journal of Lesbian Studies*, 13(3): 255–271.

Caudwell, J. (2006) 'Femme-fatale: Re-thinking the Femme-inine' in Caudwell, J. (ed.) *Sport, Sexualities and Queer/Theory*, Abingdon and New York: Routledge: 145–158.

Caudwell, J. (2003) 'Sporting Gender: Women's Footballing Bodies as Sites/Sights for the [Re]Articulation of Sex, Gender and Desire', *Sociology of Sport Journal* 20: 371–386.

Crenshaw, K. (1991) 'Mapping the Margins: Intersectionality, Identity Politics, and Violence Against Women of Color', *Stanford Law Review*, 43(6): 1241–1299.

Davis, K. (2008) 'Intersectionality as Buzzword: A Sociology of Science Perspective on What Make a Feminist Theory Successful', *Feminist Theory*, 9(1): 67–85.

Fraser, M. (1999) 'Classing Queer', *Theory, Culture and Society*, 16(2): 107–131.

Gopinath, R. (2005) *Impossible Desires: Queer Diasporas and South Asian Public Cultures*, Durham and London: Duke University Press.

Gorely, T., Holroyd, R. and Kirk, D. (2003) 'Mascularity, Habitus and the Social Construction of Gender: Towards a Gender-Relevant Physical Education', *British Journal of Sociology of Education*, 24(4): 429–448.

Grenfell, M. and James, D. with Hodkinson, P., Reay, D. and Robbins, D. (1998) *Bourdieu and Education: Acts of Practical Theory*, London: Falmer Press.

Hollows, J. (2000) *Feminism, Femininity and Popular Culture*, Manchester and New York: Manchester University Press.

McDonald, M. (2006) 'Beyond the Pale: The Whiteness of Sport Studies and Queer Scholarship' in Caudwell, J. (ed.) *Sport, Sexualities and Queer/Theory*, London and New York: Routledge: 33–46.

McDonald, M. (2002) 'Queering Whiteness: The Peculiar Case of the Women's National Basketball Association', *Sociological Perspectives*, 45: 379–396.

McLeod, J. (2005) 'Feminists Re-reading Bourdieu: Old Debates and New Questions About Gender Habitus and Gender Change', *Theory and Research in Education*, 3(1): 11–30.

McNay, L. (1999) 'Gender, Habitus and the Field: Pierre Bourdieu and the Limits of Reflexivity', *Theory, Culture and Society*, 16(1): 95–117.

Paechter, C. and Clark, S. (2007) 'Who are tomboys and how do we recognise them?' *Women's Studies International Forum* 30: 342–354.

Puwar, N. (2004) *Space Invaders: Race, Gender and Bodies Out of Place*, Oxford and New York: Berg.

Puwar, N. (2002) 'Multicultural Fashion . . . Stirrings of Another Sense of Aesthetics and Memory', *Feminist Review*, 71: 63–87.

Ratna, A. (2011) '"Who wants to make Aloo Gobi when you can Bend it Like Beckham?" British Asian Females and their Racialised Experiences of Gender and Identity in Women's Football', *Soccer and Society*, 12(3): 381–400.

Ratna, A. (2007) 'A "Fair Game?": British Asian Females' Experiences of Racism in Women's Football' in Magee, J., Caudwell, J., Liston, K. and Scraton, S. (eds.) *Women, Football and Europe: Histories, Equity and Experiences*, Oxford: Meyer and Meyer Sport: 69–88.

Rottenberg, C. (2003) 'Passing: Race, Identification and Desire', *Criticism* 45(4): 435–452.

Scraton, S., Caudwell, J. and Holland, S. (2005) '"Bend it Like Patel": Centring "Race", Ethnicity and Gender in Feminist Analysis of Women's Football in England', *International Review for the Sociology of Sport*, 40(1): 71–88.

Scraton, S. (2001) 'Reconceptualising Race, Gender and Sport: The Contribution of Black Feminism' in Carrington, B. and McDonald, I. (eds.) *'Race', Sport and British Society*, London and New York: Routledge: 170–187.

Skeggs, B. (2004) 'Context and Background: Pierre Bourdieu's Analysis of Class, Gender and Sexuality', *The Sociological Review*, 53(2): 19–34.

Spelman, E. (1982) 'Theories of Race and Gender: The Erasure of Black Women', *Quest*, 5(4), 36–62.

Valentine, G. (2007) 'Theorizing and Researching Intersectionality: A challenge for Feminist Geography', *The Sociological Review*, 59(1): 10–21.

Watson, B. and Ratna, A. (2011) 'Bollywood in the Park: Thinking Intersectionally about Public Leisure Space' *Leisure/Loisir* 35(1): 71–86.

Young, I.M. (1990) *Throwing Like a Girl and Other Essays in Feminist Philosophy and Social Theory*, Bloomington: Indiana University Press.

18

BLACK FEMALE ATHLETES AS SPACE INVADERS

L. Anima Adjepong and Ben Carrington

Introduction

Despite recent advances in women's sport participation, extensive coverage of women's sports at the Olympics, and the continuing popularity of women's football (soccer) especially in the United States of America, sport remains a terrain for the reproduction of dominant forms of white masculinity (Ferber, 2007; Long and Hylton, 2002; Walton and Butryn, 2006). In many cases, sportswomen are only noticed insofar as they are portrayed as sexually attractive to an assumed heterosexual and male audience (Bernstein, 2002; Lafferty and McKay, 2004; Mennesson, 2000). The sexualization of women athletes illustrates the anxieties many men have regarding the idea that the gender order (Connell, 2001) is in a state of flux. Within this context the very presence of female athletes challenges the idea of sport as a male preserve.

One key criticism of previous feminist scholarship is that white women have historically been seen as the quintessence of femininity,[1] the 'second sex' understood as a de-racialized category that in fact privileged the interests and concerns of white women (Maynard, 2002). As Shelia Scraton and Anne Flintoff (2013: 101) put it, within the feminist movement white women 'have not only failed to address the marginalization of black women but have failed to seriously interrogate their own whiteness'. Early figures from the black women's movement, such as Sojourner Truth, argued that black and white women experienced the world in very different ways, for example, slavery disrupted traditional gender roles within black family structures with black men often engaged in domestic labour and black women forced to work outside the home (Davis, 1981). This meant that until the women's movement addressed forms of anti-black racism within its own structures it would fail as a truly transformative project. In a speech delivered in 1851 in Ohio, entitled 'Ain't I a Woman?', Truth contrasts the image of white women who are 'helped into carriages and lifted over ditches' with herself, a black woman who has 'ploughed and planted and gathered into barns' in order to question the dominant definition of woman. As Angela Davis noted, Truth's speech highlighted the class-bias and racism of the emerging women's movement and the fact that not all women enjoyed 'the material comfort of the middle classes' (Davis, 1981, p. 63). For Truth, as for many working-class black women, her blackness was a sign of strength rather than a mark of her degeneracy.

During the early- to mid-twentieth century blackness came to be seen as a signifier of natural sporting ability (Hoberman, 1997). The invention of the idea of the natural black athlete (Carrington, 2010) means that when black women participate in sport, they often face a different set of assumptions than white women about their femininity (or lack thereof) and their sporting ability. Because black sportswomen exist at the intersections of racial, gendered, sexual, and classed oppression, they encounter a unique set of circumstances about how their bodies are sexualized on the sports field. Representations of black women within the white sports/media complex (Carrington, 2011) are mediated by stereotypes but in ways that are often multifaceted, highlighting how contemporary 'colour-blind' racisms are increasingly able to produce racist effects whilst simultaneously denying that racism exists as a meaningful aspect of contemporary 'post-racial' societies.

This chapter maps how the varying meanings of black identity and femininity come together in the body of the black female athlete, accentuating the sexualization of the black female form while at the same time black sportswomen attempt to resist those same images. We consider the notion of black women athletes as 'invading' the masculine-coded white sports field. We examine how they are 'overdetermined' as fulfilling certain myths concerning black femininity and the ways in which black women contest stereotypes surrounding their blackness and their femaleness on the sporting field. We also consider how black women in sport are 'disciplined' to remain within predetermined social roles and the moments in which they resist these roles. Using Patricia Hill Collins' (2008 [2000]) concept of 'controlling images' we explore the inscription of an asexual 'mammy' and hyper-sexual 'jezebel' stereotypes. We suggest that these controlling images serve to discipline black women, who are perceived to transgress on the sporting field. Finally we look at the ways in which black female athletes come to represent the nation; we examine the discourse around black women athletes as national representatives and the cultural politics (and possibilities for change) this generates for reclaiming the space of sports.

Black women as space invaders

Patricia Vertinsky and Gwendolyn Captain (1998) provide an overview of the 'persistent historical myths' (p. 541) that construct black female athletes as masculine, hypersexual, or sexually undesirable. In this section, we highlight specific episodes that show how black sportswomen continue to be disciplined by these myths and the complexities of anti-black forms of racism that are often expressed in subtle and nuanced ways.

After winning her third gold Olympic medal at the London 2012 summer Olympic Games, Serena Williams danced across the famous Wimbledon Centre Court. She had just defeated Maria Sharapova in a 6-0, 6-1 victory that lasted just over an hour, becoming only the second woman to complete a Career Golden Slam (Clarey, 2012).[2] After the glorious ace that won her gold medal, Williams danced with joy. The dance Williams did originates from Compton in Los Angeles, a city known for producing symbols of popular gang culture, and was first associated with the predominantly black Crip gang. Williams' 'gangster dance' on the hallowed Centre Court was interpreted by some commentators as lacking in class and somehow disrespectful. For example, political commentator Debbie Schlussel called Williams' dance 'unclassy' and glorifying of 'hardened criminals who murder each other – and innocent Americans – for sport'. Schlussel added that 'nobody likes a low-class winner who does a dance glorifying mass murderers and drug dealers, after she wins the Olympic Gold Medal for women's tennis' (Schlussel, 2012). Similarly, sports commentator Bill Plaschke tweeted, 'Serena C-walking at Wimbledon only shows how long she's been away from home, separated from violence and death associated with that dance' (Yates, 2012). Serena Williams was seen to be breaching the decorum of the All England Lawn Tennis and Croquet Club with such a 'straight outta Compton' ghetto performance. The above reactions to Williams' emotive celebration provide illuminating examples of how blackness is prefigured as associated with the ghetto, 'violence and death'. This construction of blackness stands in stark contradiction to normative white middle-class values associated with sports like tennis and is employed in the Williams' case to show her seeming unwillingness to adopt white middle-class standards of femininity (Cooky et al., 2010; Douglas, 2005; Schultz, 2005).

Williams' dance was interpreted as a 'flub', and debates erupted about how inappropriate her performance was in 'the city of kings and queens' (Forgrave, 2012). As Reid Forgrave (2012) described it, 'the woman who grew up in Compton did the crip dance . . . you couldn't help but shake your head. It was as if Serena just couldn't seem to avoid dipping into waters of controversy even as she'd ascended to the top of her sport.' Forgrave's description of Williams' dance – 'Crip-Walking all over the most lily-white place in the world' (Forgrave, 2012) – can be understood as an example of a color-blind rhetoric (Bonilla-Silva, 2010)[3] that accepts blackness only insofar as that blackness does not present itself as such, a rhetoric that has attempted to frame both Serena and her sister Venus throughout their careers (Douglas, 2011; Ifekwunigwe, 2009; Schultz, 2005; Spencer, 2004).

It is through this lens of colour-blind rhetoric that we turn to Taylor Townsend.[4] During the 2012 US Open Junior's Tournament, the *Wall Street Journal* reported that the US Tennis Association (USTA) had declined to provide funding for Townsend's trip to the tournament. When questioned about their refusal, tennis officials reported that they did not think she was in good enough shape to play; according to the organization, she needed to lose weight (Perrotta, 2012). Despite the USTA's refusal to pay for her participation in the tournament, Townsend advanced to the quarterfinals. The suggestion was that the world number one ranked player, who at the time had just won the junior girls' Australian Open, the Wimbledon Doubles, and advanced to the finals of the French Open, was in worse shape than her peers. The USTA maintained that Townsend was simply not in adequate shape to compete.

The Williams and Townsend examples might, at first glance, appear to be both idiosyncratic and unrelated to race. Athletes' bodies in general, and especially those of elite athletes, are often subject to forms of surveillance that athletes come to accept. Our argument is not that intentional and overt anti-black racism can explain the reactions to the examples given here (that would be to unduly privilege one aspect above all others) but a more complex one that suggests that racial discourses help to make sense of the particularities of the reactions and the meanings given to these events. Or more positively, that failing to understand the complexity of modern-day racism gives us an incomplete account of why these examples matter and why they often attract the attention that they do.

Townsend's case raises questions about the USTA's criteria for funding players and developing talent. The USTA had a difficult case to make since Townsend was, after all, ranked number one in the world. The debate around this young woman's supposed lack of fitness and need to lose weight is illustrative of the ways in which sporting institutions police women's bodies (Cahn, 2011; Cooky et al., 2010; Krane et al., 2004). David Leonard (2012) asks the pointed question, 'Is it just a coincidence that the two girls/women who have been chastised, ridiculed and demonized for their weight, for their body, for their appearance, are both African-American?' That the Williams sisters are the only other notable black women in US tennis, and that Serena Williams' body has often been parodied and ridiculed highlights the anxieties that black women on the tennis court provoke due to their difference from the normative whiteness of women's tennis.

The ubiquitous images of fat unfit black women makes it easy for the USTA to reasonably believe that they could refuse to support the number-one ranked junior player with no real consequence, after all, historically speaking such a body is rare on any sporting field (Brooks and Althouse, 2000; Bruening, 2012). As Jennifer Bruening (2012) shows, black women are overrepresented in sports such as basketball and track, but only appear as 'tokens' in other sports (p. 331), leading to diminishing self-esteem for these women (p. 337). When examined from the context of the controlling mammy image (Collins 2008 [2000]), it makes sense that the tennis association could so easily dismiss Townsend. Girls and women are often pressured to 'display appropriate physically-active, fit, and "thin" subjectivities in contemporary societies where consumption practices, body ideals, and obesity discourses converge on and through their bodies' (Rich and Evans, 2013, p. 192). Within western societies such 'body ideals' are implicitly framed and constructed in relation to whiteness – thus we can see how assumptions about the acceptability of female bodies (sporting or otherwise) that appear to be race-neutral may in fact draw upon and help to reinforce notions of black bodies as somehow deviant and in need of change in order to conform to white body-type ideals.

Nirmal Puwar's (2004) notion of space invaders is useful in helping to make sense of the position of black female athletes. Puwar theorizes the ways in which bodies are perceived as belonging and not belonging within certain spaces. We come to understand the 'somatic norm' as those bodies that can occupy spaces without question. If we consider that, as black women, Williams and Townsend are 'space invaders' we can begin to see why they would receive such criticism. Whereas black men have come to be accepted as athletes and sporting icons, black women must contest *both* the perceived inherent masculinity of the sporting field and the stereotypes around black femininity (Cooky et al., 2010; Withycombe, 2011). At the same time, they navigate a politics of respectability wherein they are prefigured as 'unclassy' and 'deviant' for any transgressions, however minor, and bodies that are somehow out of place, even when they win.

Sexualizing black women athletes: good woman/bad woman

Studies show that media coverage in sports continues to be extremely gendered and racialized. Despite some limited progress on how much media coverage women athletes receive, commentary on women's sports still tends to disproportionately focus on female athletes' physical attractiveness and their 'natural' beauty and grace (Cooky, Messner and Hextrum, 2013; Dworkin and Messner, 1999; Vincent, 2004). Such a framing of female athletes is not innocent or insignificant, but rather a 'discursive strategy that trivializes a sportswoman's accomplishments because her appearance has nothing to do with her athletic performance' (Duncan, 2006, p. 242). For example, although the 2012 Olympics were heralded as the end of the Anna Kournikova era,[5] this declaration must be received critically. In fact various events during the games counter this assertion and highlight the ways that media coverage of female athletes continues to sexualize them often in specifically racialized ways.

In an August 2012 *New York Times* article, 'For Lolo Jones, everything is image', sportswriter Jeré Longman comments on how black US female athlete, Jones, 'failed' to achieve a gold medal in the Beijing Olympics because she was more interested in selling her heterosexy image than in training for her Olympic events.[6] Specifically, Jones was accused of being too busy posing nude for *ESPN* Magazine and sharing with the world her decision to remain a virgin at 30 years old in order to be a successful athlete. Longman chastises Jones for failing to take advantage of her position to 'undress her opponents, not herself', characterizes Jones as a failure, and as regressing the advances of women in sport. Longman quotes Janice Forsyth, director for the International Centre for Olympic Studies at the University of Western Ontario, who compares Jones to Anna Kournikova. Forsyth suggests that the era in which women are sexualized as athletes is over and Jones' publicity attempts may undo all the work that women have done to be taken seriously as athletes.

In Longman's analysis of Jones' performance he reproduces the very sexualization he claims to be frustrated by. He describes Jones' 'exotic beauty' and her acquiescence to being 'whatever anyone wants her to be—vixen, virgin, victim'. In his characterization of her, Jones cannot simply be a savvy athlete hoping to get sponsorship in order to compete. Instead, she is supposedly intent on using her sex appeal to establish herself as an athlete. We might better understand Longman's descriptions of Jones as drawing upon the controlling image of the jezebel (Collins, 2008 [2000]). Collins describes the jezebel as representative of deviant black female sexuality and whose 'function was to relegate all Black women to the category of sexually-aggressive women' (2008 [2000]: 89). The jezebel is constructed in sharp contrast to the mammy who is 'most familiar with the skills needed for Black accommodation' (p. 80) and often depicted as asexual.

Longman unfavorably compares Jones to a fellow African-American female hurdler, Harper. Longman shows how Harper had a similar impoverished childhood to Jones. However, unlike Jones, Harper does not appear 'on the cover of *Outside* magazine seeming to wear a bathing suit made of nothing but strategically-placed ribbon' in her quest for sponsorship. Instead, Harper competed wearing borrowed spikes during the 2008 Beijing Olympics. The difference that Longman paints between the two women serves to mark one, Jones, as an 'exotic' and sexually-deviant woman, a jezebel, and the other, Harper, as mammy, an acceptable black woman who does things right.

As noted earlier, the strategies used to diminish Harper's and Jones' athletic prowess, focusing instead on their sexuality, are not specific to black women. However, particular discursive tools used to undermine their athleticism are mired in racialized tropes that draw upon the controlling images of black women. Sexualizing black female athletes is not limited to a focus on their sexual availability. This sexualization is undergirded by the possibility that should these women resist, their very femininity will be called into question.

Policing African femininity: the curious case of Caster Semenya

In 2009, after completing an 800-metre race in 1 minute 55.45 seconds, Caster Semenya was subjected to gender testing by the International Association of Athletics Federation (IAAF; www.iaaf.org/athletes). The South African born 18 year old had just improved her personal best time by eight seconds. Concerned about the increase in her performance, officials tested Semenya for performance-enhancement drugs and to determine whether or not she was a man. While 'gender verification testing' is not exclusive to black women (Cooky and Dworkin, 2012), because black women have historically been categorized as somehow closer to masculinity than white women (Cahn 1993), it is important to situate such tests, and the nature of the reaction they produce within the mass media, in the context of the history of masculinizing black women. For example, Delia Douglas recalls the 'longstanding White supremacist beliefs about the unwomanly nature of Black females' (2011: 3) that resulted in tennis player Althea Gibson being subjected to chromosome tests in the 1950s.

Semenya's case is a reminder of the racialized ways that gender is policed on the sporting field, and recalls Gargi Bhattacharyya's (1998, p. 139) words in 'The model's tale', 'whatever I wear people imagine they can see my sexual organs'. The very public way that Semenya's gender was questioned invoked for many the case of Saartjie Baartman.[7] Semenya thus illustrates how colonial myths around black women's bodies are reproduced even after the formal dismantling of western colonial regimes. These myths emphasize the ways that black women's bodies are differently sexualized in comparison to other women (Cahn, 2011; Douglas, 2011; Withycombe, 2011). As CL Cole and Michael Giardina have noted, imbedded within the discourse of suspicion that surrounded Semenya, 'was her alleged (visual) unreadability as feminine' (2013, p. 543).

On the London 2012 800-metre medal stand, Semenya proudly flexed her biceps. In some ways Semenya's flexing can be compared to Serena's crip-walking. These are open acts of defiance that, even if only for a moment, reclaim the athlete's right to take up those spaces in which they find themselves. Because black women perform these acts, the specificity of their racial location cannot be excluded from how they resist. Although black women's participation in sport is often challenged, these sportswomen confront these challenges in ways that destabilize their unquestioned exclusion from sporting space.

Representing the spirit of the nation

Despite the Olympic charter's claim that contests are between individuals or teams and not nations, national interests characterize such competitions and athletes are seen to represent their nation. Thus it is often the case that medal-counts are viewed as indicative of a country's superiority (Allison and Monnington, 2002). Recognizing the historical legacy with which these bodies navigate the world, the performances of female athletes of color are often read not just in terms of gender politics but in relation to racial progress as well.

When Cathy Freeman finished first in the 400-metre race at the 2000 Sydney Olympics, she ran her victory lap waving both the Australian *and* Aboriginal flags. For some, Freeman's success in the Olympics was an important marker of national reconciliation (Gardiner, 2003). However, there is an apparent tension in this act. As the 'Spirit of Australia', Freeman came to symbolize 'multicultural Australia and reconciliation . . . between Black and White' (Hargreaves, 2000, p. 125). At the same time her embodiment was used to deny the ongoing tensions between the Aboriginal peoples and the Australian government.

In many ways similar to Cathy Freeman, Gabby Douglas the sixteen-year-old Team USA gymnast was also thought to represent a post-racial America (Hunter, 2012; Shaw, 2012). After Douglas won her all-round gymnastics gold medal in the 2012 London Olympics, Bob Costas, host of the NBC Olympics said on TV:

> You know, it's a happy measure of how far we've come that it doesn't seem all that remarkable, but still it's noteworthy, Gabby Douglas is, as it happens, the first African-American to win the women's all-round in gymnastics. The barriers have long since been down, but sometimes there can be an imaginary barrier, based on how one might see oneself.

Here Costas' words attempted to undermine the structural barriers that black female athletes face, and instead erects self-generated 'imaginary barriers' for the (black) individual to overcome. This comment can be understood as exemplary of the sincere fictions (Feagin et al., 2001) color-blind societies tell themselves. By celebrating Douglas' success as evidence of demolished racial barriers, she becomes a symbol of progress in much the same way that Cathy Freeman was seen to represent reconciliation between Aboriginals and the Australian government (despite atrocities still directed at them). As Jennifer Hargreaves has noted, Freeman's victory 'consolidated the key themes of multiculturalism, reconciliation and unity which had saturated the ceremonies preceding the Games' (2000, p. 126).

It is important to remember that sports are contested ideological terrains. The meanings and identifications produced by sport are not static. Part of the reason why men have traditionally defended the boundaries of sport so vehemently in order to keep women from entering the playing field is the fear that gender roles are not fixed but malleable. Similarly, given the historical role in which women, at certain moments, are seen to embody (and reproduce) the nation biologically, culturally and symbolically (Yuval-Davis, 1997), sportswomen of colour like Freeman can produce powerful counter-narratives to mono-culturalist political movements. During the 2012 London Olympics, for example, and notwithstanding cyclists Bradley Wiggins, Chris Hoy and Victoria Pendleton and the athlete Mo Farah, Jessica Ennis became Britain's most celebrated Olympian. Reflecting on the 2012 sporting year, the journalist Richard Williams (2012) noted that the summer's sporting action,

> told us [Britain] a great deal about who we are and what, as a society, we have become, although there are no guarantees that the new understanding will be taken to heart . . . Ennis, the daughter of a black father and a white mother [added] a new layer of meaning to the combination of flags making up the union flag draped around her shoulders.

Williams' words highlight the ways in which sport can and is often used to produce popular anti-racist discourses even as it sometimes reifies ideas about 'race' and how black female (and not just male) athletes are increasingly at the forefront of these debates.

Conclusion: ain't I a sportswoman?

In *Tales of dark-skinned women* Gargi Bhattacharyya (1998) shares the sportswoman's tale. The sportswoman tells the story of how her physical prowess, although it brought pride to the nation, never resulted in her actually belonging. Regardless of her achievements she remained outside of the boundaries of belonging. In this tale Bhattacharyya highlights the exclusion of black people from the narrative of the imagined community. In this chapter, we explored how black female athletes continue to be framed and represented in problematic ways that reinforce sexist and racist ideas about black femininity as well as their symbolic role in helping to consolidate popular beliefs concerning the end of racism and the arrival of a post-racial, colour-blind society.

We have shown how despite the achievements of black sportswomen, they are still often framed as 'space invaders'. These women experience resistance to their right to be on the sports field, to their right to control their sexuality, and to their right to represent their nation. Black sportswomen are conditionally accepted and celebrated as long as they act, look and talk in ways deemed acceptable, codes of behavior that are implicitly modeled on notions of appropriate white middle-class femininity. At the same time, black sportswomen challenge the boundaries that exclude them and offer possibilities for different ways to understand black women as athletes and black subjectivity more generally. The entry of black sportswomen into field of sports suggests that we might actually begin to think of them as not simply 'invading' that space but increasingly creating claims of ownership and rightful belonging, a political gesture that is reconfiguring the space sports. In other words, tracing the new and varied layers of meaning produced by the very presence and success of black female athletes will help us to better understand the changing dynamics of gender and sexuality both in sport and wider society.

Notes

1   We use the terms 'femininity' and 'masculinity' throughout this chapter to describe the equation between 'men' and 'masculinities' and 'women' and 'femininities'. However, we also want to call attention to the idea that these terms are not stable; men do not inherently 'possess' what is generally understood to be masculinity, nor are women always feminine. Instead, hegemonic ideas about

masculinity and femininity serve to discipline men and women and limit the ways in which they can engage with the world.

2   This means that she had won all the Grand Slam tennis tournaments as well as a gold medal. The first woman to do this was Steffi Graf in 1988.

3   Bonilla-Silva argues that whereas Jim Crow racism explained away blacks' social position using biological arguments concerning blacks' moral and physical degeneracy, 'color-blind racism avoids such facile arguments. Instead, whites rationalize minorities' contemporary status as the product of market dynamics, naturally occurring phenomena, and blacks' imputed cultural limitations' (2010: 2).

4   At sixteen years old, Taylor Townsend was the first African-American to win the Australian Open Girls' Junior tennis championship.

5   Jay Caspian King (2012) remarks on the Anna Kournikova era as a time when everything about women's sports was also about the tennis player Anna Kournikova. Emphasis on Kournikova's sex appeal 'was held up as proof that men could take a completely unremarkable yet thoroughly hot tennis player and use her as an excuse to never say one serious word about women's sports'. However, King argues that women's success during the 2012 Olympic Games brought an end to the lack of seriousness given to women's sport.

6   It is important to recall that Jones had only recently recovered from spinal surgery.

7   Saatjie Baartman was a Southern African woman who was put on exhibition in Europe as an icon of black female sexuality. Baartman is often cited as the quintessence of how black bodies are displayed and ascribed with deviant sexualities.

References

Allison L and Monnington T (2002) Sport, prestige and international relations. *Government and Opposition* 37(1): 106–134.

Bernstein A (2002) Is it time for a victory lap? Changes in the media coverage of women in sport. *International Review for the Sociology of Sport* 37(3–4): 415–428. Retrieved July 16, 2012 from http://irs.sagepub.com/cgi/doi/10.1177/101269020203700301

Bhattacharyya G (1998) *Tales of dark-skinned women: Race, gender and global culture.* London: Routledge.

Bonilla-Silva E (2010) *Racism without racists: Color-blind racism and the persistence of racial inequality in the United States.* 3rd ed. New York, NY: Rowman and Littlefield Publishers, Inc.

Brooks DD and Althouse RC (2000). *Racism in college athletics: The African American athlete's experience.* Morgantown, WV: Fitness Information Technology.

Bruening JE (2012) Gender and racial analysis in sport: Are all the women White and all the Blacks men? *Quest* 57(3): 330–349.

Cahn SK (2011) Testing sex, attributing gender: What Caster Semenya means to women's sports. *Journal of Intercollegiate Sport* 4: 38–48.

Cahn SK (1993) From the 'Muscle Moll' to the 'Butch' ballplayer: Mannishness, lesbianism, and homophobia in U.S. women's sport. *Feminist Studies, Inc.* 19(2): 343–368.

Carrington, B. (2011) '"What I said was racist – but I'm not a racist": Anti-racism and the white sports/media complex'. In Long J and Spracklen K (eds.) *Sport and Challenges to Racism,* Basingstoke and New York, NY: Palgrave Macmillan, pp. 83–99.

Carrington B (2010) *Race, sports and politics: The sporting Black diaspora.* London, UK: Sage.

Clarey C (2012) Williams coasts to gold, and a career golden slam. *New York Times,* August 4. Retrieved August 4, 2012 from http://www.nytimes.com/2012/08/05/sports/olympics/serena-williams-beats-sharapova-for-olympic-gold-in-tennis.html

Cole CL and Giardina MD (2013). Embodying American democracy: Performing the female sporting icon. In Andrews DL and Carrington B (eds.) *A Companion to Sport,* West Sussex, UK: Wiley Blackwell.

Collins PH (2008 [2000]) *Black feminist thought.* New York, NY: Routledge

Connell RW (2001) *The men and the boys.* Berkeley, CA: University of California Press.

Cooky C and Dworkin SL (2012) Woman enough to win? *The Society Pages.* Retrieved August 10, 2012 from http://thesocietypages.org/specials/sex-testing/

Cooky C, Wachs FL, Messner M, and Dworkin SL (2010) It's not about the game: Don Imus, race, class, gender. *Sociology of Sport Journal* 27(2): 139–159.

Cooky CM, Messner MA, and Hextrum RH (2013) Women play sport, but not on TV: A longitudinal study of televised news media. *Communication and Sport*. Retrieved April 12, 2013 from http://com. sagepub.com/lookup/doi/10.1177/2167479513476947

Davis A (1981). *Women, race and class*. London: The Women's Press.

Douglas DD (2011). Venus, Serena, and the inconspicuous consumption of Blackness: A commentary on surveillance, race talk, and new racism(s). *Journal of Black Studies* XX(X): 1–19.

Douglas DD (2005) Venus, Serena, and the Women's Tennis Association: When and where 'race' enters. *Sociology of Sport Journal* 22: 256–282.

Duncan MC (2006). Gender warriors in sport: Women and the media. In Raney A and Bryant J (eds.), *Handbook of Sports and Media*, London: Routledge, pp. 231–252.

Dworkin SL and Messner MA (1999) Just do . . . what? In Ferree MM, Lorber J, and Hess BB (eds.) *Revisioning Gender*, Thousand Oaks, CA: Sage Publications

Feagin JR, Hernan V, and Pinar B (2001). *White racism: The basics*. New York, NY: Routledge.

Ferber AL (2007) The construction of Black masculinity: White supremacy now and then. *Journal of Sport & Social Issues* 31(1): 11–24. (http://jss.sagepub.com/cgi/doi/10.1177/0193723506296829).

Forgrave R (2012) Serena flubs crowning moment. *FoxSports*, August 5. Retrieved September 20, 2012 from http://msn.foxsports.com/olympics/tennis/story/serena-williams-taints-golden-slam-with-crip-walk-dance-080412

Gardiner G (2003) Running for country: Australian print media representation of Indigenous athletes in the 27th Olympiad. *Journal of Sports and Social Issues* 27(3): 233–260.

Hargreaves J (2000) *Heroines of sport: The politics of difference and identity*. London: Routledge.

Hoberman J (1997) *Darwin's athletes: How sport has damaged Black America and preserved the myth of race*. New York, NY: Houghton Mifflin

Hunter TW (2012) Olympian Gabby Douglas – the gymnast is golden but her family is obscured. *The Christian Science Monitor*. August 9, 2012.

Ifekwunigwe J (2009) Venus and Serena are 'doing it' for themselves: Theorizing sporting celebrity, class, and Black feminism for the Hip-Hop generation. In Carrington B and McDonald I (eds.) *Marxism, cultural studies and sport*. London: Routledge.

King JC (2012) The death of the Anna Kournikova era: The state of women's sports after the summer of Serena. *Grantland.com*, September 13. Retrieved November 1, 2012 from http://www.grantland.com/story/_/id/8372737/from-serena-williams-missy-franklin-gabby-douglas-summer-2012-defined-female-athletes

Krane V, Choi PYL, Baird SM, Aimar CM and Kauer KJ. (2004). Living the paradox: Female athletes negotiate femininity and muscularity. *Sex Roles* 50(5/6).

Lafferty Y and McKay J (2004). 'Suffragettes in satin shorts?' Gender and competitive boxing. *Qualitative Sociology* 27(3): 249–276. Retrieved September 25, 2013 from http://www.springerlink.com/openurl.asp?id=doi:10.1023/B:QUAS.0000037618.57141.53

Leonard D (2012). Just win? The USTA and its epic failure. *Huffington Post*, September 28. Retrieved November 1, 2012 from http://www.huffingtonpost.com/dr-david-j-leonard/utsa-taylor-townsend_b_1916047.html

Long J and Hylton K (2002). Shades of white: An examination of whiteness in sport. *Leisure Studies* 21: 87–103.

Longman J (2012) For Lolo Jones, everything is image. *New York Times*, August 4. Retrieved August 4, 2012 from http://www.nytimes.com/2012/08/05/sports/olympian-lolo-jones-draws-attention-to-beauty-not-achievement.html?_r=0)

Maynard M (2002). 'Race', gender and the concept of 'difference' in feminist thought. In Scraton S and Flintoff A (eds.) *Gender and sport: A reader*. London: Routledge.

Mennesson C (2000) 'Hard' women and 'soft' women: The social construction of identities among female boxers. *International Review for the Sociology of Sport* 35(21): 21–33. (http://irs.sagepub.com/cgi/doi/10.1177/101269000035001002).

Perrotta T (2012) Why the USTA benched America's best junior. *Wall Street Journal*, September 8. Retrieved September 20, 2012 from http://online.wsj.com/article/SB10000872396390444273704577635530959121916.html

Puwar N (2004) *Space invaders: Race, gender and bodies out of place*. Oxford: Berg.

Rich E and Evans J (2013). Physical culture, pedagogies of health, and the gendered body. In Andrews DL and Carrington B (eds.) *A companion to sport*, West Sussex, UK: Wiley Blackwell.

Schlussel D (2012) Serena Williams does crip walk after winning Olympic gold medal – classy chick! *debbieschlussel.com* August 5, 2012.

Schultz J (2005). Reading the catsuit. *Journal of Sport & Social Issues* 29: 338–357. Retrieved September 5, 2012 from http://jss.sagepub.com/cgi/content/abstract/29/3/338

Scraton S and Flintoff A (2013) Gender, feminist theory, and sport. In Andrews DL and Carrington B (eds.) *A companion to sport*, West Sussex, UK: Wiley Blackwell.

Shaw M (2012) Gabby Douglas' race narrative. *Salon*. August 4, 2012.

Spencer NE (2004) Sister Act VI: Venus and Serena Williams at Indian Wells: 'Sincere fictions' and White racism. *Journal of Sport & Social Issues* 28: 115–135. Retrieved September 5, 2012 from http://jss.sagepub.com/cgi/doi/10.1177/0193723504264411

Vertinsky P and Captain G (1998) More myth than history: American culture and representations of the Black female's athletic ability. *Journal of Sport History* 25: 532–561.

Vincent J (2004) Game, sex, and match: The construction of gender in British newspaper coverage of the 2000 Wimbledon Championships. *Sociology of Sport Journal* 21: 435–456.

Walton TA and Butryn TM (2006) Policing the race: U.S. men's distance running and the crisis of Whiteness. *Sociology of Sport Journal* 23(1): 1–28.

Williams R (2012) '2012: A truly remarkable sporting year to be relished over and over', *The Guardian*, December 28. Retrieved March 15, 2013 from http://www.guardian.co.uk/sport/blog/2012/dec/28/2012-sporting-year-review

Withycombe JL (2011) Intersecting selves: African American female athletes' experiences of sport. *Sociology of Sport Journal* 28: 478–493.

Yates C (2012) Serena Williams and the crip walk. *Washington Post*. August 5, 2012

Yuval-Davis N (1997) *Gender and Nation*. London: Sage.

19

DISABLED SPORTING BODIES AS SEXUAL BEINGS

Reflections and challenges

Andrew C. Sparkes, James Brighton and Kay Inckle

Introduction

Disabled bodies, Goodley (2011) suggests, constitute 'a sexually challenging idea' (p. 41). In general, disabled people's sexualities have been ignored, controlled, pathologised and medicalised (Shakespeare et al., 1996), and their bodies conceptualised as asexual, unruly, monstrous, and unattractive (Kim, 2011; Shildrick, 2007). Specifically, disabled men are seen as passive, weak and, by implication, impotent, while disabled women are viewed as ugly, incontinent and unfit for the desiring male gaze. Disabled sexual bodies are, therefore, framed within binary discourses of either lack and failure, or excess and perversion with a tendency to over-emphasize psychosexual (mal)functioning; explore men's sexuality rather than women's; place a lot of store on medical rehabilitation and therapeutic interventions; and assume heterosexuality.

In spite of an expanding corpus of literature on disability and sport (Berger, 2009; DePauw & Gavron, 2005; Fitzgerald, 2009; Goosey-Tolfrey, 2010; Thomas & Smith, 2009), the issue of sexuality tends to be overlooked. This chapter, therefore, attempts to foreground this crucial aspect of embodiment. We explore the complex dynamics of disability, sex and sport by drawing on life history interviews with three elite disabled athletes. These are, Jack, an athlete in his sixties; Steve, a wheelchair basketball player in his thirties; and Lindsey, a paradressage horse rider in her fifties (all names are pseudonyms). Each became disabled following a spinal cord injury (SCI). We indicate how their narratives are framed by the ideologies of heteronormativity, compulsory heterosexuality and compulsory able-bodiedness which restrict their ability to challenge a number of limiting norms that inhibit new, radical and diverse disabled body–self relationships that are pleasurable and fulfilling. Their narratives are also used to provoke some reflections on how the very 'queerness' of their bodies might provide a corporeal resource for subverting sexualities and desires in sport and other domains (Caudwell, 2006).

Doing hegemonic masculinity: restoring heteronormativity

Connell (1995) states that, 'To be an adult male is distinctly to occupy space, to have a physical presence in the world' (p. 57). A physically disabled man symbolically fails the test of masculinity and is positioned as impotent, weak, dependent, childlike and not a *real* man any-more. For 'straight' men with acquired disabilities it can appear that normative masculinity is restored through the assertion of (heteronormative) sexual prowess. Steve's social network status epitomises this restorative impulse which is formed in contrast to the mainstream interpretation of his disabled body.

> The answer to the question that people are frightened to ask is yes I can [have penetrative intercourse], why wouldn't I be able to?!!
>
> *(Steve; social network status)*

> I used to be able to pick up, I used to able to talk to all of the good looking women and meet them and go out with them and have no troubles at all. When I was playing football, and I didn't think of it at the time, but your body is quite physically attractive. Women like that. They like a nice ass just as much as men do. But now they won't give you the time of the day. Now they just rub my head, sit on my lap, have a quick chat or whatever, it's just one of them things.

Steve's narrative and online exclamation articulates his frustration both with the pathologisation of his body, and the condescending and desexualising actions that he experiences. In drawing comparisons with his previous heteronormative sporting body his comments also echo hege-monic sentiments where sex is the privilege of the heterosexual, young, non-disabled and nor-matively attractive. Steve's social network status resonates with contemporary Western society's emphasis on the functionality of the sexual organs, the ability to orgasm and the performance of (hetero)sexual acts. As Sakellariou (2006) states: 'Male sexuality in particular is perceived in an exclusive, phallocentric and oppressive way . . . the penis and its performance assume the leading role' (p. 102). Such phallocentricity is performed to excess in the jock subcultures that Steve inhabited before his SCI where objectification, misogyny and sexualisation is common. Therefore, Steve has few resources available to him to re-evaluate his sexuality and develop new disabled body–self relationships.

In the immediate aftermath of his accident Jack also interpreted his body and sexuality within this phallocentric paradigm and could see no alternative to it:

> There were two things that hit me when I came out of hospital and that was blokes were no longer afraid of me, I was no longer a threat. I was a nothing. I was a nobody, and I didn't give a shit at that point. And I never ever thought that another girl would ever find me attractive. It isn't so bad now, I don't mind now. I'm sixty bloody four, it doesn't matter now! But when you're 19 you might as well be dead. And I can remember being sat outside this local chip shop one night and this car pulled up and this absolutely stunning blonde got out and she smiled at me. And that was the first girl that smiled at me since my accident. And she went into this fish shop and she was waving at me through this fish shop window, and all my mates were in there, and she comes out of this fish shop and walks straight towards me. My heart was going 15 to the dozen. She came straight up to me . . . . and . . . she gave me money to buy chips. I was absolutely gutted. I was devastated. I thought is this going to be my life, sat on the pavement with somebody throwing money at me.

Phallocentrism also informs medical rehabilitation which attempts to restore male heterosexual-ity. Here, penis functionality is omnipotent, resulting in the administration of drugs for cyborg erections regardless of how stimulating or pleasurable the result. As Killacky (2004), a queer crip activist, former dancer and marathon runner who had a tumour removed from his spine and as a result is paraplegic, ironically observes:

> Before discharging us, Larry and I spent an overnight in a 'transitional' apartment on the medical floor, replete with videos designed for couples dealing with spinal injuries. The sexuality tape was beyond ludicrous. Not only was it completely heterosexual, it postulated that the ideal position for a man was still on top. It seemed more than a mere oxymoron for someone who has lost proprioception and feeling in the groin to be advised that thrusting and insertion still defined the sexual act.
>
> *(p. 59)*

Heteronormative discourses and able-bodied ideologies are also prevalent in disability sport. Competing in violent disability sports such as wheelchair rugby can be an attempt to restore the sense of normative masculinity which is threatened by disablement. Many disabled men seek extreme forms of behaviour in order to distance themselves from their disability and the negative identities imposed on them by others. These hypermasculine performances reiterate the misogyny and the relinquishment of intimacy found in masculine able-bodied sports as illustrated by Berger's (2009) analysis of dating patterns amongst wheelchair basketball players. He found men operated a double standard where they viewed dating able-bodied women as distancing them from their disability and restoring their masculinity. These attitudes were also echoed by Steve who experienced his own sexual identity through disableist double standards:

Friend: I saw this real fit blonde in a wheelchair last night – she would have been so lovely for you!

Steve: You what! (shocked)

Friend: Oh, real stunning blonde in a wheelchair, would have been right up your street . . .

Steve: Why do you think that she was in a wheelchair that she would be right up my street?! Why would I be interested? I am offended! I don't want to go out with anyone in a wheelchair, doesn't matter how nice or how horrible they are. I have enough problems of my own; I don't want to deal with anyone else's problems if I am honest. I wouldn't go out with anyone in a wheelchair. I wouldn't have gone out with anyone in a wheelchair when I was able bodied, so I'm not going to go out with anyone now just because I'm disabled.

Steve's comment is paradoxical. His sense of sexuality is entrenched in his previous able-bodied identity. Dating an able-bodied girl, therefore, is symbolic of restoring his sexuality as it was prior to his SCI. Conversely, by failing to recognise the reality of his altered body, Steve also reinforces attitudes others may hold towards his disability. This is potentially alienating and repressive, in terms of Steve engaging in sex but also in terms of him exploring his sexuality, the polymorphous nature of desire, friendship, love and intimacy in different ways.

The hypermasculinity embedded in normative sports culture is uncritically reiterated in these narratives where internalised disabled-phobia propels men to negotiate their masculine identities within the very structures of compulsory able-bodiedness in which they will always remain emasculated and lacking. The next section explores the similarly limiting intersections of heteronormative femininity, sport, sex and disability.

Disability as failed femininity

The ideal female sports body is defined as firm but shapely, fit but sexy, strong but thin, and, we would add, able-bodied. It does not challenge hegemonic norms of femininity. The confines of femininity mean that all women inevitably fail to measure up to heteronormative ideals in some way or at some point in their lives. However, as Garland-Thomson (2002) notes, women with disabilities are entirely 'removed from the sphere of true womanhood and feminine beauty' (p. 17). They are neither desirable to look at nor effective as objects for the expression of male desire. Their bodies, instead of drawing the desiring and affirming male gaze, attract 'the stare' which signifies revulsion and dehumanisation defining them as 'failed' women in terms of gender and sexuality. Lindsey, a Great Britain (GB) para-dressage rider describes how she felt about herself as a woman post-SCI:

> Most of the time, not much of one. I sort of try not to think of my body from the waist down because it is so revolting now and my legs are pretty much like corn beef, they are always purple and blotchy and horrible.

Lindsey's narrative reveals that her disability has deeply affected her sense of self based on the appearance of her body, leaving her unable to reconcile her transformed body with a gendered and sexual self. Richards et al. (1997) report a similar 'shutting down and shutting out of sexuality' in the narratives of women immediately post-SCI. Lindsey comments on her new sense of embodiment:

> I think if I was going somewhere I would want to sort of dress up and look nice. I do miss that a bit now, I just sort of, I don't think of my body in a sexual way anymore so I suppose I'm just a sort of blob in a chair. I always thought I was feminine even if I wasn't beautiful. But now I just think that it is so difficult because I know my body is even more horrendous than it was to start with. And I only wear trousers now and so hopefully people only sort of look at you from the waist up. But now I've turned into Michelin Man I don't want anyone to see my arms.

Lindsey's narrative is desexualising. Her unwillingness to dress up, to wear feminine clothes and being like the 'Michelin Man' illustrate the rejection of a gendered and sexual body altogether that feels unable to live up to hegemonic feminine ideals. Her comment that her body is 'more horrendous than it was to start with' highlights the multiple layers of complexity and repression in responding both to her disability and dominant ideologies of the female body-beautiful in contemporary Western society. Outside of these norms, however, the appearance and capacities of Lindsey's body would not necessarily desexualise her in the same way. For example, in sexual subcultures which operationalise an alternative sexual aesthetics and pleasure, such as the bondage, dominance, sado-masochism (BDSM) or devotee communities, Lindsey's body might be considered highly desirable and even sought after.[1]

It is easier perhaps for Aimee Mullins, the American former Paralympian and double amputee who is now a fashion model, actress and motivational speaker to challenge ableist aesthetics of the female body. Tellingly, media discourses frame her as *too pretty to be disabled*. Mullins' sensual body, shaped through her athletic career, her long blonde hair and exquisite looks exude (hetero)sexual suggestiveness. As Garland-Thomson (2002) observes, 'Photographed in her functional prosthetic legs, she embodies the sexualised jock look that women be both slender and fit' (p. 25). In highlighting that the disabled sporting body can be erotic and aesthetically sexual, Aimee Mullins offers some resistance to the erotophobic attitudes held towards other disabled bodies. However, simultaneously, the ways in which her body is represented by herself and others can undermine this resistance via its support for traditional notions of femininity that are validated by the normative gaze of the able-bodied majority. This has implications for Lindsey as evidenced by her following comment about how she attempted to explore her sexuality post-SCI:

> When I finally got home and we were brave enough to have a go, he was just so terrified of hurting me it was quite a big deal for him and, and then it sort of . . . I know people do but as far as I am concerned if there's no feeling there and if you want me to be brutally honest because you're flaccid there's nothing to keep him erect, you know. It's not the same. I think the thing I will never get used to is bowels and bladder and umm you know sort of lack of sex, feelings. I remember it was like the first time I got in the bath. I was so looking forward to getting in the bath, that lovely feeling of the hot water all over you and I suddenly thought, 'well I can only feel it from the waist up'. You know they're just floating, I don't know whether we're in hot water, cold water you know. So that was a disappointment and a shock and it's sort of the same I suppose with sex.

Lindsey's experiences reflect what Richards et al. (1997) refer to as 'sexual disenfranchisement' amongst women with SCI, resulting in feelings of relationship disconnection and disappointment. Her comment also reveals how the norm of heterosexual vaginal intercourse erases more polymorphous forms of sexuality enjoyed by those with non-normative bodies and/or desires (McRuer, 2006). Lindsey's disappointment and anxiety could be re-articulated by moving away from the phallocentric ideals of sex she has internalised which confirm that the failure of sexual pleasure is a straightforward result of her 'failed' body. It is also significant that Lindsey measures her sexuality by choosing an act which she can neither feel nor participate in. She might find that activities which fall outside of heteronormative limits are both enjoyable and empowering to her as well as novel and stimulating to herself and her partner. As Penny, a disabled woman in Shakespeare's (2000) research commented: 'If you are a sexually active disabled person, and comfortable with the sexual side of your life, it is remarkable how dull and unimaginative nondisabled people's sex lives can appear' (p. 163).

Nonetheless, for Lindsey her attempt at intercourse reiterates that she feels asexual, a 'blob' and 'not much of a' woman. It is (tragically) ironic that Lindsey views the experience of disappointment and disconnection during intercourse as quite different from the experiences of able-bodied heterosexual women. Wilton's (2004) research found that a large proportion of heterosexual women cite disappointment, disconnection and lack of stimulation as the ongoing features their sexual lives with men. Likewise, Shakespeare (2000) points out that the idea of free-flowing orgasmic eroticism is one of the pervading myths of contemporary capitalist culture which leaves many people, able-bodied and disabled alike, feeling lacking, inadequate and disappointed.

Reworking the disabled sporting body and sexuality

We now explore the ways in which the sexual, disabled sporting body, here exemplified by Jack as he reflects back on how his views of his sexuality have changed over time, can challenge and exceed hegemonic norms and offer radical and pleasurable ways of being. Though disability sport participation Jack developed a greater understanding of his body; learning new sensitivities of touching and feeling which he translated to his sexual life. This offered an alternative outlook on his sexual body and abilities enabling him to adapt to his post-SCI sexuality, creating a communicative body that transgresses hegemonic gender roles and is a source of pleasure and fulfilment:

> I was absolutely petrified of women. And we had gone out for a meal, and it was pissing it down with rain and we come back to my place like, like my heart is going a bit you know and she is a stunner, she was stunning but a brilliant personality too. We got back to my place her figure was unreal and then she said to me, and we started talking and kissing, and she said . . . and I was scared stiff, she said, can you make love and I said y-e-s! But it was brilliant, but she understood, she kind of understood but she made love to me, put me on the floor actually, put me on the floor, undressed me and she just straddled me and she gave me one. And I thought, what have I been worried about you know?

When asked how he felt about this event, Jack responded as follows:

> I think that there are two emotions. When I cum now I know I am going to cum but it isn't that massive explosion that you have before. And it's nothing to do with age or anything like that, it is the actual disability. But the bonus is that I can keep going and going and I have found out that a long time ago, that what I can't use down there sometimes, or when that goes off a bit, or if I lose my hard-on I will use my tongue and I found that equally as good. I learnt a long time ago that that was important. And talking . . . talking and touching. I have become a really touchy person, sensitive to touch. The upper part of my body has become hypersensitive and if they know which buttons to press there for me I will do the same I will reciprocate. Sex now can be as good as it ever was before my accident and stuff you know and I think a lot of it is feeling in my mind too as well.

Such adjustment of the sexual body is a crucial part of the transformative process. Although Jack holds on to the importance of the performance of sexuality (he can keep going) not only does he show willingness to relinquish the dominance of his male sexual role by letting the female partner take the lead, but also alludes to the importance of talking and intimacy in sexual interaction. By 'remapping' his erogenous zones (Sakellariou, 2006) and embracing the sensuality of his upper body, he is recognising that sex does not have to be centred on the functionality of his sexual organs. Jack's carnal articulation offers both phenomenological hope for the sexual body through exploration and poses important questions regarding the assumed biological realities of our sexualities. This reverberates with Whipple et al.'s (1996) findings that areas of the body that have remained sensate can become erogenous zones. As Shuttleworth and Sanders (2010) note with regard to sexuality this 'complicates the neat categorisation of research issues and methodologies' (p. 4). This radical remapping through self-exploration is common to disabled (and queer) sexuality as Ann a participant in a study by Gillespie-Sells et al. (1998) explains: 'My neck is my clitoris and my shoulders are my "G spot". I don't have to feel my body to get off on watching my girlfriend touching the numb parts of me' (p. 52). Likewise, living with progressive multiple sclerosis Mairs (1997) points out that with her disabled partner, even their most mundane interactions can bear an erotic change: 'he may stroke my neck when he brings me coffee. And since my wheelchair places me just at the level of his penis . . . I may nuzzle it in return' (p. 54).

Jack's narrative also reveals how explorations in sport can provide him with a positive sense of his body and improved confidence. His sense of self both included and transgressed hegemonic norms of masculinity. Jack described how through disability sports he developed a muscular self which resulted in him *feeling* more attractive. However, for Jack, acquiring disability was also an opportunity to explore new forms of sexuality and intimacy, just as it was an opportunity to take part in alternative sports and become a full-time athlete.

> After the accident I couldn't stand a woman looking at me naked, I just couldn't stand that thought of her looking at me naked. But the stupid thing is, is that that is a man thing. Because women . . . they just don't see it like that. Sport is has been great to me. You think you've got good guns [biceps], these are 64 year old fucking guns! I'm sixty bloody four now, but I still look fucking good!

The story told by Jack highlights that it is not his body, but societal attitudes towards disability and sexuality that inflict limitations. Despite the pressure to conform to hegemonic norms, sport may offer heightened opportunities for creating positive sexual and gendered identities (DePauw, 2000). Therefore, disabled athletes may be in a unique position to move beyond the limiting hegemonic norms of gender, sexuality and embody a radical politics of sex and sport which can transform sports theory, research and culture.

Reflections: connecting disability, queer and crip theories in sporting lives

In this chapter we illustrated how the experiences of three elite disabled athletes are framed by heteronormativity, compulsory heterosexuality and compulsory able-bodiedness in ways that reproduce dominant ideologies of sexuality. We also indicated that these ideologies can be resisted and that individuals can change their lives in ways that have profound implications for how they experience themselves as disabled, gendered and sexual beings. We now wish to suggest that there is much to be gained from reflecting on the experiences of Steve, Lindsey and Jack through the lenses of queer and crip theory. Here, we take our lead from Sykes (2006) who notes how disability studies have always challenged what counts as a 'normal' body and recognises how the bringing this perspective together with queer theory and crip theory offers possibilities for future interdisciplinary approaches to studying sport. Likewise, Shildrick (2007) notes that in recent years, disability studies, particularly those working with queer and feminist theory, 'have increasingly problematized the conventional parameters of sexuality, in order to explore non-normative constructions of sexual identities, pleasures and agency that more adequately encompass multifarious forms of embodied difference' (p. 227).

Queer theory, which emerged in the 1990s at the intersection of gender and sexuality studies, psychoanalysis, and HIV/AIDs activism, has provided a radical new intervention. By positing queer as a verb, rather than a sexual identity (i.e. gay, lesbian, bisexual), queer theory offers a new means of interrogating the structures of power which operate through idealised norms which appear as natural and inevitable – such as able-bodied heterosexuality (Edelman, 2004). Because of its history queer theorists have paid particular attention to the ways in which power operates through gender, sexuality and bodily norms in cultural representations. More recently queer theorists have focused on ethnicity, disability and human rights in a lived, global context (Butler, 2004).

Queer theorists challenge and transform limiting norms through recasting taken for granted positions. They operationalise a queer framework which opens up new forms of interpretation, knowledge and praxis. Queer is then, 'a suggestive rather than a prescriptive concept' (Doty, 2000, p. 7), more accurately understood as a verb, as a *doing* – or, rather, an '*un*doing' – than an identity (Butler, 2004; Edelman, 2004). Thus, in adopting queer as a political strategy, we become 'queer positioned' (Doty, 2000, p. 4) in relation to normative society and utilise queer as an interrogative, transformative force. Queer theory then, offers a powerful lens through which to re-figure the stigmatising norms which position the disabled body as failed, un-gendered and asexual.

Queer theory has been a primary influence on the emergence of crip theory which brings the 'queerness' of disabled bodies to the fore as a powerful vehicle for the interrogation and transgression of (ableist) norms. Instead of measuring the disabled body against such norms, crip theorists use the disabled body as the starting point to interrogate and undo them, exposing their limitations, contradictions and inequalities.

> Cripping spins mainstream representations or practices to reveal able-bodied assumptions and exclusionary effects. Both queering and cripping expose the arbitrary delineation between normal and defective and the negative social ramifications of attempts to homogenize humanity, and both disarm what is painful with wicked humor, including camp.
>
> *(Sandahl, 2003, p. 36)*

Utilising the lenses of crip and queer theory our analysis of the experiences of Steve, Jack and Lindsey exposes the impact of the intersections of heteronormative and ableist approaches to gender, sexuality and the body and suggests how these might be transgressed, as indeed they are in Jack's case.

Initially, their narratives illustrate how being 'fully human' (Butler, 2004) is experienced exclusively through normative bodily, gender and sexual practices. When individuals fall outside of those norms through, for example, SCI, the loss of normative gendered and sexual identity has devastating implications for their sense of self and their social and sexual relations. However, from a crip perspective, we would suggest that it is precisely this location, outside of normative structures of the body, gender and sexuality that enables radical theory and praxis. These are new ways of knowing and being which expose the limitations of heteronormativity and ablism and challenge others to think in new directions. Furthermore, the expansiveness of the bodily, gender and sexual possibilities which are celebrated within crip and queer approaches provide opportunities for individuals who experience damaged or stigmatised identities not only to transcend the limitations imposed on them but also to exemplify modes of praxis which exceed compulsory able-bodiedness and compulsory heterosexuality. This is epitomised in Jack's delight in his body and his pleasure in his sexuality.

We suggest, therefore, that crip and queer perspectives have much to offer, not simply in terms of understanding those who are disabled or LGBT, but rather, in exposing the limitations of normativity and opening out new ways of knowing and being. By their very existence sexual, disabled, sporting bodies queer hegemonic norms of body, gender and sexuality. Interrogating these norms from crip and queer perspectives is essential if sports theory and praxis is to embrace the full spectrum of human potential and avoid reiterating hierarchies of oppression and exclusion.

Acknowledgements

We wish to thank, Steve, Jack and Lindsey for sharing their stories and for their permission to use their comments in this chapter. Thanks also to Toni Williams (UWE Hartpury) for assisting in data collection and Mark Vicars (Victoria University) for enlightening and assisting our thoughts.

Note

1   This is not to uncritically endorse these aesthetics and pleasures as the devotee community remains largely heteronormative in that disabled, and particularly amputee, women's bodies are simply recast as exotic new objects of for the desiring male gaze (Aguilera, 2000).

References

Aguilera R (2000) Disability and delight: Staring back at the devotee community. *Sexuality and Disability* 18(4): 255–261.

Berger R (2009). *Hoop Dreams on Wheels: Disability and the Competitive Wheelchair Athlete*. London: Routledge.

Butler J (2004) *Undoing Gender*. London: Routledge.

Caudwell J (ed) (2006) *Sport, Sexualities and Queer Theory*. London: Routledge.

Connell R (1995) *Masculinities*. Berkeley, CA: University of California Press.

DePauw K (2000) Socio-cultural context: Implications for scientific inquiry and professional preparation. *Quest*, 52: 538–368.

DePauw K and Gavron S (2005) *Disability and Sport: 2nd Edition*. Champaign, IL: Human Kinetics.

Doty A (2000) *Flaming Classics: Queering the Film Cannon*. London: Routledge.

Edelman L (2004) *No Future: Queer Theory and the Death Drive*. London: Duke University Press.

Fitzgerald H (ed) (2009) *Disability and Youth Sport*. London: Routledge.

Garland-Thomson R (2002) Integrating disability, transforming feminist theory. *NWSA Journal*, 14(3): 1–32.

Gillespie-Sells K, Hill M and Robbins B (1998) *She Dances to Different Drums: Research into Disabled Women's Sexuality*. London: Kings Fund.

Goodley D (2011) *Disability Studies: An Interdisciplinary Introduction*. London: Sage.

Goosey-Tolfrey V (ed) (2010) *Wheelchair Sport*. Champaign, IL: Human Kinetics.

Killacky J (2004) Careering toward kensho: Ruminations on disability and community. In: Guter B and Killacky J (eds) *Queer Crips: Disabled Gay Men and their Stories*. London: Harrington Park Press, pp. 57–62.

Kim E (2011) Asexuality in disability narratives. *Sexualities*, 14(4): 479–493.

Mairs N (1997) *Waist-High in the World: A Life among the Nondisabled*. Boston, MA: Beacon Press.

McRuer R (2006) *Crip Theory: Cultural Signs of Queerness and Disability*. New York: New York University Press.

Richards E, Tepper M, Whipple B and Komisaruk B (1997) Women with complete spinal cord injury: A phenomenological study of sexuality and relationship experiences'. *Sexuality and Disability*, 15(4): 271–283.

Sakellariou D (2006) If not the disability, then what? Barriers to reclaiming sexuality following spinal cord injury. *Sexuality and Disability*, 24: 101–111.

Sandahl C (2003) Queering the crip or cripping the queer? Intersections of queer and crip identities in solo autobiographical performance. *GLQ: Journal of Lesbian and Gay Studies*, 9(1–2): 25–56.

Shakespeare T (2000) 'Disabled sexuality: Towards rights and recognition. *Sexuality and Disability* 18(3): 159–166.

Shakespeare T, Gillespie-Sells K and Davies, D (1996) *The Sexual Politics of Disability: Untold Desires*. London: Cassell.

Shildrick M (2007) Dangerous discourses: Anxiety, desire and disability. *Studies in Gender & Sexuality*, 8(3): 221–244.

Shuttleworth R and Sanders T (2010) *Sex and Disability: Politics, Identity and Access*. Leeds: The Disability Press.

Sykes H (2006) Queering theories of sexuality in sport studies. In: Caudwell J (ed) *Sport, Sexualities and Queer Theory*. London: Routledge, pp. 13–32.

Thomas N and Smith A (2009) *Disability, Sport and Society: An Introduction*. London: Routledge.

Whipple B, Richards E, Tepper M and Komisaruk B (1996) Sexual response in women with complete spinal cord injury. In: Krostoski D, Nosek M and Turk M (eds) *Women with Physical Disabilities: Achieving and Maintaining Health and Well-Being*. Baltimore, MD: Brookes Publishing, pp. 191–201.

Wilton T (2004) *Sexual (dis)orientation: Gender, Sex, Desire, and Self-fashioning*. Basingstoke: Palgrave Macmillan.

20

"MY BIGGEST DISABILITY IS I'M A MALE!"

The role of sport in negotiating the dilemma of disabled masculinity

Nikki Wedgwood

Introduction

By providing training in the embodiment of masculine ideals, sport is one of the primary practices in which young men construct their gender identities. The particular importance of sport in masculinity construction is that "[w]hat it means to be masculine is, quite literally, to embody force, to embody competence" (Connell, 1983: 27). Sport thus ritually celebrates physical abilities as well as male superiority. Yet not all men are able-bodied. Those with impairments embody a contradiction between dominant forms of masculinity (skilful, powerful) and impairment (reduced physical abilities/power). The participation in sport by men with impairments highlights this contradiction, and thus can provide important insights into how this "dilemma of disabled masculinity" (Shuttleworth, Wedgwood and Wilson, 2012) is negotiated.

One study of quad or wheelchair rugby in the US found that performing with athletic skill and embodying the hyper-masculine violence and aggression commonly seen in able-bodied sport enabled a form of gender and identity rehabilitation which helped players to go from self-loathing and self-stigmatization to acceptance and pride (Lindemann and Cherney, 2008: 120). However, in doing so, they adopted hyper-masculine attitudes and employed ableist values of strength and physical accomplishment in order to approximate normality. Conversely, in a study of English men who sustained spinal cord injuries whilst playing rugby, the participants struggled to come to terms with their disability or to reconstruct the hegemonic masculine identities they had constructed previously through able-bodied sport. They refused to participate in disability-specific sport, perceiving it to be inferior to able-bodied sport (Sparkes and Smith, 2002).

The participants in both these studies remained firmly committed to hegemonic masculine ideals after acquiring disabling injuries—a pattern consistent with one of the typologies developed by Gerschick and Miller (1994) in their seminal article on masculinity and disability. They suggest there are three dominant ways in which men with physical impairments relate to hegemonic masculinity's standards: embracing dominant conceptions of masculinity despite an inability to meet many of the ideals (reliance); redefining hegemonic characteristics on their own terms (reformulation); or renouncing these standards and either creating their own principles and practices or denying masculinity's importance in their lives (rejection). Although Gerschick and Miller (1994) stress that men use a complex combination of these three strategies within the context of a primary pattern, it is difficult to agree that this caveat helps "avoid 'labeling' men and assigning them to arbitrary categories" (p. 37).

The following study adds to the nascent research on masculinity, disability and sport, which thus far has focused on adult men, despite the fact that adolescence is a critical and formative phase of gender identity development. Through the use of life history case studies of three adolescent men with a range of impairments—congenital and acquired, mild to moderate—it considers the impact of both able-bodied and disability-specific sport on their lives, not just as a physical activity but as a powerful social institution. In particular, it explores whether playing sport is a form of cultural capital in the construction of a masculine identity for young men with impairments.

The findings presented here are from a study conducted in an Australian city in 2008. Participants were interviewed individually by the author. Whilst eliciting a narrative of their life history, the following topics were covered: family background, sporting history, adolescent development, embodiment/body, practices in which relationships are constructed, career and future plans. Interviews were recorded, transcribed, developed into narrative life histories, and then analysed in terms of the topics outlined above.

Findings

The three abridged case studies presented here focus primarily on the intersection of sport, masculinity and disability.

Carlos

Carlos (16), a lively and humorous young man, lives in a working class suburb with his parents who migrated from Latin America as adolescents, and his two older siblings, Maria (18) and Tim (21). Carlos was born with cerebral palsy (CP), greatly affecting his ability to walk and has been a chair user since he was eight. He lives in a highly-gendered household where: "the females cook and clean and males just do what they do. Just being male . . . That's what my mum says is my biggest disability, is I'm a male!" Sport also serves to demarcate gender in his family, as Carlos stressed when asked whether his family are sporty:

> Hoh! My brother and my father are but not so much my mum and my sister. They stay at home and they clean and do the dishes and stuff and cook and everything. Yeah, but me, my brother and father, we're all the sporty ones . . . we've got all the trophies.

Able-bodied team sports are something from which Carlos has been routinely excluded. He recalls that in primary school when his classmates were playing soccer: "I'd be on the sidelines and . . . have my head like this [head resting on hands] and just stare at nothing and wait for the game to be over."

Due to his father's Latino background, soccer is the sport with the most masculine kudos in their household. Indeed, in their family the role of soccer is similar to that of Australian Rules football in an earlier study of a group of able-bodied adolescents whose fathers inducted their sons into the game as: i) a masculinising institution; ii) an emotional proxy for fathers and sons; and iii) gender demarcation within families (Wedgwood, 2003). Carlos' brother Tim and his father follow Spanish-speaking teams together and play soccer every weekend while, as at school, Carlos is left on the sidelines:

> . . . it was hard because . . . I used to sit around on the couch and do nothing and wait for Mum and my brother and my dad to come home from soccer . . . I used to go watch them sometimes . . . I never really liked soccer . . . I just waited until the game was over and used to just think "I wonder if I would think differently if I could play that?"

Rather poignantly, Carlos says he does not understand "what's so great about [soccer]. It's just a couple of guys kicking a ball *with their feet* so I really wouldn't understand the glory of it but you know they enjoy it so that's the main thing."

Carlos participated in swimming and athletics from a young age but did not play disability-specific team sports until, encouraged by his mum, he took up touch football at 12. He began wheelchair basketball at 13 when his high school physical education (PE) teacher "stumbled upon it" and suggested he try it. What kept him from participating prior to that was his need to first come to terms with his disability:

> Can you imagine a four year old is . . . trying to figure this out? He is wondering "Why?" to himself and he just doesn't have the answer . . . you start feeling all these different emotions, anger, sadness and then it all explodes into one.

At the age of eight, when an operation to stop him walking with bent knees was botched, Carlos lost his ability to walk altogether, further impeding his ability to come to terms with his disability. He would spend hours alone in his room but eventually decided that if he wanted to do something like play sport he should just do so, rather than sitting around wishing he could do things and brooding that "if it wasn't for those bloody doctors cutting my legs . . . I would still be able to walk".

Carlos' mental wellbeing was already improving before he took up sport, but participating further improved his mental and physical wellbeing: "Sport was a big, big turning point because [it] gives you a great joy if you can do something in front of somebody that you never could do before." It also helped Carlos lose a lot of weight, which stopped his older brother teasing him and improved his self-esteem. Through basketball Carlos met others with physical impairments with whom he could swap advice and relate to because "You actually know that these people feel these problems." It also provided him with a crucial outlet for his anger:

> I used to get picked on by my brother when I was young and . . . I didn't really know how to handle that so I got angry and started hitting stuff and throwing my aggression this way and that way. But sport is also an outlet of aggression.

Despite the positive impact of disability-specific sport on his wellbeing, there remains an unresolved tension between Carlos' physical abilities and masculinity construction, which was manifest throughout his interview in exaggerated and defensive claims:

> If I have a really hard match and I'm getting bruised and getting smashed . . . and I'm still trying to go for the ball and I keep getting hit—that's what I love about contact sports—I keep getting hit and everything and still getting up.

Carlos displays a defensive masculinity similar to that of a small group of young men in an earlier study of able-bodied high school footballers who held tenuous positions near the bottom of the male hierarchy at school (Wedgwood, 2003). They also came from families with traditional gender regimes and displayed insecurities and defensiveness about their fragile masculine status, particularly in terms of their physical presence and skills on-field (Wedgwood, 2003).

Carlos' involvement in disability-specific sports appears to have had limited impact on his peer status, despite a visit to his school from a disability sports organisation to set up a game of wheelchair basketball with Carlos and his able-bodied peers, giving Carlos a rare opportunity to display his physical *abilities* to them:

> I was running circles around them, I was doing it in my sleep, bouncing the ball up high in the air and then running [sic] after it . . . It felt absolutely awesome because I was burning them with my speed! Everyone's trying to keep up . . . They all said to me "Look mate you're a freak. You're a freak. I don't want to ever experience that again!"

By his account, Carlos' prowess in wheelchair basketball earned him respect among his peers; important because masculinity cannot be assumed but must be conferred by one's male peers (Buchbinder, 1994: 35). Yet, the kudos earned may have been short-lived or non-transferable from the disability-specific sporting context to a broader able-bodied context because, when asked where he fitted in among the peer groups at school, he said, "I'm a drifter. I just fit in, go wherever I want to go. I march to the beat of my own drum." It was clear that Carlos has friends at school but, given that social inclusion takes a very particular form during adolescence—membership in a peer group—it might be more accurate to say Carlos is *accepted* as opposed to fully *included* by his peers:

> I've got close friends here and there. They all hang out in separate groups . . . I've got one close friend over this group and another close friend over there . . . to me there's no barrier, we're all people and we don't have to be split up. I figure I might as well join the party in every group!

Jake

Jake (18) is a mature, personable and self-assured young man. He lives in an affluent suburb with his parents and three brothers aged 5, 15 and 20. Jake says his family is close due to their Judaism, which "keeps families pretty close together and our whole community are pretty close". Despite studying at university, Jake's mum is a "stay-at-home Mum" because she had children before she could establish a career. His father, who studied law, is a manager with a successful corporate career. Jake feels he is closer to his mum than his brothers are because he developed a life-threatening condition at 13. At 14 Jake had half his hip removed and now has minimal muscle in one leg, walks with a cane and shoe-raiser, requires a wheelchair to play sport and cannot sit or stand for long periods due to constant pain.

Before his illness Jake had played many sports and was a very good all-rounder. In his family soccer is particularly highly valued. A father-and-son activity, his dad would take Jake and his brothers to their weekend soccer matches: "Basically our whole Saturdays used to be soccer [jovial]!" This has added significance given his father worked long hours and only saw his kids on weekends: "My dad's played soccer his whole life. He used to play [representative] soccer . . . we used to go kick the ball all the time on the weekend and that was just a family thing." Jake tried out for a representative team like his dad but then fell ill and "had to pull out but, yeah [struggling for words], everyone's sporty [in the family], but I was really good".

Whilst Jake's relationship with his mum is "more emotional" and he can talk to her about anything, he says he bonds with his father and brothers primarily through "physical stuff" like playing sport: "Well it's something we *used* to do [poignant pause]. Oh, we still do, I play tennis with them. I'm in the chair and they're just running around [pathos in voice]."

Due to the small size and cultural homogeneity of his high school—all the students are Jewish—most of his year hang out as one big group and, within that, smaller groups of "best friends". Upon returning to school after his illness, Jake was accepted into one of these groups comprised of around ten male and female members. He is included in most of their leisure activities. Nevertheless, his limited access to able-bodied sports has re-shaped his relationships with both his male and female peers:

> I find becoming friends with girls a bit easier than guys because like at this stage in a guy's life it's basically all sport. Like they get hyped up and start jumping around and I can't get hyped up and start jumping around [humorous]. I just click with girls.

Jake tries to find ways of joining in: "at lunchtimes, sometimes the guys play soccer . . . and I'll just be goalie . . . Just to be involved." He also swims at the beach whilst his mates surf, but there are some things he cannot do. This limits his interactions with male peers, such as his best friend with whom he used to play ice hockey: "we had that in common [hesitant, down] . . . but then I couldn't [play] any more. So other friends started . . . which was kind of bad."

Taking up wheelchair tennis at 16 has played a pivotal role in coming to terms with his impairment. Jake was very young when he became ill and probably lacked the wherewithal to deal with something so momentous as a life-threatening illness but, after struggling with depression for a long time, his outlook changed:

> there's nothing I can do about it so I should . . . still think that I'm as good as anyone else and should still be confident . . . I've only been able to think about it this way for a year and a bit. I think tennis helped a huge amount and meeting people who have been through similar things to me, well different things but they've had to go through the same thought processes and stuff; like being okay then being injured and how they deal with it.

Playing wheelchair tennis gives Jake "more confidence just because I'm winning", thus improving his mental health and self-esteem, which had been badly bruised by his impairment:

> Before tennis I was depressed for a long time because I used to be very sporty and I just couldn't do anything. Then I found out about wheelchair sport and . . . I've loved it, just being able to play sport again . . . just being active, which is what I love to do . . . it's like a thrill because I'm good at it and I've been playing for [elite team] . . . When I'm not playing sport I get down in the dumps.

Whilst wheelchair tennis has had a positive influence on many aspects of Jake's life, it does not hold the same social status or meanings as able-bodied soccer and cannot replace the role soccer played in bonding with his father, belonging to his peer group or being part of the Jewish community: "For the whole school or whole community, soccer is their sport. Yeah, so I don't get to be part of it."

Jake rarely plays tennis with able-bodied friends or family, preferring to play with other "wheelies". Wheelchair tennis has become a central part of his project to reinvent himself, as he re-establishes his identity and place among his family, peers, community and society more broadly. Jake's struggle to re-establish an identity, which had been pulled like a rug from under him, has been further complicated by no longer being able to be a straight-A student. Due to his illness, Jake missed most of Years 8, 9 and 10 and, upon his return to school, was no longer able to excel academically, due to constant pain hampering his concentration and ability to sit for extended periods. Given Jake comes from an affluent, highly-educated family, this has implications for his identity. He now aspires to be world number one in wheelchair tennis, spurred on by his coaches who tell him he has the potential.

Wheelchair tennis has replaced able-bodied soccer as the major masculinising practice for Jake. Yet, far from developing a hyper-masculine or defensive masculine identity, Jake has eschewed some culturally-defined masculine aspects of his identity. Having faced his own mortality has, he says, made him less ashamed of his emotions:

> I would say that I'm more emotional than my brothers from what I've been through. Or . . . maybe the same emotional but I show it more . . . my brothers might be emotional but they don't show it because it's like the male thing to do, but I don't really care about that [laughing].

Logan

Logan (19) is an exuberant and well-adjusted young man. He has mild cerebral palsy in one arm and leg due to being born prematurely, though his twin, Kai, was unaffected. Logan attends university in a large regional town where he lives with his family, who he describes as "just a normal family, with loving parents who are really supportive and who do a lot of things together". Both parents are busy professionals with an egalitarian division of labour. Despite this, Logan's leisure activities with his parents are gendered. He goes shopping, to lunch or for walks with his mum. With his dad he does "male bonding type stuff!" like surfing or washing their cars. Sport is not a defining feature of Logan's relationship with his father and they follow different football codes, but enjoy surfing together: "it's pretty personal when you are out in the water, which is nice because we don't really get to spend that much time together".

Logan's impairment is such that it did not prevent him from being able to excel in many able-bodied sports—playing cricket, basketball and soccer at representative level. He was introduced to able-bodied soccer when he was five by his parents who are not sporty but were keen to instil in him that he was no different from anyone else. Though Logan's father watches him play soccer, his parents "never really pushed me . . . to further my soccer career like a lot of parents do". It was Logan's desire to fit in with his male peers that had the greatest influence: "I just wanted to do it because all my mates were doing it." Able-bodied sport has remained a shared interest with his male peers throughout school and university: "a kind of a bonding thing".

Being able to play sport was not the only factor in his peer acceptance. The mildness of his impairment, coupled with his good self-image, were critical. In primary school peers would ask, "What's wrong with your leg/arm?" when they noticed his limp, compression glove and armband. Keen to "fit in", he worked hard to "complete all the tasks that everyone else does". He also worked hard at his physiotherapy and by high school no longer wore a glove, carried his arm as close to his body or limped as visibly. Peers stopped asking about his impairment so he stopped telling them.

Yet even before being able to *pass* as able-bodied, Logan felt included in every aspect of school: "I've always been accepted and a valued class member." Only bullied twice, he seems genuinely unaffected by these incidents due to his buoyant personality and the outlook on life encouraged by his parents:

> . . . having the disability never really stopped me . . . My parents had always told me to just go and do whatever . . . from a young age I've been told I was no different . . . I've always been pretty popular and always been pretty sociable and no real social inhibitions because of my CP.

Logan describes the friendship groups at high school as the sporty guys, nerds, cool nerds, drop-kicks, deros ("smoked pot and did drugs") and the cool people. Logan could talk to anyone in his year but, when pushed, modestly admitted his "constant group of friends" were the cool group. He had two long-term girlfriends in high school and experienced no difficulties dating: "I wasn't really introverted so I didn't really have a problem with talking to girls . . . my CP wasn't a factor. They didn't look at me and go, 'Oh you've got a disability so I won't give you the time of day'".

Logan continues to play soccer in an able-bodied premier league, has a girlfriend and a close group of friends at university, many of whom he knows through able-bodied soccer. Though he has encountered prejudice, like being cut from a selection trial when he said he played CP soccer, his able-bodied sporting experiences have been primarily inclusive. Despite this, Logan took up a disability-specific sport. Whilst able-bodied sport has been primarily a normalising practice for Logan—particularly in terms of peer acceptance and masculinity construction—CP soccer has played a very different role in his life and personal development.

Inspired by the Sydney Olympics, Logan took up CP soccer as a young teen, the impact of which has been positive, deep and extensive. He reports skipping much of the turmoil of adolescence due to his involvement in the game:

> The confused kind of "Where do I fit in?" period didn't really happen for me because I had a purpose and a drive so young . . . As a 13 year old getting told "If you work hard you will get in the [elite team]" . . . instilled that drive and passion for . . . playing a sport that I love . . . I had to mature quickly being on [an overseas] tour at 14 . . . They weren't going to take me if I was immature . . . I kind of skipped that . . . and didn't really have that "Who am I?" question hanging over my head. I had a place where I was comfortable.

Nor has Logan ever experienced any of the depression and anxiety that often accompanies adolescence: "It's pretty hard to be depressed when you get told you are in the [Elite] Squad and you get to compete at the highest level!" Nor did his relationship with his parents become turbulent over drugs, alcohol, girlfriends or staying out late, partly due to his parents' broad-mindedness and partly due to his involvement in CP soccer, which kept him "on the straight and narrow". After being drug tested at 14 he decided "it's not worth . . . smoking a joint . . . getting a two-year ban . . . then two years of frustration and heartache not playing my sport".

Logan's CP soccer coach and manager took him under their wings: "I suppose that confidence that they gave me did transfer into my schooling, to my social life." Indeed, whilst initially Logan adopted a "don't ask/don't tell" policy about his impairment at high school, by Year 12 he was proudly telling his peers he played in an elite CP soccer team. Some who had known him for six years said "What? You're not disabled!"

195

Logan's main reason for playing CP soccer is the opportunity to excel in a sporting arena not measured against able-bodied standards and thus being able to play at a higher level than he could reach in able-bodied soccer: "I'm a great player and I believe in my ability . . . [but] I know that there's going to be a person that's better than me that's able-bodied."

CP soccer has also made Logan realise he is "different" and provides opportunities to be around others with CP. He is friends with and goes surfing with his able-bodied soccer team mates but notes: "a deeper sense of belonging with the other squad because you are around guys that you do have that commonality of the CP and you can relate to each other a bit more". Perhaps CP soccer helps Logan re-engage with his body that he suppresses most of the time. Though his impairment is mild, Logan nevertheless grew up in an ableist society with an impairment that attracted questions from peers about what was "wrong" with his body, encouraging him to retrain his body to the point that he could pass as able-bodied from early adolescence. Like the suppression/denial of other aspects of identity, such as homosexuality in the context of a heterosexist world, perhaps "passing" as able-bodied is not without a cost to his sense of self. Participation in a disability-specific sport has provided Logan with the opportunity to reconnect and come to terms with his disability at a crucial time in the consolidation of his identity, helping define who he is—one of the most complex developmental tasks of adolescence, usually more difficult for someone with a physical impairment in an able-bodied world. In Logan's words, CP soccer has: "given me so much, it's more than just a game for me. It's part of who I am now." Indeed, Logan is not only studying for a career in sport but aspires to compete in the Paralympics, continue playing CP soccer and thereafter remain involved as a coach or in another capacity.

Logan sees his impairment as providing opportunities rather than setbacks:

> the chances and the path that I've been given because of my CP has just been unbelievable . . . I don't know if I would have had the drive that I have in life if I didn't have a disability. It's kind of a blessing in disguise . . . I love my life . . . I wouldn't change anything for the world.

Conclusions

A small-scale exploratory study like this cannot be representative of all or even most young men with physical impairments. It does, however, add to our understanding of disability and masculinity by teasing out some of the adaptations to, and lived complexities of, constructing a masculine identity in an ableist society. Whilst all three young men are redefining themselves through sport, each has developed different ways of responding to the challenges of living with the cultural contradictions between masculinity and disability. Carlos accentuates the hypermasculine aspects of wheelchair basketball to compensate for exclusion from able-bodied sport. Logan, despite the luxury of being able to pass as able-bodied, has constructed an identity and career through a disability-specific sport. Jake, whose masculinity-construction project was rudely interrupted in early adolescence and who is no longer able to construct a middle-class professional male identity due to the impact of his condition on his studies, is now also working his way towards becoming an elite disabled sportsman. Yet disability and illness have also profoundly shaped aspects of Jake's gender identity in ways inconsistent with dominant forms of masculinity; he is also developing more emotionally open and closer relationships with his mother and female peers. This is in contrast to the quad rugby players in the Lindemann and Cherney (2008) study, whose pre-disability masculine identities heavily influenced their "reliance" on dominant definitions of masculinity after becoming impaired. One reason for this difference may be age at onset of disability—Jake was 13, on the cusp of adolescence, a seminal developmental phase in terms of identity development. Whatever the reason/s, Jake has developed a "contradictory masculinity" much like that of the young men in the Wedgwood (2003) study, who also used sport to "pass" as reproducers of hegemonic masculinity whilst at the same time developing egalitarian relationships with females.

Certainly one could, somewhat arbitrarily, classify Carlos and Logan in Gerschick and Miller's terms as "reliant" and to categorise Jake as a "reformulator". Yet, doing so detracts from the in-depth insights provided by these case studies into the complex ways in which the masculinity/disability dilemma is lived and embodied. For instance, it does little justice to the complexity of Jake's new relationship with the hegemonic project—embracing some elements of it whilst rejecting others. Nor to Logan's case study, which provides empirical evidence of the importance of the body as a lived reality which cannot be completely suppressed, ignored or denied, even by passing as able-bodied.

Aside from occasional inclusion in informal games with able-bodied family members, friends or peers, disability-specific sports provided separatist experiences for the young men in this study. That is except for Logan who can pass as able-bodied and flit between the two. Moreover, as in studies of able-bodied adolescents, social inclusion and social status among peers was associated more with doing well in able-bodied sports. Thus, playing a disability-specific sport may not translate into cultural capital for young men like Carlos with moderate or severe physical impairments. It may well be that male social power constructed and conferred within a disability-specific sport has no currency in broader able-bodied society, thus is context-specific and may add little in terms of social status and inclusion in able-bodied society.

In summary, sport is a powerful normalising institution, with an impact far beyond those who play, yet it is neither a panacea for the social inclusion of young men with physical impairments, nor a masculinity factory. This is not to downplay the role of sport as an ableist and gendered institution but rather to stress that people bring to it an enormous array of factors which intersect to mediate its influence on their lives.

References

Buchbinder D (1994) *Masculinities and Identities*. Melbourne: Melbourne University Press.
Connell R (1983) Men's Bodies. In: Connell R (ed) *Which Way is Up? Essays on sex, class and culture*. Sydney: Allen & Unwin, pp. 17–32.
Gerschick TJ and Miller AS (1994) Gender Identities at the Crossroads of Masculinity and Physical Disability. *Masculinities* 2(1): 34–55.
Lindemann K and Cherney J (2008) Communicating in and through "Murderball": Masculinity and Disability in Wheelchair Rugby. *Western Journal of Communication* 72(2): 107–125.
Shuttleworth R, Wedgwood N & Wilson N (2012) The Dilemma of Disabled Masculinity. *Men and Masculinities* 15(2): 174–194.
Sparkes A and Smith B (2002) Sport, Spinal Cord Injury, Embodied Masculinities, and the Dilemmas of Narrative Identity. *Men and Masculinities* 4(3): 258–285.
Wedgwood N (2003) Aussie Rules! Schoolboy football and masculine embodiment. In: Tomsen S and Donaldson M (eds) *Male Trouble: Looking at Australian masculinities*. Melbourne: Pluto Press Australia, pp. 180–199.

21

RELIGION, CULTURE AND SPORT IN THE LIVES OF YOUNG MUSLIM WOMEN

International perspectives

Symeon Dagkas, Tansin Benn and Kelly Knez

Introduction

Muslim women have been markedly marginalised in international sport. For example, there are very low numbers of Muslim women competitors in major international sporting events, such as the Olympics. One explanation, proposed by Pfister (2010), is that the roots of modern sport are grounded within Western culture, and sport, in its current Western form, is not part of mainstream Islamic society (Pfister, 2010). Still, while there are vast differences in provision and practice for boys and men compared with those for girls and women in many countries of the world, this is particularly so in Islamic countries. This chapter therefore includes narratives of success and challenge in the physical activity experiences of Muslim girls and women in Islamic (predominantly Arabic) and Western (European) countries. It examines the participation of Muslim girls and women in sport and physical education in differing contexts: both in diaspora situations in the Western world and within Islamic countries. There is no intention to homogenize the experiences of Muslim women; instead, we hope to increase understanding of the diversity of cultural and religious influences that affect their participation in sport and physical education.

Islam, women and sport: a 'contested terrain'?

The interface of sport and faith cultures is an interesting area of study because the socio-cultural body is central to, and therefore contested in, both sport and Islam. The female sporting body is performative in culturally-specific ways. Recognised norms of sporting activities and dress codes are historically Western and increasingly globalized (Benn and Dagkas, 2012). But in a vastly different context, Islamic requirements are often embodied in the sense that values, attitudes, dress and behaviour are 'lived' in and through bodily practices. As such, denial of 'modest dress codes' or gender segregation post-puberty can be problematic for some Muslim girls and women (Benn, 2009). The centrality of the body within both sport and Islam acts as a potential site for tensions within and across physical activity locations including schools, provision in the community and at elite level.

In this chapter we examine the discourses (mainly in the Western world and also in the Middle East) of both situational and structural issues that can enable or prevent the inclusion of Muslim girls and women in sport. Situational issues relate to specific social, cultural and political contexts and structural issues relate to sport and physical education policies and regulatory decisions that can prevent the inclusion of some Muslim girls and women. Concerning the use of the term 'sport contexts', we refer to the engagement of women and girls in any form of physical activity, exercise or sport, as well as school-based physical education/sport.

Berger (1999) has used the term 'desecularisation' to emphasize that, in global terms, religion is flourishing. He argues that, with some exceptions (notably Europe), today's world 'is as furiously religious as it ever was, and in some places more so than ever' (cited in Scourfield et al., 2012: 92). Even though secularisation and its resultant decline in religiosity, especially in Christianity, has been documented in the Western world, no evidence of such decline has been seen in other religions and, significantly, the religions of ethnic minority groups globally. Bruce (1996) robustly promotes the secularisation thesis, but nonetheless acknowledges that when ethnic identity is threatened, for example, in the context of migration, religion can provide a resource for helping people to navigate a new and challenging situation and to maintain distinctive identities and places in the host society (Dagkas and Benn, 2006). Indeed, the increase of diasporic communities in the West and the rising politicization of Islam are pertinent issues across Islamic and non-Islamic countries. Globalization has also led to increased attention to the human rights agenda regarding equity and freedom in gender and religion and to discourses of inclusion in PE and sport. We therefore maintain that there is a need to recognise points of tension and different ways these have been resolved in selected recent studies in some Western and Islamic contexts.

Hargreaves (2007) argues that the Muslim female body is at the very heart of the theological struggles between Islamic fundamentalists and more moderate Islamic secular ideologies. Female body regulation in Islam has been centred on issues of body modesty and sexual propriety, largely vested in women's bodies. This has resulted in practices such as sex-segregation post-puberty and the adoption of dress codes that cover the body, arms and legs; as well as wearing of the hijab in public (used here to mean the headscarf to cover the hair – a contested symbol that is seen by some as an act of honour and empowerment and others as one of repression). These practices are regarded by some secular feminists as rigid and restricting, and, in contrast, as essential to 'embodied faith' by Islamic feminists (Benn et al., 2011; Benn and Dagkas, 2012; Pfister, 2011). In many ways, such practices are the antitheses of the Western sporting model, where dress codes allow or even demand minimal cover (as in beach volleyball and athletics) and where sports events are mixed-sex, held in public arenas and reported in the press, often bringing global visibility to elite sport events and participants. Even in recreational sports and school-based physical education, in most Western countries facilities are used for mixed-sex participation and are often open to public viewing. For some Muslim girls and women these realities mean that their families do not allow them to participate, or they make personal choices to abstain because the environments are not conducive to their religious requirements for privacy and body modesty.

There have been many examples of tensions between Islamic imperatives and Western sporting practices and requirements regarding the extent of coverage of women's bodies. For example, the Iranian women's team was banned by the Fédération Internationale de Football Association (FIFA) from the Youth Olympics in 2011 because they wore the hijab. Some feminists see this as a contradiction to discourses of inclusion and anti-discrimination; others regard religious symbols (such as the hijab) as anathema to secular sport. After much global lobbying, FIFA has negotiated a way to allow the wearing of the hijab provided it meets safety requirements. While recognising this concession is positive for the majority of Muslim women globally who, for faith reasons, may choose to wear the hijab while participating in football, we also acknowledge that political Islam, as evident in Iran, can coerce women to wear the hijab. There are no easy solutions to seeking compromise.

The issue of modesty and body cover is 'integral in the construction of a diasporic global Muslim society' (Hargreaves, 2007: 76). The tensions at the interface of religious and cultural values are exacerbated in the diaspora where the dynamic nature of cultures ensures multiple influences in shaping 'cultures of hybridity' (Dagkas and Benn, 2006). These fluid contexts influence processes of socialization and physical activity discourses, and shape dispositions towards bodies. These factors affect Muslim girls' and women's participation in sport contexts in complex and diverse ways. In Islamic and Muslim-majority countries there is also diversity in social, cultural, political and economic situations. While there is nothing within Islam that prevents women's participation in physical activity, lived experiences in the following selected examples reveal how individuals negotiate their situation with regard to sport-related participation and faith.

Sporting contexts in Islamic countries

In Islamic countries, the code of living is expressed through Islamic laws laid down in the Shari'ah. These codes imbue Islamic culture, giving meaning to the way in which Muslims make sense of their lives, behave, dress, eat and drink (Dagkas and Benn, 2012). In this chapter, we include Muslim majority states where Islamic law is used solely (for example Saudi Arabia, Iran and Sudan) or in combination with civil or common law (for example Qatar and Jordan) for the political governance of a country. The majority of these countries are located within what is known as the 'Arab world'. Islamic countries are also extended geographically to include countries such as Pakistan, Malaysia and Indonesia. In spring 2011 the civilian uprising and political tensions resulting from the Arab spring (an uprising amongst dissidents in Arab countries in pursuit of greater democracy) happened against a variegated backdrop of rapid economic and social development within the region. Examples from previous studies and literature discussed below illustrate the heterogeneity in Muslim women's sporting life chances in some of these countries.

Accounts and descriptions of the sport participation of Muslim girls and women are important, but what is often absent is attention to how different cultural and religious norms impact on them to produce multiple and sometimes contradictory embodied dispositions. By this we mean individual values and attitudes towards bodily and physical behaviours at the interface of culture, religion, gender and sport. In her well known article, 'The status of Muslim women in sport: Conflict between cultural traditions and modernization', Sfeir (1985) provided one of the first detailed descriptive accounts of Muslim women's participation in sport with considerations made to the socio-cultural context of Islam. The research was based on analysis of information collected from various documents and reports that covered an extended period from 1960s to 1980s. With the research underpinning her article spanning 29 different predominantly Islamic countries (such as Afghanistan, Egypt, Iran, Iraq, Jordan, Oman, Saudi Arabia, Qatar and Syria), it provides a descriptive account of the opportunities that were available for Muslim women living in Islamic countries to participate in sport and physical education prior to and during the 1980s. Despite relatively low participation rates at the Olympic Games, Sfeir points to formalised physical education classes across all 29 countries for girls (albeit this was taken up in different ways), and strong participation of women at regional competitions such as the African, Arab, Asian and Mediterranean Games.

There are, however, vast differences between women's sport-related opportunities in neighbouring countries. For example, the denial of physical activity for girls and women in Saudi Arabia is contrasted in neighbouring Bahrain. In Bahrain, sporting opportunities are strong with women athletes competing in global sporting events such as Ruqaya Al Ghasara, the hijab-wearing athlete who competed in the Beijing Olympics in 2008 (Al-Ansari, 2011). She chose to wear the hijab and claims that there had never been any problems for her wearing the hijab and competing. A problem, however, would arise if she were required by sporting officials to remove her hijab, as has been the case with some sports. Contrary to Ruqaya's experience, 'Zeynap', an elite athlete from Turkey, was forced to remove her hijab by laws in her secular but Muslim-majority country. Accordingly, her identity as a Muslim and career as an athlete were in conflict. When an aspiring Olympian, she chose to participate in sport, but under coercion, did so without wearing the hijab. However, she found a way to negotiate a compromise for herself by wearing a 'bandana', even though she regretted having to deny her faith (Koca and Hacisoftaoglu, 2011). Further highlighting the differences of lived experiences among Muslim athletes, El Faquir (2011) writes about the freedoms she experienced as a pioneer Moroccan athlete in the 1970s and reports on the narratives of recent elite Moroccan women athletes who tell of their internalised faith, ways in which this helps them as athletes, the family support they receive and the irrelevance of any dress code issues between sport and faith in their lives. Certainly the constant processes of change in these countries will continue to impact on the opportunities for women to take part in sport, but the women's narratives shared here illustrate the significance of the specific political, cultural and religious situations in shaping the ways in which women and girls make meaning of, and participate in, sporting contexts.

Marshall and Hardman (2000) indicated that the Middle East enjoyed a relatively 'high legal status' of physical education in schools in the 1980s (Sfeir, 1985). However, the legal and political rhetoric can also be far away from the realities in those Islamic countries caught between tradition and modernity, such as the Arabian Gulf countries of the Gulf Co-operative Countries (GCC) comprised of Oman, United Arabic Emirates, Saudi Arabia, Qatar, Bahrain and Kuwait. Examples of mismatch between rhetoric and reality regarding the inclusion of girls arose in research on Qatar in which Al-Mohannadi and Capel (2007) drew attention to the gender disparity in physical education provision, with boys receiving two lessons a week and girls only one. Al-Sinani and Benn (2011) highlighted that although Omani girls were entitled to a physical education curriculum, a lack of qualified teachers combined with the marginalisation of physical education within the larger curriculum, presented difficult challenges. Progress in sport for Muslim women is slow, which is not surprising since modern sport is a symbol of secularism and modernity and therefore a potential 'risk' to societies managing multi-levelled modernisation processes whilst trying to retain their Islamic and distinctive cultural heritage. Away from the GCC region, Hoe (2008) demonstrated a similar pattern within Malaysia, where physical education was mandated for both girls and boys, but a lack of qualified teachers and the perceived 'non-academic' status of the subject continued to marginalise the opportunities for many girls and some boys to participate in sporting contexts.

For some Muslim sportswomen manifestations of Islam, such as the wearing of the hijab and sex-segregated sporting environments are essential. If this is the case, adherence to these bodily practices positions them as active agents in shaping and reshaping their identities. 'Gender enactment', or the 'doing' of gender behaviours (Azzarito, 2012), may be paralleled with 'religious enactment', essential to Muslimness for some women. However, freedom to enact gender, ethnicity or faith depends on their political beliefs – some women are active agents, some experience 'relative freedoms', but others feel coerced into a way of life that gives them few choices about the sports they can play or the conditions under which they take part, or whether or not they take part in any physical activity at all. It is interesting that women are often seen alongside men in media coverage of the current 'Arab Spring' struggle for greater democracy. With such instability, inevitably sport will not be a priority and may, as in Iraq, regress before it regains momentum.

Negotiating sporting discourses in the Western world

This section provides insight into Muslim girls' and women's experiences of sport-related activities through research conducted in Western European countries: the UK, Germany and Denmark. The dominant discourse in the contexts explored is one of inclusion whereby policy-makers and practitioners are politically driven to seek ways to be inclusive of different groups and to meet individual needs, although processes of achieving these aims are different. Azzarito (2012) suggests that stereotypical views of Muslim girls as 'passive' or 'subordinated' by family and home can significantly influence the ways in which many of these girls are (mis)represented in sport. In the West, Muslim girls have been repeatedly reported and problematised as inactive and conforming to rigid gender stereotypes in ways that influence their participation in school sport and physical activity (Dagkas and Benn, 2006; Walseth, 2006). Furthering the idea of enactment within particular situations, such views are challenged by providing insights into diverse realities (Knez, Macdonald and Abbott, 2012). Issues of hijab and sex segregation, identified earlier, can be challenging for providers in secular societies with minority Muslim populations. Histories and traditions have resulted in sporting provision that is structured and organised in line with predominantly Eurocentric perspectives. In these contexts mixed-sex provision and Western sporting dress codes that typically provide sparse body covering are normalised (Macdonald et al, 2009).

In the Birmingham Advisory Support Service (BASS) project (UK) (Dagkas et al., 2011), empirical research was used to clarify issues and potential solutions regarding increased parental withdrawal of Muslim girls from physical education and school sport. Parents did this based on the grounds that religious preferences for dress codes (that did not cover enough of the female body to be acceptable to their faith), together with sex-segregated lessons, were not being met. Head teachers, physical education teachers, Muslim girls and their parents provided indicators of concerns regarding the inclusion of Muslim girls in physical education and school sport. The study provided insight into the characteristics of schools that were struggling to accommodate the needs of Muslim girls. These were schools which were serving diverse local communities; met high levels of religiosity and family desire for stricter codes of body modesty; were under-resourced; used local community sport facilities where staff were unwilling or unable to meet all-female environment requests; and had head teachers and physical education teachers unsure of the boundaries of Islamic cultural practices (Dagkas et al., 2011; Walseth and Fasting, 2004). Evidence showed that the schools most successful in facilitating the inclusion of Muslim girls in sporting contexts were characterized by the following factors: stability in the local community; good communication between schools and community; regular opportunities for school/home/community meetings; links with local sports partners able to provide all-female spaces; and knowledgeable teachers who were confident of Islamic requirements and what changes had been necessary to enable Muslim girls to participate.

Problems of non-participation in the BASS study, or withdrawal of Muslim girls from sport settings, were rooted in the learning environments provided. In many cases, the nature of spaces, policies and practices inside which learning took place were creating barriers for some Muslim girls. Gaps in knowledge and understanding were raised in connection with teacher training and continuing professional development, which often failed to equip teachers with sufficient confidence in their knowledge of diversity issues (Benn and Dagkas, 2006; Flintoff et al., 2008). Furthermore, the lack of Muslim women role models for pupils who were sporting stars or physical education teachers was also raised as a significant 'gap' (Dagkas et al., 2011) in providing strong messages and motivation to young Muslim children (Benn and Ahmad, 2006).

It is important to recognise the political context of the UK study where the 'multicultural-ism' discourse had moved beyond assimilation rhetoric to rhetoric of valuing cultural diversity, appreciating and making space for difference. The compulsory national curriculum for physical education placed pressure on head teachers to seek solutions where impasse situations arose. In Denmark, another culturally-diverse European country with many migrant workers and refugees now settled into communities, political emphasis is on assimilation. In contrast with the UK situation where single-sex and mixed-sex schooling co-exists, Denmark has only co-education, so meeting gender-segregation requirements for those Muslim families requesting such provision is more problematic.

Contextual insights into the situation of Denmark, which has large migrant populations, and the political and structural management of cultural diversity in relation to physical education and sport, can be found in Pfister's (2010) article. With-Nielsen and Pfister (2011) explored diversity issues in a case study of 16–17 year olds in school sport in one Danish school with. Findings indicated that their peers perceived the Muslim girls as poor in sport and lazy. In contrast, in an in-depth interview, 'Iram' (one of the participants in their study who was a hijab-wearing Muslim girl) revealed ways in which she was managing her identity differently in and out of school, because of her religious identity and cultural needs. The co-educational physical education/sport lessons meant she chose to wear the hijab to meet the requirements of her religion for body modesty. She actively withdrew from physical challenges with the boys choosing to perpetuate ways in which she saw Muslim girls as 'different' from Danish girls, remaining quiet and calm. Outside of school she was a high-level sports person, attending all-female clubs (for any woman wanting to attend) in Thai boxing and swimming. In this context she was able to remove the hijab and engage freely in her love of sport. Irma was enacting gender and Muslimness differently depending on the organizational context of specific sporting environments, motivated by wanting to adhere to the cultural requirements of her faith.

Kleindienst-Cachay (2011) provided deep insights into the German context of cultural diversity, especially the increasing number of Muslim Turkish migrant workers arriving over recent decades. Sporting activities that were popular in Turkey, such as taekwondo and karate, attracted many from this group while working in Germany. While intergenerational transmission of values continued, new opportunities also arose. One initiative was 'Integration through Sport' that led to sports clubs targeting those from different ethnic groups. While only 5% of the Muslim female population in Germany participates in sport compared with over 22% of German women, there are examples of increasing engagement by young Muslim women. Research (Benn et al., 2011; Benn and Dagkas, 2012) is providing insights into the challenges and successes of managing bi-cultural identities. The emergence of Muslim women in elite sport, and others in German sports clubs who chose to continue in sport, were also high achievers in education. These women reportedly felt empowered through sport, and enjoyed the wider social network the clubs provided. At the same time, they maintained their faith-based practices and negotiated ways of managing a family and a sporting identity.

The above studies indicate there can be issues and solutions for Muslim girls and women's engagement in physical activity from school level to elite sport. The complex intersection of diversity, ethnicity, culture, religiosity, socio-economic status, gender relations and patriarchy is acknowledged as contributing to challenges for all women in sport, depending on specific situations, relative freedoms and personal paths. Some examples have been shared in this chapter to illustrate differences, successes and challenges.

Conclusion

Any researcher engaged in trying to deepen understanding of Muslim women's experiences of sport-related activities and contexts needs to take into account cultural diversity, and the manner in which this intersects with the various ways in which individuals embody their faith and nego-tiate the faith/sport interface. Religion is not as pivotal in Western societies as it once was, but for some people, particularly those in diaspora groups, and for many in Islamic countries, faith forms the centrality of everyday life, values, beliefs, behaviours and bodily practices. Since gen-der equity and religious freedom are fundamental human rights, the position of those Muslim girls and women currently excluded from participation in physical activity should be addressed, both for health reasons and for the life-enhancement and well-being physical activity can bring. Sport and education policy-makers, teachers and coaches have a professional responsibility to meet the needs of all young people without discrimination.

Muslim women and girls live in different political, linguistic, economic and socio-cultural contexts, both in Islamic and Western countries. In many cases, as we have demonstrated in this chapter, the interface of sports practice and cultural interpretations of religion can create challenges for some Muslim girls and women as well as for sports policy-makers, coaches and teachers. We have shared examples of successful Muslim women's engagement in sport because many texts focus only on the negative aspects of this topic.

We have acknowledged that macro political and institutional forces can remove personal freedoms but, as we have shown at the micro level, exchanges between human beings and respect for personal choices and actions can lead to positive life changes. Improving participa-tion in sport-related activities for Muslim girls and women depends on increasing understand-ing amongst policy-makers and practitioners about the power of faith in the lives of some people, as well as the problems posed by political Islam. We set out to forefront diversity and illustrate that knowledge of the situation in which people live is crucial to understanding their realities.

References

Al-Ansari M (2011) Women in sport leadership in Bahrain. In: Benn T, Pfister G and Jawad H (eds) *Muslim women and sport*. London: Routledge, pp.79–91.

Al-Mohannadi A and Capel S (2007) Stress in physical education teachers in Qatar. *Social Psychology of Education* 10(1): 55–75.

Al-Sinani Y and Benn T (2011) The Sultanate of Oman and the position of girls and women in physical education and sport. In: Benn T, Pfister G and Jawad H (eds) *Muslim women and sport*. London: Rout-ledge, pp. 125–137.

Azzarito L (2012) 'I've lost my football . . .': Rethinking gender, the hidden curriculum, and sport in the global context. In: Dagkas S and Armour K (eds) *Inclusion and exclusion through youth sport*. London: Routledge

Benn T (2009) Muslim women in sport: A researcher's journey to understanding 'embodied faith'. *Bulletin 55, International Council for Sports Science and Physical Education (ICSSPE)*, pp 48–56. Available at: www.icsspe.org (accessed 28 January 2009).

Benn T and Ahmad A (2006) Alternative visions: International sporting opportunities for Muslim women and implications for British youth sport. *Youth and Policy* 92: 119–132.

Benn T and Dagkas S (2012) Olympics, the Olympic Games and Islamic culture. *International Journal of Sport Policy Special Issue: Sport Policy and the Olympic Games*.

Benn T, Dagkas S and Jawad H (2011) Embodied faith: Islam, religious freedom and educational practices in physical education. *Sport, Education and Society* 16(1): 17–34.

Benn T, Pfister G and Jawad H (2011) *Muslim women and sport*. London: Routledge.

Berger P (1999) *The desecularization of the world: Resurgent religion and world politics*. Washington, DC: Ethics and Public Policy Center; Grand Rapids: WB: Eerdmans Publishing Co.

Bruce S (1996) *Religion in the modern world: From cathedrals to cults*. New York: Oxford University Press.

Dagkas S and Benn T (2006) Young Muslim women's experiences of Islam and physical education in Greece and Britain: A comparative study. *Sport, Education and Society* 11(1): 21–38.

Dagkas S and Benn T (2012) The embodiment of religious culture and exclusionary practices in youth sport. In: Dagkas S and Armour K (eds) *Inclusion and exclusion through youth sport*. London: Routledge

El Faquir F (2011) Women and sport in North Africa: Voices of Moroccan athletes. In: Benn T, Pfister G and Jawad H (eds) *Muslim women and sport*. London: Routledge, pp. 236–248.

Flintoff A, Fitzgerald H and Scraton S (2008) The challenges of intersectionality: Researching difference in physical education. *International Studies in Sociology of Education* 18(2): 73–85.

Hargreaves J (2007) Sport, exercise and the female Muslim body: Negotiating Islam, politics, and male power. In: Hargreaves J and Vertinsky P (eds) *Physical culture, power, and the body*. London: Routledge, pp.74–100.

Henry I (2007) *Transnational and comparative research in sport: Globalisation, governance and sport policy*. London: Routledge.

Hoe WE (2008) *Innovative practices in physical education and sports in Asia*. UNESCO: Bangkok.

Knez K, Macdonald D and Abbott R (2012) Challenging stereotypes: Muslim girls talk about physical activity, physical education and sport. *Journal of Health, Sport and Physical Education* 3(2): 109–122.

Koca C and Hacisoftaoglu I (2011) Struggling for empowerment: Sport participation of women and girls in Turkey. In: Benn T, Pfister G and Jawad H (eds) *Muslim women and sport*. London: Routledge, pp. 154–166.

Macdonald D, Abbott R, Knez K and Nelson A (2009) Talking exercise: Cultural diversity and physically active lifestyles. *Sport, Education and Society* 14(1): 1–19.

Marshall J and Hardman K (2000) The state and status of physical education in schools in international context. *European Physical Education Review* 6(3): 203–229.

Pfister G (2010) Women and Sport in Islamic countries, *Forum for Idræt*.

Pfister G (2011) Muslim women and sport in diasporas: Theories, discourses and practices – analysing the case of Denmark, In: Benn T, Pfister G and Jawad H (eds) *Muslim women and sport*. London: Routledge, pp. 41–76.

Scourfield J, Taylor C, Moore G and Gilliat-Ray S (2012) The intergenerational transmission of Islam in England and Wales: Evidence from the citizenship surveys. *Sociology* 46(1): 91–108.

Sfeir L (1985) The status of Muslim women in sport: Conflict between cultural tradition and modernization. *International Review for Sociology of Sport* 20(4): 283–305.

Walseth K (2006) Young Muslim women and sport: The impact of identity work. *Leisure Studies* 25(1): 75–94.

Walseth K and Fasting K (2004) Sport as a means of integrating minority women. *Sport in Society* 7: 109–129.

With-Nielsen N and Pfister G (2011) Gender constructions and negotiations in physical education: Case studies. *Sport, Education and Society* 16(5): 645–664.

PART IV

Gender conformity and its challenges

22

INTERROGATING THE BODY IN CONTEMPORARY CHEERLEADING

Pamela Bettis and Natalie G. Adams

Introduction

In 2006 university cheerleader, Kristi Yamaoka, fell backward 15 feet onto her head from atop a human pyramid, suffering a concussion and chipped vertebra. Although laid out on a stretcher with her neck immobilized in a brace, Kristi continued to perform the fight song in a video that circulated throughout the web. Praised for her "loyalty and toughness", on NBC's *Today Show*, Kristi explained, "I'm still a cheerleader – on a stretcher or not. So as soon as I heard that fight song, I knew my job and just started to do my thing." Her biggest concern was that her accident might distract her squad and the basketball team.

Kristi's dramatic fall and concern for her team highlight the nebulous space cheerleading occupies in debates about its legitimacy as a sport. What is its primary purpose? What athletic skills are required to participate? How are team members selected? What danger does it pose to its participants? How does it compare to "real" sports? While these questions have been widely addressed in the courts, the Office of Civil Rights (OCR), the Women's Sports Foundation, and cheerleading organizations, we argue that these questions need to be augmented by a more fundamental question. What do the prevailing discourses about cheerleading say about the types of normalizing practices that continue to regulate and discipline the female body in the supposed age of "Girl Power"?

We situate our work with the few critical scholars who have taken cheerleading as a topic worthy of serious study (Anderson, 2005, 2008; Grindstaff and West, 2006, 2010). One reason for its absence is that cheerleading is typically viewed as a corporeal symbol of heterosexualized femininity and is not considered "real sport". However, as several researchers have noted (Adams and Bettis, 2003; Buzuvis, 2011; Harvard Law Review, 1997) cheerleading should not be dismissed in sports scholarship since discussions about its legitimacy as a sport are part of the current debates about Title IX[1] and gender equity in sports. The National Collegiate Athletic Association has been asked to recognise competitive cheerleading as an emerging sport, and the question of its legitimacy as a sport has even found its way to a U.S. District Court (Thomas, 2011).

Our intellectual analysis of cheerleading draws from the work of feminist poststructuralists (Azzarito, 2010; Bartky, 1990; Butler, 2009; Pringle and Markula, 2005) who use the body as a site to examine how power and status are created in everyday social practices. We contend that a critical examination of cheerleading – a social practice involving four million young people in the U.S. (primarily girls and women but also an increasing number of boys and men) – offers insight into the construction and regulation of bodies in sports and the creation of "bodies of differences" that sustain unequal power relations in society.

In this chapter we interrogate two prevailing discourses framing debates about contemporary cheerleading. We pay particular attention to what these discourses reveal about the normalizing practices that regulate and discipline the female body in the age of "Girl Power". Following Butler (2009) in her task "to examine in what ways gender is constructed through specific corporeal acts, and what possibilities exist for the cultural transformation of gender through such acts" (p. 416), we conclude by introducing a missing discourse that acknowledges the raced and classed practices of cheerleading.

"If cheerleading got any easier, it would be called football": cheerleading as sport discourse

While cheerleading has changed dramatically since the 1970s, particularly with the meteoric growth of competitive cheerleading in which squads compete against each other with precise and physically demanding routines, it is typically considered "something other than a sport". The U.S. Department of Education classifies cheerleading as an "extra-curricular activity". The official position of the Office of Civil Rights, the Women's Sports Foundation, the National Collegiate Athletic Association, Varsity Spirit (the leading cheerleading organization) and, recently, a federal court is that cheerleading is *not* a sport under Title IX guidelines (Thomas, 2011). "Athletic activity" is the classification proposed by the American Association of Cheerleading Coaches and Administrators (n.d.) – the primary organization in the United States for promoting cheerleading safety. They assert that cheerleading requires its participants to perform physically demanding feats that "challenge the limits of the body". The "body" being referenced here has no signifier. However, as feminist researchers (Bartky, 1990; Butler, 2009) remind us, bodies are never "just bodies". They are gendered, raced, classed, and sexualized so that they are culturally scripted with particular meanings in particular social contexts. The debate about whether or not cheerleading is a sport is embroiled in normative assumptions about the female body, although rarely is the gendered argument articulated publicly. Should the cheerleading body be a docile body, relegated to the sidelines in a position of service to "real" athletes or should the cheerleading body be recognised as a physically strong instrument able to withstand pain, injury, and abuse in the pursuit of sporting glory?

Sports have long served as the primary institution for adult men to initiate boys into a certain way of thinking about their bodies (Anderson, 2008; Bryson, 1987; Colburn, 1985; Messner and Sabo, 1994). As part of the sport ethic, male athletes accept pain and injury as a normal part of participation (Pringle and Markula, 2005; Young, White, and McTeer, 1994). To gain credibility, some female athletes assume signifiers of masculinity, including the adoption of pain as a way to prove one is a real athlete (Adams, Schmitke, and Franklin, 2005; Malcolm, 2006; Theberge, 1997; Young and White, 1995). Cheerleaders are no different from other female athletes in that they are constantly measured against the standards of male sport in order to gain legitimacy. However, unlike most other sports that girls play, no masculine counterpart to cheerleading exists. Thus, cheerleading-as-sport advocates work diligently to demonstrate how their sport rivals both male and female sports in terms of pain, injury, and danger. Eric Pearson, Chairman of the American Sports Council, mobilized a discourse of pain and injury to protest the federal court ruling in 2010 that competitive cheerleading could not count as an intercollegiate sport under Title IX. He wrote:

> More female athletes suffer catastrophic injuries from competitive cheer than from any other women's sport. Competitive cheer is one of the nation's fastest growing sports for women, and in the interest of the safety of the athletes there is no logical reason not to allow schools to recognize it as a varsity sport.
>
> *(Saving Sports, 2010)*

Pearson drew from data compiled by the National Center for Catastrophic Sport Injury Research, which defines catastrophic injuries as those sport injuries which result in a brain or spinal cord injury or skull or spinal fracture. Such statistics are routinely cited in discussions about why cheerleading should be a sport, and are attributed to the changes in cheerleading over the last twenty-five years which have made it a more athletic endeavour (Mueller and Cantu, n.d.).

The title of this chapter – "Pain is temporary. Pride is forever" – is displayed on just one of hundreds of t-shirts worn by cheerleaders espousing the physical, and often painful, facet of cheerleading. In our own observations of the preparation leading up to the tryouts for a middle-school squad in a small city in the Midwest, we routinely observed girls practising with sprained ankles, broken bones and torn ligaments. During the cheer preparation class offered at their school to help girls prepare for the upcoming tryouts, one girl suffered a torn ligament that sent her to the emergency room, and another was on crutches for two weeks because of a severe ankle sprain. Neither saw their injuries as a deterrent to their trying out for the squad. As athletes encultured into the dominant model of men's sport, they knew that disciplining one's body to endure pain was expected and rewarded. A third girl explained:

> On the day of tryouts, I had 104 degrees fever; I had pneumonia. I had been sick for days and lost six pounds before tryouts. At tryouts, I fell on my head during my back handspring. It was like my wrists just collapsed. But I scored number one. I couldn't even come to school the next day because I was so sick. My dad said he was proud of me because I showed determination.

Cheerleaders, rankled by the notion that what they do is not considered a sport, typically compare themselves to male athletes, particularly football players, as a way to prove their sport-worthiness. Cheerleading t-shirts abound with such sayings as: "If cheerleading got any easier, it would be called football" and "In any other sport, if you miss the catch, all you lose is the ball".

Using pain and injuries to garner respect and acknowledgement as a sport is meant to challenge normative assumptions about the cheerleader body since it is so closely associated with heterosexualized femininity. Indeed most media accounts of cheerleading injuries typically begin their story with references to pompoms, short skirts, and big smiles. "For decades, they stood by safe and smiling, a fixture on America's sporting sidelines. But today's young cheerleaders, who perform tricks once reserved for trapeze artists, may be in more peril than any female athletes in the country," begins a 2007 *New York Times* article about the dangers of cheerleading (Pennington, 2007). The situating of the cheerleader body as strong, athletic, confident, and risk-defying offers an empowering image of girls that seems to personify a new form of femininity that will help them achieve success in a post-industrial, global economy (Azzarito, 2010; Kindlon, 2006).

However, unlike other sports in which girls participate, girls who cheer have seen their "sport" dramatically curtailed precisely because of too close an identification with masculinity. In a counter move to dissociate cheerleading from any semblance of sport, detractors have used statistics about injury and risky behaviour to return cheerleading to a clearly-defined feminine activity whose primary purpose is to serve the athletes for whom they are cheering. This move is a poignant reminder of how the "body" in the cheerleading discourse is quite resoundingly a gendered body inscribed with a host of cultural assumptions about femininity. Following a spate of serious cheerleading injuries and public discussions of how dangerous cheerleading has become, many state high school athletic associations, school districts, and colleges and universities have responded by greatly restricting the kinds of tumbling, stunting, and pyramid building cheerleaders can do. For example, the University of Nebraska (UN) at one point "ground bound" the cheerleading squad after one of their cheerleaders was seriously injured. This meant that the UN squad could not perform any stunts in which both hands and feet left the ground.

While one could certainly question why cheerleading has adopted the male model of sport with its acceptance of pain and injury as the price one pays to play the game, policies restricting how cheerleaders can use their bodies can be read as reinforcing a hierarchy of gendered power in which female bodies need more protecting than male bodies. Given the number of injuries and deaths incurred by practising football in extremely hot temperatures (Raven, 2012), why are football players permitted to practice during the summer? "Groundbounding" is a poignant example of how "docile" female bodies are created through regulatory policies aimed at constructing normative gendered bodies. These polices also remind us of how bodies can be disciplined and punished (Foucault, 1977) for being transgressive. When the cheerleading body interlopes too freely and closely into the masculine sphere of sports, power, and dominance, it can be quickly curtailed and brought back into its proper place, that of ideal sexualized femininity.

Cheerleaders gone wild: the cheerleader as erotic icon

Interspersed between debates on whether cheerleading should be considered a sport is a very different discourse: the erotic and sexually promiscuous cheerleader (Kurman, 1986). For all of the promotion of cheerleading as a skilled, athletic, and physically dangerous endeavour, its association with feminine sexuality continues to undermine cheerleaders' quest for sport recognition. Although the hypersexualization of cheerleaders began in the 1970s with the popularity of the Dallas Cowboys Cheerleaders (Hanson, 1995), it has expanded to include more than just revealing uniforms and sexy dance moves. The fact that *Debbie Does Dallas* was and is still one of the best selling pornographic movies along with the more recent award-winning *Cheerleaders* highlights the eroticism that cheerleading symbolically conveys.

Certainly, women volleyball and basketball players engage in "inappropriate behaviours", but their behaviours do not necessarily reflect on their sports. Because cheerleading's history is steeped in idealized, heterosexualized femininity, any behaviours that transgress that status not only malign the individual girls but also the activity itself, particularly when the transgressions occur in uniform. Thus, cheerleading cannot be understood as only an athletic activity; it is also one of the most visible and well-known symbols of girlhood/young womanhood in the United States (Adams and Bettis, 2003), and the uniform is central to that identity, as seen in the movie, *American Beauty*.

In the following discussion, we use the cheerleading uniform as a primary text with which to examine practices of femininity, expectations for athleticism and the ideal body, and girls' own understandings of themselves as sexual beings. We expand the concept of the uniform to include the cheerleading body and smile which are also an integral part of what it means to be a cheer-leader. Just as the common sense belief that pain and injury rates legitimize cheerleading, so too do assumptions about cheerleaders' sexual desirability contribute to its denigration. Upon being asked whether cheerleading should become a sport on a nationally syndicated radio programme, one response was, "Cheerleading can't be a sport because the scoring takes place after the game is over" (Adams and Bettis, 2003, p. 60). Making it with a cheerleader has become a mainstay of American male fantasy, and central to this fantasy is the cheerleading uniform.

The pleasure and discipline of cheerleading uniform

School athletes throughout the U.S. "dress up" on game days and then switch to their uniforms for the actual athletic event. Cheerleaders, however, wear their uniforms during the day and during the games for every school sport, which means that they wear them a lot, as seen in the popular U.S. television series, *Glee*. There is no other athletic activity in which the uniform plays such an iconic and controversial role. Often cheerleading uniforms worn during the school day do not adhere to the school dress codes for girls' due to their skirt lengths and the size and shape of the short tops (Bettis and Adams, 2006). All those worries disappear, however, during game nights when cheerleaders across the United States don their uniforms, smiles, and make-up to motivate the fans. A brief historical peek at cheerleading uniforms reveals their enduring importance.

Early yell leaders, as they were called, did not wear uniforms since the activity was not organized enough to have them (Hanson, 1995), but that changed after university administrators began to supervise school athletics. In a 1924 *New York Times* editorial the cheerleaders, who were mostly male at the time, were described as "lithe, white-sweatered and flannel-trousered youths in front of the bleachers" (cited in Hanson, 1995, p. 2). Thirty years later, Gonzales (1956) describes coed cheerleaders who were beginning to dominate squads as: "Pretty young things in vestigial skirts, (and) amply-filled sweaters" (p. 104). Long skirts, pleated or full, and sweaters were the mainstay of female cheerleader attire for many years. The skirts shortened as a result of changes in women's fashion beginning in the 1960s, but it was the Dallas Cowboys Cheerleaders, professional cheerleaders who cheered for a Texas professional football team, who contributed to major changes in cheerleading uniforms. The "amply filled" part of Gonzales' description remained, but the squad added short shorts, boots, and cleavage-revealing shirts which disrupted the chaste and good-girl image that had been associated with cheerleading since the activity was feminized in the late 1940s and 1950s. University and high school cheerleading squads began to change their attire as well but also as a response to the changing nature of the activity.

In the past, girls' cheerleading did not require athleticism; physical coordination and good looks were the major criteria, and even these were not absolute since many student bodies elected their squads. That changed in the 1970s when cheerleading companies and advocates aligned cheerleading with the societal emphasis on fitness and the development of women's sports. Cheerleading camps and gyms promoted routines that incorporated back handsprings, human pyramids, and gymnastic stunts. This focus on physically demanding moves required that girls wear different kinds of uniforms that would accommodate the new physicality of the activity. Cheerleading uniforms made of stretchy materials and designed to be smaller to allow for physically demanding routines became the new cheerleading look.

The ubiquitous cheerleading skirt remains short and continues to be the staple of cheerlead-ing attire. The short skirt, coupled with a sometimes midriff revealing top, emphasizes the femi-ninity of the activity. Generally, cheerleaders embrace the short cheerleading skirt as part of the allure of the activity. Along with make-up and the ever-present cheerleader smile (Grindstaff and West, 2010), the skirt allows girls and young women to be the sexy athlete, one who is fearless, physically fit and yet sexually appealing. Although national cheerleading organizations have attempted to reign in the shrinking uniform and some high school cheerleaders themselves have refused to wear what they considered inappropriate uniforms, such as a few of the Central High School squad in New Jersey (Pegues, 2010), the short skirts and tiny tops remain.

The struggle over the meaning and appropriateness of the cheerleading uniform itself is not just relegated to styles or lack of bodily coverage. The uniform itself holds such iconic status that engaging in inappropriate behaviour while wearing it turns those girls and women into villains. In a case that swept major news organizations, five Texas high school cheerleaders, known as the Fab Five, posted photos of themselves in uniform at a Condoms to Go shop while holding a large penis candle. The following exchange in a made-for-television movie between the leader of the Fab Five and her coach highlights the traditional meaning of the cheerleading uniform.

Coach: Why are you a cheerleader?

Brook: Because I'm good. I am a cheerleader for me. That's what people notice. Me.

Coach: A cheerleader is being a certain kind of person, a person who cares about her squad, her fellow students, her school. Look at your uniform. Your name or number are not on the back. The uniform is not about you, Brook.

Contrary to Brook's coach, our research findings suggest that it is the allure of the uniform, specifically the skirt, which entices young girls to cheerleading. One middle-school girl claimed, "Girls want to be cheerleaders because they believe that guys will like them more – they will see them as cute women in short skirts." This comment captures one facet of the continuing popularity of cheerleading for younger girls – it offers a way for them to perform adult heterosexualized femininity in a socially-sanctioned space. Far from distancing themselves from the sexualized nature of cheerleading, the middle and high school girls from our research embraced that sexuality, and the short skirt was central to it. A cheerleader who made the squad commented, "I'm in it for the short skirts, the guys, getting in front of everybody and making a total fool of myself."

The baggy jerseys and shorts sported by basketball and soccer players are not typically considered sexy by those who wear them or watch them and can't be found in pin-up calendars, popular movies, or pornographic web sites. Images of cheerleaders, however, can be easily located in all of these venues, but it is not only because of the cheerleading uniform; what also counts is the ideal body and cheerleading smile.

The cheerleader smile is not natural nor is it a spontaneous emotional response to the dynamics of the game being cheered for; rather the ability to plaster a smile on one's face at a moment's notice and under physically-challenging circumstances also requires a form of discipline, one that is easily overlooked. In contrast to cheerleaders, there are no public expectations for athletes to smile. However, the smile is a required part of the cheerleading "uniform" for girls and women.

Much of the early training that cheerleaders receive focuses on the smile. A middle-school coach certainly understood the importance of the "smile" and even provided advice on how to emphasize it when trying out for the squad, "Put Vaseline on your teeth." Twelve- and thirteen-year-old girls who were trying out for the squad understood its importance as well: "You've got to have fake smiles all the time. You know, cheesy. It takes practice to smile without it looking fake. I practice all the time in front of my mirror. It's hard work." While athletes playing at all levels of sports express their emotions during games, the cheerleaders' facial expressions remain fixed in a smile and are a reminder that cheerleaders have a separate code of emotional behaviour, no matter the score, unfair referees, or their own physical pain. But not all girls are willing to sublimate their own emotions for the good of the school. As one African American girl in our study commented, "Sometimes I have a smile on my face; sometimes, I don't."

The missing discourse of cheerleading

Although rarely acknowledged by those involved in the sport, cheerleading is a practice, the culture and expense of which often excludes girls of colour and low-income girls. One of the primary reasons that white, middle-class girls disproportionately fill cheerleading squads is economic. Uniforms, camps, camp attire, camp accessories, and private tumbling lessons are financially prohibitive. However, the prevailing discourse that links cheerleading with a certain type of body and bodily presentation is equally powerful in determining the complexion of cheerleading squads (Bettis and Adams, 2003).

The construction of cheerleading as an activity primarily for white girls is based on certain assumptions about the normative cheerleading body. Julie, a white seventh-grade girl in our study, explains why one of the few African American girls trying out for the squad is ill-suited for being a cheerleader:

> Her toe touches are . . . they are really good. . . But I don't know if she'll make it or not, just because she's like not really the cheerleading type at all. She's more like the sports type. . . You wouldn't picture her as a cheerleader. . . She's on the basketball team.

Julie's comment draws on racialized essentialist notions of sports participation to rationalize why more Black girls are not represented on cheerleading squads. They do not have the "look" of a cheerleader – the inference being they do not embody the markers of white, middle-class heterosexualized femininity. Black, Brown, Native, queer, poor, and overweight girls disrupt the ideal feminine image of cheerleading in their physical appearance, their muscularity or lack of, and their differing emotional expression.

Conclusion

Cheerleading is understood today as a feminine, heterosexual performance for the pleasure of the heterosexual male gaze or as an athletic performance with risk of injury. These contemporary discourses simplify what is a complicated and shifting gender performance, one in which girls may be athletes yet still embody traditional markers of heterosexual femininity with short skirts and lipstick smiles. For many of those who participate in cheerleading along with feminist post-structuralists such as Butler and Kenway et al., gender performance does not necessarily equate to gender subordination. Kenway et al. (1994, p. 205) speak to the possibilities of performance.

> The performance metaphor allows the girls to feel a sense of control over different performance genres, to pick up, discard, play and take risks within them, and even to go beyond them through improvisation, collage, and carnival. Femininity can then become a source of power and pleasure rather than a source of control.

In our own research, we have listened to young girls and women describe the pleasures and power of cheerleading derived from taking physical risks, trying on an overt sexuality with adult approval, making lifelong friends, commanding an audience to follow their lead and the pure joy and fun of the activity. Besides the pleasure and power found in cheerleading by its participants, what is also missed in dominant cheerleading discourses is that the signifying cheerleading body is usually white, middle-class, heterosexual, and able-bodied. This norm of middle-class whiteness serves an exclusionary purpose by defining in very narrow terms the desirable and uniformed cheerleading body, thus determining who can and cannot be a cheerleader. We argue that prevailing discourses of cheerleading have "real effects", whether intentional or not, on the lives of all adolescent girls and limit the possibilities of who can cheer and what cheerleading might become.

Note

1 Title IX was enacted in 1972 and prohibits any public programme that receives federal aid to discriminate based on sex. Its implementation has been highly contentious in college and high school athletics.

References

Adams N and Bettis PJ (2003) *Cheerleader: An American Icon*. New York: Palgrave.

Adams N, Schmitke A and Franklin A (2005) Tomboys, dykes, and girly girls: interrogating the subjectivities of adolescent female athletes. *Women's Studies Quarterly* 33 (1 & 2): 17–34.

American Association of Cheerleading Coaches and Administrators (n.d.) Cheerleading as a sport. Available at: http://aacca.org/content.aspx?item=Resources/Test.xml (accessed 5 January 2012).

Anderson E (2005) Orthodox and inclusive masculinity: competing masculinities among heterosexual men in a femininized terrain. *Sociological Perspectives* 48: 337–355.

Anderson E (2008) 'I used to think women were weak': orthodox masculinity, gender segregation, and sport. *Sociological Forum* 23: 257–280.

Azzarito L (2010) New girls, transcendent femininities, and new pedagogies: towards girls hybrid bodies? *Sport, Education and Society* 15: 261–276.

Bartky S (1990) *Femininity and Domination: Studies in the Phenomenology of Oppression*. New York: Routledge.

Bettis P and Adams NG (2003) The power of the preps and a cheerleading equity policy. *Sociology of Education* 76(2): 128–142.

Bettis P and Adams NG (2006) Short skirts and breast juts: cheerleading, eroticism and schools. *Sex Education* 6(2): 121–133.

Bryson L (1987) Sport and the maintenance of masculine hegemony. *Women's Studies International Forum* 10(4): 349–360.

Butler J (2009) Performative acts and gender constitution: an essay in phenomenology and feminist theory. In C McCann and Seung-Kyung Kim (Eds.) *Feminist Theory Reader*. (pp. 415–427). New York: Routledge.

Buzuvis E (2011) The feminist case for the NCAA's recognition of competitive cheer as an emerging sport for women. *Boston College Law Review* 52: 439–464.

Colburn K (1985) Honor, ritual and violence in ice hockey. *Canadian Journal of Sociology*, 10(2): 153–170.

Foucault M (1977) *Discipline and Punish: The Birth of the Prison* (A.M. Sheridan, Trans.). New York: Pantheon Books.

Gonzales A (1956) The first college cheer. *American Mercury* 83: 101–104.

Grindstaff L and West E (2006) Cheerleading and the gendered politics of sport. *Social Problems*, 53(4): 500–518.

Grindstaff L and West E (2010) "Hands on hips, smiles on lips": gender, race, and the performance of spirit in cheerleading. *Text and Performance Quarterly* 30 (2): 143–162.

Hanson M (1995) *Go! Fight! Win! Cheerleading in American Culture*. Bowling Green, OH: Bowling Green State University Popular Press.

Harvard Law Review (1997) Cheering on women and girls in sports: using Title IX to fight gender role oppression. *Harvard Law Review* 110: 1627–1644.

Kenway J, Willis S, Blackmore J, and Rennie L (1994) Making hope practical rather than "despair convincing": feminist poststructuralism, gender reform, and educational change. *British Journal of Sociology of Education, 15*(2): 187–210.

Kindlon D (2006) *Alpha Girls: Understanding the New American Girl and How She is Changing the World.* New York: Rodale.

Kurman G (1986) What does girls' cheerleading communicate? *Journal of Popular Culture,* 20: 57–63.

Malcolm N (2006) "Shaking it off" and "toughing it out": socialization to pain and injury in girls' softball. *Journal of Contemporary Ethnography,* 35(5): 495–525.

Messner D and Sabo D (1994) *Sex, Violence and Power in Sports.* Freedom, CA: Crossing.

Mueller, G and Cantu, R (n.d.) National Center for Catastrophic Sport Injury Research. Available at: http://www.unc.edu/depts./nccsi/allSport.htlm (accessed 5 January 2012).

Pegues J (2010) Cheerleaders refuse to wear "skimpy" uniforms. Available at: http://abclocal.go.com/wabc/story?section=news/local&id=7708482 (accessed 22 June 2012).

Pennington B (2007) As cheerleaders soar higher, so does the danger. *New York Times,* Available at: www.nytimes.com/2007/03/31/sports/31cheerleader.html? . . . all (accessed 5 January 2012).

Pringle R and Markula P (2005) No pain is sane after all: a Foucauldian analysis of masculinities and men's experiences of rugby. *Sociology of Sport Journal* 22: 472–497.

Raven K (2012) Deaths triple among football players. Available at: http://.www.sciencedaily.com/releases/2012/120227162658.html (accessed 22 June 2012).

Saving Sports (2010) CSC statement on Quinnipiac University, competitive cheer, and Title IX. Available at: http://savingsport.blogspot.com/2010/07/csc-statement-on-quinnipiac-university.html (accessed 5 January 2012).

Theberge N (1997) "It's part of the game": physicality and the production of gender in women's hockey. *Gender & Society* 11(1): 69–87.

Thomas K (2011) Born on sideline, cheerleading clamors to be sport. *The New York Times.* Available at: http://www.nytimes.com/2011/05/23/sports/gender-games-born-on-sideline-cheering-clamo . . . (accessed 5 January 2012).

Young K and White P (1995) Sport, physical danger, and injury: the experiences of elite women athletes. *Journal of Sport and Social Issues* 19(1): 45–61.

Young K, White P, and McTeer W, (1994) Body talk: male athletes reflect on sport, injury, and pain. *Sociology of Sport Journal* 11: 175–194.

23

SEXUALITY AND THE MUSCULAR MALE BODY

Kenneth R. Dutton[1]

Though it had long been implicit in the artistic depiction of the powerful body, the association between the male sexual drive and the impetus towards the exercise of power (physical or otherwise) was not subjected to scientific scrutiny until the late nineteenth century, when Freud's concept of 'castration anxiety' brought together the fear of sexual impotence and a more generally diffused fear of powerlessness. It was perhaps not entirely fortuitous that the pioneering work of Freud, Havelock Ellis, Krafft-Ebing and other analysts of male and female sexuality began towards the end of the nineteenth century, amid the first stirrings of female emancipation and men's consequent psycho-sexual anxieties.

It took the eccentric but well-attuned American physical culture advocate Bernarr Macfadden (1868–1955) to recognise the nature of this male anxiety and to name it openly. In his 1900 work *The Virile Powers of Superb Manhood*, he took up and enthusiastically bandied about the term 'virility', redolent as it was with suggestions of sexual confidence and energy, and certainly more seemingly scientific in connotation than Walt Whitman's use of terms such as 'amativeness' and 'mettle' to refer to his own identification of physical muscularity with sexual potency (see Stacy, 2009: xxxviii). Macfadden's influence on the world of muscular development was of long duration, and for the generations that followed the code-word 'virility' was a feature of advertisements for books, equipment and food supplements aimed at fostering the development of a muscular body. Though given a curious new twist in more recent times, when steroids and other androgenic drugs may have the effect of lowering the body's own testosterone production and causing temporary impotence, the appeal of bodybuilding as a supposed enhancer of sexual prowess has had a powerful effect on many of its adherents and promoters.

The world's largest-selling bodybuilding magazine, *Muscle and Fitness*, for years owed much of its circulation success to the association of muscular development with increased sexual potency. Unlike most similar magazines,[2] with their covers depicting a prominent male bodybuilder exercising or posing for the camera, *Muscle and Fitness* almost invariably had a cover-shot of a male and female bodybuilder, or male bodybuilder and swimsuited female model, posing together, the woman usually running her hands over the male physique; on occasion there was a suggestion of an erotic embrace. The cover was liberally sprinkled with conventional bodybuilding slogans ('king-size delts', 'giant thighs', 'washboard abs'), but included among them were strategically-placed messages such as: 'Hard bodies are sexy', 'Trim, strong, sexy you', 'Strengthen your sexual muscles', 'Shaping a hard, sexy body', 'Stronger is sexier', and even 'Magic sex in muscles'.

These cover-slogans were clearly intended to convey the message of bodybuilding as an enhancer of sexual drive: the recurring word 'sexy' can be understood as referring primarily to sexual potency rather than sexual attractiveness. Occasional slogans made the point more explicitly: 'Don't Droop: Put Virility Power Into Your Body', proclaimed the April 1987 cover, just below the caption 'Getting Big!' The cover-phrases often bore no relationship to the articles contained within the magazine itself, though occasional features with titles such as 'Exercise Makes You Sexy', 'Sex and Bodybuilding', or 'So you Want a Hard, Sexy Body' extolled the benefits of exercise in hormone production and improved self-confidence. Reassuring or ego-boosting statements such as that in the January 1990 edition ('Our bodybuilding lifestyle puts you in tune with all the sensations and movements of your body that can make the sex act the ultimate thrill') encouraged the belief that bodybuilding was 'a short-cut to increased sexuality'.

The message of improved sexual prowess, whether obliquely hinted at or openly proclaimed, undoubtedly accounts for much of the fascination of bodybuilding amongst adolescent and young adult males, particularly in the primacy accorded to sheer muscular size over such qualities as proportion, symmetry and balance of development. The obsession with 'twenty-inch arms', for example, which haunts many enthusiastic adherents of the sport, is one of the signs of a more generalised adulation of sheer muscular bulk which perhaps has its origins in that identification of physical dominance with tribal leadership (and sexual rights over female members of the tribe) that can be observed in a number of 'primitive' cultures and among the higher apes (Morris, 1971: 42). Such a theory does much to indicate the basically non-homoerotic nature of the fascination of heterosexual male bodybuilders with the more highly developed bodies of other males.

An example of the male interest in other male bodies can be found in men's common fascination with comparisons of penis size and length. The penis and its operations are a constant source of male anxiety and insecurity in a context where the ability to 'perform' is a sign of masculinity and male adequacy. Curiosity about the sexual organs of others can thus be aimed at self-reassurance or a validation of one's own gender identity. As with the penis sheaths worn by some New Guinea tribesmen, the possession and display of a large penis is seen as a sign of sexual prowess or status, aimed (if only implicitly) at other men. Given the well-established symbolism that associates the hard, muscular body with the engorged, erect and potent phallus, the need for reassurance and confirmation of male adequacy (whether of the sexual organs or of the body as a whole) can be seen as grounded not so much in homosexual attraction as in heterosexual status rivalry and its attendant performance anxiety.

The association of muscular development with heightened sexual capacity goes hand in hand with the image of visible muscularity as an erotically attractive signal. Just as sexual vigour is marketed by magazines and the purveyors of gym equipment and bodybuilding diet supplements, so the promise of sexual desirability is held out to muscle-builders by the manufacturers of designer workout clothing on the implicit premise that appearance in the weight-room is a form of seductive display. Even outside the 'gym culture', the motivation to take up some form of physical exercise is often grounded in the desire to make the body more physically attractive rather than in the quest for better health or improved fitness. In this context, the relationship between heightened muscularity and the transmission of sexually-oriented visual messages becomes so intimate as to raise the question whether the display of the muscular body is primarily, even exclusively, an erotic transaction.

This is, of course, by no means a peculiarly modern issue, and the difficulty of identifying a completely unequivocal significance in the 'messages' of bodily display has haunted the Western consciousness for centuries. Even in a culture where religious belief has waned and secular values predominate, the inheritance of the Christian cultural tradition has invested the body with an ambiguous status. Nowhere is this more apparent than in the world of art, where the nude body was both – and often at one and the same time – the supreme symbol of proportion and reason, and the most effective vehicle for the expression of sexual feeling. Thus, the human body could be depicted nude in the Western artistic tradition – and even carry more than a hint of eroticism – while the apparent 'subject' of the painting was a moralising scene from mythology or Biblical history (Lucie-Smith, 1982: 30). Here as elsewhere, a single image may permit two or more quite different readings, the beholder's particular frame of reference determining which of them prevails.

The messages emitted by the body, in fact, depend for their significance at least as much on their recipients as on their senders. Without a recipient who reacts to the message, it is not a message at all but merely an unsuccessful attempt at communication. If sender and recipient do not share the same cultural language or the same expectations, then either no message is conveyed or else the message received differs from that which was intended. If we Westerners fail to see anything erotic in a Japanese painting of a love-scene, it is because our cultural language differs from that of Japan and we have not learned to read that country's traditional pictorial language. Equally, some early European travellers in the Pacific found the mere sight of bare-breasted island maidens so erotically stimulating that they remained for a time in a state of constant sexual arousal, whereas the local males (scarcely an impotent breed of men) managed to go about their daily work with equanimity. Though the 'senders' emitted similar messages to both groups, the cultural background of the recipients differed markedly and the messages deviated accordingly

These observations underscore the difficulty of making valid or even moderately defensible statements about the specific messages emitted by the developed body. More particularly, the extent to which the display of a muscular body is an erotic transaction – while it may to some degree depend on its originator's intentions, its specific form and the context of its presentation – will ultimately be determined by the psycho-sexual make-up of those who are at the viewing end of the display. Some people, we are told, are 'turned on' by Sumo wrestlers, while still others find the sight of nurses in starched uniforms irresistibly erotic. There is simply no accounting for the vast array of human sexual preferences and fantasies, and the message received may bear no relationship to the intrinsic purposes of the sender or the activity in which he or she engages.

With the above provisos, however, some general propositions may be advanced concerning the language of advanced muscularity, and an attempt may usefully be made to explore the at times tenuous lines of demarcation which *in principle* separate the muscular and the erotic modes of bodily display. The issue is posed in acute form in competitive bodybuilding, an activity in which a number of performers appear in public in a near-nude state, and move through a sequence of poses designed for no other purpose than to display their physical attributes to a group of interested spectators. The recipients of the bodily messages conveyed are in attendance precisely because they derive some form of satisfaction from observing the relatively unclothed bodies of (usually young) athletic men and, in some cases, women. Put in such stark terms, the question of erotic attraction can hardly be avoided.

The issue is further complicated by the visual media which convey to the public the pictorial image of the bodybuilder. Some of the publicity photographs found in bodybuilding journals are hard to distinguish from those in soft-core erotic magazines, and indeed some erotic publications specialise in photographs of bodybuilders. In particular, there is a well-established section of the market aimed at the homosexual community which concentrates on photographs of well-muscled young men. Even well-known and successful professional bodybuilders, including the 1982 Mr Olympia Chris Dickerson and internationally placed professionals such as Bill Grant and Tony Pearson, have posed for nude photographs or videos targeted primarily at the gay community. It is clear that there is a recognisable market segment which finds muscular development erotically stimulating: while the 'legitimate' bodybuilding magazines pander mainly to the sexual response of heterosexual males through mildly erotic photographs of female bodybuilders, the alternative market catering for homosexual readers and viewers is a good deal more explicit.

The use of muscularity as an erotic signal is not of recent origin. The 'father of bodybuilding', Eugen Sandow (1867–1925), was not averse to displaying his body for the purpose of eliciting an overtly sexual response, and although in his public appearances this took a heterosexual form in the performances billed as 'for ladies only', where he would pose dressed only in a silk posing-strap (Chapman, 1994: 83–84), it is probable that photographs of the classical poses in which he appeared clad in a false fig-leaf were being circulated in the English homosexual community towards the turn of the twentieth century (Walters, 1978: 289). It is also worthy of note that the three main periods in which the portrayal of the nude male body in Western art was pursued with most vigour – the age of classical Greece, the Renaissance and the latter part of the nineteenth century – were periods in which homosexuality had a more than usually observable profile in public life.

The overtones of homoerotic display which had dogged bodybuilding since its inception were magnified in the period from the late 1940s to the late 1960s, owing largely to the images conveyed by photographs of 'artistic' male posing following the work of Edwin Townsend and others. The most successful bodybuilding photographer of this period was Alonzo Hannagan, known as 'Lon'. In the late 1940s, his work was appearing in physique photo albums with titles such as *Masculine Perfection*, where well-known bodybuilders of the time such as John Grimek were shown in aesthetic poses. Other bodybuilders were even described, without apparent irony, as master *poseurs*, and their photographs were for sale as 'athletic poses' or 'artistic pose arrangements'. Lon was the chief exponent of this type of photography, and by the 1960s he had opened studios in London and several cities in the USA. Occasionally, two bodybuilders were photographed together in dual poses, perhaps in mock combat or wrestling, as if to stress the element of homosexual attraction. Even mainstream bodybuilding magazines such as the *British Amateur Weightlifter and Body-Builder* and the *Reg Park Journal* carried such material, which along with photographs of recognised and professional bodybuilders included 'studies' of nude or near-nude young men who had visibly never been near a barbell in their lives.

On the basis of this evidence, it is tempting to conclude that male bodybuilding is largely, if not entirely, a form of erotic display, directed chiefly if not exclusively at other males. However, the problem of interpretation here resides in an over-preoccupation with the recipients of bodily messages rather than the messages themselves. If some homosexuals are attracted by the sight of muscular male bodies, it is concluded, then the point of bodybuilding must be homosexual voyeurism. This is rather like arguing that if some men are sexually aroused by the sight of women such as nurses in starched uniforms, then the point of nursing must be sado-masochistic sexual arousal. While the analogy is far from perfect – bodybuilding, unlike nursing, is essentially a form of bodily display – it nonetheless serves to shift our attention away from the assumption that the message received by some is a key to the nature of the message itself.

Finally, it is relevant to point out (even in the absence of hard statistical evidence) that the opinion of those involved in the administration and practice of contemporary bodybuilding is overwhelmingly to the effect that homosexuality is no more prevalent in the bodybuilding world than in the community at large. The great majority of bodybuilders and their audiences are visibly heterosexual in orientation, at times even aggressively so. In the top professional ranks, a few bodybuilders have been known to be gay, though to date only one internationally-placed competitor (Bob Paris) has openly admitted his homosexuality.

Although a distinction can be drawn in principle between the public display of muscularity and the erotic stimulation it may evoke in some individual spectators, the fact remains that the line between the erotic and the non-erotic display of the body is always, at best, tenuous. In the world of high art where the distinction cannot always readily be drawn between erotic and non-erotic nudes, as in the world of nudism where the limits of propriety are an ever-present issue, the sexual messages of the disclosed body are so potent that they can never be entirely denied. While this is certainly the case, it is worth noting that the change in legal regulations and censorship requirements which took place in the 1970s brought about the demise of the pseudo-art magazine and helped clarify the difference *in principle* which separates the bodybuilding and the erotic display, as well as the audiences at which they are directed.

To draw this distinction of principle may appear over-defensive, and it must be conceded that it does not always apply in practice. Although we have attempted to analyse the male bodybuilder–male audience relationship primarily in terms of the dominance-display theory of behaviour, the gradations of human sexuality are such that it makes little sense in practice to divide responses into two entirely discrete categories (homosexual/non-homosexual). It is manifestly not the case that predominantly homosexual males can respond to the bodybuilding display only in erotic terms, totally different from those in which it is viewed by predominantly heterosexual males. The corollary of this proposition would suggest that, even for the latter group, it is difficult to separate out an element of repressed or sublimated sexual interest from the total spectrum of imaginative constructs, fantasies and personal obsessions of which their interest in muscular development is composed.

There is some evidence to suggest that the contemporary re-appraisal of gender roles following the Women's Liberation movement has significantly altered the context of erotic or quasi-erotic display of the male body. The traditional distinction – men are 'the sex that looks' whereas women are 'the sex that is looked at' – no longer appears to hold true in liberal Western cultures. The first stirrings of a change in attitude can be traced back to Sandow, whose 'ladies only' posing sessions (significantly contemporaneous with the age of women's emancipation) first established the unclad male figure as an object of public female scrutiny. The double legitimisation involved (for women, the legitimacy of looking; for men, the legitimacy of being looked at) meant a profound change in socio-sexual expectations, though not till more recent times has the shift in general social values given widespread currency to the newer understanding.

Since the mid-1980s, the concept of 'Men for Women' has gained increasing acceptance in the presentation of the sexually attractive male body. The popularity of male stripping with female audiences, and particularly with younger women, has become well established, while symbols of undoubted masculinity such as football players now have no hesitation about being photographed in various states of undress for pin-up 'hunk' calendars, no longer inhibited by the suggestion that such photography is aimed at homophile audiences. The male strip show and the 'hunk' calendar have their antecedents in the two traditional forms of expression of bodybuilding (the live display and the photographed pose), and it may well be that the renewed popularity of bodybuilding in the later 1970s, associated with the rise of the super-masculine Arnold Schwarzenegger, is equally related to the re-appraisal of gender roles which occurred at that time.

For most of its hundred years of history, the bodybuilding exhibition – the chief forum for the public demonstration of muscular development – has occupied a curiously uncertain zone lying somewhere between sporting activity, entertainment and erotic display. For the last fifty of those years, sporadic attempts have been made at the organisational level to dissipate some of the aura of ambiguity, notably by emphasising the sporting character of organised competition. The recognition of bodybuilding by the US Amateur Athletic Union in 1940 was accompanied by the formulation of competition rules which remain basically similar from one organisation to another, those laid down by the International Federation of Bodybuilders (IFBB) being the most commonly applied.

In addition to an extensive set of rules covering judging criteria and procedures and the accreditation of official judges, an important factor in the attempt to classify bodybuilding as a respectable sporting activity was the regulation of acceptable costume. In earlier years, male competitors had at times appeared in states of semi-undress which were to say the least questionable: underpants, jock-straps and G-strings had all made their appearance on the contest stage, to the delight or outrage of audiences depending on individual taste. The IFBB rules set out to abolish such aberrant practices: 'Men competitors', they stated, 'must wear trunks which are clean and decent. Men are not allowed to wear bikini-type trunks'; in the later rules for women the costume 'must conform to accepted standards of taste and decency'. Over the last twenty years, costumes for both men and women have tended to become briefer and higher-cut at the rear, a fact which officials might well put down to a change in 'acceptable standards' over that time.

A further move on the part of officials, aimed at establishing the bodybuilder as a 'sporting' figure rather than an object of erotic interest, was the provision of earnest moral advice that he or she was expected to serve as an example, both morally and physically, in order to inspire other young people to participate in the sport. In support of this exhortation, the IFBB stipulated that it was a serious offence for any bodybuilder to allow themselves to be photographed nude, or to show any genitalia, on pain of suspension from the organisation. The rule appears not to have always been applied in practice, or at least not to have adversely affected the careers of a number of male and female bodybuilders who have posed for nude photographs or even made erotic videos ranging from nude posing to various forms of soft-core pornography. Whether a blind eye was turned by officials or whether such activities did not come to their attention, the existence of the rule is a significant reminder of the peculiar susceptibility of bodybuilding to turn into a form of erotic exhibition and of the obvious sensitivity of officials and organisers on this score. It is hard to think of any other sporting activity in which such a rule would be conceivable, let alone necessary.

While official vigilance had some effect in minimising or at least reducing the erotic overtones of muscle display at the organised competitive level, perhaps a more significant development in the overall image of bodybuilding lay in the greater liberty of social expression and open publication which was becoming accepted by the 1970s, especially in relation to sexually-oriented material. Magazines intended for erotic interest could now be published for what they in fact were, and it was no longer necessary for them to masquerade as collections of 'physique studies' of bodybuilders – or, for that matter, publications intended for dedicated naturists or sun-lovers. Whatever one's judgment on the emergence of this specialised literature, we have already noted its effect in separating out the serious market for bodybuilding publications from that aimed purely at sexual gratification. From the 1970s onwards, any sexual (and particularly homosexual) overtones in mainstream bodybuilding magazines would at most be implicit, and the 'athletic young models' had disappeared from their pages, though an element of homosexual voyeurism is still evident in some men's 'lifestyle' and fitness magazines.

In varying degrees, the above developments have reduced the aura of uncertainty surrounding bodybuilding and in particular its identification as a form of conspicuous erotic display. They have not, however, been entirely successful in freeing it from its traditional representation as an abnormal mode of quasi-sexual behaviour or enabled it to achieve an undisputed status as a sporting activity: 'A big contest like Mr Olympia or Mr Universe,' writes Margaret Walters, '[is] a beauty pageant . . ., with the strongman, just like the beauty queen, offering up his body as an object to be admired. He deforms his body even more than she does; the irony is that these grotesquely developed muscles are for display, not use' (Walters, 1978: 295).

This view would probably be echoed by most of those observers of the world of competitive bodybuilding who are not attracted towards its cultural paradigms. Even more than for most sports (assuming that the term 'sport' is justified), it is a world apart, a world of its own. It is an autonomous subculture which has its own rituals and system of demeanour – a world in which arcane terms of jargon such as striated glutes, diamond calves, abdominal vacuums and pumped lats all have meaning and significance, and where the relative merits of high reps, pre-exhaustion, staggered sets, split routines and a multitude of other techniques are eagerly debated by insiders while to those outside they seem meaningless or futile.

In attempting some kind of objective appraisal of bodybuilding as an autonomous activity, it is useful to refer to the terms of Margaret Walters' illuminating if critical analysis quoted above. Her comparison with weightlifting ('the muscles are for display, not use') implies that the move from instrumental to representational muscularity which marked the birth of bodybuilding underlines the 'uselessness' of muscular display, a view often advanced in order to contest the sporting status of bodybuilding. But, as Johan Huizinga's authoritative study of games and sport (*Homo Ludens*) has argued, the very 'uselessness' of all sporting activity – from golf to pigeon-racing – is precisely what constitutes them as sports or pastimes (Huizinga, 1970: 19–29). Christopher Lasch, who disputes a number of Huizinga's conclusions, agrees that the point of sporting mastery is 'to ratify a supremely difficult accomplishment [. . .] to forget a bond between [the sportsman] and his audience, which consists in a shared appreciation of a ritual executed flawlessly' (Lasch, 1978: 104–105). The element of display and representation, Lasch argues (in a passage which has particular relevance to bodybuilding) is a vitally important reminder of the former connections between play, ritual and drama. Ceremony requires witnesses (in this case spectators) who are conversant with the rules of the performance and its underlying meaning.

As to Walters' categorisation of bodybuilding as a beauty pageant, the lines of demarcation may perhaps be better understood by a comparison with the male strip show, particularly as in most male stripping the final state of undress of the performer approximates closely to that of the bodybuilder. A comparison of the two forms of activity may help us to clarify further the contextual (if not always actual) difference of bodybuilding display and erotic display.

Male strip shows, originally restricted to the seedier clubs and cabarets and intended largely for homosexual audiences, were to see a significant rise in popularity in the 1980s, and leading groups of strippers such as the 'Chippendales' currently attract audiences (mainly female) of over 50,000 per week in appearances throughout the world. No longer restricted to back-street clubs and gay bars, they perform before women's tennis clubs, social and recreational clubs, charity organisations and even old-age pensioner groups. Male stripping has been the subject of movies (*For Ladies Only*) and stage-plays (*Ladies' Night Out*), and can now be seen regularly on TV in many Western countries; even in relatively small provincial centres it can provide a lucrative source of income for those adept at it. At least in those cases where it stops short of total nudity, it has become a socially acceptable form of display in liberal Western cultures.

Like bodybuilding, the male strip show often (if not always) employs muscularity as a form of expression, and many male strippers are also enthusiastic bodybuilders. What distinguishes the male bodybuilding display from the male strip show is primarily the context of display. It is an understood convention that mild (and thus, nowadays, acceptable) sexual titillation is the purpose of the stripper's activity and that this is the expectation of the audience as well as the aim of the performers: the gestures, attitudes and activity are all designed to suggest or mimic sexual attraction and desire. The unambiguous nature of the messages emitted, conveyed and received by the stripper's form of bodily disclosure bring into sharp contrast the more elusive and ill-defined act of communication involved in the bodybuilder's 'pseudo-classical posing'.

If the bodybuilder (like the stripper) offers himself to the audience, he equally offers himself to the judges who separate him both physically and symbolically from that audience. He is literally 'distanced' from the spectators, and never leaves the podium to strut around the auditorium. He is never touched, and no one throws money or under-garments at him. He enters and leaves the stage as directed by the officials. Whatever the implicit suggestions of his choreographed routine, its aim is not to evoke desire; it is to lose fewer points than his opponents. The contextual signs of competitive bodybuilding are modelled on those of individual competitive sport, bearing some similarity to gymnastics, diving and other forms of sporting activity in which the language of subjective aesthetic appreciation is applied by judges with a dispassionate, almost clinical technicality.

Neither strength display nor beauty contest – though often understood as a failed attempt at one or the other, or both – bodybuilding is still seeking its identity as a sport. Whether it will ever gain widespread public acceptance in these terms seems at least open to doubt, notwithstanding the efforts of official organisations. As long as the body remains both the focus and the organ of human sexual desire, no activity which focuses so intently upon the body itself can ever achieve the degree of social legitimisation accorded to sporting activity in general.

The attempted de-sexualising of bodybuilding has distanced it from the more overt forms of erotic display by providing it with a degree of contextual autonomy. To do more would be impossible, since it would be to deny one of the most fundamental components of our fascination with the body and its enduring power over us. The developed body may speak to the mind, but it speaks in the language of the senses.

Notes

1   This chapter is based on Chapter 8, 'The Sexual Body', from his book, *The Perfectible Body: The Western Ideal of Physical Development*, published in 1995.
2   For example, *Mandate* (1975–2009), *Honcho* (1978–) and *Torso* (1982–), all published by the Mavety Media Group.

References

Chapman, D (1994) *Sandow the Magnificent: Eugen Sandow and the Beginnings of Bodybuilding*. Urbana and Chicago: University of Illinois Press.

Huizinga, J (1970) *Homo Ludens: A Study of the Play Element in Culture*. London: Granada Publishing, Paladin.

Lasch, C (1978) *The Culture of Narcissism: American Life in an Age of Diminishing Expectations*. New York: Norton.

Lucie-Smith, E (1982) *The Body: Images of the Nude*. London: Thames & Hudson.

Macfadden, B (1900) *The Virile Powers of Superb Manhood: How Developed, How Lost, How Regained*. New York: Physical Culture Publishing Co.

Morris, D (1971) *The Human Zoo*. London: Corgi Books.

Stacy, J (ed) (2009) *Leaves of Grass, 1860: The 150th Anniversary Facsimile Edition*. Iowa City: University of Iowa Press.

Walters, M (1978) *The Nude Male: A New Perspective*. London and New York: Paddington Press.

24

CAN GENDER EQUALITY BECOME AN ENCUMBRANCE?

The case of sport in the Nordic countries

Håkan Larsson

Introduction

The development of competitive sport in the Nordic countries – Denmark, Finland, Iceland, Norway and Sweden – to a great extent parallels that of the United States and United Kingdom. Frequently, however, the Nordic countries are considered to be forerunners concerning gender-equality issues. This might be true in a way, but the picture is not unambiguous. Does the gender-equality success story really deliver what it promises within a Nordic sports context?

Gender issues have had a fairly prominent position within sport studies in the Nordic countries. A number of researchers have contributed substantially to the knowledge formation, and many of them have also played an important part in creating gender-equality policies for sport both in their countries and internationally (see e.g. Fasting and Sisjord, 1981; Laine, 1989; Olofsson, 1989; Pfister, 1980; Trangbæk and Kruger, 1999). However, they have also demonstrated that gender equality as a political endeavour in sport is sometimes ambiguous and contradictory. A lot has been done in sport in the name of equality, but these initiatives have had only limited impact on changing gender power relations. At best, gender-equality initiatives improve the situation within existing power relations in sport. On occasions, they might even become an encumbrance to the endeavour for fundamental change should they fail to include a critical approach to sex/gender.

There are great cultural similarities between all the Nordic countries, but to some extent, for instance the way competitive sport is organised at a national level (see Seippel, et al., 2010), they are not identical. Each one of the countries has specific characteristics and for this reason I will comment on common developments and then use Sweden as a particular example.

Gender equality in sport – an ambiguous endeavour

In contemporary Nordic societies, *gender-neutral legislation*, based on the premise that individuals of both genders are socially and legally interchangeable, is seen to promote gender equality in the best manner. Little by little, legislation within post-WWII labour law, civil law, family law, etc., has changed from being differentiated by gender to being gender neutral. However, in competitive sport this is not the case. Here, the genders are not interchangeable. Gender matters, and to such extent that men and women are consistently separated in competitions in most sports (and also often in training). This separation is officially justified as follows in the Swedish Sport Confederation's (SSC) general policy:

> Sport is as important for women as for men, for girls as for boys. And women and men are equally important for sport. Hence, gender-equality is important to sport. Due to the different physical conditions, there are reasons to separate men and women when competing in a number of sports. [. . .] Further, one must account for differences between boys and girls and the increased importance of gender difference during adolescence.
>
> *(SSC, 2005)*

'Different physical conditions', which are arguably valid at a statistical group level, are deemed valid also at an individual level. This legitimises a separation of the genders and quite often also a differentiation of the rules in a way that makes the female competition class an 'easier', 'lighter' version of the male class – even though women and men do not compete against each other – while the male class is more 'severe' as it requires/allows greater physical force.

The situation opens up an interesting problem: by creating a common competition class or removing gender differentiation (regarding e.g. the weight of throwing implements and hurdle heights in athletics or the height of the net in volleyball) gender-neutral rules are simply not considered a means to promote gender equality in competitive sport in the same way as they do in other social arenas. However, this seemingly paradoxical situation is rarely contemplated within sport or elsewhere. If it were, a critical gaze on gender patterns like these might be met with surprise. In fact, the sports culture of the Nordic countries is characterised by marked gender differentiation patterns in many ways. These patterns are, however, chiefly not, at least not among a majority of representatives of the sport organisations, considered to denote inequalities. As an expression of neoliberal political discourses, they are rather interpreted as unproblematic choices made by autonomous individuals (Klausen, 1996). For instance, that many sports attract a lot of boys *or* a lot of girls, or that boys *or* (perhaps more often) girls drop out of sport at an early age, is certainly seen as a problem among coaches and leaders within these sports, *but not necessarily as a gender-equality problem*. Neither is the relatively low share of women in the special sport federation boards.

Researchers have tried to problematise this situation through the use of feminist theorising (e.g. Larsson, 2003; Olofsson, 1989; Ottesen et al., 2010). Their results have indicated that the quest for gender-equality in sport has followed mainly two approaches, both, however, falling somewhat flat in the endeavour to challenge gender stereotypes and the cultural significance of sex. These strategies will be illustrated and problematised further on in the chapter. The aim is to illuminate how different approaches to gender equality might even become an encumbrance should it not include a critical perspective on gender and a problematisation of the category sex and to discuss why a critical approach to sex/gender seems to be at odds with a basic rationale about gender in competitive sport.

Sport in the Nordic countries – from a male activity to gender equality

Today, overall sports participation is more or less equal among women and men in the Nordic countries. In the main, the legislation surrounding male and female leisure-time sports participation has followed the overarching idea that equal numbers of male and female participants signify that 'gender does not matter', i.e. that the conditions are co-equal. When the share of women/men is within the range of 40–60 percent, whether in terms of participation in a particular sport, in terms of sport leadership in federations or clubs, or in terms of governing bodies, the conditions are, at least formally, considered to be equal. This said, it is worth noticing that co-education is the dominant teaching method in physical education (PE) at all levels, although this situation has not always been the case. However, examples of female dominance are rarely seen to evoke gender-equality initiatives, only male dominance.

About a century ago, sport, and competitive sport in particular, was considered to be a male activity, being too strenuous, and even dangerous, for women to enjoy (see e.g. Annerstedt, 1984; Laine, 1991; Olofsson, 1989; Trangbæk, 2005). Taking part in competitive sport has been, and still is to a large extent, related to developing a masculine identity (see e.g. Andreasson, 2007; Bonde, 1991; 2010; Fundberg, 2003). In the early 1900s, women were mainly restricted to female gymnastics, a dynamic, flexible and in fact highly successful form of gymnastics that developed out of the traditional and often rigid Swedish gymnastics. Ideas of the time about female physiology restricted women's sport participation to specific forms of physical activity that, though marginal, are still applied to some sports and exercise cultures today (Laine and Gurholt, 2006; Trangbæk, 2000). For instance, the present-day dominant approach to fitness training (e.g. 'aerobics') where the aim is first and foremost fitness-as-looking-good rather than fitness-for-performance bears traces of this development (Waaler Loland, 1999).

Male dominance in competitive sport remained until well after WWII and it was not until the 1960s that it was radically challenged, as more and more girls and women started to take part. The equalising of male and female participation in sport in the Nordic countries developed largely into a child and youth movement, a development that was spearheaded by the idea that sport was an appropriate educational arena (Støckel et al., 2010). As a result of this, it began to receive substantial financial and/or material public support (Bergsgard and Norberg, 2010). At first, women mainly took part in individual sports, such as athletics, swimming and skiing. During the 1970s, the breakthrough of women's football and other team games meant that the sports movement could be considered to be progressively more co-equal (Olofsson, 1989). In recent decades women have advanced their cause even further and started to take part to a reasonable extent also in motorsports and martial arts (statistics published by SSC, www.rf.se, accessed March 2013).

That women in contemporary Nordic societies participate in sport almost to the same extent as men can be explained by both societal changes, above all women entering the labour market giving them increased resources, including increased leisure time, and by the explicit struggle for gender equality. The last hundred years has seen a number of different gender-equality policies put into practice in sport, aiming sometimes at separating the genders and sometimes at removing gender(ed) boundaries. A century ago, while female participation in competitive sport was not on the political agenda, efforts were put into forming a gymnastics system that was clearly *distinguished* from male gymnastics, and which promoted a decidedly feminine identity and female leadership (Laine and Gurholt, 2006; Trangbæk, 2000). During the 1960s and 1970s, however, when it became politically viable to promote women's participation in competitive sport, an opposite strategy – a *participation strategy* – was launched where the guiding principle was the pursuit of women's rights to do sports, i.e. the same sports as men pursued (Larsson, 2003; Olofsson, 1989). On the face of it, this strategy was successful, as it strengthened women's rights to *participate* in competitive sport. It is more doubtful, however, to what extent it managed to radically challenge gender power relations in sport. Superficially, it seemed that gender equality was reached during the 1980s once women gained the same *rights* as men in competitive sport, and since they overall participated in sport virtually to the same extent as men. However, the pursuit of gender equality was not entirely successful. The traditional pattern, where men took part in competitive sport, while women did not, was succeeded by a new pattern, where men dominate in some sports while women dominate in others. For instance:

- women dominate in equestrian sport and 'aesthetic sports' such as gymnastics, dance and figure skating, while men dominate in a whole range of sports, including team games and sports like weight lifting, boxing and wrestling (statistics from SSC, www.rf.se, accessed March 2013);
- men dominate as leaders and coaches at an élite level (for both genders), while women coach girls (and to some extent boys, if they are young) at a 'lower' level (Redelius, 2002).

Typically, however, these patterns are *not* viewed as signs of gender inequalities, especially since both women and men have the *right* to do whatever sport they choose. Sparse attention is directed to whether these patterns mirror for instance stereotypical gender identities or how they relate to social values and media attention. The participation strategy also guided gender-equality efforts in PE.

Co-education in physical education – with unexpected consequences

Altogether in line with a gender-neutral equality policy, co-education has replaced gender-separate teaching in PE in all of the Nordic countries. In Sweden, co-education was formally decreed in PE at the national level in 1980. Gender-separate teaching was abandoned mainly because it was considered to prevent girls from taking part in sport activities that were pursued by boys (Carli, 2004). Prior to 1980, the boys' PE curriculum was oriented towards competition and physical training, while the girls' curriculum was more oriented towards 'aesthetic movement' (Lundquist Wanneberg, 2004). Although co-education was explicitly introduced for gender-equality reasons, a number of problems immediately arose from this change.

Virtually overnight, boys, as compared to girls, started to get higher grades in PE, developed a more positive attitude towards the subject, became more physically active during class, and began to feel they had greater opportunities to influence lesson content and pedagogy (Larsson & Redelius, 2008). In addition, the gymnastics-based curriculum that had dominated the girls' programme prior to 1980 more or less disappeared, leaving aesthetic and expressive movements to be nearly absent in the new co-education curriculum (Carli, 2004; Lundvall & Meckbach, 2003). Instead, the boys' curriculum prior to 1980, based on sports (mainly games) and physical training came to dominate the new co-education curriculum. This situation has been virtually unchanged over the last three decades (Quennerstedt et al., 2008). Simply put, gender-integrated PE gave boys an advantage over girls, and this as a result of an intended gender-equality intervention.

As an attempt to reinforce the gender-neutral policy, PE teachers, along with all Swedish teachers, have since 1994 been expected to 'counteract traditional gender roles' when teaching (SNAE, 1994). It seems, though, as if PE teachers have difficulties with seeing the point of 'counteracting gender roles'. Or rather, quite a few teachers seem to interpret this objective as 'counteracting sex differences', i.e. 'work against nature', which does not make any sense to them (Larsson et al., 2010). To teachers who do not see the genders as interchangeable, the gender-neutral policy is difficult to come to terms with. What, then, happened in competitive sport as the SSC adopted the first equality policy in 1989?

Gender-equality work becomes an encumbrance

It should be noted here that gender equality in sport has been an important issue at policy level in the Nordic countries. In Sweden, the year 1989 stands out as a milestone concerning both gender-equality policies in sport and feminist sport studies. That year, sports pedagogy researcher, Eva Olofsson, published the first Swedish feminist doctoral thesis on sport (Olofsson, 1989). Olofsson also took part in creating the first gender-equality policy adopted by the SSC that same year. These events mark an interesting intersection between sports policy and research. In her thesis, Olofsson concluded that competitive sport was 'created by men for men' (p. 182, my translation), and that women consistently have had to relate to – and often subordinate themselves to – men's sport and masculine values (competitiveness, perseverance, a total devotion to sport, etc.). *The Sport Equality Plan (Idrottens jämställdhetsplan)* of 1989 was supposed to change this situation. The plan challenged the hegemonic position of 'male values' in sport. It stated that:

> We live in a society for men, a society where men's experiences and values are normative, and where women are 'different'. [. . .] Sport rules and organisation are shaped to fit men.
>
> *(SSC, 1989, p. 1 and 6; my translation)*

An overall ambition with the plan was to challenge the male dominance of sport. The former endeavour to promote 'women's rights to do sport' was changed to the promotion of *women's rights to do sport – on their own terms*. This ambition includes what could be called a 'female perspective' and it can be interpreted as a move away from a gender-neutral equality policy. How, then, does such a policy turn out in practice? To answer that question, it is necessary to take a closer look on *what has been done* within sport in the name of 'gender-equality from a female perspective' ('her-story').

Several Swedish studies (Fagrell, 2000; Grahn, 2008; Larsson, 2003; Redelius, 2002; Svender et al., 2011) highlight that interventions and support in the name of 'gender equality' since 1989 have been made first and foremost 'for girls and women'. In fact, the concept 'gender' seems chiefly to mean 'girls' or 'women'. For instance, when sports representatives discuss 'gender', it is mainly about the conditions under which *girls and women* participate in sport (see e.g. Grahn, 2008; Larsson et al., 2011). Boys' and men's sport is rarely designated as a 'gender' issue. Instead, it serves as the – often implicit – normative foundation for reflections on girls' and women's sport. Thus, not including boys' and men's sport in a discussion on gender equality is effectively a way of not challenging gender power relations. It follows that the endeavour to support girls' and women's sport seems to have difficulties both with challenging the hegemonic position of male sport and stereotypical views on women *and* men in sport. The following passages from textbooks published by the SSC's publishing house during the 1990s signify how attempts to support girls' and women's sport run the risk of reinforcing gender stereotypes in relation to sport:

> Recent research shows that the motives for participating in sport differ between girls and boys. The studies show that girls are less interested in competition than the boys. Girls are more oriented towards social relations.
>
> *(Mogren, 1997, p.12, cited in Larsson, 2003, p. 17)*

> [. . .] the most important motive for girls [to participate in sport; my note] are social relations, i.e. to socialise and have fun together. To the boys, competition is the main thing.
>
> *(SSC textbook for the education of coaches, 1998, p.49, cited in Larsson, 2003, p. 17)*

Of course, the quotations illustrate well-intended attempts to upgrade the significance of social relations (considered to be 'female') in sport in contrast to competitiveness (considered to be 'male'). However, linking 'social relations' tightly to girls and 'competition' to boys, as well as seeing 'social relations' as opposite to 'competition' (or them both as being mutually exclusive) turned out to be counterproductive in terms of gender equality, since it reproduced rather than challenged stereotypical views on gender. With the following example I illustrate how similar approaches can be problematised in order to deconstruct the gendered discourse of femininity that constitutes the rationale for girls' physical and sport:

> Puberty is often problematic. Especially for girls. They develop into women and start to menstruate. The body changes and many girls get a negative body image. They search for an identity. Role models have a big influence [. . .] Friendliness is important to girls. Closeness and intimacy is more important than competition and individuality. The group is more important than one's own success. These qualities, so important to girls, are not always acknowledged in the sports movement.
>
> *(Pamphlet circulated by the SSC in 1989, cited in Larsson, 2003, p. 17)*

Let me picture my reading of this quotation as me interviewing the text (after Larsson, 2003). This is done in order for the commonplace ideas about gender that the text is based on to stand out more clearly: *For whom is puberty problematic?* – Especially for girls! – Why not also for boys? *Why is it so problematic?* – Girls develop into women; the problem is inscribed *within* the adolescent girl growing into womanhood. *What is so problematic about that?* – They start to menstruate; again it seems as if it is the adolescent female body that poses the problem. And so on. The second part of the quotation is interesting because it gives us a hint about the alleged 'normal' sportsperson, the sports*man*. He seems not to be so keen on friendliness, closeness and intimacy. Competition and individuality, on the other hand, is paramount, as is personal success. And these characteristics are, incidentally, seen both as manly traits and as necessary values in competitive sport. Hence, competitive sport is seen as inherently male, rather than as a social construction which relays not only gender stereotypes, but also a heterosexist understanding of gender, i.e. that the category gender is homogenous, that female is opposite to or different from, or complementary to male, and that these characteristics imply heterosexuality which is taken to be natural and desired (Eng, 2006). The 'female perspective' also constitutes the construction of the modern sportswoman, which is illustrated in the next, and last, quotation from the literature on gender equality published by the SSC's publishing house:

> For the girls, it does not suffice to compete and be the best one. We are humans first, only then athletes. Our female players *want* to achieve, and they *are* good, but they focus on entirely other things compared to boys. For them (the girls; my note), it is also about finding one's personality, a deeper motive for one's sporting activities. The achievements are, one could say, a bonus.
>
> *(SSC textbook for the education of coaches, 1993, p. 9, cited in Larsson, 2003, p. 18)*

What, then, is the significance of sport to boys and men? Let me paraphrase the above passage, changing it slightly:

> For the boys, competing to be the best one is the primary thing. We are sportsmen first, only then humans. Our male players achieve, and they are good, and they focus entirely on this task. For them, it is not so much about finding one's own personality; they already have one as a sportsman.
>
> *(after Larsson, 2003)*

The quoted passages illustrate how a gender-equality policy unintentionally might turn out to relay gender stereotypes and heteronormativity when put into practice. Should it not include a critical view of sex/gender? The analysis reveals that gender equality is a difficult endeavour to achieve if the genders are *a priori* seen as either interchangeable or different. But what other strategies might there be?

Beyond gender (equality)?

The efforts to promote gender equality in sport have been significant in the Nordic countries, and successful too. However, gender equality has ultimately proven to be somewhat elusive. A gender-neutral approach to equality – a participation strategy – was to some extent successful, although it failed to radically challenge and change power relations between male and female sports, between men and women in sport, and between what are considered to be 'masculine' and 'feminine' sports (e.g. that aesthetic sports are typically considered to be feminine while team games are considered to be masculine). It also seemed to promote a somewhat fraudulent perception of individual choice. Further, this approach to equality failed to take into account that the prevailing idea is that sex matters in sport. A gender-specific approach to equality – including a 'female perspective' – matches this idea about the significance of sex differences in sport. On the other hand, a gender-specific approach seems to have promoted stereotypical views on gender; hence, it has also failed to radically challenge and change gender power relations in sport. Consequently, overall, the conditions for women (in male-dominated sports) and men (in female-dominated sports) has improved over the years, but there are few signs indicating that traditional views on women and men, i.e. girls and women being more socially-oriented and reliant on a coach, and boys and men being more competitive and confident in competitive situations, are challenged. The existing strategies have not problematised the category sex.

Research during the last decade suggests a need for a more critical approach to sex/gender in order to destabilise gender power orders. Such an approach would include a questioning of some very self-evident truths in competitive sport, for instance the existence of two clearly distinguishable sexes. The research indicate that the ideas, within sport as in society broadly speaking, about sex differences is clearly linked to heteronormativity in the sense that what is seen to be 'naturally' female (being socially-oriented and reliant on a coach) and 'male' (being competitive and confident) is also to be a heterosexual – and to be otherwise is to be a homosexual (Andreasson, 2007; Eng, 2006; Fundberg, 2003; Larsson, 2003). Some might think that such a *queer* approach, i.e. an approach that challenges the given assumption that people are heterosexuals 'until proven otherwise', to sport would be beneficial primarily for lesbian, gay and bisexual persons, but I argue that it would be beneficial for everyone, since gender stereotypes and heteronormativity affects – and limits – everyone, regardless of sexual identity.

In relation to gender stereotypes and heteronormativity, American scholar Kevin Kumashiro has suggested teachers should teach paradoxically (Kumashiro, 2004). This means that teachers should question their own practice, and in particular how practice reproduces or challenges gender stereotypes. Teachers might ask: How does my way of teaching challenge stereotypes? 'How does it reinforce them? What does it leave unchallenged? Does it raise critical questions? Whom does it leave invisible? Whom does it call on to contest my own privileges?' (Kumashiro, 2004, p. 113). I have been involved with promoting such a strategy both within a PE context (Larsson et al., 2011) and within a sports context (Larsson, 2005). However, this queer strategy seems to clash with the conventional approach not only to gender, but also to competitive sport (i.e. propensity to classify participants, the demands for accuracy, etc.). In the end, the demands of competitive sport, as it is now played out, produce not only accurately measurable competition results but also individuals that are classified as either male or female. In simple terms, a critical approach to the sex/gender question should be accompanied by a critical approach to how competitive sport is performed and what it demands of individuals. This is what the SSC will have to deal with should it want to take the *Sport Equality Plan* one step further.

References

Andreasson, J. (2007) *Idrottens kön. Genus, kropp och sexualitet i lagidrottens vardag* [The gender of sport. Gender, body and sexuality in the everyday of team sports]. PhD Thesis, Lund University, Sweden.

Annerstedt, C. (1984) *Kvinnoidrottens utveckling i Sverige* [The development of women's sport in Sweden]. Malmö: Liber.

Bergsgard, N.A. and Norberg, J.R. (2010) Sports policy and politics – The Scandinavian way, *Sport in Society*, 13(4), 567–582.

Bonde, H. (1991) *Mandighed of sport* [Manhood and sport]. Odense University studies in history and social sciences, 146.

Bonde, H. (2010) *The Politics of the Male Body in Global Sport. The Danish Involvement.* London: Routledge.

Carli, B. (2004) *The Making and Breaking of a Female Culture. The history of Swedish physical education 'in a different voice'.* PhD Thesis, University of Gothenburg, Sweden

Eng, H. (2006). Queer athletes and queering sport. In J. Caudwell (Ed) *Sport, Sexualities and Queer/Theory* (pp. 49–61). London: Routledge.

Fagrell, B. (2000) *De små konstruktörerna. Flickor och pojkar om kvinnligt och manligt i relation till kropp, idrott, familj och arbete* [The little constructors. Girls and boys on feminine and masculine in relation to body, sport, family and labour]. PhD Thesis, Stockholm Institute of Education, Sweden.

Fasting, K. and Sisjord, M.-K. (1981) Gender, verbal behavior and power in sports organizations, *Scandinavian Journal of Sports Sciences*, 8(2), 81–85.

Fundberg, J. (2003) *Kom igen gubbar! Om pojkfotboll och maskuliniteter* [Come on, guys! On masculinity in boys' football]. PhD Thesis, Stockholm University, Sweden.

Grahn, K. (2008) *Flickor och pojkar i idrottens läromedel. Konstruktioner av genus i ungdomstränarutbildningen* [Girls and boys in sport education material. Constructions of gender in coach education]. PhD Thesis, University of Gothenburg, Sweden.

Klausen, K.K. (1996) Women and sport in Scandinavia: Policy, participation and representation. *Scandinavian Political Studies*, 19(2), 111–131.

Kumashiro, K. (2004) Uncertain beginnings: Learning to teach paradoxically. *Theory into Practice*, 43(2): 111–115.

Laine, L. (1989) In search of a physical culture for women. Elli Björkstén and women's gymnastics, *Scandinavian Journal of Sports Sciences*, 11(1), 15–20.

Laine, L. (1991) Kropp, idrott och kvinnohistoria [Body, sport and women's history], *Kvinnovetenskaplig tidskrift*, 12(4), 48–58.

Laine, L. and Gurholt, K. (2006) Gymnastics, dance and the formation of femininities in the Nordic countries: An introduction. *Moving Bodies*, 4(1), 9–16.

Larsson, H. (2003) A history of the present on the 'sportsman' and the 'sportswoman'. *Forum Qualitative Research*, 4(1), http://www.qualitative-research.net/index.php/fqs/article/view/751/1629

Larsson, H. (2005) Queer idrott [Queer sport]. In D. Kulick (Ed.) *Queersverige [Queer Sweden]* (pp. 110–135). Stockholm: Natur och kultur.

Larsson, H. and Redelius, K. (2008) Swedish physical education research questioned – current situation and future directions. *Physical Education and Sport Pedagogy*, 3(4), 381–398.

Larsson, H., Fagrell, B., Johansson, S., Lundvall, S., Meckbach, J. and Redelius, K. (2010) *Jämställda villkor i idrott och hälsa med fokus på flickors och pojkars måluppfyllelse* [Equal conditions in physical education with a focus on girls' and boys' performance]. Unpublished report to the Swedish National Agency of Education.

Larsson, H., Fagrell, B. and Redelius, K. (2011) Challenging gender in physical education. A queer lens on PE teaching, *Swedish Journal of Sport Research 2011*, 27–48.

Lundquist Wanneberg, P. (2004) *Kroppens medborgarfostran. Kropp, klass och genus i skolans fysiska fostran 1919–1962* [The civic education of the body. Body, class and gender in physical education schooling 1919–1962]. PhD Thesis, Stockholm University, Sweden.

Lundvall, S. and Meckbach, J. (2003) *Ett ämne i rörelse?* [A subject in movement?] PhD Thesis, Stockholm Institute of Education, Sweden.

Olofsson, E. (1989) *Har kvinnorna en sportslig chans? Den svenska idrottsrörelsen och kvinnorna under 1900-talet* [Do women have a sporting chance? The Swedish sports movement and the women during the 20th century]. PhD Thesis, Umeå University, Sweden.

Ottesen, L., Skirstad, B., Pfister, G. and Habermann, U. (2010) Gender relations in Scandinavian sport organizations – a comparison of the situation and the policies in Denmark, Norway and Sweden. *Sport in Society*, 13(4), 657–675.

Pfister, G. (Ed.) (1980) *Frau und Sport* [Woman and Sport]. Frankfurt: Fischer Taschenbücher.

Quennerstedt, M., Eriksson, C. and Öhman, M. (2008) Physical education in Sweden – a national evaluation. E-published on *Education-line*. Accessed 2 January 2012.

Redelius, K. (2002) *Ledarna och barnidrotten. Idrottsledarnas syn på idrott, barn och fostran* [The leaders and the child sport. The sport leaders' view of sport, children and up-bringing]. PhD Thesis, Stockholm Institute of Education, Sweden.

SSC (1989) *Idrottens jämställdhetsplan* [Sport equality plan]. The Swedish Sport Confederation, Stockholm.

SSC (2005) *Idrottens jämställdhetsplan* [Sport equality plan]. The Swedish Sport Confederation, Stockholm, http://rf.se/ImageVault/Images/id_1793/ImageVaultHandler.aspx (accessed March 2013)

Seippel, Ø., Ibsen, B. and Norberg, J.R. (2010) Introduction: Sport in Scandinavian societies. *Sport in Society*, 13(4), 563–566.

SNAE (1994) *Curriculum for the Compulsory School System, the Pre-school Class and the Leisure-Time Centre Lpo 94*. Stockholm: Swedish National Agency of Education.

Støckel, J.T., Strandbu, Å., Solenes, O., Jørgensen, P. and Fransson, K. (2010) Sport for children and youth in the Scandinavian countries. *Sport in Society*, 13(4), 625–642.

Svender, J., Larsson, H. and Redelius, K. (2011) Promoting girls' participation in sports: discursive constructions of girls in a sports initiative. *Sport, Education and Society*, DOI:10.1080/13573322.2011.608947.

Trangbæk, E. (2000) Svensk gymnastik og de kvindelige pionerer [Swedish gymnastics and the female pioneers]. *Studier i idrott, historia och samhälle*, 2000, 253–279.

Trangbæk, E. (2005) *Kvindernes idræt – fra rødder til top* [Women's sport – from its roots to its height]. København: Gyldendal.

Trangbæk, E. and Kruger, I. (1999) *Gender and Sport from European Perspectives*. Copenhagen: CESH.

Waaler Loland, N. (1999) *Body Image and Physical Activity*. PhD Thesis, The Norwegian School of Sport Sciences, Norway.

25

WOMEN AND SURFING SPACES IN NEWQUAY, UK

Georgina Roy and Jayne Caudwell

Introduction

The female (hetero-sexy) surfer is currently one of the most valuable 'icons' of the surf industry (Heywood, 2008). She has helped bridge the gap between female consumers and 'macho' surfer culture with consistently lucrative results. In the waves, women account for more than half of those attending surf lessons, and it is estimated that around 20% of the British surfing population are female (Barkham, 2006). In surfing nations like Australia, it is closer to a third (Booth, 2001a). However, as the editor of *Surfer* magazine has acknowledged, despite this so-called 'boom' in surfing amongst women, women's professional surfing has hardly prospered:

> No single group has had a greater struggle for respect and acceptance than female pro competitors, whose course since the mid-1970s has been undermined by pitfalls: gender bias, industry apathy, indifferent media coverage [and] outright hostility from the male pros . . .
>
> *(Surfer Magazine, 2010).*

Scenarios like this form part of what Booth (2001a) refers to as the 'paradoxes of surfing culture' (p. 3). The women's Association of Surfing Professionals (ASP) world tour has been troubled by a lack of sponsorship and a significant disparity between prize money for men and women. Furthermore, discourses of exclusion which serve to maintain masculine heterosexuality remain valued within surfing culture. This continues to perpetuate what Evers (2009) refers to as 'an ever-present overt homophobia in surfing spaces' (p. 896).

Given the ever-increasing popularity of surfing amongst women, it seems appropriate and timely that feminist scholars explore the significance of this 'new' sporting context in terms of sexualized subjectivities. Existing critical studies of surfing have emerged from a range of academic disciplines, including cultural studies (Heywood, 2008; Comer, 2010), media studies (Henderson, 2001; Ormrod, 2007), history (Booth, 2001a; Ormrod, 2007), sociology (Ford and Brown, 2006) and geography (Waitt, 2008; Evers, 2009). However, there is 'remarkably little research that has focused on the experiences and subjectivities of the female surfer' (Wheaton, 2010, p. 1068). Recent literature addressing issues surrounding gender and sexualities includes work on competitive female surfers in Brazil (Knijnik, Horton and Cruz, 2010), mother surfers in New Zealand (Spowart, Burrows and Shaw, 2010) and 'women-who-surf' in Australia (Waitt, 2008). This chapter offers a critical view of surfing, gender and sexualities in England. We map out some of the key ways in which gendered surf culture has come to be defined by, and aligned with, standards of whiteness and heteronormativity. We then reflect, briefly, on existing literature and theoretical trends, before focusing specifically on how gendered and sexualized subjectivities are negotiated by women surfers in the UK-surf hotspot: Newquay, Cornwall.

Gendered surf culture

In the last five decades, gender and sexuality have developed as central to struggles over surfing styles, identities and subjectivities. These struggles have been played out, predominantly, in modern surfing's cultural and commercial hotbeds: California, USA and east coast, Australia (cf. Stedman, 1997; Comer, 2010).

In westernised accounts of surfing histories, the 1950s and 1960s are key periods of growth. During this era of expansion, developments in surfing were aided by the emerging significance of youth culture and concomitant processes of Americanisation (Booth, 2001b). The popularity of iconic surf films such as *The Endless Summer* and *Gidget*—films commonly known collectively as *Beach Blanket* and music like that of the *Beach Boys*—functioned to firmly secure the 'surf lifestyle' in the popular culture imaginary. This process, as Ormrod (2002) has recognized, romanticized 'surf lifestyle' and helped define a distinctly gendered, raced and classed image of beach culture as middle-class, white and heteronormative.

The term 'heteronormativity' is 'widely used as shorthand for the numerous ways in which heterosexual privilege is woven into the fabric of social life, pervasively and insidiously ordering everyday existence' (Jackson, 2006, p. 108). From the 1960s onwards, as surfing rose in popularity, the performative and repetitive gendering of surf culture became more closely aligned with white-male aggression and power, and surf spaces became socially marked—and contested (Stedman, 1997).

Male machismo, masculinity and virility are evidenced in Stedman's (1997) case study of Australian surfing culture and she demonstrates how women's surfing subjectivities shift during the 1960s to 1990s. In particular, she notes a marked difference in the gendered representations within the popular surf magazine *Tracks*. She describes the 1970s as a time when gender boundaries were relatively 'blurred'; women were recognized as a small but active contingent in the surfing community, and 'for a while, even gay male surfers were tolerated' (p. 81). However, by the late 1980s this recognition had given way to 'continuous and strenuous attempts to assert an image of masculinity'. Stedman writes:

> Obviously, the gay male surfer had not ceased to exist by 1989. He had merely been rendered invisible and irrelevant, in preparation for the next target of the same tactic – women . . . Any 'mainstream' tolerance of feminists or homosexual men is now regarded by many male surfers as evidence of the weakness of non-surfing men.
>
> *(pp. 81–82)*

Representations of the female surfer all but vanished from 1980s dominant surfer cultures, replaced instead by images of bikini-clad models. Discourses of 'extreme sexism' (Stedman, 1997, p. 80) actively operated to deny women access to the waves. Stedman attributes this increasingly misogynistic, homophobic and white-male-dominated surf culture to 'accelerated individualisation', 'hyper-commodification' and 'mass consumption' (p. 75).

As Heywood (2008) and Comer (2004) suggest, in the fight to be recognized as serious contenders, women surfers often proved themselves by becoming 'one of the guys'. World tour winner, Layne Beachley, claims that 'back in the late '80s and early '90s women's surfing seemed to lack a sense of identity due to the fact that women felt the need to act and dress like men to earn their respect' (Beachley, 2009). This largely remained the case until Lisa Andersen rose to prominence in the early 1990s. A four-time world champion, Lisa surfed 'like a man', but with 'feminine grace and fluidity': 'Her smooth, refined surfing style presented a whole new image, demanded reverence from her peers, and gave the surfing world a revived appreciation of the power of a woman in the waves (Beachley, 2009).

Andersen's aggressive approach, read here as male, was balanced out—in the now familiar processes of 'gender apologetic'—by her feminine looks and her role as a mother. In 1994, Andersen became the poster girl for Roxy, Quiksilver's now hugely successful sister brand. This commercially-savvy move increased Roxy sales, as well as the exposure of women's surfing (Booth, 2001a; Comer, 2004). From the 1990s onwards, surfing was increasingly drawn to corporate-generated and commercially-produced popular culture (Rinehart and Sydnor, 2003; Wheaton, 2004). And, the figure of the surfer-girl has been a central commodity in globalised processes of [post-]subcultural consumption (Heywood, 2008).

Theoretical waves in surf research

Theoretically, particular ways of exploring women's surfing are emerging. For instance, Waitt (2008) maintains that surfing spaces and subjectivities are mutually constituted. Drawing on interviews with women surfers in Australia, he argues that despite the ways 'the heteronormative qualities of surf space reconfirm [surf] breaks as a seemingly natural heteromasculine domain' (p. 92), some women disrupt this domain because they move between normative and alternative-gendered discourses and embodiments. These shifting gendered locations invite us 'to rethink gender practices and gendered meanings of surf space' (p. 92).

Furthering this line of enquiry, Knijnik, Horton and Cruz (2010) make use of Markula's (2006) discussions of Deleuze's rhizome metaphor and apply it as a conceptual device for thinking about surfing bodies. They consider how surfing females challenge, explore and diversify embodied femininities by 'living in and through their changing bodies that are no longer dichotomized but "rhizomatized" ones' (p. 1181). Rhizomatized bodies are ones which resist gender norms and instead seek out ways in which gender might be differently lived. According to Knijnik, Horton and Cruz, competitive female surfers in Brazil are 'simultaneously reproducing and assaulting entrenched gender attitudes and practices'; they are 'opening up new possibilities for all Brazilian girls and women' (p. 1181). As the authors argue, this is particularly important in their country, where heterosexualized norms are highly valued; and 'skimpy bikinis, semi-nude people . . . physical exercise and eroticism are essential elements of the life on the beach' (p. 1173).

Clifton Evers (2009) also references Deleuzian theory in exploring how surfing bodies might be viewed as 'affective assemblages' (Grosz, 1994, in Evers, 2009). He demonstrates how surfing bodies make assembled connections with other bodies, nature, equipment and affects. In doing so, he argues, surfing bodies can, at times, escape significations of gender, even sex. For instance, when water, board and limbs momentarily blur into a 'falling body' . . . 'Gendered discourses actually have to catch up to work out if it is a "male" or "female" body, and a "masculine" or "feminine" experience' (p. 897).

Similarly, Roy (2011) highlights the value of a Deleuzian-influenced exploration of how female surfers activate the 'opening up'—rupturing, or deterritorialising—of traditional gendered and sexualized subjectivities. Sydnor (2003) has also applied these terms within the context of skysurfing and Laviolette (2010) has recognized Deleuze's own observation that surfing 'take[s] the form of entering into an existing wave. There's no longer an origin as starting point . . . The key thing is how to get taken up in the motion of a big wave . . .' (Deleuze, 1995, p. 121). Essentially, unlike institutionalized sports involving starter guns, targets, obstacles, boundaries and final whistles, surfing can only ever exist *in between*; between earth, sea and sky, and the constant swells of the ocean. This inherent connection between surfing, motion and mobility makes it distinct from more traditional sporting cultures in ways that allow for rhizomatic ruptures. In this chapter, we adopt this Deleuzian perspective.

Gender, sexualities and Newquay surf spaces

Ethnographic fieldwork, including participant observation and seven in-depth interviews with female surfers, was carried out by Georgina Roy who lived in Newquay, Cornwall, for six months in 2011.[1] Six of the women were previously known to the researcher through surfing, and field notes are based on her participation. Significantly, some of the women owned and/or worked for a small adventure sports business, positioning them within local commercial as well as socio-cultural relations.[2] All the women had moved, separately, to Newquay:

> Everyone's congregated here, there's not many people that are originally from Cornwall . . . they've all sort of travelled there, visited, and end up staying.
>
> *(Laura)*

> Just packed my van . . . drove down one day . . . Followed signs to Fistral beach . . . 'Surf capital' and all that.
>
> *(Jen)*

Since moving to Newquay, the women became socially intertwined in a range of ways. There is not a discernible group of seven surfers, because the connections between them constantly alter and shift. These connections are, like the waters they surf, emergent, organic, unpredictable; sometimes fickle, sometimes powerful, but always immanent.

Geographical characteristics define each and every surf location. Physical geography intertwines with the social and cultural geography of each space (Waitt, 2008; Evers, 2009). An important physical feature of surfing in the UK is that it is done in cold water. Consequently, in contrast to Brazilian culture, surfing is not tied as strongly to dominant images of 'beach culture' that are widely depicted in subcultural and popular media. Furthermore, Newquay itself has come to be associated with certain defining characteristics:

> Newquay is Britain's self-styled surf capital . . . There are surf shops on every corner and shapers[3] galore . . . It has good surfing beaches and crowds to match. It's also a real party town, not for the shy and retiring – summer nights are a throng of stag nights, hen parties and a rainbow spectrum of football shirts.
>
> *(Nelson and Taylor, 2008, p. 56)*

The life-blood of Newquay is tourism. In line with the exponential growth in surfing, the commercial development of Newquay has been considerable and rapid. The area now attracts around 750,000 people a year, about 30% of all tourist visitors to Cornwall. During the summer, the population of the Newquay increases from about 20,000 to 100,000 (Duchy of Cornwall, 2012).

Newquay is considered the birthplace of British surfing (Mansfield, 2009). Its reputation is wholly characterised by surfing and, significantly, by partying. It is a particularly popular destination for groups of young people. In the summer, Newquay's town centre echoes until the early hours with the noise of drunken partiers (tourists and locals). In the daytime, the streets and beaches become busy with people of all ages and backgrounds. Families, couples and groups mill around the town's main strip, and claim their space on Newquay's various beaches, which become occupied by sun and sea bathers; clusters of people building walls with windbreakers, children marking out football pitches, families playing cricket, and groups of people (predominantly men) spreading out to play rugby, Frisbee, or football. Jen describes Newquay as:

> . . . a very seasonal thing . . . it's living the high life all summer, but you know that the winter's gonna come, and then it'll all be like 'hmm', it's all unpredictable, and unsecure, like where are you gonna get a job, where you gonna live, you go through all that rigmarole.

When the buzz of summer gives way to winter, the population of Newquay dwindles. Bars and pubs become almost empty, half the shops close, and the rest strip back their stock to a minimum. Jen adds 'there's not much money to be made . . . and the winters are hard. . . .'

Newquay is undeniably a dominantly heterosexual, white, British space. It is evident in all of its most visible guises—as a holiday space for families, a party space for stag and hen groups, a commercial space for businesses, and as a surfing space. In many respects it epitomises the traditions of English seaside holiday towns, although its reputation as a tourist destination does contribute to the diversification of its demographics. 'The sort of people that live in Newquay, they're not born and bred here, I mean . . . [people] born in Newquay . . . they're very thin on the ground . . . it's quite a unique thing, to be a local' (Jen). Many visitors heard both on the streets and in the surf have travelled from various parts of the UK or from overseas, and although residents and visitors from ethnic minorities are vastly under-represented, they are less marginalised in Newquay than in many other parts of Cornwall. 'When I am here, I don't . . . have problems because . . . I am German, [or] because I am black' (Olivia).

The growing popularity of surfing in Britain can be evidenced by walking the length of Newquay's Fistral beach in summer. Observing Fistral beach, and the numerous surf schools operating there, it is apparent that surfing is creating opportunities for women to become active participants. However, what can also be gauged is that the numbers of males and females sitting 'out back' (behind the breaking waves and learning surfers) is much less evenly weighted than it is in the surf lessons. Here, to estimate, women make up around 10% of surfers, 20% at most.

> I always have a quick scan for women. Out back at North Fistral there was maybe one woman to every 20 men. I see a small woman with long dark hair on a shortboard. We make eye contact. She turns to the male surfer she is surfing with, puts her index finger in the air and then points towards me with her thumb. It appears, like me, she has noticed how many other women are out in the surf.
>
> *(Field notes, June 2011)*

Lesbian surfers in Newquay: making a difference?

Feminist and queer geographers have demonstrated the ways in which public social and sporting spaces come to be normalised as heterosexual (Valentine, 1996). As van Ingen notes, 'spaces are inexorably linked to the social construction of dominant ideologies and to the politics of identity' (2003, p. 210). Social norms act as powerful forces upon us in ways that are not necessarily *apparent*, but are nonetheless spatially present (Deleuze, 2004). They are 'woven into the fabric of social life' (Jackson, 2006, p. 108). The beach spaces in Newquay reflect a type of spatial gendering (evident in the ways in which men and boys dominate). The surf, however, is—literally—much more fluid, and this impacts on how gendered power relations infuse surfing spaces. The changing nature of the gendered connections between surfers is reflected in the conflicting experiences of female surfers when asked whether they thought they were treated differently by male surfers:

> Yeah, I think people tend to like, paddle round you more, sort of don't respect your position in the line up . . . but a lot of the time, if you just catch a wave, and then . . . sort of, show 'em you can surf [then they will respect your ability].
>
> *(Julia)*

> Er . . . only in a positive way . . . they'll let you take waves, that they probably wouldn't have let a guy do . . . they're a little bit more forgiving if you do drop in on them . . . it's a little bit patronising, but erm . . . quite handy (smiles) . . . they seem to be quite encouraging of women in the water.
>
> *(Jen)*

Surfing is not precisely spatially and temporally located as most other sports. The power relations that infuse surfing spaces are less fixed. Despite the fact that women still remain vastly outnumbered by men in surfing spaces, the numbers of competent female surfers has certainly grown (although it would be difficult to calculate a gendered ratio). The mix of men and women in the surf varies according to the surf conditions, the size and power of the swell, and the speed of the breaking wave. All these factors impact on who surfs on any given day, depending on the spot:

> North and South Fistral for example, if you were talking about Fistral as quite different, North is very pros and they might get a bit pissed off if you were in their way, whereas South is a little bit more forgiving and a little bit more chilled.
>
> *(Jen)*

The constantly changing features of surfing spaces in Newquay mean that, in the surf, it is difficult for gendered and sexualized power relations to take root. Therefore, whilst dominant configurations of gender and sexuality might emerge in Newquay surf, they are not often maintained. They are instead rhizomatic; in a constant state of change, and in this sense, surfing allows for the creation of alternatively gendered spaces. '. . . it's what men have said, it's good to have girls out there, it's less testosterone . . . little do they know that [a lot of] girl surfers are gay [in her experience]' (Jen).

Citing Podmore (2001) and Peace (2002), Brown et al. (2010) contend that queer geographers have tended to overlook the less visible and more subtle ways in which lesbian and queer women appropriate space. They propose that 'geographies of lesbian space can only be advanced through an attention to women's social networks' (Brown, Browne, and Lim, 2010, p. 8).

> I've never really experienced any homophobia wherever I've been . . . maybe one or two name calling . . . it's never really affected me in any way, cos I've always got all my friends around me, who I adore, so . . . but, I guess, I wouldn't walk around Wakefield

holding my girlfriend's hand . . . as I would do in Newquay . . . so I am aware that there's more homophobia in different places . . .

(Laura)

G: Do you think there are any lesbian spaces in Newquay?
Julia: On the spot I'd say no . . . Define lesbian space . . . is the space intentionally designed for lesbians? Is the 'space' a byproduct of lesbians using it? I think 'spaces' are made by the presence of people . . . five lesbians go for a surf, it's a lesbian space, but then that's like power in numbers.

Pink (2009) has considered the fluid nature of lived space. She quotes Casey (1996) when suggesting that '*lived bodies belong to places* and help to constitute them' in the same way that '*places belong to lived bodies* and depend on them' (cited in Pink, 2009, p. 30, original italics). Pink (2009) explores the idea that 'place', rather than being a specifically located space, might alternatively be conceptualized as an 'event'.

The girls that I surf with, pretty much, are all gay . . .

(Tammy)

In Brighton as a gay person, you'd be on the scene [gay scene] and that culture . . . fashion and music. Here it's ['gay scene' is] . . . having a surf . . . fire on the beach.

(Jen)

The women surfers in Newquay do not have lesbian and or queer places (e.g. bars, clubs, coffee shops) in which to meet. Sarah recognizes that Newquay 'doesn't really have a scene-scene, but then there are, it's just that sort of place, you can go out, and, yeah, I guess there are quite a few lesbians here. . . .' For this group of women, rather than places being available for lesbians, spaces are created *by* lesbians and at times *through* lesbian bodies (kissing, holding hands). Surfing is enabling the 'opening up' and activation of these social spaces, and surf spaces.

Julia: . . . five lesbians go for a surf, it's a lesbian space?
G: So . . . by that definition, are there any lesbian spaces in Newquay?
Julia: I suppose so, they are transient . . . What I would say, there is a community of lesbians as far as I am aware, there are no specific 'places' for lesbians to go, maybe because it is a small town there doesn't need to be . . . Presence creates space, it's the community . . . a lot of lesbians know each other and if enough of them go out at the same time it's a space.

Unlike the gay scene, or Gay Games, and even lesbian sports teams, which provide localized and/or bounded meeting places for lesbians, surfing spaces are more mobile, transient and nomadic. As Ingold (2008, p. 13) has suggested, it is not the case 'that living beings exist in places . . . [rather] places occur along the life paths of beings. . . .' These contexts provide instances where heteronormative surfing spaces might momentarily, transiently become re-configured as different spaces, potentially queer spaces. These moments of rhizomatic rupture might only be subtle ones, but they are visible, as is evident here:

I am quite affectionate with Sally in the water, and on the beach, and when I get out of the surf and she's waiting for me, we'll have a kiss and stuff, and it doesn't bother me . . . but it doesn't bother me in public either . . . in Newquay it doesn't bother me, if I'm out of Newquay, I'm more aware of it. I don't like people watching me and staring, and 'oh my god she's gay'.

(Jen)

Jen catches a few, then spends some time with Sally in the shallows. I see them leaning on a board together. They look at each other and kiss. It is a comfortable and relaxed kiss. They don't look around to see who's watching, no signs of un-comfort. As if it is their space.

(Field notes, 2011)

As Deleuze (1995, p. 176) comments, ruptures of the dominant 'appear for a moment, and it's that moment that matters, it's the chance we must seize'. Such moments matter because of, in this instance, the queer challenge to heteronormativity. They are an 'opening up' of space to different ways of doing surfing sexualities and reflect the rupturing of surfing's heteronormative culture.

Concluding comments

When surfers surf, they are not channeling, manipulating or harnessing power, but rather negotiating the force of the waves and sliding, joining its orbits momentarily in order to move in a slightly different direction.

(Ishiwata, 2002, p. 266)

The ways the lesbian surfers in this research occupy spaces is akin to the act of wave-riding itself. It is not a matter of blatant resistance, but is subtle—slight at times—rather than obvious and obstructive. This is what Ishiwata refers to as an 'other' form of politics, 'one that does not simply react to a set of constraints but instead develops an "other" sensitivity to them', one which is 'subtle enough to convert them into opportunities' (Ishiwata, 2002, p. 265, quoting Massumi, 1992).

As we highlight, Newquay is distinctly gendered and sexualized. This is especially notice-able during the tourist season, when the town and its beaches are configured through het-eronormative practices and cultures. And yet, lesbians are maneuvering within Newquay's spaces, 'opening up' opportunities to transform its gendered and sexualized spatiality. Wave-riding offers prime site/sight for these transformative flows because, as Deleuze recognized, it is always 'in motion'. Fiske (1989) describes this further: 'The wave is the text of bliss to the surfie . . . constantly shifting, needing retreading . . . It contradicts, defines, momentarily the ideological subjectivity through which discourses exert their control' (in Lewis, 2003, p. 65).

In this chapter, we discussed some of the ways lesbian surfers are instigating 'events', moments, ruptures, 'however inconspicuous, that elude control, [and engender] new space-times . . .' (Deleuze, 1995, p. 176). Our discussions provide support for the notion that subjectivities inter-twine with the 'process and production' of space and place (Probyn, 2003, in Waitt, 2008). We centre emergent theoretical flows (i.e. the ideas of Gilles Deleuze) to explore the potential for some women to choreograph gender and sexuality in non-normative ways, especially in and through the surf.

Notes

1 Six of the women self-identify as either lesbian or gay, one woman commented that she would not call herself 'completely straight'.
2 Four of the women owned or worked part-time for local businesses. One woman was a student and two women worked full-time.
3 Shapers are people who shape surf boards.

References

Barkham, P. (2006) A bigger splash, a lot more cash, *The Guardian* [online] 17 July. Available at: http://www.guardian.co.uk/travel/2006/jul/17/travelnews.watersportsholidays.unitedkingdom [accessed 17 December 2011].

Beachley, L. (2009) #22: Lisa Andersen: Surfer celebrates the 50 greatest surfers of All Time, Surfermag.com (accessed 30 October 2009; no longer available).

Booth, D. (2001a) From bikinis to boardshorts: *Wahines* and the paradoxes of surfing culture, *Journal of Sport History*, 28(1): 3–22.

Booth, D. (2001b) *Australian beach cultures: The history of sun, sand and surf*, London: Frank Cass.

Brown, G., Browne, K., and Lim, J. (2010) Introduction, or why have a book on geographies of sexualities, in Browne, K., Lim, J., and Brown, G. (Eds.) *Geographies of sexualities: theory, practices, and politics* (pp. pp. 53–69), London: Ashgate.

Comer, K. (2010) *Surfer girls in the new world order*, Durham: Duke University Press.

Comer, K. (2004) Wanting to be Lisa: Generational rifts, girl power and the globalisation of surf culture, in Campbell, N. (Eds.) *American youth cultures*, New York: Routledge.

Deleuze, G. (2004) *Difference and repetition*, London: The Athlone Press.

Deleuze, G. (1995) *Negotiations*, New York: Columbia University Press.

Duchy of Cornwall (2012) *Design and development: Newquay growth area* [online].Available at: http://www.duchyofcornwall.org/designanddevelopment_newquay.htm (accessed 20 January 2012).

Evers, C. (2009) 'The Point': surfing, geography and a sensual life of men and masculinity on the Gold Coast, Australia, *Social & Cultural Geography*, 10(8): 893–908.

Fiske, J. (1989) *Reading the popular*, Boston: Unwin-Hyman.

Ford N. and Brown, D.H.K. (2006). *Surfing and social theory: Experience, embodiment and narrative of the dream glide*, London: Routledge.

Henderson, M. (2001) A shifting line up: Men, women, and *Tracks* surfing magazine, *Continuum: Journal of Media and Cultural Studies*, 15(3): 319–332.

Heywood, L. (2008) Third wave feminism, the global economy, and women's surfing: Sport as stealth feminism in girls' surf culture, in Harris, A. (Ed.) *Next wave cultures feminism, subcultures, activism*, London: Routledge.

Ingold, T. (2008) Bindings against boundaries: Entanglements of life in an open world, *Environment and Planning A*, Advance Online Publication.

Ishiwata, E. (2002) Local motions: Surfing and the politics of wave sliding', *Journal for Cultural Research*, 6(3): 257–272.

Jackson, S. (2006) Gender, sexuality and heterosexuality: The complexity (and limits) of heteronormativity, *Feminist Theory*, 7(1): 105–121.

Knijnik, J.D., Horton, P., and Cruz, L.O. (2010) Rhizomatic bodies, gendered waves: Transitional femininities in Brazilian surf, *Sport in Society*, 13(7): 1170–1185.

Laviolette, P. (2010) *Extreme landscapes of leisure: Not a hap-hazardous sport*. Farnham: Ashgate.

Lewis, J. (2003) In search of the postmodern surfer: Territory, terror and masculinity, in Skinner, J., Gilbert, K. and Edwards, A. (Eds.) *Some like it hot: The beach as a cultural dimension*, Oxford: Meyer and Meyer.

Mansfield, R. (2009) *The surfing tribe: A history of surfing in Britain*, Cornwall: Orca Publications.

Markula, P. (2006) Deleuze and the body without organs: Disreading the fit feminine identity, *Journal of Sport and Social Issues*, 30(1): 29–44.

Nelson, C. and Taylor, D. (2008) *Surfing Britain and Ireland*, Bath: Footprint Handbooks.

Ormrod, J. (2007) Surf rhetoric in American and British surfing magazines Between 1965 and 1976, *Sport in History*, 27(1): 88–109.

Ormrod, J. (2002) Issues of gender in muscle beach party (1964). *Scope Online Journal of Film Studies*, http://www.nottingham.ac.uk/film/journal/ (no longer available).

Pink, S. (2009) *Doing sensory ethnography*, London: Sage.

Rinehart, R. and Sydnor, S. (Eds.) (2003) *To the extreme: Alternative sports, inside and out*, Albany: State University of New York Press.

Roy, G. (2011) Exploring the feminist potential of the female surfer: Surfing, spaces and subjectivities, in Watson, B. Harpin, J. (Eds.) *Identities, cultures and voices in sport and leisure* (pp. 141–158), Eastbourne: LSA Publication (no. 116).

Spowart, L., Burrows, L., and Shaw, S. (2010) 'I just eat, sleep and dream of surfing': When surfing meets motherhood, *Sport in Society*, 13(7–8): 1186–1203.

Stedman, L. (1997) From Gidget to Gonad Man: Surfers, feminists and postmodernisation, *Journal of Sociology*, 33(1): 75–90.

Surfer Magazine (2010) Pro surfing: THE SHARP END [online] Available at: http://www.surfermag.com/features/prssrfing/ (accessed 13 November 2011).

Sydnor, S. (2003) Soaring, in Rinehart, R. and Sydnor, S. (Eds.) *To the extreme: Alternative sports, inside and out*, Albany: State University of New York Press.

Valentine, G. (1996) (Re)negotiating the 'heterosexual street': Lesbian productions of space, in Duncan, N. (Ed.) *BodySpace: Destabilizing geographies of gender and sexuality*, London: Routledge

van Ingen, C. (2003) Geographies of gender, sexuality and race. Reframing the focus on space in sport sociology, *International Review for the Sociology of Sport*, 38(2): 201–216.

Waitt, G. (2008) Killing waves: Surfing, space and gender, *Social and Cultural Geography*, 9: 75–94.

Wheaton, B. (2010) Introducing the consumption and representation of lifestyle sports, *Sport in Society*, 13(7–8): 1057–1081.

Wheaton, B. (Ed.) (2004) *Understanding lifestyle sports: Consumption, identity and difference* (pp. 131–153), London: Routledge.

26

FEMALE FOOTBALL FANS AND GENDER PERFORMANCE

Stacey Pope

Introduction

This chapter focuses on the experiences of female football (soccer) fans in England, thus aiming to redress the dearth of research in the field. Drawing on a 'grounded theory' approach (Glaser and Strauss, 2008), 51 interviews were conducted with three generations of female fans of men's football. I categorised two different kinds of gender performances displayed by female football fans: 'masculine' femininities and 'feminine' femininities, focusing here upon the experiences of those women who typically performed 'masculine' femininities. I outline characteristics of these women, before examining the complexities for female fans in balancing their gender and sporting identities.

The dearth of research on female fandom

Although it has been widely assumed that the female football fan is a relatively new phenomenon, there is evidence that a small but significant number of women attended football matches in England from the 1880s onwards (Lewis, 2009). However, changes over the past two decades have opened up opportunities for women to attend matches as live fans, leading to the so-called 'feminization' of English football (Pope, 2011).

A shift in the gendered nature of professional football can be examined through the Hillsborough Stadium disaster of 1989, which saw 96 Liverpool supporters crushed to death. This symbolises the shift from the 'hooligan' years of the 1970s and 1980s to the supposedly new family-orientated, 'friendly' atmosphere at football today (Taylor, 1991). The instigation of all-seater stadia for clubs in the top two divisions of the sport, and the England national team reaching the semi-finals at the 1990 World Cup, prompted an upsurge of interest amongst women (Lopez, 1997). The formation of the FA Premier League in 1992, and the subsequent income from satellite television and other sponsorships, led to the new ubiquitous nature of elite football and the 'celebrity' status of players, described by Blackshaw and Crabbe (2004: 112) as a form of 'soap opera'. These developments are likely to have stimulated further female (and male) interest in the sport.

These changes have coincided with major transformations in women's working and leisure lives (Kay, 2000) leading to a greater equalisation of power relations between the sexes, enabling females to become more involved in 'former' predominantly male preserves such as sport (Liston, 2006: 371). Accordingly, the numbers of female fans have increased in recent years, with women now estimated to make up 19 per cent of the Premier League crowd (European Professional Football Leagues, 2012). However, only a handful of studies have explored women's experiences of watching men's football (see, for example, Jones, 2008). Instead, studies have largely focused upon the importance of football for constructing men's hegemonic masculinities, reflected in the large body of work which has centred upon hooliganism and male supporter subcultures (see, for example, Armstrong, 1998; Spaaij, 2008). This male-centric approach to the study of sports fandom provided the impetus for my research.

Performances of femininity in sport

A number of studies have examined the ways in which female athletes negotiate their approaches to femininity in sport. Many of these centre upon how females who participate in 'male defined' sports feel that they must clearly demarcate their conventional heterosexual femininity (Cox and Thompson, 2000). Here I draw upon Ussher's (1997) typology of gender performance and Sisjord and Kristiansen's (2009) application of this to the life world of female wrestlers. Ussher's typology provides a useful framework to consider the different ways in which heterosexual female sports fans might 'perform' femininities in what is largely regarded as a male domain.

Ussher (1997: 445–61) proposes that women actively negotiate the various 'scripts' of femininity in order to take up or resist the position of woman; thus, becoming 'woman' is something that women *do* rather than something women *are*. She suggests that there are at least four 'performances' of femininity available to most women. 'Being girl' refers to the archetypal position of 'woman' taken up when women want to 'be' rather than 'do' femininity. 'Doing girl' describes the position of performing the 'feminine masquerade' but knowing that this is 'playing a part', thus women taking up this position possess the ability to shift between 'appearing to be girl and ridiculing the very performance of femininity'. 'Resisting girl' refers to women who deny the traditionally signified 'femininity', such as the necessity for body discipline or the adoption of the mask of beauty. 'Subverting femininity' is associated with women who knowingly play with gender as a performance. The scripts outlined in Ussher's (1997) typology are neither concrete nor fixed – her aim is to capture the complexity of the continuous process of negotiation and resistance, with women moving between different positions at different points in their lives or in different situations.

Sisjord and Kristiansen (2009: 244) use Ussher's idea to explore the different ways in which heterosexual female wrestlers 'perform' femininity. They argue that women wrestlers exhibit a kind of 'resistant' femininity through 'transgressing traditional social norms by entering one of the most masculine arenas in the sport world – wrestling'. However, they also highlight a distinction between junior and senior wrestlers in their gender performances. Junior wrestlers mainly positioned themselves within the 'being' and 'doing' girl categorisations – 'doing' because of their participation in a masculine sport and so ridiculing the very performance of conventional femininity, but 'being' when holding back in workouts, thus complying with narrow scripts of femininity/muscularity. The seniors, however, performed 'doing girl' and 'resisting girl' performances – they 'resisted' or neglected 'body discipline' according to traditional scripts of femininity and were consequently more likely to gain respect from males as 'serious' wrestlers.

Methods

The findings for this chapter have been extracted from a wider comparative project on female football and rugby union fans in the English East Midlands city of Leicester (Pope, 2010). I draw on 51 semi-structured interviews conducted with three generations of Leicester City female football fans. The sampling frame used to select the respondents was a local questionnaire survey (Williams, 2004a), and potential interviewees were divided into three broad age groups using the age delineations from the survey.

Systematic sampling techniques (selecting every fifth questionnaire returned) were used to select potential interviewees and the final sample was made up of 10 'younger group' fans (aged 20–27 years), 25 'middle group' fans (aged 28–59) and 16 'older group' supporters (over 60 years old). Although Leicester is an ethnically diverse city, ethnic minority fans are not typically well represented in sports crowds in the UK (Williams, 2004b) and as a consequence, nearly all women in the sample were white. All of the women who agreed to participate in the research were also heterosexual. Many respondents were Season Ticket Holders (STHs) who attend all home matches or club members who attend the majority of home matches, but there were also some occasional attendees. Interviews were typically rich in detail and averaged around two hours in length, with a small number verging on life-history interviews and lasting four hours.

A 'grounded theory' approach was adopted so there was an emphasis upon 'the discovery of theory from data' throughout the research (Glaser and Strauss, 2008: 1). The research largely produced 'substantive theory', but also drew upon other sources where appropriate, such as Ussher's (1997) typology, thus incorporating 'formal theory' into the analysis (Glaser and Strauss, 2008: 32). After fully transcribing the interviews, the data was coded drawing upon the 'constant comparative method'; data collection and analysis continued until 'theoretical saturation' was reached (Corbin and Strauss, 2008). Pseudonyms are used to protect participant anonymity.

Findings

Female fandom and performing 'masculine' femininities

Drawing upon Giulianotti's (2002) 'hot' and 'cool' axis which is used to indicate the different degrees to which the club is central to football fans' self-formation or self-identity, my findings revealed two ideal fan types: 'hot' committed fans (for whom the club was a central life interest) and 'cool', more casual supporters (who did not express an intense identification with the club and instead viewed sports fandom as one of many leisure activities). There was a continuum between 'hot' and 'cool' fans with varying levels of fan attachment. Nearly 85 per cent (43/51) of fans were most suited to the 'hot' fan category, with football fandom forming a crucial aspect of their identities.

Ussher's (1997) four performances of femininity and Sisjord and Kristiansen's (2009) application of this model to research on female wrestlers was useful in my analysis of the multiplicity of supporter styles revealed amongst the sample of female football fans. Like Sisjord and Kristiansen's (2009) wrestlers, many female football fans could be understood to be exhibiting a kind of 'resistant' femininity due to their participation in a highly masculine sport, and also performed 'doing girl' as this could be said to ridicule the performance of femininity.

I have synthesised Ussher's categories into two different kinds of gender performance which helped to connote female fan types (Pope, 2013): 'masculine' femininities (those characterised by 'doing girl' and 'resisting girl' approaches to presentation of self and displayed by 'hot' fans) and 'feminine' femininities (those characterised by 'doing girl' and 'being girl' approaches and exhibited by 'cool' fans). This may serve as a useful framework in future research on female fans.

There was some overlap between the female fan types – not all 'hot' fans, for example, performed 'masculine' femininities. But crudely speaking, 'hot' fans were more likely to adopt the position of 'resisting girl'; typically exhibiting 'masculine' characteristics. However, 'cooler', less committed fans more typically performed 'being girl' approaches, thus emphasising traditional 'femininity'. Here I focus my discussion primarily upon women who performed 'masculine' femininities.

Paechter and Clark (2007) discuss how taking part in a stereotypically masculine activity is regarded as a defining feature of a tomboy identity. Many of the fans who performed 'masculine' femininities had adopted a tomboy persona when younger. Other studies have found links between females playing sport and a tomboy identity (Cox and Thompson, 2000; Liston, 2006) and in this research female fans who had early experiences of playing football with males invariably explored this option with comments such as 'I was a real tomboy' (Eileen, age 50, occasional attendee) or 'I used to be a tomboy' (Rachel, age 23, occasional attendee).

Paechter (2006) suggests that tomboys who reject the conventions of femininity and enjoy identifying with boys are claiming a share of male power. This seems to be supported by my findings where more adventurous leisure activities were favoured by tomboys, and although many tomboys reported how they were seen as 'odd' by 'more feminine' girls, and were aware that playing football was generally perceived as unusual, they gained confidence and enjoyment from this activity. As Williams (2003: 97) suggests, this 'she-bloke' attitude amongst female football players offers both liberation from the perceived limits of femininity (a fear of being hurt) and a form of male emulation.

Three of the younger women who eventually graduated to play in women's football teams felt that they had benefited most from competing against males and Rachel explained that, 'They didn't see me as though I was just a girl, it was just a team mate' (Rachel, age 23, occasional attendee). This seems to echo Sisjord and Kristiansen's (2009) findings that senior wrestlers were compatible with Ussher's 'resistant girl' performance, as they transgressed traditional perceptions of feminine behaviour and were 'respected' when they trained with male seniors. The use of the tomboy label demonstrates the identity work that was necessary for young females to gain access to football. Inhabiting and performing a tomboy identity seemed to be one of the main ways in which girls could render more socially acceptable their interest in and access to sport.

Nearly all the women who described themselves as tomboys discussed how this marked them out as *different* from other girls, and many of the women maintained aspects of this tomboy identity into adulthood. Rachel (age 23, occasional attendee) proposed that women who follow football as fans are regarded as tomboys as, unlike hockey or netball, football is not typically perceived as 'a woman's sport'. Some women identified more strongly with men and male fans than with other women and this was usually attributed to their continued involvement in football:

> I was sort of brought up as one of the lads . . . I've always got on with the lads better as I've grown up and I think it's because of the interest in football. And even at work now it's the same.
>
> *(Charlie, age 37, STH)*

> I've always had a lot of male friends throughout my life, just 'cos, obviously, I do have this sporting side inside of me, which they can relate to.
>
> *(Rosie, age 20, STH)*

Sharing an interest in football also served as an important social facilitator. Football was described as an 'international language' that could prompt conversations – usually with men. Many female fans who performed 'masculine' femininities often discussed football with male fans beyond match days; for example, with colleagues in the workplace, with friends and family members, or when they spontaneously encountered football fans that they had never met before in another city or country.

Anita described how none of her female friends were interested in football, initially labelling her interest as 'mad'. But her sporting knowledge was an important form of cultural capital that gave her an advantage in the workplace: unlike most women, she could use this as a form of communication in the male-dominated world of business:

> You still see it now in business; there are no other women that I work with that can talk about football or even go down. So that makes me different in business, I can talk to men about football and golf and I think that's one of the reasons why they took me on, 'cos I think they realised that predominantly a lot of the people that I meet with were going to be men, therefore there was a high chance they were going to be into golf and football. [. . .] You can get closer to people very quickly when you start talking about football.
>
> *(Anita, age 35, occasional attendee, sales manager)*

These women often expressed hostility to what they perceived to be extreme forms of conventional femininity – to those women who performed 'feminine' femininities and who were characterised by 'being girl' approaches to presentation of self. Jones (2008: 528) has argued that some female fans rejected women who in their eyes did not 'do fandom properly', for example, by emphasising their femininity through feminine dress and make-up, expressing a sexual interest in the male players, and not possessing an understanding of the rules of the sport.

My research lends weight to these findings. Some 'hot' committed fans were frustrated by 'cooler' fans who performed 'feminine' femininities, and criticized how these women lacked sporting knowledge as they 'haven't got a clue what they are talking about' (Katie, age 26, STH). It was suggested that these (other) women were not fully focused on the match and treated this as an 'afternoon out'; in the words of Deborah (age 51, member): 'They don't get as involved . . . they're probably doing their lipstick and things like that. And I'm thinking "What the hell do you come for?"'

Studies have shown that female fans complain about perceptions (from male fans) that they lack sporting knowledge and commitment, which is often closely tied to the accusation that they only attend sporting events to 'lust' after male players (Crawford and Gosling, 2004: 477). Although some women who performed 'masculine' femininities in my study did express sexual interest in players, they were also aggravated by female fans who said that their main interest in the sport was the pleasure they derived from looking at male athletic bodies. Toffoletti and Mewett's (2012) findings suggest that female Australian Football League fans will stress their knowledge and commitment to sport over any voyeuristic pleasure they might experience. My respondents were frustrated by those women who 'played up' their sexual interest in male players, especially as this meant that they would consequently have to defend their own position as a 'real' fan. In the words of Janet (age 26, STH): 'The ideal way to tease a woman [at football] is to tease her about only going because they fancy the players. I don't want to be a victim of that, so I just wish women would shut up about it.'

Balancing gender and sporting identities

For women who are involved in football as 'hot' committed fans, some complex issues were raised surrounding their gender identities. Russell and Tyler (2002), in their study of identity construction of younger girls (aged 10–11 years), found that 'doing' femininity was a complex process at this age. Girls defined themselves as 'half-girlie' because although they participated in the 'girlie' activity of shopping and were already conscious of their appearance, they also played football. Thus, a blurring of conventional forms of the 'masculine' and 'feminine' led to some early identity confusion, which was only 'rectified' when girls grew older and felt compelled to choose a side. However, some of my (especially younger) female fans were able to accommodate the different gendered facets of their identities into adulthood. Janet (age 26, STH) described how, 'I certainly don't think that going to the football and being feminine are mutually exclusive at all', and whilst she self-defined as a 'tomboy' who is interested in so-called 'male' activities such as football and snowboarding, she also discussed some stereotypically 'feminine' attributes: 'I do preen in front of the mirror all of the time . . . I'm just really vain.' Thus, some women successfully managed potentially conflicting aspects of gender identity skilfully and with confidence:

> I'm not like a girl football fan, who isn't into anything else. I love shopping, absolutely obsessed with it . . . I've always been the girlie girl but I've just always been football . . . I've only ever been described by one person as a 'ladette' . . . I have proper in-depth conversations with him about the football, and he's like 'Ohh, you're such a tomboy.' And I'm like 'Yeah, but I'm not really, am I?' Maybe that's people's stereotypes or opinions on women who like football . . . Maybe what they expect a woman who likes football to be, is not what I am. [. . .] I was a little bit shocked by that. [. . .] But I think maybe it's 'cos I've got a bit of confidence when it comes to talking about stuff, especially football.
>
> *(Helena, age 23, STH)*

However, some female fans struggled to balance their gender and sporting identities and their different identity traits. This was especially the case when their performances of 'masculine' femininities conflicted with traditional gender roles and expectations. For example, women's commitment to their football club was perceived as 'strange' and 'odd' by others, especially if their male partner did not share this interest. Andrea (age 78, STH) described how 'They always say to him "We can't believe it, it's usually the man going to the match" . . . People find it hard because I'm that wrapped up in it.' This sort of gender transgression or role dissonance could lead to abuse towards female fans – or towards their male partners. This is illustrated by Helena's experiences (age 23, STH) as when she challenged the heterosexual role division by attending football matches without her (now ex) boyfriend, they were both ridiculed. This could herald serious life impacts for women, such as refusing to enter a relationship with a non-Leicester City fan. As Deborah (age 51, member) put it: 'It's a big part of my life, and if he can't accept me as a Leicester fan then I'm afraid I don't want to know you, sort of thing.'

Other extreme examples of the role of football in heterosexual relationships included female fans threatening to split up if their male partners did not accompany them to matches. For Sabrina (age 46, STH), although a general interest in football initially brought her and her husband together, she later found that she 'needed somebody who liked football, Leicester City basically, *as much as I did*'. Their marriage problems were exacerbated by Leicester City's manager joining the club her husband supported, and following her divorce she entered a relationship with a man who supported the same club.

Women also encountered difficulties in balancing their involvement in football as 'hot' committed fans with the expectations of motherhood. Although some respondents were firmly rooted as 'hot' or 'cool' fans, the typical heterosexual female life cycle also meant in some cases there was some considerable shifting between the 'hot' and 'cool' modes. Bialeschki (1994) suggests that women's lack of leisure is often perceived as inevitable, as many women are pressed to defer to the needs of other family members until later in life when their 'caring' roles are presumed to be rather less restrictive. In my research, having children was one of the main factors which affected movement from a 'hot' to a rather 'cooler' fan affiliation – and then perhaps back up to 'hot' (or planning to return) after offspring were older. Others found it difficult, emotionally, to invest strongly in sport when their children were young, so they postponed their active, committed fandom until their children were older. This is unlike some male partners who continued to attend matches whilst female fans were compelled to take 'fan breaks'. Thus, women's sporting fan 'careers' follow very different paths from those of male fans who, broadly speaking, have not been shown to face the same competing demands or to adjust their involvement as football spectators at different stages of the life cycle. Supporting this, Giulianotti (1999) describes how male hooligans adopt other roles such as parents and partners, alongside their involvement in football.

Even for those women who did not take time away from attending matches after having children, thus maintaining their involvement in football as 'hot' committed fans, there was often a conscious repression of performing 'masculine' femininities in order to conform to the social expectations of the role of mother. For example, Anita described how, before she had children, football was 'all important and you lived your life by it'; and she would attend matches to 'shout my head off and absolutely get rid of all the aggression and the anger'. But as her children now accompany her to matches she did not feel that she could use football as a stress outlet.

Whereas women are likely to be defined by their enduring and essentialist responsibility as the primary home carer, sport is typically seen as one of the key definers of acceptable masculinities and a release from the feminising constraints of children and home, and so it is perhaps unlikely that many male fans will share these kinds of restrictions. Similarly, Sisjord and Kristiansen (2009: 242) describe the difficulties for senior wrestlers of balancing the divergent expectations of training 'like a man' but also demonstrating their traditional femininity outside of wrestling. In my research, adopting a dual identity was one way for women to try and balance their interest in football with the expectations of being a mother. For Sabrina this enabled her to interact with other mothers and avoid being socially alienated:

> It became quite awkward being a female football supporter being around lots of mums who didn't really have any interest in football and I had to learn almost to talk about something other than sport and football to be able to fit in with the group. Because obviously my children needed to mix with other mums and kids. [. . .] You have to become something else to a certain extent, you have no choice; they [children] don't want the mum that's a weirdo. [. . .] It's almost like being two people in a funny sort of way, to be as daft about football as I was, I had to compromise to some extent . . . I was still going to do it, I just wasn't going to let it be quite as badly known what I was up to.
>
> *(Sabrina, age 46, STH)*

Summary

This chapter makes a contribution towards redressing the gender imbalance in research on sports fandom. Female fans could be said to demonstrate a kind of 'resistant' femininity through their involvement in the male dominated sport of football. I have argued that two different kinds of gender 'performance' helped to connote fan types for female sports fans: 'masculine' femininities (typically displayed by 'hot' fans and characterised by 'doing girl' and 'resisting girl' approaches) and 'feminine' femininities (exhibited by 'cool' fans adopting 'doing girl' and 'being girl' approaches).

For those women performing 'masculine' femininities, many had played competitive sports when younger, and adopted a tomboy identity that they maintained into adulthood. These were 'hot' committed fans, whose knowledge of sport could even be used to give them an advantage in male dominated work spaces. They were hostile to women who performed 'feminine' femininities or 'being girl' approaches as this threatened to undermine their own status as legitimate sports fans (see also Jones, 2008).

Performing 'masculine' femininities could in some ways open up opportunities for female fans to access spaces and behaviours that would be strictly off limits to those who subscribed to conventional forms of femininity and thus could to some extent be regarded as potentially liberating. However, for some women, their identity as football fans threatened to disrupt other areas of their lives such as heterosexual relationships or their role as mothers. The complexities of female fans' lives required them to construct a particular lifestyle to enable them to encompass different interests and identity facets and combine their sporting interest with the social expectations of conventional femininity. Thus, despite recent changes which have opened up opportunities for women to enter the 'former' male preserve of football, female fans are still required to negotiate their involvement in football with other competing demands and to balance this with conventional gender role expectations.

Acknowledgements

This work was supported by the Economic and Social Research Council (grant PTA-030-2005-00310).

References

Armstrong G (1998) *Football hooligans: Knowing the score*. Oxford: Berg.
Bialeschki D (1994) Re-entering leisure: Transition within the role of motherhood. *Journal of Leisure Research*, 26(1): 57–74.
Blackshaw T and Crabbe T (2004) *New perspectives on sport and 'deviance': Consumption, performativity and social control*. Abingdon: Routledge.
Corbin J and Strauss A (2008) *Basics of qualitative research: Techniques and procedures for developing grounded theory*. London: Sage Publications Ltd.
Cox B and Thompson S (2000) Multiple bodies: Sportswomen, soccer and sexuality. *International Review for the Sociology of Sport*, 35(1): 5–20.
Crawford G and Gosling V (2004) The myth of the 'puck bunny': Female fans and men's ice hockey. *Sociology*, 38(3): 477–93.
European Professional Football Leagues Website (2012) The changing face of the premier league. Available at http://www.epfl-europeanleagues.com/changing_face.htm (accessed 15 February 2012).
Giulianotti R (1999) *Football: A sociology of the global game*. Cambridge: Polity Press.
Giulianotti R (2002) Supporters, followers, fans, and flâneurs. *Journal of Sport and Social Issues*, 26(1): 25–46.
Glaser B and Strauss A (2008) *The discovery of grounded theory: Strategies for qualitative research*. London: AldineTransaction.
Jones K (2008) Female fandom: Identity, sexism, and men's professional football in England. *Sociology of Sport Journal*, 25: 516–37.
Kay T (2000) Leisure, gender and the family: The influence of social policy. *Leisure Studies*, 19: 247–65.
Lewis R (2009) 'Our lady specialists at Pike Lane': Female spectators in early English professional football, 1880–1914. *The International Journal of the History of Sport*, 26(15): 2161–81.
Liston K (2006) Women's soccer in the Republic of Ireland: Some preliminary sociological comments. *Soccer and Society*, 7(2–3): 364–84.

Lopez S (1997) *Women on the ball*. London: Scarlet Press.

Paechter C (2006) Masculine femininities/feminine masculinities: Power, identities and gender. *Gender and Education*, 18(3): 253–63.

Paechter C and Clark S (2007) Who are tomboys and how do we recognise them? *Women's Studies International Forum*, 30: 342–54.

Pope S (2010) *Female fandom in an English 'sports city': A sociological study of female spectating and consumption around sport*. PhD Thesis, University of Leicester, UK.

Pope S (2011) 'Like pulling down Durham cathedral and building a brothel': Women as 'new consumer' fans. *International Review for the Sociology of Sport*, 46(4): 471–87.

Pope S (2013) 'The love of my life': The meaning and importance of sport for female fans. *Journal of Sport and Social Issues*, 37(2): 176–195.

Russell R and Tyler M (2002) Thank heaven for little girls: 'Girl heaven' and the commercial context of feminine childhood. *Sociology*, 36(3): 619–37.

Sisjord M and Kristiansen E (2009) Elite women wrestlers' muscles: Physical strength and a social burden. *International Review for the Sociology of Sport*, 44(2): 231–46.

Spaaij R (2008) Men like us, boys like them: Violence, masculinity and collective identity in football hooliganism. *Journal of Sport and Social Issues*, 32(4): 369–92.

Taylor I (1991) English football in the 1990s: Taking Hillsborough seriously?. In: Williams J and Wagg S (eds) *British football and social change: Getting into Europe*. Leicester: Leicester University Press, pp.3–24.

Toffoletti K and Mewett P (2012) 'Oh yes, he is hot': Female football fans and the sexual objectification of sportsmen's bodies. In: Toffoletti K and Mewett P (eds) *Sport and its female fans*. London: Routledge.

Ussher J (1997) *Fantasies of femininity: Reframing the boundaries of sex*. London: Penguin Books.

Williams J (2003) *A game for rough girls? A history of women's football in Britain*. London: Routledge.

Williams J (2004a) *A survey of Leicester City FC football fans*. Report, University of Leicester, UK.

Williams J (2004b) *A Research Survey of Leicester City FC Supporters*. Report, University of Leicester, UK.

27

WATCHING WOMEN BOX

Kasia Boddy

Boxers Hit Harder When Women Are Around', the title of a 1939 poem by Kenneth Patchen (1968, p.71), sums up the all-too-familiar scenario (at least in Hollywood) of male boxers performing anxiously before women whose love is conditional on the knockout blow that will provide a definitive physical and financial proof of masculinity. Boxing, says Joyce Carol Oates, 'is for men, and is about men, and *is* men' (2006, p.72). But not always. What happens to the story when the boxers themselves are women? Who watches the women and what do they see?

The first descriptions of women fighters are by Roman poets dreaming of a long-past (and largely imaginary) idyllic time in which naked men and women competed together, 'covered in dust' and with 'thongs for boxing' attached to their arms (Propertius, 1994, p.90). The poet Ovid envisages Theseus, King of Athens, coming upon the beautiful Helen, Queen of Sparta, competing in the *palaestra[0]* (gymnasium), 'a naked maiden with naked men' (1990, p.153), while Propertius fantasizes about two bare-breasted Amazons: 'One soon to be prize boxer, the other horseman / Between whom Helen with bare nipples took up arms.' Roman women, on the other hand, he complained, pay 'boring attention to perfumed hair' (p. 91). If these poets were the first, they were certainly not the last men to suggest that the attraction of women's boxing did not lie in its demonstration of skill or power but rather in the opportunities it afforded to expose bare flesh. 'Nation finally coming round to the idea of sweaty, underdressed young women', joked the American satirical newspaper *The Onion* of the 'increased interest in women's boxing' in the 1990s (Anon, 1999).[1] From classical to modern times, women's boxing has always had to contend with this kind of response and one of the purposes of this essay will be to consider how women boxers themselves have reacted and what alternative images have been offered over the last two hundred years.

Boxing's first proto-modern manifestation was in eighteenth-century England when bare-knuckle prize fighting became a professional working-class sport and gloved sparring a fashion-able recreation for the upper classes. While women played no part in sparring, Dianne Dugaw argues that there was 'casual acceptance of women combatants' in fights for money (1989, p.126). 'Scarce a week passes', reported *The London Journal* in August 1723, 'but we have a Box-ing-Match at the Bear-Garden between women' (Johnson, 1996, p.343). Two of the most pop-ular fighters were Elizabeth Stokes and Mrs. Sutton, who fought with quarter-staffs (short sticks) as well as their fists, and sometimes, in what we might call mixed doubles, with their husbands. Men and women weren't expected to fight differently, Dugaw argues, and female participation 'in "masculine" sports seems not to have been considered a violation of their "natural" female abilities or inclinations' (p.126). Certainly no humour or sensationalism accompanied the report that, in August 1725, 'Sutton the champion of Kent and female heroine of that county fought Stokes and *his much admired* consort of London' (Dugaw, 1989, p.125).

And yet, for all the press coverage given to these fighters, descriptions of their contests (especially by foreign visitors) tended to concentrate on the state of their dress rather than the blows they exchanged. Recalling a trip to London in 1710, Zacharias Conrad von Uffenbach described a fight between two women 'without stays and in nothing but a shift' (1934, pp.90–91), while the only point of pugilistic interest that Martin Nogüe noted of the women he observed was that they were '*dépouillées jusqu'à la ceinture*' (stripped to the waist) (1728, p.364). William Hickey too, coming upon two women boxing near Drury Lane in 1749, simply reported that 'their faces [were] entirely covered in blood, bosoms bare, and the clothes nearly torn from their bodies' (1913, pp.82–83). Fiction's depiction of 'Amazonian heroines' fond of 'fisticuff-war' – such as Molly Seagrim in Henry Fielding's *Tom Jones* (originally published in 1749) – also paid most attention to the striptease that fisticuff-war entails. A fight begins and, Fielding assures his readers, 'in a very few minutes they were both naked to the middle' (1996, p.156).

One of Molly Seagrim's opponents is Goody Brown, a woman who, we are told, has the advantage of having no bosom; her breasts are 'an ancient parchment, upon which one might have drummed a considerable while without doing her any damage'. Molly is 'differently formed in those parts' and therefore susceptible to 'a fatal blow had not the lucky arrival of Tom Jones at this point put an immediate end to the bloody scene' (p.156). Tom now fights Goody; perhaps, Fielding suggests, he forgot she was a woman, 'for, in reality, she had no feminine appearance but a petticoat' (p.157). I mention this scene because, in just a few words, Fielding presents the two stereotypes with which female boxers ever since have had to contend. Molly represents the kind of feminine (that is, busty) woman for whom fighting is a kind of sexual display. She performs lustily if not particularly effectively, but her lack of success serves merely to emphasise her femininity. Goody is presented as unfeminine (encapsulated in her flat chest) and therefore as a better if less appealing fighter. 'Have you not heard of fighting Females / Whom you rather think be Males?', Fielding had asked in an earlier poem, in which he burlesques Elizabeth Stokes and Mrs Sutton (Fielding, 1972, p.111). On this reading, the woman boxer, if not exactly male, represents a kind of parody of masculinity.

By the beginning of the nineteenth century, the woman boxer had become an established figure in both feminist and anti-feminist discourses. Women who challenged gender distinctions (in the name of 'rights for women') were satirised as aspirant men, longing for nothing less (or more) than the day 'when the sex would acquire high renown in boxing matches' (Bisset, 1804, p. 200). But fame was not the only reward for female boxing skills. A more practical application was suggested by William H. Bishop's 1895 novel, *The Garden of Eden, USA*. Set in a utopia of sexual and economic equality in which cooking and housework are done by centralized machinery, *The Garden of Eden, USA* was perhaps the first novel to discuss rape as a social problem and certainly the first to advocate boxing training as a potential response. In the world outside utopia, Bishop argues, 'the power of self-defence or of indignant protest is more necessary to women than to men' (p.148). But even in Eden, women box 'in bravado of conventional prejudices' (p.198).

Those prejudices would prove hard to shift, even as a small number of women found a place in the modern mass spectator sport of gloved and regulated boxing that was beginning to establish itself in the United States at this time. In 1880, the *Police Gazette* – one of the great forces behind boxing promotion – announced that a Miss Libbie Ross was 'champion female boxer of America' and in 1884, Hattie Stewart was declared world female champion. Unlike the crowns held by their male equivalents, these titles were not, however, taken very seriously.

With an almost eighteenth-century relish, the *Police Gazette* tended to prefer stories in which women fought over men 'according to pugilistic rules' (Smith and Smith, 1972, p.120) and in skimpy clothes.

Early films, such as Thomas Edison's 1898 *Comedy Set-To*, also viewed women's boxing as a reliable source of amusement and titillation for male spectators. Starring the *Police Gazette* 'Champion Lady Bag Puncher', Belle Gordon, against Billy Curtis, *Comedy Set-To* was, according to one magazine, a 'refined, scientific, and genuine comedy'. 'Belle Gordon is as frisky a little lady as ever donned a boxing outfit, and her abbreviated skirt, short sleeves and low necked waist make a very jaunty costume'(Toulmin, 1999, p.33).[2]

In Britain, America and Australia, professional women's boxing – or 'Lady Boxing Attractions' – remained closely aligned to the worlds of vaudeville and fairground entertainment until well into the second half of the twentieth century (Toulmin, 1999, p.29). The 1950s (often considered the decade which sent women back from the workplace into the kitchen) saw the first small stirrings of a professional boxing circuit in the United States. At the forefront was Yorkshire-born Barbara Buttrick, the undefeated Women's World Fly and Bantamweight champion from 1950 to 1960. After several years touring Britain's boxing booths, Buttrick immigrated to the United States where she fought in both competitive bouts and exhibition matches. She was the first woman boxer to have a fight broadcast on television (in 1954), to appear in *The Ring* magazine (in 1957) and, with Phyllis Kugler, to obtain a Texan boxing license, also in 1957 (Hargreaves, 1996, p.127; Toulmin, 1999, pp.40–42; Dunn, 2009, pp.130–31).

While the second-wave women's movement established further milestones during the 1970s, it wasn't really until the 1980s and 1990s that the sport's appeal, and accessibility, began to widen. Various explanations have been given for boxing's development at this time. The major impetus was amateur and middle class, as women sampled the sport's techniques and training methods in the boxerobics or self-defence classes that mushroomed in the US and in Europe during the 1980s fitness boom (Dunn, 2009, p.19). Gleason's Gym in Brooklyn, for many the archetypal boxing gym, first admitted women in 1986 and by 2000, it had 116 (that is 15%) women members (Hass, 2000, p.7). Some women were attracted by the 'total body workout' offered by the sport, as a Gleason's 2006 how-to-guide put it (Roca and Silverglad, 2006); others were drawn to its romantically 'gritty' atmosphere (Picket, 2000, p.1). After going to a 'proper' gym, Leah Hager Cohen found the pink hand wraps and wicker baskets offered by a 'spiffy' women's health club unsatisfying (2005, p.222). Some of these women were attracted to the boxing gym as one of the 'traditional proving grounds of masculinity' (Rotella, 2002, p.32). What better place in which to challenge traditional gender stereotypes, except perhaps in the ring itself?

In 1970, the artist Judy Chicago placed an advertisement for her upcoming show in the major American art magazine *Artforum*. The full-page photograph presented the gloved artist leaning on the ropes on a boxing ring with the new name that she had adopted (in preference to her birth name, Cohen, or her married name, Gerowitz) blazened across her chest like a boxer's *nom de guerre*. On the wall above her head is a large image of Jack Johnson, the first black heavyweight champion; the implication is that Chicago is similarly taboo-breaking and trailblazing. She later said the advertisement 'marked the moment when women all over the country came out fighting in an effort to somehow effect a change in the intense discrimination of the art world' (Chicago, 1996, p.21). Whether or not that effort was successful is not for this essay to judge, but Chicago's pose certainly inspired a generation of feminist artists to go one step further and enter the ring for real. Cindy Sherman's sparring partner describes her as a 'pit bull terrier' in the ring and 'just as tenacious' about her work (Berne, 2003, p.37). In this context, it was hardly surprising that Annie Liebovitz chose an image of a naked woman in boxing stance (with red gloves and a feminist text painted on her blacked-up body) to advertise an exhibition of photographs of American women at the beginning of the twenty-first century.

More recently, the symbolic emphasis has shifted from the political to the personal. Since the 1990s, several women amateur boxers have published memoirs which explore 'what happens when you transpose generic female motivations and confusions into the boxing ring' (Sekules, 2001b, p.8). Kate Sekules, for example, reports that she had no problem fighting men, but had to work hard to overcome her reluctance to hit other women (2001a, p.70), while Leah Hager Cohen describes how boxing helped her to come to terms with anorexic and suicidal feelings and, finally, allowed her to fuse 'erotic and aggressive impulses' (p.225). Lynn Snowden Picket took up the sport because it helped her express anger at her cheating ex-husband (p.7), while psychotherapist Bonnie Klein found, through boxing, that she was able both to 'get out of [her] head and into [her] body' and to reconnect to her Jewish heritage (2010, p.193). Like many boxing memoirs written by men in this period, these stories draw on the therapeutic language of self-help: boxing is presented less in terms of jabbing, feinting and punching than (as Laila Ali's (2003) book *Reach!* put it) 'finding strength, spirit, and personal power'. A similar motivational message has driven recent Hollywood films about women boxing, which mostly just substitutes a girl for a boy in a conventional plot. In *Blonde Fist* (1991), *Knockout* (2003) and *Million Dollar Baby* (2004), girls fulfil their father's thwarted ambitions by winning a belt or find in their coach a new, better father; in *Girlfight* (2000), *The Opponent* (2000) and *Honeybee* (2002), they dispense with their abusive boyfriends, both in and out of the ring. Singers such as Christina Aguilera and Pink regularly dress up as boxers to suggest that they're feisty and in control, an image that advertisers also use to sell a variety of products from deodorant with 'a different kind of strength' to vitamins with 'extra PUNCH'.

Other women, however, were less interested in the symbolism of boxing or the life lessons it offered than in the challenges of the sport itself. What they wanted to do was compete; but before they could enter the ring, they needed to go to court. The first legal challenge came in 1993 when an American teenager, Dallas Malloy, successfully sued USA Boxing, the national amateur boxing association, for gender discrimination. The association quickly implemented a series of rules and regulations governing women's boxing and by July 1994, 260 American women had registered as amateur boxers (Dunn, 2009, pp.19–20). The following year, women took part in the New York *Daily News* Golden Gloves tournament and in 1997 the first US Women's National Championships was held, with the first Women's World Championships following in 2001. In a few short years, then, women's amateur boxing established a strong institutional basis with an increasingly wide international reach, culminating in the decision of the International Olympic Committee (IOC) to include the sport (at three weight categories) in the 2012 Olympic Games.[3]

Professional boxing had a rather different trajectory. The breakthrough came in 1995 when Christy Martin ('The Coal Miner's Daughter' from West Virginia) fought an Irish fighter called Deirdre Gogarty on the undercard of the Mike Tyson–Frank Bruno heavyweight title fight in Las Vegas. The main event was a desultory affair and sportswriters focused, with relief, on the competitive and exciting women's contest. Martin appeared to much acclaim on the cover of *Sports Illustrated*; inside, photographed with a vacuum cleaner, she said that she was 'not out to make a statement about women in boxing . . . This is about Christy Martin' (Hoffer, 1996). Nevertheless, the fight provided an impetus to many novice fighters, many of whom, initially, were offered fights despite their lack of experience. Women boxers had a novelty value and, by 1999, Carlo Rotella was complaining that promoters opted for 'comely incompetents' who had little knowledge of 'defense and technique':

Women's boxing often pleases crowds because it looks, paradoxically, both conventionally manlier than men's boxing and more womanly. It looks more like the way men pretend to fight in movies . . . [or a] catfight.

(p.34)

Ten years on, a small number of professional women boxers have managed to make a career, although, now that the novelty has worn off, very few make much money at the sport. Some, like Lucia Rijker, came to boxing from the martial arts; others, like Laila Ali, Jacqui Frazier and Freeda Foreman, capitalized on their famous fathers' names and often fought each other. The language used to describe these celebrity fixtures was either humorously patronising – Laila Ali was 'a manicurist on a mission' who 'stings like a butterfly' – or, more usually, spitting with moral outrage (Lindsey, 2000). The *New York Post* described the US$2 million fight between Ali and Jacqui Frazier as a 'perversion' (Usborne, 2001), while the London *Daily Mail* complained that the debut of 'fat girl' Freeda Foreman meant that boxing finally had reached the (long-anticipated) 'depths of depravity' (Woodridge, 2000).

It was to prove hard for women to break the association with catfights and other 'titillating novelty acts' (Dunn, 2009, p.127). Part of the problem, argued the veteran boxing commentator Harry Mullan, was the paucity of women spectators at women's fight. 'It is the edge of sexual voyeurism which heightens my discomfort' (1998, p.6).

Women boxers themselves have struggled with their own self-image. The Irish boxer Deirdre Gogarty's 'main fear' was being thought of as 'butch' or 'unfeminine' (Hargreaves, 1996, p.130), a not unreasonable anxiety at a time when Christy Martin was taunting Lucia Rijker with demands for a sex test (Dunn, 2009, p.234). Such slurs are not uncommon in women's sport more generally and yet they seem particularly common in a sport so often imagined as 'purely masculine' (Oates, 2006, p.70). In order to 'defend' Riker, her promoter, Bob Aram, felt obliged to inform the press that for one fight, they had to 'get a special medical clearance . . . because she was menstruating' (Dunn, 2009, pp.145–46). More generally, a 'feminine' and 'seemingly heterosexual boxer', argues Christy Halbert (currently coach of the US women's boxing team), is seen as 'more marketable than a seemingly gay boxer' (Halbert, 1997; Henneman, 2005, p.51)

Opposition to women's boxing has often focused on the sport's impact on femininity's prime assets and vulnerabilities – a woman's breasts and face. 'Would anyone like to go out with a girl sporting two lovely purple-black eyes?' asked Peter Wilson in 1948: 'What a monstrous, degrading, disgusting idea!' (Murphy, 2010). Similar remarks greeted women boxers fifty years later. Asked why Cuba was not sending women boxers to the 2012 Olympics, the national boxing coach Pedro Roque declared that women should be 'showing off their beautiful faces, not getting punched in the face' (Anon, 2012).

But even more incompatible with boxing, it seemed, was the female psyche. Boxers did not only need flat, hard bodies, they needed to be aggressive. For many feminists, the real value of boxing was that, unlike other sports, it demonstrated 'women's capacity for aggression' (Dunn, 2009, p.20). The novelist Katherine Dunn was one of many who saw women's boxing as a challenge to American feminism's traditional unwillingness to embrace the full range of women's experiences. Boxing, she argued, revealed two things: firstly, that there was a considerable 'variability' among women in 'the form and context in which aggression is expressed' (p.109) and second, that the expression depended on 'learned and cultural factors' rather than biology (p.115).

Learning to box, in other words, could offer women an education in a particular cultural practice – that is, the disciplined expression of aggression (or, as it tends to be called, empowerment). That seems to be the idea behind various recent US and European initiatives to introduce boxing into countries in which women (and their bodies) are most restricted. For example, the charity Oxfam supported the development of 'Fighting for Peace', a boxing programme for women in Kabul that challenged 'preconceived notions about Afghan women'. The programme is perhaps the reason why the only woman on the 2012 Afghan national Olympic team was a boxer, Sadaf Rahimi.[4] 'Who would have thought', asked the American boxer and filmmaker Katya Bankowsky, 'that women in Afghanistan would be training for the Olympics in the same auditorium where the Taliban were executing women just a few years ago?' (Parker, 2012).

For Bankowsky and others, women's boxing serves as a synecdoche for various forms of freedom of expression that women in the democratic West enjoy (albeit only recently) and boxers like Rahimi are lauded as inspirational role models. The extent to which the achievements of individual sportswomen can effect (as well as reflect) broad cultural change is a question that goes beyond boxing and yet it is always worth paying attention to the discourses and images that surround them.

It is perhaps, therefore, salutary to note that as the 2012 Olympic Games approached, most of the discussion about women's boxing has focused on the clothes the fighters will wear. One concern related to Islamic codes of feminine modesty – resulting in what Bankowsky calls 'burkha boxers' (Parker, 2012). Another was about Western codes of feminine attractiveness. During the 2010 Women's World Championships, the Amateur International Boxing Association (AIBA) handed out skirts to all the semi-finalists and finalists, and Ching-Kuo Wu, President of AIBA, also suggested that skirts be worn by all competitors at the next meeting. Wu was not worried about modesty so much as television ratings:

> I have heard many times, people say, 'We can't tell the difference between the men and the women,' especially on TV, since they're in the same uniforms and are wearing headgear.
>
> *(Bourgon, 2012)*

Fighters from Poland and Romania wore skirts in the 2011 Championships but most other national federations rejected the idea. Nearly 60,000 people signed a petition attacking the AIBA for their intention of keeping boxing 'in the Victorian era':

> Female athletes should wear whatever uniform best suits their sport. Suggesting that female boxers should wear skirts reduces these skilled athletes to sexual objects. It undermines the respect they have long fought for.
>
> *(Plank, 2012)*

In early March 2012, the AIBA ruled that either a skirt or shorts would be acceptable.

Reading these stories of empowerment, on the one hand, and skirts, on the other hand, I am reminded of Angelo Dundee's description of Barbara Butterick as 'a perfect English lady outside the ring but a lioness when she climbed through the ropes' (Bunce, 2003, p.28). Beyond sporting ability, women boxers are sometimes expected to embody a utopian conjunction of gender identities: the 'frame of a pugilist in the person of a girl not yet out of her teens' (Norris, 1996, p.240); 'an impression of virility with none of the womanly left out' (London, 1906, p.60). Altogether too much has been asked of them.

Notes

1   We might compare recent responses to beach volleyball: 'What first attracted you to the sport in which women in tiny bikinis leap about in the sand, Mr President?' (Barnett, 2012).

2   Other women's boxing movies of this period include *Gordon Sisters Boxing* (Edison, 1901), based on Bessie and Minnie Gordon's stage act; *The Physical Culture Girl* (Edison, 1903), in which a young woman wakes up, stretches, and hits a punch bag; and *Boxing Ladies* (Mitchell and Kenyon, early 1900s) in which two women fairground boxers rescue a man from a gang of thieves.

3   The categories are flyweight (48–51kg); lightweight (56–60kg) and middleweight (69–75kg).

4   Sadaf Rahimi and her sister Shabnam also feature in Ariel Nasr's 2009 documentary *The Boxing Girls of Kabul*.

References

Ali L with Ritz D (2003) *Reach! Finding Strength, Spirit and Personal Power*. New York: Hyperion Books.

Anon (1999) Women's Boxing on the Rise. *The Onion*, 27 October. Available at: http://www.theonion.com/articles/womens-boxing-on-the-rise,7837 (accessed 28 March 2012).

Anon (2012) Female Boxers Allowed to Wear Skirts at 2012 Olympics. *Sports Illustrated Vault*, 1 March. Available at: http://sportsillustrated.cnn.com/vault/article/web/COM1195542/index.htm (accessed 28 March 2012).

Barnett L (2012) What's the Allure of Beach Volleyball for Politicians and Civil Servants? *The Guardian Shortcuts Blog*, 25 January. Available at: http://www.guardian.co.uk/sport/shortcuts/2012/jan/25/beach-volleyball-politicians-civil-servants (accessed 28 March 2012).

Berne B (2003) Cindy Sherman: Studio Visit. *Tate Arts and Culture*, 5 (May/June), pp.37–41.

Bishop WH (1895) *The Garden of Eden, USA: A Very Possible Story*. Chicago: Charles H. Kerr.

Bisset R (1804) *Modern Literature: A Novel*, vol 3. London: T.N. Longman and O. Rees.

Bourgon L (2012) Why Women Boxers Shouldn't Have to Wear Skirts. *Slate*, 18 January.

Bunce S (2003) Ladies Who Punch. *The Observer Sports Monthly* (March), pp.26–31.

Chicago J (1996) *Through the Flower: My Struggle as a Woman Artist*. New York: Viking.

Cohen LH (2005) *Without Apology: Girls, Women and the Desire to Fight*. New York: Random House.

Dugaw D (1989) *Warrior Women and Popular Balladry, 1650–1850*. Cambridge: Cambridge University Press.

Dunn K (2009) *One Ring Circus: Dispatches from the World of Boxing*. Tuscon, AZ: Schaffner Press.

Fielding H (1972) *Miscellanies*, vol 1. Oxford: Clarendon Press.

Fielding H (1996) *Tom Jones*. Oxford: Oxford University Press.

Halbert C (1997) Tough Enough and Woman Enough: Stereotypes, Discrimination and Impression Management among Women Professional Boxers. *Journal of Sport and Social Issues*, 21 (1): 7–36.

Hargreaves J (1996) Bruising Peg to Boxerobics: Gendered Boxing - Images and Meaning. In: Chandler D, Gill J, Guha T, and Tawadros, G (eds) *Boxer: An Anthology of Writings on Boxing and Visual Culture*. London: Institute of International Visual Arts, pp.120–31.

Hass N (2000) When Women Step into the Ring. *New York Times*, 1 October, 1, 7.

Henneman T (2005). A Knockout Role. *The Advocate*, 1 March, 51–52.

Hickey W (1913) *Memoirs*, vol 1. London: Hurst and Blacken.

Hoffer R (1996) Gritty Woman. *Sports Illustrated*, 15 April 15, 56–62.

Johnson C (1996) 'British Championism': Early Pugilism and the Works of Fielding. *Review of English Studies*, 47: 331–51.

Klein B (2010) *Blows to the Head: How Boxing Changed My Mind*. Albany, NY: State University of New York Press.

Lindsey E (2000) She Stings Like a Butterfly. *The Independent on Sunday Review*, 2 July, 4–8.

London J (1906) Amateur Night. In: *Moon-Face and Other Stories*. New York: Macmillan.

Mullan H (1998) You Can Box, Girl, But I Can't Watch. *Independent on Sunday*, 15 February, 6.

Murphy V (2010) Barbara Buttick: World Pays Tribute to Brit Champ Boxer. *Daily Mirror*, 30 October.

Nogüe M (1728) *Voyages et Aventures*. The Hague: Adrien Moetjens.

Norris F (1996) A Girl of Twenty Who has the Frame of a Sandow. In: McElrath JR Jr and Burgess DK (eds) *The Apprenticeship Writings of Frank Norris*, vol. 1. Philadelphia: The American Philosophical Society, pp. 238–40.

Oates JC (2006) *On Boxing*. New York: HarperPerennial.

Ovid (1990) Letter XVI: Paris to Helen. In: *Heroides* trans. H Isbell. Harmondsworth: Penguin Books.

Parker G (2012) US Women's Boxing Trials: The Winners. *The Guardian Sport Blog*, 20 February. Available at: http://www.guardian.co.uk/sport/blog/2012/feb/20/us-women-boxing-trials-winners-2012 (accessed 28 March 2012).

Patchen K (1968) *The Collected Poems*. New York: New Directions.

Picket LS (2000) *Looking for a Fight*. New York: The Dial Press.

Plank E (2012) Tell AIBA: Play Fair, Don't Ask Women Athletes to Wear Skirts. Available at: https://www.change.org/petitions/tell-aiba-play-fair-dont-ask-female-boxers-to-wear-skirts (accessed 28 March 2012).

Propertius (1994) The Advantage of Spartan Athletics. In: *The Poems* trans. G Lee. Oxford: Oxford University Press.

Roca H and Silverglad B (2006) *The Gleason's Gym Total Body Workout for Women*. New York: Simon and Schuster.

Rotella C (2002) *Good with Their Hands*. Berkeley, CA: University of California Press.

Sekules K (2001a) *The Boxer's Heart: How I Fell in Love with the Ring*. London: Arum Press.

Sekules K (2001b) Glove Story. *The Guardian*, 20 March, G2, 8.

Smith G and Smith JB (1972) *The Police Gazette*. New York: Simon and Schuster.

Toulmin V (1999) *A Fair Fight: An Illustrated Review of Boxing on British Fairgrounds*. Oldham: World's Fair Publications.

Usborne D (2001) Daughters Degrade the Ali-Frazier Legend. *Independent on Sunday*, 16 June, 16.

von Uffenbach ZC (1934) *London in 1710* trans. W.H. Quarrell and M. Mare. London: Faber and Faber.

Woodridge I (2000) In the Name of the Father, These Girls Will Drag Boxing Down Even Lower Than Tyson. *Daily Mail*, 23 February, 88.

PART V

Homosexuality

Issues and challenges

28

OVERCOMING SEXISM AND HOMOPHOBIA IN WOMEN'S SPORTS

Two steps forward and one step back

Pat Griffin

History

In 1981 Marilyn Barnett sued Billie Jean King for alimony, claiming she had been in a relationship with Billie Jean for seven years. The news quickly dominated sports and mainstream media. Billie Jean was not only a tennis champion, she was also a well-known and revered feminist speaker for a variety of women's equality issues. After initial denials, Billie Jean acknowledged the relationship, calling it a "mistake" and posed for *People* magazine with her husband.

Prior to this public "scandal," the topic of lesbians in sports was primarily confined to whisper and innuendo. No lesbian athletes were publicly out. The Ladies' Professional Golf Association and the Women's Tennis Association, the most prominent professional women's sports organizations of the day, went to great lengths to silence lesbians out of fear that the social stigma associated with lesbians would dampen or destroy support for women's sports. This fear was affirmed when Billie Jean lost her commercial endorsements following her revelation.

In 1982, tennis champion, Martina Navratilova was outed as lesbian in a *New York Post* article. Martina had come out to the reporter, but asked that the article not be published until after she had successfully petitioned for United States citizenship. According to Martina, the *Post* printed the article without approval. Martina was at her competitive prime at the time and, like Billie Jean, lost most of her commercial endorsements. Throughout the 1980s, in her rivalry with Chris Evert, Martina was cast as the "Beast" to Evert's "Beauty." Martina was called "masculine" and, with a mix of sexism and homophobia, some of her opponents, and many tennis fans, attributed her tennis accomplishments as much to her sexuality and assumed masculinity as to her training regimen.

It is for these reasons that I suggest that lesbian athletes 30 years ago were the bogeywomen of women's sport. The lesbian label, along with accompanying unsavoury stereotypes, was an effective social control mechanism to trivialize, marginalize and stigmatize women athletes and women's sports. And there were no notable heterosexual allies who would speak publicly against homophobia or heterosexism in sport. Lesbian athletes and coaches played out their careers locked firmly in a professional, and sometimes personal, closet. As Billie Jean and Martina found out, their fear was justified.

In another American example, in 1980 infamous (former) Penn State University women's basketball coach, Rene Portland, instituted her "no drugs, no alcohol, no lesbians" policy, leading to a 25-year reign of terror and discrimination against anyone on her team she suspected was a lesbian. In 2005, a player sued Portland and Penn State to challenge Portland's discriminatory practices. By that time, several young athletes (over the course of Portland's 27-year tenure at Penn State), had lost their scholarships, left the team and forfeited their dreams of playing college basketball. After much negative publicity for Penn State, the lawsuit was resolved with a confidential settlement in 2007. Soon after the settlement was announced, Portland resigned.

In the early 1980s only one state (Wisconsin) had a law prohibiting discrimination based on sexual orientation. Few colleges or universities included sexual orientation in their non-discrimination policies or coach-education diversity programmes. No lesbian, gay, bisexual or transgender (LGBT), or feminist advocacy organization focused on athletics as an arena in which discrimination based on sexual orientation needed to be addressed. Furthermore, scholars interested in writing about or researching heterosexism/homophobia in sport did so at great risk to their academic careers.

LGBT coaches and athletes learned quickly that the way to survive in an overwhelmingly heterosexual male-dominated sports world was to adapt to the culture of the closet by hiding their sexual orientation. In the 1980s, LGBT students were an invisible minority. No advocacy groups championed the rights of young people or challenged discrimination and harassment in schools based on sexual orientation or gender identity. Instead, LGBT advocacy organizations focused on adult discrimination issues. Thus, LGBT athletes and coaches in school sports suffered discrimination and harassment in silence and fear with no legal recourse.

Fast forward 30 years to 2012, the year of writing this chapter. How are homophobia and heterosexism in women's sport different or the same? Where have we made progress in addressing homophobia, heterosexism and sexism in sport? And more importantly, what challenges remained?

This chapter highlights both progress and challenges in addressing heterosexism and homophobia in women's sports in the United States, exploring the effects of sexism on how women athletes experience homophobia and heterosexism differently from their male counterparts. The effects of race and religion on homophobia and heterosexism will also be addressed.

Progress

Much of the progress in eliminating homophobia and heterosexism in women's sports in the United States is a reflection of broader social change. The visibility of LGBT issues and people has increased greatly since the 1980s. Not only are LGBT people publicly out in most professions (and in the mainstream media), but we have made tremendous progress on the legal recognition of same-sex relationships and families, the elimination of sodomy laws, the death of the military's Don't Ask, Don't Tell policy, as well as the increasing addition of "sexual orientation" and "gender identity/expression" as protected categories in non-discrimination laws and organizational policies. These cultural and institutional changes are the backdrop for the progress we see in addressing homophobia and heterosexism in sports today.

The emergence of the Internet and social media as sources of information and support have made it possible for LGBT young people to make connections with others in ways unavailable to previous generations. Moreover, a number of education, legal and advocacy organizations that focus on addressing LGBT discrimination in schools and in the workplace are now available, where there were none 30 years ago.

Against this backdrop of broader social change, we can identify several important points of progress in addressing LGBT discrimination in sports. In the mid-1990s the National Collegiate Athletic Association (NCAA) adopted a policy for its employees prohibiting discrimination on the basis of sexual orientation. It now offers training on sexual orientation to college athletic departments. These institutional actions are essential to making the collegiate athletic climate more inclusive for LGBT coaches and athletes. Second, increasing numbers of male and female athletes and coaches are coming out at younger ages (Anderson, 2011; Fink, Burton, Farrell & Parker, 2012). In response, more of their heterosexual teammates and coaches are comfortable with and supportive of their LGBT teammates. Third, parents of LGBT student-athletes are increasing likely to accept their children's LGBT identity and advocate for them.

Furthermore, organizations, such as the National Center of Lesbian Rights (www.nclrights. org) and The Gay Lesbian Straight Education Network (http://sports.glsen.org), have instigated projects that address homophobia and heterosexism in sport, offering education and legal resources to athletes, coaches, sports administrators and parents. Websites like Outsports.com and www.competenetwork.com (Compete), though catering mainly to a gay male sports audience, provide information and news. Similarly, GO! Athletes (www.goathletes.org) is a national network of LGBT and heterosexual ally high school and college athletes who encourage the development of school-based support and advocacy groups in athletics dedicated to changing the climate on school teams. These changes provide education, advocacy and support for athletes and coaches who are targeted by discrimination based on sexual orientation, enabling them to challenge this treatment personally and in the courts.

Finally, one of the most welcome changes concerns the increasing number of heterosexual professional male athletes who are speaking out publicly for the inclusion of LGBT athletes and coaches on sports teams. Hudson Taylor's Athlete Ally, Patrick Burke's You Can Play and Ben Cohen's Stand Up Foundation take the fight against homophobia and heterosexism by appealing to heterosexual coaches and athletes to take a personal stand against LGBT discrimination and bullying on their teams and in their schools. Other athletes – Chris Kluwe, Scott Fujita and Brendon Ayanbadejo of the National Football League (NFL), Grant Hill and Steve Nash of the National Basketball Association (NBA), and Sean Avery of the National Hockey League (NHL) – have also been visible. In response to LGBT youth suicides, several professional sports teams, such as the Boston Red Sox, San Francisco Giants and Chicago Cubs, have participated in the Internet-based "It Gets Better" video campaign.

The year 2011 brought unprecedented visibility and attention to heterosexism and homophobia in sport. In 2011 alone, the following actions occurred:

- The Gay Lesbian Straight Education Network (GLSEN), the "go to" national organization for making K-12 schools safe and respectful for LGBT youth, unveiled a sports project focused on K-12 athletics and physical education.
- The NCAA released policy and best practice recommendations for including transgender students on college sports teams.
- The NFL, NBA and Major League Baseball have joined the Women's National Basketball League in adding "sexual orientation" to their non-discrimination policies.
- The founding of Athlete Ally (www.athleteally.org), an organization led by a heterosexual former All-American wrestler at the University of Maryland and dedicated to encouraging heterosexual athletes in particular to take a pledge to stop anti-LGBT discrimination in sport.

- The formation of the Stand Up Foundation (www.standupfoundation.com) by Ben Cohen, a heterosexual former British Professional Rugby star, dedicated to spreading an anti-bullying message to athletes and coaches.
- Nike hosted several programmes focused on addressing homophobia and heterosexism in sports culminating with a National Coming Out Week Panel highlighting the role of straight allies.

The Internet has also facilitated advocacy on those with less media presence. The Equality Coaching Alliance is, for example, a Facebook-based group that offers professional and personal support for LGBT coaches. Campus Pride (www.campuspride.org), is a national advocacy and education organization focused on making college campuses welcoming and inclusive for LGBT students, initiating a campaign to provide resources and speakers to collegiate athletic programmes. Br{ache The Silence (www.freedomsounds.org) is an education and awareness initiative also focused on addressing heterosexism and homophobia in sports. The You Can Play Project (www.youcanplayproject.org) is an initiative based in professional men's ice hockey, promoting collaboration among gay and straight athletes and enlisting heterosexual athletes to become allies to their gay teammates.

The development of advocacy organizations and the adoption of policy and programming at the institutional and school levels of sport are accompanied by an increase in research on LGBT issues and heterosexism and homophobia. Where faculty researchers and their graduate students were once reluctant to take on what they perceived to be controversial and professionally risky topics, homosexuality (including in sport) is now accepted as valid and serious areas of inquiry in most institutions.

A new generation of sport research in sociology, psychology, history, legal studies and sports management is making important contributions to the body of knowledge we have available about heterosexism and homophobia in sports (Anderson, 2005, 2012; Krane, Ross, Miller, Rowse, Ganoe, Andrzejczyk & Lucas, 2010; Sartore & Cunningham, 2010). In 2008 Ithaca College hosted the first-ever conference on sports and sexuality during which established researchers and graduate students shared their work.

From the vantage point of 2012, it is difficult to ignore the changes we have seen in how homophobia and heterosexism in sport are addressed. From the pervasive silence, scandal and fear of the 1980s, we have emerged into 2012 where more LGBT and straight ally sportspeople are publicly out, more organizations are addressing LGBT issues in sport and more support systems, professional and personal, for LGBT athletes and coaches are in place. Noting this progress is important because it provides a benchmark to assess and celebrate what changes have been made and to identify challenges that remain.

Challenges

Before we can claim that anti-LGBT discrimination, bullying and name-calling in sport are eliminated, and before we can expect to see more openly LGBT coaches and athletes participating at all levels of sport, several entrenched challenges need to be addressed.

Holding college athletics accountable to basic educational values of equality and fairness

Big time college sports, particularly men's football and basketball at Division 1 schools, are engaged in an "arms race" in which schools spend billions of dollars on coaches' salaries, scholarships, new arenas, special athletic training and office facilities, tricked-out locker rooms and any number of other perks in pursuit of top high school recruits, television revenues, athletic apparel contracts and, of course, fans in the stands. Sport at this level is big business, scouting ethical corners is endemic. How can we keep programmes accountable for fairness and inclusion when winning coaches are given broad discretion concerning their treatment of athletes? Here, money trumps educational values (Pappano, 2012). Until we take action to rein in the insanity of the 'arms race' in men's sports, particularly men's football and basketball, all college sports will suffer from the disconnect from basic educational values of fairness, equal access and the right to safety and respect.

Understanding the manifestations of homophobia and heterosexism in women's and men's sports

Addressing the differences in how homophobia and heterosexism are manifested in women's and men's sport is an important challenge that needs attention from LGBT sports advocates and allies. Simply put, sexism and how it affects women in sports must be factored into any comprehensive understanding of homophobia and heterosexism (Griffin, 1998).

Perceptions of women and men athletes have always been embedded in cultural expectations of masculinity and femininity. Whereas athletic prowess, physical strength and competitive toughness in a man are expected and celebrated, the same qualities in a woman are regarded with suspicion, unless she can counterbalance these qualities with exhibitions of femininity and heterosexuality. As a result, women's sports and women athletes are often trivialized and marginalized as second rate imitations of male athletes and men's sports. At the same time, women who are athletic, strong and tough are stigmatized as unfeminine/not sexy at best and lesbian at worst.

From gender differences in sport flow many consequences. College and high school women's sports, despite the changes over the last 40 years of post-Title IX advances, are still underfunded and under-resourced. Women are a minority within the ranks of sports administrators and coaches (even among coaches of women's teams). Sports media provide little coverage of women's sporting events at any level (Messner & Cooky, 2010): professional women's sports teams struggle for survival, while men's professional sports thrive.

From a feminist perspective, perhaps one of the most frustrating consequences is the defensiveness exhibited by many women athletes and advocates about their image. Early sport feminists coined "the apologetic" to describe the ways that women's sports advocates and the athletes themselves have attempted to present themselves as "normal" women despite their athleticism as a way to gain social approval (Felshin, 1974). Normal is, of course, a code for heterosexual women primarily interested in marriage and family.

Failure to see the lesbian label as a means of social control effectively used to contain and intimidate women's sports advocates and women athletes themselves, leads female athletes to respond to insinuations and accusations with defensiveness and apology rather than confidence and power. Women who succumb to the myth that by presenting themselves as sex objects for men will increase the popularity and acceptability of women's sports, fail to see that these presentations do not increase the appeal of women's sports at all. Instead, they further trivialize women's athleticism by reinforcing the belief that women athletes and sports are only acceptable if they can be sexualized for male consumption (Kane, 2011).

At the same time, defensiveness and apology leave discrimination against lesbian athletes and stereotypes of lesbians unchallenged. In a perverse kind of sexism, even when a woman athlete comes out as a lesbian, the public response is often indifferent, reflecting both a lack of interest in women's sports and an assumption that, given associations between female athleticism and lesbians, a woman athlete proclaiming she is gay is not news. The difference in public reaction to the coming out of professional basketball players Sheryl Swoopes and John Amaechi illustrate this point. When Swoopes (arguably one of the greatest women to play the game) came out, the media flurry was short, compared to when John Amaechi, a journeyman player of modest accomplishment, came out in the NBL (Kian and Anderson, 2009).

Male athletes, who epitomize rather than contradict the accepted gender narrative for men, do not live with the conflicting expectations and suspicions placed upon women athletes (Anderson, 2005). Quite the opposite: such are the cultural expectations of male athletes that the general public reacts with surprise when a male athlete comes out as a gay man (Anderson, 2002). Sexism is also present in conversations among LGBT sports activists and advocates when they assume that talking about "gay" athletes applies to both men and women. Assuming that gay male athletes' experiences are the same as lesbian athletes' experiences discounts all of the effects of sexism outlined here.

Perhaps the greatest manifestation of sexism among LGBT sports advocates is evident when they intentionally focus on men's sports without addressing homophobia and heterosexism in women's sports. Sometimes this omission is rationalized by the mistaken belief that homophobia and heterosexism are no longer a problem in women's sports. While it is true that there are no publicly out active gay athletes in the major men's professional sports in the United States, it is equally important to be aware that homophobia is alive and well in women's sports, too. Only one NCAA Division 1 women's basketball coach is publicly out – Sherri Murrell at Portland State University in Oregon. A handful of other college women's coaches are publicly out as lesbian or gay, but the number is still small compared with the number of coaches locked firmly in the back of their professional closets.

Homophobia is also still used as a recruiting tool in college women's sports, both blatantly and subtlety (Cyphers & Fagan, 2011). Women coaches lose their jobs (or are eliminated from the applicant pool) because of the perception or actuality that they are lesbian. Athletes perceived to be or who are lesbians are dismissed from teams or find their playing time diminished. These are the realities of homophobia and heterosexism in women's sports despite sexist assumptions that discrimination on the basis of sexual orientation is no longer a problem for women in sport. It is for these reasons that Anderson (2005) suggests that homophobia in women's sport likely has a broader-reaching negative impact than homophobia in men's sport. Understanding the cumulative effects of sexism and homophobia on women athletes and women's sports is essential to thoughtful and sophisticated conversations about homophobia and heterosexism in sport.

Changing institutional policies and practices

Despite the LGBT sports "moment" we enjoyed in 2011–12, actual change at the institutional level among individual schools, athletic conferences and sport governing organizations is slow. Instituting proactive non-discrimination and anti-harassment or anti-bullying policies that include "sexual orientation" and "gender identity/expression" at all institutional levels is essential to eliminating homophobia and heterosexism in sports. Until comprehensive policies that include consequences for non-compliance, changing the athletic climate for LGBT people will be hindered.

Gaining administrative support for policies and practices

Backing policies up with administrative commitment is even more challenging. Policy that is ignored is akin to no policy at all. Unfortunately, as a default response, many athletic administrators back up coaches who are accused of discriminating against LGBT athletes. It is often an uphill battle for athletes and their parents to force athletic departments to take action against a coach, or rectify discrimination, without resulting in the termination of the athlete's career. Administrators who condone, ignore or support coaches who discriminate or engage in bullying behaviour perpetuate the problem and the fear associated with it. Administrators who themselves discriminate against LGBT coaches often disguise and legitimize their discriminatory practices in unfair performance evaluations or manipulations of hiring processes.

Instituting procedures for educating coaches, student-athletes and other athletic personnel about non-discrimination policies and practices

To be effective, policy and best practice expectations must be communicated to all coaches. New coaches should participate in an orientation programme that includes information about non-discrimination policies and department and school expectations for the treatment of all athletes. Coaches should be made aware of legal obligations imposed by federal and state non-discrimination laws. To be most effective, these policy and legal requirements should be communicated as they relate to the athletic context. Coaches need to have specific examples of what is acceptable and unacceptable team policy and practice. In addition to communicating broad expectations for adherence to non-discriminatory actions and policies, coaches need to know that such practices as negative recruiting based on sexual orientation, highlighting the heterosexual family status of coaches in media guides and on recruiting trips, intruding on an athlete's privacy by investigating their sexual orientation, treating LGBT athletes differently from other athletes because of their sexual orientation or gender identity or dismissing team members from the team because of their sexual orientation are unacceptable.

Closing the generation gap between coaches and athletes

As noted earlier, one of the signs of progress in addressing heterosexism and homophobia in sports is heterosexual young people's increasing comfort with and acceptance of LGBT peers and coaches. At the same time that LGBT youth are coming out at younger ages, their heterosexual peers are more likely to respond positively or at least neutrally to them. Though many heterosexual coaches are also changing their perspectives and are comfortable with LGBT members in their teams, many others are not (Anderson, 2005). These coaches have spent their careers in an athletic climate where LGBT people were expected to remain in the closet. Openness about being LGBT was not accepted and was, in fact, grounds for dismissal from teams. The generation gap between coaches and athletes creates a problem in that coaches who have negative perspectives about LGBT people and reflect this perspective in their treatment of LGBT athletes create dissonance on teams. Because coaches maintain power over their athletes, they can make or break an athlete's career. Until coaches catch up with the accepting attitudes of athletes on their teams, the potential for discrimination remains despite wider acceptance among young people and in the larger culture.

Restricting institutionally-sponsored religious practice in public school-based athletic programmes

The separation of church and state is one of the founding principles of the United States. In athletics, particularly athletic programmes not affiliated to religious institutions, administrators and coaches have a responsibility to ensure that athletes are not required or pressured to participate in religious activities. Individual expressions of faith by athletes are acceptable according to Federal guidelines; however, when coaches or administrators who are employed by public and/or secular institutions lead team prayers, encourage Bible studies, or post religious quotes in the locker room, they violate Federal guidelines. These practices are unfair to those who do not share the religious perspectives of the coach and they pressure athletes to participate or risk creating conflict with the coach.

The importance of the separation of church (including synagogue or mosque) and state is related to the issue of LGBT inclusion in sport to the extent that some specific faith traditions regard LGBT people as sinners who need to be "saved," and heterosexual people as needing protection from their influence. When coaches in public athletic programmes discriminate against LGBT athletes or when administrators, on the basis of their personal religious convictions, discriminate against coaches, a conflict arises that affects the climate of athletics and the rights of LGBT athletes and coaches to participate in sports without harassment or judgment.

Evangelical sport ministries, such as Athletes in Action and the Fellowship of Christian Athletes, encourage Christian athletes and coaches to use their sports participation as a vehicle to bring others to Christ. The official position of these organizations is that homosexuality is a sin and spiritual sickness and that finding Christ is the cure. When a person in a position of authority expresses these beliefs, they create an environment where it is not acceptable to be LGBT.

Increasing the visibility of female heterosexual allies in sport

As noted earlier, sexism imposes different restrictions on women and men in sport. Heterosexism and homophobia are used as social control mechanisms to devalue and trivialize women's athletic accomplishments and women's sports in general, in ways not experienced by male athletes or men's sports (Anderson, 2005). One of the most unfortunate effects of sexism and homophobia in women's sports is the relative silence of heterosexual allies. While increasing numbers of heterosexual male athletes, at all levels, are speaking out against homophobia and bullying in sports, the silence of heterosexual women athletes is deafening.

This imbalance can be attributed to several possible explanations, including that heterosexual women allies in sport are overlooked by the media. Whether the gay press or mainstream sports media, both dominated by men, don't know about women allies, or don't value them enough to cover these stories, the result is the same: many more male allies speak out against homophobia in men's sport, than women do in women's sport. It is also probable that, because the lesbian label can be deployed to affect heterosexual women as well as lesbians in sport, all women, regardless of their sexual orientation or their personal commitments to equality in sports, are held hostage to fear of being called a lesbian. Innuendo about lesbians on teams or speculations about coaches' sexual orientations affect all women and sports teams who are targeted by them. As long as the lesbian label carries a negative stigma in the eyes of athletes, parents, fans and the general public, it is an effective silencer of heterosexual women allies in sports. While heterosexual male athlete allies may also face challenges to their heterosexuality, they do not experience the institutionally-sanctioned consequences for their advocacy that silence women.

Integrating race and racism into LGBT advocacy efforts

Just as we need to avoid assuming a "male default" in addressing homophobia and heterosexism in sports, we must also take care to avoid a "white default" in our efforts. Coaches and athletes of colour, who also may identify as LGBT, experience heterosexism and homophobia in the context of racism. Ignorance of the ways that race, racism and white privilege affect

LGBT sports advocacy work renders it incomplete at best and insulting at worst. This omission, whether intentional or unintentional, weakens our claims of commitment to equality in sport and makes our efforts less effective. Rather than assuming that heterosexism and homophobia affect whites and people of colour in the same ways, it is essential that LGBT sports advocates also do their homework on the effects of intersecting social justice issues such as racism and sexism (Crenshaw, 1991).

Addressing biphobia and bisexuality in sports

We typically include the "B" when we speak of LGBT issues in sports, but there is rarely any substantive effort to back up this nominal inclusion with tangible efforts to address biphobia and the experiences of bisexual people in sport. Though LGBT rolls off of our tongues easily, efforts to differentiate biphobia from homophobia and the experiences of lesbian and gay athletes or coaches from those of bisexual athletes and coaches are rare. With some recent exceptions the same claim can be made with regard to the "T" in LGBT, but Helen Carroll addresses this issue in a separate chapter in this volume, so I will merely note the importance of addressing it here.

As with any social justice movement, the LGBT sports-equality movement has pioneers. Dave Kopay, Billie Jean King, Martina Navratilova and Rene Richards all came out and called attention to homophobia and transphobia in sports at a time when doing so required great personal courage and conviction. These pioneers led the way for all the rest of us without the benefit of advocacy organizations, positive shifts in public perspectives on LGBT rights and awareness of LGBT people or the increasing legal protections we enjoy today.

Without a doubt they see a sports world today that is much improved over the one in which they fought for their rights to compete openly as LGBT. However, we still have much work to do. The struggle for LGBT equality in sport is on-going. Yes, progress is evident, but we have many challenges remaining. To finish the job of eliminating homophobia and heterosexism in sports requires thoughtful attention to the intersections of multiple forms of social injustice and the practical work of education, policy development and expanding legal protection. It takes collaborative efforts on a grand scale to create and maintain an inclusive vision of sports in which sexual orientation and gender identity or expression are accepted as merely two more ways in which sportswomen and men may differ from each other. We've come far, but we still have a long way to go.

References

Anderson E (2002). Openly gay athletes: Contesting hegemonic masculinity in a homophobic environment. *Gender and Society* 16: 860–877.

Anderson, E (2005). *In the game: Gay athletes and the cult of masculinity.* Albany, NY: State University of New York Press.

Anderson, E (2011). Updating the outcome: Gay athletes, straight teams, and coming out at the end of the decade. *Gender & Society* 25(2): 250–268.

Anderson, E (2012). Shifting masculinities in Anglo-American countries. *Masculinities and Social Change* 1(1): 60–79.

Crenshaw, B (1991). Mapping the margins: Intersectionality, identity politics and violence against women of color. *Stanford Law Review* 43: 1241–1299.

Cyphers, L & Fagan, K (2011). On homophobia and recruiting. *ESPN: The Magazine.* January 26.

Felshin, J (1974). The dialectic of woman and sport. In Gerber, E, Felshin, J, Berlin, P & Wyrick, W *The American Woman in Sport.* Reading: MA, Addison-Wesley.

Fink, J, Burton, L, Farrell, A & Parker, H (2012). Playing it out. Female collegiate athletes' experiences in revealing their sexual identities. *Journal for the Study of Sports and Athletes in Education,* 6 (1): 83–106.

Griffin, P (1998). *Strong women, deep closets: Lesbians and homophobia in sport*. Champaign: IL, Human Kinetics.

Kane, MJ (2011) Sex sells sex, not women's sports. *The Nation*. August 15–22, http://www.thenation.com/article/162390/sex-sells-sex-not-womens-sports

Kian, E & Anderson, E (2009) John Amaechi: Changing the way sport reporters examine gay athletes. *Journal of Homosexuality* 56(7): 1–20.

Krane, V, Ross, S, Miller, M, Rowse, J, Ganoe, K, Andrzejczyk, J & Lucas, C (2010). Power and focus: Self-representations of female college athletes. *Qualitative Research in Sport and Exercise*, 2(2): 175–195.

Messner, M & Cooky, C (2010). *Gender in televised sports. Center for feminist research*, University of Southern California. http://www.nytimes.com/2012/01/22/education/edlife/how-big-time-sports-ate-college-life.html?pagewanted=all

Pappano, L (2012). How big time sports ate college life. *The New York Times*. January 20, http://www.nytimes.com/2012/01/22/education/edlife/how-big-time-sports-ate-college-life.html?pagewanted=all

Sartore, M & Cunningham, G (2010). The lesbian label as a component of women's stigmatization in sport organizations: A comparison of two health and kinesiology departments. *Journal of Sport Management*, 24: 481–501.

29

CHANGING THE GAME

Sport and a cultural shift away from homohysteria

Rachael Bullingham, Rory Magrath and Eric Anderson

Introduction

Since the foundation of organised sport in the late nineteenth and early twentieth century within the Western world, sport has traditionally served as a masculine preserve through the regulation of gendered behaviours. It has maintained the purpose of turning young boys towards a hegemonic perspective of male heterosexuality; one distanced from femininity and homosexuality. The construction of a dominating form of heterosexual masculinity was accomplished through multiple mechanisms, including socialising boys into the physical violence, sexism and homophobia indicative of organised, competitive sport (Anderson, 2009). Adams et al. (2010) add that to construct an esteemed and 'acceptable' masculine identity, it is not just necessary to display one's heterosexuality, but also to 'police' the gendered behaviours of one's peers. Policing is conducted through specific discourses used to question men's heteromasculinity. Epithets such as 'fags', 'sissies', and 'poofs' are often used to emasculate and feminise those who do not comply with supposed traditional hetero-masculine norms.

With sport's traditional function of masculinising and heterosexualising boys—and subsequently marginalising effeminacy—it is unsurprising that homophobia and anti-femininity have been commonly employed among athletes in the construction of gender-normative performances (Anderson and McGuire, 2010). This was particularly true of the purpose of sport (in the Western world) in the 1980s. Here, sport took on renewed importance for boys and young men as it was a central tool in heterosexualising men in a culture that Anderson (2009) calls 'homohysteric'.

In describing the construction of masculinities, Anderson (2011a) describes a culture of homohysteria as a 'homosexually-panicked culture in which suspicion [of homosexuality] permeates' (p. 83). He argues that in order for a culture of homohysteria to exist, three social factors must coincide: 1) the mass cultural awareness that homosexuality exists as a static sexual orientation within a significant portion of the population; 2) a cultural zeitgeist of disapproval towards homosexuality; 3) and disapproval of men's femininity or women's masculinity, as they are associated with homosexuality.

Anderson (2011a) describes homohysteria as a concept to analyse the history of one's own culture, or for making cross-cultural comparisions. Either way, he describes three conditions that a culture (might) move through. The first is homosexual erasure. Here, the culture is highly homophobic, but the citizens do not readily believe that homosexuality exists as an immutable sexual orientation of a significant portion of their population. Exemplifying this condition, Anderson argues that in much of the Islamic world today, as well as throughout much of Africa, homosexuality is thought to be 'only' a Western phenomenon (Frank et al., 2010). In contrast, in a homohysteric culture, there is widespread awareness that a significant percentage of the population can be gay (even if closeted) and if this culture also looks poorly upon homosexuality, the stage for homohysteria is set.

Exemplyfing this last position, Anderson suggests that homohysteria manifested in the United States during the 1980s because of the increased awareness of the growing normalcy and frequency of homosexuality, alongside extreme homophobia. Anderson adds that, in the United States, homohysteria was heightened by an increasingly noisy fundamentalist Christianity that was opposed to and consequently demonised homosexuality (Anderson, 2011a), which was made culturally salient through HIV/AIDS and the large percentage of even gender-typical men who acquired it through same-sex sex. In this homohysteric culture boys and young men (particularly those who were unmarried) needed to establish and re-establish themselves as heterosexual by aligning their gendered behaviours with idealised notions of masculinity. This is something that Kimmel (1994) describes as 'masculinity as homophobia'. It is especially between the years 1983 to 1993 that Anderson argues that boys in Western cultures needed to use sport in order to prove their *heteromasculinity* (Pronger, 1990). This is because, Anderson (2009) suggests, homosexuality is not readily visible (like gender or race): ostensibly, anyone can be gay.

Anderson continues to explain that because men's masculinity is/was associated with heterosexuality in Western, industralised cultures, boys in a culture of homohysteria are/were required to elevate their display of masculinity to prove that they are/were not gay. In other words, they used culturally-endorsed sports to distance themsleves from what Anderson (2009) calls 'the spectre of the fag':

> Men attempt to associate with masculinity and disassociate with femininity. They self-segregate into masculine enclaves within the larger feminized space and perceive that excluding women and gay men from their peer circles raises their masculine capital.
>
> *(p. 51)*

Anderson suggests further that participation in organised team sports is less important for the construction of heterosexuality in a culture where homosexuality is not believed to exist as a significant demographic of the population. He uses Iran as an example. While homophobia is intensely high in Iran, in 2007, Iranian president Mahmoud Ahmadinejad claimed to an American audience that, '. . . in Iran we don't have homosexuals like in your country'. Anderson suggests that homophobia is so high in Iran that few people come out of the closet, leaving the perception that homosexuals constitute too small a proportion of the population to raise suspicion that one's friends or family members could be one of them. Accordingly, boys in Iran will have less need to distance themselves from cultural suspicion of homosexuality. It is this mass denial that homosexuals exist in large numbers which permits Iranian men to walk together in public holding hands.

Finally, homohysteria cannot exist in a culture that is not homophobic. In contemporary Western culture for example, and particularly for youth, a large body of research has shown that homophobia has dramatically decreased (Anderson, 2009, 2012; Keleher and Smith, 2012;

Loftus, 2001). Consequently, the gendered behaviours of boys and men are likely to be radically different if/when they no longer fear being culturally homosexualised (McCormack, 2012). This is something that Anderson (2011a) describes as a culture of inclusivity.

Evidencing the Western shift into a culture of inclusivity he focused in his research on sport team initiation rituals in the United Kingdom, where he monitored behaviours over a seven year period (Anderson et al., 2011). During this time, same-sex activities as part of these imitations were phased out in line with the decrease in cultural homohysteria. Early in the study, male athletes were forced to kiss one another as a form of doing something that was normally stigmatised in order to prove their worth, loyalty and desire to be on the team. But by the end of the study, team members willingly engaged in same-sex kissing, not as a form of hazing, but as a mode of homosocial bonding and support. Thus, Anderson argues, (for male adolescents) Britain has moved from a disposition of pre-homohysteria and post-homohysteria to homosexual erasure and a culture of inclusivity. And while Anderson's notion of homohysteria proves a useful heuristic tool in understanding cultural shifts that lead *men* to fear association with homosexuality, his concept has yet to be applied to the experiences of women in sport. That is the purpose of this chapter.

Homohysteria in women's sport

Because sport has been defined as 'the last bastion of male domination' (Burton Nelson, 1994: 6), it has created not only a problem for effeminate and/or gay men, but also for women. Although women challenge traditional gender boundaries in sport by simply taking part, only certain sports are seen as feminine-appropriate; mainly those not requiring physical contact. Writing specifically about rugby, Wright and Clarke (1999) suggested that women's participation 'could therefore be expected to challenge fundamentally what it means to be a male and female' (p. 229). Hence, women playing male-dominated team sports, such as football and rugby, face particular confrontation and questioning about their involvement.

Wright and Clarke's research was, however, carried out in the 1990s, and the sporting terrain has changed for women since that time. In the United Kingdom, the Football Association launched the Women's Soccer League, with international sponsors such as Umbro and Vauxhall (www.thefa.com). Football has the largest female participation rates of any team sport in the United Kingdom with 1.38 million women of all ages regularly playing (www.thefa.com). Similarly, women's rugby has seen an increase in players: '2,000 players in 1988 to 8,000 players by 1998, to near 15,000 in 2008' (www.rfu.com). The media have also begun to cover women's sport: ESPN TV, in the United States, covers the Women's Soccer League, and Sky Sports shows the Women's Rugby World Cup live.

In this chapter, we highlight that despite social science research into the relationship between sportswomen and sexuality in sport during the1980s and 1990s (Cahn, 1994; Griffin, 1998; Hargreaves, 1994; Lenskyj, 1986, 1995), there remains a need for a comprehensive theory to explain the sporting arena's historical relationship to homosexuality.

Hargreaves (1994: 171) argued that when women participated in male-dominated sports they faced 'the greatest criticism and exposure to ridicule'. Lenskyj (1986: 95) summarised that the central issues concerning women's participation in sport were that, 'femininity and heterosexuality [were] seen as incompatible with sporting excellence: either sport made women masculine or sportswomen were masculine from the outset'. Griffin (1998) argued that in order to limit controversy about their participation, women have been shown to promote heterosexual images (heterosexy) and use overt homophobia as a way to socially distance themselves from being thought lesbian. Even early in the twenty-first century Cox and Thompson (2001) found that female footballers were assumed to be lesbian because of their choice to play a traditional male team sport. Shire et al. (2000) describe the behaviour of heterosexual women within one hockey team, saying, 'They joked about the lesbian women in order to reinforce their heterosexuality to others' (p. 49).

Just as playing sport permitted men some cultural transgression of rigid masculinity norms (Anderson, 2005), the promotion of a feminine image allowed women playing men's sports to do so with less lesbian suspicion. Griffin (1998, p. 68), wrote that 'femininity has become a code word for heterosexuality', just as Kimmel (1994) described that masculinity was heterosexuality for males. Thus the conditions described by Anderson of homohysteria for men in sport, also existed for women in sport. Just as a 1980s and 1990s culture of homohysteria presented a problem for both gay and straight men, the homohysteria of women's sport also created a problem for both lesbian and straight women. Women were understood as being pressured into presenting an image of hyper-feminine heterosexuality in order to gain and maintain public support of their new found sporting freedoms (Lenskyj, 2003). This can either be understood as a form of denial, or it might also be viewed as a survival strategy to compete without homosexual suspicion and the discrimination that comes with it (Lenskyj, 1995). Either way, the silence and denial of lesbianism in sport permits stereotypes and discrimination to continue unopposed (Krane and Barber, 2003).

The erasure of lesbianism through the promotion of femininity and heterosexuality is known as the 'apologetic'. Apologetic behaviour occurs because women are participating in a male domain. Felshin (1974) argues that: 'because women cannot be excluded from sport and have chosen not to reject sport, apologetics develop to account for their sport involvement in the face of its social unacceptability' (p. 36). Scholars explain that apologetic behaviour occurs in numerous ways: creating a feminine image, or apologising for on field behaviour, such as aggression (Davis-Delano et al., 2009; Ezzell, 2009). So while it seems that homohysteria is falling in men's sport, it remains rife within women's sport.

Decreasing homophobia for men in contemporary sport

The increased awareness of homosexuality (made visible through HIV/AIDS) led to homophobia hitting an apex in 1988. During this epoch, the 1987 British Social Attitude Survey reported that 63.6 per cent of the population thought homosexuality was wrong, a sharp increase in relation to results of the same survey in 1983. A similar trend has been shown in the American social attitude surveys (Anderson, 2011a).

Scholars of this time (Clarke, 1998; Hekma, 1998; Pronger, 1990) described men's sport as an arena for the development and emphasising of men's masculinity, with heterosexual athletes, 'unwilling to confront and accept homosexuality' (Wolf-Wendel et al., 2001: 470). Indeed, Hekma (1998) argued that, 'gay men who are seen as queer and effeminate are granted no space whatsoever in what is generally considered to be a masculine preserve and a macho enterprise' (p. 2). This has been predominantly shown by the use of homophobic discourse and derogatory name-calling. For example, Hekma (1998) described how, when a member of a team looked gay and missed the ball, his teammates immediately called him a 'dirty queer' (p. 4).

Surprisingly, however, in 2002 Anderson found that none of his sample of openly gay male athletes was derided or verbally abused when they came out. Indeed, the reception the athletes received when coming out was either neutral or positive. Since this time, other research has shown that gay men are increasingly accepted within competitive sport (Adams, 2011; Adams et al., 2010; Anderson, 2005, 2009; Cashmore and Cleland, 2011, 2012; McCormack and Anderson, 2010a). In his research on gay athletes, for example, Anderson (2011b) found that, regardless of the sport played, when athletes came out to their team they were not treated any differently. Participants were surprised at the inclusivity they experienced from their teammates, many regretting not coming out sooner.

Anderson (2005) even shows that in the context of American university cheerleading, traditionally perceived as a female activity, it is acceptable for gay participants to portray a feminised image. Additionally, there is also a belief that some straight men can still exhibit effeminate behaviours without being socially perceived as gay. In other words, the corpus of this research shows that men's masculinity is softening and becoming more inclusive of homosexuality: men in many sporting contexts are culturally aware of homosexuality existing, but they are no longer concerned or show objection to it. Greater acceptance of homosexuality therefore permits straight men to modify their behaviours, too. Effeminate behaviours once stigmatised are now considered a normal operation of heterosexual masculinity; all without homosocial suspicion (Anderson, 2009; McCormack and Anderson, 2010b). This can be described as an epoch of post-homohysteria or homosexual inclusivity.

Decreasing homophobia for women

While Griffin noted in 1998, 'the winds of change can be heard in the comments of some young lesbian athletes' (p. 161), there has been a dearth of research examining the experience of lesbian athletes since that time. Outside a few post-structuralist pieces with small sample sizes (Krane, 1996; Krane & Barber, 2003), there has been no empirical investigation of the experiences of lesbian athletes on ostensibly heterosexual teams.

Still, there is evidence for some cultural progress toward the acceptance of lesbianism in sport. More women are coming out, and it is likely that their experiences are better than those of lesbian athletes who came out in previous years. For example, most are familiar with Billie Jean King and Martina Navratilova, who both had a hostile reception when they were 'outed' in the 1980s in the sport of tennis (see Chapter 28); however, significantly more lesbian athletes have been open about their sexuality in more recent times without disastrous consequences: Amelie Mauresmo (tennis) came out in 1999, Women's National Basketball Association (WNBA) players Michele Van Gorp came out in 2004, Sheryl Swoopes in 2005, Seimone Augustus in 2012 and Brittney Griner (WNBA) in 2013).

However, while there are more openly lesbian athletes today, on the whole, elite sportswomen still seem reluctant to come out. Fortunately, more positive results have been found within collegiate environments (Fink et al., 2012). College athletes noted the importance of trailblazers and greater numbers of players coming out compared to the findings of previous research. Fink et al. (2012) conclude that teammates come out not to make a political statement, nor to bring about change, but simply to 'be themselves' (p. 92).

It is clear that more research needs to be carried out to discover whether there have been widespread changes within Western women's sporting cultures, as Anderson's body of work has shown among men (Anderson, 2009). Although Fink et al. (2012) show some positive changes, they only interviewed 11 lesbian participants and three bisexual athletes. So while Anderson has systemically demonstrated a lessening of homophobia male sports, more detailed and extended research is needed to see if this is also the case for females.

Discussion

Anderson (2009) has suggested that the 1980s were a unique period for men and sport in Western cultures—ushering in a period of unprecedented homohysteria. He demonstrates that heterosexual and closeted gay men used competitive team sport in order to bolster their masculine capital and therefore stave off homosexual suspicion. Anderson (2009) argues further, however, that homohysteria has rapidly reduced within men's team sport in recent years, evidencing this with both qualitative and quantitative work. However, the application of Anderson's notion of homohysteria has yet to be applied to women's sport.

The myth that female athletes (particularly those in masculinised sports) are all lesbians might remain an enduring misconception, suggesting cultural differences between men's and women's sports. With Anderson's (2002, 2005, 2011a, 2011b) research suggesting that sport is ready to accept gay athletes, more research is required to monitor changes in acceptance for lesbian athletes. Just because homophobia and homohysteria have decreased on men's teams does not necessarily mean that the same is true for women's teams. Making this point salient, Anderson (2005) argues that whereas a gay male athlete coming out to his soccer team does not call the other players' heterosexuality into question, a lesbian coming out to her team does.

We can speculate that homophobia has decreased to some extent for women in sport. This is because Anderson (2005) has argued that the change to men's sport has not come from sport itself, but instead from the larger cultural milieu surrounding sport. Unless women's sports are immune from changes to youth culture, it holds that there should also be linear improvements since the 1980s.

However, there remains one other condition that might impact upon the levels of homophobia and homohysteria within women's sport: there is deeply ingrained sexism that surrounds women's participation in sport, and most women's sports remain controlled by men. For example, the majority of coaches in the American collegiate system are men, and there has been a significant increase in the number of male coaches who coach women's sports teams (Acosta and Carpenter, 2010). Most sports administrators are men; and the members of the sports media are also dominated by men. Furthermore, Lapchick and colleagues (2011) show that 94 per cent of sports editors in the United States are men, as are 90 per cent of assistant sports editors, 90 per cent of columnists and 89 per cent of reporters. This male-controlled media provide a sexualised view of female athletes. Lack of control of their own image means that women are somewhat hindered in making changes to their own sport culture. This is perhaps one reason why Lenskyj (2003) argues that, 'although advances have been made . . . since the 1980s the situation for women, especially lesbians, in mainstream sport has remained stubbornly woman-hating and homophobic' (p. 33). Unfortunately, the scarcity of contemporary research in women's sport leaves us unable to make definitive statements about the level of homohysteria in women's sport today. More research is required.

References

Acosta VR and Carpenter LJ (2010) Women in intercollegiate sport: A longitudinal study thirty-three year update 1977–2010. Unpublished document. Brooklyn, NY: Brooklyn College.

Adams A (2011). 'Josh wears pink cleats': Inclusive masculinity on the soccer field. *Journal of Homosexuality* 58: 579–596.

Adams A, Anderson E and McCormack M (2010) Establishing and challenging masculinity: The influence of gendered discourses in organised sport. *Journal of Language and Social Psychology* 29: 278–300.

Anderson E (2002) Openly gay athletes. Contesting hegemonic masculinity in a homophobic environment. *Gender & Society* 16: 860–877.

Anderson E (2005) *In the game: Gay athletes and the cult of masculinity.* Albany, NY: State University of New York Press.

Anderson E (2009) *Inclusive masculinity the changing nature of masculinities.* London: Routledge

Anderson E (2011a) The rise and fall of Western homohysteria. *Journal of Feminist Scholarship* 1: 80–94.

Anderson E (2011b) Updating the outcome: Gay athletes, straight teams, and coming out in educationally based sport teams. *Gender and Society* 25: 250–268.

Anderson E (2012) Shifting masculinities in Anglo-American cultures. *Masculinities and Social Change* 1: 40–60.

Anderson E and McGuire R (2010) Inclusive masculinity and the gendered politics of men's rugby. *The Journal of Gender Studies* 19: 249–261.

Anderson E, McCormack M and Lee H (2011) Male team sport hazing initiations in culture of decreasing homohysteria. *Journal of Adolescent Research* 20: 1–22.

Burton Nelson M (1994) *The stronger women get, the more men love football.* New York: Avon Books.

Cahn SK (1994) *Coming on Strong: Gender and sexuality in twenith century women's sport.* London: Harvard University Press.

Cashmore E and Cleland J (2011) Glasswing butterflies: Gay professional footballers and their culture. *Journal of Sport and Social Issues* 20: 1–17.

Cashmore E and Cleland J (2012) Fans, homophobia and masculinities in association football: Evidence of a more inclusive environment. *The British Journal of Sociology* 63: 370–387.

Clarke G (1998) Queering the pitch and coming out to play: Lesbians and physical education in sport. *Sport, Education and Society* 3: 145–160.

Cox B and Thompson S (2001) Facing the bogey: Women, football and sexuality. *Football Studies* 4: 7–24.

Davis-Delano L, Pollock A and Ellsworth Vose J (2009) Apologetic behaviour among female athletes. *International Review for the Sociology of Sport* 2–3: 131–150.

Ezzell MB (2009) 'Barbie Dolls' on the pitch: Identity work, defensive othering, and inequality in women's rugby. *Social Problems* 56: 111–131.

Felshin J (1974) The triple option . . . for Women in sport. *Quest* 21: 36–40.

Fink JS, Burton LJ, Farrell AO and Parker HM (2012) Female intercollegiate athletes' experiences in revealing their sexual identities. *Journal for the Study of Sports and Athletes in Education* 6: 83–106.

Frank DJ, Camp BJ and Boutcher SA (2010) 'Worldwide Trends in the Criminal Regulation of Sex, 1945 to 2005'. *American Sociological Review* 75: 867–893.

Griffin P (1998) *Strong women, deep closets.* Leeds: Human Kinetics.

Hargreaves JA (1994) *Sporting females.* London: Routledge.

Hargreaves JA (2000) *Heroines of sport.* London: Routledge.

Hekma G (1998) 'As long as they don't make an issue of it . . .': Gay men and lesbians in organised sports in the Netherlands. *Journal of Homosexuality* 35: 1–23.

Keleher A and Smith ERAN (2012) Growing support for gay and lesbian equality since 1990. *Journal of Homosexuality* 59: 1307–1326.

Kimmel M (1994) Homophobia as masculinity: Fear, shame and silence in the construction of gender identity. In: Brod H and Kaufman M (eds) *Theorizing masculinities*, Thousand Oaks, CA: Sage Publications, pp. 223–242.

Krane V (1996) Lesbians in sport: Toward acknowledgement, understanding, and theory. *Journal of Sport & Exercise Psychology* 18: 237–246.

Krane V and Barber H (2003) Lesbian experiences in sport: A social identity perspective. *Quest* 55: 328–346.

Lapchick R, Moss A, Russell C and Scearce R (2011). The 2010–11 Associated Press Sports Editors from University of Central Florida, Institute for Diversity and Ethics in Sport Web site: http://www.tidesport.org/RGRC/2011/2011_APSE_RGRC_FINAL.pdf?page=lapchick/11051 (Accessed June 2012).

Lenskyj HJ (1986) *Out of bounds. Women, sport and sexuality.* Ontario: The Women's Press.

Lenskyj HJ (1995) Sport and the threat to gender boundaries. *Sporting Traditions* 12: 47–50.

Lenskyj HJ (2003) *Out on the field. Women, sport and sexualities.* Toronto: Women's Press.

Loftus J (2001) America's liberalization in attitudes toward homosexuality, 1973 to 1998. *American Sociological Review* 66: 762–782

McCormack M (2012) *The declining significance of homophobia: How teenage boys are redefining masculinity and heterosexuality.* Oxford: Oxford University Press.

McCormack M and Anderson E (2010a) The re-production of homosexuality-themed discourse in educationally-based organised sport. *Culture, Health and Sexuality* 12: 913–927.

McCormack M and Anderson E (2010b) 'It's just not acceptable anymore': The erosion of homophobia and the softening of masculinity at an English sixth form. *Sociology* 44: 843–859.

Pronger B (1990) *The arena of masculinity: Sports, homosexuality, and the meaning of sex*. London: GMP Publishers Limited.

Shire J, Brackenridge, C and Fuller M (2000) Changing positions: The sexual politics of a women's field hockey team 1986–1996. *Women in Sport and Physical Activity Journal* 9: 35–64.

Wolf-Wendel L, Toma D and Morphew C (2001) How much difference is too much difference? Perceptions of gay men and lesbians in intercollegiate athletics. *Journal of College Student Development* 42: 465–479.

Wright J and Clarke G (1999) Sport, the media and construction of compulsory heterosexuality. *International Review for the Sociology of Sport* 34: 227–248.

30

CONTEXTUALIZING HOMOPHOBIC LANGUAGE IN SPORT

Mark McCormack

Introduction

Throughout the 1990s, men's sports—particularly men's team sports—were characterised by high levels of homophobia. Researchers who examined the relationship between gay men and sport largely agreed that organized sport existed as a hostile environment for gay men (Pronger, 1990). However, cultural attitudes have undergone significant transformation in recent years, both outside (McCormack, 2012a) and inside (Anderson, 2011b) sport. Supporting this argument, research documents a remarkable change in the attitudes of fans toward gay players in football (Cashmore and Cleland, 2012; Magrath, 2012) and improved attitudes of heterosexual athletes toward gay men in sport (Anderson and McGuire, 2010), as well as improving experiences of openly gay male athletes (Anderson, 2011a, 2011b).

In this chapter, I examine how decreasing levels of homophobia influence homophobic language within sport, arguing that we need to broaden our understanding of such language. Drawing on literature that highlights the regulatory power of homophobic language in policing men's gendered behaviours, I draw on contemporary research in the sociology of sport to show how decreasing cultural homophobia has led to a fluid and contextually specific understanding of homosexually themed language within sport.

Sport, homophobia and the regulation of masculinity

As other chapters in this handbook illustrate, sport has traditionally served as a social institution that reproduces and consolidates patriarchal relations, as well as defining and celebrating orthodox forms of masculinity (see also Nauright and Chandler, 1996). Research documents that one of the key motives of sporting participation for men is to distance themselves from the stigma of being perceived as feminine and/or gay (Anderson, 2005). Accordingly, as part of their masculinity-making process (Adams, Anderson and McCormack, 2010), male athletes often discursively stigmatize gay and gender non-conforming men (Muir and Seitz, 2004), as well as women (Schacht, 1996). It is through these processes of marginalisation and domination that one form of masculinity, often described as 'the jock', achieves social dominance among other archetypal groups of men.

Colleagues and I have previously discussed the role of language in establishing hegemonic dominance among male athletes (Adams, Anderson and McCormack, 2010). This is something we described as 'masculinity establishing discourse'. Drawing on the ethnographic data of a British football team, we showed how football was demarcated as a 'man's game' where men were required to be 'warriors'—embodying the orthodox masculine traits of aggression, self-sacrifice and the denial of pain. In addition to showing how a particular form of masculinity is established in sport, we then documented how masculinity is *regulated*—through 'masculinity challenging discourse'. This discourse is described as a systematic set of practices where masculinity was questioned through the use of homophobic and misogynist comments/jibes and by linking these with suggestions of deficiencies in the male body—for example, by asserting that particular men had 'no bollocks'. By use of the combination of masculinity-establishing and masculinity-challenging discourse, we found that homophobia and misogyny combined to reproduce a particular form of masculinity within sport.

While recognising masculinity to be policed by a number of factors, scholars argue that homophobia is the most significant mechanism by which men regulate masculinity (Anderson, 2005; Pronger, 1990). This is because, unlike race or gender, homosexuality is an invisible characteristic; with the result that assertions that another who identifies as heterosexual is actually gay cannot be disproved. Accordingly, a number of scholars find that in a culture of homophobia, the primary way to subordinate a young male is to call him a 'fag', or accuse him of being gay—even if one does not believe he is (Plummer, 1999). Accusing someone of homosexuality demonstrates one's heteromasculinity at the expense of that person.

Interviewing 32 openly gay athletes between 1998 and 2001, Anderson (2002) found that homophobic language was present in all types of men's sports. He argued that both explicit and covert forms of prejudice were enacted because gay athletes did not fit into the heteromasculine ethos of sport where homophobic language restricts the life experiences of sexual minorities, polices gendered behaviours, and stigmatizes youth who do not conform to orthodox notions of masculinity (see also Parker, 1996). Anderson (2002) therefore suggested that homophobic language acted as a barrier against the establishment of a gay subculture, serving to maintain men's sport as an institution in which a heterosexual identity is pre-requisite, and masculinity is strictly regulated.

However, in the decade since Anderson's (2002) study, there has been a remarkable decrease in homophobia in sport (Anderson, 2011b; Cashmore and Cleland, 2012; McCormack and Anderson, 2010a, 2010b). On the surface, this seems to be in contradiction with the continuation of homosexually-themed language in contemporary sport cultures. This chapter examines the continued prevalence of words that were once used to stigmatize, by analysing the shifting meanings of language use.

Theorising homophobic language

Much of the literature that has examined the use of homophobic language has often used definitions that are implicit or imprecise (e.g. Anderson, 2002). This is not to criticise this body of work, much of which was providing the first analysis of homophobic language in the sporting arena, but to highlight that it is necessary to develop a comprehensive definition of homophobic language. Reviewing the literature, I identify two necessary features for language to be considered homophobic: first, that it is said with pernicious intent (Armstrong, 1997; Thurlow, 2001); and second, that it has a negative social effect (Brackenridge et al., 2008; Plummer, 1999).

Pernicious intent recognises that the speaker is intending to degrade or marginalize a person or their behaviour by association with homosexuality. Evidencing this, Thurlow (2001) examined 'intensifiers'—additional words like 'fucking—to argue that homophobic language has negative intent. He found that homophobic language was accompanied by an intensifier more frequently than any other form of insult; for example by saying 'you fucking queer' rather than 'you queer'.

In order to understand negative social effect, one need only consider the centrality of homophobia in bullying behaviours (Rivers, 2011). Retrospective accounts of schooling and youth experiences by gay and lesbian adults frequently refer to the emotional trauma caused by homophobic bullying (Flowers and Buston, 2001; Plummer, 1999) and the negative social impact it has on students and athletes (Brackenridge et al., 2008). It is argued that homophobic language is often also used to regulate gendered behaviours, rather than to explicitly seek to stigmatize an individual (Mac an Ghaill, 1994). Yet even when this is the case, such language still reproduces homophobia because users intend to stigmatize same-sex desire (Hillier and Harrison, 2004). For example, using explicitly anti-gay epithets to regulate heterosexual athletes who do not conform to orthodox gender stereotypes reproduces the unequal stratification of masculinities, as well as wounding the recipient of the abuse. Accordingly, homophobic language has a negative social effect and can contribute to a hostile sports culture for all male youth.

While pernicious intent and negative social effect are the two key factors that have been used to determine if language is homophobic, there is an implicit assumption made in literature on the topic that homophobic language occurs within a homophobic environment. That is, there is an assumption that when people use homophobic language, they do so in a local culture where people maintain homophobic sentiments. But I would maintain that whereas this assumption once made sense, recent social changes have been profound and this has had a significant effect on the meanings and nuances of homosexually themed language.

The assumption of a homophobic environment is understandable given that the vast majority of the research on homophobic language occurred between 1980 and 2000 (Anderson, 2002; Davis, 1990; Plummer, 1999; Thurlow, 2001), when British and American cultures were highly homophobic (Anderson, 2009; Keleher and Smith, 2012). Yet the marked decrease in levels of homophobia in recent years necessitates that the importance of cultural context be understood. We need a new model for understanding the use of this type of discourse in contemporary times. It is for this reason that I build on our understandings of the complexity of homophobic language by proposing that we first consider the social environment in which the discourse occurs, before discussing the motivations, intensity and effects of such language.

Pro-gay language and its links to masculinity

I have documented that the homophobia and violence traditionally associated with sport has eroded in some sporting cultures. For example, in a recent article on rugby players (McCormack and Anderson, 2010b), unlike earlier work on rugby men (Nauright and Chandler, 1996; Schacht, 1996), Anderson and I found that rugby players espoused support of gay rights and rejected explicit forms of homophobia. One of the players, Graham, exemplified the positive association that the players have with homosexuality, when asked if he would mind having an openly gay player on the team. He said, 'Maybe my coach would, but I wouldn't.' Another player, John, agreed, 'I wouldn't give a shit. Not in the slightest.' Tim added, 'Seriously, what kind of people do you think we are?' These statements were not exceptions to the team's sentiment, but the consensus view of the players; not a single one of whom maintained negative attitudes toward sexual minorities.

Rather than rejecting any engagement with homosexually-themed language, though, these young sportsmen used language in a way that we described as 'flirting with gayness'. For example, the athletes would often say to each other 'hey gay boy', but this was done in what we could only describe as a welcoming manner. When asked about the 'gay' content of this banter, participants argued that their pro-gay attitudes prevented gay banter from being interpreted as homophobic. Mike said, 'It's simply banter. We don't mean anything by it.' Alex clarifies that this type of gay banter is understood as indicative of close friendship. When asked if he would banter with someone on the team he disliked, he responds, 'No. Of course not! You only banter with those you like.' This use of language is part of a larger project of masculine bantering, serving as a form of homosocial bonding between friends; in my research on English sixth-form students in the south of England, openly gay students participated in this banter and argued that it was a way of social bonding (McCormack, 2012b).

These men also did not exhibit the self-sacrificing behaviours or misogynistic attitudes previously identified with rugby men, either (Dunning and Sheard, 1979). Also collecting data with a rugby team, Anderson and McGuire (2010) found that not only did they reject violence and refuse to play through injury, but that they also rejected their coach's more orthodox, homophobic, behaviours. In their study, they report how Mark talked about the support that athletes gave each other in the face of bullying from the coaches: 'the other guys are there for you when the coach screams this shit at you. They give you a hug and say, "Don't listen to him, he's a jerk"' (p. 256).

It is within this context of valuing social support and espousing positive attitudes regarding homosexuality that one needs to analyse new forms of homosexually-themed language. In my book, *The declining significance of homophobia* (2012a), I conceptualise 'pro-gay language' as a way of understanding homosexually themed language which has a *positive* social effect. I define it as 'the use of homosexually themed language that is used to bond people together in socio-positive ways or to demonstrate pro-gay attitudes'. One example of this bonding occurred in an English lesson, when openly gay student, Max, was working with his heterosexual friends, Cooper and James. While Cooper was doodling in his book, he looked up and asked, 'Is this really gay what I'm doing?' Max started laughing, and said, 'Yeah, it's pretty gay.' Not only do these students bond, they expunge some of the negativity from the word. This is perhaps why these youth do not hear 'that's so gay' as homophobic, whereas adults do. Youth have been socialised into hearing a different meaning, whereas adults have not. Interestingly, this again supports the heterosexual rugby players' contention that their language use was not homophobic (McCormack and Anderson, 2010b).

I also documented a second form of pro-gay language: one where heterosexual male students casually call their close friends 'lover' or 'boyfriend'. Here, heterosexual male students used language as a sign of homosocial affection, without any discernible attempt to consolidate their heterosexual standing. Proclaiming close friends as boyfriends was understood by the students as a way of demonstrating emotional intimacy. Importantly, these students (athletes and non-athletes alike) did not think that labelling each other this way would homosexualise them. The ability for boys to express their emotions in such an open way is clearly a positive development. Moreover, just as homophobic language once contributed to a homophobic school environment, this form of pro-gay language now helps promote gay-friendly cultures of inclusivity.

Modelling the changing nature of homosexually themed language

In order to understand the changes in meanings and effects of homosexually themed language, it is vital to look to the broader culture—and specifically the declining significance of homophobia for younger men (McCormack, 2012a, 2012b). And, in order to do this, it is necessary to understand how homophobia operates as a social mechanism in the regulation of gendered behaviour. This has been best theorised through Anderson's (2009) concept, homohysteria.

Defined as the fear of being socially perceived as gay, there are three factors that determine the level of homohysteria within a culture: 1) widespread awareness that homosexuality exists as a constant sexual orientation within that culture; 2) homophobic attitudes and beliefs in that culture; and 3) the conflation of male homosexuality with femininity. According to Anderson, a culture is homohysteric if all three characteristics are present (Anderson, 2011c). In America in the 1980s a perfect storm of the rise of conservative right wing politics, the politicisation of evangelical religion and the AIDS crisis coalesced to produce an exceptionally homohysteric era in American history (Anderson, 2009). This created a moral panic against homosexuality, with dominant media and political discourses reactionary in their attempts to promote 'traditional family values' (Anderson, 2011c).

Homohysteria is a useful concept for distinguishing between cultures where homophobia regulates gendered behaviours and those where it does not. Anderson (2011a) highlights this by contrasting homophobic but non-homohysteric countries, like Iran, with homohysteric cultures, like Britain and the US in the 1980s.

In Iran, despite extremely homophobic attitudes, homosocial tactility including two males holding hands occurs without social regulation. This is because such behaviours do not connote homosexuality (Frank, Camp and Boutcher, 2010)—the result of Iran not being homohysteric. The combination of high levels of homophobia and a lack of homohysteria leads to a state of what we call *homoerasure* (Anderson, 2014). A stage prior to homohysteria where it is stated that homosexuality does not or cannot exist within the population (the President of Iran has said homosexuality does not exist in his country), and homosexuality is cast as a Western perversion. If Western notions of gay rights are imported into Iranian culture, it will be a test of homohysteria as a concept to see if homophobia becomes a policing agent of masculinity.

However, in the UK and US, where the three conditions for homohysteria are met, homophobia is an effective policing mechanism of masculinity. This means that homosexual suspicion can be cast on anyone, and same-sex touch has to be accompanied by behaviours that prevent the action from being socially coded as gay. Accordingly, when tactile behaviours occurred in male institutions such as in the military and in sport during homohysteric periods, they were frequently accompanied by homophobic abuse (Plummer, 1999).

Cultural context, and specifically the level of homohysteria, is therefore key to understanding and categorizing types of homosexually themed language in my work. In times of high homohysteria, where boys use homophobic language to consolidate their own heterosexual identity, phrases like 'that's so gay' have pernicious intent and negative social effect and would be appropriately classified as homophobic. But in a culture that is non-homohysteric because they are aware that homosexuality exists but do not hold antipathy toward it (something Anderson describes as post homohysteria), such as those discussed in my research (McCormack 2012a), men do not police their behaviours to live up to a heteromasculine ideal. Here, homosexually-themed language is used in a way that has *positive* social effects, and 'that's so gay' won't have damaging connotations.

I have developed a model (Figure 30.1) to understand the diverse meanings of homosexually themed language in different contexts (McCormack, 2012a), where I argue there are four distinct phases that have occurred with regards to homosexually themed language. First, in a highly homohysteric culture, boys use homophobic language to consolidate their own heterosexual identity and masculine standing (Plummer, 1999). In this stage, homosexually themed language is indeed homophobic, as it is used with pernicious intent and has a very negative social effect.

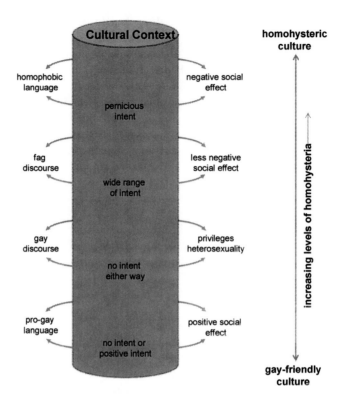

Figure 30.1 A model of homosexually themed language

The second framework, fag discourse, occurs in settings which are slightly less homohysteric. Here, it is likely that many gay people have negative sport and educational experiences, and the setting is homophobic; but it is also likely that there will be people who support gay rights. In this stage, some young men who use fag discourse will insist that it is not meant to stigmatize homosexuality, while others will use it with pernicious intent. It will continue to have negative social effects, however, including the regulation and restriction of acceptable masculine behaviours, because the intent of language use is not always clear (Anderson, 2002).

In the third framework gay discourse occurs in settings where young men are not particularly concerned about whether they are socially perceived as gay. In these settings of low homohysteria, boys say phrases like 'that's so gay' as expressions of dissatisfaction and frustration. Importantly, there is no intent to marginalize or wound people with this use of language. And while this is not necessarily pro-gay, young men maintain that the word 'gay' does not connote same-sex desire in this context (see McCormack and Anderson, 2010a).

Finally, in gay-friendly cultures such as the high schools discussed in my book, men are not part of a homohysteric culture. While they might prefer to be thought of as heterosexual, they do not police their behaviours to live up to a heteromasculine ideal. Instead, homosexually-themed language is used in a way that has *positive* social effects. Sometimes pro-gay language is said without any specific intention, but it is also used as a mechanism for bonding students by demonstrating emotional intimacy or inclusion of openly gay students. The fun and fundamentally friendly way this language is used—that is, the ease these students have with gay peers—helps contribute toward a gay friendly environment (see McCormack, 2012a).

The use of language is always complex and tricky. There will be some overlap between types of language, as well as exceptions to the framework. For example, while a person can use homophobic language in a gay-friendly setting, this would be an anomalous result and would not fit with general conceptualizations of homophobic language in the wider literature. For example, if a student were to shout 'you fucking poof' at another boy on a gay-friendly sports team, it is highly likely that the athlete would be reprimanded by both his fellow teammates and the coach; and apart from the impact it would have on the recipient, it would have marginal if any negative social effect on the broader culture. Likewise, saying 'that's so gay' in a highly homophobic setting would probably be interpreted as homophobic, while it would not in a gay-friendly one. In understanding this form of language, context is all-important (see McCormack and Anderson, 2010a). In summary, the meanings of words change. It is therefore necessary to take account of this complexity when seeking to understand the use of language related to homosexuality in future sport research.

References

Adams A, Anderson E, and McCormack M (2010) Establishing and challenging masculinity: The influence of gendered discourses in organized sport. *Journal of Language and Social Psychology* 29(3): 278–295.

Anderson E (2002) Openly gay athletes. *Gender & Society* 16(6): 860–877.

Anderson E (2005) *In the game: Gay athletes and the cult of masculinity.* New York: Suny Press.

Anderson E (2009) *Inclusive masculinity.* London: Routledge.

Anderson E (2011a) Openly gay athletes: Updating the outcome. *Gender & Society* 25(2): 250–268.

Anderson E (2011b) Masculinities and sexualities in sport and physical cultures: Three decades of evolving research. *Journal of Homosexuality* 58(5): 565–578.

Anderson E (2011c) The rise and fall of Western homohysteria. *Journal of Feminist Studies* 1(Fall): 80–94.

Anderson E (2014) *21st century jocks.* London: Palgrave MacMillan.

Anderson E and McGuire R (2010). Inclusive masculinity theory and the politics of men's rugby. *Journal of Gender Studies* 19(3): 249–262.

Armstrong J (1997) Homophobic slang as coercive discourse among college students. In Livia A and Hall K (Eds.) *Queerly phrased: Language, gender and sexuality* New York: Oxford University Press, pp. 326–334.

Brackenridge C, Allred P, Jarvis A, Maddocks K, and Rivers I (2008) *A literature review of sexual orientation in sport.* London: UK Sport.

Cashmore E and Cleland J (2012) Fans, homophobia and masculinities in association football: Evidence of a more inclusive environment. *British Journal of Sociology* 63(2): 370–387.

Davis L (1990) Male cheerleaders and the naturalisation of gender. In Messner MA and Sabo D (eds) *Sport, men and the gender order* Champaign, IL: Human Kinetics, pp. 153–161.

Dunning E and Sheard K (1979) *Barbarians, gentlemen and players.* Oxford: Martin Robertson.

Flowers P and Buston K (2001) 'I was terrified of being different': Exploring gay men's accounts of growing-up in a heterosexist society *Journal of Adolescence* 24: 51–65.

Frank DJ, Camp B, and Boutcher S (2010) Worldwide trends in the criminal regulation of sex, 1945 to 2005. *American Sociological Review* 75: 867–893.

Hillier L and Harrison L (2004) Homophobia and the production of shame: Young people and same-sex attraction. *Culture, Health & Sexuality* 6(1): 79–94.

Keleher A and Smith E (2012) Growing support for gay and lesbian equality since 1990. *Journal of Homosexuality* 59(9): 1307–1326.

Mac an Ghaill M (1994). *The making of men.* Buckingham: Open University Press.

McCormack M (2012a) *The declining significance of homophobia: How teenage boys are redefining masculinity and heterosexuality.* New York: Oxford University Press.

McCormack M (2012b) The positive experiences of lesbian, gay, bisexual and transgendered students in a Christian sixth form college. *Sociological Research Online,* 17(3), 5.

McCormack M and Anderson E (2010a) 'It's just not acceptable any more': The erosion of homophobia and softening of masculinity at an English sixth form. *Sociology* 44(5): 843–859.

McCormack M and Anderson E (2010b) The re-production of homosexually-themed discourse in educationally based organised sport. *Culture, Health & Sexuality* 12: 913–927.

Magrath R (2012) 'To try and put them off their game': The use of homophobic discourse among gay-friendly football fans. *BSA Youth Study Group, Changing Masculinities*, Friday 2nd November, London.

Muir KB and Seitz T (2004) Machismo, misogyny, and homophobia in a male athletic subculture: A participant observation study of deviant rituals in collegiate rugby. *Deviant Behavior* 25: 303–327.

Nauright J and Chandler T (1996) *Making men: Rugby and masculine identity*. London: Frank Cass.

Parker A (1996) The construction of masculinity within boys' physical education [1]. *Gender and Education* 8(2): 141–158.

Plummer D (1999) *One of the boys: Masculinity, homophobia and modern manhood*. New York: Harrington Park Press.

Pronger B (1990) *The arena of masculinity*. New York: St Martin's Press.

Rivers I (2011) *Homophobic bullying: Research and theoretical perspectives*. New York: Oxford University Press.

Schacht S (1996) Misogyny on and off the 'pitch': The gendered world of male rugby players. *Gender & Society* 10: 550–565.

Thurlow C (2001) Naming the 'outsider within': Homophobic pejoratives and the verbal abuse of LGB high-school pupils. *Journal of Adolescence* 24: 25–38.

31

100 MISSING MEN

Participation, selection, and silence of gay athletes

Scott Ogawa

Introduction

Jason Collins recently became the only current professional male athletes in the top four American leagues (American football, baseball, basketball, and ice hockey) to publicly come out as gay. Conventional wisdom presumes that many more gay athletes exist and that they will come out of the closet in the coming years as tolerance for homosexuality spreads into the locker room. This chapter challenges this presumption. I instead argue that the reason there are so few openly gay male athletes is because so few exist, not because so many are in the closet.

I understand that this claim may strike you as implausible, or perhaps even offensive, for it is readily understood that when we overcome intolerance toward sexual minorities we discover homosexuality is typical everywhere. This even appears to be the case for the lower levels of competitive sport (Anderson, 2002, 2005, 2011). Thus, is it possible that among elite athletes in certain sports homosexuality is remarkably atypical? The social dynamics of professional athletes and homosexuality is difficult to observe. Nevertheless, accurately inferring the lack of sexual minorities at this level of sport might accelerate, not thwart, the promotion of tolerance within the professional locker room. If we insist that what we see (few openly gay athletes) is self-evident proof of homophobia, we might deny the anti-homophobia efforts and attitudes within this space.

What we observe

Using game-day rosters as the criteria, there are 3,496 men in the four major North American leagues: National Football League (NFL, 32 teams, 53 players in each team); Major League Baseball (MLB, 30, 25); National Basketball Association (NBA, 30, 12); and National Hockey League (NHL, 30, 23). Assuming the proportion of gay athletes is similar to the proportion in the general population, and using the oft-cited rate of 2.8% male homosexuality (Laumann et al., 1994), we should observe approximately 100 gay men at this level of sport.

Over the previous 40 years these leagues have had 10 men that are publicly known to be gay. Six are in football (Jerry Smith, David Kopay, Roy Simmons, Esura Tuaolo, Wade Davis, and

Kwame Harris); two in baseball (Glenn Burke and Billie Bean); and two in basketball (Collins and John Amaechi). There have been none in hockey. As mentioned, Collins came out publicly at the age of 34 while seeking a new contract in 2013. Burke appears to have been partially out during his career in the late 1970s. Smith died of AIDS without ever publicly declaring his sexuality, though it was confirmed by Kopay. Harris's sexual orientation was revealed by court documents, though he followed up with a public interview. The remaining players came out voluntarily after retirement.

The numbers are continuously changing, with news of Collins and Harris occurring within the last year. Nevertheless, as this chapter goes to press, these figures indicate that about 0.05% of professional contracts have been signed by men known to be gay. Similar patterns hold for major European soccer leagues and individual sports such as tennis and boxing. In all cases, we know of exceptionally few gay athletes. Even if 50 more current and former athletes were to come out as gay, the known rate of homosexuality in sport would be 0.3%, an order magnitude less than what we might expect (2.8%) given typical sexuality estimates in the general population. No statistical techniques are needed to confidently assert that this is more than sampling error. An explanation is warranted.

There are at least three potential hypotheses: (1) gay men in these leagues remain silent about their sexuality – the "silence" hypothesis; (2) gay men choose not to play sports – the "non-participation" hypothesis; (3) gay men are less likely than straight men to achieve professional status – the "selection" hypothesis. Anderson (2005) has also highlighted that there are multiple possibilities for the lack of openly gay athletes at this level of sport. I collectively refer to the second and third hypotheses as the "non-existence" hypothesis since both imply non-existence of professional gay male athletes.

Unfortunately we have no conclusive evidence for any of the three hypotheses. Also, there does not have to be only one reason that there are far fewer known gay male athletes than we might expect. Nonetheless, we can ask which hypothesis is the most likely to account for most of the 100 missing men given the collaborating evidence.

We start with the knowledge that the non-existence hypothesis is not absolute, given the aforementioned gay men in professional sports. It therefore appears that most journalists assume the silence hypothesis (Kian and Anderson, 2009). However, I scrutinize the silence hypothesis as an untenable way of understanding the silence among *so many* athletes in the four major North American leagues. I next examine recent findings that highlight that gay male youth opt out of sport in relatively large numbers. I argue that while this ostensibly supports the non-participation hypothesis, at a deeper level it is unlikely to be the principal reason we see so few gay male athletes at the elite level. I finish by providing evidence in support of the selection hypothesis by demonstrating that it explains several patterns we see among professional athletes, both male and female.

Limits of the silence hypothesis

There is little doubt that gay men face pressure to remain silent about their sexuality, especially in an environment like a locker room. Yet despite the strength of the silence hypothesis, it has difficulty accounting for every pattern we observe among elite athletes; the situation is likely more complicated. We should not be surprised that some gay athletes remain silent during their professional careers. It is puzzling, however, that each year roughly 100 gay men have chosen to keep their sexuality a public secret and succeeded in doing so. In critically examining the silence hypothesis, there are three observations that led me to believe that it does not tell the entire story.

Pockets of tolerance

Before homosexuality finds universal acceptance in competitive sport, we should expect pockets of tolerance to gay male athletes. Two of the most recent players to be revealed as gay (Harris and Collins) both attended Stanford, a large liberal university which is at least outwardly perceived to be gay friendly. Many NFL and NBA players attend relatively liberal institutions before signing professional contracts. The fact that some university climates are perceived to be gay friendly does not, of course, mean that all gay men at these schools are out. However, at such universities, there certainly are many openly gay students.

Now consider the fact that liberal universities attract students, including athletes, from across the nation, and that these institutions offer full scholarships to recruits that have professional-level potential. A portion of the gay male superstars would likely desire to attend overtly tolerant universities on the West coast where they could contemplate living openly. Yet tolerance for homosexuality over the past 10 years at liberal universities that serve as a gateway to the professional ranks has not attracted a noticeable number of gay male athletes who choose to live openly. This suggests that even if we achieve universal tolerance for homosexuality in the next 10 years, the 100 missing men may, for the most part, remain missing.

Athletic achievement as an objective metric

Another conundrum stems from the observation that athletes are largely judged by some known metric. Relative to other endeavours, perception is *less* important in sport. This is because on-field performance is objective (albeit imperfectly). People choose which politician to vote for and which entertainer to watch, but they do not choose which athlete crosses the finish line first. This is the value of athletic capital in sport. As Anderson (2005) has previously stated, athletic ability mitigates stigma. Athletes, especially those not on the margin of being cut from the team, have less to lose since they have more (their athletic talent) to fall back on.

If we focus attention on this aspect of sport, we would expect politicians and entertainers to lag behind athletes in revealing their sexuality. I find it noteworthy that athletes have not only failed to lead these other celebrities in terms of revealing their sexuality, but have instead lagged in a severe way.

The "one missing man" in the Internet age

Consider for a moment the life of the highest-profile 36 superstar athletes in the digital age. They represent multi-millionaire men with high facial recognition. They are easily identified by most people that they meet on the street, and by most of the men they have sex with. The public – including high-paying tabloids – already show an interest in the sex lives of men (gay or straight) of such high status. This calls into question the proposition that one of these extremely famous men could keep his sex life completely private if he happened to be gay. He would have a difficult time suppressing photos and rumours from circulating online. Furthermore, today's male sex partners would probably be less likely than those in the past to have anything to hide. I speculate that many would find requests by the superstar athlete not to mention encounters to friends and family to be unreasonable.

If a superstar athlete were gay I therefore find it difficult to explain the general absence of indirect signs on the Internet. And most of the online rumours that do exist are largely based on juvenile stereotypes regarding appearance; not explicit accounts by scorned lovers or good-natured innuendo by famous friends. Information is limited, but this reasoning does suggest that there is a decent chance that a gay male superstar, at least one that is sexually active, does not currently exist. This creates a problem of "one missing man": among the top 36 superstars we would expect roughly one to be gay. For me, the most plausible hypothesis is that this man does not currently exist, not that he remains silent.

Alternative explanations?

In order for the silence hypothesis to generate the data that we observe on its own, homophobia and conformity would need to: (1) prevent the vast majority of approximately 100 gay men from seeking ever more available environments (such as liberal universities) that might allow them to live openly; (2) outweigh the fact that the most talented athletes who come out publicly would have more to fall back on relative to politicians and celebrities; (3) produce a silence among sexually active superstars that it has survived the rise of Twitter, message boards, and a gay community with increasingly less to hide.

On top of all this, what if there actually is not much homophobia in the locker room? Each of these conundrums becomes that much more puzzling. In fact, Cyd Zeigler (2012) from Outsports.com writes that "the stereotype of professional athletes as homophobic is as outdated as the stereotype of gay men as theater queens". Zeigler, a leader in understanding homosexuality and sports, makes a strong case that we should expect several gay male athletes to come out. Furthermore, as the recent reaction to Jason Collins' public declaration has made quite clear, many professional players are willing to voice explicit and public support for gay athletes.

The silence hypothesis is nevertheless an important part of explaining why we do not know of many gay men in pro sports. However, is it the full story? I argue that there exists an alternative hypothesis that is as important – or perhaps even more important – for understanding the patterns that we observe among elite athletes.

Participation by gay male youth

One alternative to the silence hypothesis is that very few gay men actually exist in professional sports because gay male youth either opt out or never participate in the first place. In this section I argue that even if gay boys opt out at high rates, this non-participation hypothesis is unlikely to fully explain what we see among *professional* athletes.

Zipp (2011) looked at data from the National Longitudinal Study of Adolescent Health (Add Health) in the United States and found that self-identified gay boys are in fact more likely to drop out of sports while in high school, something Anderson (2005) shows qualitatively. While this evidence is compelling, it cannot explain *all* of the missing gay men. Even if fully half of all gay males voluntarily dropped out of sports (and all straight boys remained), there would still be about 50 gay men in the professional ranks of these four sports. Yet retrospectively, no year has seen more than three known gay men playing professionally at the same time.

More importantly, looking at the *average* dropout rates for boys playing sports is problematic because it assumes the decision to drop out is the same for boys of average ability as it is for boys of exceptional ability. Yet the 100 missing men, to the extent they exist, are all of exceptional ability. The potential cost of foregoing sports, both in terms of future earnings and current peer-admiration, is much higher for the typical athlete who shows NBA potential at a young age. Would so many exceptionally-talented boys choose to forego so much, not only in American professional sport, but in professional sport throughout the world?

Finally, the non-participation hypothesis corresponds to the existence of gay adults who have the undeniable physical gifts to play professional football or basketball, yet claim to have quit sport in high school or college due to sexuality. It is thus informative that no publicized accounts currently exist.

Selection due to differences in the populations

I conclude my chapter with a proposition that may strike you as radical and perhaps quite offensive: the reason we see so few gay men in professional sport is because so few have the talent to play at the most elite levels. In other words, gay men are in fact slightly less athletic than straight men, and this manifests itself in an exaggerated way at the elite level. This is only an argument about averages, and the difference is so small that we do not notice it from everyday experience. Nevertheless, regardless of how distasteful you find this claim, it provides the basis for a plausible way to account for the majority of the 100 missing men. Furthermore, there is evidence in support of this proposition.

Some research has been conducted on body-type differences between gay and straight men, and while results are not conclusive, they are suggestive. Bogaert and Blanchard (1996) compare 318 gay men to 318 straight men and find that gay men are on average smaller and less physically demonstrative. They also show that gay men are less muscular and have worse spatial reasoning. "Compared with heterosexual men", they write, "homosexual men are shorter, lighter and younger at the onset of puberty." This is consistent with findings by Blanchard, Dickey, and Jones (1995) who show that one group of homosexual men were "shorter, lighter, and lighter in proportion to their height". Rahman and Wilson (2003) and McCormick and Witelson (1991) find a difference in the spatial reasoning ability between gay and straight men, with gay men scoring closer on average to women than to straight men. Finally, Evans (1972) compared 44 homosexual men to 111 heterosexual men, finding that homosexual's "shoulders were narrower in relation to pelvic width, and their muscle strength was less". Each of these studies suffers from selection bias, but nevertheless, the fact that they point to the possibility that gay men are slightly less athletic on average is both surprising and informative.

Findings like these imply that we should fully *expect* to observe a higher rate of heterosexuality in populations of men that are *above* average in strength. The question thus becomes whether this effect is large enough to explain just how few gay men we observe in a population of highly-talented professional athletes. Can a small difference in the averages between gay and straight men really create such a stark outcome in a professional league?

The nature of extreme selection

Humans have poor intuition for the power of selection when it isolates extreme slices of the population. The following example is purely illustrative, but nevertheless shows how a relatively small difference between the averages of two groups can lead to very stark outcomes within selected samples.

Assume height follows a normal distribution (the "bell curve"). Suppose also that there is a minority group that comprises 20% of a population and is shorter on average when compared with the rest of the population (5'8" rather than 5'10"). If we select all individuals of above average height then members of the minority will account for roughly 10% of this selected population, even though they are 20% of the overall population. This means everybody will know plenty of tall people from the shorter group. However, if we consider only people in the top 1% in terms of height (6'5"), then members of the minority group will constitute only 2.5%. If we limit the slice to the tallest 0.01% (6'9") then the minority group will be *less than 1%*. We thus see that a relatively small difference in population averages leads to a stark outcome when severe forms of selection are applied. This outcome, however, is impossible to comprehend from everyday experience since most people are unlikely to have multiple acquaintances in the top 0.01% of the population along any dimension.

The aforementioned example begins with a minority of 20%, and reduces it to under 1% by the selection process that is most severe at the tail end of the distribution. Can this framework pull the rate of homosexuality in the general population of 3% all the way down to anything close to the currently known historical rate of 0.05% in pro sports? We have evidence that gay and straight men are different physically, but we do not know the size of this difference, along which dimensions it is most pronounced, or any other details about the distributions of ability. Thus we cannot be certain. However, the selection hypothesis *has the potential* to account for most of the 100 missing gay men. In contrast, the silence and non-participation hypotheses each help account for some of the missing 100 gay men, but are most likely insufficient as the sole mechanisms.

1,748 missing women

Additional support for the selection hypothesis comes from another area where we see very stark outcomes based on differences in athletic ability. Among the 3,496 aforementioned professional athletes each year, *all are male*, even though fully half of the population is female (thus we would expect to observe 1,748 women). The only reason this does not strike us as preposterous is because it is so utterly familiar. We understand that while not all men are better than all women in football, at the tail end of the talent distribution, men at the professional level are better than all women.

Attraction to females

Finally, consider the following relationships: first, strength (X) is correlated with being a man (Y) – on average men are stronger. Second, being a man (Y) is correlated with the tendency to find females attractive (Z). Neither of these correlations is absolute. Some women are stronger than some men, and some people are attracted to others of the same sex. Yet both correlations are not disputed. If X is positively correlated with Y, and Y is positively correlated with Z, should we be surprised if X turns out to be positively correlated with Z? In other words, should we be surprised if being strong is associated with finding females attractive?

We can replace "being a man" with "testosterone level". In this framework there is concrete evidence to support my thesis. In his review of the literature, Simon LeVay (2003) notes a widespread finding based on studies that manipulate hormones in the womb of animals: "High prenatal testosterone levels organize the brain in a male-specific fashion; low levels of testosterone permit it to organize in a female-specific fashion." Given a link between testosterone and muscle production, this suggests that strength is ultimately about which sex people are attracted to in absolute terms. People (of either sex) who are *attracted to women* will be slightly more athletic on average. Supporting this proposition, in a study with 5,500 women, Bogaert (1998) finds that lesbians are taller and heavier than heterosexual women.

Testable predictions

To summarize the selection hypothesis: (1) we see few openly gay professional male athletes because few exist; (2) few exist because few are athletic enough to compete at the highest levels; and (3) few are athletic enough to compete at the highest level because of a rather mild correlation in the population between athleticism and attraction to females. Again, this hypothesis does not preclude the silence and non-participation hypotheses, and it is likely that all three are important for understanding what we observe. However, the selection hypothesis does produce distinct predictions that are not part of the silence or non-participation hypotheses.

Prediction 1: trickle, not flood, and on the margin

There have been some gay athletes at the professional level. One way to make sense of this observation is to assume it is the tip of the iceberg. However, we can also interpret what we observe as precisely what we might expect from a population with a particularly low rate of homosexuality. According to the selection hypothesis, among the men who are gay, they are more likely to come from the lower ranks of pro teams in terms of athletic achievement. We should also expect to see a higher rate of gay men playing college sports each year, and even higher rates of gay boys in high school sports.

All of the most recent male athletes known to be gay confirm the prediction that gay athletes are more like to come from the margins of the professional ranks. Collins is arguably the most accomplished of all known gay athletes, yet he has primarily been a role player during his 12 years in the NBA. Robbie Rogers is a footballer who recently came out publicly as he simultaneously temporarily stepped away from the game. Rogers was not a star and had recently been released by a second-tier English club. And Alan Gendreau is an openly gay American-football kicker from Middle Tennessee State. He entered the NFL draft last year but was not selected by any team. Like the majority of athletes, these men are quite talented yet face an exceedingly competitive labor market, so there is nothing atypical about their experiences. Nevertheless, each year there are also hundreds of all-star caliber athletes across the top four North American leagues. Thus far, not one, past or present, is publicly known to be gay. This argument can be formalized. Suppose we define "all-star caliber" to be any athlete in the top third of the talent distribution within the professional ranks. While open to debate, none of the aforementioned 10 gay athletes were all-star caliber during their career. The probability that 10 observations will all come from the bottom two thirds of the distribution of talent is under 2%. Thus either all-star caliber athletes are less likely to come out publicly, or within the professional ranks there is a correlation between talent and sexuality.

Prediction 2: many lesbian stars

The selection hypothesis is centered on sexual attraction. For both sexes it implies that people attracted to females tend to be slightly more athletic on average. This implies that among elite female athletes we should expect to see a higher proportion of lesbians than we see in the general population. Furthermore, this higher rate of homosexuality will be most pronounced amongst the *most* elite female athletes, such as Billie Jean King and Martina Navratilova, two of the greatest female tennis players of all time.

Reading about the Women's National Basketball Association (WNBA) online produces many unsubstantiated rumours, some claiming close to half of the league is lesbian or bisexual. This is quite unlike the NBA, in which such rumours are nearly impossible to find. At the very least, several of the very best WNBA players have officially come out of the closet. This list includes stars such as Sheryl Swoopes, Seimone Augustus, and recently Brittney Griner – arguably the most talented female player of all time. This fact problematizes the silence hypothesis in another way: any argument about why locker-room culture keeps male athletes especially silent must be nuanced as to allow for a preponderance of openly gay elite female athletes.

Anderson (2012) argues that homophobia may be worse for women's sports than for men's, and Bullingham, Magrath and Anderson argue (in another chapter of this handbook) that this is because there is more homohysteria in women's sports. In other words, when a man comes out in sport, it does not implicate his teammates as also being gay; but when a woman comes out, it does. If homophobia is worse in women's sports because of homohysteria, it fails to explain why there are many openly lesbian athletes, but no openly gay male athletes.

Prediction 3: fewer gay men in sports predicated on size, strength and speed

If the selection hypothesis is valid, we should see more elite gay men in sports in which men as a population far outperform women as a population. This is typical in sports predicated primarily on size, strength and speed, and less so in sports requiring acquired skill, aesthetic performance, or ultra-endurance. Highlighting this implication, consider the 2012 Olympics. According to the website Outsport.com (Buzinski, 2012), in a sample of just over 10,000 athletes, there were three openly gay male athletes. Two were in equestrian and one was in diving. Horse-riding and acrobatics are two activities in which being big is a disadvantage, so observing gay men in these sports is consistent with the hypothesis.

Prediction 4: fewer gay male athletes over time

The final implication of the selection hypothesis is that even if homophobia fully dissipates there may be fewer, rather than more, gay professional athletes over time. Population and athletic talent-identification continue to expand, yet the size of the pro leagues has stayed relatively fixed. This implies that elite athletes (gay or straight) are becoming ever more elite. The population of the United States has grown from 200 million to 300 million in the last 40 years, yet the NFL is roughly the same size. Thus 33% of the men in the NFL in 1970 would not be good enough to play today since they would be outperformed by the best players in that extra pool of 100 million people. This reasoning holds even when combined with ongoing improvements due to training, technology and nutrition – or even performance-enhancing drugs.

As the margins shrink, the stark consequences at the tails of the mildly unequal talent distributions become ever more pronounced. Roy Simmons, one of the few NFL players to come out, was a 264 pound offensive guard in the early 1980s. Thirty years later nearly all offensive guards in the NFL weigh 300 pounds or more. If Simmons had been born 30 years later he may have never have had the chance to come out as an active NFL player, but not because of homophobia. The NFL of today may have mixed tolerance for gay athletes, but it has zero tolerance for an offensive guard that weighs only 264 pounds.

Conclusion

I have provided statistical and logical support for the selection hypothesis as the most likely primary explanation for why we observe so few professional gay male athletes. Specifically, the selection hypothesis explains why none of the 10 known gay male athletes (past or present) have been all-star caliber. It also explains why patterns of sexuality among elite female athletes are reversed relative to elite male athletes. Furthermore, this hypothesis is consistent with few openly gay athletes amidst a backdrop of overtly tolerant rhetoric from teammates, club executives, and even many fans. Finally, the selection hypothesis is more than a post hoc explanation of current observation since it also makes the refutable prediction that the number of elite gay athletes will actually decrease over the long term. I do not preclude silence or non-participation by gay athletes, but I do claim that these are likely to be of lesser importance for accounting for the 100 missing men.

I conclude this chapter with two thoughts. First, just because different groups demonstrate different levels of collective achievement does not imply we should discourage some kids from participating in sports. The failure of female athletes to outperform male athletes has not stopped us from providing athletic opportunities for girls, or from pursuing gender equality in many other aspects of life.

Second, and more important, it is possible that the lack of gay male athletes (due to physical reasons) might mean that homophobia in men's sport is not as bad as we assume it to be. If we put unsubstantiated faith in the silence hypothesis, it leads us to falsely assume that latent homophobia must still exist among professional male athletes. Alternatively, if we acknowledge that there may be few gay men at this level of sport it sheds light onto what academics (see Anderson, 2011) and sport journalists (see Outsports.com) have been saying in recent years: that homophobia among team-sport players is lower than we think. The recent public declarations of support for Jason Collins by fellow athletes shows that like the rest of us, athletes have progressed a long way towards tolerance; there have simply not been many gay teammates to prove it.

References

Anderson E (2002) Openly Gay Athletes: Contesting Hegemonic Masculinity in a Homophobic Environment. *Gender & Society* 16(6): 860–877.

Anderson E (2005) *In the Game: Gay Athletes and the Cult of Masculinity*. Albany, NY: SUNY Press.

Anderson E (2011) Updating the Outcome: Gay Athletes, Straight Teams, and Coming Out in Educationally Based Sport Teams. *Gender & Society* 25: 250.

Anderson E (2012) *Sport, Men and Masculinities*. New York, NY: Routledge.

Blanchard R, Dickey R and Jones CL (1995) Comparison of height and weight in homosexual versus nonhomosexual male gender dysphorics. *Archives of Sexual Behavior* 25(5): 543–554.

Bogaert A (1998) Physical development and sexual orientation in women: Height, weight, and age of puberty comparisons. *Personality and Individual Differences* 24(1): 115–124.

Bogaert A and Blanchard R (1996) Physical Development and Sexual Orientation in Men: Height, Weight, and Age of Puberty Differences. *Personality and Individual Differences* 21(1): 77–84.

Buzinski J (2012, July 18) 23 Openly Gay and Lesbian Athletes at 2012 London Summer Olympics. Available at: http://outsports.com/jocktalkblog/2012/07/18/9-openly-gay-and-lesbian-athletes-at-2012-london-summer-olympics/

Evans R (1972) Physical and biochemical characteristics of homosexual men. *Journal of Consulting and Clinical Psychology* 39(1): 140–147.

Kian T and Anderson E (2009) John Amaechi: Changing the Way Sport Reporters Examine Gay Athletes. *Journal of Homosexuality* 56(7): 1–20.

Laumann EO, Gagnon JH, Michael RT, and Michaels S (1994) *The Social Organization of Sexuality. Sexual Practices in the United States.* Chicago: University of Chicago Press.

LeVay S (2003) The Biology of Sexual Orientation. Available at: http://www.simonlevay.com/the-biology-of-sexual-orientation

McCormick CM and Witelson SF (1991) A Cognitive Profile of Homosexual Men Compared to Heterosexual Men and Women. *Psychoneuroendocrinology* 16(6): 459–473.

Rahman Q and Wilson G (2003) Large Sexual-Orientation-Related Differences in Performance on Mental Rotation and Judgment of Line Orientation Tasks. *Neuropsychology*.17(1): 25–31.

Zeigler C (2012) Pro Sports Are Finally Ready for a Gay Athlete. Available at: http://www.huffingtonpost.com/cyd-zeigler/pro-sports-are-finally-re_b_1927873.html

Zipp J (2011) Sport and Sexuality: Athletic Participation by Sexual Minority and Sexual Majority Adolescents in the U.S. *Sex Roles* 64: 19–31.

32

I DON'T "LOOK GAY"

Different disclosures of sexual identity in men's, women's, and co-ed sport

Elizabeth Cavalier

Introduction

Research has demonstrated mixed narratives about the experiences of sexual minorities in sport, with most recent evidence suggesting that the atmosphere is improving (Anderson, 2011). While much of the research focuses on the experiences of athletes, there has also been some focus on the experiences of employees (Anderson 2009; Cavalier, 2011; Griffin, 1998; Kauer 2009; Maurer-Starks, Clemons and Whalen, 2008). This chapter is based on a research project comparing the experiences of sexual minority employees in the USA working in men's, women's and co-ed sport, before focusing specifically on the gender-conforming strategies that employees in men's sport use as they negotiate their coming out decision-making at work.

Coming out in sport

There is an expansive body of literature discussing the process by which people deal with being a sexual minority at work. Strategies range from staying in the closet (Degges-White and Shoffner, 202; Griffin, 1998; Henderson, 1995), omitting personal details, or outright disclosure. Higgs and Schell (1998, p. 67) utilise Goffman's "front stage, backstage" analogy to analyse the closet, noting, "one mechanism often used by closeted lesbians to appear normal [sic] in their work situation involves creating and maintaining a personal front that does not call attention to her true sexual identity".

In more recent literature, disclosing a non-heteronormative sexual identity in the workplace is understood as maintaining social value. Researchers overwhelmingly suggest that it is important to come out, not only for individual happiness, but also in order to create social change around issues of sexual identity discrimination in the workplace (Bredemeier et al. 1999; Carroll and Gilroy 2001; Degges-White and Shoffner 2002; Gough 2007; Griffin 1998; Griffith and Hebl 2002; Ragins, Singh and Cornwell 2007; Rees-Turyn 2007; Ward and Winstanley 2005). While this is not the only way to create an inclusive environment, the argument is often that it is the *most* effective.

Finally, Anderson (2009, p. 4) argues that while most research regarding sport focuses on the experiences of the athletes, "sport stakeholders", by whom he means "those who train the athletes, those who hire and manage the coaches, those who market and promote sports, and those who report on the successes and failures of athletes through the sport media" are also important. He argues "despite the gains of feminism and the mandates of Title IX, and despite the increased acceptance of gay men in sport . . . there has been little change in the gatekeeping practices of the occupations within the sport industry" (p. 5). Discussing this in relation to men, he suggests that the "ethos of masculinity" pervades men's organised sport, creating a climate of hegemonic masculinity and homophobia. The climate of hegemonic masculinity leads to a context for sexual minorities in the sport workplace that can be fraught with anxiety and insecurity (Cavalier, 2011). This leads to disparities in experiences and strategies for negotiating the sport employment environment.

Sample and methods

There were 37 participants in the study (10 men and 27 women). All but two of the participants identified as gay or lesbian (two women identified as bisexual). Nearly all participants were white (two participants were Hispanic), all were college-educated, and they ranged in age from 22–68, with an average age of 33.75. They worked in both front-office jobs with little or no direct contact with athletes (n = 21) and on-field or direct-contact jobs (n = 16). Seventeen participants worked in professional sport, including the National Hockey League (NHL), Major League Baseball (MLB), the National Football League (NFL), the National Basketball Association (NBA), and the Women's National Basketball Association (WNBA). Fourteen participants worked in collegiate athletics (National Collegiate Athletic Association; NCAA), and the remaining six participants worked in club-level (non-youth, non-collegiate) sport.

Participants were split into three categories: those working in men's sport exclusively, those working in women's sport exclusively, and those working in co-ed sport. Fifteen participants worked in men's sport (six men and nine women). One participant worked in an NCAA position; the other 14 participants worked in professional sport. Five of the men worked in on-field positions, while one man and all of the women worked in off-field positions. They ranged in age from 22–68, and the average age was 35.8.

Thirteen participants worked in women's sport (all women). Seven of these participants worked in NCAA sport, three in club-level sport, and three in the WNBA. Ten women worked in on-field positions, while three worked in off-field positions. They ranged in age from 23–46, with an average age of 31.7.

The remaining nine participants worked in co-ed sport, in both NCAA sport (n = 6) and club-level sport (n = 3). Four men and five women worked in co-ed sport. Only one worked in an on-field position. They ranged in age from 23–53, with an average age of 31.5.

Participants were recruited using snowball sampling, then later in data collection, through targeted network sampling. I relied upon flyers, internet posts, and key informants to identify and recruit subjects who met the following criteria: they 1) regularly received a pay check for work in professional, collegiate, or club sport for at least two years in the last five years; and 2) identified as gay, lesbian, bisexual, or any sexual identity other than heterosexual while they were employed in sport.

Thirty-seven people participated in data collection over a two-year period, engaging in face-to-face or telephone interviews that lasted between one and four hours. I recorded, transcribed, coded, and analysed interviews using a modified grounded theoretical approach (Glaser & Strauss, 1967). I utilised Strauss and Corbin's (1998) process of microanalysis throughout the analysis stage. Microanalysis is defined as "the detailed line-by-line analysis necessary at the beginning of a study to generate initial categories (within their properties and dimensions) and to suggest relationships among categories" (p. 57). Through microanalysis and open coding, distinct categories developed from the data, which became theoretically saturated after repeated interviews with all respondents.

Results

This chapter focuses on two intertwined issues: 1) how employees differed in their discussion of the atmosphere of sport based upon their employment in men's, women's, or co-ed sport; and 2) how that atmosphere affected their decision-making about coming out. For those working in men's sport in particular, there was a hyper-awareness of gender conformity and appearance as a strategy to stay closeted or semi-closeted at work.

The dividing line between "out" and "closeted" is not easily discernible. There were wide variations between those who identified as explicitly out at work and those who went through significant steps to conceal their sexual identity. Coming out is not a one-time event; it is instead an ongoing negotiation that shifts based on audience, self-comfort, and other circumstances. Participants' decisions about coming out at work varied for men and women, employment in professional, college or club sport, and employment in men's, women's or co-ed sport. Coming out disclosures also varied based on an employees' position in the workplace hierarchy, their job requirements, their experiences coming out in other parts of their life, and their experiences as former athletes.

Despite definitional difficulties, participants were nonetheless split into three categories, all based on self-report: whether they were "out" at work, whether they were "not out" at work, or whether they fell somewhere in between. Of the ten men in the sample, four identified as "out", three as "in-between", and three as "not out". Of the 27 women, 9 considered themselves "out", 13 reported they were "somewhere in between", and 5 reported they were "not out". Men and women utilised different strategies for disclosing their sexual identity, and had different perceptions of the sport atmosphere. However, for all but four employees, their actual *experiences* at work regarding sexual identity were neutral to positive.

Although I hypothesised that men and women would have significantly different experiences working in sport, and would thus have different perceptions of the atmosphere of sport and utilise different disclosure strategies, the data makes apparent that the more salient category was not whether the participant was male or female, but whether they worked in men's, women's, or co-ed sport.

While there were nearly equal numbers of men's sport employees who were out, not out, or in-between, only one employee each in women's sport and co-ed sport identified as "not out". This supports the contention of researchers (Anderson 2002, 2005; Gough 2007; Harry 1995; Messner 1992, 2002; Muir and Seitz 2004; Woog 1998, 2002) that men's sport is a unique site of homophobia, predicated around hyper-masculinity. Both men and women who worked in men's sport expressed more reluctance to come out than those working in women's or co-ed sport. One conflating factor, however, is that those working in men's sport were also more likely to be working in professional sport as well. Thus, they expressed a sense that they had more "at stake" that those working in NCAA or club levels of sport.

Men's sport

The 15 participants who worked exclusively in men's sport repeatedly discussed two issues. For many of these participants, the concept of "the closet" was a particularly relevant construct.

They expressed a substantial awareness of the role their appearance played in their ability to "pass" as heterosexual if they chose to (or, alternately, the role their appearance played in outing them whether they wanted to be out or not). Secondly, the participants reported an atmosphere in men's sport that reflects the dominant literature of men's sport as a site that reinforces hegemonic masculinity. This was expressed through both the objectification of women (by men) and through competitive behaviour among women.

Participants working in men's sport discussed an overt awareness of their appearance as a way to keep their sexual identity hidden. John, an on-field employee in the NFL, discussed how he did not want to be seen as gay:

> Oh there's no question employees don't want to be seen [as gay]. I mean, I'll be honest, I'm one of them. I've been doing this for 10 years in professional sports, and it's never been brought up, "why don't you have a girlfriend?" Who are you going out with? People don't say, "you haven't dated anyone in nine years, are you gay?" They haven't asked me that because of how masculine I am.

Tina, an off-field NFL employee, discussed a hyper-awareness of her appearance back when she was a college athlete and started coming out:

> I would call myself sort of a sporty femme . . . I had long hair, I wore dresses when I felt like it. I had short hair, but it was the cute little weird pixie, and I always wore a barrette with it. I was never someone who was butch, if you want to use a term like that. But I definitely became far more aware of how I looked once I realised I was gay. I never would have been nervous about it before I realised it.

While employees discussed their appearance as having an impact on whether or not they were out at work, they also discussed the role that partners played in their disclosures. Many employees used the presence or lack of a partner as a tool in their coming out decision-making process. Some discussed defaulting to being in the closet only because they didn't have a partner to discuss. Other participants noted how their partner's appearance and outward gender conformity could end up being either an asset or a liability in their ability to be closeted at work. For example, John discussed an ex-boyfriend who was "straight-acting", so that if he brought him around work colleagues they would never know that either of them was gay. Tina discussed bringing her girlfriend to work on several occasions, "She was like me, pretty sporty, pretty femme. She was often wearing a skirt, so from a physical standpoint people might not have guessed it." For other participants, however, their partners lacked the standard gender-conforming appearance, and thus outed the couple. Marcus, an NFL on-field employee, discussed how he assumed some players knew he was gay because he ran into them at brunch one morning with his partner. "Some players saw us . . . and he wasn't the most masculine guy in the world. So they probably put two and two together because by this time I'm over 40 and I'm single."

While discussing the role of appearance at work, some participants acknowledged an awareness of the overall atmosphere of men's sport as sexist, and couched their discussions of appearance in that context. Tina, an NFL employee, noted that there seemed to be a competitive atmosphere between the women working for the team.

> Women get real catty with each other when there's the opportunity for success for one woman. If someone was having success, or if attention was paid to them by a player, it automatically started getting talked about a little bit, that she might be slutty, or that

she was probably being more than just a friend to people. If you were a young woman that was cute, then chances are that people were going to think that you were there to sleep with players . . . And, I think that it's kind of a jealousy thing. And I don't know if it is fair for me to say it's a gender thing, because the men assumed it too. But I feel like women were always the ones to start that conversation.

Several employees discussed how the atmosphere of men's sport was predicated on an objectification of women. Alex, an MLB on-field employee, describes the environment of baseball:

You're dealing with a frat house mentality, you really are. They're all young guys, they're all cocky and tacky; they're very competitive. You've got a lot of freedom, you don't have anybody looking over your shoulder, so there's a lot of booze involved. There's a lot of guys cheating on their wives, cheating on their girlfriends, it's not uncommon.

Other employees discussed a similar working environment, including the role of heteromasculine socializing after work: strip clubs, alcohol, and a social atmosphere that could be oppressive if one wasn't willing to go along with the culture. In this overarching context, female employees were extremely aware of the role of the traditionally feminine standards of appearance as a way to project an image of heterosexuality. Rachel, an NFL on-field employee, discussed her hiring process. She was hired to replace someone who, she inferred, did not meet acceptable standards.

And [the bosses were] like, "we need someone totally opposite; we need some hot blonde to work for us". And [the boss laughed and said] "you walked through the doors and we're like, oh we're gonna have to hire her". So like right out of the gate, I was like, okay, being gay is unacceptable, and I'm gonna be stereotyped from the start. But I thought I could handle it, because I was working for an NFL team!

Both male and female employees discussed the overall atmosphere of men's sport in heterosexual terms. The objectification of women, the hyper-masculine standards of behaviour for men, and the traditionally feminine standards of behaviour for women were commonplace and taken-for-granted in the sport environments. Of interest, however, when the participants discussed this with me, they discussed it in neutral, matter-of-fact terms. Instead of lamenting the atmosphere, they accepted it, and oftentimes used the atmosphere as the context for not coming out. Conversely, employees in co-ed and women's sport had significantly different experiences.

Women's sport

In contrast to men's sport, data derived from the 13 women who worked exclusively in women's sport shows it to be a substantially more welcoming place than men's sport. This appeared to be the narrative regardless as to whether these employees were out or not. These employees suggested that women's sport was a sort of "safe haven" for lesbians, should they choose to be out, acknowledging that they had it better than their counterparts in men's sport—whether those counterparts were male or female.

For example, Sheri, an off-field WNBA employee, described the atmosphere:

I mean I think that people know in the WNBA you're gonna have gay athletes, you're gonna have gay Chief Operating Officers, gay administrators, gay sales managers and directors, so I definitely think that people get that when they're working in the WNBA and that's just a given that there are gonna be people that are out and they need to get comfortable with it.

Nearly every participant cited the presence of openly gay women working in women's sport, as well as openly lesbian athletes in women's sport, as evidence that the atmosphere in women's sport was markedly different from men's sport. This effect appears to be cyclical: the presence of lesbians indicated that the atmosphere was friendly for gay employees, which attracted gay employees to women's sport, thus continuing a positive atmosphere for sexual minorities.

Alicia, who worked for the NFL in an off-field position but had extensive experience working in women's NCAA sport, noted the differences between men's and women's sport. She focused on the fact that women who grew up playing sport had been exposed to the idea of lesbianism, whether or not they were gay themselves:

> I think for females it's become more accepted just because there are more gay coaches in women's sport, for example. It's definitely something where people realise that maybe the majority of players, college or professional, are gay so you kind of have to accept it. You can't be against it because then you'll have a pretty good amount of your teammates that hate you . . . So you grow up to accept those people as your friends, as your peers, as your teammates . . . In general, it just becomes even more accepted as you get older and get into positions as a coach or president or something.

Alicia illustrates a point that repeatedly emerged in my data: employees in sport drew on their entire lifetime of experiences in sport—for nearly all employees this included time as former athletes. For most female employees, this meant exposure to lesbianism and tolerance early in their playing careers. This impacted on their perceptions of sport, and continued as a sort of self-fulfilling prophecy as they became employed in sport.

Finally, participants discussed women's sport as a unique and special environment for sexual minorities precisely because women dominated the field.

When Sheri started making hiring decisions, she said she "worked her ass off" to hire well-qualified men in the WNBA, but had a difficult time doing so. The female-dominated staff of women's sport contributed to the positive atmosphere she reported. Sheri noted, "I think women tend to be more open than men, just in general, more accepting, more open, more interested to ask questions and learn."

Women working in women's sport spoke nearly universally of women's sport as a welcoming and affirming environment for sexual minorities. However, this did not necessarily translate directly into coming-out behaviours; while only one participant referred to herself as "not out", more participants were "in-between" than "out", by their own self-report. However, their coming-out disclosures were affected by a myriad of other factors, and nearly all of them discussed that they *could* come out in women's sport if they wanted to.

Co-ed sport

The five women who worked in co-ed sport did not report substantially different experiences than the women who worked in women's sport. They felt the atmosphere of co-ed sport was a welcoming one for lesbians (and they hypothesised that it was welcoming for all sexual minorities). The four men who worked in co-ed sport had significantly more positive experiences in sport than their counterparts in men's sport, but that seemed to be primarily because of the greater presence of women in their work environment. Greg, an off-field NCAA employee, came out to several people at work, but his first, and easiest, disclosures were to lesbian coworkers. He notes:

> The easiest ones to come out to are the gay ones (laugh)! [Most of the people I have come out to have been women.] You hear through the rumors [that someone is a] lesbian or yes, she's dating someone, and then in the right social gathering, you say, hey, that guy over there's hot and they all turn their heads like what? What are you talking about?

Greg relied upon cues in determining which fellow employees were "safe" to come out to at work. He was out to several co-workers, but nearly all of them were straight women or lesbians. He noted that there was a disconnect in his athletic department between the men and the women.

> There's a clique at work with our top-level male administrators. If you are married with kids you're in that clique and me being single with no kids, it's like I have no way of getting into that clique, yet they're the power brokers. They're mediocre at what they do, but yet they keep getting promoted because they're in the right little clique. In that regard, it's tough being the gay guy.

Steven, an off-field NCAA employee, noted that part of what made his experience positive was his openness and acknowledgement of "jock banter". He did not report significant differences between men's and women's teams. He notes:

> The male student athletes that I work with are probably more comfortable knowing and dealing with the fact that I'm gay than the female student athletes I work with . . . and I think that's because I'm just honest with them, I don't tell them any lies. I'm also not overly sensitive, so I don't take anything that they were to say as being personal . . . in other words, if they get this jock talk banter, and something might slip, I don't take it personally only because I don't think it's intended personally.

As with women working in women's sport, those working in co-ed sport were more likely to be out or "somewhat out", with only one male employee reporting being "not out". Those who were out spoke positively about the atmosphere; the presence of women seemed to be the overriding factor in whether or not they felt the environment was a positive one for sexual minorities.

Discussion

The differences in the environment between men's sport and women's/co-ed sport is striking. The experiences of employees in men's sport, whether men or women, are coloured by an impression of men's sport as an "unsafe space" for sexual minorities. In contrast, both women's sport and co-ed sport are understood as safe havens for sexual minorities. However, a crucial difference in this sample was that nearly all of the employees working in men's sport worked in professional sport; those working in women's and co-ed sport were primarily NCAA and club sport employees. It is likely that the high-stakes of professional men's sport impacted on both employee decision-making and their perceptions of the sport environment.

It was perhaps due to the hyper-masculinized nature of men's sport that the employees (of both sexes) were uncritical of the environment. As Rachel pointed out, they were instead willing to go along with sexism or homophobia in exchange for the opportunity to work in the upper echelon of sport. The employees were willing to sacrifice their personal life for their professional life; much for the same reason Anderson (2005) argues that gay professional athletes remain closeted.

It remains to be seen if this safe space for sexual minorities in the NCAA and club levels translates to a more open environment in professional leagues for both men's and women's sport. More research is needed to examine the nuances between coming out disclosures and the atmosphere of sport for sexual minorities. The lessons from women's sport can only have positive impacts on the masculinist models of sport that currently dictate the operation of men's professional leagues.

References

Anderson, E., 2002. Openly gay athletes: Contesting hegemonic masculinity in a homophobic environment. *Gender and Society* 16 (6), 860–877.

Anderson, E., 2005. *In the game: Gay athletes and the cult of masculinity.* Albany: SUNY Press.

Anderson, E., 2009. The maintenance of masculinity among the stakeholders of sport. *Sport Management Review* 12 (1), 3–14.

Anderson, E., 2011. Updating the outcome: Gay athletes, straight teams, and coming out at the end of the decade. *Gender and Society* 25 (2), 250–268.

Bredemeier, B., Carlton, E., Hills, L., and Oglesby, C., 1999. Changers and the changed: Moral aspects of coming out in physical education. *Quest* 51, 418–431.

Carroll, L., and Gilroy, P., 2001. Being out: The behavioral language of self-disclosure. *Journal of Gay and Lesbian Psychotherapy* 4 (1), 69–86.

Cavalier, E., 2011. Men at sport: Gay men's experiences in the sport workplace. *Journal of Homosexuality* 58 (5), 626–646.

Degges-White, S., and Shoffner, M., 2002. Career counseling with lesbian clients: Using the theory of work adjustment as a framework. *The Career Development Quarterly* 51, 87–96.

Glaser, B., and Strauss, A. 1967. *The discovery of grounded theory: Strategies for qualitative research.* New York: Aldine Transaction.

Gough, B., 2007. Coming out in the heterosexist world of sport: A qualitative analysis of web postings by gay athletes. *Journal of Gay and Lesbian Psychotherapy* 11 (1), 153–174.

Griffin, P., 1998. *Strong women, deep closets: Lesbians and homophobia in sport.* Champaign: Human Kinetics Publishers.

Griffith, K., and Hebl, M., 2002. The disclosure dilemma for gay men and lesbians: "Coming out" at work. *Journal of Applied Psychology* 87 (6), 1191–1199.

Harry, J., 1995. Sports ideology, attitudes towards women, and anti-homosexual attitudes. *Sex Roles* 32 (1), 109–116.

Henderson, K., 1995. Lesbian, gay and bisexual employees in the workplace: Ethical implications for leisure service organizations. *Journal of Applied Recreation Research* 20 (2), 141–156.

Higgs, C., and Schell, L., 1998. Backstage, frontstage: An analysis of work and leisure roles of women recreational softball players. *Journal of Homosexuality* 36 (1), 63–77.

Kauer, K.J., 2009. Queering lesbian sexualities in collegiate sporting spaces. *Journal of Lesbian Studies* 13 (3), 306–318.

Maurer-Starks, S.S., Clemons, H.L., & Whalen, S., 2008. Managing heteronormativity and homonegativity in athletic training: In and beyond the classroom. *Journal of Athletic Training* 43 (3), 326–336.

Messner, M., 1992. *Power at play: Sports and the problem of masculinity, (2nd Edition).* Boston: Beacon.

Messner, M., 2002. *Taking the field: Women, men and sports.* Minneapolis: University of Minnesota.

Muir, K., and Seitz, T., 2004. Machismo, misogyny, and homophobia in a male athletic subculture: A participant-observation study of deviant rituals in collegiate rugby. *Deviant Behavior* 25(4), 303–327.

Ragins, B., Singh, R., and Cornwell, J., 2007. Making the invisible visible: Fear and disclosure of sexual orientation at work. *Journal of Applied Psychology* 92 (4), 1103–1118.

Rees-Turyn, A., 2007. Coming out and being out as activism: Challenges and opportunities for mental health professionals in red and blue states. *Journal of Gay and Lesbian Psychotherapy* 11 (3), 155–172.

Strauss, A., and Corbin, J., 1998. *The basics of qualitative research: Techniques and procedures for developing grounded theory (2nd edition)*. Thousand Oaks: Sage.

Ward, J., and Winstanley, D., 2005. Coming out at work: Performativity and the recognition and renegotiation of identity. *The Sociological Review* 53 (3), 447–475.

Woog, D., 1998. *Jocks: True stories of America's gay male athletes*. Los Angeles: Alyson.

Woog, D., 2002. *Jocks 2: Coming out to play*. Los Angeles: Alyson.

33

GAY SPORTS SPACES

Transgressing hetero(/homo)normativity and transforming sport?

Scarlett Drury

Introduction

Homophobia and heteronormativity are central to the culture of sport. Though the effects of the discourses surrounding them are far-reaching and impact on all individuals involved in sport, they have particularly damaging implications for the participation of non-heterosexual athletes. The impact of homophobia on gay- and lesbian-identified sportspeople has been widely documented (Griffin, 1998; Lenskyj, 2003; Anderson, 2005, 2011). Early studies highlighted the silence surrounding homosexuality and the subsequent pressure experienced by non-heterosexual sportspeople to conceal their identities for fear of homophobic abuse. More recently, studies into the ways in which gay and lesbian athletes negotiate homophobic discourses have uncovered examples of resistance – one of the most noteworthy of which has been the development of 'gay sports cultures'. However, recent scholarship has uncovered a number of tensions associated with the politics of gay sports spaces that threaten their potential to transform homophobia and heteronormativity (e.g. Wellard, 2009).

This chapter draws on ethnographic research into the experiences of men and women affiliated with gay- or lesbian-identified football clubs and organisations within the UK. It examines the extent to which heteronormativity remains influential in shaping the culture of gay sport. 'Gay football' provides not only a unique environment for the tensions of gay sports culture to be understood (Drury, 2011), but also a lens through which broader issues of heteronormativity can be explored. Whilst football in general has been widely cited as a sport in which homophobia is most deeply entrenched, it is simultaneously one of the most prominent sports to have been co-opted into gay sports culture. Data is presented in the form of excerpts from interviews with a total of fifteen participants, which took place as part of a broader ethnographic study spanning eighteen months of participatory involvement in 'gay football'. The majority of the accounts presented come from players who are actively involved in gay- or lesbian-identified teams. However, three participants were asked about their specific roles within related organisations. These were Chris, the chairperson of the Gay Football Supporters' Network (GFSN), and Jason and Darren, the founding director and director of The Justin Campaign (2009), a prominent anti-homophobia initiative. Before turning to this data, the next section examines some of the tensions associated with gay sports culture that have been uncovered by previous literature.

The discursive dynamics of gay sports spaces

Although gay sport was initially set up to offer a 'safe' space for non-heterosexual athletes, as Lenskyj (2002) notes, many gay sports organisations also encompass a strong political and cultural agenda, initiated by the engagement of gay activists who realised the potential for sport to deliver broader political messages associated with the liberation of sexual minorities. Gay sport has also pursued a broader quest for social justice, challenging other forms of discrimination and exclusion, particularly those related to ability and sporting prowess (Hargreaves, 2000). The focus for those involved in the development of gay sport has been less about including gay and lesbian athletes into mainstream discourses and more to do with fostering a unique alternative; notably, one that is based around the principles of inclusion. A prominent feature of many gay sports spaces is a rejection of hyper-masculine practices and the decentring of sport's competitive ethos.

The politics of gay sports culture, however, are by no means straightforward (Pronger, 2000). There has been considerable debate around gay sport's transformative potential in relation to two issues in particular: the first concerns the extent to which it is able to be truly inclusive; and the second relates to its ability to pose any significant challenge to the homophobic and heteronormative discourses of mainstream sport (Drury, 2011). One of the first and most obvious criticisms faced by gay sports communities is that they constitute separate and potentially ghettoised spaces that fail to pose any real threat to the institution of sport because they remain marginal to it. Symons (2007) suggests that rather than challenging homophobia, the very existence of gay sport further reinforces the boundaries between gay and mainstream culture. For Eng (2006), the ghettoised nature of gay sport poses even greater problems by presenting homosexuality as the deviant 'other' to normative heterosexuality.

As Pronger (2000) notes, attempts to establish the relative inclusivity or transformative potential of gay sports spaces are complicated by the increasing diversification in the ethos of gay sports culture. While the discourse of inclusion continues to be a driving force at policy level, there has been a gradual trend within some organisations towards the sanctioning, legitimising, codifying and, increasingly, mainstreaming of lesbian and gay sports events. This has created a number of tensions. On the surface, it would seem that the legitimation of gay sport might go some way towards challenging negative stereotypes surrounding the perceived incompatibility of gay men and competitive sport. Similarly, the visibility of gay athletes in mainstream contexts clearly has the potential to disrupt heteronormativity. However, the more closely aligned with mainstream practices it becomes, the less power gay sport will have to challenge and transform the way that sport is played (Pronger, 2000).

The pervasive concern for homosexual visibility, which forms the bedrock of the philosophies of many gay sports organisations, may be to blame. Whilst this may offer some level of disruption to heteronormativity, it is also problematic. Related to the potential ghettoisation of gay sport, the first difficulty comes in determining the extent to which the visibility of 'out' homosexuals within gay identified sports spaces can impact upon mainstream culture. Perhaps a bigger concern, however, is not the lack of mainstream visibility but the *type* of visibility that is being promoted. Although the philosophies of many gay sports organisations purport to be inclusive of all genders and sexualities, there is evidence to suggest that 'negative' stereotypes of camp men or butch women are simultaneously discouraged (Symons, 2007). This presents something of a contradiction: non-normative identities are permitted, but only those deemed 'normative' enough to present an 'appropriate' or 'acceptable' image of gay and lesbian identities. This has significant implications for the discourse of inclusion surrounding gay sport. Indeed research has indicated that gay sports culture does not incorporate the level of diversity that its inclusive philosophy would suggest. Studies show that the gender dynamic of many gay sports spaces is somewhat reflective of that of mainstream sport (Lenskyj, 2002; Wellard, 2009; Drury, 2011). In relation to ethnicity and social class, both Van Ingen (2004) and Waitt (2006) have also identified the propensity for white, affluent, Western gay male identities to dominate gay sports spaces.

Pronger (2000) points to the problem of visibility being more deeply rooted, noting that it is the emphasis on normalising gay and lesbian identities that is particularly problematic. Gay culture in general is dependent upon visibility, and as a result the act of 'coming out' is promoted as an important political strategy (Gutterman, 1994). Rather than breaking down sexual boundaries, the position of 'outness' reinforces the homo/hetero binary. Gay sports spaces undoubtedly subvert heteronormativity, but in place of this, 'homonormativity' (Duggan, 2003, cited in King, 2008) emerges as the dominant discourse. It may be that rather than transcending hetero (/homo)normativity, the politics of gay sport remain firmly rooted in the hetero/homonormative binary. Though this may create limitations in terms of gay sport's transformative potential, it is still important that it is viewed as a logical and understandable symptom of a broader heteronormative culture.

Research has offered valuable insight into the experiences of participants competing within gay- or lesbian-identified clubs. However, responding to the growth and increasing diversity of gay sports culture there is a clear need for continued empirical research in order to further unpack the theoretical and political tensions and to consider how gay sport might be instrumental in challenging homophobia and heteronormativity. The remaining part of the chapter considers some of these issues in relation to the specific context of football. Data is presented in two sections: the first addresses the notion of gay football as a positive and transformative space for the inclusion of non-heterosexual identities; the second explores some of the challenges that gay football faces with respect to transforming the culture of football.

Gay football as a transformative sports space

Football is widely cited as one of most influential institutions involved in the (re)production of homophobia within the UK (e.g. Caudwell, 2011). Mainstream men's football in particular represents one of the most significant institutions involved in the construction of heteronormative notions of masculinity. Male footballers who fail to maintain an adequate display of appropriate football masculinity risk homophobic abuse. For women, on the other hand, the close association between football and masculinity means that their very involvement in the game often results in their (hetero)sexuality being called into question.

This climate of homophobia and hostility towards homosexuality in mainstream football contexts was acknowledged by many participants in the study. As Chris pointed out, this has led many gay men to feel 'disenfranchised' from the game. Similarly, Darren discussed the sense of 'alienation' and 'isolation' felt by young males caused by homophobia:

> I think there'd be a massive gay following for football if the institution wasn't so homophobic. People are alienated by it because if they're seen to be shit at tackling or if you can't kick it properly or if you're last in line to be picked, then you're a poof, you're a queer, you're a faggot, you know what I mean? And straight away you're alienated from the game. I think when you grow up you just become so kind of oblivious to the world of football because you think that you don't belong there, and it's amazing because football is supposedly so community focused, but with the

institution being so homophobic, pushing LGBT [lesbian, gay, bisexual, and trans-gender] people out of that kind of community culture leaves people feeling really isolated.

However, very few of the players indicated that their involvement with gay football had stemmed directly from experiences of homophobic abuse in mainstream football. Whilst football in general was perceived as a largely homophobic institution, there were clear pockets of resistance. Many of the male participants had been involved in mainstream football in some capacity prior to joining a gay team. Supporting the findings of Anderson (2011), although some had kept their sexuality hidden, those who were 'out' suggested that knowledge of their sexuality was received relatively positively by straight male team mates. However, it seemed that this was largely managed through what Dan described as 'homophobic banter'. Discussing one of his team mates who plays for both gay and mainstream teams, Paul, for instance, described how members of the 'straight' team 'took the piss' out of him by buying him a pink goalkeeper shirt and calling him 'pinky'. Rather than constituting homophobia, this was interpreted as an indication of the team's openness to discuss his sexuality and make him feel an accepted part of the team. For Dan, 'homophobic banter' was also interpreted positively: 'On the pitch it'd be like you'd drop your shoulder and go past a defender and score and one of your team mates shouts "what's it feel like to get beaten by a poof?"'

Dan went on to describe how he found that ridiculing stereotypes of gay men himself also helped to break down the boundaries between him and heterosexual team mates. Though other participants suggested that they found this type of 'homophobic banter' unacceptable, Dan argued that it was all about context. Further reinforcing Chris and Darren's narratives, many of these men indicated that they felt 'turned off' football due to their perceptions of the heteronormative culture of the game.

For women, experiences of negotiating discourses of gender and sexuality in mainstream teams were markedly different from those of the male respondents. Supporting the work of Caudwell (1999) many of the women had experienced homophobia from individuals outside their football communities as a result of the widespread discursive association between women's football and lesbian identity. Kim acknowledged that women's football in general was 'perceived as gay', and that this resulted in the sexuality of all women players being questioned. However, participants reported that women's football teams were generally welcoming of diverse sexualities, and can offer a space for the acceptance and protection of non-heterosexual players. For many, early involvement in mainstream football was cited as an instrumental factor in helping to reaffirm their 'lesbian' identity, supporting the assertion that that women's sports communities are able to challenge and subvert heteronormativity (Ravel and Rail, 2007).

Though few of the participants interviewed became involved with 'gay football' as a direct result of mainstream homophobia, it was clear that gay football culture offered something that players were unable to gain elsewhere. When discussing reasons for participation in gay-identified teams, two closely linked themes emerged: the first was the social aspect of participation in gay sports communities; the second related to the non-competitive and inclusive ethos that underpinned many gay football teams.

Players frequently referred to their experiences of gay football in relation to notions of 'community'. Reflecting the findings of Jones and McCarthy (2010), gay football provided a space to socialise with 'like-minded' people and to create 'support networks', in which gay and lesbian identities were normalised. Some went as far as to refer to their football club as an 'extended family' in which they felt unconditionally accepted:

With my straight mates we have lots of banter, which is great, but certain things you're not too comfortable talking about for their sake. But if you've got a gay mate who you can just have a pint with or whatever, it just helps, and it's helped me no end. My social confidence went, you know, from zero to maximum.

Ashley agreed:

It has helped me a lot. I've met new friends through football, lesbians, which I did not meet in [home country] or before actually I came out here. When I was in [home country] I was still 'heterosexual', so yeah that has helped me a lot. I'm glad I found different friends who are lesbians.

Echoing the findings of Van Ingen (2004) and Owen (2006), the notion of gay football as an alternative to 'the scene' was also commonplace. Many of the male participants indicated that they had felt excluded from commercial gay culture. Chris spoke of implicit pressure within LGBT communities to conform to gay stereotypes:

I was trying to find common ground with people in the LGBT [society], but other than sexuality I was struggling, apart from that we went to the same university. I tried talking to them about sports and indie music. I wanted to talk about you know, every-day stuff, and one of them took me to one side and said 'Chris, you're gay now, you can stop these ridiculous straight obsessions', and I thought there's something not quite right here. I don't see why because I was gay I had to conform to the gay stereotype. I don't conform to the straight stereotype, I don't conform to the gay stereotype. I'm just . . . I am who I am and I hope our organisation [Gay Football Supporter's Net-work] helps people be who they are.

Paul also described how he 'never found acceptance' on the scene.

It's just you come out and you look for something that reflects what you're into, where you're going to feel comfortable, and there's at least half a dozen people who will probably say similar to me, who didn't really bother with the scene, wasn't too sure about themselves. All they really wanted was gay mates, and mates that liked football.

The concept of gay football as an 'alternative' football space was also frequently cited as a major factor in players' motives to compete within gay- or lesbian-identified football clubs. In keeping with the ethos that underpins many larger gay sports organisations, the majority of the teams that were encountered throughout the research operated on a predominantly 'friendly', 'non-competitive', or 'inclusive' basis. When asked about the differences between gay and main-stream football, participants primarily referred to issues around inclusivity rather than sexuality. They indicated that it was not the game itself that they had previously disliked, but the culture of exclusion that surrounded the sport. For the men who had previously avoided involvement in football, gay-identified clubs provided their first experience of gaining a sense of enjoyment from sport. Given their absence from the game and subsequent lack of football-playing experi-ence, this was something that was not available to them as novice players entering mainstream football. The appeal of gay football was clear: where mainstream football rewards skill and physi-cal prowess, in gay football contexts levels of skill are inconsequential to a players' acceptance within the team. Tom said, 'I go along on a Sunday to have a kick around, when I can and when I'm able, and you know, I don't care, and if I drop a ball when I'm in goal or anything, who cares?'

The decentring of competition within gay football clubs was also cited as a major appeal for more experienced and skilful players. For Paul, who had previously competed at semi-professional level, the style of play adopted by gay teams provided a welcome point of departure from some of the more hostile approaches adopted by mainstream teams:

> First game I took deadly serious, so I'm running around kicking the ball as hard as possible and I quickly realised that this wasn't what they were about. So I stopped and from that point on just played differently, you know, just trying to get people involved and stuff. Then I saw it as my responsibility to make the whole thing as welcoming as possible to anyone coming in on every level.

The importance of fostering a welcoming and inclusive playing environment was also highly significant to the female players. Lindsie, the founding member of one of the main teams involved in the research was particularly influential in creating this dynamic:

> When I got it off the ground I just wanted somewhere to play football without having to fit in with a clique or without having to be able to run as fast as a fifteen year old. I wanted that to be available to me when I'm like knocking on in my forties and fifties. So just thought there must be a huge market for all those people who've been pushed out of the game.

In addition to issues related to sexuality, many of the clubs involved in the research were positioned as inclusive with respect to other identity markers. Gay sports spaces have previously been critiqued for their absence of diversity along axes of difference other than those associated with sexuality. Van Ingen (2004) and Waitt (2006) both note the propensity for gay sports communities to perpetuate a norm of affluent white Western gay masculinity. However, my research participants stressed their emphasis on providing an 'open' space for *all* individuals to compete. The visible inclusion of a disabled British-Asian female goalkeeper on an otherwise male-dominated team during a tournament was testament to this. Acknowledging the strict adherence to single sex-competition regulations in mainstream football, importance was also placed on including transsexual players. Similarly, the emphasis on providing 'outreach' funding for teams from parts of the world with harsh laws on homosexuality demonstrated the commitment of the International Gay and Lesbian Football Association towards displacing the white Western normativity that otherwise permeates commercial gay spaces.

My findings suggest that gay football undoubtedly has the potential to offer an alternative sports space that is capable of transcending the oppressive discourses of mainstream football. Providing a 'safe' space for non-heterosexual players, it clearly offers some level of resistance to homophobia and provides a context in which homonormativity becomes the dominant discourse. However, it does not follow that this constitutes a full transformation of homophobia and heteronormativity, or indeed a threat to the dominance of mainstream sports ethos.

The limits of gay football

Eng (2006) argues that gay and lesbian sports clubs are able to provide a queer alternative to mainstream sport by virtue of their ability to subvert heteronormativity. However, like

Caudwell (2006), Eng (2006) suggests that this does not necessarily constitute a full challenge to normative discursive practices. On the contrary, the appropriation of gay space 'can run the danger of strengthening heteronormative existence as the "normal" by constituting as queer refuge as an alternative for the "deviants"' (Eng, 2006: 54). Rather than transforming heteronormativity then, this would only serve to reinforce the homo/hetero binary, and thus the 'othered' status of homosexuality.

The notion of gay space as ghettoised space would support this theory. When asked about the potential that gay football has to challenge homophobia, many of the participants referred to concerns over the 'separatist' nature of gay football communities. Jo said, 'I think it's the whole enclave thing, pushing yourself away and just closing it off. There is a certain place for it, but I do find it problematic.'

Others also referred to the problems of 'segregation' and 'divisions' between gay and straight communities. Dan suggested that this critique came from both within and outside of the gay community. However, whilst players acknowledged the validity of these criticisms, they were quick to highlight the need for gay space. It was clear that no one wanted to distance themselves from heterosexual footballers, but that there was a need to create a space in which players could feel 'safe'. Dan said:

> It's like why do we have gay bars and why do we have gay clubs and all the rest of it? They don't generally turn straight people away, but it's somewhere where gay people can feel comfortable, and it's the same with the league, you know. We don't turn straight people away but it's somewhere we can feel comfortable.

Participants were also critical of the concept of gay football in relation to the limited amount of visibility that it has within mainstream football culture. This was cited as a factor that may inhibit any real challenge to homophobia. Kim said:

> Any gay group in society is helping to tackle homophobia in society, but how much are we really changing things? Not significantly. How many people know about us? You have to be gay or search gay football to find us, and you wouldn't do that if you weren't gay.

However, many players commented on the role of gay football in challenging negative stereotypes. A number of female players suggested that their club was instrumental in demonstrating the diversity of lesbian identity and presenting a 'positive' image of 'successful' women. For the men, there was an emphasis on the role of gay football in distancing gay male sexuality from the 'camp' stereotype. Dan said:

> The stereotypical image of the gay person has changed completely, you know, we don't all do our hair, as you can tell, and we don't shave every day. We're all different. Some of us even drink bitter, so you know . . . it's all changed.

For David, this was also about sending out a clear message that gay men and football prowess were not incompatible; that football skill was not contingent upon heterosexual identity:

> They think that everybody fits the stereotype, but that's now being broken down, drastically, and that's where we need it to continue so the general public see that there are players at all levels.

However, reminiscent of the work of both Owen (2006) and Wellard (2009), it seems that any attempt to challenge stereotypes was invariably framed within a desire to conform to normative notions of athletic masculinity. This would indicate that even the 'safe' spaces of a gay football clubs are not entirely free from the discourse of heteronormativity. This has particular implications for the discourse of inclusion that is said to underpin gay football spaces.

The trend towards the mainstream legitimation of gay sport was also evident. Whilst legitimation was welcomed by some clubs as a means of 'proving' the athletic capabilities of non-heterosexual athletes, a major result of such legitimation is the inevitable shift in emphasis towards a competitive ethos. This, in turn, results in the appropriation of a mainstream sports discourse and undermines the discourse of inclusion. This was a central topic in the narratives of many male participants. Chris said 'there is a constant balancing act to have in each regional team between the recreational players and the competitive players, and unfortunately there are some teams that have collapsed because of that'.

Pronger (2000) argues that we must question boundaries – or limits – of gay sports culture. Understanding these boundaries means that we are able to see who is included within gay sports culture and, more importantly, who or what is positioned outside. Duggan's (2003, cited in King, 2008) concept of 'homonormativity' is also beneficial here. If we accept that gay football is a homonormative space, then what becomes clear is that a homosexual identity is given precedence over other sexual identities. With respect to inclusion, an account from one of the female players summed up this tension: 'it seems really inclusive in some ways, but . . . inclusive just for people who identify as lesbian'. These views were not isolated; the othering of heterosexuality and bisexuality became a recurrent theme throughout the research. A number of the women players questioned the exclusion of 'gay friendly' heterosexual footballers, and others indicated that although their club was positioned as welcoming of bisexual women, their sexuality was rarely acknowledged in the social dynamics of the club. The open inclusion of heterosexual players in men's clubs was more prominent. Most teams competing within the GFSN league acknowledge the presence of straight men, and many participants spoke positively of this dynamic. For many it was viewed as an indication of the changing attitudes towards sexuality within society, and additionally as a sign perhaps that mainstream sport has something to learn from the gay alternative. However, this did not detract from the fact that gay football was positioned first and foremost as a gay space; there was a level of discontent and concern amongst some players that some teams were allowing too many straight players to compete, resulting in a diluting of an otherwise homonormative space.

Although the silencing of heterosexuality and bisexuality within some clubs indicates a challenge to homophobia and heteronormativity, as I have argued previously (Drury, 2011), this does not reflect a transformation, but a subversion of heteronormativity. In the same way that heteronormativity is contingent upon the presence of a homosexual 'other', homonormativity can only prevail in gay sports spaces if non-homosexual identities are positioned as marginal. However, that is not to say that the dynamics of homonormativity are straightforward. Homosexuality was undoubtedly normalised, yet the narratives indicate a degree of discursive distancing from certain aspects of gay culture, particularly in those related to 'transgressive' gender identities. Exclusionary boundaries around the enactment of 'camp' male and 'butch' female identities were evident. This of course signifies something of a problem for alleged 'inclusivity', but in addition, presents another interesting paradox: with this distancing from gay stereotypes comes the inevitable association with (hetero)normative constructs of gender. So whilst homosexual identities may be normalised, only those that conform to 'acceptable' representations of masculinity and femininity are permitted. This indicates that the dynamics of homonormativity and heteronormativity are more complex than a simplistic dichotomy.

Theoretical and political tensions aside, this does not mean that progress is not being made. While hetero(/homo)normativity may be difficult to fully transcend, the activism from many involved in the gay football community has forged positive links with mainstream football organisations and fuelled a growing concern to tackle homophobic discrimination within the game. The intervention of groups such as the GFSN and the increasingly prominent 'Football v Homophobia' initiative associated with The Justin Campaign (2009), are two such examples.

References

Anderson E (2005) *In the Game: Gay Athletes and the Cult of Masculinity*. New York: SUNY.

Anderson E (2011) Updating the outcome: Gay athletes, straight teams, and coming out in educationally based sports teams. *Gender and Society*, 25(2): 250–268.

Caudwell J (1999) Women's football in the United Kingdom: Theorising gender and unpacking the butch lesbian image. *Journal of Sport and Social Issues*, 23(4): 390–402.

Caudwell J (2006). Femme-fatale: Re-thinking the femme-Inine. In: Caudwell J (ed.) *Sport, Sexualities and Queer/Theory*. London: Routledge, pp.145–158.

Caudwell J (2011) 'Does your boyfriend know you're here?' The spatiality of homophobia in men's football culture in the UK. *Leisure Studies*, 30(2): 123–138.

Drury S (2011) 'It seems really inclusive in some ways, but . . . inclusive just for people who identify as lesbian': Discourses of gender and sexuality in a lesbian identified football club. *Soccer & Society*, 12(3): 421–442.

Eng H (2006) Queer Athletes and Queering in Sport. In: Caudwell J (ed.) *Sport, Sexualities and Queer/Theory*. London: Routledge, pp.49–61.

Griffin P (1998) *Strong Women, Deep Closets: Lesbians and Homophobia in Sport*. Leeds: Human Kinetics.

Gutterman DS (1994) Postmodernism and the Interrogation of Masculinity. In: Brod H & Kaufman M (eds) *Theorising Masculinities*. London: Sage, pp.219–238.

Hargreaves J (2000) *Heroines of Sport: The Politics of Difference and Identity*. London: Routledge.

Jones L and McCarthy M (2010) Mapping the landscape of gay men's football. *Leisure Studies*, 29(2): 161–173.

King S (2008) What's queer about (queer) sport sociology now? A review essay. *Sociology of Sport Journal*, 25(4): 419–442.

Lenskyj HJ (2002) Gay Games or Gay Olympics? Implications for lesbian inclusion. *Canadian Women's Studies*, 21(3): 24–28.

Lenskyj HJ (2003) *Out on the Field: Gender, Sport and Sexualities*. Toronto: Women's Press.

Owen G (2006) Catching Crabs: Bodies, Emotions and Gay Identities in Mainstream Competitive Rowing. In: Caudwell J (ed.) *Sport, Sexualities and Queer/Theory*. London: Routledge, pp.129–144.

Pronger B (2000) Homosexuality in Sport: Who's Winning? In: McKay J et al. (eds) *Masculinities, Gender Relations, and Sport*. London: Sage, pp.222–244.

Ravel B and Rail G (2007) One the limits of 'gaie' spaces: Discursive constructions of women's sport in Quebec. *Sociology of Sport Journal*, 24(4): 402–420.

Symons C (2007) Challenging Homophobia and Heterosexism in Sport: The Promise of the Gay Games. In: Carmichael Aitchison, C (ed.) *Sport and Gender Identities: Masculinities, Femininities and Sexualities*. London: Routledge, pp.140–159.

The Justin Campaign (2009) *Campaigning against homophobia in football*. Available at: www.thejustincampaign.com (accessed 25th Jan 2009).

Van Ingen C (2004) Therapeutic landscapes and the regulated body in the Toronto front runners. *Sociology of Sport Journal*, 21(3): 253–269.

Waitt GR (2006) Boundaries of desire: Becoming sexual through the spaces of Sydney's 2002 Gay Games. *Annals of the Association of American Geographers*, 96(4): 773–787.

Wellard I (2009) *Sport, Masculinities and the Body*. London: Routledge.

34

THE GAY GAMES

A beacon of inclusion in sport?

Caroline Symons

Introduction

The Gay Games is the largest international lesbian, gay, bisexual, transgender, intersex and queer (LGBTIQ) sport and cultural event, engaging up to 15,000 athletes and cultural performers, and many more attendees, from all continents of the world. It stands out as a uniquely inclusive major sporting event with a history of proactive policies and programming in order to enable people of all ages (18 and over), abilities, sporting backgrounds, health statuses, sexuality and gender identities to participate. Inclusiveness was foundational to the Gay Games and has been elaborated upon through identity and coalition politics of host communities and Games organisers over the past quarter century. The Gay Games has also championed normalisation of LGBT peoples through the emulation of certain features of mainstream sport and the successful commercialisation of the Games. Through historical analysis of Gay Games I (San Francisco, US, 1982), IV (New York, US, 1994), V (Amsterdam, Netherlands, 1998) and VI (Sydney, Australia, 2002), I will argue that notwithstanding assimilationist tendencies, the Gay Games offer alternative, diverse, even radical and always inclusive ways of expressing sporting communities, identities and practices.[1]

Alternative visions of Gay Games I

The first Gay Games was held in San Francisco in 1982, an internationally renowned haven for gays and lesbians. San Francisco was ideally placed to host these first Gay Games, having a large enough gay and lesbian population to supply volunteers and leaders, as well as positive backing from local government and essential services (Symons, 2010: 44–45). The principle founder of the Gay Games, Dr Tom Waddell, had spent most of his athletic career, including his years as an Olympian, using sport as his closet, only 'coming out' whilst living in San Francisco during the late 1960s. The power of the Olympics to bring diverse peoples together through sport and ceremonial rituals impressed Waddell. However, he was critical of the hyper-commercialism, politicisation, chauvinistic nationalism, racism, drug taking and winning at all costs ethos that seemed to permeate them. The Gay Olympic Games (as originally termed) was to be an 'exemplary' alternative sports festival based on inclusion, participation and doing one's best. Waddell envisaged that through the common international language of sport, gay men, lesbians, bisexuals, heterosexuals, as well as people of different ages, abilities, socio-economic, ethnic, cultural, religious, and political backgrounds could be brought together to experience and learn from each other's similarities and differences in a positive and celebratory Games' atmosphere (Messner and Sabo, 1994: 19).

The Games successfully accommodated differences. Anyone aged over 18 could participate and gender parity was pursued. There were men's and women's co-chairs for significant organisational positions, an active Outreach committee that successfully recruited women locally and from across the US, and an equalised sports programme for women and men (Gildersleeve and Wardlaw, 1982). Lesbians and gay men usually led quite separate social and political lives at this time and it was a passion of the early Gay Games organisers to bring together these disparate communities. Strong women on the Board of Directors of the Games emphasised the perspectives of lesbians during meetings, recruited friends and raised funds. An outreach committee was also active in recruiting people from minority ethnic and racial groups to participate in the Games (Interview with Sara Lewinstein, member of the Board of Management of Gay Games 1 and II and co-Chair of Sport for Gay Games II, 13 November 1996).

Chauvinistic nationalism that often accompanied major sports events was muted at the first Gay Games, accomplished through having participants represent their city of origin rather than their country. Medal tallies and the displaying and keeping of records of athletics feats were also banned. Medal ceremonies, speeches and Games literature emphasised individual effort rather than national success. In fact, competition was revised. It wasn't about dominating one's opponents and exulting in the victory, rather, the emphasis was placed on 'healthy' challenge and self-fulfilment achieved through sport. The relationship between competitors became one of mutual striving in a friendly atmosphere, the performance of one spurring on and enhancing the other (Interview with Dr Tom Waddell, key visionary and foundational leader of the early Gay Games, cited in Messner and Sabo, 1994: 126).

New-left critics of mainstream sport that advocated more playful and humanistic approaches originated in California during the 1970s. Radical sport psychologist, Jack Scott (1971), provided one of the first critical analyses of modern sport arguing that deeper benefits came from playing for its own sake, for enjoyment, self-expression, friendships and personal growth and that these benefits were undermined in the capitalist and exploitative professional sport world. Waddell trained with Scott during the 1970s. The popularisation of health and fitness and the beginnings of the masters' sport movement were also centred in California at this time. This all provided fertile soil for an alternative vision for sport at the Gay Games. Gay pride, and the growth and consolidation of a broad gay culture and community, especially in San Francisco at the time, provided the foundations for the Gay Games.

Normalisation through sport

Contrasting these transforming foundations of the first Gay Games were strong assimilationist policies and practices. Waddell and other Games pioneers used a vision of the Olympics as an important promotional strategy to connect sporting gays and lesbians from the US and other Western nations to a fledgling Gay Olympic Games. Ironically, legal proceedings by the United States Olympic Committee (USOC) against San Francisco Arts and Athletics (SFAA), for their use of Olympics in the title for their Games, lead to increased exposure, boosted solidarity and attendance, and ensured strong gay and mainstream media interest (Symons and Warren, 2006). At this time, homophobia in sport was widespread and pernicious and I have documented numerous cases in which gay and lesbian sportspeople were fearful of 'outing' themselves at such an explicitly gay sport event (Symons, 2010: 43–45). San Francisco itself was considered as a very 'out' and brash gay city – 'an opulent experience for other US teams, let alone teams from overseas' (*Metra*, 1982). The concentration on healthy physical contest and achievement that emulated a number of the trappings of the Olympics was considered by Gay Games organisers as vital in the quest for normalisation and respectability for lesbians and gay men.

In media interviews, organisers explicitly emphasized the 'normalising' purpose of the Gay Games and the need to transform negative gay stereotypes. For Waddell, gay men could validate their masculinity; sport was not for 'sissies'. This corresponded with the predominant gay-male style originating in San Francisco during the late 70s – the super macho – more masculine in appearance than heterosexual men (Altman, 1983: 1). Free sexual expression during sport competitions and official ceremonies was deemed inappropriate and the Games' image was carefully managed by the organisers, resulting in the banning of drag and leather and the control of press images so as not to be used for 'pornographic purposes' (Carlson, 1982: 4). Conventional sport events, run by registered officials, with locally-sanctioned rules and the wearing of sporting uniforms, were central enactments of this mainstreaming conservatism.

Inclusion at the first Gay Games was conditional – camp and queenie men, drag queens and the leather community had to 'straighten up' (Symons, 2010: 41–43). Lesbians were assumed to play sport anyway, so no stereotypes were thought to need questioning here. In fact the Games provided lesbians with the opportunity to enjoy and be celebrated for their participation in all sorts of sports, including the more rugged rugby and weightlifting (Symons, 2010: 41–43, 61–62). From the Gay Games' inception there was an abiding tension between its mainstreaming and transformative potentials. By Gay Games IV, held in New York in 1994, these tensions had taken on different forms and emphases, and inclusiveness was more radical and representative of the diverse LGBT communities from this Games onwards.

Gay Games IV – international, diverse and commercial

The New York Gay Games was a major multi-sport and cultural event with international media profile, sponsorship breakthrough and commercialisation, professional organisation, celebrity endorsement and diverse community involvement. The Games had grown eleven-fold since Gay Games I, attracting around 15,000 sport and cultural participants from forty-five countries spanning six continents (Unity '94, 1994a). These were an unapologetically GAY Games. Drag queens acted as city-placard carriers during the Opening ceremony and a host of lesbigay sports and entertainment celebrities promoted, fundraised and performed. Gay Games IV was held in conjunction with the twenty-five-year celebration of the Stonewall riot – the watershed event in New York that is recognised internationally as marking gay liberation. Stonewall 25 and the New York Gay Games involved one of the largest queer-pride events and parade ever to be held (*Outrage*, 1994).

Inclusive and pioneering policies and practices that were part of the community and the professional basis of these Games enabled diverse participation in the sports and cultural programmes. The organisational structure involved paid staff as well as thirteen policy-making committees made up of volunteer community members covering diverse organisational areas. In the six-month lead-up to the Games, staff and volunteer numbers grew exponentially (6,000), the majority coming from local LGBT communities (Interview with Operations Manager Quarto, 1 December 1996). The politics of diversity and difference was an integral feature of day-to-day life of the Gay Games office and management and along with the community-based committee-structure drove inclusive policy making.

Radical inclusion: Gay Games IV–VI

Inclusiveness was enacted in policy and practice in a variety of ways. Firstly, the sexuality/gender diversity of the LGBT communities was well represented. Lesbian, gay and queer gender styles were evident at the sports, cultural, human rights and pride events, as well as at ceremonies and parties: butch, dyke, designer dyke, lipstick lesbian, lesbian chic, androgynous, bi, radical lesbian, leather, sado-masochism (S&M), punk, suburban middle class, queenie, camp, straight-playing, macho, bear, young, buffed and hairless, pierced and tattooed, drag – the whole multitude of sexual orientations, expressions and lifestyles (Labrecque, 1994). Heterosexual participants were also included, but they were definitely in the minority.

The first transgender participation policy of any major multi-sports event was enacted at the Games. Deb-Ann Thompson, Vice President of the Federation of Gay Games (FGG), consulted one of the leading bodies representing transgender people within the US to develop this policy (Interview with Thompson, 3 June 2001). The intent of the policy was to include people who lived their lives fully as the sex they had transitioned to – with or without surgery. Proof of complete legal name-change to match the gender lived, as well as documentation from medical and mental health professionals to verify active involvement in hormone therapy and emotional and psychological transition into the desired gender was also required. Whilst transgender inclusion was pioneering, it was also prescribed in policy to guide action in the spirit of competitive fairness. Changing ones name was not possible in many countries. Quarto reports that the Sports Co-Chairs of these Games raised concerns about the practicalities of including transgenders in sport when the sanctioning bodies of the sports themselves had no policy and still viewed sex and gender in essentialistic and dualistic terms. It wasn't until 2003 that the International Olympic Committee (IOC) formulated any policy on transgender participation in the Olympics (IOC, 2003).

A number of lesbian and gay Sports Co-Chairs were also concerned that transgender inclusion could generate negative publicity and jeopardise the sanctioning of gay sport by mainstream organisations and the corporate funding that was needed to finance a US$6 million budgeted major event. Concern was also raised about insurance coverage and litigation in the event that a female athlete in a contact sport could be injured by a presumably stronger male–female (M–F) transitioning athlete. Some of these concerns were very practical. The Gay Games consisted of thirty-two sports played in multiple venues, with up to a thousand athletes and/or large numbers of teams in any one sport and with each having major logistical, health, safety and legal, as well as officiating and volunteer requirements. The Games could not be run by local lesbian and gay sporting clubs alone.

Partnerships with mainstream sports bodies had major benefits including the instigation of rules and procedures familiar to global sporting communities. Participants prepared for the Gay Games with training, knowledge of their sport and its rules and investment in time, resources and emotions. Furthermore, valuable bridges were built between mainstream and queer-identified sport clubs and events when the sharing of common sporting passions forged positive relationships and dispelled misinformed and damaging stereotypes of LGBT peoples (Borrie, 2003: 7). Skills, knowledge, networks and membership were also developed within queer sports organisations and events. However, sanctioning did have its challenges for transgender inclusion and there were also relatively conservative, less transgender-inclusive perspectives among the leadership of sport at Gay Games IV. As I observed, 'organisers were attempting to balance the competition and participation ethos and be responsive to the needs and interests of a growing number of sexualities in the Games, all in a world that was still deeply prejudiced against gays and lesbians, let alone transgenders' (Symons, 2010: 210).

In contrast, there was celebration of queer sports culture as well as a pervasive ethos of encouragement and support for people of all levels of ability. Seasoned Gay Games participant, Terry Allison, talks about the playful nature of the Games for participants:

> . . . but they can also participate in sport that is not so competitive, where the goal isn't crushing your opponent . . . little scenes captured it for me when I was in New York. I visited a volleyball game and you see some really queeny acting guys giving each other five with limp wrists. I thought it was fabulous because they were playing having a good time but also not worried about presenting a macho image connected to sport.
>
> *(Interview with Allison, 20 November 1996)*

In sports such as figure-skating and ballroom dancing, the spirit of same-sex attraction, love, playfulness and sexiness was expressed especially through the pair events and the strict rules on gender-appropriate costuming were largely ignored. The Gay Games pioneered these events, as well as the first international women's wrestling competition (Symons, 2010: 121,152–156). The Pink Flamingo – a playful, queer aquatic theatrical team event – has become a highlight of the Gay Games. By Sydney 2002, these and other body-displaying sports events, such as the physique competition and water polo finals, followed by 'synchronised swimming, drag relays and diving exhibitions', were ticketed events, celebrating and commercialising the playful, aesthetic and often irreverent LGBT culture (Sydney 2002, 2002: 21). The heterosexist and gender-limiting traditions of mainstream sport were played with and critiqued in these Gay Games sports.

Inclusiveness was also manifest through policies, programmes and promotional efforts directed at other disadvantaged minority groups within the broader gay community, including women, blacks, people with disabilities and HIV and AIDS. The latter had had a significant impact on the LGBT community within the US and internationally. According to the *New York Times*, 'despite two world wars, the Depression and epidemics, nothing this century has affected the life expectancy for New Yorkers as greatly as AIDS' and over 60 per cent of those afflicted were gay and bisexual men (Firestone, 1996: 25). Involvement in sporting and cultural activities as athletes, volunteers, spectators and organisational leaders provided opportunities for people living with HIV/AIDS to connect with a larger caring community and to engage in enriching and health-promoting experiences, gain validation and a sense of achievement. The health-promotion aspect of the Gay Games, especially for those living with HIV/AIDS, was recognised from Gay Games II onwards and one of the first-ever safe-sex campaigns occurred at these Games. People with other disabilities were also integrated into the sport programme from these Games onward. Less physically demanding activities such as chess, billiards and croquet were introduced to the programme of Gay Games III in Vancouver in order to broaden participation. This continued at Gay Games IV and V (Symons, 2010: 78–87).

Numerous HIV-positive athletes of Gay Games IV achieved personal best performances. Two broke world masters' swimming records and another – Brent Nicholson Earle – acted as the human torch of the Games by rollerblading an ultra-marathon that finished with the opening ceremony. He did so in order to raise funds and awareness about HIV/AIDS and to remember those who had died (Symons, 2010: 82–86). Gay Games cycling competitor, Gary Reese, reflected that:

> The Games offered a rare chance to simultaneously celebrate our lives and mourn our losses. For once I did not feel the push-pull of trying to do one without the other, as

if we had to isolate AIDS and everything it means to us before we can feel good about ourselves and our future.

(cited in Labreque, 1994: 78–79)

Differently-abled people and those living with HIV and AIDs were made welcome through a 'safe Games' and 'open-accessibility' organisation and policy for those with special needs. Policy initiatives included the provision of a Persons With Aids (PWA) Resource/Hospitality Centre, rest areas at Games headquarters and various sports and the main ceremony venues. Access to medical and pharmacy services, wheelchair access, transportation to ceremonies and crisis intervention were provided to support PWA (Unity '94, 1994b). Venue managers, volunteers and paid staff received training and resources to ensure the needs of PWA were met. Similarly, during Gay Games V in Amsterdam, measures were in place to welcome and support all peoples with special needs (deaf, hard of hearing, visually impaired, mobility impaired, or with chronic conditions such as HIV/AIDS, diabetes, asthma . . .). Furthermore, differently-abled communities were empowered to define their needs and participate directly in the formulation of inclusive policies and practices (Symons, 2010: 88–90).

In the lead up to Gay Games IV, the Co-Presidents of the FGG and numerous gay and lesbian lawyers successfully worked through the Health and Human Services Department of the US government to make the Games a special event so that it would qualify for a thirty-day waiver of US immigration law that banned non-US citizens from entering the country on the basis that they had a 'communicable disease of public health significance'. The USOC assisted with these efforts as a goodwill gesture and to gain important information from the FGG on how to better cater for Olympic athletes who were HIV positive (Interview with Susan Kennedy, co-President of the Federation of Gay Games (1991–1998), 17 November 1996; and Derek Lieckty, Director of Facilities during Gay Games II as well as long serving director on the Federation of Gay Games, 30 September 1996). The Gay Games was regarded by the USOC as providing a model of best practice in this area. The radical inclusion of athletes living with HIV/AIDS contrasted strongly with that of the mainstream sports world at this time, in which silence, fear, homophobia, exclusion and erasure were the primary responses (Messner and Sabo, 1994: 120–124; Keyser 1999; Burke, 2002: 57–64; Symons, 2010: 95–97).

Gay Games IV implemented a hosted-housing scheme to make accommodation in New York City more accessible and a scholarship programme to subsidise economically-disadvantaged people who wanted to participate in the Games. However, regardless of intention, policies in themselves cannot overcome significant systemic socio-economic, cultural and political differences that disadvantage women and minority groups within society and sport and limit their capacity to attend the Games. For instance, in the early 1990s women in the US earned on average 70 per cent of the male average wage and were also more likely to be looking after dependents (Jacobs, 1997: 169–172). The female participation rate for sport in Gay Games IV was 38 per cent, favourable when compared with other multi-sports events, but also reflective of socio-economic difference and promotional efforts that tended to concentrate on the richer white, gay male demographic.

Through the most systematic effort of any Gay Games to include women more equally, Gay Games V boasted that women made up 42 per cent of all participants, workers and visitors and women's cultures and interests were well represented in the ceremonies, cultural, human rights and sports programmes. An activist Women's Advisory Committee, and a full-time and paid Women's Promotion Officer were central in achieving this remarkable result. Gender parity was sought in leadership positions, committee representation, staffing and volunteers. Proactive recruitment through women's networks and events was considered essential to address male domination in the Games. Affirmative action was used in selection and 46 per cent of paid staff and just under half the management personal were women. Extensive, targeted and sophisticated marketing campaigns that were in tune with lesbian cultures, politics and socio-economic considerations were also employed successfully.

Another strategy used to achieve greater gender equity was the creation of the International Women's Festival – involving theatre, dance and music to explore the themes of 'role models, dress codes, sexuality and gender crossing'. Women's sports participation in Gay Games V was also greater than at any previous Games (van Leeuwen 1999). Gender parity and co-leadership has been a central tenant of the Gay Games from its inception. Strong lesbian leaders as well as supportive gay men have kept gender equity and inclusion on the Games agenda. Researchers have demonstrated that the international sports world is largely male dominated and that such vigorous and proactive gender equity policies and outcomes in sport leadership are rare (McKay, 1997; Sundstrom, Marchant and Symons, 2011: 107–126). Gender politics are abiding features of LGBT and mainstream sport and although able-bodied, white and middle-class men still dominate both contexts, more radical and inclusive policies and outcomes for women and minorities have been achieved at the Gay Games.

The inclusion of racially and culturally diverse participants in the Gay Games occurred on the local and international level though targeted promotion, outreach efforts and scholarships. Whilst ethnic and racial background was not officially recorded (only nationality for overseas visitors), Hargreaves (2000) suggests that there 'has been a higher representation of Black, Asian and Latina lesbians from the US in the Gay Games than there are Black, Asian and Latina women in the mainstream Olympics' (p. 159). Comparative demographics for men are also unclear. The Marketing Manager for the Chicago 2006 Gay Games, Kevin Boyer, highlighted the promotional efforts made to engage the significant Black lesbigay population in and around Chicago (Interview with Boyer, 16 January 2007).

Gay Games VI was the first to occur in the Southern Hemisphere and the provision of promotional materials as well as financial (180 scholarships) and human support to indigenous people from Australia and the Asia Pacific was a key focus of Sydney 2002. In fact, Sydney 2002 broke new ground in its recognition of indigenous peoples and their Western and non-Western ways of thinking and living gender and sexuality. There were indigenous transgender teams and individuals playing sport under the most open gender participation policy of any Gay Games. I collected evidence (Symons, 2010: 192) that:

> (A) team from Palm Island, off Australia's northern-most coastline, made up of Aboriginal players who identified as sistergirls – boys who had been brought up as girls and live as females within their indigenous communities – received scholarships to play in the netball competition. Sistergirls don't see themselves as suffering from gender dysphoria that needs treatment through Western medicine. Nor do they see themselves as they are frequently viewed – as gay men. Western cultural understandings do not work here.

There were numerous indigenous and Pacific islander transgender teams playing in netball and volleyball (non-sanctioned) competitions of these Gay Games, enabled by the broadening of cultural understanding of sexuality and gender, as well as greater flexibility of rule-making on the borders of sex/gender. The ceremonies of Sydney 2002 also recognised the significance of indigenous culture as well as the ongoing struggle and double oppression experienced by LGBT indigenous people. Trans and intersex representation on the committee responsible for gender policy also demonstrated commitment to inclusion. In sports that involved body contact such as wrestling, record-breaking and the management of safety was in the hands of mainstream sports technical officials. This amounted to a pragmatic accommodation of difference rather than a radical transformation or queering of sport since dualistic determinations of sex/gender could be applied (Symons, 2010: 212–215).

Gay Games IV, V and VI had large and diverse international participation traversing every continent of the globe, although LGBT people from developing countries, as well as nations with repressive laws and attitudes against homosexuality, were a small minority. It can be challenging economically and politically for them to attend a Gay Games. Some feared reprisals in their home country if they were seen at the Games. In her 2011 landmark speech calling for the recognition of LGBT rights as human rights at the United Nations, US Secretary of State, Hillary Clinton spoke of LGBT human rights that:

> are denied in too many parts of the world today . . . They [LGBT] are arrested, beaten, terrorized, even executed. Many are treated with contempt and violence by their fellow citizens while authorities empowered to protect them look the other way or, too often, even join in the abuse. They are denied opportunities to work and learn, driven from their homes and countries, and forced to suppress or deny who they are to protect themselves from harm.
>
> *(Clinton, 2011)*

These Games had human rights as well as sports and cultural programmes, the former paying particular attention to LGBT rights abuses and widespread discrimination from governments and societies, as well as providing opportunities for people to tell their stories, share activist strategies and take political action to raise awareness and promote change (Symons, 2010: 143–146, 157–161, 191–192).

Normalisation through commercialisation

Critics of Gay Games diversity outcomes could readily point to the fact that the majority of Games participants are relatively well-off, white, gay men and to a lesser extent, women, from North America, Europe and Australia. Sponsorship breakthroughs were achieved to fund Gay Games IV using affluent Western LGBT people not representative of the diverse LGBT community, who could now be normalised as good consumers in this late-capitalist marketplace. According to the New York Games Sponsorship Manager, Harold Levine, sponsoring companies were mainly after the single, urban, well-educated and affluent gay man who 'spends freely on vacations, travel, clothing, alcohol and entertainment' (Interview, 3 December 1996). Most Games advertising featured this same demographic, a marketing pattern well replicated in subsequent Games as well as in the mainstream Western gay and lesbian press. Gay Games growth in participation and programming has also involved increasing sponsorship, commercialisation, marketing and professionalisation, which in turn has created lively tensions within the Games' community base. Furthermore, the overwhelming 'out and proud' lesbian and gayness celebrated at the Gay Games is a universalising one derivative of Western, late capitalist society, circulated by international marketing, media and travel trends of which the Gay Games are a prime exemplar.

Conclusion

The Gay Games has largely lived up to its transformative promise of gender and sexuality diversity and inclusion in sport and culture. The heteronormative traditions of a number of sports at the Games are played with and proactive inclusion policies and practices are pursued, enabling diverse LGBT communities and individuals from across the world to participate, marking the Gay Games as a beacon of inclusion in sport. However, radical ways of envisioning sport have also been tempered at the Games by the practicalities of staging a major global multi-sports event, and the strong commitment many LGBT sportspeople have to mainstream sport organisations and practices. The latter could certainly learn and be enriched from the proactive and creative endeavour of the Gay Games' movement to be radically inclusive.

Note

1   This history is based on over sixty in-depth interviews with key Gay Games organisers and some participants spanning all Gay Games until 2007, extensive archival analysis and participant observation of the Amsterdam (1998), Sydney (2002) and Chicago (2006) Gay Games, and the 1st World Outgames held in Montreal (2006) (see Symons, 2010).

References

Altman D (1983) *The Homosexualisation of America*. Boston, MA: Beacon Press.

Borrie S (2003) *Sydney 2002 Gay Games and Cultural Festival Sports Department Final Report – March '03*. Sydney: Sydney 2002.

Burke M (2002) 'Can Sport Cope with a "Wimpy Virus"? Using Questions Not Asked in the HIV and Sport Discourse to Resist Discrimination', *Journal of the Philosophy of Sport, Champaign, Illinios*, 29 (1): 54–65.

Carlson C (1982) 'Commentary', *The Voice*, San Francisco (Gay Press), 10 September, 4 (18): 4.

Clinton HR (2011) 'Remarks in Recognition of International Human Rights Day', Palais de Nations, Geneva, Switzerland, 6 December, http://www.state.gov/secretary/rm/2011/12/178368.htm (accessed 13 October 2013).

Firestone D (1996) 'Life Span Dips for Men Born in New York: AIDS is the Main Reason for Decline, Report Says', *New York Times*, 27 April: 25.

Gildersleeve J and Wardlaw L (1982) *Gay Games 1 Newsletter – Gay Olympiad 1 in 'Coming Up' – August 1982, San Francisco*, Archived in San Francisco Public Library (SFPL): Federation of Gay Games Archive (FGGA), Box 1, Series I, Gay Games I folder.

Hargreaves J (2000) *Heroines of Sport: The Politics of Difference and Identity*. London and New York: Routledge.

IOC (2003) Statement of the Stockholm consensus on sex reassignment in sport, www.olympic.org/Documents/Reports?EN/en_report_905.pdf (accessed 2 May 2012).

Jacobs M (1997) 'Do gay men have a stake in male privilege? The political economy of gay men's contradictory relationship to feminism'. In Gluckman A and Reed B (eds.) *Homoeconomics. Capitalism, Community and Lesbian and Gay Life*. New York: Routledge, pp. 165–184.

Keyser D (1999) 'Living with HIV/AIDS: The voices of sports professionals'. In Sankaran G, Volkwein K and Bonsall D (eds.) *HIV/AIDS in Sport. Impacts, Issues and Challenges*. Champaign, IL: Human Kinetics, pp. 57–64.

Labrecque L (ed.) (1994) *Unity: A Celebration of Gay Games IV and Stonewall*, San Francisco. CA: Labrecque Publishing.

McKay J (1997) *Managing Gender: Affirmative Action and Organizational Power in Australian, Canadian, and New Zealand Sport*. Albany, NY: State University of New York Press.

Messner M A and Sabo D F (eds.) (1994) *Sex, Violence & Power in Sports: Rethinking Masculinity*. Freedom, CA: Crossing Press.

Metra (1982) 'San Francisco – a very "out" and brash gay city', Gay Games Issue, 10 September: 24.

Outrage (1994) 'First we take Manhattan. Gay Games and Stonewall 25 taught the world about tolerance, diversity and friendly competition', August: 20

Scott J W (1971) *The Athletics Revolution*. New York: The Free Press.

Sydney 2002 (2002) *Official Guide to the Sydney 2002 Gay Games and Cultural Festival*. Sydney: Sydney 2002.

Sundstrom L, Marchant D and Symons C (2011) 'Play, but don't stay: Women leaders in Australian sport'. In Burke M, Hanlon C, Hess R and Thomen C (eds.) *Sport, Culture and Society, Approaches, Methods and Perspectives*. Melbourne: Maribyrnong Press, pp. 107–126.

Symons C (2010) *The Gay Games. A History*, London: Routledge

Symons C and Warren I (2006) David v. Goliath: Engagement, the Gay Games and the Ownership of Language. *The Entertainment and Sports Journal*, April, 4 (1).

Unity '94 (1994a) *Gay Games IV Policies' Gay Games IV and Cultural Festival. Athletes Registration Book.* Archived in SFPL: FGGA, Box 2, Series V, folder 10.

Unity '94 (1994b) *Gay Games IV Policy Document Special Needs are Human Needs*. Archived in SFPL: FGGA, Box 2, Series IV, folder 56.

Van Leeuwen I (1999) *Final Report – Gay Games Amsterdam 1998: Equal Gay and Lesbian Event? The Efforts of the Feminine Politics*. Translated from Dutch to English by Paulien Ingen-Housz. Archived at Victoria University: Caroline Symons Personal Gay Games Archive.

35

THE PINK FLAMINGO

A gay aquatic spectacle

Terry L. Allison

Introduction

The Gay Games, a promising idea to challenge mainstream conceptions of athletic competitions, have fostered little formal innovation in sport. For the greatest part, the Gay Games have sought legitimisation through official sanctioning by national and international sporting associations. Rather than spoofing sport or bending regulation, except for rare events, the Gay Games have sought to demonstrate that lesbians and gays can play by the same rules and succeed (Symons 2010: 51). From the first Games in 1982, Tom Waddell's principles of "participation, inclusion, personal best" were meant to challenge the masculine, heterosexist, and competitive nature of mainstream sports and to address social divisions of gender, race, and socioeconomic status. Adherence to these principles has been meaningful to participants and has changed athlete, spectator, and mainstream officials' views of lesbian, gay, bisexual, transgender, and queer (LGBTQ) people.[1] At the same time, if "The Games" are to be "Gay", one might expect that the sports events themselves might be queered, questioning traditional binary sex and gender roles by perverting rules, intermixing play, parody, kitsch, camp, gender questioning, or even by introducing social and political commentary into sport.

The Pink Flamingo, which began as an informal performance, developed into a fun relay and then evolved into a multifaceted aquatic spectacle, has provided one instance in the Gay Games' movement when athletes have "queered" sport. The Pink Flamingo goes beyond LGBTQ people and their allies performing mainstream sport in a public venue. Through creation of an event that springs particularly, but not exclusively, from gay men's history of camp, the Pink Flamingo queers mainstream sport, creating spaces for LGBTQ people to create community and common traditions, play with gender and sexuality, develop sociopolitical satire and reverent commemoration, as well as explore relationships with national and transnational identities.

This chapter, part of an ongoing in-depth work co-authored with Caroline Symons on the history and meaning of this spectacle, examines the Pink Flamingo as a site in which sexual minorities explore gendering of aquatic sport. As spectacle, the Pink Flamingo also illustrates how male domination within the Gay Games' movement can alienate or exclude lesbian and feminist participants seeking an equal presence, voice, and space. At the same time, this spectacular event demonstrates how participants productively address gendered tensions and explore innovative, creative ways to play.

Methodology

Caroline Symons and I conducted 21 interviews during Gay Games VII in Chicago 2006, and at the first Outgames in Montreal in 2006. Shortly thereafter we followed with more than a dozen interviews in Melbourne, New York, and at the International Gay and Lesbian Aquatics (IGLA) championships in Honolulu in 2011. During these years, we separately recorded interviews using set questions while maintaining a conversational tone. We found native and non-native English speakers from North America, Europe, Australia, and New Zealand, chosen primarily because of their knowledge and involvement in the Pink Flamingo or Outsplash.[2] We deliberately sought gender diversity among interviewees and somewhat by chance (as aquatic sport participants are predominantly white), were able to achieve some ethnic/racial diversity. Interviewees are a highly-educated sector of professionals, some with international jobs, reflecting the ability of participants to travel nationally or internationally to participate in LGBTQ athletic competitions. Some interviewees did not give clear permission to use their full names, so we have given them pseudonyms, indicated by placing the name in quotation marks. We have observed a number of Pink Flamingos in person and on film, are participant observers, and have used our observation or participation to exchange ideas with our interviewees as well as with each other during our analytical process.

Origins and history of the Pink Flamingo

As Symons (2010) describes in *The Gay Games: A history*, the initial impulse of the Gay Games was to normalize lesbian and gay male athletes as not "other" and not different; queering athletics was suppressed in favour of mainstreaming sexual and gender minorities in sport. Every team was expected to present itself in uniforms and the lead organizers modelled their dress on that of the U.S. Olympic Committee, crisp blazers and ties. No official space was created for the Gay Games to reflect LGBTQ culture or traditions such as leather or drag (Symons 2010: 42). But how could one gather over 50,000 LGBTQ athletes, volunteers, and spectators and expect no manifestations of queerdom to erupt? In Gay Games I (1982) and II (1986) *public manifestations of the queer, in particular cross dressing*, were suppressed, but individuals within various private party settings surrounding the Gay Games still managed to express their outsider status. One such manifestation came when New York swimmer, Charlie Carson, camped it up at a post-competition swimmers' party:

> Charlie actually brought a, he had a women's swim suit and a bathing cap and it was kind of Esther Williams . . . he had tied his medals into like a leash and he had two of the West Hollywood swimmers as I remember it down on their hands and knees . . . and put the medals around them as almost leashes, and he walked in dressed in his sunglasses and his Carmen Miranda cap and looked very Esther Williams and his two lap boys scantily clad, muscular lap boys, took him to the edge of the pool and he dove in and did an Esther Williams routine and everyone was just howling.
>
> *(Interview, Mark Wussler)*

This campy fun was not the kind of portrait that the Gay Games I organizers wanted to display but many interviewees knew of this episode and point to it as a source of the Pink Flamingo.

The next significant step towards the Pink Flamingo came directly after Gay Games II at the newly formed IGLA championships, held in San Diego in 1987 and 1988. At the first IGLA meet, Charlie Carson and teammates representing New York Aquatic Homosexuals (NYAH) showed up at the traditional final relay event in long, stretchy dresses, with Statue of Liberty crowns. During this time, cities and regions began to stage regular LGBT single or multi-sport competitions in order to provide regular competition, health and fitness, and community building. As well as San Diego and its nascent IGLA competitions, the northwest of the United States and southwest of Canada took leadership in sustaining LGBT athletics between the quadrennial Gay Games. Several of our interviewees first locate the use of a pink flamingo to a dual meet between Vancouver and Seattle. Ralph Doore of San Francisco, who has a large pictorial and video archive as well as detailed recall of a great number of Pink Flamingos (by 2006 he had witnessed about 20), confirms the timing and location:

> It actually started in the dual meets between Seattle and Vancouver before 1987. Or I should say probably 1987 . . . It started out simply as strapping a leg-pulled-off lawn flamingo on your head, swimming a length, passing it to a partner, then swimming, and, that's you know, swimming in any style. Most of the, all of the other teams really got introduced to it that July 4th weekend in '87 when [Seattle] hosted that first Northwest Gay and Lesbian Sports Festival.

As a number of interviewees agree, the camp aspect of the Pink Flamingo Relay started with simple drag. Several teams of men appeared as "the East German women's relay team", a spoof on the well-documented concern, eventually confirmed, that East German women swimmers gained muscle strength through doping (Jankofsky 1991). A few interviewees described the muscled men in women's competition tank suits as a "Russian women's team", perhaps a comment on the Soviet athletic machine or perhaps confusing one Soviet-bloc programme with another. This particular form of muscular men dressing as women recalls the "pony ballet", a set piece of U.S. military drag shows during World War II (Bérubé 1990: 70).

The Pink Flamingo in the 1989 IGLA championships was large, costumed, and complex, including four swimmers per team divided into tandem pairs in which both time and costume determined medals. But 1989 was a mere lead-up to the 1990 Gay Games III competition, again in Vancouver, described here in an interview by "Ethan Donald":

> . . . by 1990 it became this huge costumed event that had far more than just four people and really elaborate costumes and people put hundreds of hours of effort by that point and I think it blew people away. Certainly with our local officials and the straight swim community, it just blew them away; they were astounded and captivated by it all. I think for all us it was just amazing.

Several interviewees pointed to NYAH whole-team effort as a key point in the event's history. Most teams promenaded just four members for the relay while some, like San Francisco Tsunami, involved more of the team in elaborate display (e.g., "Les fruits de la mer" with sea creatures, sailors, mermaids, etc.—Interview, Doore). NYAH originally sent out four men in matching outfits representing actress Marlo Thomas in the U.S. television series, *That Girl* (1966–1971). The humour of four men identically outfitted in signature A-line dresses and shoulder-length flipped 60s wigs was camp-intensified by the New York-specific connection and knowledge that many male swimmers were posing as "That Girl". Even if one missed this specificity, the audience could appreciate the humour as the four-man squad (the Marlos) began to appear from all corners, jumping off the ten-meter dive, cavorting on the deck, and approximately sixty in all massing in their lane to start the relay. As more than one interviewee expressed, the Marlos changed everything. "It was an explosion of love and energy and excitement and gayness; that was just the entrance!" (Interview, "Steven Randall"). NYAH raised the stakes in costuming and spectacle, but because of the length of their promenade and wigs getting stuck in the pool-filtering system (along with other teams' use of sequin and glitter), this performance fostered development of a set of rules governing the event. These rules became codified through IGLA, which developed a small handbook for teams seeking to host the IGLA championships (International Gay & Lesbian Aquatics 2009: 48–50).

In future work Symons and I will provide a fuller history and description of how the relay gave way to water ballet, poolside choreography, and eventually to synchronized swimming. We will expand her previous descriptions of the most memorable Pink Flamingos including: the stunning AIDS commemorations in New York in 1994; the tribute to Princess Diana in 1997; and the meeting of the respective "queens" of England and the Netherlands at Gay Games V in Amsterdam (Symons 2010: 125–126, 156, 188). For now, I discuss how the Pink Flamingo, with its elements of cross-dressing, cultural references to female stars, and other gendered performance developed from gay men's historical relationship to camp. I examine the impact of camp humour as a means of community formation among male participants and spectators while potentially being exclusive of women who may find drag alienating, if not offensive.

Why aquatic sports?

While the Gay Games has promoted the inclusion of women in formerly male-only sports (e.g., wrestling) and for the first time provided international competition in formerly heterosexualised couple sports (i.e., figure skating pairs and ballroom dancing; Symons 2010: 156), the Pink Flamingo is the unique new event in Gay Games' history. Certainly the camp inspirations of Charlie Carson and others fostered the creation of this event, but we find it no accident that the Pink Flamingo was born in aquatic sports rather than in another arena.[3] This is because swimmers and divers have a long history of making spectacles of themselves, combining sport with entertainment.

The most significant early proponent of swimming as performance was Australian Annette Kellerman, whose biopic, *Million Dollar Mermaid*, starred Esther Williams. Although Kellerman insisted that her displays served only to promote the healthiness of swimming, regular exercise, diet and alcohol abstinence, publicity and other materials from the era indicate that the ability to see Kellerman's "perfect body" in what was for the time a very revealing one piece suit, drew the crowds as much as her athletic/aesthetic display (Gibson and Firth 2005). Now largely forgotten, and not cited by the interviewees, Kellerman paved the way for later well-known Hollywood stars, Johnny Weissmuller and Esther Williams, who parlayed competitive swimming into major live performance and cinematic careers. Several of our interviewees invoked the name of Esther Williams as an inspiration for the Pink Flamingo, drawing upon shared visual history of aquatic sport as cinematic spectacle. Significantly, the gay men and lesbians we interviewed did not cite Weissmuller, a five-time Olympic champion swimmer and Hollywood star of the 1930s and 1940s, a tall, handsome swimmer who appeared in very revealing costume, most notably as Tarzan. Although Weissmuller may fail to serve as camp inspiration, male aquatic sport participants are also clad scantily and during competition perform a parallel masculine ideal. Instead of Weissmuller, interviewees spoke of Busby Berkeley (a director of film dance spectacles who choreographed *Million Dollar Mermaid* at Williams' request, Williams 1999: p. 217), Carmen Miranda, or Bette Midler, each with a unique, spectacular aesthetic.

This cultural citation derives from gay men's relationship to camp, humour that depends on gender exaggeration, inversion, and sexual innuendo. Esther Williams was promoted as an ideal of femininity and is not usually considered representative of the exaggerated sexuality of Mae

West or Bette Midler, both queens of camp. Whatever Williams' screen persona, her spectacular aquatic scenes almost define camp: kitsch, artifice, frivolity and excess, all elements recognised by our interviewees as central to a Pink Flamingo performance (Sontag 2001). I am not saying that aquatic athletes in the LGBT sports movement are inherently campier than other athletes. Instead, I am claiming that aquatic athletes had a camp aesthetic history on which to draw to create a new event—a shared visual history relatively unique to swimming and diving—and that this history featured a starring female athlete–performer whom cross-dressing male swimmers could emulate.

In addition, several of the interviewees cited the individual nature of swimming as a reason that a team-building event like the Pink Flamingo was initiated and why it was important to sustain it. Interviewees said "of course we do have relays" or cited team scoring as having the potential for team building, and some cities also have water polo teams whom they cheer. Still, they found the Pink Flamingo uniquely successful in promoting inclusivity and belonging. Kaye Gravell, from Melbourne, said:

> . . . I thought this would be an opportunity to just get to meet different people 'cause I guess the down side of swimming is you talk to people in your lane, and it's not like other sports where you can perhaps have more opportunity to mix. So, I thought this would be an opportunity to actually speak to other people, and I like the performance, dance and other stuff . . . yeah, but it was mainly, probably the main motivation was just to get to know other people in the club.

Participants consistently discussed search for community as a reason for engaging in LGBTQ sports. Lou Theunissen, a male swimmer from Amsterdam, described this well: "So the corporate environment is hostile. Everywhere in the world. On the contrary, swim teams, gay swim teams, wherever I meet them, in every country, are very warm. It's a warm bath."[4] Kaye Gravell's remarks above indicate that some women find a place in this warm bath, but as Symons (2002) found, women still must assert themselves to claim space in male-dominated LGBTQ aquatics. (pp. 108–109)

Is the Pink Flamingo successful?

The Pink Flamingo is largely successful in community building. Greg Retter, from London, describes what several interviewees named as the highlight of its twenty-five-year history, a moving tribute to Princess Diana that Out to Swim performed after an IGLA championship:

> And the team itself got this amazing buzz from it, this huge sense of achievement for what was a fairly simple piece and everyone came back from that and years later of "We remember your Pink Flamingo from San Diego—it was fantastic, it was beautiful." The team as a whole really achieved something quite special at that moment, it really pulled everyone together. . . . It wasn't too difficult to organize but it was the catalyst for them going forward for the bigger Pink Flamingo which we wanted to include as many people in the club and to try and get the same sort of feeling of togetherness and try to bring the whole club to a focal point at the end of the swim meet. And that was in Amsterdam in the Gay Games in 1998.

Not only did this performance have a lasting impact within the London team, the Princess Diana tribute, like the Montreal AIDS ribbon water ballet in New York '94, provides a shared visual history across clubs and national boundaries, creating an imagined transnational community with common lore (Anderson 1983).

"Adrian Mitchell" from Toronto also emphasizes the inclusive nature of the Pink Flamingo:

> . . . It's so fun! They're so excited! Especially if someone is not a very strong swimmer. They can be part of the team and almost be part of the foundation, that pillar that helps make the team. I think that's very rewarding. For me, that's the most fun, seeing someone happy. Just being part of it. Being included.

Most said that the Pink Flamingo would not happen at a "straight" meet. Lucille Thirlby called the Pink Flamingo "just pure fun" and a "bonding experience". When queried about the possibility of Pink Flamingo in other team sports including, for example, "straight soccer", she responded: "Oh no, no, no, no. If I was a swimmer with straight people that wouldn't work at all . . . I think it's about, I think we are quite good at expressing our flamboyance and allowing ourselves to be freer than some straight people . . . "[5] Thus, while the Pink Flamingo epitomises the spirit of inclusiveness of the Gay Games by integrating athletes at all performance levels across aquatic sports into a shared enterprise, it also serves to reinforce the participants' perceptions of a community apart from the mainstream with its own customs, humour, and sensibilities. The event assumes a shared set of references, particularly to the arts and politics, and shared conventions such as drag, to reinforce its subcultural credentials and integrate new participants and observers.

The interviewees and our own observations reveal a more mixed story of success in playing with gender identities. The Pink Flamingo has encouraged some individuals to begin playing with gender and sexual identities and the heteronormative conventions of sport, and sometimes even incorporates heterosexuals into play that completely blurs sex and gender roles. As "Steven Randall" said: "Men can play. Gay men can play. I've never seen another sport with this interpretative element." This same interviewee applauded the evolution of the event: "Drag queens used to be the norm. That's why I'm so impressed that it evolved. Because it now shows more of our culture, of our values, of our wounds."

But interviewees also described the difficulty of fostering women's participation in LGBTQ aquatics and their full incorporation as team members. Interviewee "Tim Howard" said: "It's still basically men. I think the gender dynamics are basically the same in any other event involving gay men and gay women. Men primarily want to be with other men and women want to be with women." Women often constitute 10–20% of an aquatic team, much lower than women's overall participation in the Gay Games. Some teams have no female members.[6] At the Sydney 2002 Gay Games, as a result of their decided minority status on aquatic teams, women from a number of teams, while also performing for their home city, joined together to stage a women's Pink Flamingo. In discussing the imbalance of gender, Benoit Ethier said: "It's always the same story. I wish for more women to take part in those things." Several interviewees responded similarly, describing the Pink Flamingo not as an event that has created division among aquatic athletes, but as a reflection of the lack of gender balance in LGBT swimming, diving, and water polo.

Others perceived the drag elements of Pink Flamingo as demarcating differences between gay and lesbian cultures, describing the Pink Flamingo as primarily a men's camp convention not particularly inviting to women. One woman interviewee, "Samantha Teller", expressed it as follows: "I can imagine that as a woman it's hard to make more of a statement in Pink Flamingo . . . when it's really dominated by men . . . " She continued: "The guys are expected in a way to be creative and the lesbians are kind of, just do your sport." Still, some interviewees did not believe that gay men were naturally inclined to cross-dressing and saw the Pink Flamingo as a way for men to begin to explore gender play that they had not previously found attractive. "I noticed that more and more of my fellow teammates don't have a problem to wear a transvestite outfit during an Upstream party . . . People have become more liberal, more free to dare; more daring" (Theunissen).

In *Vested Interests* (1993), Marjorie Garber encourages us to look at transvestism as a thing unto itself, encouraging us to see drag not as men dressed as women or vice versa, but a third term which troubles gender identities. Still, Garber agrees with Lisa Duggan's assessment that drag typically does not appeal to lesbians: "When lesbians sponsor strip shows, or other fem erotic performances, it is very difficult to 'code' it as lesbian, to make it feel queer. The result looks just like a heterosexual performance, and lesbian audiences don't respond to it as subversively sexual, specifically ours" (Duggan 1988, cited in Garber 1993: 152). In reference to her team's 2002 Sydney performance, Lucille Thirlby describes how some women have contested male teammates' emphasis on drag:

> I think [the Pink Flamingo] is dominated by camp men, but . . . within our team we had quite a lot of assertion of the women that this is not just going to be a men's sort of thing. Within our Pink Flamingo—for the Sydney one—the dancers, they wanted to have men all dressed as women and the women dressed as men. We were all like, "Oh come on, that just doesn't work for us", and so we had the women dressed as women and the men dressed as men except for two of us. So I dressed as a man and he dressed as a woman, so we allowed that a bit.

Garber (1993) describes lesbian use of the monocle, cigarette, cigar, or pipe as "pieces" in female to male (F2M) transvestism rather than wigs, fake breasts, or lingerie familiar to male to female (M2F) cross-dressing (pp. 152–161). But in a Pink Flamingo pool-side performance, these small props don't deliver. Occasionally, women participants have performed in male bathing suits or even emphasised their difference as women through baring or partial exposure of breasts. Within the U.S., women's partial nudity in several Pink Flamingos became a substantial problem. Lou Theunissen, from the Netherlands described the Pink Flamingo in 1995:

> TA: Can you describe any controversies or can you recall any controversies related to Pink Flamingo or Outsplash?
>
> LT: (Pause) Yeah, there was in Atlanta, if I remember well, there was a controversy about showing nudity. A lesbian had painted her breasts in the shape of a, how do you call it?
>
> TA: A bra.
>
> LT: A bra. Exactly. That was funny. And I think it is a little bit silly. But typical American.[7]

At the Easter Pink Flamingo (Long Beach, California, 1991), four West Hollywood women participated with only inflatable guitars covering their breasts. However, when the Toronto team engaged in sacrilegious parody of the crucifixion that included topless women as Roman soldiers, the performance was interrupted and site managers threw IGLA out of the pool, citing "nudity" that disrupted the family atmosphere of the plunge ("Steven Randall"). While "no nudity" frequently was mentioned among our interviewees as one of the rules of the Pink Flamingo, all instances of nudity they identified as controversial were of bare female breasts; no male nudity or semi-nudity was cited as controversial. One interviewee, "Michael James", celebrated how Paris Aquatique played with male partial undress: "They were wearing thongs or something with their butts hanging out but they carried waiters' trays and it was choreographed so they were hiding each other's bottoms with the trays." This dichotomous view of semi-nudity reinforces the Pink Flamingo as an uneven field, one much more supportive of men's gender and sexuality play.

Still, men and women have found creative ways to play together. Greg Retter, from London, described a Pink Flamingo in 1998 Amsterdam in which the team deliberately engaged women in their gender play:

> We didn't want to have a lot of drag, we wanted a show. That's why it was called the Fuller Monty rather than the Full Monty, because we had five guys and five women stripping down to the G strings and bras and they looked sexy.

Thus while there are tensions about gendered roles and gay male conventions of drag, Pink Flamingo staging has also served as a productive venue for lesbians and gay men to explore their cultural differences and negotiate them successfully.

At times, teams' Pink Flamingo performances have deliberately played with gender and sex in more striking ways than drag. Doore described a performance that others also recalled in which the athletes switched body parts:

> I think it was '94, Toronto did one where they wore suits, tops and bottoms, men and women, and they had Velcro in all the naughty bits and they had rubber parts that they interchanged with other people in the show. There were dongs and rubber tits and rubber vaginas and they all had the other parts.

And gender confusion can develop from less graphic display. Phil Vogel from Montreal describes how the Pink Flamingo generated gender confusion for a female heterosexual participant, the only woman on an all-male swim team:

> And it was very funny because during one of our practices [for Pink Flamingo] all the synchro swimmers are girls and at one point they were saying, okay we want everyone to mix up . . . and they were saying, okay, girls mix with the guys and she was confused because she wasn't sure, am I with the guys on the team or am I one of the girls?

These are but two brief examples of how the Pink Flamingo has exceeded its camp origins, queering sport's traditional division into two sexes and providing space for women and men to play with gender. Still, the Pink Flamingo, with its reliance on camp cross-dressing, lacks connection to women's cultural histories of gender play. This uneven dynamic reflects the dominance of men in aquatic sport and, in an American context, the constraints against women baring breasts, a women's convention in some LGBTQ pride parades. The Pink Flamingo, this "funny and nice and stupid event", is usually nicer for male participants who draw on a camp cross-dressing aesthetic and more challenging for women athletes who still seek avenues to become full partners in gender play and performance.

Notes

1 As one example, see Symons (2010: 107). Although it should be noted that master's sports, which grew rapidly in parallel to the Gay Games, foster a similar ethos of self-development and camaraderie rather than unstinting competition.

2 For previous discussion of the Pink Flamingo, see Symons (2010), notably her discussion of the schism in international LGBT sports which led to the first Outgames, which were not permitted to use the newly trademarked "Pink Flamingo", thus created "Outsplash" (p. 234).

3 Charlie Carson is the aforementioned individual who dressed in drag after Gay Games I; he remains active in IGLA and the Gay Games movement. Daniel Collins of Vancouver is credited with inspiration from a series of television commercials for using the pink flamingo (Interview, "Ethan Donald").

4 See also Symons (2002: 108) for a discussion of the Pink Flamingo and community building in LGBT sports.

5 Kristian Nergaard from San Francisco also said "Absolutely not" when asked if he could imagine a Pink Flamingo taking place at the US Masters Swimming national championships.

6 For gender equality at the Games see Symons (2010: 166–170).

7 Note that Symons (2010) description of the closing ceremonies at Gay Games V, Amsterdam (1998) included "leather clad and bare-breasted 'dykes' on large motorbikes who kissed and caressed each other during a romantic song" (p. 171), supporting the notion that women's partial undress and play has proven more acceptable outside the U.S.

References

Anderson, B (1983) *Imagined Communities: Reflections on the Origin and Spread of Nationalism*. London: Verso.

Bérubé, A (1990) *Coming Out Under Fire: The History of Gay Men and Women in World War Two*. New York: Penguin.

Duggan, L (1988) The Anguished Cry of an 80's Fem: "I want to be a drag queen". *Out/Look* 1: 64.

Garber, M (1993) *Vested Interests: Cross-dressing & cultural anxiety*. New York: Harper Perennial.

Gibson, E and Firth, B (2005) *The Original Million Dollar Mermaid: The Annette Kellerman Story*. Crows Nest, NSW: Allen & Unwin.

International Gay & Lesbian Aquatics (2009) Rules and Recommendations for IGLA Championships and Gay Games Aquatics Competitions. http://www.igla.org/online-documents/publications/2009.00.00. IGLA-Championship-Rules.pdf (Accessed June 2012).

Jankofsky, M (1991) OLYMPICS; Coaches Concede That Steroids Fueled East Germany's Success in Swimming. *New York Times* 3 December.

Sontag, S (2001) *Against Interpretation and Other Essays*. New York: Picador (pp. 275–292).

Symons, C (2002) The Gay Games and Community. In: Hemphill, D and Symons, C (eds) *Gender, Sexuality and Sport: A Dangerous Mix*. Petersham, NSW: Walla Walla Press.

Symons, C (2010) *The Gay Games: A History*. London: Routledge.

Williams, E with Diehl, D (1999) *The Million Dollar Mermaid*. New York: Simon & Schuster.

PART VI

Questioning and transgressing sex

36

SUBJECTIVE SEX

Science, medicine and sex tests in sports

Vanessa Heggie

The maintenance of sex-segregated sports in the twentieth century has been based on two assumptions: that human beings come in two sexual forms, male and female, and that one of these forms has significant biological advantages in terms of sporting performance. From the 1930s sports organisations have increasingly turned to biomedical experts to provide 'objective' scientific tests to maintain segregation in sports, an activity nearly always justified by an appeal to the notion of fair competition. Ironically, through the same period a range of scientific disciplines – including genetics, endocrinology and forensic psychology – as well as social sciences such as anthropology and sociology, began to describe human gender identities as flexible and continuous, and identified not a binary sex system, but a complex identity built of many kinds of sex (e.g. Fausto-Sterling, 1992).

This chapter outlines the medical and scientific tests used to determine whether athletes were eligible to compete in women's sporting events in the twentieth century. Variously called tests for 'sex', 'gender' and 'femininity', these surveillance regimes had to satisfy competing and often contradictory demands from sports organising bodies, scientific professionals, advocacy groups and the athletes themselves. Such tests were discussed by sports organisations and medical professionals in the early 1930s, and were relatively common in Western sports by the 1940s, undergoing significant political and procedural changes throughout the second half of the twentieth century. Examining these tests demonstrates the shifting balance of power and authority in sports sciences, as well as highlighting clear conflicts between biological, social and cultural ways of understanding bodily difference.

Histories of sex testing in sports have tended to localise the origins of the tests in the games of the 1950s, where in the shadow of a Cold War successful female athletes from behind the iron curtain were accused of gender fraud. More recent studies have shown that this gender anxiety was in fact clearly present as early as the 1930s, leading to systematic requirements for female athletes to prove they were eligible to compete in women's events (Heggie, 2010). These concerns matched broader social fears about the apparent mutability of biological sex, fed by popular understandings of newly discovered sex hormones. In particular it was the phenomenon of the female-to-male transition that provoked popular coverage and interest, and several examples were drawn from the world of sport. Through the twentieth century the concern within sport remained fixed on this transformation, from female into male; whereas in the worlds of sexology, endocrinology and reassignment technologies quite the opposite happened, with the male-to-female transition becoming the focus of attention (Meyerowitz, 2002). The ongoing demand for a binary sex system, and a focus on female transgression, meant that the needs of sports were not well met by the scientific sex and gender tests which were introduced, since these were the products of quite different understandings of biology and psychology, as this chapter will show.

The most well known cases of gender ambiguity in the first third of the twentieth century are Stella Walsh (born Stanisława Walasiewicz in Poland, Walsh's family emigrated to the US before she was a year old) and the German-born Heinrich Ratjen. Ratjen is the only documented case of straightforward gender fraud; the dramatic version of his story that he was compelled by corrupt Nazi sports officials to compete fraudulently is almost certainly a myth, rather his story seems to be one of gender confusion at birth and an ongoing inability to negotiate a new sexual or gender identity once he had mistakenly been registered as female (Heggie,2010). Ratjen's case was resolved in 1938 when he was given new papers and a new identity as a man. Walsh, on the other hand, lived her entire life as a woman, and only had her gender questioned after her violent death, when in 1980 an autopsy revealed some ambiguous sexual features. The autopsy had no effect whatsoever on the introduction of sex tests, and her frequent appearance in articles relating to the topic of sex testing was driven more by authors' senses of dramatic irony than a desire to explain a chain of causes and consequences. (Claims that Walsh was 'suspected' of 'being a man' during her years as a competitive athlete appear to be an invention by modern authors (Heggie, 2010).)

Walsh took second place in the women's 100m race at the 1936 Olympic Games in Berlin; first place went to the American Helen Stephens. Questions were raised – by whom it is not clear – about Stephens' gender, and she was subject to an unspecified sex test by the German authorities, who confirmed her eligibility and her right to the gold medal. Outraged by this accusation, chair of the US Olympic Committee, Avery Brundage – who disapproved of women's competitive athletics in general – complained bitterly about the indignity of an accusation of manliness followed by an intrusive test, and argued that female competitors should bring their own certificates to events to prove their eligibility. He pointed, not to Walsh, but to two other successful female athletes who had undergone surgical procedures and were now living as men, as evidence that there was a gender problem in modern sports. Zdenek Koubkov had competed as Zdenka Koubkova for Czechoslovakia, and Mark Weston had won world records competing as Mary Weston for Britain. To this short list of widely known sporting transsexuals we should also add the famous case of Willy (Elvira) de Bruyne, a Belgian cyclist who transitioned in 1935 (Meyerowitz, 1998).

By the 1930s Germany had become the centre of expertise for those wanting to transition from one sex to another, using a combination of hormone therapy and surgical intervention – and the first account of a case of surgical transition was published by a German surgeon in 1931, a few years before Koubkov, Weston and de Bruyne transitioned (Abraham, 1931). While doctors and scientists talked of restoring 'true' sex or of 'fixing nature's mistakes', as if there were underlying gender identities which could be confidently medically established, this work took place in an era when hormonal and endocrinological theories of sex promoted more mutable notions of sexual identity, which had strong cultural penetration. From the scandalous claims of Charles Eduard Brown-Séquard in 1889 that extracts of guinea-pig testicles were returning his lost virility, the use of 'gland extracts' (the specific hormones of progesterone, oestrogen and testosterone were only identified in 1929, 1934 and 1935, respectively) was widely discussed in Europe and North America. Gland therapy and its extraordinary – and usually sexual – effects was used by popular writers, such as Conan Doyle, in the 1929 Sherlock Holmes story *The Adventure of the Creeping Man*. It was also covered in popular newspapers, for example, in the late 1930s the coach of the Wolverhampton Wanderers' football club announced that he was giving 'gland extracts' to his players to improve their performances (Heggie, 2011, p. 81).

While titillating, the use of 'male hormones' to augment male performance – sexual or sporting – did not seem particularly problematic (in the case of Wolverhampton Wanderers, media coverage was concerned for the health of the players, but ambivalent about cheating). Similar attitudes did not extend to women. Female sport, already a transgressive activity, by the early twentieth century had its strong supporters, including social reformers, doctors and politicians, although female participation in vigorous or competitive exercise was still limited by gender expectations. Whether it was the political danger of publicly visible, independent women (particularly associated with cycling), or the medical danger of vigorous exercise to the more fragile female organism, or the social danger of encouraging women to be competitive and aggressive, limits were put on women's right to participate in sport (Hargreaves, 1994).

By the 1930s mainstream biomedical authorities appear to have been, in general, more positively disposed towards female sport (and female robustness) than sports organisations themselves – particularly the International Olympic Committee (IOC). Nonetheless, the internationally reported presence of female-to-male transsexuals in sport certainly contributed to popular and sporting suspicions that even if sport did not 'make' women into men, the sorts of women who were successful in sports might 'really' be men, or manly. The earliest 'sex tests' were therefore generally physical, phenotypical[1], or physiological tests – that is, sex was determined by the possession of a certificate of femininity signed by a doctor, usually one's family doctor (team doctors were still not common for sports organisations in the 1930s). This requirement was brought in by the International Amateur Athletics Federation in the late 1930s (Rule 17 Paragraph 3) and adopted by the IOC, so that the first post-war Games, in 1948 in London, were the first to include this requirement for female athletes.

Gender controversies at mid-century make more sense when we see them in the longer context. Focusing on the Ukranian sisters Irina (1939–2004) and Tamara Press (b.1937), sports coverage sometimes suggested that they were 'really' men, but as frequently discussed, it was more likely that 'substances', possibly hormones, were used to create male-like body types and high-level sporting success. This was explicitly the way the IOC saw the problem, as an article in its *Bulletin* in 1961 makes clear:

> a particularly revolting form of doping. . .[involves taking] male hormones which lead[s] to castration of the functional cycle of women amount[ing] sometimes to an atrophy of the ovaries which may cause a chronic disease in the long run.
>
> *(Eyquem, 1961, p.50)*

The associations between hormonal doping and gender anxiety continued into the twenty-first century – as Davis and Delano (1992) have shown, anti-doping campaigns focusing on steroids act to reinforce the binary nature of gender, representing gender-transgressive or gender-ambiguous bodies as evidence/consequence of drug use.

Crucially, though, at mid-century science could not yet offer an effective test for the use of hormones; what it could offer was a test for *sex* (Shackleton, 2008). Although the IOC had specifically highlighted the problem of doping with sexual hormones, the preventive measures it introduced examined only the problem of *naturally occurring* transgressive bodies. This ambiguity was admitted by the IOC

> . . . certain medicasters have not hesitated to render women champions . . . more *virile* in order, that during international competitions, they may achieve results which are over and above their normal capacities . . . However dangerous this may be for the feminine organism and however reprehensible it may be from a moral point of view, these 'treatments' in no way change the basic sexual characteristics, for it has been scientifically proved that hermaphroditism does not exist. One is born a man or a woman and one remains of that sex.
>
> *(Berlioux, 1967, p.1)*

Instead of introducing tests for substances which increased 'virility', the IOC attempted to find tests which would provide a simple, comprehensive, *objective* measure of someone's birth sex, that is, their unchangeable, natural gender identity.

Accusations of gender fraud increased through the 1950s – importantly, not just aimed at the women we remember, such as the Press sisters, but also to other, forgotten athletes. One member of the British team at the 1960 Rome Olympics was charged by two other teams with being a man. In response, an indignant Jack Crump, secretary of the British Amateur Athletic Board, insisted that all his team had the 'proper form', signed by both himself and a medical practitioner, '[i]t would be unthinkable', he argued, 'for us and for anybody else to challenge the integrity and capability of a registered practitioner' (Anon, 1960). But such a challenge is exactly what occurred in the 1960s, as the level of suspicion, and the stakes of competition, meant that the word of medical practitioners from athletes' home nations were no longer to be trusted in international competition.

The first *systematic* at-event sex testing was introduced at the 1966 European Athletics Championship, held in Budapest, and then taken up widely at other international sports events. Initially these tests were a continuation of the practices of the 1930s and 1940s, that is, a physical and phenotypical test. But what might have been acceptable when practised by one's family doctor, or a familiar team doctor, was quite a different experience when practised by unsympathetic strangers. Participants in women's sports in the 1960s later gave highly critical accounts of the processes. Maren Siedler, an American shot putter said that at the 1967 Pan-American Games in Winnipeg '[t]hey lined us up outside a room where there were three doctors sitting in a row behind desks. You had to go in and pull up your shirt and push down your pants. Then they just looked while you waited for them to confer and decide if you were OK' (Larned, 1976, p.8). At other events even more invasive systems of testing were chosen, for example sex-testing at the 1966 Commonwealth Games in Jamaica was described by British pentathlete Mary Peters:

> [it was] the most crude and degrading experience I have ever known in my life . . . [I was] ordered to lie on the couch and pull my knees up. The doctors then proceeded to undertake an examination which, in modern parlance, amounted to a grope. Presumably they were searching for hidden testes. They found none and I left.
>
> *(Larned, 1976, p.8)*

The unpleasantness and invasiveness of the test meant it was not going to be a sustainable practice; in addition, it also appeared alarmingly arbitrary. Ewa Kłobukowska, a Polish sprinter, passed the test in Budapest in 1966, but then failed it in 1967 at the European Cup Track and Field Event in Kiev. Clearly the phonotypical test for sex was too subjective – different panels of doctors might reach different decisions. Since, as the IOC had insisted, we were all born either male or female, and could not change over our lifetime, a test was sought which could distinguish between men and women conclusively. The test chosen was the Barr Body test – used on Kłobukowska in 1967 after she failed a 'close up visual inspection of the genitalia', and which she also 'failed', leading to her disqualification for life from women's sports (Anon, 1967).

The Barr Body test had been developed in the 1950s by Canadian microanatomist Murray Barr. He and a research student first spotted this deeply staining cellular artefact whilst studying cats in the late 1940s, and published on the topic in *Nature* in 1949 (Barr and Bertram, 1949). The Barr Body was only present in the cells of female cats, and Barr developed a theory that this artefact was actually stained heterochromatin[2] and therefore evidence of two condensed X chromosomes. If that were the case, then the fairly easily visualised Barr Body could be used as a proxy for establishing chromosomal sex, at a time when more extensive karyotyping was difficult and unreliable. In mammals, at least, a Barr Body could be taken as evidence of an XX sex-chromosome karyotype, and therefore femininity, while its absence indicated the organism was XY, and therefore male.

To prove this was the case Barr and his assistants engaged in a series of experiments with hormones and the removal and transplant of sexual organs, in an attempt to prove that the Barr Body was an indicator of chromosomal sex at conception, rather than being an artefact produced by, say, high levels of female hormones. By the early 1950s he had concluded that these experiments were a success, and that Barr Bodies were proxies for female chromosomal sex. At this time, the prevailing understanding of sex determination assumed that male identity was the default for mammalian foetuses, controlled by the non-sex chromosomes (the autosomes). It was only where a 'double dose' of 'female-making' sex chromosome was present – that is in XX individuals – that an embryo would shift course and become female instead of male. In this reading the Y chromosome was generally considered inert and inactive.

Barr's team wrote in 1953 that '[o]ur hope is that the chromosomal sex will prove to be a reliable indicator of the dominant sex of the patient as a whole' (Moore et al., 1953, p.641). However, before the end of the decade flaws in the system had already been discovered, most notably through studies of people with various sex chromosome disorders, i.e. those whose sex chromosomes are XXY (Barr Body female, phenotypically male) or XO (Barr Body male, phenotypically female). Two of Barr's assumptions were also overturned: firstly that the Barr Body itself was formed of both X chromosomes. Instead it was found to be a single X chromosome; since only one X chromosome is necessary to fulfil genetic functions, in people with two copies of the X one becomes inactivated and appears as the dense ball that constitutes the Barr Body. Secondly it was discovered that the Y chromosome was not inert, but played a role in sex determination and development.

Despite this, it was the Barr Body test that the IOC chose as its 'femininity test' of choice in the late 1960s. As the article, quoted above, in the IOC's own bulletin-cum-newsletter (later the *Olympic Review*) goes on to say: '[t]he chromosome formula indicates quite definitely the sex of a person and, some years ago, it was discovered that a simple saliva test will reveal its composition' (Berlioux, 1967, p.1). This is a significant overstatement of the competencies of the Barr Body test, and it is not clear from the published sources why this, already critiqued, test for sex was so eagerly taken up by the IOC. I would suggest three factors may have played a role in this choice: firstly, the test seemed both scientific and objective, and gave a straightforward negative or positive outcome, which meant it had significant advantages over the apparently subjective, human process of assessing phenotypical and physical sex. Secondly, the test was largely non-invasive, involving initially a cheek swab (buccal smear) and later a hair sample, reducing the need for the deeply unpopular and unpleasant visual and manual tests. Thirdly, the committee tasked with organising sex testing was not a specialist committee, but a subcommittee of the newly formed Committee on Doping. No permanent Medical Committee was formed by the IOC until 1967, and as Alison Wrynn (2004) has shown, this organisation was riven in its early years by disputes about authority, remit and funding.

It is clear that many of those tasked with organising and carrying out early sex testing – including doctors and scientists – had very poor understandings of the clinical and psychological consequences. For example, this rather naïve quotation comes from a report to the IOC, drawn up by the doctor in charge of the trials of the Barr Body test at the Winter Games in 1968 (which disqualified one downhill skier): 'I do not exactly know why some personages are unwilling to tolerate this examination; the main obstacle would seem to be the fear of seeing the young adolescent's psychism [sic] traumatized. Considering the harmless nature of the swab, I fail to understand where the traumatism comes in' (Thiebault, 1967).

Meanwhile, geneticists and other scientists were actively criticising the choice of the Barr Body test. It is worth quoting at length from one critique, as it was written by Dr Keith Moore, who was supervised through his MSc and PhD by Barr himself, and had been a co-author on some of the papers relating to the Barr Body in the 1950s:

> The question of whether certain female athletes are in fact female will certainly arise during medical examinations at the Olympics, even though the obviously doubtful cases will likely remain at home. The rapid advances registered during the last decade in our understanding of sex and its aberrations have resulted in confusion in the minds of some, however, concerning the contribution of various factors (genetic, gonadal, hormonal) towards the sexual identity of an individual. As a result, females have been declared ineligible for athletic competition for no other apparent reason than the presence of an extra chromosome . . . [these tests] cannot be used as indicators of 'true sex'.
>
> *(Moore, 1968, p.787)*

Despite these protests, the IOC stuck with the Barr Body test; in part I would suggest because the internal struggles over the role and responsibility of the Medical Committee left little time for high-tech or psycho-sociological discussions of issues as complicated as sex testing. Since many sports organisations followed the lead of the IOC in terms of eligibility and the organisation of competition, the consequence was that tests for chromosomal sex were used widely as a means of establishing an athlete's eligibility to compete as a woman – despite scientific opposition. The only significant change in the 1970s was a switch to hair samples rather than buccal smears, and in some cases the use of a fluorescent dye test for the presence of the Y chromosome (in part to deal with the possibility of XXY and XO competitors).

The consequences of the use of this test are impossible to measure, because although some records are kept of at-event tests, and scandals are well known, thousands of women were tested quietly, secretly, 'at home'. In 1970 the British Association of Sport and Medicine (later the British Association of Sport and Exercise Medicine) funded a 'sex test' and a 'chromatin count service' for the use of any British governing bodies of sport who wanted to check their athletes' chromosomes before attending a major sporting event and it did not fund counselling or medical support for athletes found to be chromosomally 'abnormal' (Anon, 1970).

The first significant challenge to these testing regimes came in the 1980s. Spanish hurdler, Maria Martinez-Patino, underwent a sex test at the 1983 World Track and Field Championships in Helsinki, passed, and was given a certificate of eligibility. In 1985 she went to Kobe, Japan, to compete in the World University Games. She forgot her certificate and the authorities insisted on retesting her. This time she failed, and her coach advised her to fake an injury and go home, which she did. When she tried to compete again the following year her story was leaked to the press; she was banned from her teams, her medals and records were revoked, and her fiancé left her (Patino, 2005).

Patino began a three-year campaign for reinstatement. She found sympathetic Spanish doctors willing to write reports about her medical condition, and was championed by Finish geneticist Albert de la Chapelle, who challenged routine sex testing on ethical and human rights grounds. Chapelle had received a PhD in human genetics from the University of Helsinki in 1962, and spent much of that decade investigating the phenomenon of XX males; that is, people who are chromosomally 'female', but physiologically and hormonally 'male'. At exactly the time that Patino was mounting a challenge to the use of chromosomal sex tests, Chapelle was effectively developing a test for *genetic* sex. Between 1984 and 1987 he and colleagues published a series of papers in extremely high profile journals (including *Nature* and *Science*) demonstrating that the Y chromosome plays a crucial role in sex determination.

In this reworked understanding of sex determination in mammals, the female is now the 'default' developmental pathway for a foetus. Instead of a 'double dose' XX signal directing female development, a signal from a specific region of the Y chromosome (later known as the Sex Determining Region, or SDR) starts a cascade of events which lead to male phenotypical development. Further, the X and the Y chromosomes can sometimes exchange genetic material through a process of 'crossing over' during cell division (meiosis)[3] which means that the SDR can end up on an X chromosome, hence the phenomenon of XX males.

With this support, Patino was reinstated in 1988, on the grounds that she had Androgen Insensitivity Syndrome; that is, a fault in the testosterone receptors in the body such that, as a foetus, the signals for male development had no effect, and she continued through a near-normal female developmental pathway. In the same year the International Association of Athletics Federations (IAAF) dropped chromosomal testing, reverting instead to a reliance on the physical examination conducted by the team doctor (in other words, a reversion to the 1940s system of sex testing). The IAAF abandoned all forms of systematic sex testing in 1992, arguing that because athletes had to pass urine in front of witnesses for drugs testing, and because of the revealing nature of tight sports clothes, it did not consider sex fraud a genuine threat to sport.

The IOC did not drop its testing protocols; it remained steadfast in its assertion that this was the right way to ensure fair competition, and 'remov[e] scandal and innuendo from international sport' (Ferguson-Smith and Ferris, 1991, p.20). By 1991 official objections to the IOC's testing regime had been issued by the American Medical Association, American College of Physicians, ACP Division of Internal Medicine, American College of Obstetrics and Gynaecology, the Endocrine Society, the American Society of Human Genetics, the genetic societies of Canada and Australia, and many other organisations. In 1992 the IOC switched from tests for chromosomal sex to tests for genetic sex. A new sex test was introduced, looking for two specific regions of DNA usually found in the SDR on the Y chromosome. Although this test used cutting-edge research, rather than something a decade old (as had been the case for the Barr Body test), it still did not give the precision and the objective answers the IOC needed; all eight women who 'failed' the test at Atlanta in 1996 were reinstated after a physical examination. Finally, under increasing pressure from scientists and other lobby groups, the IOC announced in 1999 that it would no longer routinely test for sex at the Olympic Games.

Of course, sports organisations — including the IOC and IAAF — have reserved the right to insist on sex testing for athletes if specific accusations are made, or suspicions raised about their 'true' sex. Despite the growing scientific evidence that gender and sex are multifaceted and graduated identities, not binaries, and despite growing social acceptance of transgender and intersex identities, sport still functions on a principle of binary, simple, sexual identity. It is hardly surprising that biomedicine failed to provide an adequate testing regime; not only was there no consensus on which 'sort' of sex (genetic, nuclear, chromosomal, phenotypical, hormonal, genital, psychological) really mattered, but the IOC and other sports organisations also had competing aims for sex testing.

On the one hand the IOC and others talked about the need to ensure fairness in competition; an ethically complicated aim, given that competitive sport itself depends upon inherent differences between athlete's abilities. The need to divide into gender categories was a social need, not a sporting or scientific one – tests were not introduced for any other hormonal, physiological or genetic sporting advantage, and we do not segregate by height, race or possession of any of dozens of gene variants which have significant impacts on peoples' potential performance. On the other hand, a great deal of concern was also expressed about the need to protect female athletes from public criticism or negative evaluations of their physical appearance. It is quite clear that no testing regime has solved the problem that the successful athletic body often does not neatly match contemporary Western cultural ideals of femininity. Attempts to rely on scientific authority to 'prove' an athlete's 'true' sex, regardless of appearance, have failed. If anything, the current system emphasises this clash of goals; selective gender testing, that is, testing only of 'suspicious'-looking athletes, can only act to reinforce a hegemonic vision of acceptable, heterosexually attractive, female appearances.

> It comes into everybody's mind . . . that when a woman takes advantage of her size and her body build in sports and gets national recognition, she must be more of a man than a woman.
>
> *(Larned, 1976, p.41)*

Notes

1 Phenotypical. An organism's phenotype is the sum of its observable characteristics, physical and behavioural. This is used in contrast to its 'genotype' which is simply the genetic code of the organism which does not include the possible effects of environment, variations in the process of development, etc.

2 Heterochromatin. Chromatin is the collective name for the material that forms chromosomes, consisting of DNA and associated proteins. It can come in two forms, euchromatin which is the most common, and the more unusual heterochromatin which is particularly dense.

3 Meiosis. Meiosis is the term given to the first cell division after conception. Unlike normal cell division (mitosis), in meiosis the chromosomes – one set from each parent – exchange genetic material. This 'shuffling' process ensures that children are not clones of their parents, and maintains genetic diversity in a population.

References

Abraham, F (1931) Genitalumwandlung an zwei männlichen Transvestiten. *Zeitschrift Für Sexualwissenschaft und Sexualpolitik.* 18: 223–226.

Anon (1960) Olympic Women 'have medical certificates'. *Times* (London) 22 Aug: 4.

Anon (1967) Girl athlete to have new sex tests. *Daily Mirror* (London) 20 Sept: 6.

Anon (1970) Minutes of the Executive Committee of the BAS(E)M, 7 Mar. Wellcome Library Archives, SA/BSM.

Barr ML and Bertram EG (1949) A morphological distinction between neurones of the male and female, and the behaviour of the nucleolar satellite during accelerated nucleoprotein synthesis. *Nature* 163: 676–677.

Berlioux, M (1967) Feminity [sic]. *Olympic Review*. 3: 1–2.

Davis LR and Delano LC (1992) Fixing the boundaries of physical gender: Side effects of anti-drug campaigns on athletics. *Sociology of Sport Journal* 9: 1–19.

Eyquem MT (1961) Women sports and the Olympic games. *Bulletin du Comite International Olympique* 73: 48–50.

Fausto-Sterling A (1992) *Myths of Gender: Biological Theories about Men and Women*. New York: Basic Books.

Ferguson-Smith MA and Ferris EA (1991) Gender verification in sport: The need for change. *British Journal of Sports Medicine* 25: 17–20.

Hargreaves J (1994) *Sporting Females: Critical Issues in the History and Sociology of Women's Sport*. London: Routledge.

Heggie V (2010) Testing sex and gender in sports; reinventing, reimagining and reconstructing histories. *Endeavour* 34: 157–163.

Heggie V (2011) *A History of British Sports Medicine*. Manchester: Manchester University Press.

Larned D (1976) The femininity test: A woman's first Olympic hurdle. *Womensports* 3: 8–11 and 41.

Meyerowitz J (1998) Sex change and the popular press: Historical notes on transsexuality in the United States, 1930-1955. *GLQ: A Journal of Lesbian and Gay Studies* 4: 159–187.

Meyerowitz J (2002) *How Sex Changed: A History of Transsexuality in the United States*. Cambridge, MA: Harvard University Press.

Moore K (1968) The sexual identity of athletes. *Journal of the American Medical Association* 205: 787–788.

Moore KL et al. (1953) The detection of chromosomal sex in hermaphrodites from a skin biopsy. *Surgery, Gynecology and Obstetrics* 96: 641–648.

Patino MM (2005) A woman tried and tested. *Lancet* 366s: 38–39.

Shackleton C (2008) Steroid analysis and doping control 1960-1980. *Steroids* 74: 288–295.

Thiebault (1967) Medical Commission of the International Olympic Committee Reports. IOC Historical Archives, Olympic Studies Centre, Lausanne.

Wrynn A (2004) The human factor: Science, medicine and the International Olympic Committee, 1900–70. *Sport in Society* 7: 211–231.

37

AFFECTIVE FORMS

Neuroscience, gender, and sport

Leslie Heywood

Introduction

In her book, *Time Travels: Feminism, Nature, Power*, Elizabeth Grosz (2005) wrote:

> I believe that it is time to move beyond the very language of identity and gender, to look at other issues left untouched, questions unasked, assumptions unelaborated . . .to [look to] messy biology, matter, materiality . . . force, energy, affect.

Although I take issue with the language of "moving beyond" above, feminist philosopher Elizabeth Grosz nonetheless points to a problem that has come to characterize much work coming out of the humanities and many of the social sciences. The twentieth-century dedication to cultural analysis in these academic areas produced nuanced work on categories like identity and questions of agency as they related to self-construction in particular historical locations, as these are inflected by the intersectionality of many variables: gender, race, ethnicity, class, and, most recently, positionality within a globalized world. Social constructionism asked how objects of consciousness develop in these social contexts, exploring the constitutive role of language and the defining role of ideology as a mechanism of power. As part of a turn away from biological essentialism, in some contexts biology itself came to be seen as a non-signifying category, the "raw matter" cultures shaped to their particular ends.

Technological developments in the twenty-first century, however, such as functional magnetic resonance imaging (fMRI) devices in the field of neuroscience have brought biophysiological characteristics back into focus, but with a different emphasis (Panksepp 1998; Damasio 2005). Instead of essentialism, evolutionary theory has shifted to incorporate what are termed interactionist, co-evolutionary, or biocultural models. There has been a marked turn away from the kind of genetic determinism associated with the "selfish gene" theory (Dawkins 1976) to the frameworks of epigenetics, evolutionary development, and dual inheritance theory often subsumed under the name of the "Extended Synthesis" that emphasize the interaction effects between biology and culture, genes and environment (Jablonka & Lamb 2005; Pigliucci & Muller 2010). In this sense, interactionist research is doing the kind of work Grosz (2005) calls for, focused on "messy biology, matter . . . affect," and because it is focused on this, can forget the social dimension. Those of us who have been trained in social constructivist models—and this includes many working in gender and sport studies—need to keep insisting on the performative, culturally constituted aspects of gender while simultaneously taking biophysi-ological models into consideration in an interrelational frame—or what psychologist Cordelia Fine (2010) has termed the new "neurosexism" may come to define contemporary (essentialist) ideas about gender.

So what *can* recent research on the brain—especially that from affective neuroscience—give us for a non-essentialist perspective on gender and sport? In order to establish the utility of this research, Knoppers' and McDonald's (2010) account of the "levels of analysis" concept in sport research is useful: "we apply the concept 'levels of analysis' that has been used in other feminist reviews regarding the changing state of scholarship about gender and sport. These scholars conceptualized gender at three levels: individual/categorical, institutional/dis-tributive, and symbolic/ideological/relational" (Knoppers & McDonald 2010, p. 312). In this account, the individual level of analysis was an early stage that assumed innate gender differ-ence and used quantitative methodologies to study those "differences." Institutional/distribu-tive research was more concerned with structural inequality in terms of opportunity: differen-tial access to resources such as athletic sponsorships, media coverage, sport participation, and jobs within sport industries. Symbolic/ideological/relational research looks at the social and historical production of sport as a function of power relations that are intersectional, involving multiple positionalities inflected by sexuality, gender, race, class, ethnicity, and other vari-ables, a "(re)imagining of gender within a matrix of social relations" (Knoppers & McDonald 2010, p. 318). This account shows how sport sociology has tended to focus on the large, macro-level, culturally-derived aspects of sport such as economics, the ways sport contributes to nationalistic ideologies, and the intersectional politics of gender. On the other hand, more physiologically oriented disciplines such as sport psychology and kinesiology have tended to focus on the micro-level aspects of clinical psychology and performance enhancement for the individual athlete. Each of these models cannot fully account for embodied experience, particularly an embodied theory of the emotions as they contribute to sport. A neuroscientific perspective on the emotions can provide an account of embodiment, and the way biological mechanisms are shaped by and shape cultural formulations that impact a gendered experience of sport.

Affective neuroscience: an alternative model of embodiment

Over the years there have been many calls to "bring the body back in" to sport studies via a focus on embodiment. In *Embodied Sporting Practices*, for instance, Kath Woodward (2009) shows how a feminist analysis of sport can provide a model in which bodies are "embodied" and "enfleshed," with the lens of sport providing a site for the exploration of such "enfleshment." Other approaches to embodiment utilize the perspective of phenomenology (Allen-Collinson 2009), in particular the existential phenomenology of Merleau-Ponty, a French philosopher who emphasized the body as the primary site of knowing the world. Although Merleau-Ponty's work was, among other things, a critique of positivism, his work has recently been utilized in neurophysiological accounts of cognition (Varela, Thompson & Rosch 1991). Using neuro-scientific work that focuses on the primary process mechanisms associated with pre-cognitive affect (the experience of emotion in response to stimuli), I will develop an alternative theory of embodiment in relation to sport practice and the ways forms of practice (models of sport) have historically been gendered.

Jaak Panksepp, a neuroscientist, psychologist, and psychobiologist, founded the field of affec-tive neuroscience, which studies the neural mechanisms of emotion, and claims that "all basic psychological processes are thoroughly dependent on brain biophysical processes, working in concert with body, environment, and culture" (Panksepp 2008, p. 59). Much of the cultur-ally-based work done in sport studies might be profitably supplemented by attention to neural mechanisms in conjunction with the normative objects of study. Panksepp's work shows how affective primary processes, which influence behavior and action, influence secondary-process cognition and behavior that is associated with memory and cultural learning. Panksepp (2010) terms the relationship between primary and secondary process the "BrainMind," which, he says,

> has to be envisioned as an evolutionarily layered organ system, with all higher devel-opments still anchored to the lower primary processes of the brain . . . The original foundations of mind remain critically important for the ability of higher processes to function.
>
> *(Panksepp 2010, p. 263)*

Panksepp (1998) identifies seven core emotional systems that provide a neurobiology of affect: SEEKING, RAGE, FEAR, LUST, CARE, PANIC, and PLAY. The systems most relevant to affect in sport are SEEKING, RAGE, and PLAY (Panksepp uses all caps to designate the primary process nature of these systems). The SEEKING system is the appetitive motivational system that "energizes engagement with the world as individuals seek goods from the environ-ment as well as meaning in everyday life" (Panksepp 2009, p. 9), and is a generalized substrate for all other emotional processes. It is located in the hypothalmus and the mesolimbic dopamine system arising from the ventral tegmental area (VTA), and extends through the lateral hypoth-almus to the ventral striatal nuclei, in particular the nucleus accumbens, olfactory tubercle, and further up to medial cortical regions (Panksepp 2009).

The "RAGE" system's expression can be linked to feelings of empowerment and assertion-activation based in a perception (real or imagined) of threat in an organism's environment. It is located in the corticomedial areas of the amygdala and descends to the medial hypothalamus via the stria terminalus, and is linked to the FEAR/PANIC system. The RAGE system is acti-vated in response to threat, and evolutionarily speaking, being held immobile as prey (Panksepp 2000).

The third system most relevant to sport is the "PLAY" system. It is located within medial zones of the thalamus, and provides a safe context for young (human and non-human) animals to learn what they can or cannot do to each other. It can provide a physical engagement with others that is experienced as joyous, with therapeutic indications for adults, whose play urges can be re-energized by bodily activities such as dance or sport (Panksepp 2009). The PLAY system has effects on the cortex, facilitating social development (Panksepp 1998; 2000). An important function of sport is therefore to help the brain become socially oriented. Panksepp (2010) writes that "play is one of the major ways that the complex social brain emerges from the experiences of living within various ecological and cultural constraints" (p. 268). For Panksepp, particular experiences in interaction with primary process urges such as play catalyze secondary process functions. All of the primary process affective systems help to provide an alternative frame-work for understanding embodiment, linking our deep evolutionary histories and physiological responses with the cultural factors of our specifically contextualized environments.

"Neurosexism": gender and play in evolutionary accounts

Panksepp's work on play does not fall into the gender essentialism in biologically based research areas that ignore contextual factors. While "rough and tumble play" has often been posited as "naturally" more characteristic of boys, feminist theories of embodiment have persuasively shown how historically, girls' physicality is inhibited while boys' is encouraged (Young 1990; Whitson 1994). Models from evolutionary psychology, for instance, tend to ignore these social factors, despite claiming to utilize an interactionist framework. For instance, in a paper that claims a framework in which "sex differentials emerge from an interaction of characteristics shaped by sexual selection and environmental conditions of development," Daniel Kruger and Carey Fitzgerald state that

> rough and tumble play is three to six times more frequent in boys than girls, consisting of chasing, capturing, wrestling, and restraining. This form of play appears to be a mechanism for establishing social dominance, something boys consider more important than girls do.
>
> *(Kruger & Fitzgerald 2011, pp. 9, 16)*

Yet there is no consideration of "environmental conditions of development" anywhere in the paper, and parental investment theory (the idea that women invest much more in offspring than men do because female reproduction is more "metabolically costly") is utilized as a default explanation for the gender differences the paper asserts.

Gendered discussions of play often proceed this way. Evolutionary psychologist Peter La Freniere, for instance, argues

> the organizing effects of hormones secreted during prenatal development shape sex differences in both brain structures and social behavior, particularly in play. These steroids help direct the organization and wiring of the brain during development, and they influence the structure and neuronal density of various regions. Several researchers have reported sex differences in a variety of brain structures, including the amygdala and hypothalamus, both of which are involved in play behavior. These two parts of the brain appear to be implicated in gender-differentiated patterns of rough-and-tumble play.
>
> *(LaFreniere 2011 p. 476)*

LaFreniere's formulations point to reasons why sport studies has tended to be critical of physiological explanations—here fetal hormones would seem to "organize" sex differences that result in boys being more physically active than girls, an explanation that more than fifty years worth of feminist research on sport can easily discredit.

Such explanations, however, seem to be having their historical moment, particularly in relation to the cultural authority granted to work in neuroscience. Psychologist Cordelia Fine writes:

> Neuroscience is used . . . to reinforce, with all the authority of science, old-fashioned stereotypes and roles . . . Gender stereotypes are legitimated by these pseudo-scientific explanations. Suddenly, one is being modern and scientific, rather than old-fashioned and sexist.
>
> *(Fine 2010, pp. 237, 172)*

Fine (2010) calls this kind of research "neurosexism," and discusses why it has gained popularity: "There's something special about neuroscientific information. It sounds so unassailable, so very . . . well, *scientific*, that we privilege it over boring, old-fashioned behavior evidence"

(p. 168). Popular neuroscientific theories about sexual dimorphism in the brain, usually said to be caused by fetal testosterone, are linked to gender dimorphism in behavior (boys are better at math, boys and men are more active "risk-takers"). Feminists who criticize this are said to be hostile to science:

> In the interminable sex differences debate it always seems to be those who are critical of scientific claims of essential differences who are accused of allowing political desires to blinker them to the facts of the case . . . When criticisms are dismissed as "political"—to be contrasted with one's own, value-free scientific judgment—we learn nothing about the quality of the scientific evidence [or] the hidden work of political values in the scientific debate.
>
> *(Fine 2011)*

Evolutionary analysis, then, can be used to confirm the very stereotypes that feminist sport studies have denaturalized, but it need not be. Panksepp's work, for instance, cannot be characterized as "neurosexist" in the same ways, as he emphasizes that difference doesn't necessarily correspond to morphology. In the case of the impact of fetal testosterone on development, Panksepp writes that

> we now understand why intrinsic gender identity and body morphology do not always match up. . . humans . . . can have female-type brains in male-type bodies (if DHT [dihydrotestosterone] was present in sufficient quantities but estrogen was not) or male-type brains in female-type bodies (where estrogen was present but DHT was not).
>
> *(Panksepp 1998, p. 234)*

His own studies of rough and tumble play in children did not replicate the gender essentialism seen in LaFreniere: "The major findings show only modest gender differences . . . the main difference is that boys engaged in slightly more physical play solicitations than girls" (Panksepp & Scott 2003). When differences are found in the ways boys and girls play, feminist theories of embodiment can account for them through structural explanations: "how differently the childhoods of girls and boys come to be structured: by discourses of femininity and masculinity and by gendered practices of play that teach us to inhabit and experience our bodies in profoundly different ways" (Whitson 1994, p. 353). I will argue that work in the neurosciences such as Panksepp's, if examined in conjunction with this kind of culturally-related work in feminist sport studies, can provide a fuller model of sport and athletic experience than those which are solely physiologically or culturally based.

Models of sport where core emotional systems manifest

The alternative framework for embodiment offered by affective neuroscience has particular applications to the study of sport. Historically, there have been two primary models or modalities of sport, the competitive and the participatory. The competitive model has explicit goals and quantifiable achievements, and is philosophically aligned with a mechanistic instrumentality expressed in the carefully structured, goal-directed use of time: the sport is useful for something, a means to an end. Sport practiced competitively is therefore an instrumental activity with use value, and might be psychologically linked to a sense of threat—having to overcome something in one's environment. Sport practiced in this modality most engages the SEEKING/RAGE systems. In contemporary terms, the competitive model has stood as the dominant cultural definition of "sport" in the developed world, even though those who "prefer to play for fun" represent the majority demographically speaking. In distinction, the participatory model implements a non-instrumental modality based in play, and is practiced in the context of a sense of safety within one's group or individually. In the participatory model, there are no threats to an individual's status, whereas in the competitive model, status within a prestige hierarchy is always at stake. In the participatory mode, sport is a non-instrumental activity done for itself, not as a means to a goal/end. The participatory model has residual contemporary status in concepts like recreational sports leagues or "fun runs." It is directly aligned with what Panksepp defines as the PLAY system, but it is also, like the other systems, is activated by the SEEKING system.

Gender in the competitive and participatory models of sport

According to sports historian Susan K. Cahn, beginning with the professionalization of physical education at the turn of the twentieth century in the U.S., women's physical educators began to advocate for a "participatory" model of their own, in direct contrast to the male-defined competitive model. "Participatory" sport should center around the concepts of democracy, equal access, and sport for the sake of play, not winning (Cahn 1994). This countered what women's physical educators saw as problems with the competitive model in that the competitive model was seen to subordinate values such as sportsmanship (consideration and respect for others), loyalty, and health to a "win at all costs" mentality. Jennifer Hargreaves (1994) notes that the Women's Division of the American Amateur Athletic Federation planned an alternative festival to the Olympics in 1932 that emphasized "'play for play's sake', in direct contrast to the stress and over-specialization associated with individual sporting accomplishment" (p. 215).

The competitive model was seen to over-value ability to a degree that excluded the majority of sport participants, who weren't particularly talented at sports and who enjoyed movement for movement's sake, "playing for fun." Women's intercollegiate physical educators organized "Play Days" in colleges in the U.S. starting in the 1920s to promote this philosophy, but the development of competitive varsity programs occurred simultaneously (Hult 1994). In these ways, the competitive model was seen to inculcate masculine values, and the participatory model was based on a "feminine" alternative, but many female athletes wanted to seriously compete and not have their options limited (Cahn 1994). A more recent example of the distinction between sport as practiced in competitive and participatory modes is provided by the sport of surfing, which is often split into those who participate for the pure joy of surfing ("soul" surfing) and those who compete to win surfing contests and showcase their prowess and mastery of the waves (Heywood & Montgomery 2008). Feminist alternatives to mainstream competitive sport are also particularly visible in women's softball leagues, which promoted an "anti-rationalist view of sport" that emphasized enjoying the process of play over winning (Birrell & Richter 1994).

A third model: sport as immersive practice

A third model of sport, what I am calling the immersive, combines elements of the competitive and participatory (Heywood, 2006; Heywood and Montgomery, 2008; Whitson 1994, p. 354). It is critical of the competitive model, but asserts that competition provides a number of positive effects, from in-group bonding to the empowerment of disenfranchised individuals or groups. In terms of gender, the immersive model is based on the idea of sport on a gender continuum, with some men excelling less at sports than some women and some women excelling more than some men at particular kinds of sports, with some men embracing participatory values and some women competitive ones (Kane 1995). Sport formulated as exclusively competitive or partici-patory excludes some of the core affective systems or forces the suppression of one to facilitate the other. The immersive model accounts for more of our core motivations, and how these inform sport participation. It also allows for a wider expression of gender variability—men who want to "just play," women who want to fiercely compete, and everything in between.

A key feature of this model is focused attention, the same kind of absorption seen by a hunter stalking prey or in a parent caring for an infant. The athlete experiences a sense of being "out of time," and is so focussed on the movement of the body in the moment that all other considera-tions fall away. This resembles what Mihali Csíkszentmihályi (1990) discusses as "flow" or peak experience, a completely focussed motivation, single-minded immersion in the activity itself. The immersive model, including the experience of flow, can contain elements of the competi-tive model as well as participatory, but the key determinant is that the activity is performed in the context of safety, not threat/humiliation. As we will see, it is around the question of safety that an athlete's social and familial contexts become crucial.

Informing the "immersive sport" model: Polyvagal Theory and the evolutionary question of safety

In order to understand how sport in the immersive model is experienced physiologically, Pank-sepp's work on the subcortical regions of the central nervous system (CNS) needs to be extended to the autonomic nervous system (ANS). The work of Stephen W. Porges, a neuroscientist specializing in psychophysiology, performs this extension. Porges's "Polyvagal Theory" argues that an individual's ANS response to environmental challenges follows a phylogenetic hierarchy facilitated by "neuroception"—"a neural process, distinct from perception, that is capable of distinguishing environmental (and visceral) features that are safe, dangerous, or life-threatening" (Porges 2009, p. 45). We react to real-world, environmental challenges with three neural cir-cuits, in this order: 1) the evolutionarily newest system, the Social Engagement System (SES), a parasympathetic neural circuit that is expressed in the newer myelinated vagus nerve (ventral vagal complex) that promotes pro-social behavior and helps maintain calm behavioral states. 2) If we evaluate an environment/situation as threatening, we react spontaneously with the older, sympathetic nervous system that supports fight/flight behaviors. This system mediates between the two vagal circuits. 3) If fight/flight fails, and we perceive ourselves to be in life-threaten-ing conditions, we resort to the oldest vagal circuit, a parasympathetic circuit expressed in the older, unmyelinated vagus nerve that inhibits motion and is linked to disassociation in response to trauma—playing dead, and having the sensation of floating out of your body (Porges 2009; 2011).

Polyvagal Theory has important applications to the various models of sport. If the practice of sport harkens back to our evolutionary heritage as both predators and prey, immersive sport can only be practised in a context of safety in which there are no direct needs/threats operational at the time. The competitive model is more linked to competing for resources in a context of scarcity—we compete because there is an environmental need to get resources/establish dominance, and is therefore linked to what Porges formulates as the second-level, flight/fight response: one's identity/position are under threat. Athletic dominance contains that threat, so this response provides powerful motivation to act.

By contrast, the participatory model of sport is linked to the first-level response of the SES, and the motivation is the activity itself practiced in a safe context. There is no need to "prove" oneself: acceptance is assumed, and the pro-social behaviour of others cues the individual that the environment is safe. This is also where an individual athlete's particular social and familial contexts become important to their ability to perform. Negative experiences like war or domestic violence, or suffering stigmas associated with socially-devalued group identities, can disrupt an athlete's affective balance long-term, thereby unsettling their ability to dampen their flight/fight response (Panksepp 2009; Porges 2009; 2011). This in turn blocks their ability to reach higher levels of performance. Similarly, Panksepp's conceptualization of "joyous" PLAY is only possible in the context of this kind of first-level response to one's environment—a context of safety where sport isn't practiced as humiliation and ridicule as it can sometimes be in the competitive model.

Toward a cultural neuropsychology of immersive sport

Polyvagal Theory and the seven core primary process affective systems, then, provide a neurophysiological basis for understanding the different sport modalities. The competitive model of sport engages the SEEKING and RAGE systems, provoking a neuroception of danger, and thereby a fight/flight response that has the extrinsic motivation of overcoming the threat of competitors through dominating them athletically. By contrast, the participatory model of sport engages the SEEKING and PLAY systems, triggering a neuroception of safety that facilitates a state of calm engagement and has the intrinsic motivation of participating in the activity itself, rather than overcoming rivals. While the competitive model has traditionally been associated with men's sports and values and the participatory with women's, today many women are involved in competitive sport while many men participate more recreationally. Furthermore, in the contemporary networked world of a globalized economy, the pro-social values of the participatory model seem to be gaining social status.

What I am calling a cultural neuropsychology of sport would then incorporate the context of cultural support for or against sport (resistance to women's sports in certain countries; lack of infrastructure in underdeveloped countries; opportunities to play/receive training in developed countries—inflected by sexuality, race, gender, class, ability, etc.—all of which would induce a neuroception of threat rather than safety). Within these broader contexts, a cultural neuropsychology of sport would also examine psychological dimensions such as an individual athlete's environment and cultural/familial context, including issues such as individual trauma response (informed by disrupted neuroception) and personality differences.

To return to the "levels of analysis" concept referenced by Knoppers and McDonald (2010), the model of embodiment I am proposing would link the individual, structural, and symbolic levels in an indissociable relation with a body's affective experience. While the basic physiological substrates of that experience are the same across bodies, a particular body's intersectional positioning catalyzes affect, and produces the particular behavioral responses that are then manifested and regulated in sport. To succeed at the highest levels, or to experience sport as enjoyable, an athlete can't be worried about jockeying for position—the fight response has to be calmed.

This model of embodiment has important implications for the feminist "anti-rationalist" challenges to the competitive model of sport (Birrell & Richter 1994). For the ANS to respond in more positive ways, and for the SEEKING and PLAY systems to engage more than the RAGE system, pro-social behaviour among athletes should be encouraged more than it currently is within many athletic cultures in the developed world. Starting with youth sports, coaches and media should reinvigorate the ideal of "sportsmanship" and give it real weight. Play should be encouraged more than mechanized learning and competition (and parents should be encouraged to emphasize these aspects as well). Currently, many people don't participate in sports because the competitive model makes them uncomfortable, and the calls to increase sport participation in order to achieve public health goals could be facilitated by more emphasis on pro-sociality. The evolutionary perspective supplements feminist work on the reformation of sport, providing additional reasons why the purely results-focused, "win-at-all-costs" coaching model should be replaced by a model that creates a context of safety and cohesion that triggers each athletes' SES, thereby facilitating better performance and experience on all levels, whether competitive or participatory.

References

Allen-Collinson, J (2009) Sporting embodiment: sports studies and the (continuing) promise of phenomenology. *Qualitative Research in Sport and Exercise* 1(3): 279–296.

Birrell, S & Richter, D (1994) Is a diamond forever?: feminist transformations of sport. In Birrell, S & Cole, CL (eds) *Women, Sport, and Culture*. Champaign, IL: Human Kinetics Press, pp. 221–244.

Cahn, SK (1994) *Coming on Strong: Gender and Sexuality in Twentieth Century Women's Sport*. Cambridge, MA: Harvard University Press.

Csíkszentmihályi, M (1990) *Flow: The Psychology of Optimal Experience*. New York: Harper.

Damasio, A (2005) *Descartes' Error: Emotion, Reason, and the Human Brain*. New York: Penguin.

Dawkins, R (1976) *The Selfish Gene*. New York: Oxford University Press.

Fine, C (2010) *Delusions of Gender: How Our Minds, Society, and Neurosexism Create Difference*. New York: Norton.

Fine, C (2011) Let's say goodbye to the straw feminist blogs.plos.org/2011/02/11/lets-say-goodbye-to-the-straw-feminist/

Grosz, E (2005) *Time Travels: Feminism, Nature, Power*. Durham, NC: Duke University Press.

Hargreaves, J (1994) *Sporting Females: Critical Issues in the History and Sociology of Women's Sports*. London: Routledge.

Heywood, L (2006) Immanence, transcendance, and immersive practices: female athletes in U.S. neoliberalism. In Glenney, GE & Jakobsen, J (eds) *The Scholar and the Feminist Online*, Vol 4, no.3, http://barnard.edu/sfonline/sport/heywood_01.htm

Heywood, L & Montgomery, M (2008) Ambassadors of the last wilderness?: surfers, environmental ethics, and activism in America. In Atkinson, M & Young, K (eds) *Tribal Play: Subcultural Journeys Through Sport*. London: Emerald Group Publishing, pp.153–172.

Hult, J (1994) The story of women's athletics. In Costa DM & Guthrie SR (eds) *Women in Sport: Interdisciplinary Perspectives*. Champaign, IL: Human Kinetics, pp. 83–106.

Jablonka, E & Lamb, M (2005) *Evolution in Four Dimensions: Genetic, Epigenetic, Behavioral, and Symbolic Variation in the History of Life*. Cambridge, MA: MIT Press.

Kane, M (1995) Resistance/transformation of the oppositional binary: exposing sport as a continuum. *Journal of Sport & Social Issues* 19: 191–218.

Knoppers, A & McDonald, M (2010) Scholarship on gender and sport in *Sex Roles* and beyond. *Sex Roles* 63, 311–323.

Kruger, D & Fitzgerald, C (2011) Understanding sex differences in human mortality rates through Tinbergen's four questions. *Human Ethology Bulletin* 26(2), 8–24.

LaFreniere, P (2011) Evolutionary functions of social play: life histories, sex differences, and emotion regulation. *American Journal of Play* 3(4), 464–488.

Panksepp, J (1998) *Affective Neuroscience: The Foundations of Human and Animal Emotions*. New York: Oxford University Press.

Panksepp, J (2000). The neuro-evolutionary cusp between emotions and cognitions: implications for understanding consciousness and the emergence of a unified mind science. *Consciousness and Emotion* 1(1), 15–54.

Panksepp, J (2008) The affective brain and core consciousness: how does neural activity generate emotional feelings? In Lewis, M, Haviland-Jones, J and Feldman Barrett, L (eds) *Handbook of Emotions*. New York: The Guilford Press, pp. 47–67.

Panksepp, J (2009) Brain emotional systems and qualities of mental life. In Fosha, D Siegel, D and Solomon, M (eds) *The Healing Power of Emotions: Affective Neuroscience, Development, and Clinical Practice*. New York: Norton, pp. 1–26.

Panksepp, J (2010) Science of the brain as a gateway to understanding play: an interview with Jaak Panksepp. *American Journal of Play* 2(3), 245–277.

Panksepp, J & Scott, E (2003) Rough and tumble play in human children. *Aggressive Behavior* 29(6), 539–551.

Pigliucci, M & Muller G (eds) (2010). *Evolution: The Extended Synthesis*, Cambridge, MA: MIT Press.

Porges, S (2009) Reciprocal influences between body and brain in the perception and expression of affect. In Fosha, D Siegel, D and Solomon, M (eds) *The Healing Power of Emotions: Affective Neuroscience, Development, and Clinical Practice*, New York: Norton, pp. 27–54.

Porges, S (2011) *The Polyvagal Theory: Neurophysiological Foundation of Emotions, Attachment, Communication, and Self-Regulation*. New York: Norton.

Varela, FJ, Thompson, E and Rosch, E (1991) *The Embodied Mind: Cognitive Science and Human Experience*. Cambridge, MA: MIT Press.

Whitson, D (1994) The embodiment of gender: discipline, domination, and empowerment. In Birell, S & Cole, C (eds) *Women, Sport, and Culture*, Champaign, IL: Human Kinetics Press, pp. 353–371.

Woodward, K (2009) *Embodied Sporting Practices: Regulating and Regulatory Bodies*. New York: Palgrave.

Young, IM (1990) *Throwing Like a Girl and Other Essays in Feminist Philosophy and Social Theory*. Bloomington, IN: University of Indiana Press.

38

QUEER GENES?

The Bio-Amazons project: a response to critics

Claudio Tamburrini

In modern societies, sexual segregation is rejected in most areas of social life. Within sports, however, this practice is seldom questioned, not even by radical feminists.[1]

Together with Tännsjö, I have elsewhere pleaded for eliminating sexual segregation in (elite) sports competitions (Tamburrini and Tännsjö, 2005) so that women and men could compete against each another on equal terms in sport arenas. How could this be achieved? Roughly, the strategy that we favoured was offering women the possibility to genetically modify their physical constitution in order to become as strong as men. The resultant irruption of Bio-Amazons, if such a project ever became scientifically viable, would be desirable as a step towards substantial equality of opportunities in sports. In general, female athletes do not attain equal fame and fortune as male athletes do in professional elite sport. The reason is simple: elite sport is a male-biased activity. Physical attributes historically monopolised by males – strength, muscle volume, speed and height – are much more valued in the sport market than typically female physical traits as balance, rhythm and resistance. This fact renders a situation of sex inequality in elite sports, as women athletes in general get less economic rewards and social recognition than sportsmen.

The traditional (sport) feminist answer to gender inequalities is to keep sex segregation in sports and increase women athletes' share of prizes and rewards (English, 1978). In my view, this is not a rational strategy. First, it would perpetuate the division between male and female sport gender stereotypes and might contribute to cement male chauvinism and power. Second, to increase female athletes' revenues could be perceived by the public as unwarranted positive discrimination. Equal rewards would be overwhelmingly hard to sustain in a situation in which male sport performances are most valued by the market. Instead, we affirmed in our article "the need for women to conquer powerful spaces in male, well-paid sports, not by imposed benefits redistribution, but instead, if necessary, through genetically adapting their physique to market requirements" (Tamburrini and Tännsjö, 2005, p. 183). By offering women the possibility to catch up with men in the most rewarded and popular sports, the Bio-Amazons project might also be expected to generate more appealing female role models for present and future generations of boys and girls, who would experience that women can become physically equally strong, or even stronger, than men.

A discussion on the potential for Bio-Amazons is increasingly necessary as science, particularly sports medicine, is advancing so fast that the prospect of genetically (or by other means) transforming sex-related physiological traits in athletes might become a reality in a relatively near future. Without repeating all the arguments Tännsjö and I have already advanced in support of the Bio-Amazons project, I will present the main thrust of our proposal and then proceed to answer the critical reactions to its formulation.

(a) We started from the following assumption ("the conjecture"): "if, in a certain area, one sex is genetically disadvantaged, then, in this area, it is easier for the disadvantaged sex to catch up with the advantaged one, than it is for the more advantaged one to move further ahead. If this conjecture is borne by realities, it means that genetic enhancement is indeed a feasible means of levelling out differences" (Tamburrini and Tännsjö, 2005, p. 188).

Furthermore, we provided an answer to the most common objections to the Amazons project.

(b) Against the claim that such a programme would be too risky from a medical point of view, we argued that by the time the genetic modification of women athletes becomes a reality, genetic technology will have been so widely tested as to be relatively safe, at least as safe as any medical technique can be.
(c) Regarding the objection that the programme implies revisiting the Eastern European experiment with women athletes, we underlined that the association often made between genetic enhancement and racial or elitist eugenic programmes disregards the fact that, in the Bio-Amazons' world, it is the individual athletes themselves, not State or sport officials, who decide whether or not to undergo genetic empowerment.
(d) We also provided an answer to the criticism that genetic engineering of women athletes amounts to a misuse of medical expertise and resources, as these women are not sick but rather healthy individuals who wish to enhance their physical traits. In our view, a private, sponsor-supported genetic programme would not burden the State treasury.
(e) Finally, we met the objection that the Bio-Amazons would increase unfairness in competition by pointing out that, on the contrary, the genetic modification of women athletes will contribute to a fairer sport world in two senses: by allowing (at least some) women to compete on more equal terms with men and thereby attain rewards and benefits until now exclusively enjoyed by males, and by equalising competing conditions between them and other female athletes (recall the Caster Semenya case and intersex female athletes[2]) who, by the work of the genetic lottery, enjoy a more powerful physical condition.[3]

However, it turned out that this defence of the Bio-Amazons proposal was not enough. Further criticism against the project was raised and an intensive discussion started on biologically-induced (not culturally- promoted) gender equality in sports. In this article I will try to answer the objections to the Bio-Amazons project.

The best among their class?

In the anthology referred to above, Sherwin and Schwartz argue that the sport public are not merely interested in the most accomplished athletes ("the best male exemplars") but rather in the best athletes *among their class*. And for this ". . . separate competitions for men and women are legitimate, as they are for different age groups (and sometimes different weight classes), and for athletes with various types of disability (e.g., the Special Olympics)" (Sherwin and Schwartz, 2005, p. 200)

To begin with, Sherwin and Schwartz' objection is advanced as a factual statement but, to my knowledge, no empirical research has been conducted on the matter. My impression, however, is that their view rests not so much on what sport spectators actually do but instead on what Sherwin and Schwartz hope sport spectators do or what they think they should do. Their assumption that the sport public are not merely interested in the most accomplished athletes but rather in the best athletes *among their class* is most probably wrong. Our interest in the "local best" seems to rest on our interest – indeed, our uncritical admiration – for "the best, period".[4]

But there is another aspect of sex classes that shows even more clearly that Sherwin and Schwarz' argument does not hit the mark. Sex differences are different in the sense that, unlike age, weight and physical disabilities, they are only *indirectly* relevant for sport performance. If you are a heavy-weight boxer, then you automatically have a competitive advantage over a fly-weight. If you are a male boxer, however, you might or might not have an advantage over a female competitor: other things being equal (for instance, technical skills), that would ultimately depend on how the two physiques are constituted.

Furthermore, sex is also different in another, ethically and socially more interesting way. While separate competitions between people of different weight and age do not solidify social prejudices against the lower performing group, they certainly do regarding women. As a result of sex-segregated sport, *all* women are perceived as less powerful ("the weaker sex" was the term used in the past) and therefore separated in order to flourish.

Something similar appears to happen regarding the Paralympics. Segregating physically fully capable and disabled persons probably reinforces negative attitudes toward people with different types of disabilities. Thus, a corollary of our proposal for sex-integrated sport competitions is that the same policy should be advocated regarding disabled sports. I shall return to this issue later in the article.

The objection from male chauvinism

Our proposal has also been charged with being male chauvinistic. Simona Giordano and John Harris, for instance, write that, "Equality is compatible with both levelling down and levelling up. In order to abolish the distinction between male and female sports, we could make males weaker, rather than women stronger" (Giordano and Harris, 2005, pp. 210–211). Related to this, they also argue that the ideology expressed in our article:

> ... presupposes distinctively males attributes as the equivalent of "health" and "wholeness" in body. Many disabled groups reject the idea that the non-disabled embody a better paradigm of the good life. . . . The fact that they [Tamburrini and Tännsjö] suggest that women should be allowed (or encouraged?) to make genetic modifications to their body (rather than the other way around) shows that they are implicitly endorsing a male chauvinistic and sexist ideology.
>
> *(Ibid, p. 212)*

Also Sherwin and Schwartz seem to endorse this criticism when they maintain that equality should not be equated with sameness. According to them, in our proposal the "best" in sports is defined in terms of male talents. But to require women to become as men is to accept and reinforce this sexist bias. Instead, they advance the view that "Gender justice sometimes requires that men and women be treated differently precisely in order to ensure that they have equal opportunities" (Sherwin and Schwartz, 2005, p. 201). In a similar vein, Giordano and Harris (2005, p. 212) say that: ". . . the moral force of appeals to equality derives not from notions of equal competition or equal opportunity, but rather from the obligation to treat people with equal concern and respect".

So, there seems to be an overwhelming consensus among our critics regarding the sexist and male chauvinistic character of the Bio-Amazons proposal. I will attempt now to answer their criticism.

Are "levelling down" and "levelling up" morally equivalent?

To start with the most obvious defence against the charges above, that there is a morally relevant difference between levelling down and levelling up. While the proposal of allowing women to level up to men's level of performance would rest on a voluntary basis, the counter-proposal of levelling down male athletes' performance would obviously have to be implemented by force. How else would male athletes accept going through genetic modifications that would make them perform at lower levels? It was this difference, rather than a sexist bias, that made us favour increasing women's performance levels instead of decreasing men's. This is compatible with allowing male athletes who might wish to transform their genetic make-up with a view to developing physiological characteristics hitherto considered as typically female. But such a radical transformation of the sporting landscape should never be implemented by force.

Is being a woman a disability?

Here our critics might retort that there is an important moral objection to certain forms of "levelling up". Maybe raising the strength and level of performance of a fly-weight boxer would not incite social prejudices; but raising women and handicapped athletes to the level of performance of male, full physically-able sport practitioners certainly would do. According to Giordano and Harris, for instance, our proposal presupposes male attributes as equivalent to bodily "health" and "wholeness". But, they object, being a woman cannot qualify as being disabled! By encouraging women to transform their genome in order to acquire male physiological traits we would be sanctioning male standards as superior; and this means telling women that the only way to avoid being discriminated against is to become (at least as strong as) men. Fixing gender discrimination by means of genetics, Harris and Giordano tell us, would be exacerbating the problem as well as insulting to women and this "would be the equivalent of proposing a remedy for racism which involved a genetic alteration in skin pigmentation rather than a comprehensive assault on prejudice and unfair discrimination" (Giordano and Harris, 2005, p.216)

I do not think such a comparison is appropriate. A black person who undergoes treatment of whatever kind to get white skin ceases to be black and could be seen as assimilating to the standard values of a predominantly white society. But why should we consider that a woman who develops strong muscles ceases to be a woman or in any way renounces her female condition? Giordano and Harris seem to be equating being a female with having a physically inferior condition. Not only that, their sex essentialism renders the unpalatable consequence of depriving women of the right and the possibility of developing the kind of physique they desire: it is contradicted by facts. There are men who are (physically) weaker than the average female as well as women who are stronger than average male exemplars.

Giordano and Harris' argument appears, however, to be stronger when restricted exclusively to sports. If transforming the female physique is necessary to achieve men's level of performance, being a woman must be seen as a disability *in the context of sports*. Would that not be an insult to (sports)women?

In the context of sports, excepting a few disciplines which are best adapted to female physiology, I believe that being a woman is a disability. But, unlike Giordano and Harris, I see no insult in this recognition. Historically, sport disciplines were designed to measure typically male physical traits. Thus, most sportswomen are at a disadvantage in relation to most sportsmen, as they compete in disciplines which are better suited to the male physiology. In that regard, the most rewarding and popular sports are male-biased, and the best-performing athletes in absolute terms will almost always be a man. I feel that allowing women the possibility to reduce this performance gap through technology implies annulling the male bias that characterises the sport market in the most rewarding and popular sports.

This technological move might also be effective in speeding up the process of equalising competitive opportunities between the sexes. As we don't know how much of "the muscle gap" between the sexes depends on physiological factors, and how much of it originates in culture, we should be open to changes in the physiological status quo (even technologically-induced ones) with the potential to change the public's perception on men's and women's physical prowess.

Giordano and Harris also argue that the Bio-Amazons project seems to imply that we should extend the possibility of bodily transformation (either technologically or genetically) to the disabled or, alternatively, deny women athletes that possibility.

I am convinced that we should let both the disabled and women athletes do what they want with their bodies. As a matter of fact, they already do. In the Special Olympics, disabled athletes try, with the assistance of different technical devices and coping strategies, to overcome their physical handicap in order to achieve sport performances as near as possible to those of non-disabled athletes. And women resort to weightlifting in order to increase their muscle volume as part of their training programmes. Why should it be different regarding similar, though genetically-induced, enhancements?

The fact that both women and the disabled have always tried to emulate the performance standards of fully physically capable males in elite sports, speaks in favour of extending that possibility to both groups.

"The tyranny of the normal"

It could perhaps also be argued that allowing lower-performing individuals to modify themselves in order to get characteristics (physical, cognitive or other characteristics) that belong to the best-situated part of a population implies reinforcing "the tyranny of the normal" and that instead of showing respect for what all individuals do, by letting women become genetically modified we would be indirectly encouraging them to adopt male standards as a condition for admiring and rewarding their sport results. Again, this phenomenon is particularly evident in the disability debate. As it has been explicitly stated in the discussion on deafness culture, many disabled people refuse to emulate, sometimes even to adapt to, "normal" standards and demand instead to be recognised for what they are (Padden and Humphries, 1988)

I do not think that allowing disabled or female athletes to reach the levels of performance that hitherto have been achieved by male athletes would necessarily imply any form of disrespect for the lower performers. It is not a question of respect, but rather of securing equal opportunity for all participants in sport competitions. Male and female athletes will not be competing on equal terms in sports as long as we do not equalise men's and women's physiological standards. Respecting lower performances for the effort and sacrifice they no doubt demand should not be confused with considering them as equally good as the best ones. There is no logical incompatibility between showing respect for those who do not reach high standards and allowing them to improve their performances by the means they prefer. From this perspective, it becomes clear that Giordano and Harris are confusing "respect" with "equal value". In physically-demanding sports, we have reason to respect different levels of performance, but this does not mean that the lower ones should be considered as equally valuable. After all, we want sportspersons to reach higher and higher levels of performance. So, even if "respect" does not require equalising levels of performance, "equal opportunity" does. A notion of equality that had no bearing at all on fairness in competition would indeed be a rather empty one.

Fairness in competition

Contributing to fairer competitions is what Sherwin and Schwartz seem to have in mind when they propose treating men and women athletes differently. According to them, gender equality should not be interpreted in terms of making men and women equal, and we should try to abolish sexism in society and treat women athletes differently by giving them the same or more resources than we give men (Sherwin and Schwartz, 2005, p. 203).

Besides, according to Sherwin and Schwartz, there is also a further, global aspect of fairness in competition that might be negatively affected if the Bio-Amazons ever became a reality. They argue that genetic interventions aimed at transgressing biological sex-boundaries will probably be too expensive for the poor as well as for developing countries. Sponsorship, they say, is not a solution to this problem, as genetic alterations would be required before athletes gained recognition from the sport market. In their words:

> Legitimizing expensive interventions for the sake of reducing gender inequality is likely to exacerbate inequality due to income both nationally and internationally. Tamburrini and Tännsjö imply that athletes would pay for these genetic enhancements themselves, rather than relying on the State treasury. They see this as a fair suggestion since lucrative sports sponsorship allows athletes the luxury of paying for elite medical services. We submit that this proposal is confounding since the genetic alterations would likely occur before the athlete had gained international success and secured these sponsorships. . . . Currently, success in sports is regarded as a way out of poverty for some underprivileged children who see their poor background reflected in the history of some sports stars. If Tamburrini and Tännsjö's proposal were to become a reality, this avenue of hope may be closed, as successful athletes would increasingly come from families that could afford these expensive technologies. This problem would also be reflected internationally, where it would be unlikely that poor countries would continue to be able to enter athletes in international competition against genetic Amazons.

> *(Sherwin and Schwartz, 2005, pp. 201–202)*

This is a very impressive criticism. However, I believe it has less substance than seems to be the case at first sight. To begin with, why would we suppose that only the rich children will be genetically enhanced? Many offspring of the rich lack the necessary physical endowments required for a successful and meaningful genetic intervention. And, the other way around, why would we assume that no children of the have-nots would be properly supported by sponsors? Sherwin and Schwartz's criticism shows they are unaware of the fact that the sport market, and the enterprises acting in it, is becoming more and more aggressive in discovering young sport talents. Often we read of children/adolescents contracted by a football club for many years to come. No matter what we think and how we feel about talent-spotting, the current tendency of the sport market suggests the objection advanced by Sherwin and Schwartz can be neutralised at national and international level. There is no reason to suppose that sport agents' hunting of young talent will stop at the national boundaries.

Besides, even granting that the Bio-Amazons project might bring about some social inequality, it should be seen in light of the increases in *gender* equality it might contribute to. Perhaps Sherwin and Schwartz are right in that the rich man's offspring will get an unfair advantage over the children of the have-nots, but that unfair advantage will also favour the rich man's daughters to the detriment of, certainly both the sons and daughters of the poor, but also the rich man's sons. Why would it be wrong to trade-off some *social* inequality (related to different social groups' access to a sporting career) for more *gender* equality (that will probably have positive effects upon the whole social body and not only in the world of sports)?

In relation to fairness in competition, I wish to comment on how Sherwin and Schwartz believe we might come to terms with unequal distribution of the benefits and rewards of elite sports. They argue that "equality requires equal resources and equal opportunity, not the requirement to change one's genetic makeup to more closely approximate the physical advantages men have for particular sports" (Sherwin and Schwartz, 2005, pp. 203–204).

Sherwin and Schwartz' proposal has the merit of going further than merely requiring equal concern and respect for male and female athletes' performances.[5] As I argued before, equal opportunity demands more substantial measures than merely adopting a particular mental attitude towards a person or a social group and their achievements. But I think they fail to realise that no matter how much we try to level out resources and opportunities (for instance, coaching and training facilities, sport grants, etc.), there will still be a substantial physiological inequality between the sexes in sports. Short of re-distributing rewards in elite sports, we should instead go for equalising the conditions of competition, *biologically*. Otherwise, treating women differently by giving them extra rewards (as distinct from resources), we might be risking consolidating general prejudices regarding women's supposed inferiority when it comes to physical performances.

Is the Bio-Amazons project too conservative?

Our proposal has also been charged with being not radical enough. In that regard, Kutte Jönsson has argued that:

> Although their [Tamburrini and Tännsjö's] argument works in favour of the idea of individuals crossing sex/gender barriers, it still entails the acceptance of the concept of gender, and the concept of gender differentiates bodies into certain (gender) norms, and that involves and promotes (gender) discrimination.
>
> *(Jönsson, 2009, p. 136)*

Thus, in Jönsson's view, it is only in a world of asexual cyborgs that gender discrimination – both in sport and in society – can be successfully neutralised. Rather than trying to abolish sex and gender discrimination by social, cultural and political means (as our critics argue against us) or by biological means (as we propose), he believes that we should abolish sex and gender as normative and discriminating categorisations.

Jönsson's argument is well-taken. In the past, there were *some* sex differences that might have been considered as essential. Mainly they were related to one activity that women, but not men, could perform: childbearing. But things have changed. Some men can today give birth.[6] In the future, ectogenesis (that is, pregnancy outside the womb) might also help women to liberate themselves from "the tyranny of reproduction" (Firestone, 2002, p. 185)

The sport world, however, is not evolving so fast. Sex segregation forces sport practitioners into one of two different sex categories, no matter how their physiological constitution looks.[7] Sportspersons are not seen, much less categorised, as asexual cyborgs, either by the public or by sport officials. Starting from this categorisation, men (on average) still jump higher, run faster and lift heavier weights than women (Cheuvront et al., 2005; Holden, 2004). Given this context, the Bio-Amazons project might be a healthy contribution to abolishing sex categorisations in sport and society. Making women stronger than men through genetic modifications is the next step to take at the present stage of our scientific development.

Concluding remarks

The outcome of my discussion seems favourable to the Bio-Amazons project. In the preceding sections I set out to answer the objections raised by our original proposal of allowing female athletes to (genetically) transform their physiques in order to catch up the physiological advantage men have in certain sport disciplines. I will not repeat my arguments here; the critical reader will be the final judge of my defence of the Bio-Amazons project.

However, it might still be asked, why is there resistance to the Bio-Amazons? In my view, part of the explanation rests on our strongly-cemented prejudices that make us perceive any kind of transcending sexual barriers as threatening. This applies even to people who, on behalf of their profession, have devoted themselves to critically scrutinise those very prejudices. In some way or another, we all are sex-blind.

But the Bio-Amazons project is not only part of a sex-equalising programme; it also expresses a secular, science-based libertarian model according to which the deliberate adaptation of our biological nature is the individuals' prerogative, not God's or any other worldly authorities'. Within such a model, moulding our biology implies transcending the limitations imposed upon us by the genetic lottery (some people are born with more or less favourable physiological and intellectual conditions than others) as well as the sex lottery (people are born with physical characteristics that differ from those belonging to the other/s sex/es). We are now entering into an era in which the whimsical limitations imposed upon individuals by these natural lotteries might be modified according to our desires. This prospect will of course add further negative reactions to those expressed against the Bio-Amazons.

I hope this resistance can be overcome.

Notes

1 Exceptions to this are Anderson (2010) (particularly Chapter, 6 Sport's Use in Marginalizing Women, pp. 121–134), and McDonagh and Pappano (2008). However, even if other authors have proposed making structural changes in sports in order to promote sex integration, our proposal is, as far as I know, unique in that it purports to attain sex equality by changing women's physiological condition, rather than the ideological and cultural fundamentals of (elite) sports.

2 The South African middle-distance runner Caster Semenya won the 800 m women race at the 2009 World Championship in Athletics in Berlin. A few hours after her victory, it was announced that she had been subjected to "gender testing" and was suspended from international competition by the International Association of Athletics Federations (IAAF). After having been examined for more than a year, Semenya was allowed to compete again on 6 July 2010. Her case brought to the light the situation of so called intersex (female) athletes, that is, sportswomen who have higher than average levels of male hormones (mainly testosterone). As a direct consequence of the Semenya case, new regulations

were introduced by the International Olympic Committee (IOC) and IAAF that set an upper limit to androgen levels for women athletes. Although indirectly, these new regulations imply intersex women should undergo medical treatment (for instance, with estrogen) in order to be allowed to compete with other women.

3   For a more detailed discussion on these objections, see Tamburrini and Tännsjö, 2005.

4   Being "the best, period" has to be understood in absolute, not relative, terms. That means that, on average, most men run and swim faster, lift heavier weights, etc., than most women. I will return to this question in the section, "Is being a woman a disability?".

5   In that sense, Giordano and Harris (2005) are wrong as well when they refer to "equal opportunity" as simply requiring "equal concern and respect".

6   In 2008, an Oregon couple redefined division of labour in marital life. Thomas Beatie, a man who was born a woman gave birth to a child after undergoing sex change surgery to become a man 10 years earlier, while retaining his female reproductive organs, just in case. His wife Nancy was unable to have children due to a hysterectomy. Thomas – who is legally a man and legally married – stopped taking testosterone injections and started having periods again, allowing him to become pregnant by artificial insemination. After that, Thomas gave birth to two more children (Perth Now, 2010)

7   Recall the decision taken by the IOC and the IAAF that, although indirectly, compels intersex female athletes to undergo estrogen treatment to be allowed to compete with other women. Intersex athletes illustrate the fact that sex is a continuum with clear-cut females and males on both extremes of the scale, but with many less easily judged cases in between.

References

Anderson E (2010) *Sport, Theory and Social Problems – A Critical Introduction.* London and New York: Routledge.

Cheuvront SN, Carter R, Deruisseau KC and Moffatt RJ (2005) Running performance differences between men and women. *Sports Medicine* 35: 1017–1024.

English J (1978) Sex equality in sports. *Philosophy and Public Affairs* 7 (3): 269–277.

Firestone S (2002) The dialectic of sex. In: *The Case for Feminist Revolution.* New York: Farrar, Strauss & Giroux (originally published 1970).

Giordano S and Harris J (2005) What is gender equality in sports? In: Tamburrini C and Tännsjö (eds) *Genetic Technology and Sport – Ethical Questions.* London and New York: Routledge, Chapter 18.

Holden C (2004) An everlasting gender gap?. *Science* 305: 639–640.

Jönsson K (2009) Who's afraid of Stella Walsh? On gender, "gene cheaters", and the promises of cyborg athletes. In: Tamburrini C and Tännsjö T (eds) *The Ethics of Sports Medicine.* London and New York: Routledge, Chapter 10.

McDonagh E and Pappano L (2008) *Playing with the Boys: Why Separate is Not Equal in Sports.* Oxford: Oxford University Press.

Padden C and Humphries T (1988) *Deaf in America: Voices from a Culture.* Cambridge: Harvard University Press.

Perth Now (2010) First known transgender man to give birth delivers third child. 3 August.

Sherwin S and Schwartz M (2005) Resisting the emergence of Bio-Amazons. In: Tamburrini C and Tännsjö T (eds) *Genetic Technology and Sport – Ethical Questions.* London and New York: Routledge, Chapter 16.

Tamburrini C and Tännsjö T (2005) The genetic design of a new Amazon. In: Tamburrini C and Tännsjö T (eds) *Genetic Technology and Sport – Ethical Questions.* London and New York: Routledge, Chapter 15.

Tamburrini C and Tännsjö T (2009) *The Ethics of Sports Medicine.* London and New York: Routledge.

39

JOINING THE TEAM

The inclusion of transgender students in United States school-based athletics

Helen J. Carroll

Introduction

An increasing number of young people in schools are identifying as transgender, meaning that their internal sense of gender identity is different from the gender they were assigned at birth. These students challenge many parents and educators to rethink their understanding of gender as universally fixed at birth, simultaneously challenging them to create educational institutions that value and meet the needs of all students. Educators must ensure that these students have equal access to opportunities in all academic and extracurricular activities in safe and respectful school environments.

It is particularly important for school sports to be open to transgender students. School sport programmes are integral parts of the high school and college experience, particularly in the United States. The benefits of school athletic participation include many positive effects, and participation in high school sport improves chances of acceptance into college. For some students, playing on high school teams leads to future careers in athletics, either as competitors or in ancillary occupations. All students, including those who are transgender, deserve access to these benefits. Thus, schools must identify effective and fair policies to ensure equal access.

Though the needs of transgender students in high school and college have received some attention in recent years, this issue has not been adequately addressed in the context of athletics. Few high school or collegiate athletic programmes, administrators, or coaches are prepared to fairly, systematically, and effectively facilitate a transgender student's interest in participating in a sport. The majority of school sport programmes have no policy governing the inclusion of transgender student athletes. In fact, most school athletic programmes are unprepared to address even basic accommodations such as knowing what pronouns or names to use when referring to a transgender student, where a transgender student should change clothes for practice or competition, or what bathroom or shower that student should use.

In response to this need, the National Center for Lesbian Rights Sports Project and the Women's Sports Foundation initiative 'It Takes a Team! Education Campaign for Lesbian, Gay, Bisexual and Transgender Issues in Sport' convened a national think tank in October 2009 called 'Equal Opportunities for Transgender Student Athletes. Think tank participants included leaders from the National Collegiate Athletic Association (NCAA) and the National High School Federation, transgender student athletes, and an impressive array of experts on transgender issues from a range of disciplines—including law, medicine, advocacy, and athletics.

Think tank participants were committed to a set of guiding principles based on core values of inclusion, fairness, and equal opportunity in sport. The think tank goals were to develop model policies and identify best practices for high school and collegiate athletic programmes to ensure the full inclusion of transgender student athletes.

In October 2010, the think tank released a report titled *On the Team: Equal Opportunity for Transgender Student Athletes* (Caroll and Griffen, 2010). In August 2011, the NCAA published an organizational policy and best practices guide about the inclusion of transgender collegiate student athletes, which it distributed to its 1,200 member institutions across the country.

It is important for school-based athletic leaders to learn about the basic issues facing transgender students so they can adopt and implement inclusive policies.

What does 'transgender' mean?

'Transgender' describes an individual whose gender identity (one's internal psychological identification as a boy/man or girl/woman) does not match the person's sex at birth. For example, a male-to-female (MTF) transgender woman or girl is someone who was born with a male body, but who identifies as a girl or a woman. A female-to-male (FTM) transgender man or boy is someone who was born with a female body, but who identifies as a boy or a man (Gender Spectrum, no date).

Some transgender people choose to share the fact that they are transgender with others. Other transgender people prefer to keep the fact that they are transgender private.

It is important that other people recognise and respect a transgender person's identification as a man or a woman. In order to feel comfortable and express their gender identities to other people, transgender people may take a variety of steps, including: changing their names and self-referencing pronouns to better match their gender identity; choosing clothes, hairstyles, or other aspects of self-presentation that reflect their gender identity; and generally living and presenting themselves to others in a manner consistent with their gender identity. Some, but not all, transgender people take hormones or undergo surgical procedures to change their bodies to better reflect their gender identity.

Some people are confused by the difference between transgender people and people who have intersex conditions. Apart from having a gender identity that is different than their bodies, transgender people are not born with physical characteristics that distinguish them from others. In contrast, people with intersex conditions (which may also be called 'Differences of Sex Development', DSD), are born with physically mixed or atypical bodies with respect to sexual characteristics such as chromosomes, internal reproductive organs and genitalia, and external genitalia (Intersex Society of America, 2008). An estimated one in 2,000 people are born with an anatomy or chromosome pattern that doesn't fit typical definitions of male or female. The conditions that cause these variations are sometimes grouped under the terms 'intersex' or 'DSD'.

Most people with intersex conditions clearly identify as male or female and do not experience confusion or ambiguity about their gender identities. In fact, most intersex conditions are not visible, and many intersex people are unaware of having an intersex condition unless it is discovered during medical procedures. Though there may be some similar issues related to sports participation between transgender and intersex individuals, there are also significant differences. This chapter will focus on the participation of transgender people in sports.

Why address transgender issues in school sport programmes?

Core values of equal opportunity and inclusion demand that educational leaders adopt thoughtful and effective policies that enable all students to participate fully in school athletic programmes. Schools have learned over the past years the value and necessity of accommodating the sport participation interests of students of color, girls and women, students with disabilities, and lesbian, gay, and bisexual students. These are all issues of basic fairness and equity that demand the expansion of our thinking about equal opportunity in sports. The right of transgender students to participate in sports calls for similar considerations of fairness and equal access.

Addressing the needs of transgender students is an important, emerging equal opportunity issue that must be taken seriously by school leaders. Because a more complex understanding of gender may be new and challenging for some people, there is a danger that misinformation and stereotypes will guide policy decisions rather than accurate and up-to-date information. Athletic leaders who are charged with policy development need guidance to avoid creating policies based on misconceptions and misinformation that, ultimately, create more problems than they solve.

Why focus on high school and college sport?

Providing equal opportunities in all aspects of school programming is a core value in education. As an integral part of educational institutions, high school and college sport programmes are responsible and accountable for reflecting the goals and values of the educational institutions of which they are a part. It follows that school athletic programmes must reflect the value of equal opportunity in all policies and practices.

Sport programmes affiliated with educational institutions have a responsibility, beyond those of adult amateur or professional sports programmes, to look beyond the value of competition to promote broader educational goals of participation, inclusion, and equal opportunity. Because high schools and colleges must be committed to those broader educational goals, they should not unthinkingly adopt policies developed for adult Olympic and professional athletes. Recognising the need to address the participation of transgender athletes, a few leading international and professional sport governing organizations have developed policies based on overly stringent, invasive, and rigid medical requirements. These policies are not workable or advisable for high school and college athletes for a number of reasons.

For example, in 2004 the International Olympic Committee (IOC) developed a policy addressing the eligibility of transgender athletes to compete in IOC sanctioned events (International Olympic Committee, 2003: 1). While the IOC deserves credit for its pioneering effort to address the inclusion of transgender athletes, medical experts have identified serious flaws in the IOC policy, especially its requirement of genital reconstructive surgery, which lacks a well-founded medical or policy basis. Most transgender people—even as adults—do not have genital reconstructive surgery, which can be very costly and is rarely covered by insurance (Mottet, 2010). In addition, whether a transgender person has genital reconstructive surgery has no bearing on his or her athletic ability. The IOC policy also fails to provide sufficient protections for the privacy and dignity of transgender athletes. Because of these serious flaws, high schools and colleges should not adopt or look to the IOC policy as a model (Dreger, 2010).

High school and college student athletes have needs that differ from those of adults. A core purpose of high school and college is to teach students how to participate and be good citizens in an increasingly diverse society, as well as how to interact respectfully with others. In addition, high school and college sporting programmes impose limits on how many years a student athlete can compete that do not exist in adult sporting competitions, where athletes can compete as long as their performances are viable or, in the case of most amateur sports, as long as they wish to.

High school and younger transgender students are also subject to different medical protocols than adults because of their age and physical and psychological development (Brill and Pepper, 2008). The World Professional Association for Transgender Health (WPATH) has established guiding medical protocols for transitioning—the process by which transgender people live consistent with their gender identities, and which may include treatments to have the person's physical presentation more closely align with his or her identity (2001). Those protocols vary based on the age and psychological readiness of the young person. For children and youth, transition typically consists entirely of permitting the child to dress, live, and function socially consistently with the child's gender identity. For youth who are approaching puberty, hormone blockers may be prescribed to delay puberty in order to prevent the youth from going through the traumatic experience of acquiring secondary sex characteristics that conflict with his or her core gender identity. For older youth, cross-gender hormones or even some sex-reassignment surgeries may be prescribed. Given these different stages of emotional and physical development, it is essential that policies related to transgender athletes are tailored to the ages of the participants.

Should the participation of transgender student athletes on school teams raise concerns about competitive equity?

Concern about creating an 'unfair competitive advantage' on sex-separated teams is the primary reason administrators provide when they resist policies ensuring equal participation of transgender student athletes. This concern is cited most often in discussions about transgender women or girls competing on a women's or girls' team. Some advocates for gender equality in high school and college sports are concerned that allowing transgender girls or women—that is, MTF transgender athletes who were born male, but who identify as female—to compete on women's teams will take away opportunities for other girls and women, or that transgender girls or women will have a competitive advantage over other non-transgender competitors.

These concerns are based on three assumptions: one, that transgender girls and women are not 'real' girls or women and therefore do not deserve an equal competitive opportunity; two, that being born with a male body automatically gives a transgender girl or woman an unfair advantage when competing against non-transgender girls and women; and three, that boys or men might be tempted to pretend to be transgender in order to compete in competition with girls or women.

These assumptions are problematic for several reasons. First, the decision to transition from one gender to the other—to align one's external gender presentation with one's internal sense of gender identity—is a deeply significant and difficult choice that is made only after careful consideration and for the most compelling of reasons. Gender identity is a core aspect of a person's identity, and it is just as deep-seated, authentic, and real for a transgender person as for others. For many transgender people, gender transition is a psychological and social necessity. It is essential that educators in and out of athletics understand this.

Second, while some people fear that transgender women will have an unfair advantage over non-transgender women, it is important to place that fear in context. When examined carefully, the realities underlying this issue are more complex than they may seem at first blush. The basis of this concern is that transgender girls or women who have gone through male puberty may have an unfair advantage due to the growth in long bones, muscle mass, and strength that is triggered by testosterone. However, a growing number of transgender youth are undergoing medically guided hormonal treatment prior to puberty, thus effectively neutralising this concern. Increasingly, doctors who specialize in treating transgender people are prescribing hormone blockers to protect children who clearly identify as the other gender from the trauma of undergoing puberty in the wrong gender and acquiring unwanted secondary sex characteristics. When the youth is old enough to make an informed decision, he or she can choose whether to begin cross-gender hormones. Transgender girls who transition in this way do not go through a male puberty, and therefore their participation in athletics as girls does not raise the same equity concerns that might otherwise be present.

In addition, even transgender girls who do not access hormone blockers or cross-gender hormones display a great deal of physical variation, just as there is a great deal of natural variation in physical size and ability among non-transgender girls and boys. Many people may have a stereotype that all transgender girls and women are unusually tall and have large bones and muscles. But that is not true. A MTF transgender girl may be small and slight, even if she is not on hormone blockers or taking estrogen. It is important not to over-generalise: the assumption that all male-bodied people are taller, stronger, and more highly skilled in a sport than all female-bodied people is not accurate and is often based on sex stereotyping. This assumption is especially unreliable when applied to youth, who are still developing physically and who therefore display a significantly broader range of variation in size, strength, and skill than older youth and adults.[1]

It is also important to know that any athletic advantages a transgender girl or woman arguably may have as a result of her prior testosterone levels dissipate after about one year of estrogen therapy. According to medical experts, the belief that a transgender girl or woman competing on a women's team has a competitive advantage outside the range of performance and competitive advantage (or disadvantage) that already exists among female athletes is simply not supported by medical evidence (Wagman, 2009). As one survey of the existing research concludes, 'the data available does not appear to suggest that transitioned athletes would compete at an advantage or disadvantage as compared with physically born men and women' (Devries, 2008).

Finally, fears that boys or men will pretend to be female to compete on a girls' or women's team are unwarranted given that in the entire 40 year history of 'sex verification' procedures in international sport competitions, no instances of such 'fraud' have been revealed (Buzuvis, 2011). Instead, 'sex verification' tests have been misused to humiliate and unfairly exclude women with intersex conditions (Simpson, 2000). The apparent failure of such tests to serve their stated purpose of deterring fraud—and the terrible damage they have caused to individual women athletes—should be taken into account when developing policies for the inclusion of transgender athletes.

Rather than repeating the mistakes of the past, educators in high school and collegiate athletics programmes must develop thoughtful and informed policies that provide opportunities for all students, including transgender students, to participate in sports. These policies must be based on sound medical science, which shows that MTF transgender athletes do not have any automatic advantage over other women and girls. These policies must also be based on the educational values of sports and the reasons why sports are included as a vital component of the educational environment: promoting the physical and psychological well-being of all students, and teaching students the values of equality, participation, inclusion, teamwork, discipline, and respect for diversity.

What are the benefits of adopting inclusive policies and practices regarding transgender student athletes?

All stakeholders in high school and collegiate athletics will benefit from adopting fair and inclusive policies that enable transgender student athletes to participate on school sports teams. School-based sports, even at the most competitive levels, remain an integral part of the process of education and development of young people, especially emerging leaders in our society. Adopting fair and inclusive participation policies will allow school and athletic leaders to fulfill their commitment to create an environment in which all students can thrive, develop their full potential, and learn how to interact with persons from diverse groups.

Many schools and athletic departments identify diversity as a strength and have included sexual orientation and gender identity/expression in their non-discrimination policies. Athletic departments and personnel are responsible for creating and maintaining an inclusive and non-discriminatory climate in the areas they oversee. Adopting inclusive participation policies provides school athletic leaders with a concrete opportunity to fulfill that mandate, and to demonstrate their commitment to fair play and inclusion.

Moreover, when all participants in sport are committed to fair play, inclusion, and respect, student athletes are free to focus on performing their best in athletic competition and in the classroom. This climate promotes the well-being and achievement potential of all student athletes. Every student athlete and coach will benefit from meeting the challenge of overcoming fear and prejudice about social groups of which they are not members. This respect for difference will be invaluable to all student athletes as they graduate and enter an increasingly diverse workforce that requires people to work effectively and closely with people of varied and wide-ranging backgrounds.

What are the harmful, potential consequences of failing to adopt transgender-inclusive policies and practices?

When schools fail to adopt inclusive participation policies, they are not living up to the educational ideals of equality and inclusion, and may reinforce the image of athletics as a privileged activity not accountable to broad institutional and societal ideals of inclusion and respect for difference. Moreover, this failure puts schools, athletic conferences, and sport governing organizations at risk of costly discrimination lawsuits and negative media attention.

Failure to adopt inclusive participation policies also hurts non-transgender students by conveying a message that the values of non-discrimination and inclusion are less important than values based on competition and winning. Schools must model and educate about non-discrimination values in all aspects of school programming, not only for students, but for parents and community members as well.

Last but not least, failure to adopt policies that ensure equal opportunities for transgender student athletes may also result in costly and divisive litigation. A growing number of states and localities are adopting specific legal protections for transgender students. In addition, state and federal courts are increasingly applying sex discrimination laws to prohibit discrimination against transgender people.

Several studies show that schools are often hostile places for transgender students and other students who do not conform to stereotypical gender expectations (Greytak et al., 2009). These students are frequently subjected to peer harassment and bullying which stigmatizes and isolates them. This mistreatment can lead to feelings of hopelessness, depression, and low self-esteem. When a school or athletic organization denies transgender students the ability to participate in sports because of their gender identity or expression, it condones, reinforces, and affirms the students' social status as outsiders or misfits who somehow deserve the hostility they experience from peers.

Finally, the absence of transgender-inclusive policies and practices reinforces stereotypes and fears about gender diversity. When transgender students are stigmatized and excluded, even non-transgender students may experience pressure to conform to gender-role stereotypes as a way to avoid being bullied or harassed themselves.

Policy recommendations for including transgender student athletes

The policies below are recommended for competitive athletic participation on teams and in organized extramural competition, comprised of leagues with state and national championships, among high school and collegiate schools. It is recommended that participation within schools (intramural and recreational participation) be open to participants without discrimination on the basis of race, color, religion, age, sex, sexual orientation, gender identity, gender expression, or national origin and without the requirement of any medical intervention for transgender participants. Bates College of Lewiston, Maine adopted a model intramural/recreational policy in 2011 that encompasses these values: people participating in any intramural sports or other athletic programmes, such as physical education courses, may participate in accordance with their gender identity, should that be relevant, regardless of any medical treatment.

Guiding principles

In addition to the organization's stated values, it is recommended that the following principles be included in any transgender student athlete policy statement:

1. Participation in interscholastic and intercollegiate athletics is a valuable part of the education experience for all students.
2. Transgender student athletes should have equal opportunity to participate in sports.
3. The integrity of women's sports should be preserved.
4. Policies governing sports should be based on sound medical knowledge and scientific validity.
5. Policies governing sports should be objective, workable, and practical; they should also be written, available, and equitably enforced.
6. The legitimate privacy interests of all student athletes should be protected.
7. The medical privacy of transgender students should be preserved.
8. Athletic administrators, staff, parents of athletes, and student athletes should have access to sound and effective educational resources and training related to the participation of transgender and gender-variant students in athletics.
9. Policies governing the participation of transgender students in athletics should comply with state and federal laws protecting students from discrimination based on sex, disability, and gender identity and expression.

Recommended policy for high school athletics

A transgender student athlete at the high school level shall be allowed to participate in a sports activity in accordance with his or her gender identity irrespective of the gender listed on the student's birth certificate or other student records, and regardless of whether the student has undergone any medical treatment. This policy shall not prevent a transgender student athlete from electing to participate in a sports activity according to his or her assigned birth gender.

Recommended policy for college athletics within the United States

A transgender student athlete participating at the elite intercollegiate competitive level should be allowed to participate in any sex-separated sports activity so long as that athlete's use of hormone therapy, if any, is consistent with the National Governing Body's (NGB's) existing policies on banned medications. Specifically, a transgender student athlete should be allowed to participate in sex-separated sports activities under the following conditions:

1. Transgender student athletes who are undergoing hormone treatment

    1. A MTF transgender student athlete who is taking medically prescribed hormone treatment related to gender transition may participate on a men's team at any time, but must complete one year of hormone treatment related to gender transition before competing on a women's team.[2]
    2. A FTM transgender student athlete who is taking medically prescribed testosterone related to gender transition may *not* participate on a women's team after beginning hormone treatment, and must request a medical exception from the NGB prior to competing on a men's team because testosterone is a banned substance.
    3. A FTM transgender student athlete who is taking medically prescribed testosterone for the purposes of gender transition may compete on a men's team.
    4. In any case where a student athlete is taking hormone treatment related to gender transition, that treatment must be monitored by a physician, and the NGB must receive regular reports about the athlete's eligibility according to these guidelines.

2. Transgender student athletes who are *not* undergoing hormone treatment

    1. Any transgender student athlete who is not taking hormone treatment related to gender transition may participate in sex-separated sports activities in accordance with his or her assigned birth gender.
    2. A FTM transgender student athlete who is not taking testosterone related to gender transition may participate on a men's or women's team.
    3. A MTF transgender student athlete who is not taking hormone treatments related to gender transition may not compete on a women's team.

The recommended U.S. collegiate transgender policy for participation of skilled, elite student athletes, which requires a MTF transitional time of one year of hormonal therapy and no surgery, allows for the maximum number of participants to become eligible within their playing career. International competition, including the Olympics, could use these standards and achieve a level playing field for all competitors throughout the world.

Notes

1   Assuming that boys have an automatic advantage over girls is particularly false with respect to pre-pubescent children, where gender plays virtually no role in determining relative athletic ability. For that

reason, we strongly recommend that school and recreational sports adopt the policy recommended by the Transgender Law and Policy Institute (2009) and endorsed by Gender Spectrum.

2   Recent research indicates that most salient physical changes likely to affect athletic performance occur during the first year of hormone treatment, making a longer waiting period unnecessary (see Goorin and Bunck, 2004).

References

Brill S and Pepper R (2008) *The Transgender Child: A Handbook for Families and Professionals*. San Francisco, CA: Cleis Press.

Buzuvis E (2011) 'Transgender Student-Athletes and Sex-Segregated Sport: Developing Policies of Inclusion for Intercollegiate and Interscholastic Athletics', *Seton Hall Journal of Sports and Entertainment Law* 21: 1: 1–59. http://law.shu.edu/Students/academics/journals/sports-entertainment/upload/Buzuvis-Transgender-Athletes-3.pdf

Caroll H and Griffen P (2010) *On the Team: Equal Opportunity for Transgender Student Athletes*. Available at: http://www.nclrights.org

Devries M (2008) Do Transitioned Athletes Compete at an Advantage or Disadvantage? Available at: http://www.caaws.ca/e/resources/pdfs/Devries_lit_review(2).pdf

Dreger A (2010) Sex Typing for Sport. *Hastings Center Report*. March–April. Available at: http://www.thehastingscenter.org/Publications/HCR/Detail.aspx?id=4548

Gender Spectrum (no date) A Word about Words. Available at: http://www.genderspectrum.org

Goorin L and Bunck M (2004) Transsexuals and competitive sports. *European Journal of Endocrinology* 151: 425–429. Available at: http://www.eje.org/cgi/reprint/151/4/425.pdf

Greytak E, Kosciw J and Diaz E (2009) Gay Lesbian Straight Education Network. *Harsh Realities: The Experiences of Transgender Youth in our Nation's Schools*. New York: GLSEN.

International Olympic Committee (2003) Statement of the Stockholm Consensus on Sex Reassignment Surgery in Sport. Available at: http://www.olympic.org/Documents/Reports/EN/en_report_905.pdf

Intersex Society of America (2008) What's the Difference Between Being Transgender or Transsexual and having an Intersex Condition? Available at: http://www.isna.org/faq/transgender

Mottet L (2010) National Transgender Discrimination Survey. National Gay and Lesbian Task Force Policy Institute and National Center for Transgender Equality. Washington, DC: NGLTF.

Simpson J (2000) Gender Verification in the Olympics. *JAMA* 284: 1568–1569.

Transgender Law and Policy Institute (2009) Guidelines for Creating Policies for Transgender Children in Recreational Sports. Available at: http://www.transgenderlaw.org/resources/TLPI_GuidlinesforCreatingPoliciesforTransChildreninRecSports.pdf

Wagman B (2009) Including Transitioning and Transitioned Athletes in Sport – Issues, Facts and Perspectives – Discussion Paper. Available at: http://www.caaws.ca/e/resources/pdfs/Wagman_discussion_paper_THE_FINAL.pdf

World Professional Association for Transgender Health (2001) *The Harry Benjamin International Gender Dysphoria Association's Standard of Care for Gender Identity Disorders, Sixth Version (2001)*. Available at: http://wpath.org

40

TRANSGENDER EXCLUSION AND INCLUSION IN SPORT

Adam Love

Introduction

Few institutions maintain a sex-segregated structure more rigidly than sport. This strict adherence to a system based upon a static and binary understanding of sex has presented considerable barriers to the participation of transgender athletes, who have traditionally been faced with policies of overt exclusion by sport organisations. However, in response to challenges from transgender athletes and other activist groups, many sporting bodies have begun to adopt policies that appear, at least ostensibly, to be designed to include transgender athletes. This chapter provides an overview and analysis of this shift from policies of overt exclusion to supposed inclusion. In doing so, I suggest that while such policies may appear inclusive on the surface, closer scrutiny reveals them to conform to conservative views of sex and gender in important ways. Ultimately, I argue that scholars and sporting officials should seek more inclusive, non-sex-binary-based models for organising sporting competition.

I proceed with the understanding that – as will become apparent in discussion about the practice of sex-verification testing in sport – anatomical, chromosomal, and hormonal complexities involved in differentiating men from women make sex, like gender, a socially and historically-constructed category (Schultz, 2011; Wackwitz, 2003). My call for non-sex-binary-based strategies for organising sport is broadly informed by the ideas of queer feminist scholars, such as Burke (1996) and Fausto-Sterling (2000), whose deconstruction of sex and gender has highlighted how the two-sex system itself reproduces a hierarchy upon which transphobia specifically, and sexism more generally, are based. In addition, it should be clarified that the term *transgender* is used generally in this chapter to include individuals who have a gender identity other than that which was assigned to them at birth as well as those who may not entirely identify with a particular sex. Some transgender individuals may seek medical procedures, such as surgery or hormone therapy to *transition* to a particular sex, while others may not. In contrast to transgender, the term *cisgender* refers to 'individuals who have a match between the gender they were assigned at birth, their bodies, and their personal identity' (Schilt and Westbrook, 2009: 461). Transgender must also be distinguished from *intersex*, which includes individuals with 'atypical combinations of chromosomes, hormones, genitalia, and other physical features' (Buzuvis, 2011: 11). Although intersex athletes have significantly been affected by sporting bodies' exclusionary policies, the primary focus of this chapter is on policy developments related to transgender athletes. The analysis is limited by my status as a white cisgender man, who has experienced the privilege of not directly suffering the effects of exclusionary gender policies in sport. With these points in mind, I begin by discussing the history of overt exclusion encountered by many individuals who do not so neatly fit into a static and binary model of sex.

Policies of overt exclusion

The general hostility of key figures in sport to those who may transgress the sex binary is vividly illustrated by the history of sex-verification testing. Because the practice has been more rigorously examined by others (e.g., Schultz, 2011; Sullivan, 2011; Wackwitz, 2003), I provide only a brief overview of sex testing here as it directly relates to the participation of transgender athletes. Although Wackwitz (2003) points to the deep roots of the practice by suggesting that the requirement for men to compete naked at the Olympics in ancient Greece was the first recorded instance of sex testing, the formalised policy of sex testing in modern elite sport was initiated in the 1960s. This initially consisted of requiring participants in women's events to submit to visual and gynaecological examinations at competitions governed by the International Association of Athletics Federations (IAAF). The introduction of chromosomal testing for competitors in women's events by the International Olympic Committee (IOC), meanwhile, occurred at the 1968 Olympic Games. During the next three decades, testing included methods designed to identify the presence of a second X chromosome (Barr Body test) or the presence of a Y chromosome (polymerase chain reaction test) and were mandated by the IOC to determine who was and was not allowed to compete in women's events. However, due in part to the ineffectiveness and ambiguity involved in determining sex through such procedures, mandatory sex testing for women's events was abandoned prior to the 2000 Summer Olympics.

While sex testing was outwardly justified by an interest in maintaining a climate of fair play, motivated in part by a fear that men might seek to 'pass' as women in hopes of achieving victory, feminist scholars have suggested that it also illuminates the unease created when women's accomplishments in sport conflict with dominant beliefs about female inferiority (Sullivan, 2011; Wackwitz, 2003). Due to the fact that muscles and strength (key ingredients of sport success) are gendered as masculine, Cavanagh and Sykes (2006: 83) argue that there is a 'psychic need to regulate female bodies entering into the masculinised arena of sport'. Sex testing provides one such means of regulation. The ineffectiveness of testing, however, demonstrates that sex is not as simple as women = XX and men = XY. Rather, each mode of sex testing has 'revealed subtle differences between male and female genders, as opposed to clearly delineated "opposite" sexes' (Cavanagh and Sykes, 2006: 81). In fact, the impossibility of unambiguously defining sex through anatomical, chromosomal, or hormonal testing shows it to be historically and culturally constructed much like the concept of gender (Schultz, 2011).

Although organisations such as the IOC and IAAF no longer practise compulsory sex testing, they still allow for testing on a case-by-case basis 'in response to suspicion of gender fraud' (Buzuvis, 2011: 20). Notably, while sex-verification testing has made numerous intersex athletes aware of their condition and, in turn, disqualified many of them from competition, it has failed to catch athletes seeking to perpetrate gender fraud (Buzuvis, 2011). Although the IOC and IAAF may not have instituted sex-verification testing with the specific purpose of excluding transgender athletes, the history of such testing illustrates the extent to which sport organisations have invested in a segregated system organised around a binary understanding of sex.

Other sporting organisations, however, have implemented policies that appear to be specifically aimed at excluding transgender competitors. The United States Tennis Association (USTA), for example, introduced chromosome-based sex testing in 1977 in response to transitioned woman Renee Richards' attempts to compete in women's events. Richards sued the USTA and was ultimately allowed to participate in the women's competition at the US Open after a New York state court ruled in her favour. Notably, this marks the only instance in which a court has held that a sex discrimination statute – in this case the New York Human Rights Law – protects a transgender athlete's right to participate in a sex-segregated sport competition (Buzuvis, 2011). However, it does not appear as though the decision ushered in an increased acceptance of transgender athletes in the broader sport context. For instance, a decade after the Richards decision, the United States Golf Association responded to the increased success of Charlotte Ann Woods, a transitioned woman, by introducing a policy requiring that competitors in women's events be 'female at birth' (Sykes, 2006). Further, unlike the court's interpretation of human rights law in the Richards decision, in some cases anti-discrimination statutes ostensibly designed to prevent unfair treatment of transgender citizens have specifically exempted sport organisations. For example, the UK's Gender Recognition Act of 2004 allows sporting organisations to exclude transgender participants to promote 'fair competition' or 'the safety of competitors' (see McArdle, 2008: 47). Sport organisations have also been exempted from a transgender non-discrimination law in New South Wales, Australia (Buzuvis, 2011). Such policies again demonstrate how sport organisations are often induced to maintain a binary and static model of sex. As McArdle (2008: 40) notes, the existence of such statutes is 'symptomatic of the confused and incoherent approach to transgendered participation in sports – an approach that is, in its turn, a consequence of the sporting field's equally confused and incoherent antipathy towards most forms of difference'. However, despite this antipathy, numerous sporting organisations have begun to formulate policies that are, at least on the surface, intended to include transgender athletes. In the next section of this chapter, I subject several of these policies to critical scrutiny.

Policies of inclusion?

Policy discussions and developments regarding the participation of transgender athletes in sport have tended to centre on concerns of 'fair play' and assumptions about how testosterone may confer an unfair advantage upon some competitors. Concerns about testosterone are clearly demonstrated in the guidelines set forth by the 'Stockholm Consensus' – a policy approved by the IOC Executive Committee prior to the 2004 Summer Olympic Games. Specifically, the Stockholm Consensus allowed transgender athletes to complete if they had (a) undergone sex reassignment surgery (including external genitalia and gonadectomy), (b) been given legal recognition of their sex by their country of citizenship, and (c) undertaken hormone therapy and lived in their newly-assigned gender for two years (Cavanagh and Sykes, 2006). The policy was notable not only because of the high profile of the IOC, but also because prior to the Stockholm Consensus, most sporting bodies either had no policies designed to include transgender participants or simply relied upon requirements that all competitors in women's events be 'female at birth' (Cavanagh and Sykes, 2006). Indeed, the Stockholm Consensus appears to have acted as somewhat of a model, as numerous sporting organisations have adopted policies governing the participation of transgender athletes since its implementation. These organisations include the Ladies European Golf Tour, Ladies Golf Union, Ladies Professional Golf Association, USA Hockey, USA Rugby, USA Track and Field, United States Golf Association (USGA), and Women's Golf Australia (Buzuvis, 2011).

Although it has often been hailed as a progressive measure that can serve as a catalyst for the increased inclusion of transgender athletes, the Stockholm Consensus (and the extent to which it has served as a model for subsequent policy) is concerning for a number of reasons.

Accompanying the focus on testosterone in policy discourse is the assumption that all men (whether they are born or 'made') have a physical advantage over women (Sullivan, 2011). Such discourse works to obscure the continuum upon which human performance lies – a continuum in which many women routinely out-perform men (Kane, 1995). Further, a model such as that established by the Stockholm Consensus continues to rely on a conservative, binary understanding of sex, which stands in opposition to reality, as was highlighted in the difficulties associated with sex-verification testing. While policies modelled on the one adopted by the IOC may provide a certain level of inclusion for some individuals, they do so in a way that is gender-conforming rather than gender-transforming (Travers, 2006).

By relying on the most conservative, medicalised criteria to determine access, such policies continue to exclude many transgender athletes and erase 'all local, economic, cultural, and racial differences in how transsexual athletes have access to sex reassignment surgeries or hormone usage' (Sykes, 2006: 11). Further, even those who could be included by such policies may view them as being unnecessarily invasive, treating transgender athletes as 'others'. As golfer Mianne Bagger, a transitioned woman, commented about the USGA's policy, which required her to allow the organisation unrestricted access to her medical and psychiatric records, 'we are treated as a complete freak, and we are treated so differently to any other competitor with complete disregard to the real facts and medical conditions involved in our treatment and the person who we are' (cited in Love, Lim, and DeSensi, 2009: 73–74).

Ultimately, such policies reassert the notion that there are 'two and only two choices when it comes to one's sexual identity, thereby ignoring the range of social and biological possibilities that exist along the continuum between these two seemingly pure categories' (Schultz, 2011: 235). In fact, it may be that the concern with neutralising an alleged masculine advantage in sport is, in reality, more about managing the gender binary at a time when there is growing evidence of its insufficiency and when transgender persons are gaining increased access to basic civil rights in numerous areas of social and cultural life (Cavanagh and Sykes, 2006). Given this state of affairs, continued scrutiny, of the ways in which the sex binary is reasserted and certain lived realities are excluded from participation, is merited as sporting officials formalise policies, such as the Stockholm Consensus, that are ostensibly designed to include transgender athletes.

However, as we enter the second decade of the 21st century, there are signs that some sporting organisations may be departing from certain aspects of the policy model established by the Stockholm Consensus. The National Collegiate Athletic Association (NCAA) of the United States, for example, adopted a policy in September of 2011 that had the stated goal of creating the 'opportunity for transgender student-athletes to participate in accordance with their gender identity while maintaining the relative balance of competitive equity within sports teams' (Lawrence, 2011: paragraph 6). Specifically, the policy states that 'a trans male (female to male) student-athlete who has received a medical exception for treatment with testosterone for gender transition may compete on a men's team but is no longer eligible to compete on a women's team' (Lawrence, 2011: paragraph 4). In contrast, 'a trans female (male to female) student-athlete being treated with testosterone suppression medication for gender transition may continue to compete on a men's team but may not compete on a women's team . . . until completing one calendar year of documented testosterone-suppression treatment' (Lawrence, 2011: paragraph 5).

In its press release announcing the policy, the NCAA highlighted the fact that it was aided by a report co-authored by the National Center for Lesbian Rights' Director of the Sports Project, Helen Carroll, and Gay, Lesbian and Straight Education Network project director, Pat Griffin. In an entry on her blog, Griffin (2011) specifically stated that the NCAA 'got this one right' and advocated that administrators at all levels of collegiate sport should adopt the same policy.

In some ways, the policy provides a greater level of inclusion than the Stockholm Consensus in that it does not require surgical intervention, and it requires hormone treatment for only one year as opposed to two. However, it still maintains a focus on hormones, above and beyond other physical and environmental considerations, as being the key factor determining eligibility. It also embraces, perhaps even more explicitly than the Stockholm Consensus, a language of female physical inferiority, as it allows male to female transsexuals to continue their participation on men's teams, but does not grant similar rights for female to male transsexuals to continue participating on women's teams.

In addition to policies being formulated by sporting organisations, such as the IOC and NCAA, rules concerning the participation of transgender athletes have also developed at the youth and scholastic levels of sport competition. For example, in 2007 the Washington Inter-scholastic Activities Association (WIAA) became the first interscholastic sport governing body in the United States to adopt a formal policy on participation by transgender athletes (Buzuvis, 2011). Specifically, the WIAA policy allows students to participate in sports 'in a manner that is consistent with their gender identity, irrespective of the gender listed on a student's records' (Washington Interscholastic Activities Association, 2011–2012: 49). In cases where questions arise about whether a student's gender identity is 'bona fide', the policy outlines an appeals process in which the student must appear in front of an eligibility committee composed of such officials as physicians, mental health professionals, administrators, WIAA staff members, and/or advocates 'familiar with Gender Identity and Expression issues' (Washington Interscholastic Activities Association, 2011–2012: 49–50). The committee, rather than requiring medical evidence, considers such documentation as affirmed written statements from the student, a parent/guardian, and/or a health care provider. While the WIAA policy might be seen as signalling a new level of inclusiveness, other states that have adopted policies for transgender participation in interscholastic sports appear to have followed a model more similar to that of the IOC. Specifically, the Connecticut Interscholastic Athletic Conference adopted a policy under which students are required to participate as a member of their 'birth sex' unless they have had sex-reassignment surgery, undergone hormone treatment, received legal recognition of their new sex, and completed a two year post-surgery waiting period (Buzuvis, 2011). In the state of Colorado, a policy adopted in 2009 has similar requirements regarding surgical and hormonal transition for transgender students seeking to participate in sports (Buzuvis, 2011). Such widely-varying policies at the state level create an uneven field and paint a somewhat clouded picture regarding the future directions that may be taken as organisations consider the status of transgender youth in sporting activities.

The extent to which the status of transgender athletes is tenuous in sport is further demonstrated by the fact that even the Gay Games, which explicitly states its mission as being to empower lesbian, gay, bisexual, and transgender (LGBT) athletes, seems to have struggled with the inclusion of transgender competitors. For example, organisers of the 1994 Gay Games were met with protests over rules that required individuals to have had surgery and lived for two years with hormone therapy in their gender of identity (Sykes, 2006). As a result, the Gay Games has changed its stance on transgender athletes in the subsequent two decades. At the 2010 Gay Games, participants in sports that were organised with separate men's and women's competitions were allowed to choose the competition in which they wished to participate, but documentation (e.g., passports, birth certificates) was required to verify gender identity (Federation of Gay Games, 2010). For instances in which people's identity documents indicated a sex other than that in which they wished to compete, and the sport they were registering for could 'accommodate them without creating an undue safety risk and without breaching any required sanctioning rules', organisers could allow them to participate in their chosen gender if the athletes were able to provide either (a) a letter from a medical practitioner 'stating that the participant had been actively involved in hormone treatment for a minimum of two full years' or (b) proof (e.g., driver's licence, passport, personal letters, testimonials, bank accounts, leases) that they have lived in their self-identified gender for a minimum of two years (Federation of Gay Games, 2010). Recognising the 'challenges that may be involved in changing legal documents in some countries', the policy allows officials to exercise 'discretion' when evaluating the adequacy of a person's documentation (Federation of Gay Games, 2010). However, the policy stipulates that copies of all documents must be provided in English with certified translations.

While all of the policies discussed in this section provide some level of inclusion for certain transgender athletes, they all still work to exclude some individuals and maintain the practice of enforcing a binary view of sex through written policy.

Toward a more radically-inclusive system

I began by highlighting how sex-verification testing illustrates the extent to which many sport governing bodies have operated (with a static and binary understanding of sex), creating an environment that has been quite hostile to the participation of transgender athletes. Indeed, some sport organisations seem to have implemented sex-testing policies with the specific intent of excluding transgender athletes. In the past decade, however, particularly since the implementation of the IOC's Stockholm Consensus, a growing number of sport governing bodies have adopted policies ostensibly intended to include transgender athletes. However, policies that rely on specific medicalised criteria for inclusion, such as surgery and hormone treatment, are insensitive to cultural or economic differences in how transgender athletes might have access to such procedures and therefore work to exclude many individuals. Further, the invasiveness of such policies may also work to discourage some transgender athletes from participation who are not directly excluded by the language of the policy itself.

There are, however, sport organisations that have developed seemingly more inclusive policies that do not rely solely on medical criteria to determine sex. In fact, policies such as that of the NCAA have received praise from some feminist groups. What all the aforementioned policies have in common, though, is the practice of reproducing a segregated system based upon a binary model of sex – a constructed and socially-imposed system that is 'designed against the reality of life as it is lived' (Wackwitz, 2003: 558).

Feminists should be cautious in supporting the sex-segregated model of sport, as it works to reproduce an ideology of men's superiority and women's inferiority in many ways (Love and Kelly, 2011; McDonagh and Pappano, 2008; Travers, 2008). In particular, the ideology of women's inferiority is often perpetuated by discourse about the inclusion of transgender athletes in sex-segregated sport. For example, transitioned women who are seeking to be included in women's sporting events often discuss how they have become physically weaker after transitioning. While such weakness may be the result of adjusting to a new anatomical form, hormone injections, and other complications associated with surgery (Cavanagh and Sykes, 2006), such discourse, particularly when interpreted uncritically, operates to reinforce the idea that women are forever biologically and physically destined to be inferior to men. Such uncritical interpretation was noted by Birrell and Cole (1990) in their observations about media coverage of Renee Richards, which focused on men's 'natural' ability rather than the years of privileged access to sport that Richards enjoyed prior to transitioning, thus foregrounding physical definitions of sex while obscuring cultural considerations.

As an alternative to the segregated two-sex model of sport, Travers and Deri (2011) have discussed how some lesbian softball leagues in North America have adopted more radical, non-sex-binary-based trans-inclusive policies. Specifically, such policies go far beyond the others highlighted in this chapter to include 'transwomen and transmen of all variations and stages of transition (in terms of surgery and hormones) as well as transgender individuals whose gender identities lie between or outside the gender binary' (Travers and Deri, 2011: 493). Perhaps providing reason for optimism about the future possibilities of such reform, the authors suggest that 'ten years ago it was unthinkable . . . that a bearded man or a pre-operative transsexual woman would be playing on a lesbian softball team but now, if not exactly commonplace, it is increasingly unremarkable' (Travers and Deri, 2011: 493–494). They suggest that the presence of transsexual, transgender and genderqueer players on teams is important because it provides visual evidence of a shift away from dyadic sex boundaries.

There are many possible benefits to be realised from such radically-inclusive policies. For example, trans-inclusive teams can serve as valuable sites of support for transgender individuals (Travers and Deri, 2011). This is particularly important, because members of the transgender community suffer disproportionately from health problems (Cuypere et al., 2005) that could perhaps be ameliorated by sport participation in a welcoming environment (McArdle, 2008). Additionally, interaction between transgender and cisgender athletes in a supportive sporting environment may work to reduce prejudice against members of the transgender community (Buzuvis, 2011). Of course, in addition to the direct benefits for transgender athletes who might be included by such policies, a move away from the segregated two-sex model of sport may help alleviate the damaging effects of orthodox masculinity in sport (Anderson, 2008) and disrupt the ideology of unquestioned male superiority that is frequently reproduced in and through sport.

There would be, however, important issues to be considered in any move to more radically-inclusive, non-sex-binary-based models in sport. For example, in the softball leagues studied by Travers and Deri (2011), some lesbian participants feared that transinclusion might take away from the empowering women-only spaces free of men and sexism that they valued so much. Indeed, support for Renee Richards in her efforts to participate in women's tennis often tended to take an anti-feminist and anti-woman tone (Birrell and Cole, 1990). Such tendencies highlight legitimate concerns about advocating integration under conditions of deep-seated gender inequality in sport. These concerns certainly pose important challenges that must be considered in formulating and advocating more radically-inclusive, non-sex-binary-based models in sport. Thus, I do not call for the naïve or careless adoption of such radically-inclusive models immediately at all levels of sport. I do, however, suggest that moving away from the segregated two-sex system as much as possible is desirable, not only for the inclusion of transgender athletes but also as a means of promoting gender equity more broadly. Thus, I urge scholars and sporting officials to consider more radically-inclusive approaches as policy is formed in the future.

References

Anderson E (2008) 'I used to think women were weak': Orthodox masculinity, gender segregation, and sport. *Sociological Forum* 23: 257–280.

Birrell S and Cole CL (1990) Double fault: Renee Richards and the construction and naturalization of difference. *Sociology of Sport Journal* 7: 1–21.

Burke P (1996) *Gender shock: Exploding the myths of male and female.* New York: Anchor Books/Doubleday.

Buzuvis EE (2011) Transgender student-athletes and sex-segregated sport: Developing policies of inclusion for intercollegiate and interscholastic athletics. *Seton Hall Journal of Sports and Entertainment Law* 21: 1–59.

Cavanagh SL and Sykes H (2006) Transsexual bodies at the Olympics: The International Olympic Committee's policy on transsexual athletes at the 2004 Athens Summer Games. *Body & Society* 12: 75–102.

Cuypere G, T'Sjoen G, Beerten R, Selvaggi G, Sutter P, Hoebeke P, Monstrey S, Vansteenwegen A and Rubens R (2005) Sexual and physical health after sex reassignment surgery. *Archives of Sexual Behavior* 34: 679–690.

Fausto-Sterling A (2000) *Sexing the body: Gender politics and the construction of sexuality.* New York: Basic Books.

Federation of Gay Games (2010) Gay Games VIII Gender Identity Policy. Available at: www.transgender-law.org/resources/FederationGayGamesPolicy.pdf (accessed 1 May 2012).

Griffin P (2011) NCAA adopts trans-inclusive policy. Available at: ittakesateam.blogspot.com/2011/09/ncaa-adopts-trans-inclusive-policy.html (accessed 1 May 2012).

Kane MJ (1995) Resistance/transformation of the oppositional binary: Exposing sport as a continuum. *Journal of Sport and Social Issues* 19: 191–218.

Lawrence M (2011) Transgender policy approved. Available at: www.ncaa.org/wps/wcm/connect/public/NCAA/Resources/Latest+News/2011/September/Transgender+policy+approved (accessed 1 May 2012).

Love A and Kelly K (2011) Equity or essentialism? U.S. courts and the legitimation of girls' teams in high school sport. *Gender & Society* 25: 227–249.

Love A, Lim S and DeSensi JT (2009) Mianne Bagger: A transitioned woman's efforts for inclusion in professional golf. *Women in Sport and Physical Activity Journal* 18: 68–77.

McArdle D (2008) Swallows and Amazons, or the sporting exception to the Gender Recognition Act. *Social Legal Studies* 17: 39–57.

McDonagh E and Pappano L (2008) *Playing with the boys: Why separate is not equal in sports.* New York: Oxford University Press.

Schilt K and Westbrook L (2009) Doing gender, doing heteronormativity: 'Gender normals', transgender people, and the social maintenance of heterosexuality. *Gender & Society* 23: 440–464.

Schultz J (2011) Caster Semenya and the 'question of too': Sex testing in elite women's sport and the issue of advantage. *Quest* 63: 228–243.

Sullivan CF (2011) Gender verification and gender policies in elite sport: Eligibility and 'fair play'. *Journal of Sport and Social Issues* 35: 400–419.

Sykes H (2006) Transsexual and transgender policies in sport. *Women in Sport and Physical Activity Journal* 15: 3–13.

Travers A (2006) Queering sport: Lesbian softball leagues and the transgender challenge. *International Review for the Sociology of Sport* 41: 431–446.

Travers A (2008) The sport nexus and gender injustice. *Studies in Social Justice* 2: 79–101.

Travers A and Deri J (2011) Transgender inclusion and the changing face of lesbian softball leagues. *International Review for the Sociology of Sport* 46: 488–507.

Wackwitz LA (2003) Verifying the myth: Olympic sex testing and the category 'woman'. *Women's Studies International Forum* 26: 553–560.

Washington Interscholastic Activities Association (2011–2012) Washington Interscholastic Activities Association Official Handbook (2011-2012) Available at: wiaa.com/ConDocs/Con951/Handbook (Web). pdf (accessed 1 May 2012).

41

MALE/FEMALE OR OTHER

The untold stories of female athletes with intersex variations in India

Payoshni Mitra

The gender-verification test, a procedure that has been contested by feminist sport scholars (Griffin, 2010; see Adam Love in this *Handbook*) was introduced by the International Olympic Committee (IOC) in 1968. So-called 'scientific' sex testing conducted by the IOC was deemed indispensable when rumours about East European male competitors masquerading as females became widespread. At the height of the Cold War, it was feared that Eastern Bloc countries were trying to win medals by cheating, having men disguise themselves as women to gain unfair advantage in the sporting field. However, the tests that were originally supposed to catch cheats have subsequently become a 'clumsy model for detecting disorders of sexual development' (Hercher, 2010).

The term intersex[1] has been used in this chapter in place of 'Disorders of Sex Development' – the medically-used term that pathologizes people with intersex variations in a way that is contradictory to the fundamental tenets of intersex activism (Reis, 2009).[2] The first international sports body to address issues related to the inclusion of athletes from sexual minority communities was the International Association of Athletics Federations (IAAF) in 1990. Later, in 2003, the IOC created what was considered to be 'a progressive access policy designed to include transsexuals'[3] (Cavanagh & Sykes, 2006), but remained remarkably silent about inclusion of intersex people in sport. In 2006 the IAAF again focused on transsexual athletes and sex reassignment, listing medical conditions which 'should be allowed' (IAAF Medical and Anti-Doping Commission, 2006), but were far from comprehensive. The ineffectiveness of the policy came to the forefront during the shoddily-handled case of South African athlete Caster Semenya in 2009, whose gender was questioned during the World Championships in Berlin where she won the athletics gold medal in the 800 metres, reportedly lowering her time 'significantly'. The IAAF banned her from competing and then after much debate and speculation, revoked the decision in July 2010.

Following the particular case of Caster Semenya, the subject of intersexuality has also received unprecedented attention from sports organizations, journalists and scholars worldwide. Feminist sport scholars and advocates argued that male athletes with genetic advantages have been eulogized, whereas female athletes with genetic advantages have always been looked at with suspicion.[4] The oldest recorded example where an athlete of exceptional quality was subjected to unfair suspicion is probably that of Babe Didrickson in 1932.[5] Another related question concerns competitive advantage – specifically, if there is a difference between the possible competitive advantage gained due to height or longer upper body or limbs and that gained by producing excess testosterone. This issue questions the essentialist binary sex model, whether the strict male–female division in sport should be replaced with a more just approach based on other physical attributes.

Keeping the theoretical debates about sex tests and competitive advantage to one side, this paper examines three cases[6] of Indian athletes with intersex variations who were publicly humiliated, their efforts trivialized, their intentions doubted, and their identities questioned for being born different.

The story of Santhi Soundarajan

The first case study is of Santhi Soundarajan, an Indian athlete who remains in the public memory today as someone who failed a sex test in the Asian Games at Doha in 2006. Born in 1981, Santhi was assigned female sex at birth at a government hospital in Pudukkottai. Accordingly, she was reared as a girl child. She grew up with no clear idea about her condition that she now refers to as a 'problem'. She wore dresses and *salwar kameez*,[7] as all other girls, and identified herself as a girl. However, as an adolescent, she realized she was different. In an interview, she said:

> At puberty, my friends will have the *Poopunitha Neeraattu Vizha* – the Tamil puberty ceremony. I used to wonder why my body was not changing like other girls. My breasts did not develop. I did not menstruate. I realised I was different.[8]

She continued:

> I used to wear what other girls would wear. I used to look like a boy in them. My school friends used to say 'Santhi is both a girl and a boy.' Everyone used to laugh at me. It is at this point that I began to take sports seriously. And like most athletes, I began to wear track pants. I felt a lot more accepted as an athlete.[9]

Santhi's grandfather introduced Santhi to sports. Sports in rural India are often looked at as a stepping stone for social upward mobility. The lure of a potential job at a governmental institution under a sports quota[10] often motivates athletes from economically underprivileged backgrounds to train hard in order to do well in sports. And for Santhi, success helped her attain a new identity, respect among friends and, more importantly, social acceptance. By 2005, Santhi began to represent the nation, a dream that she cherished from the very beginning.[11]

And then, in December 2006, she ran the last formal race of her career – the 800 metres final at the Asian Games in Doha – and won a silver medal. Soon after, Santhi's sexual identity was questioned and she was summoned by a medical board that declared that clinically and genetically she was male. At the time, the IAAF's policy indicated that:

> If there is any 'suspicion' or if there is a challenge then the athlete concerned can be asked to attend a medical evaluation before a panel comprising gynaecologist, endocrinologist, psychologist, internal medicine specialist, expert on gender/transgender issues.
>
> *(IAAF Medical and Anti-Doping Commission, 2006)*

Santhi's Gender Verification Report[12] suggested that the panel that examined her, comprised of physicians from the Hamad Medical Corporation, did not include any expert on gender/

transgender issues, but what bothered Santhi the most was how the entire sporting fraternity abandoned her after the episode. The Indian Olympic Association (IOA) notified the media about the results of the sex test informing them that Santhi 'did not possess any characteristics of a woman'.[13] And the media took no time to sensationalize the issue.

The science

In *Myths of Gender: Biological Theories about Women and Men* (1992), Anne Fausto-Sterling, noted biologist, feminist and social activist, refers to some cases where the concerned individuals have male genes and gonads, a somewhat abnormal fetal hormonal sex, a female infant anatomical sex, and a male adult hormonal and anatomical sex (p.84). Fausto-Sterling uses this example to challenge the binary sex model. She asks:

> At what point in its growth do we stop calling the genital tubercle a clitoris and start calling it a penis? How small does a penis have to be before we call it a clitoris?[14]

One of the main targets of the Intersex Rights Movement in the West has been the medical community. Intersex management, gender assignment and surgery were based on John Money's findings during more than four decades from the 1950s. Money said 'the conclusion that emerges is that sexual behaviour and orientation as male or female does not have an innate instinctive basis' (Money & Hampson, 1955). Fausto-Sterling argued that since Money's study of intersex people was directed at finding more about 'normal' development, he failed to notice, perhaps deliberately, the other point that his research findings were indicating: that male/female categories have no biological basis (Fausto-Sterling, 2000). Money later said that gender identity becomes fixed during the first three years of a child's life, depending primarily on the sex of rearing, rather than on such details as the presence or absence of a Y chromosome, ovaries or testes (Money & Ehrhardt, 1972). Money, therefore, recommended that sex assignment and required surgery should be conducted as early in life as possible.

In the context of the athletes I have been working with, modern medical facilities of gender assignment were inaccessible. Following the tradition of intersex management since the time of John Money, sex is assigned mainly on the basis of the size of the phallus or the positioning of the urethral opening to newborns with ambiguous genitalia. Doctors I have interviewed in the course of this research admitted that it was preferable to assign female sex in cases of ambiguity because it was surgically easier to create a female genitalia rather than male genitalia.[15] In *Myths of Gender*, Fausto-Sterling (1992) discussed the work of endocrinologist Julianne Imperato-Mcginley and her associates. They concluded that gender identity is not unalterably fixed in childhood but is continually evolving. According to Imperato-Mcginley, when the sex of rearing is contrary to the testosterone-mediated biologic sex, the biologic sex prevails. To such persons, the sex of rearing remains less important than the hormonal influence that appears during adolescence (Imperato-Mcginley, Guerrero, Gautier, & Peterson, 1974).

The case of Bandana Pal

It is interesting to study the case of Bandana (Bany) Pal, in the light of Imperato-Mcginley's inference. A former footballer from Bengal, Pal has successfully embraced her biologic sex. Pal was born with ambiguous genitals and was assigned female gender at birth. She began to play football at a young age and became an important player in the Bengal women's football team. But as she began to draw attention to her promise as a young striker, her sex was questioned.

Football officials took Pal to see a gynecologist who diagnosed her as having Partial Androgen Insensitivity Syndrome (PAIS) and conducted a gonadectomy.[16] By then, Pal had already signed a contract with the Income Tax football team and the management was desperate to have her in the team. The senior officials therefore convinced Pal's family that the birth of rearing should prevail as changing her sex from female to male may mean humiliation for the family as well as an end to her promising football career. Then sixteen, Pal was not offered counseling, was not properly informed about the surgery, and medical reports and procedures were leaked. Furthermore, sport journalists were informed and some popular Bengali-language newspapers carried her unusual story. Overnight, Pal was deserted by the family, the federation and the football community. She went back to the doctor to tell him that she would like to embrace 'maleness'. After a few months of expensive hormone therapy, Pal had to discontinue having medication because it was unaffordable.[17]

Today, Bandana lives as Bany, hundreds of miles away from his family with a female partner. Though they call themselves man and wife, Bany is legally still a woman and in need of further treatment to repair the damage done to him through surgery.[18]

Pal's case indicates that John Money's recommendations led to what many called mutilation or butchery. Since the 1990s, adults in North America on whom genital surgery has been performed have challenged the necessity of corrective surgery at an early stage. They argue that the choice to undergo surgery should be one's own (Karkazis, 2008). While in advanced countries 'normalizing' atypical genitalia to match the assigned gender inspired a decade-long debate against medical management of intersexuality, in the case of the athletes described in this chapter, the debate is not restricted to medical treatment because the nation and the national sport governing bodies complicate the situation.

Official interventions and complexities

South Africa, as a nation, stood by Caster Semenya after she was banned by the IAAF in 2009. This was evident in 2012 when Semenya carried her nation's flag at the inaugural ceremony of the London Olympics. Initially when Semenya was banned, South Africa's Sports Minister, Makhenkesi Arnold Stofile declared,

> We (would) go to the highest levels in contesting such a decision . . . .We have referred the matter to our lawyers to see how best her rights and interests can be protected. Caster is a woman, she remains our heroine. We must protect her.
>
> *(Ori & Johnsson, 2009)*

The South African politicians' interpretations of Semenya's sex, gender and embodiment were mainly induced by an anti-imperial, nationalist politics (Munro, 2010). In contrast, after Santhi was banned from competitive sport, Indian sports officials, politicians and the media did not support her. Unlike the sense of pride among South Africans about Caster's achievements, coupled with an urge to protect her from being tagged 'male', Santhi's efforts were belittled by the sense of national shame that followed her 'sex test' failure. Federations deserted her and national newspapers discussed her case calling it 'mysterious' or 'strange'.[19] There was only a reluctant attempt at showing her as a victim in the national media, especially after she tried to commit suicide in 2007. However *Dalit Marasuru*, a Tamil magazine for the rights of Dalit (low caste) people, saw her case as an example of oppression of Dalit people by those from upper castes[20] and Santhi received support from the DMK-led[21] Tamil Nadu government. A parallel to the South African Sport Minister's comments were found in the then Chief Minister of

Tamil Nadu, Karunanidhi's words. When most of the country deserted her and called her a cheat, the Tamil Nadu state government made a unique gesture. Soon after Santhi won the 800 metres silver medal at the Asian games in 2006, Karunannidhi promised to give her a big sum of money and a colour television. When her medal was withdrawn by the Olympic Council of Asia (OCA), amidst much controversy Karunanidhi decided to stick to his promise. He argued, 'It does not matter. This is the same body that ran the race' (cited in Mitra, 2010). Karunanidhi did not try to argue about whether Santhi was male or female, as if Santhi's sex did not matter. Perhaps he attempted to destigmatize bodily difference. Significantly, it was during this time that the transgender rights movement in Tamil Nadu flourished.

Karunanidhi's daughter, Kanimozhi, also a Member of Parliament, is reported to have played an important role in her father's actions. In 2006, the state Department of Social Welfare passed a landmark order stating that 'admission in schools and colleges should not be denied based on sex identity' (Harrington, 2008). The Tamil Nadu Transgender Welfare Board (Baudh, Vasudevan, & Chugani, 2009), the first of its kind, was created, and social welfare schemes to support transgender people were introduced (May 2006–May 2011). Activists believe that this would not have been possible without the many years of relentless work from members of the transgender community of Tamil Nadu (Doorairaj, 2009). Though the initiatives, many believe, favoured male to female transgender people[22] – traditionally called *aravanis* or *hijras* – the awareness raised through such initiatives had a positive impact on Santhi's case. By giving support to Santhi, largely considered to have been victimized on the basis of her 'low caste' identity, as well as her ambiguous sexual identity, Karunanidhi tried to please both the Dalit people and those belonging to the 'third sex' in Tamil Nadu.

In contrast, born and brought up in Bengal, Bany Pal has been left alone since 1999. The transgender rights movement had not had an impact in Bengal at that time. Even today, there is no political will to address such issues. The football federation treated Pal as an instrument to support better team performance, and to help the team to win medals and trophies internationally. They forced her to undergo damaging surgery and then deserted her. The state government did not stand by her. And neither did the nation.

The case of Pinki Pramanik

Pinki Pramanik, a former female Indian track athlete, presents a more recent case of ambiguous gender identity, which arose when a woman she lived with accused her of rape. It was years after Pramanik had formally retired from competitive sport. One of the most promising Indian athletes of the last decade, Pramanik retired from athletics surprisingly early. There are claims that she was advised by Indian sports officials to silently withdraw her name after Santhi Soundarajan failed the 'sex test'.

When Pramanik was arrested in June 2012, the police and other state government institutions looked at the whole case from a point of suspicion. The media also began to question whether Pinki Pramanik was male or female. At this point, along with some non-profit organizations, I became increasingly involved in shifting the public debate from the question of 'whether male or female' to that of the violation of Pramanik's human rights. Finally, Pramanik was granted bail on July 10, 2012 and the news was welcomed by most. At the time of writing, the court case has not been resolved.

In Pinki Pramanik's case the police in the station where the complaint was lodged, the journalists who covered the case, the court lawyers, and members of the medical board could not disconnect Pramanik's athletic past with the current allegations. The following questions were raised: Was the medical board set up at the Barasat District Hospital trying to see if the accused was capable of raping a woman? If so, why did they need to know Pramanik's genotype or her hormone levels, which used to be important components of the redundant 'gender-verification test' in international athletics, but were of no significance in a rape charge. The utter confusion that has been created by drawing our attention to whether the medals Pramanik won years ago should be retained or returned could be avoided only if the allegations of rape are disconnected from her former achievements.

The manhandling of Pramanik demonstrated how brutality towards the non-normative could be a weapon to secure space for the normative. Many different forces joined hands to disgrace Pramanik and demonize someone who is looked at as different. The police were able to humiliate Pramanik publicly, grope her chest to see if she had breasts, take her to a private nursing home without a court order and forcefully conduct a physical examination of her genitals without reproof. Because Pramanik was characterized as deviant, she became an acceptable object of curiosity and abuse. A section of the judiciary pushed her to undergo repeated 'sex-determination tests' and, without Pramanik's consent, members of the medical boards as well as the police shared information with reporters about her phenotype and other personal details. During a live Bengali TV programme,[23] when Pramanik was a member of the panel, I directly challenged a reporter about discussing details of her 'sex determination test'. He retorted that it was his duty to do so as the public is curious to know. Without hesitation, newspaper reports also speculated about her specific condition, including her genitals. Following the submission of the charge sheet by the police, the media 'created a monster out of the former athlete, labeling her as not only an aberration but also conclusively declaring her to be an imposter, a rapist and a potential murderer – above all "A MAN"' (Mitra, 2013).

All three of these athletes have a story to tell – a story of severe abuse and misuse by insensitive, corrupt and ruthless officials, the medical community, the government, the society and their own families. However, in some ways, Santhi's case sends a clear message. Increased mobilization of people with gender variance, if not particularly those born intersex, can have a positive impact on governmental policies and can in turn protect such individuals. The public debate surrounding Pinki Pramanik's case also had some positive impact at a national level. Currently, the Ministry of Youth Affairs and Sports, the Government of India, together with the All India Institute of Medical Sciences are in the final stages of developing a national protocol to cover disputes regarding the eligibility of female athletes with hyperandrogenism.[24] The aim is better management of female athletes with intersex variations in India.[25]

Conclusion

Scholars and historians have argued that the binary sex model was not as integral to the cultures of traditional Indian societies as to those in the West. Nivedita Menon argues that neither prior to the sixteenth century in Europe, nor until the early nineteenth century in India, was it believed that bodies are naturally completely one sex or another, that intersexuality was considered to be a disease, or that desire naturally flows only between different sexes (Menon, 2011). She further argues that 'normative' male and female bodies and 'normative' male and female behaviours were constructed by modernizing nationalist elites in an effort to embrace colonial modernity in India in the nineteenth and twentieth centuries.

Even though there is ample evidence of the presence of a 'third sex', of *hijras* and *aravanis*, in history and traditional literature (Reddy, 2005), the process of delegitimization of the third category of gender/sex began during colonization. Therefore, the current efforts to accommodate alternative identities in application forms or formal identity cards[26] by the Tamil Nadu government (Baudh, Vasudevan, & Chugani, 2009) or the Indian government should not merely be interpreted as modernizing policies. These efforts to legitimize the presence of the *aravani* community in Tamil Nadu are in reality an attempt to embrace tradition over Western concepts of modernity.

Medical science in twentieth century Europe and America portrayed intersex bodies as different and in need of treatment. Scientists believed that in order to accommodate such bodies in society, it was important to categorize them as either male or female, and therefore surgery and other forms of treatment were prescribed. In the cases of both Santhi, who was born in a government hospital, and Pal, who was born at home in an *atur ghar* or the labour room, without the presence of a doctor, the doctor and midwife felt no obligation to make them look 'normal'. One way of explaining this phenomenon is to blame lack of access to 'modern' medical facilities in remote corners of India. But it can also be interpreted as a rejection of any necessity for correction or repair, a process of embracing what is natural at the cost of being deemed pre-modern.

None of the athletes' families felt the obligation to repair their respective child's atypical genitals. They definitely realized that their child was born different but they did not try to surgically 'normalize' the child's body. Intersex people in India, who receive treatment or undergo surgery when young, mostly belong to that section of the society that has access to and has been influenced by the medical science of twentieth century Europe and North America. The IOC and the IAAF are overtly concerned to shape bodies to suit medical notions of male and female, popular in the West. Bandana Pal is a victim of butchery in the name of advanced science whereas Santhi Soundarajan is a victim for not wanting to look 'normal' and for not succumbing to modern medical science. Pinki Pramanik on the other hand, is still unshakable, even after her body was investigated publicly, images of her naked body were circulated, and her integrity was questioned. In a personal interview, she said, 'What I am, I am. No one has the right to tell me what I am or how I should be'.[27] Although both Santhi's and Pramanik's parents may not have had access to modern technology and science, they did not feel obliged to shape their child's body to fit Western notions of gender normality.

While recent constructions of sex and sexuality by medical science are drawing our attention to the inadequacy of popular notions of sex, gender and sexuality, the recent policies of the IOC and the IAAF still pose problems for athletes born different. Their current position, focusing on hyperandrogenism, suggests that female athletes who naturally produce androgen in the male range and do not have androgen resistance are not eligible to run and can compete in the women's events only after their hyperandrogenism is 'treated' or their androgen level is lowered to a certain level in order to ensure a level playing field for all female athletes. Treatment may include hormone therapy and in some cases even gonadectomy.

The emphasis on providing a level playing field to all female athletes and therefore subjecting them to surveillance resulting in a ban from their sport until 'treated' is clearly discriminatory. In the Play the Game 2011 Conference, Professor Arne Ljungqvist, Chairman of the IOC Medical Commission, claimed that the discriminatory 'gender-verification tests' have been abolished and described the current policy on hyperandrogensim as a 'matter of eligibility for participation in female competition'. However, he admits that the policy is 'not perfect'. I argue that the current policy is no better than the routine 'gender verification tests' previously conducted by the IOC. Professor Bruce Kidd, Faculty of Kinesiology and Physical Education, University of Toronto, a former Olympian and Chair of the Commonwealth Advisory Board on Sport, posed a question at the same conference last year: 'How can the Olympic Movement, which encourages and affirms the right of self-expression through sport, deny the right of self-identity to some humans?' Professor Kidd recommends that international athletic competition should have self-declaration as the rule where athletes declare in writing what they believe to be their sex, gender and identity and be allowed to compete on that basis.[28]

Professor Rebbeca Jordan-Young, a sociomedical scientist from Barnard College, and Dr. Katrina Karkazis, an anthropologist and bioethicist from Stanford University, have been campaigning against the IOC/IAAF policies and wanted them to be withdrawn immediately. According to them, endogenous testosterone does not confer athletic advantage in a predictable way, an assumption that the new policy is based upon.[29]

A study conducted in 2000 by British endocrinologist, Peter Sonksen, examined 650 Olympian athletes across sports.[30] A scatterplot of his data has been published in a report which clearly demonstrates that about 5% of the women have testosterone in the male range and 6% of the men have testosterone in the female range, suggesting that testosterone cannot be a marker of sex or of athletic capacity. Dr. Karkazis and Professor Jordan-Young also say that there is hardly any research that suggests that elite athletes with naturally high levels of testosterone perform better than those with low levels, which also points to the lack of credibility of IOC/IAAF policies.

What the current policy and the practice of 'gender-verification tests' (now abolished) successfully indicate is the IAAF and the IOC's desperation at maintaining the 'gender gap' in sports. Even though they are suggesting that the current policy is a step forward from the notorious 'gender-verification tests' of the past, this policy reinstates the popular notion that female athletes should look 'feminine'. On the pretext of providing a level playing field to all female athletes, the IAAF policy (IAAF, 2012) attempts to identify female athletes with 'masculine traits' and 'uncommon athletic capacity' and forces them to undergo detailed medical examination and subsequent medical intervention.

What is also alarming is that powerful international organizations encourage national sport governing bodies to ensure that their athletes are eligible for selection in accordance with IOC rules and regulations. The IOC policy (IOC, 2012) urges each NOC to 'actively investigate any perceived deviation in sex characteristics' and keep complete documentation of the findings prior to registration of their athletes in international competitions like the Olympics. Worryingly, this gives national sport administrators an excuse to conduct tests on any female athlete they perceive to be deviant. Female athletes in India are therefore at risk of undergoing increased scrutiny, exploitation and forceful medical treatment.

What is most alarming is the tendency among sport governing bodies and the media to consider the IOC/IAAF policies as absolute and the final answer to an athlete's sexuality or sexual identity. The IOC has bestowed policy responsibility on its Medical Commission encouraging uncritical acceptance of recommendations made by medical scientists. These international sports organizations have expressed a reluctance to accept intersex bodies as they are, subjecting them to severe scrutiny and mockery, forcing them to feel inadequate and in need of repair. It is an approach that is viciously exclusionary and incapable of addressing multiplicities not only of different bodies but also of cultures and traditions. It is time that such organizations and their policies are subjected to 'our' scrutiny.

Notes

1 'Intersex people' have a biological makeup (genetic, hormonal and physical features), which is neither exclusively male nor exclusively female, but is typical of both at once or not clearly defined as either. These features can manifest themselves in secondary sexual characteristics such as muscle mass, hair distribution, breasts and stature; primary sexual characteristics such as reproductive organs and genitalia; and/or in chromosomal structures and hormones. The term intersex has replaced the term 'hermaphrodite', used extensively by medical practitioners during the eighteenth and nineteenth centuries. Intersex generally refers to variation in genital anatomy, but not all intersex variations involve ambiguous genitalia. Some intersex people have typical external genitals but the internal anatomy of the other sex.

In simpler words, bodies that have a mixture of female and male parts or characteristics may be called intersex bodies.

2 In *Bodies in Doubt: An American History of Intersex*, Elizabeth Reis (2009) suggests a new name, Divergence in Sex Development, in place of Disorder of Sex Development.

3 'Transsexual people' identify with the gender role opposite to the sex assigned to them at birth and seek to live permanently in the preferred gender role. This is often accompanied by strong rejection of their physical primary and secondary sex characteristics.

4 See 'Caught in the middle', Samantha Shapiro, August 1, 2012. http://espn.go.com/olympics/story/_/id/8192977/failed-gender-test-forces-olympian-redefine-athletic-career-espn-magazine

5 Babe Didrikson was an outstanding American athlete who excelled in different sports. In the 1932 Olympics she did phenomenally well. However, her muscular build and exceptional athletic ability led to media speculation, labeling her as 'mannish', 'unfeminine', 'not-quite-female', a 'Muscle Moll'. See http://www.bakerdonelson.com/celebrating-womens-history-month-wonder-girl-05-31-2012/ or *Coming on Strong: Gender and Sexuality in Twentieth Century Women's Sports* by Susan Cahn (Freepress, New York 1994).

6 I have met all three athletes as part of an independent research project conducted after the completion of my doctoral thesis. My work has not been restricted to research but included sustained involvement in the struggle against the very institutions that exploited them. The work, which began in 2010, is still in progress.

7 *Salwar kameez* is a traditional dress worn in India mostly by women. In Tamil Nadu young women are more likely to wear *salwar kameez* than trousers and shirts.

8 Personal interview, January 2011.

9 Ibid.

10 'Lure of government jobs draws them to sports', Vineet Gill, *The Times of India*, July 2, 2012. http://articles.timesofindia.indiatimes.com/2012-07-02/gurgaon/32507699_1_neetu-bhiwani-boxing-club-vijender-singh

11 Personal interviews, July 2010.

12 The Gender Verification Reports were not given to Santhi until she applied for them from the Athletics Federation of India (AFI) in 2011 under the Right to Information Act of 2005. When interrogated, the Olympic Council of Asia staff responded in a telephonic interview in 2010 that the athlete's copy of the report should have been handed over to her by the National Olympic Committee (NOC), the Indian Olympic Association. With Santhi's approval, I had contacted concerned officials from the Medical Commission of the IOA and the AFI in 2010. When they refused to send the reports to Santhi, we (Santhi and I) took a Human Rights lawyer's advice and sent a formal Right to Information application on January 10, 2011[0] and received the documents within two months.

13 See 'Indian's Soundarajan likely to lose medal', Anthony Caruso, Universal Sports, December 18, 2006. http://preview.universalsports.com/news-blogs/article/newsid=277801.html

14 See 'Of Genes and Gender', in *The Myths of Gender: Biological Theories about Women and Men* by A. Fausto-Sterling (Basic Books, New York, 1992).

15 Among the factors that were stated as important were (1) whether the child born with ambiguous genitalia will be able to stand and urinate as a grown up boy. Doctors also argued that (2) girl children are brought up in a more protective way and therefore there is a reduced chance of being noticed and subsequently humiliated by friends or others.

16 Gonadectomy can be defined as excision of gonads (testes/ovaries).

17 Personal interviews in 2011 in 2012 with the athlete, the family members of the athlete and doctors who treated the athlete.

18 See 'Bonny Pal strikes a new goal', Krishnendu Bandopadhyay, *The Times of India*, August 14, 2012. http://articles.timesofindia.indiatimes.com/2012-08-14/kolkata/33200410_1_bandana-bonny-football-team/2

19 See 'The mysterious case of Santhi Soundarajan and other stories', December 26, 2006. http://sportsnob.wordpress.com/2006/12/26/the-mysterious-case-of-santhi-soundarajan-and-the-y-chromosome/

20 Personal interviews with journalists writing on *Dalit* issues, 2011. See Santhi Soundarajan's interview by Meena Mayil, 'I am ashamed to be born in India' (translated from Tamil) in *Dalit Marasuru*, October 2010 and November 2010.

21 Dravida Munnettra Kazhagam is a political party in Tamil Nadu.

22 Personal interviews with development workers in Tamil Nadu, transgender rights activists and mainly female to male transgender activists in Tamil Nadu and elsewhere in India, 2012.

23 ABP Ananda, July 11, 2012.
24 Hyperandrogenism is a condition of excessive secretion of androgen from adrenal cortex, ovaries or testes. According to the IOC, androgenic hormones have performance enhancing effects.
25 I am involved in this process as a Consultant to the Department of Sports, Ministry of Youth Affairs and Sports and am trying to help create a protocol that is sensitive and progressive.
26 Identity cards include ration cards in Tamil Nadu, passport and voter's ID card in India.
27 In one of many conversations I had with Pinki Pramanik in Kolkata in 2012.
28 See *For Gender Self-declaration* by Bruce Kidd, Play the Game 2011. http://www.playthegame.org/fileadmin/image/PTG2011/Presentation/Wednesday/Kidd_Bruce_The_intersex_challenge_to_sport.pdf
29 See Karkazis, K., Jordan-Young, R., Davis, G., & Camporesi, S. (2012). Out of Bounds? A Critique of the New Policies on Hyperandrogenism in Elite Female Athletes. *The American Journal of Bioethics, 12* (7), 3–16.
30 See 'Gender games', Amanda Schaffer, *Slate*, July 25, 2012. http://www.slate.com/sidebars/2012/07/scatterplot_of_testosterone_levels_for_around_650_olympic_athletes_representing_a_random_selection_across_sports_.html

References

Baudh, S., Vasudevan, A., & Chugani, B. (2009). *Documenting the Growth of Community Action among Sexual Minority Groups in India*. India: United Nations Development Programme.

Cavanagh, S. L., & Sykes, H. (2006). Transexual Bodies at the Olympics: The International Olympic Committee's Policy on Transsexual Athletes at the 2004 Athens Summer Games. *Body & Society, 12* (3), 75–102.

Doorairaj, S. (2009, December 19). Seeking Identity. *Frontline, 26* (26). http://www.hindu.com/the-hindu/thscrip/print.pl?file=20100101262610000.htm&date=fl2626/&prd=fline&

Fausto-Sterling, A. (1992). *Myths of Gender: Biological Theories about Women and Men*. New York: Basic Books.

Fausto-Sterling, A. (2000). *Sexing the Body: Gender Politics and the Construction of Sexuality*. New York: Basic Books.

Griffin, P. (2010). *IOC releases 'New' 'Gender' Verification Policy*. Pat Griffin's LGBT Sport Blog.

Harrington, M. (2008, April 19). The Rationing of Rights. *Tehelka Magazine, 5* (15). http://archive.tehelka.com/story_main38.asp?filename=hub190408The_Rationing.asp

Hercher, L. (2010). Gender Verification: A Term whose Time Has Come and Gone. *Journal of Genetic Counseling, 19*, 551–553.

IAAF. (2012). *IAAF Regulations Governing Female Athletes with Hyperandrogenism to Compete in Women's Competition*. IAAF.

IAAF Medical and Anti-Doping Commission. (2006). *IAAF Policy on Gender Verification*. International Association of Athletics Federation. http://oii.org.au/wp-content/uploads/downloads/2009/iaaf_policy_on_gender_verification.pdf

Imperato-Mcginley, J., Guerrero, L., Gautier, T., & Peterson, R. (1974). Steroid 5α-reductase Deficiency in Man: An Inherited Form of Male Pseudohermaphroditism. *Science, 186*, 1213–1215.

IOC (2012). *IOC Regulations on Female Hyperandrogenism*. International Olympic Committee. http://www.olympic.org/Documents/Commissions_PDFfiles/Medical_commission/2012-06-22-IOC-Regulations-on-Female-Hyperandrogenism-eng.pdf

Karkazis, K. (2008). *Fixing Sex: Intersex, Medical Authority, and Lived Experience*. London: Duke University Press.

Karkazis, K., Jordan-Young, R., Davis, G., & Camporesi, S. (2012). Out of Bounds? A Critique of the New Policies on Hyperandrogenism in Elite Female Athletes. *The American Journal of Bioethics, 12* (7), 3–16.

Menon, N. (2011, February 18). The Disappearing Body and Feminist Thought. *Kafila*.

Mitra, P. (2010). *Y can't I run? The Story of Santhi Soundarajan*. Kolkata.

Mitra, P. (2013). *Gender Bender: The Case of Pinki Pramanik and the Role of the Media*. Kolkata: Sappho for Equality.

Money, J., & Ehrhardt, A. A. (1972). *Man and Woman, Boy and Girl: Differentiation and Dimorphism of Gender Identity from Conception to Maturity*. Baltimore: Johns Hopkins University Press.

Money, J., & Hampson, J. (1955). An Examination of Some Basic Sexual Concepts: The Evidence of Human Hermaphroditism. *Bulletin Johns Hopkins Hospital*, 308.

Munro, B. (2010). Caster Semenya: Gods and Monsters. *The Journal of South African and American Studies*, *11* (4), 383–396.

Ori, K. O., & Johnsson, P. K. (2009, September 12). Caster Semenya Enigma: IAAF Tests Will Disqualify Most Women Athletes. www.afrik-news.com.

Reddy, G. (2005). *With Respect to Sex: Negotiating Hijra Identity in South India*. Chicago: University of Chicago Press.

Reis, E. (2009). *Bodies in Doubt: An American History of Intersex*. Baltimore: The Johns Hopkins University Press.

PART VII

Power, control and abuse

42

FOUCAULDIAN EXAMINATIONS OF SPORT, GENDER AND SEXUALITY

Richard Pringle

Introduction

French scholar Michel Foucault is regarded by many as one of the most influential social theorists of contemporary times and his oeuvre is well recognised within sport sociology. In presenting a keynote address to delegates attending the North American Society for the Sociology of Sport annual conference, for example, Toby Miller (2010) rhetorically asked: 'Is anyone here who is not a paid up member of the Foucault fan club?' His question reflects the contemporary significance of Foucauldian theorising within sociological studies of sport but also the now seemingly conventional manner within which Foucault is drawn upon.

Yet the utility of Foucault's theoretical toolbox took a relatively long time for sport sociologists to discover. Richard Gruneau (1991), as an example, was 'long . . . struck by the comparative absence of Foucauldian analyses in English language writing on sport' (p.180). Gruneau's observation was apt, as Francophone scholars such as Jean Harvey (1983) and Jean–Marie Brohm (1981) had previously drawn on Foucault to critically examine aspects of sport.

By the late 1980s and early 1990s and in relation to the growing theoretical interest in the 'body', Foucauldian theorising gained more widespread attention (e.g. see Andrews, 1993; Cole, 1993; Hargreaves, 1986; Harvey and Sparks, 1991; Heikkala, 1993; Theberge, 1991; Whitson, 1989). Foucauldian theorising was further promoted via the publication of special editions in *Quest* (1991) and the *Sociology of Sport Journal* (1995), which both aimed to theorise the body and 'shed some light on the sociology of sport in "la Francophonie"' (Harvey and Rail, 1995, p. 119).

At the same time that Foucault's significance was gaining increased recognition, resistance to his ideas was also evident. William Morgan (1995) critiqued what he claimed to be the somewhat insidious intrusion of postmodern/poststructural ideas within sport sociology. With specific attention to Foucault, Morgan was concerned that the associated 'attack on normal inquiry' (p. 31) risked endangering 'the venerable practice of social criticism' while simultaneously promoting 'a partisan, and rather trendy, championing of the beliefs of certain groups' (p. 31). Ann Hall (1993) also raised concerns with Foucault via a critique of Cole's (1993) promotion of feminist cultural studies. Hall argued that theory had overtaken Cole's 'insights' and her use of 'complicated language' and lack of theoretical 'clarity' served 'no useful purpose' (p. 104). Regardless of the soundness or otherwise of Morgan and Hall's concerns, the internal debates reinforced the need to take Foucauldian theorising seriously.

Foucault's influence within sport sociology is now somewhat ubiquitous with his ideas drawn upon to examine an eclectic range of topics, including, as examples: coaching, disability, drug testing, embodiment, government control, health/fitness, obesity, pain and pleasure, public policy, racism, sexuality and sport pedagogy. Importantly, however, the sport scholars who first appropriated Foucault and who have led the way in 'enhancing the interpretive powers and sophistication' (Andrews, 1993, p. 162) of his ideas have been feminists. Their initiatives, according to Andrews (2000) have 'generated some of the most vibrant and incisive work related to the cultural politics of gender and sex' (p. 125).

However, the links between Foucault and feminism have not been without tension. Indeed, many feminists have raised concerns about Foucault's androcentric focus and writing style. Foucault (1983), nevertheless, was aware of how his theoretical ideas could be appropriated for the advances of feminist scholarship. He expressed, as an example, concern about 'the power of men over women' (p. 211) and illustrated how this relationship was linked to a form of power that categorises bodies and makes them subject 'to someone else by control and dependence' (p. 212). Moreover, he intended to expand his genealogical examinations concerning biopower and sexuality, by writing a text with the working title *Woman, Mother, Hysteric*. This text did not eventuate, however, as he recognised that through using a similar methodological and theoretical approach to his earlier work on sexuality, his broad argument would have been similar. It was left, therefore, for poststructural feminists to appropriate Foucauldian theorising.

Diamond and Quinby (1988) highlighted four prime complementary links between Foucault and feminism: they both (i) locate the body as important for the workings of power, (ii) focus on the local for examinations of power, (iii) are concerned with revealing marginalised discourses or knowledges, and, (iv) critique how humanism has privileged masculine ways of knowing via the seemingly neutral voice of science.

In this review chapter, I focus on the political convergences between feminism and Foucault to illustrate how sport feminists have drawn on Foucauldian theorising for projects of social justice. My broad aim is to provide an overview of Foucault's theoretical underpinnings and illustrate how his iconoclastic ideas have been used to produce insightful critiques of sport and the social construction of gendered and sexualised bodies. I introduce key Foucauldian ideas through reviewing six papers that exemplify prime aspects of sport feminist scholarship. These papers examine the following topics: the discursive construction of multiple identities (Cox and Thompson, 2000), disciplinary power and the making of elite gendered athletes (Shogan, 1999), the panoptic gaze on the female body (Duncan, 1994), the construction of normalised *and* transformative sporting bodies (Chase, 2006), the resurrection of marginalised knowledge to allow possibilities of social change (Pringle, 2008), and mindful fitness as a technology of self (Markula, 2004). Each of these papers was selected in part as they were underpinned by Foucault's anti-essentialist perspective or, more specifically, his desire to 'circumvent the anthropological universals . . . in order to examine them as historical constructs' (Florence, 1998, p. 464). The critical Foucauldian tenets introduced should not be read as recipes for social transformation but as starting points for thinking differently that allow possibilities for change.

Be skeptical of essentialist notions of the self

Foucault (1988a) summarised that his prime research objective had 'been to sketch out a history of the different ways in our culture that humans develop knowledge about themselves' (pp.17–18).

He examined the production of these forms of knowledge, particularly within the human sciences, as he believed that they acted as a form of power that defined, ordered, categorised, constituted and differentially valued individuals. Obesity scientists, as an example, have developed various ways for measuring the percentages of adipose tissue in a body (e.g. skin-fold calipers, under water weighing) and have subsequently classified certain body types into various groups (e.g. obese, overweight, normal, underweight). The scientific assertion that certain bodies are at risk of poor health has subsequently impacted on how some bodies are known and valued.

To help examine the linkages between forms of knowledge and the workings of power, Foucault (1978) developed his concept of 'discourse' and suggested, 'it is in discourse that power and knowledge are joined together' (p. 100). Foucault (1972) considered that discourses were more than linguistic phenomena and maintained that they should be treated as 'practices that systematically form the objects of which they speak' (p. 49). Various social practices and associated discourses within New Zealand, for example, work to 'objectify' ballet as a feminine activity and rugby as masculine. Discourse, accordingly, can be regarded as constraining or structuring how people perceive reality, including knowledge of self and others. Given the conjunction of knowledge and power, Foucault (1978) stressed the importance of analysing the complex interplay of discourses to help understand the complexities of social life.

Cox and Thompson (2000), in a much cited paper, drew from Foucault to explore how 16 members of a premier women's football (soccer) team 'experienced their bodies within the discourses of sport, gender and heterosexuality' (p. 5). They focused their analysis on 'the contradictions and complexities among the various discourses that surround women's sport, as well as sportswomen's own experiences and perception of their bodies' (p. 6). Via in-depth interviews they found that an array of discursive binaries (e.g. male/female sport, masculinity/femininity, thin/fat, and heterosexuality/homosexuality) created various tensions and frustrations for the female players. Cox and Thompson, for example, stated: 'while playing soccer has given the players physical fitness, strength and confidence, the bodies they have developed are also marginalised and constructed as "different" from those of other women through the heterosexual mechanisms of tomboyism and female-appropriateness in sport' (p. 12). In order to try and alleviate some of these frustrations, the football players adopted various strategies, including: the wearing of a feminine hair-style (i.e. pony tails) to create an impression of conventional femininity, not showering in front of team mates, and various attempts to 'prove' heterosexuality or disassociate from perceived lesbians.

Cox and Thompson (2000) concluded that their results supported Butler's (1990) notion of the heterosexual matrix in that the 'homophobic climate of sport puts pressure on *all* female athletes to present a heterosexual image of femininity' (p. 16).

Their study further reinforced the Foucauldian notion that the 'self' is produced in specific socio-historic contexts via the workings of multiple discourses and relations of power and, therefore, the self should not be considered as stable, whole, and unified. In contrast, they suggested that their results reinforced Judith Butler's idea that gender could be considered 'as a set of repeated performances that congeal over time to produce the appearance of a natural sort of being' (Cox and Thompson, 2000, p. 17). This conclusion could be liberating, they informed, as individuals might recognise that they do not have to perform a 'restrictive set of 'natural' traits' (p. 18).

Reveal techniques that discipline and produce the 'body'

In order to examine social struggles, Foucault (1983) deemed it important to analyse *how* power is exercised and, as a result, 'what happens'? (p. 217). He, accordingly, encouraged *empirical* analyses of the workings of power and focused on examining relationships between people (i.e. power relations) in order to understand the 'way in which certain actions modify others' (p. 219). These actions, he explained, did not always act directly and immediately on others but could also relate to the circulation of ideas (e.g. workings of discourse) and systems of communication. Foucault (1977) theorised that power was always present within human relations and correspondingly argued that the body was 'directly involved in a political field' (p. 25). His focus on the body rather than the individual reflected his anti-essentialist philosophy. The individual, according to Foucault (1980), was already the *effect* of the workings of a form of power. In this respect, he examined how this form of power was exercised to understand how 'certain bodies, certain gestures, certain discourses, certain desires, come to be identified and constituted as individuals' (p. 98).

Although Foucault (1980) acknowledged multiple forms of power, he focused extensively on what he called *disciplinary power*: a form of power that controlled and normalised individuals so that they were 'destined to a certain mode of living' (p. 94). As an anti-essentialist, he accepted that disciplinary technologies were not inherently good or bad. In this manner, his critical target of concern was not the disciplinary techniques per se, but their power effect (or what they produced).

Sport scholars who have drawn on Foucault's ideas of disciplinary technologies have similarly aimed to raise critical awareness about how these techniques are employed in sport or exercise settings to produce normalised bodies (e.g. Cole, 1993; Theberge, 1991). Debra Shogan (1999) provided an exemplary overview of the workings of disciplinary technologies in relation to the making of high-performance athletes. She drew from Foucault's (1977) work on *Discipline and punish* to illustrate how the technologies of disciplinary power 'map well onto sport' (Shogan, 1999, p. 19). These technologies included the 'individuation of private space; codification of "correct" actions in relation to a strict timetable; routinization of activities according to a training schedule of increasing difficulty, followed by an examination to test abilities; and sychronization of individuals into a collective' (Shogan, 1999, p. 19). These technologies are commonly employed in sport training contexts, for example: fitness work is often based on the overload principle, coaches plan periodised timetables, athletic ability is measured via the stopwatch, and coaches video athletes to access and develop correct technique. These various training technologies help produce, what Shogan called, the *docile* athletic body, that is, a body that is a highly efficient sport performer but also one that conforms to athletic conventions, ignores degrees of pain, provides automatic responses in sporting situations, and is subject to repetitive and often tedious training sessions.

Shogan (1999) extended her analysis of the making of high-performance athletes to illustrate how disciplinary technologies produce what she called 'hybrid athletes' (p. 45), who are simultaneously subject to multiple and competing identity discourses, such as those related to gender, sexuality and ethnicity. She acknowledged that although the sporting world can still be regarded as a modernist project, athletes exist in a broader postmodern context and are subject to greater discursive tensions.

With respect to gender, Shogan asserted: 'Disciplined athletic bodies are not "natural" or "normal", and there is nothing "natural" or "normal" about a body that has been disciplined as feminine or masculine. Femininity and masculinity, like sport skills, are acts or performances that must be learned' (p. 51). In this respect, she argued that the process of becoming identified as 'female' or 'male' could similarly be thought of as a disciplinary process that requires an extended period of training, conforming and (self) examining in relation to a specialized form of embodied knowledges. Cole (1993), for example, suggested that the 'technologies of femininity refer to those knowledges, practices, and strategies that manufacture and normalize the feminine body: those techniques, actions, and structures deployed to sculpt, fashion, and secure bodily shapes, gestures, and adornments that are recognizably female' (p. 87). Shogan added, however, that competitive institutionalized sport is a discursive context within which masculine values, gestures, actions and interactions 'are practised and normalized' (p. 54). Accordingly, although there is nothing natural about an athletic body, Shogan illustrated how female athletic embodiment could pose greater discursive conflict than male athletic embodiment. For example, female sporting bodies that display performances of aggression, strength and pain tolerance, risk condemnation as masculine as opposed to feminine.

Yet rather than concluding that the sporting context is inherently problematic for females, Shogan (1999) discussed how disciplinary technologies fail to produce homogeneous athletes within postmodern societies. Similar to Foucault's (1977) suggestion that the disciplinary systems employed in jails have high rates of failure (e.g. the number of recidivists), Shogan pointed to the disciplinary failures within sport. These failures, she added, allow opportunities for athletes to critically reflect on the costs of their high-performance involvement and potentially retire or change their sporting (or gendered) performances. She concluded that the sporting and exercising context can be viewed as a significant discursive environment, which can allow individuals to perform identities differently. Shogan (1999) pointed out, 'even committed heterosexual women experience in sport what it is like to cross-dress and perform conventional masculine skills' (p. 63). Thus, although the disciplinary technologies employed in sport are still, in many respects, relentless, the sporting context can offer possibilities for critical reflection and social transformation.

Body politics and the panoptic gaze

Margaret Duncan (1994) was also concerned with how the female body is disciplined by various 'practices such as exercising, dieting, comporting one's body in "female appropriate" styles (e.g., taking up as little space as possible), applying cosmetics, shaving, dressing in constricting clothes, curling or straightening one's hair, submitting to plastic surgery and/or liposuction . . .' (p. 49). These various practices, Duncan argued, problematically act to shape the body in conjunction with a feminine beauty ideal that 'is nearly impossible to achieve . . . naturally' (p. 49). She subsequently examined: 'How is it that such a body standard is inculcated in girls and women?' (p. 49).

To examine this question, Duncan drew from Foucault's (1977) metaphor of the panopticon, which refers to the plan of a jail with a guard tower at its centre and prisoners located in a circular position around the tower. The prime effect of the panopticon was to induce for each inmate 'a state of consciousness and permanent visibility that assures the automatic functioning of power' (p. 200). In other words, the inmates develop an understanding that they are permanently subject to a gaze of authority and subsequently discipline or police their own behaviour. The panopticon is therefore a form of disciplinary power.

Duncan (1994) argued, in an analogous way, that women were subject to a panoptic gaze with respect to potential transgressions 'against the patriarchal ideals of femininity' (p. 50). This panoptic gaze she suggested works through 'public discourses of health, fitness, exercise, dieting, and beauty' (p. 51) that are circulated, in part, via the media. Duncan subsequently conducted a textual analysis of *Shape*, a fitness magazine which typically included stories of dieting, exercise strategies and glossy images of female models. She concluded that the magazine typically encouraged women to survey their own bodies for signs of abnormality and to *confess* their sins. Although this panoptic gaze might cause distress for many women, Duncan suggested, that women may find it difficult to resist as 'the disciplinarian is a disembodied authority' (p. 50). She explained:

The invisibility and ambiguity of the source of that gaze encourage women to believe that the body standards they apply to their own bodies are personal and private standards. Thus women may blame themselves – instead of social institutions and public practices – for their anguished relationships with 'their own bodies' . . .

(p. 50)

Duncan's research provides a useful understanding of how unrealistic body standards can be inculcated in women via the circulation of particular bodily discourses in the media. Moreover, it illustrates how the body is produced through relations of power, so that the body can be thought of as a cultural product rather than as a 'natural' object.

Be skeptical of processes of normalisation

Foucault (1977) was concerned about *normalising judgment* as it can divide humans into different categories, produce a hierarchy of 'the "good" and the "bad" subjects in relation to one another' (p. 181) and reward and punish accordingly. He explained: 'The perpetual penalty that traverses all points and supervises every instant in the disciplinary institutions compares, differentiates, hierarchizes, homogenizes, excludes. In short, it *normalizes*' (p. 183). Normalisation, Foucault concluded, was one of the 'great instruments of power at the end of the classical age' (p. 184). His concern, more specifically, was the subsequent production of the abnormal.

Laura Chase's (2006) ethnographic research on female rugby players revealed a similar concern with processes of normalisation as related to the production of athletic and gendered bodies. In drawing from Shogan (1999), Chase was interested in how rugby players negotiated the seemingly competing disciplinary demands of being female and a rugby player. Her results revealed that the athletes became docile, normative, sporting bodies and were, therefore, disciplined by the technologies of dominance employed in training. Yet Chase stated that their 'bruised, battered, and bleeding bodies present a very striking contradiction to images of ideal female bodies' (p. 239). Importantly, many of the players reported that rugby participation had changed how they 'felt and thought about their body and its performance' (p. 239). They felt 'strong, confident and powerful' (p. 240) and proud of who they had become. Moreover, Chase reported that many were critically aware of how their bodies challenged 'images of the ideal female body (and disturbed) the boundaries of what is appropriate for women' (p. 241). She concluded that their bodies were shaped by competing discourses and disciplinary practices to 'produce docile, resistant and transformative bodies' (p. 245).

Resurrection of marginalised forms of knowledge

Disciplinary power, according to Foucault (1977), can only be exercised in relation to production and circulation of a functioning discourse. As a strategy to disrupt the workings of disciplinary powers and normalising judgments, Foucault encouraged the promotion of marginalised forms of knowledge: as these forms circulate a greater range of discursive resources that promote possibilities for the production of different self-understandings. His genealogical examinations, accordingly, were based on a 'reactivation of local knowledges . . . in opposition to the scientific hierarchisation of knowledges and the effects intrinsic to their power' (Foucault, 1980, pp. 83–85).

I drew on Foucault's strategy of resurrecting marginalised knowledge in my research concerning the dominant place of rugby in New Zealand schools (Pringle, 2008). Through collecting a range of men's stories about their rugby experiences via in-depth interviews, I became aware of how a celebrated discourse of rugby circulated in schools that allowed talented male rugby players to exercise more power and gain favourable self-understandings. Conversely, the dominance of rugby and its discursive articulations with tough and aggressive masculinities acted to 'limit alternative discursive resources for the construction of a range of respected masculinities, while also limiting abilities to express discontent towards rugby' (Pringle, 2008, p. 219). I accordingly aimed to resurrect the marginalised knowledges of rugby as a strategy to challenge the 'truth' that bruising rugby participation unequivocally turns boys into respectful men.

My interviewees' accounts of the adverse influence of rugby in their lives – (e.g. the fear of pain, the public *failing* to be a normal boy, the experiences of bullying and marginalisation, the humiliation of social isolation, and the realization of abnormality) – were published as a 'collective story' (see Richardson, 1997) and presented to secondary school students. In a classroom setting, the students were encouraged to critically analyse and discuss the collective story. Results revealed that the majority of the students had an empathetic response to the narrative and were subsequently encouraged to critically reflect on the relationship between rugby and gender production. In this manner, the resurrection of marginalised knowledges helped break the silence that surrounded the dominance of rugby and allowed for differing discursive resources to circulate (at least in the short term). The results supported the need for students to be able to critically discuss the relationships between sport, gender and sexuality within school settings.

Acknowledge that humans have ability to critically reflect and change themselves

The Foucauldian theorising discussed thus far has primarily focused on technologies of dominance, which 'determine the conduct of individuals and submit them to certain ends or domination' (Foucault, 1988b, p. 18). Foucault's later work on the 'technologies of self', in contrast, focused on the practices and codes of conduct that individuals could use to transform themselves. This work has, at times, been interpreted as a strategy of resistance yet Foucault did not explicitly conceptualise the 'technologies of self' as a form of resistance. In contrast, Foucault was concerned with how individuals can recognise themselves within relations of power (as an object or form), how they can problematise the codes of conduct or power relations that constitute this form or identity, and subsequently work to transform themselves via specific techniques or practices of self. Such self-transformations may have little influence on broader power relations but could provide individuals with a 'certain state of happiness, purity, wisdom, perfection, or immortality' (Foucault, 1988b, p. 18). In this respect, the technologies of self can help individuals who have been coerced by normative gender practices.

An awareness of how fitness practices in commercial clubs can 'effectively discipline participants into docile bodies' (p. 303), encouraged Pirkko Markula (2004) to examine the possibilities of whether 'mindful fitness' (e.g. Pilates, yoga and T'ai Chi) instructors could develop programmes that did not act as technologies of dominance but encouraged participants to actively problematise existing fitness/gender knowledges and practices. Her ethnographic research revealed the complexities of power relations and subsequent barriers to self-transformations that instructors of mindful-fitness faced. Overall, Markula did not endorse 'mindful-fitness' as an inherently beneficial fitness practice but stressed its possibilities for transgressing the limitations of normative gender ideals. She concluded that 'Foucault's concept of technologies of the self [was] very helpful in terms of sketching how change might take place in the present condition of the fitness industry' (p. 319). Yet, she acknowledged that the unresolved issue was how to encourage a greater critical awareness amongst fitness consumers and instructors.

Final words

This chapter has illustrated how sport feminists have drawn upon Foucauldian concepts associated with discourse, disciplinary power, and the technologies of self to understand the construction of the sporting body and associated relations of power. More specifically, this review chapter has revealed how the sporting body is gendered and sexed within specific socio-historic contexts so that one can understand, in the words of Foucault (1977), how 'power relations have an immediate hold upon it; they invest it; mark it, train it, torture it, force it to carry out tasks, to perform ceremonies, to emit signs' (p. 25). Although Foucauldian concepts can be difficult to grasp, an advantage of drawing on Foucault's oppositional imagination is that it encourages one to think differently. Indeed, it is only through thinking differently that possibilities for social change can occur.

References

Andrews DL (1993) Desperately seeking Michel: Foucault's genealogy, the body, and critical sport sociology. *Sociology of Sport Journal*, 10: 148–167.

Andrews DL (2000) Posting up: French post-structuralism and the critical analysis of contemporary sporting cultures. In: Coakley J and Dunning E (eds) *Handbook of sports studies*. London: Sage, pp. 106–137.

Brohm J (1981) Theses toward a political sociology of sport. In: Hart M and Birrell S (eds) *Sport in the sociocultural process*. Dubuque, IA: Wm. C. Brown Company.

Butler J (1990) *Gender trouble: feminism and the subversion of identity*. New York: Routledge.

Chase LF (2006) (Un)disciplined bodies: a Foucauldian analysis of women's rugby. *Sociology of Sport Journal*, 23: 229–247.

Cole CL (1993) Resisting the canon: feminist cultural studies, sport, and technologies of the body. *Journal of Sport and Social Issues*, 17(2): 77–97.

Cox B and Thompson S (2000) Multiple bodies: sportswomen, soccer and sexuality. *International Review for the Sociology of Sport*, 35(1): 5–20.

Diamond I and Quinby L (eds) (1988) *Feminism and Foucault: reflections of resistance*. Boston, MA: North Easton University Press.

Duncan MC (1994) The politics of women's body images and practices: Foucault, the panopticon, and shape magazine. *Journal of Sport & Social Issues*, 18(1): 48–65.

Florence M (1998) Foucault. In: Faubion JD (ed) *Michel Foucault aesthetics: essential works of Foucault 1954–1984, volume 2*. London: Penguin Books, pp. 459–463.

Foucault M (1972) *The archaeology of knowledge*. London: Tavistock.

Foucault M (1977) *Discipline and punish: the birth of the prison*. Translated from French by AM Sheridan. New York: Pantheon Books.

Foucault M (1978) *The history of sexuality, Volume 1: an introduction*. Translated from French by R Hurley. New York: Random House.

Foucault M (1980) Two lectures. In: Gordon C (ed) *Power/knowledge*. Brighton: Harvestor, pp. 78–108.

Foucault M (1983) The subject and power. In: Dreyfus HL and Rabinow R (eds) *Michel Foucault: beyond structuralism and hermeneutics*, 2nd edn, Chicago, IL: University of Chicago Press, pp. 208–226.

Foucault M (1988a) Technologies of the self. In: Martin L, Gutman H and Hutton P (eds) *Technologies of the self: a seminar with Michel Foucault*. Amherst, MA: University of Massachusetts Press, pp. 16–49.

Foucault M (1988b) The ethic of care for the self as a practice of freedom: an interview with Michel Foucault on January 20, 1984. In: Bernauer J and Rasmussen D (eds) *The final Foucault*. Cambridge, MA: The MIT Press, pp. 1–20.

Gruneau R (1991) Sport and 'esprit de corps': Notes on power, culture and the politics of the body. In: Landry F, Yerles M and Landry M (eds) *Sport: The third millennium*. Sainte Foy, Quebec: Presses de l'Universite Laval, pp. 169–186.

Hall A (1993) Feminism, theory and the body: a response to Cole. *Journal of Sport and Social Issues*, 17(2): 98–105.

Hargreaves J (1986) *Sport, power and culture: a social and historical analysis of popular sports in Britain*. Cambridge: Polity Press.

Harvey J (1983) *Le corps programme' ou la rhitorique de Kino-Qukbec*. Montreal: Albert Saint-Martin.

Harvey J and Rail G (1995) Sociology of sport in la 'Francophone'. *Sociology of Sport Journal*, 12(2): 119–120.

Harvey J and Sparks R (1991) The politics of the body in the context of modernity. *Quest*, 43: 164–189.

Heikkala J (1993) An introduction to a (non)fascist sporting life. In: Laine L (ed) *On the fringes of sport*. Sankt Augustin: Academia Verlag, pp.78–83.

Markula P (2004) "Tuning into one's self": Foucault's technologies of the self and mindful fitness, *Sociology of Sport Journal*, 21: 302–321.

Miller T (2010) Alan Ingham Memorial Address. In: North American Sociology of Sport 31st Annual Conference, *Producing knowledge, producing bodies*. San Diego, USA, November 3–6.

Morgan WJ (1995) Incredulity towards metanarratives and normative suicide: a critique of postmodernist drift in critical sport theory. *International Review for the Sociology of Sport*, 30(1): 25–44.

Pringle R (2008) 'No rugby – no fear': Collective stories, masculinities and transformative possibilities in schools. *Sport, Education and Society*, 13(2): 215–237.

Richardson L (1997) *Fields of play: constructing an academic life*. New Brunswick, NJ: Rutgers Press.

Shogan D (1999) *The making of high performance athletes: discipline, diversity, and Ethics*. Toronto: University of Toronto Press.

Theberge N (1991) Reflections on the body in the sociology of sport. *Quest*, 43: 148–167.

Whitson D (1989) Discourses of critique in sport sociology: a response to Deem and Sparks. *Sociology of Sport Journal*, 6: 60–65.

43

PSYCHOLOGICAL SAFETY AND THE EXPRESSION OF SEXUAL ORIENTATION AND PERSONAL IDENTITY

George B. Cunningham, Andrew C. Pickett, E. Nicole Melton,
Woojun Lee and Kathi Miner

Introduction

While there have been notable improvements over time, many lesbian and bisexual women within the sport and physical activity context experience sexual prejudice, as they work within a strongly heterosexist culture (Griffin, 2012). US researchers have observed, for instance, that lesbians, and even women presumed to be lesbian, have negative work experiences, facing various forms of discrimination from their supervisors and co-workers (Krane and Barber, 2005; Sartore and Cunningham, 2010). As a result, many lesbian coaches and administrators in the US are reluctant to disclose their sexual orientation to others (see Krane and Barber, 2005). These dynamics are not limited to coaches and administrators, though, as bisexual and lesbian athletes also report they conceal their sexual orientation from others, including teammates, believing they would face negative consequences if such information was revealed (Gough, 2007). Such fears are not unfounded, as American female athletes have told of their coaches threatening to disclose the player's sexual orientation to others for lack of performance and compliance (Melton and Cunningham, 2012).

The institutionalized nature of sport's gendered and heterosexist culture (Anderson, 2010) brings to light the primacy of personal sexual orientation identity and the freedom to express it. As articulated in social identity theory (Tajfel and Turner, 1979), personal identity represents an identity people hold that is critical to their self-concept within a particular context. It constitutes a key element of people's self-image, represents who they are as a person, and helps shape how people feel about themselves (Luhtanen and Crocker, 1992; Randle and Jaussi, 2003). As Brewer (1991) notes, personal identity represents the key elements or characteristics that help distinguish one person from others within a particular social setting (e.g., while participating on a collegiate basketball teams). Note, too, that sexual orientation personal identity is conceptually distinct from some authors' (e.g., Fink et al., 2012) use of the term 'sexual identity', which is synonymous with sexual orientation. Indeed, it is possible for two women to both identify as lesbian (representative of their sexual identity) *and* have very different levels of sexual orientation personal identity. That is, the degree to which being a lesbian is central to how they see themselves and represents a key element of their self-concept might vary considerably.

Ragins (2004) notes that feeling compelled to conceal one's sexual orientation in a social setting can stunt one's sexual orientation personal identity development. Furthermore, when others fail to recognize an important part of one's identity, psychological withdrawal and stress are likely to follow (Pinel and Swann, 2000). Thus, despite the benefits of expressing one's sexual orientation personal identity, women frequently operate in sporting environments where they cannot readily do so, and consequently, the importance to them of their identity might be diminished. In this chapter, we argue that psychologically safe environments are fundamental to changing these patterns. Specifically, in drawing from Ragins' (2004) work related to safe havens, we suggest that when lesbian and bisexual athletes participate on inclusive, psychologically safe teams, the salience of their sexual orientation personal identity is likely to increase. In the following space, we present the theoretical rationale for this position and then examine these relationships using data collected from National Collegiate Athletic Association (NCAA) women's basketball players.

Identity and identity expression

There are a number of benefits for lesbians and bisexual women expressing a strong sexual orientation personal identity. For instance, sexual minorities who have a strong sexual orientation personal identity have come to embrace their sexual minority status and to incorporate it as a key part of the self. Their sexual orientation represents an important part of their self-image and how they see themselves as a person. This might impact how they negotiate sexual minority-related issues in their own lives, including, among other things, sexual orientation disclosure to others. Indeed, various researchers have demonstrated a positive relationship between sexual orientation personal identity strength and outness (Button, 2001; Griffith and Hebl, 2002). From a different perspective, personal identity expression and salience might also be associated with stronger social networks and ties with the lesbian, gay, and bisexual (LGB) community (cf. Tajfel and Turner, 1979). These connections might help, at least partially, to assuage the heterosexism and sexual prejudice they encounter (for similar effects with race, see Branscombe et al., 1999). In addition, Krane et al. (2002) found that participation in the Gay Games helped increase lesbian and bisexual athletes' sexual orientation personal identity, and this increase was associated with subsequent improvements in pride and self-confidence. These improvements were met with other positive outcomes, too, including an increased desire to engage in social change activities (see also Fink et al. 2012).

Just as there are many benefits to possessing a strong sexual orientation personal identity, there are also negative outcomes associated with not being able to do so. In drawing from social identity theory (Tajfel and Turner, 1979), sexual minorities with a low sexual orientation personal identity might be less likely to engage with the LGB community or interact with other sexual minorities. Additionally, lesbians and bisexual women who feel compelled to suppress or minimize their sexual orientation personal identity might subsequently experience feelings of guilt, stress, or shame (Meyer, 2007). They might also develop internalized stigma associated with their identity. When this occurs, sexual minorities are likely to experience negative psychological outcomes, including decreases in self-esteem, depressive symptoms, and anxiousness (Herek et al., 2009). Melton and Cunningham (2012) observed as much in their study of lesbian and bisexual US college athletes who internalized stigma and also conveyed feelings of guilt, shame, and self-hate. Finally, sexual minorities might also express frustration and anger when feeling compelled to suppress their sexual orientation personal identity (see Pennekamp et al., 2009), as people routinely express a desire for others to recognize and value identities that are important to them (Swann, 1983).

Supportive environments

The benefits of expressing a strong sexual orientation personal identity highlight the importance of understanding factors that facilitate such expressions. From a multilevel perspective, one's personal identity is likely to be shaped by a variety of elements, including those at the societal, organization, team, and individual levels. While there is value in understanding and exploring the effects of factors at each level of analysis, in this chapter we focus on the team level of analysis, and specifically, the role of supportive environments that foster psychological safety. This decision is based largely on the premise that this is the level of analysis over which coaches and administrators have the most influence (Doherty et al., 2010). With this in mind, in the following space, we seek to demonstrate the importance of diverse and inclusive environments for sexual minorities in sport, and then focus specifically on the role of psychological safety in fostering a strong sexual orientation personal identity.

A number of authors have theorized about the benefits of diverse and inclusive organizations and teams. For instance, in their review of the literature, Joshi and Roh (2007) identified a number of contextual factors all affecting the role of diversity within a particular setting. Of particular interest here, they concluded that collaborative team environments where people feel both empowered and safe to voice differences can foster a number of positive outcomes, such as creativity and innovation. Similarly, van Knippenberg and Schippers (2007) theorized that teams whose members have pro-diversity mind-sets are more likely to reap diversity's benefits than are their counterparts. They note:

> The effects of diversity should be more positive where individuals, groups, and organizations have more favourable beliefs about and attitudes toward diversity, are more focused on harvesting the benefits of diversity, and have a better understanding of how to realize these benefits.
>
> *(p. 531)*

As a final example, Shore et al. (2011) developed a theoretical framework in which they conceptualized inclusion as involving both the sense one feels of belonging to a group *and* the degree to which one's uniqueness is valued. They argue that when both belongingness and uniqueness are present, diversity's benefits to the workplace are most likely to be realized.

In addition to these theoretical advances, other authors have provided empirical support for the benefits of inclusive work environments. Ely and Thomas's (2001) qualitative investigation provides one of the most-cited examples. The authors observed that some organizations followed an integration and learning perspective, such that diversity informed and positively contributed to the organization's core functions, differences were seen as a source of learning and growth, and as a result, shared leadership, product innovation, and a sense of learning and growth among the employees all emerged. Other studies also point to the benefits of workplace and team inclusiveness, with such environments holding a positive association with retention of racial minority employees (McKay et al., 2007), connection with the group (van Knippenberg et al., 2007), and work performance of diverse groups (Homan et al., 2007), among others.

Importantly, the same pattern of findings has emerged in investigations focusing on sexual orientation diversity. For instance, Anderson (2011), in his qualitative investigation of men's sport teams, observed that players' inclusive attitudes helped turn gay men's sexual orientation disclosure into a source of growth and cohesion for the team. Furthermore, Cunningham conducted two studies of NCAA athletic departments and observed that when such workplaces were inclusive of diversity, sexual orientation held a positive association with the presence of a creative work environment (Cunningham, 2011a) and objective measures of performance (Cunningham, 2011b).

Collectively, this literature provides robust support for the influence of inclusiveness on subsequent group and organizational outcomes. We extend this understanding by focusing on a specific element of inclusiveness—psychological safety—and its role on the individual and her or his sexual orientation personal identity expression.

Psychological safety

According to Kahn (1990, p. 708), psychological safety refers to, 'feeling able to show and employ one's self without fear of negative consequences to self-image, status, or career'. People are likely to perceive psychologically safe environments as secure places where they can trust others, and settings where there are clear, predictable patterns of behaviour (Kahn, 1990). Edmondson (1999) later extended this conceptualization to describe psychological safety in teams and groups as the degree to which group members feel (a) they can take risks, (b) others value their ideas and perspectives, and (c) other group members are respectful and supportive of their efforts. Illustrative of these dynamics, researchers have shown that psychologically safe environments allow differences to manifest themselves and be a source of learning and effectiveness. For instance, in Bradley et al.'s (2012) study of work groups in the US, the authors found that disagreements and disputes about how to best accomplish the work task (i.e., task conflict) was associated with greater team performance when psychological safety was high; however, when the groups were characterized by low levels of psychological safety, such disputes significantly hindered performance.

Ragins (2004) highlighted the importance of psychologically safe climates in her conceptualization of safe havens. Housed within a discussion of how human resource practices impacted LGB employees, she described safe havens as 'occupations, organizations and work groups that support the disclosure of a gay identity and are a refuge from discrimination in the workplace' (108). She argued that sexual minorities frequently seek to work in organizations described as safe havens because doing so provides them with an environment free from discrimination, as well as a space where they can express and develop their sexual orientation personal identity. As these work environments are both highly desirable and relatively rare, LGB employees will frequently remain in safe havens, even when other opportunities become available.

Unfortunately, systematic investigation of Ragins' (2004) safe-haven hypothesis and the influence of such environments on sexual minorities' identity development is lacking. We found two studies, though, that provide support for her position. In the first, Button (2001) collected data from lesbian and gay employees and observed a positive relationship between an advanced sexual orientation personal identity (what he referred to as internalization) and the presence of lesbian, gay, bisexual, and transgender (LGBT)-inclusive organizational policies. In the second study, Griffith and Hebl (2002) collected data from lesbian and gay employees and found that the centrality of a person's sexual orientation to her or his self-concept (which is akin to our conceptualization of a sexual orientation personal identity) was positively associated with a climate supportive of LGBT employees.

In sum, this literature points to the importance of inclusive, psychologically safe environments for sexual minorities and their personal identity development. Thus, when lesbian and bisexual athletes participate on teams where they feel secure and free to express themselves, we suspect that they are also more likely to develop a strong sexual orientation personal identity. On the other hand, in the absence of such inclusive environments, sexual minority athletes are unlikely to develop their identity or perceive their sexual orientation as a central part of their self-concept. This theorizing suggests that psychological safety moderates the relationship between a person's sexual orientation and the strength of that person's sexual orientation personal identity. In the following section, we examine this possibility with a dataset collected from NCAA Division I women's basketball players.

Sample and background information

In this chapter, we draw on a larger study aimed at understanding the experiences of NCAA athletes (for more information related to the procedures and data collection, see Cunningham et al., in press). We collected data from women ($n = 229$) participating on NCAA Division I basketball teams. Our sample was comprised of 124 Whites (54.1%), 88 African Americans (38.4%), 5 Asian Americans (2.2%), 3 Hispanics (1.3%), 4 athletes who listed 'other' (1.8%), and 5 persons who did not provide information related to their race. The average age was 20.53 years ($SD = 1.33$), and there was a wide distribution based on classification in school: 17 first year students (7.4%), 55 sophomores (24.0%), 45 juniors (19.7%), 91 seniors (39.7%), and 20 people who listed 'other' (8.7%). Finally, in an approach similar to Kinsey (1948), we asked participants, 'how do you define your sexual orientation?' and response options ranged from 1 (*completely homosexual*) to 5 (*completely heterosexual*). We then classified persons who provided responses from 1–3 as lesbian or bisexual, and those who provided responses from 4–5 as heterosexual. Others (Sartore and Cunningham, 2009) have adopted a similar approach.

For this portion of the analysis, we focus on the responses to questions related to psychological safety and sexual orientation personal identity. We measured psychological safety using Edmondson's (1999) 7-item scale ($\alpha = .75$) and sexual orientation personal identity using a 3-item measure adapted from previous studies (Cunningham et al., 2008; Randle and Jaussi, 2003; = .76). We also wanted to control for other factors that might impact the players' sexual orientation personal identity, including player race, negative affect, and team identity. Race was measured by categorizing participants as White or racial minority, negative affect using Watson et al.'s (1988) scale ($\alpha = .85$), and identity using an adapted version of previous identity scales (Cunningham et al., 2008; Randle and Jaussi, 2003; $\alpha = .78$).

Study results

Means, standard deviations, and bivariate correlations are available in Table 43.1, and we highlight several findings here. First, sexual orientation personal identity scores ranged from 1–7 for the entire sample and was only slightly more restricted for lesbian and bisexual athletes (2–7 range). This supports our previously articulated position that sexual minorities vary among one another in the centrality of their sexual orientation in their lives. Second, the mean score for both sexual orientation personal identity ($M = 4.72$, $SD = 1.42$) and psychological safety

Table 43.1 Descriptive statistics

Item	1	2	3	4	5	6
Race	—					
Negative affect	.15	—				
Team personal identity	.30★	.03	—			
Sexual orientation	.16★	.01	−.15	—		
Psychological safety	.07	−.20★	.31★	.03	—	
Sexual orientation personal identity	.11	.07	.29★	.05	.01	—
M (%)	.58	2.36	5.42	.76	3.30	4.72
SD	—	.50	1.16	—	.66	1.42

Notes

★ *p* < .05.

Race coded as 0 = racial minority, 1 = White.

Sexual orientation coded as 0 = lesbian or bisexual, 1 = heterosexual.

Negative affect and psychological safety measured on 5-point scales.

Team personal identity and sexual orientation personal identity measured on 7-point scales.

($M = 3.30$, $SD = .66$) were both significantly higher than the midpoints of the scale: t (133) = 5.87, $p < .001$, and t (192) = 6.14, $p < .001$, respectively. Finally, when not considering other factors, lesbians and bisexual athletes expressed the same sexual orientation personal identity ($M = 4.59$, $SD = 1.53$) as heterosexual athletes did ($M = 4.77$, $SD = 1.40$), F (1, 131) = .38, $p = .54$.

We predicted that psychological safety would moderate the relationship between sexual orientation and sexual orientation personal identity and examined this possibility by way of moderated regression, following Cohen et al.'s (2003) guidelines. Table 43.2 provides a summary of the results. The controls accounted for 11% of the variance, and the first order effects then accounted for an additional 1% of the variance. Finally, the sexual orientation × psychological safety interaction term accounted for a significant portion of unique variance ($\Delta R^2 = .03$, $p = .05$). We then plotted the interactions to interpret the nature of the interactions. As seen in Figure 43.1, lesbian and bisexual athletes expressed much stronger sexual orientation personal identity when in a psychologically safe team environment than when they were not; however, the differences among heterosexual athletes were less pronounced.

Table 43.2 Results of moderated regression analysis

Variable	Model 1	Model 2	Model 3
Race	.01	−.01	−.02
Negative affect	.07	.06	.07
Team personal identity	.32★	.35★	.33★
Sexual orientation		.10	.09
Psychological safety		−.04	.27
Sexual orientation personal identity			−.35★
R^2	.11	.12	.15
ΔR^2	.11★	.01	.03★

Notes

★ *p* < .05. Standardized beta coefficients represented.

Race coded as 0 = racial minority, 1 = White.

Sexual orientation coded as 0 = lesbian or bisexual, 1 = heterosexual.

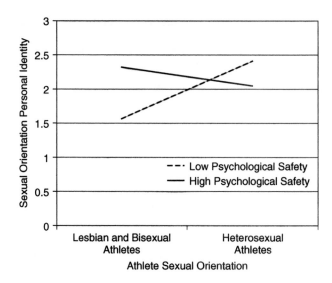

Figure 43.1 Effects of sexual orientation and psychological safety on the expression of sexual orientation psychological safety

Discussion

The findings from our research suggest (a) that there exists considerable variability in the sexual orientation personal identity of lesbian and bisexual basketball players, and (b) these differences are a function, at least in part, of the climate for psychological safety on their teams. When athletes feel safe, that they can openly and freely express themselves to others, and that their individual differences will not be held against them—all elements of psychological safety (Edmondson, 1999; Kahn, 1990)—they are likely to consider their sexual orientation as an important part of who they are as a person. However, absent such an environment, the salience of their sexual orientation personal identity diminishes. These findings are supportive of Ragins' (2004) theorizing related to safe havens, as well as the broader research pointing to the benefits of psychologically safe and inclusive environments (Anderson, 2011; Ely and Thomas, 2001; Joshi and Roh, 2007).

Given these findings, we turn to a discussion of how coaches can create and maintain psychologically safe team environments. Day and Greene (2008) argue that top leadership support, 'should be obvious, early, consistent, and comprehensive' (p. 646). In drawing from the literature (Edmondson, 1999; Joshi and Roh, 2007; Kahn, 1990; Ragins, 2004; Shore et al., 2011), we submit that coaches need to establish environments where (a) athletes and coaches trust one another; (b) athletes feel a sense of security, respect, and supportiveness; (c) athletes can take risks; (d) team members are not penalized or scrutinized for being different from others; and (e) athletes and coaches can freely express and develop identities important to them, including their sexual orientation personal identity. Coaches can create such environments by modelling inclusive behaviour, advocating on behalf of LGB athletes on the team and in the department, setting clear norms and expectations for inclusive language and behaviour, and creating formal statements of acceptance and inclusion for all persons on the team (see also Shore et al., 2011).

All of these actions help establish a team culture of diversity and inclusion. When such a culture is deeply embedded within the team, all members of the team—coaches, trainers, and players—take a role in maintaining those values. Fink et al. (2012) demonstrated as much in their study of sexual orientation disclosure on women's NCAA athletic teams, as veteran players helped pass along the cultural norms and expectations of inclusion to younger ones; further, coaches quickly engaged in behaviours (e.g., modelling, individual meetings with players) to reinforce the culture and take corrective actions when they identified player behaviours counter to the culture of inclusiveness. Anderson's (2011) work also supports these relationships, as teammates in his study collectively reinforced a culture that was inclusive of various forms and expression of masculinity. Finally, Melton and Cunningham (2012), in their qualitative study of lesbian and bisexual athletes in the US, showed that teammate actions were key in setting the culture of inclusion on the team. Thus, while coaches are influential in setting a culture of inclusiveness, others associated with the team help reproduce the culture and socialize newcomers.

Finally, recall that we opened our chapter by arguing that while there had been improvements over time, many sexual minorities participating in sport and physical activity still encounter sexual prejudice and operate within heterosexist environments. As a result, LGB athletes might feel compelled to hide or diminish the importance of their sexual orientation personal identity. That is the bad news. But, the good news is that there are real, tangible changes in which coaches can engage to make sport more inclusive. Our theorizing and empirical findings both point to the importance of psychological safety in allowing for the expression and development of sexual orientation personal identity. Coaches can readily establish such team environments—places where athletes feel a connection and sense of belongingness to the team, while also perceiving the team as a place where they can freely express who they are as a person, with their uniqueness being valued and appreciated (see also Shore et al., 2011). Given the important social, psychological, and physiological benefits of maintaining strong sexual orientation personal identity, such team cultures are sorely needed.

References

Anderson E (2010) The maintenance of masculinity among the stakeholders of sport. *Sport Management Review 12*: 3–14.

Anderson E (2011) Updating the outcome: Gay athletes, straight teams, and coming out in educationally based team sports. *Gender & Society 25*: 250–268.

Bradley BH, Postlethwaite BE, Klotz AC, Hamdani MR and Brown KG (2012) Reaping the benefits of task conflict in teams: The critical role of team psychological safety climate. *Journal of Applied Psychology, 97*: 151–158.

Branscombe NR, Schmitt MT and Harvey RD (1999) Perceiving pervasive discrimination among African Americans: Implications for group identification and well-being. *Journal of Personality and Social Psychology, 77*: 135–149.

Brewer MB (1991) The social self: On being the same and different at the same time. *Personality and Social Psychology Bulletin, 17*: 475–482.

Button SB (2001) Organizational efforts to affirm sexual diversity: A cross-level examination. *Journal of Applied Psychology, 86*: 17–28.

Cohen J, Cohen P, West SG and Aiken LS (2003) *Applied multiple regression/correlation analysis for the behavioural sciences* (3rd ed). Mahwah, NJ: Lawrence Erlbaum Associates.

Cunningham GB (2011a) Creative work environments in sport organizations: The influence of sexual orientation diversity and commitment to diversity. *Journal of Homosexuality, 58*: 1041–1057.

Cunningham GB (2011b) The LGBT advantage: Examining the relationship among sexual orientation diversity, diversity strategy, and performance. *Sport Management Review 14*: 453–461.

Cunningham GB, Choi JH and Sagas M (2008) Personal identity and perceived dissimilarity among college athletes. *Group Dynamics: Theory, Research, & Practice 12*: 167–177.

Cunningham GB, Miner K and McDonald J (in press) Being different and suffering the consequences: The influence of head coach-player racial dissimilarity on experienced incivility. *International Review for the Sociology of Sport*.

Day NE and Greene PG (2008) A case for sexual orientation diversity management in small and large organizations. *Human Resource Management 47*: 637–654.

Doherty A, Fink JS, Inglis S and Pastore D (2010) Understanding a culture of diversity through frameworks of power and change. *Sport Management Review 13*: 368–381.

Edmondson AC (1999) Psychological safety and learning behaviour in work teams. *Administrative Science Quarterly 44*: 350–383.

Ely RJ and Thomas DA (2001) Cultural diversity at work: The effects of diversity perspectives on work group processes and outcomes. *Administrative Science Quarterly 46*: 229–273.

Fink JS, Burton LJ, Farrell AO and Parker HM (2012) Playing it out: Female intercollegiate athletes' experiences in revealing their sexual identities. *Journal for the Study of Sports and Athletes in Education 6*: 83–106.

Gough B (2007) Coming out in the heterosexist world of sport: A qualitative analysis of web postings by gay athletes. *Journal of Gay and Lesbian Psychotherapy 11*: 153–174.

Griffin P (2012) LGBT equality in sports: Celebrating our successes and facing our challenges. In Cunningham GB (ed.) *Sexual Orientation and Gender Identity in Sport: Essays from Activists, Coaches, and Scholars*. College Station, TX: Centre for Sport Management Research and Education, pp. 1–12.

Griffith KH and Hebl MR (2002) The disclosure dilemma for gay men and lesbians: 'Coming out' at work. *Journal of Applied Psychology 87*: 1191–1199.

Herek GM, Gillis JR and Cogan JC (2009) Internalized stigma among sexual minority adults: Insights from a social psychological perspective. *Journal of Counselling Psychology 56*: 32–43.

Homan AC, van Knippenberg D, Van Kleef GA and De Dreu CKW (2007) Bridging faultlines by valuing diversity: Diversity beliefs, information elaboration, and performance in diverse work groups. *Journal of Applied Psychology 92*: 1189–1199.

Joshi A and Roh H (2007) Context matters: A multilevel framework for work team diversity research. *Research in Personnel and Human Resources Management 26*: 1–48.

Kahn WA (1990) Psychological conditions of personal engagement and disengagement at work. *Academy of Management Journal 33*: 692–724.

Kinsey AC (1948) Sexual behaviour in the human male. Philadelphia, PA: W. B. Saunders.

Krane V and Barber H (2005) Identity tensions in lesbian intercollegiate coaches. *Research Quarterly for Exercise and Sport 76*: 67–81.

Krane V, Barber H and McClung LR (2002) Social psychological benefits of Gay Games participation: A social identity theory explanation. *Journal of Applied Sport Psychology 14*: 27–42.

Luhtanen R and Crocker J (1992) A collective self-esteem scale: Self-evaluation of one's social identity. *Personality and Social Psychology Bulletin 18*: 302–318.

McKay PF, Avery DR, Tonidandel S, Morris MA, Hernandez M and Hebl MR (2007) Racial differences in employee retention: Are diversity climate perceptions the key? *Personnel Psychology 60*: 35–62.

Melton EN and Cunningham GB (2012) When identities collide: Exploring minority stress and resilience among college athletes with multiple marginalized identities. *Journal for the Study of Sports and Athletes in Education 6*: 45–66.

Meyer IH (2007) Prejudice and discrimination as social stressors. In Meyer IH and Northridge ME (eds) *The Health of Sexual Minorities: Public Health Perspectives on Lesbian, Gay, and Transgender Populations*. New York: Springer, pp. 244–267.

Pennekamp SF, Doosje B, Zebel S and Henriquez AA (2009) In matters of opinion, what matters is the group: Minority group members' emotional reactions to messages about identity expression. *Journal of Experimental Social Psychology 45*: 778–787.

Pinel EC and Swann, WB Jr (2000) Finding the self through others: Self-verification and social movement participation. In Stryker S, Owens TJ and White RW (eds) *Self, Identity, and Social Movements*. Minneapolis, MN: University of Minnesota Press, pp. 132–152.

Ragins BR (2004) Sexual orientation in the workplace: The unique work and career experiences of gay, lesbian, and bisexual workers. *Research in Personnel and Human Resources Management 23*: 35–120.

Randle AE and Jaussi KS (2003) Functional background identity, diversity, and individual performance in cross-functional teams. *Academy of Management Journal 46*: 763–774.

Sartore ML and Cunningham GB (2009) Sexual prejudice, participatory decisions, and panoptic control: Implications for sexual minorities in sport. *Sex Roles 60*: 100–113.

Sartore ML and Cunningham GB (2010) The lesbian label as a component of women's stigmatization in sport organizations: A comparison of two health and kinesiology departments. *Journal of Sport Management 24*: 481–501.

Shore LM, Randel AE, Chung BG, Dean MA, Ehrhart KH and Singh G (2011) Inclusion and diversity in work groups: A review and model for future research. *Journal of Management 37*: 1262–1289.

Swann WB Jr. (1983) Self-verification: Brining social reality into harmony with the self. In Suls J and Greenwald G (eds) *Psychological Perspectives on the Self* (vol. 2). Hillsdale, NJ: Erlbaum, pp. 33–66.

Tajfel H and Turner JC (1979) An integrative theory of intergroup conflict. In Austin WG and Worchel S (eds) *The Social Psychology of Intergroup Relations*. Monterey, CA: Brooks/Cole, pp. 33–47.

van Knippenberg D and Schippers M (2007) Work group diversity. *Annual Review of Psychology 58*: 515–541.

van Knippenberg D, Haslam SA and Platow MJ (2007) Unity through diversity: Value-in-diversity beliefs, work group diversity, and group identification. *Group Dynamics: Theory, Research, & Practice 11*: 207–222.

Watson D, Clark LA and Tellegen A (1988) Development and validation of brief measures of positive and negative affect: The PANAS scales. *Journal of Personality and Social Psychology 54*: 1063–1070.

44

SPORTSWORK

The role of sports in the work place

Michele R. Gregory

The sports-fan thing at the White House could become annoying and . . . her relative indifference to athletics could be mildly alienating, [said one of President Obama's female staffers] while another [female staffer] defended Obama's "all-boys network," adding that she recently hosted a baby shower for an administration official and that no men from the office were invited. She is comfortable with that—just as she is fine with never playing basketball with the president: That is just part of the culture here that I am excluded from, and I don't care.

(Leibovich, 2009: p. A1)

Introduction

In 2009 *The New York Times* reported on President Obama's all-male basketball games at the White House and all-male golf outings. In records kept by Mark Knoller of the American broadcasting organisation, CBS, during the President's first year in office he played twenty-three rounds of golf, none of which included women (Leibovich, 2009). The above quotation by female staffers in the Obama White House describes an organisational culture in which male sport can construct gender inclusion and exclusion, and the staffers' observations also reveal the importance of sport in non-sport institutions.

Using qualitative data and news articles, this chapter illustrates a theoretical construct that I call sportswork, which denotes the intersection of sport, especially male sport, and male-dominated workplaces, and signifies that in some service sector organisations highly skilled employees' engagement with sport is an important feature in their job relations, performance and opportunities. Sportswork exists in non-sport workplaces, such as banks, and includes employees talking about sport, playing sport with colleagues and clients or embodying competitive athletic behaviour, which becomes part of their performance at work, and thus part of an organisation's culture. Additionally, what emerges from this theoretical construction is a taxonomy of "practices" that illustrates the different roles that sport can play at work and the effects on non-hegemonic employees.

Research referring to competitive sport in white-collar, non-sport occupations, either as part of the construction of masculine hegemony (Pierce, 1996) or as male bonding and gender inequality (Morgan and Martin, 2006; Roth, 2006), indicates that aspects of male sport are important in being successful at work. However, researching sportswork in ethnically-diverse organisations reveals that an analysis of gender alone is not always adequate in accounting for some minorities' experiences. An intersectional analysis (Crenshaw, 1991) is crucial for describing comprehensive lived experiences of the powerful and less powerful, as well as their conflicts and resistances in social spaces. The data in this chapter focus primarily on interviews from three managers and subsequently illustrate how these employees' experiences of sportswork are framed by their gender, race and immigrant status.

Sportswork

Sportswork exists to varying degrees in private and public non-sport organisations, such as financial institutions and government departments. The concept is used to describe employees who are not professional athletes, but who, as part of their job performance: (1) talk sport, by referring to games, strategies, players and the use of sport metaphors, (2) play sport, such as golf or basketball with colleagues, and (3) use their sport experience and abilities. What emerges from these three types of activities is a taxonomy of organisational and employee practices. These practices illustrate the fluidity of sportswork, as detailed in the list that follows, which is not exhaustive:

Symbolic practices. Organisations or departments strongly identify with the combative and aggressive conduct common in competitive sport. For example, exploiting opponents' weaknesses, common in competitive sport, is considered acceptable at work. Work, like sport, is a space in which opponents, opposing teams or companies are typically dominated and employees, like athletes, must learn how to deal with and even inflict this behaviour on others in the pursuit of organisational and personal work goals.

Actual practices. (1) Employees play sport with colleagues, clients, sometimes as part of company teams or sponsored events. (2) Employees apply useful skills, such as indefatigability, learned through playing sport, to enhance their job performance. (3) Employees display sport knowledge to colleagues or clients about important games, players or their own athletic achievements.

Exclusionary practices. The symbolic or actual practices unconsciously or consciously result in the exclusion of employees from non-dominant groups, such as women, ethnic minorities, the disabled or immigrants, as well as non-athletic men.

These practices are complementary and overlapping, and each is a site for the creation of social and cultural capital (Bourdieu, 1986). Sportswork involves the construction of and use of private and public spaces and is largely enacted by men on male territory, be it in offices, hallways, sport bars or athletic grounds. Power is a feature of sportswork, and those who have had access to a society's most dominant sports are more likely to capitalise on the use of sport at work.

In male-dominated non-sport organisations, it is important to examine which sports are valued and used in the construction of hegemonic masculinity (Connell, 1987). Although Leibovich (2009) cited staffers in the Obama Administration who claimed that the President's all-male sport outings were not meant to privilege men at the expense of women, evidence suggests that women's concerns about sport, especially golf, and exclusion are not exaggerated. In their study of sales professionals in the US, Morgan and Martin (2006) found that women encountered *exclusionary practices* because they were either excluded from certain golf courses or made to tee off at different times and in different areas from men. They also discovered that when women did play golf they were sometimes humiliated and mocked by male colleagues. These findings indicate that women's *actual practice* of golf is inferior to men's *actual practice* of golf. In addition, the authors show that women who did not play golf were accused by men of not being tough enough and not prepared to do what men do to get ahead. Such arguments suggest that golf is a form of cultural and gender capital in the workplace. As white men are by far the largest group of golfers in the US at 64.4%, compared to white women (20.6%), African-Americans (6.3%) and Asian-Americans (4.1%) (African American Golfer's Digest, 2012), it is also important to analyse the roles of race and ethnicity in the construction of workplace opportunities through playing golf.

American media have revealed that golf and forms of athletic masculine embodiment have also been used to create *exclusionary practices* through male networks, and hence career opportunities for men in venerable Wall Street institutions. In 2007 Morgan Stanley settled a class action sex discrimination lawsuit for US$46 million involving 2,700 women at the firm. At the heart of the case was a "power ranking system" controlled by retail branch (sales) managers who provided client referrals and new accounts to "friends and golf buddies" (Anderson, 2007: p. C18). In 2010, a discrimination lawsuit filed by three former female employees of Goldman Sachs, two of whom were executives, alleged that the firm "systematically discriminates against women", citing evidence suggesting a relationship between the use of organisational space and the performance of athletic masculinities (Lattman, 2010: p. B1). Sections of the affidavit read:

> Ms. Orlich . . . portrays a male-dominated trading-floor culture centred on golf and other physical pursuits. Ms. Orlich . . . says in an affidavit that Goldman's management would challenge one of her male colleagues, a former member of the Navy Seals, to do push-up contests and "other displays of masculinity".
>
> *(p. B1)*

> [One of the plaintiffs] claims to have never been invited to frequent golf outings, even though she was a varsity player in high school.
>
> *(p. B13)*

It remains to be seen whether the allegations against Goldman Sachs are true. However, in *Selling Women Short: Gender Inequality on Wall Street*, a qualitative study on pay disparities among elite male and female MBA graduates at the most prestigious Wall Street firms, Louise Marie Roth (2006) found that having similar interests, including sport, with managers and co-workers was sometimes used to construct a sense of belonging. Roth's interviewees revealed that these affiliations were significant in employees' job evaluations, and gender is certainly a factor:

> Sunday night was basketball night where everybody in the department goes and plays basketball. I don't play basketball. So there was a big social network there that revolved around men's sports and men's activities, and to be on the outside of that really impacted my ability to develop relationships with people.
>
> *(p. 85)*

Although these studies and media reports do not address the role of sport beyond how it is used to exclude women as equal participants with men at work, what can be inferred is that sport can be a form of cultural capital and a factor in how organisations construct hegemonic masculinities.

Sport and the assimilation of immigrants and racial minorities

Displays of hegemonic masculinity maintain, reinforce and expand hegemonic men's dominance over women, and also over non-hegemonic men (Cheng, 1996; Collinson and Hearn, 1996). Does sport, then, help men from marginalised groups assimilate into the dominant culture at work? Cliff Cheng's (1996) study of university students' perceptions of the ideal manager revealed that those – largely European-American males – who performed hegemonic masculinity, which included features such as athleticism, competitiveness and aggression, were overwhelmingly selected as leaders, while women and Asian and Asian-American males were considered less likely to embody these leadership traits. Additionally, in his ethnographic study of American hegemonic sport cultures and the assimilation of male Southeast Asian refugees and Latino immigrants, Mark Grey (1999) found that American sport represented a form of capital, used to "discriminate against" those who do not have it:

> For many in the school – students, teachers and administrators – participation in mainstream sports became a kind of litmus test to determine whether immigrant and refugee students were serious about assimilating into American culture. Because of their lack of interest in most established sports, immigrant and refugee students were seen as outsiders.
>
> *(p. 29)*

Although neither Grey nor Cheng examines sport and hegemonic masculine embodiment among employers or employees, they do provide valuable insight into other patterns of assimilation, hegemony, opportunity and resistance in educational institutions. Additionally, their research illustrates that intersections of gender, race and immigrant status are important in understanding how the perceived non-athletic bodies of Asian and Asian-American men and the sport played by non-native males can lead to these groups "falling short" of an idealised American masculine model – a form of *exclusionary practice*. As sport can be a factor in the marginalisation of certain groups, it therefore becomes important to evaluate what American male sport symbolises at work.

Sport and expressions of dominance

Athletic masculinities symbolise much of what Western hegemony represents: strength, aggression and domination of territory. In competitive sport, domination through the taking and occupying of space is rewarded. Thus, space is about power, whether on the basketball court, football field, golf course, or at work, because in sporting contests and in many instances at work, athletes' and employees' ability to use effective game plans requires attention to their "spatial position" and that of others (Gregory, 2010: p. 307). Feminist sport geographer Cathy van Ingen (2003) argues that the existence of sport in social spaces, such as stadiums, is not neutral, but is part of "the social construction of dominant ideologies and the politics of identity" (p. 210). Van Ingen examines how bodies and space relative to sport can construct dominant and subordinate gendered, sexual and racial identities and experiences. I argue that a similar analysis of sport is useful as a way of ascertaining forms of *symbolic practices* in the workplace.

Dominating others at work is wonderfully depicted in Jennifer Pierce's (1996) ethnography of American trial litigators, in which the interaction between attorneys resembles a gladiator sport. Pierce observes that the goal is to annihilate the opponent, "'To wipe out the other side', and that this is a 'macho blast,' or 'something men get into' – a form of hegemonic masculinity, as litigators who fail to gain their adversaries' submission are viewed as 'sissies' and 'wimps'" (p. 24). van Ingen's work is relevant here, as litigators can either construct narratives of themselves as masculine and authoritative or be constructed as effeminate and weak. Pierce shows the *process* of litigation to be like a game, in that a trial usually results in a winner or a loser. Her work, however, does not analyse how talking or playing sport, such as American football or golf, is related to the job of being a litigator, or how sport is a form of cultural capital. On the other hand, Knoppers (2009) found that playing sport helped senior male managers in non-profit organisations become more effective leaders and to persevere when faced with adversity.

Data indicate that the use of sport, symbolically, verbally or physically, is a feature of the workplace, and the objective of this chapter is to provide a systematic analysis of the practices of sportswork.

Methodology

The data presented in this chapter are from the on-going sportswork project that I began in 2008. Employees from a range of white-collar professions in New York and London were interviewed about their experiences of sport at work. The objective is to use these employees' experiences and observations to understand their relationship to sportswork, a concept that has evolved inductively using qualitative research. In this chapter I focus primarily on three of the thirty-two interviews conducted thus far: two women and one man in New York City, who are middle-aged and ethnic minorities. Two of the interviewees are Chinese immigrants, and all three are either middle- or upper-middle class. The three work or worked as managers in male-dominated divisions in high-profile financial services firms or local government. Interviewees were asked open-ended questions about their sport background, the importance of sport in their department and organisation, in terms of talking sport, playing sport and the relationship between sport metaphors and organisational and employee strategies. All names have been changed to protect identities. Due to the small number of interviewees, no attempt is made to generalize from their experiences.

The goal of the chapter is not just to reveal how sport is actually used by employees to construct layers of inclusion and exclusion, but also to examine what competitive male sport symbolises at work and how it operates in organisational cultures. Additionally, as very little research exists on sportswork and race or immigrant status, it is important to understand how employers and employees use sport specifically to embody hegemonic masculinities.

Actual practice and the sport dividend

Data from the thirty-two interviews reveal variations in the amount of sportswork in different organisations; however, every interviewee maintained that men largely perform sportswork. Subsequently, few of the women I interviewed fully understood the relationship between sport and workplace culture. Sheila (African-American), who worked as a senior administrator in one of the largest divisions for the city of New York, is the only woman in the study who is a sport enthusiast, having played competitive sport, such as football and basketball, with boys in her youth. In her former position, which few other women had attained, Sheila emphasises that her sport background helped her to develop an unassailable mentality, a requirement in highly political, competitive and sometimes acrimonious environments:

> The role between sports and competition is crucial at work. The big difference between women and men at work is that women discuss domestic stuff but men talk

about sports, cars and who's zooming [American slang for having sex with] whom. This is a problem for women. Sports taught me how to compete without getting my feelings hurt. When someone calls you a motherfucker [at work], you can't blush. Through sports you learn about competition and not to take things personally. You get hit on the field and are embarrassed, but you have to get back up.

Sheila's quotation suggests that being hit, even metaphorically, or verbally assaulted by an opponent, and then quickly recovering, has value in cultures beyond competitive sport – and that aspects of work are like competitive sport or *symbolic practice*. This feature of competitive sport reinforces the importance of being not just physically but also mentally resilient, or what Knoppers's (2009) male managers referred to as having "perseverance". Withstanding visceral attacks and comments about one's performance is a requirement in organisations like Sheila's, and her sport background has provided her with invaluable knowledge. Through *actual practice*, by playing male sport and applying the skills she learned through sport, Sheila is embodying the values of hegemonic athletic masculinity in order to compete successfully with male colleagues. Although Sheila is a woman, her experience provides her with a "patriarchal dividend", an advantage that Connell (2005) argues accrues to many men due to the "inferiority" of women generally (p. 79). Playing male, not female, sport provides Sheila with an advantage that her female colleagues do not appear to have. Although Sheila no longer plays competitive sport, the dividend at work remains apparent.

Symbolic practice and striking out of the game

Feminist geographer Doreen Massey (1998) argues that gendered identities vary according to geographical locations (p. 178); therefore, the immigrant status of employees, including country of origin, versus native-born employees, can be just as important in discourses of hegemony at work. Sportswork can be a particularly peculiar phenomenon for those who are not familiar with Americans' insatiable interest in and media worship of male sport, especially American football, basketball, baseball, ice hockey and golf. The intersection of gender and native-born or immigrant status can thus determine how much of an "outsider" an employee feels when sport is a common part of the workplace culture.

Unlike Sheila who was born in the US and grew up playing the most popular American sport, Elisabeth immigrated from China many years ago with virtually no background or interest in sport. Like Sheila, Elisabeth is a manager in a male-dominated environment. She works on Wall Street for one of the largest financial services firms in the world. During an exchange of emails I had with her, Elisabeth wrote: "Everyone here says sports are wars without physically hurting your enemies. This is the mentality that people carry here. How you approach people."

During our interview, Elisabeth clarified that in her organisation it is acceptable for employees to weaken and undermine their competitors so as to render them ineffective and no longer a threat. The mentality, and presumably behaviour, of some employees is aggressive with the ultimate goal of dominating (winning) other workplace professionals, competing firms and even clients. This is similar to Pierce's (1996) study of trial attorneys where submission of one's opponents is the desired outcome. Elisabeth admitted to being baffled by this behaviour: "Don't quite understand why people [in the US], always want to win not lose, otherwise game is meaningless. True for business [in the US], also you always want to win position with competition."

Elisabeth expresses her unease over how her organisation and its employees are always ready to battle – and aim to win. Although Sheila's and Elisabeth's work experiences are in two very different professions and institutions, Sheila's acknowledgement of the benefits – aggression and resilience – that male sport has provided for her work in competitive environments seems extremely relevant to Elisabeth's observations of her organisation's *symbolic practice*. However, Sheila's *actual practice* often resulted in a positive outcome while Elisabeth views her firm's association with *symbolic practice* as negative.

The "sport as war" mentality at work is an emotional and intellectual endeavour that can be applied across a range of institutions to convey supremacy. As Elisabeth is unfamiliar with the cultural use and significance of competitive sport, she has little to draw upon which will provide her with the hegemonic sport capital that she lacks. Sportswork produces resistances to domination, as in Sheila's experience, but can also be used to construct identity-inferiority similar to Cheng's (1996) findings on women, and Asian and Asian-American men. Elisabeth observes that many of the meetings she attends are not only male dominated, but sometimes occur in sport bars, a space she does not find welcoming. However, Elisabeth's manager has indicated that she needs to become more "American" in her tastes and habits – which includes taking an interest in or participating in sport. This is not surprising, because if *symbolic practice* is the norm then employee conformity is expected.

If behaving like a highly competitive athlete is a valuable skill and symbolises dominance in the workplace, what importance is attributed to playing sport with colleagues and superiors? Additionally, how does playing a sport embody hegemonic masculinity at work?

Exclusionary practice: no game, no inclusion

Having athletic prowess, be it knowledge or skill, can become associated with occupational and professional prowess at work. But in whose image? When employers unconsciously or consciously use sport to exclude employees from valuable activities, this illustrates that work-related technical skills alone go only so far in the construction of knowledge – and opportunity. Similarly, men who are not part of the hegemonic masculine sport culture and who are viewed as unathletic may be surprised to find that their "sport quotient", or lack thereof, is used to determine leadership and promotion opportunities. Consequently, the intersection of gender, race, ethnicity, class and native-born and non-native-born status can produce different levels of exclusion for employees at work. As Sheila explains:

> Sports was a way to open up meetings; it creates lots of bonding and networking. My son played football and I would refer to this during this period. However, as much as I could talk sports, the game played at work was golf and I didn't play, and I'd have to say that I lost out. A lot of clubs didn't allow women, Blacks, Jews and other ethnic minorities. In fact my boss was Italian from a working-class background, and he was invited by his boss to his country club to play golf. Country club golf is key – it's not just about playing nine holes anywhere.

Sheila positions herself at work to capitalise on her sport knowledge and her son's experience as a football player, forms of *actual practice*. Yet knowledge of American football does not earn her access to golf – a sport that is held in the highest esteem in her organisation. Additionally, her comments about golf stress how important gender, race, ethnicity and class are in the construction of opportunities at work through certain sports. Sheila's comments about "country club golf" suggest that it is a form of hegemony, and that *actual practice* for women is not always a guarantee of acceptance.

Unlike Sheila, who was not invited to play golf with her boss, David, a Chinese immigrant who works for a financial multinational, was asked to play golf with his boss, although the occasion was not altogether a success:

> Men talk a lot about football and baseball, analyse the games. Sports is so much more important in the US than China. And golf, playing golf is important. My boss is very interested in watching golf tournaments and playing golf. Every weekend my boss will play golf, and I think this is a good way for career success and networking. Once my boss invited me to join him for golf in New Jersey and problem is it didn't work out, too left-handed. Sports is important and if want to get promoted, higher management always have sports.

David's experiences and observations indicate how gendered workplace discussions about sport are commonplace in his firm. David's comments also show that those who aspire to senior-level positions would be wise to invest in playing sport, especially golf, given the current atmosphere. Although David was not initially excluded from playing golf with his boss, despite never having played, his lack of athleticism meant that he was not asked to play again – which could mean that David's opportunities for advancement are limited. Wellard (2009) argues that "professional sport" exemplifies how a sport "should be played" (p. 4), and David falls quite short of the ideal.

Does David, as an Asian male lack the perceived athleticism that has sometimes been a feature in the construction of management (Knoppers and Anthonissen, 2005)? Cheng (1996) found that Asian and Asian-American males who did not embody mainstream American hegemonic masculinity, including athleticism, were less likely to be selected as ideal managers. Cheng's conversations with some of the Asian and Asian-American male subjects in his study revealed that they revered politeness, not competitiveness with others, similar to what Cheng indicates is common among those influenced by or familiar with Confucian philosophy. According to Chen (1995), Confucian ethics include "collectivism, harmony, consensus, absence of open ego displays that may invite criticism and relationship-centred capitalism" (pp. 29–30). Cheng therefore questions why those who are "socialized as Asians" should be expected to perform Western hegemonic masculinity (p. 193). Elisabeth's unease and David's surprise over the importance of competitive sport in their respective firms is clearly linked to their Chinese origins.

Conclusion

The concept of sportswork illustrates how embodying competitive athletic behaviour at work can be used by employers and employees to construct workplace performance, opportunity and hegemonic masculinity in non-sport organisations. Furthermore, classifying sportswork as *symbolic*, *actual* or *exclusionary practices* defines the type of relationship that organisations and employees have with sport at work. Previous studies on white-collar, highly-skilled employees in non-sport organisations (Pierce, 1996) have rarely situated sportswork, as performed by employees, as a key component of workplace culture. Data in this chapter illustrate that when employers use sportswork as a form of currency to determine competency, or to achieve organisational goals – such as conducting sales meetings with clients at golf country clubs – it becomes a form of cultural capital.

Although sportswork, especially golf, promotes male bonding and has been a factor in the exclusion of female employees from vital business opportunities (Morgan and Martin, 2006; Roth, 2006), immigrants and ethnic minorities may also find that they are excluded. Sometimes this is because of cultural differences (Elisabeth and David), and other times because of discrimination (Sheila). All three managers' experiences illustrate that sport is a factor in how members of non-hegemonic groups can assimilate – sometimes. As Sheila's experience illustrates, engaging in sportswork, albeit important, is not a panacea for members of the non-hegemonic culture. These managers' experiences indicate that gender, race, ethnicity and non-native status need to be examined more closely in any analysis of sportswork, as do other areas of difference, such as disabilities. Moreover, the concept of sportswork highlights the problematic nature of using sports to evaluate performance and determine career advancement.

Acknowledgments

The author extends her thanks to Jeff Hearn and Frances Tomlinson for their invaluable comments.

References

African American Golfer's Digest (2012) Available at: http://www.africanamericangolfersdigest.com/ (accessed on 8 May 2012).

Anderson J (2007) Wall St. Firm Will Settle Sex Bias Suit. *New York Times*, 25 April, C1, C18.

Bourdieu P (1986) *Distinction. A Social Critique of the Judgement of Taste*. London and New York: Routledge & Kegan Paul.

Chen M (1995) *Asian Management Systems: Chinese, Japanese and Korean Styles of Business*. London: Routledge.

Cheng C (1996) "We Choose Not to Compete": The "Merit" Discourse in the Selection Process, and Asian and Asian American Men and Their Masculinity. In: Cheng C (ed) *Masculinities in Organizations*. Thousand Oaks, CA: Sage, pp. 177–200.

Collinson DL and Hearn J (1996) Breaking the Silence: On Men, Masculinities and Managements. In: Collinson DL and Hearn J (eds) *Men as Managers, Managers as Men: Critical Perspectives on Men, Masculinities and Managements*. London, Thousand Oaks, New Delhi: Sage Publications, pp. 1–24.

Connell RW (1987) *Gender & Power. Society, the Person and Sexual Politics*. Stanford, CA: Stanford University Press.

Connell RW (2005) *Masculinities*, 2nd edn. Berkeley, CA: University of California Press.

Crenshaw K (1991) Mapping the Margins: Intersectionality, Identity Politics, and Violence Against Women of Color. *Stanford Law Review* 43(6): 1241–1299.

Gregory MR (2010) Slam Dunk: Sport Metaphors, Strategies and the Construction of Masculine Embodiment At Work. In: Segal MT (ed) *Advances in Gender Research, Volume 14. Interactions and Intersections of Gendered Bodies at Work, at Home, and at Play*. Bingley, UK: Emerald Group Publishing Ltd., pp. 297–318.

Grey MA (1999) Playing Sports and Social Acceptance. The Experiences of Immigrant and Refugee Students in Garden City, Kansas. In: Coakley J and Donnelly P (eds) *Inside Sports*. London and New York: Routledge, pp. 28–36.

Knoppers A (2009) Giving Meaning to Sport. Involvement in Managerial Work. *Gender, Work and Organization*. DOI:10.1111/j.1468-0432.2009.00467.x, September, pp. 1–22.

Knoppers A and Anthonissen A (2005) Male Athletic and Managerial Masculinities: Congruencies in Discursive Practices? *Journal of Gender Studies* 14(2): 123–135.

Lattman M (2010) 3 Women Claim Bias at Goldman. *New York Times*, 16 September, B1, B13.

Leibovich M (2009) Man's World at White House? No Harm, No Foul, Aides Say. *New York Times*, 25 October, A1.

Massey D (1998) *Space, Place and Gender*. Padstow, UK: Polity Press.

Morgan LA and Martin KA (2006) Taking Women Professionals out of the Office. The Case of Women in Sales. *Gender and Society* 20(1): 108–128.

Pierce J (1996) Rambo Litigators: Emotional Labor in a Male-Dominated Occupation. In: Cheng C (ed) *Masculinities in Organizations*. Thousand Oaks: Sage, pp. 1–28.

Roth LM (2006) *Selling Women Short. Gender Inequality on Wall Street.* Princeton, NJ and Oxford: Princeton University Press.

van Ingen C (2003) Geographies of Gender, Sexuality and Race. Reframing the Focus on Space in Sport Sociology. *International Review for the Sociology of Sport* 38(2): 201–216.

Wellard I (2009) *Sport, Masculinities and the Body.* New York and London: Routledge.

45

SUFFERING IN GRATITUDE

Sport and the sexually abused male child

Mike Hartill

Introduction

Childhood sexual abuse (CSA) has been a topic for sports scholarship for approximately 25 years. During that time, academics and advocates have been engaged in a number of overlapping key tasks: campaigning to convince sports organisations that child abuse in sport was both *a* problem, as well as *their* problem; generating the 'evidence' (such as prevalence data) demanded by policymakers; initiating and developing policy responses; and evaluating those responses. As a result of these endeavours, CSA in sport is a problem which has been acknowledged at the highest level within the global sports community (e.g. IOC, 2007). Aside from the central task of developing the empirical base, the issue of how child sexual abuse in sports (CSAS) should be theorised has also been a vital, though somewhat unacknowledged, aspect of the recent groundbreaking work in this field (e.g. Brackenridge, 2001).

In her seminal work *Spoilsports* Brackenridge (2001) argued that a theory of sexual exploitation and abuse in sport was possible and necessary, but also set down some key challenges for researchers about the way in which it should be conceptualised. In particular, Brackenridge argued that it is not possible to arrive at anything like a comprehensive understanding of sexual exploitation in sport without engaging with theories of power. Over a decade after its publication, a response to the challenges she presented is well overdue. Whilst this task is beyond the scope of a single chapter, the following discussion offers a contribution towards this effort whilst also serving as an introduction to key areas of debate within the field.

Socio-cultural and feminist perspectives on the problem of child sexual abuse

During the 1980s critical attention was paid to the deeply gendered context of sport and the subordination of females within it (e.g. Hargreaves, 1986). Following early feminist publications on sexual abuse (e.g. Rush, 1980) sport researchers began to pay more explicit attention to the problem of sexual violence and exploitation (e.g. Brackenridge, 1992), arguing that it was much more widespread than had previously been acknowledged. They also pointed out that it was perpetrated principally by men against women and girls. As Herman (1990, p. 188) argued, 'organized male groups which foster traditional sexist attitudes should be considered high risk, since such misogynist attitudes have been shown to be associated with sexually exploitative behaviour'.

Thus, feminist perspectives explicitly demand that explanations of sexual violence must incorporate and flow from an understanding of power relations within the social world. Therefore 'sexual assault is understood to be intrinsic to a system of male supremacy' (Herman, 1990, p. 177–178) where 'males learn that their needs are primary and to be fulfilled at the expense of others, particularly females' (Seymour, 1998, p. 416). Furthermore, according to Doan (2005, p. 304) 'feminist understandings . . . compel an analysis that connects [CSA] to the hegemonic constructions of family and masculinity that support it' and often stand in opposition to 'medico-legal discourses [which] minimize sexual violence by individualizing and pathologizing this kind of behaviour, thereby diverting attention from addressing its underlying social causes and links to hegemonic masculinity' (Cowburn and Dominelli, 2001, p. 402). Yet the 'medical model' remains dominant and in popular accounts of CSA it can be observed that men are 'rarely called men, rather they are beasts, evil, paeds, psychos and perverts' (Wykes and Welsh, 2009, p. 57).

However, according to Seymour (1998, p. 418) 'the feminist perspective has tended to develop as a critique of other theories rather than as a theory in itself'. The issue which persists is that whilst structural analyses offer convincing accounts of the preponderance of male perpetrators (and female victims), they have much more trouble explaining (within a theoretically cohesive account) the fact that most men do not sexually abuse children. As McNay (2000, p. 16) argues, the focus on macro socio-cultural structures generates an overly determinist analysis which 'lacks an understanding of how these structural forces are worked through at the level of subject formation and agency'. On the other hand, as Brackenridge (2001, p. 127) highlights within *Spoilsports*, individualised, therapy-based perspectives 'pathologize sexual abuse . . . detach the perpetrator from responsibility for his actions and overlook how human agency is accounted for'.

These are particularly thorny issues for social science, but it is evident that those who wish to contribute to a deeper understanding of sexual violence in sports, including the sexual abuse of children, must take account of these challenges and attempt to provide the 'theoretical linkage' between wider social forces and the 'more local details of everyday sexual politics . . . ' (Liddle, 1993, p. 105).

Problematizing sport: Celia Brackenridge

As Brackenridge points out, CSA does not happen by accident, but how we resolve the problem of choice and action influences our understanding of it. Reference factors such as 'poor genetic inheritance' and 'biological insults' (Ward et al., 2006) tend to explain away the social, cultural and historical antecedents of CSA. The challenge, then, is to account for CSA in a way that does not diminish perpetrator agency, thus responsibility, yet locates the socio-cultural (gendered) context at the heart of analysis.

Brackenridge (2001, p. 241) argues 'Much more work is required to develop a seamless theoretical analysis of sexual exploitation in sport' but she offers 'two major imperatives': first, researchers must be wary of avoiding moral judgement and must 'connect with the everyday understandings of most practising sports coaches, athletes and administrators'; second, 'any theoretical resolution will have to incorporate both the organisational sexuality of sport and its interpersonal sex-gender relations in ways which expose the problem of men' (Brackenridge, 2001, p. 241). As a deeply gendered, male-dominated, hetero-patriarchal field, sport has been a particularly conducive vehicle for the expression of male (heterosexual) domination over females and a cultural context supportive of sexual violence (e.g. Benedict, 1997). Thus,

Brackenridge (2001, p. 95) likens sport to the patriarchal family (the main site of men's sexual violence). As Anderson (2010) observes, the power wielded by coaches is paralleled only by military commanders and parents. The notion of sport as a surrogate family also applies to boys who are, perhaps even more than girls, encouraged to view their (male) sports coaches as role models. I return to this below.

Brackenridge and Kirby (1997) developed a specific concept in relation to the sexually abused child-athlete. They 'suggested that there is a higher risk of sexual abuse to an athlete at the "stage of imminent achievement" (SIA), just prior to elite level, especially where this coincides with puberty' (Brackenridge, 2001, p. 117). Thus, when the stakes are highest, a young athlete is most susceptible to coercion. A key objective of this discussion is to provide a theoretical frame for this empirical concept.

The notion of 'grooming' has been used to explain both how children and young people are coerced, or tricked, into sexual activity, and their apparent consent. Brackenridge and Fasting (2005) have investigated this idea through qualitative interviews. Setting aside instances where overt force is used, in many instances the perpetrator will manipulate a child's feelings and circumstances so that their capacity to resist sexual advances is considerably weakened. In my own interviews with male victims, one participant, who had been sexually abused for over a year by his male rugby coach/teacher at age 11, described both the grooming process and also his feelings of complicity:

> . . . if you became part of the elite [1st team] you were allowed into his room . . . He'd then share smutty stories with you about how he'd been 'poking' mothers. And so it became, almost became acceptable behaviour . . .
>
> *(Hartill, 2011, p. 191)*

> . . . but the first time I ever ejaculated was at the hands of this man. Whatever one says, the process of orgasm is quite pleasurable. And of course when that happens – you know, you have this immense guilt that comes with it. You know . . . are you encouraging the man? Are you? I mean – I felt complicit, and that *silenced* me.
>
> *(Hartill, 2011, p. 219)*

The average duration between abuse and disclosure for male victims of CSA is 27 years; for this man it was 39 years before he felt able to talk about his abuse. Prior to counselling, he had suicidal thoughts and was placed in a secure unit for his own safety, which he attributes directly to his childhood abuse. It is, then, not only the child's coerced feelings of compulsion to 'go along with' abusive sexual activity that must be central to theory development, but also her/his determined silence into and through adulthood.

The notion of 'grooming' helps to frame the coercive strategies that perpetrators employ to blur the child's understanding of the boundaries between what is acceptable and what is not. Yet whilst 'grooming' may offer a descriptive frame, it is not an explanatory account, even though it is often used in this way. Aside from being rather disagreeable in this context, the term itself encourages a focus on the abnormality of the perpetrator in the sense that it implies a *groomer*. This inserts an unhelpful distance between 'the problem of men' and (their centrality to) the socio-cultural spaces and milieu which frequently endorse sexual violence. It also provides little, if any room, for a substantial account of the child (and childhood agency) reducing her/him to a *groomed victim*. It is to the child-victim that I now turn.

Accounting for the child in child sexual abuse

A key issue within theorising CSA is that the other social agent in this encounter – the child – is too often absent, in any substantial sense, and thus (relatively speaking) objectified. Establishing children as victims of abuse and encouraging the voicing of survivor stories has been and continues to be a vital element in the effort to both understand and prevent CSA. But such accounts also make it clear that children are far more than passive recipients of abusive sexual behaviour. Within the sociology of childhood, the notion of the child-as-social-agent (e.g. James et al., 1998) is a core feature of recent theoretical developments. Thus, in recent years the notion of childhood empowerment *through* sport has become widespread in policy statements at all levels and is increasingly associated with the 'safeguarding' agenda.

As in other relationships of power, it is evident from victim testimonies that children resist their perpetrators in a host of different ways, including some which may intensify the abuse. Ex-National Hockey League (NHL) players Sheldon Kennedy and Thoeren Fleury both refer to how they would ridicule, even threaten, their abuser Graham James, yet the abuse continued as did their silence. So whilst resistance, however it is manifest, may or may not lead to a cessation of the sexual activity (and indeed the child may express a preference for its continuance), it is nevertheless crucial that this feature is accounted for in the way we conceptualise CSA. To do otherwise would be to fail to recognise the struggles of children, across the generations and throughout the history of sport, against those who would subject them to sexual activity, as well as to negate the wider complicity of non-perpetrating adults in its persistence. The inclusion of an explicit acknowledgment of children's capacity for action and resistance within an account of sexual victimisation is, then, both a moral, political and epistemological issue.

This is far from simply a theoretical matter. The way in which we 'construct' the sporting *child* and *childhood* pave the way for how we view and treat children. Our notions of the adult–child relation shape both our capacity to *see* abuse and (providing we not only see it but also *believe* it) our subsequent attempts to prevent it. Both recognition and prevention are new developments within the global sports community. If we are to avoid an impoverished account of the child-in-sport and CSA-in-sport, any 'theoretical resolution' must be capable of incorporating a more active sense of the child without returning to earlier simplistic and polemical notions of the child as either pure (innocent) or sinful (corrupting).

Finally, the issue of gender is also important in relation to the victim. Studies show that victims are more likely to be female and, as noted above, feminist theory has been well equipped to explain these findings. However 'up to 5% of boys are exposed to penetrative sexual abuse, and up to three times this number are exposed to any type of sexual abuse' (Gilbert et al., 2009, p. 68). Boyhood sexual abuse in sport has been an especially neglected topic and so it is crucial that we also explore ways of understanding their experiences specifically rather than relying on theory developed in relation to females. The following discussion pays particular attention to the sexually victimised sports-boy.

Some notes towards a socio-cultural account of boyhood sexual abuse in sport

For Brackenridge (2001, p. 135) 'all instances of sexual exploitation arise from expressions of agency within structural limits and cultural contexts'. In order to account for both the individual and structural aspects, Brackenridge offers a 'contingency model of sexual exploitation in sport' which revolves around three key elements, the *coach*, the *athlete* and the *sport*, for which she develops a matrix of risk, based on case study analyses. This 'represents work-in-progress towards finding a comprehensive theory' (Brackenridge, 2001, p. 145). If we accept

Brackenridge's argument that power is central to understanding and framing sexual violence, it is to social theory that we must continually return in order to refine and clarify our conceptualisation of CSAS. I have found the ideas of Pierre Bourdieu to be helpful in approaching the relation between sport and the sexual abuse of children.

A key feature of Bourdieu's theoretical framework is that choice and action are always understood through the organics of the cultural *field* within which they are situated. Fields can be defined as 'a series of institutions, rules, conventions, categories . . . and titles which constitute an objective hierarchy' (Webb et al., 2002, p. 21). By these terms, sport (and individual sports) can be understood as cultural fields. All *fields* overlap and interconnect with other fields, whilst each is distinguished by its own 'patterned set of organizing forces and principles' which are 'imposed on all those entering its parameters' (Shilling, 2004, p. 475). As a simple illustration it can be easily observed that the adult and child in sport are most often referred to through context-specific labels, usually 'coach/athlete' (or some variation). So, in a rather obvious yet almost imperceptible way, the *field* operates to reconfigure the terms within which we express the adult–child relation; it imposes its own logic. One potential effect of this is to dilute the (only recently granted) rights of the child (see United Nations, 1989; also David, 2005).

For Bourdieu (1993, p. 126) sport is an 'extremely economical means of mobilizing, occupying and controlling adolescents' thus he requires us to ask: what are the organizing forces and principles of the field of *sports* (and the *fields* of sport)? In Bourdieu's theoretical framework the imposition of forces and principles through our active engagement in fields is also productive of dispositions, or *habitus*, and it is from *habitus* that action is generated. These dispositions are neither superficial nor permanent, but rather they are installed through our engagement within fields and are, therefore, durable. Bourdieu uses a sports metaphor – *'feel for the game'* – to express the relation between the subjective and the objective in which the agent acquires a sense for how to play 'the game'. This is one way in which Bourdieu provides a theoretical linkage between social forces and individual action which acknowledges strategic creativity and choice but always within fields that impose their own distinctive logic.

For the purposes of this discussion I want to consider a particular feature of Bourdieu's philosophy of action, along with the work of Lewis Hyde (1983), principally (but not exclusively) in relation to the sexually abused *male*-child.

Gift exchange, symbolic violence and the sexually abused male-child in sport

Both Bourdieu and Hyde (1983) see *gift exchange* as a fundamental feature of social life. That is, all cultures place considerable significance on the exchange of 'gifts', thus we come to understand this as a fundamental cultural practice from a very young age (obvious examples include birthdays, Christmas, Easter, Thanks*giving*). Hyde (1983) offers a thorough exploration of gift exchange within traditional societies which may help to further illuminate contemporary youth-sport: 'In the simplest examples, gifts carry an identity with them, and to accept the gift amounts to incorporating the new identity. It is as if such a gift passes through the body and leaves us altered' (Hyde, 1983, p. 46). This notion chimes with the dominant narrative of sport, where the idea that something extremely valuable (even character building) is being given to the child is a fundamental premise. Yet (whilst he pays them less attention) Hyde (1983, p. xix) acknowledges that there are also 'gifts that leave an oppressive sense of obligation, gifts that manipulate or humiliate'.

Bourdieu develops this point through his notion of *symbolic violence*. Here the giving of a gift is seen to establish relations of power because the gift creates an obligation to reciprocate *'beyond the original gift . . . it is a way to possess, by creating people obliged to reciprocate'* (Bourdieu

1998, p. 94, emphasis added). I suggest, then, that one product of the widespread 'delivery' of sport to children within a narrative of passing on something of great value is the creation of obligation and indebtedness.

The potential for social control inherent within this sporting relation has long been recognised by governing authorities, keen to produce fully engaged, conforming and productive citizens. However, in considering *sexual* abuse, it is interesting to note Hyde's claim that 'the gift is an emanation of Eros' (Hyde, 1983, p. 22); it is intrinsically erotic, sensual. It might be argued then that the sporting 'gift' is both erotic and seductive. However, given each field has 'its own historicity and logic' (McNay, 2000, p. 57) we must recognise the distinct stakes (or *capital*) within each field. This requires detailed empirical study, but as Pronger (1999, p. 382) argues, 'Boys raised on competitive sport learn to desire, learn to make connections according to the imperative to take space away from others . . . this is the conquest logic of competitive sport.'

The erotic and seductive gift of sport, with all its potential for life-changing self-fulfilment, may nevertheless be set within a brutal economy where dominating others so that one can take from them, or more simply *take them*, is written in to the game itself. Of course such propositions clearly need to be explored within individual fields (the gender structure of sports is particularly important). However, the young child will not comprehend the true character of the *athleticist field* (although I suspect many that 'drop out' have a good sense of it) and this is unsurprising given the overwhelmingly positive and euphemistic terms in which it is presented – the stuff of dreams. Thus, s/he could not fail to be aware of the life altering potential of the sports gift. As such it resembles a seductive relation, where much is hidden from view to enable the narrow interests of seduction, thereby creating the conditions for oppression and exploitation. As Hyde (1983, p. 50) puts it '. . . we can feel the proffered future . . . The gift is not ours yet but the fullness of the gift is felt, and we respond with gratitude and with desire.'

Through these ideas, we may be better equipped to frame the accounts, and questions, of CSAS victims. For example, Simon, a man now in his 40s, was sexually abused by his rugby teacher for several years, from the age of nine, and has entered counselling programmes to help him come to terms with his childhood experiences. He recalled:

> . . . a lot of us tried to excel in the sport, and in the training, and in the coaching and in the whole thing, to be more and more attractive to our abusers . . . when you did something good, you did a good tackle or something, and [he] would give you a smile or pat you on the back, it would be like '*oh my god*,' that's just like – *that thing*.

Hyde (1983, p. 75) observes that 'Gifts from evil people must also be refused lest we be bound to evil . . . it is because gift exchange *is* an erotic form that so many gifts must be refused.' But children in sport, especially those heavily invested in sport, are deeply limited in their capacity to refuse those whose 'gifts' they (and often their parents) so value and desire. Thus 'if the teaching begins to "take," the recipient feels gratitude . . . we suffer gratitude' (Hyde, 1983, p. 48). In relation to the sexually abused child-athlete, this analysis takes on a much darker meaning than that intended by Hyde, but the notion of 'suffering in gratitude' seems apposite in light of Simon's observation that he and many other boys tried to be *more* (rather than less) attractive to their abusers. Of course, survivors express their experiences of CSA in many different ways.

Gift exchange is the foundation of symbolic violence, which 'extorts submission' (Bourdieu, 1998, p. 103) when our subjective realm (the *habitus*) is in unison with the objective (the *field*). The young male athlete, successful and ambitious, and trained for a single purpose since early childhood, is perhaps a perfect exemplar of this unity. But we might also say that this unity is exactly the purpose of the field (to reproduce *sport*men and *sport*women) and that its capacity to regenerate itself depends upon the persistent inculcation of this unity. Thus, within male-sport, boys are persistently urged not only to *play* sport, but to become *sports-like* – to become *sportsmen*, *athletes* (labels so familiar and positive we forget to question the coercive power they may contain). Thus, young boys (searching for ways to do masculinity in approved ways) are encouraged not simply to play sport, but to embody it, to believe in it, to *be it* – but certainly not to question it (Anderson, 2010). For Bourdieu, this is the *illusio*: being 'caught up in and by the game', *believing* in it.

In the increasing intensity of the moralistic urging of children into sport, they are quickly subjected to a field efficiently disposed to ('scientifically') observing, examining and exploiting their bodies. This is the symbolic violence of 'youth-sport' where, in a relentless pursuit of conquest (for social, political and material gain), children are required not only to do sport, but to embody the values of athleticism[1]; to *become* the field 'made flesh'– the *athleticist habitus*. Sport, then, has an advantage over other fields in that it is inherently 'of the body'; embodiment *is* the game. As such their capacity for action that questions or contravenes the field (and those dominant in it) is eroded by their full investment and belief in the game. Despite appearances, they are not empowered, but rather *enchanted* and the greater their investment, the more encompassing their enchantment.

It may be suggested then that the gift exchange relation within male-sport is underpinned by a master–apprentice dynamic (Messner and Sabo, 1994). In his thesis on *Masculine domination* Bourdieu (2001) refers to a *libido dominandi* – the desire to dominate – and a *libido dominantis* – a desire for the dominant. For Bourdieu (2001, pp. 79–80) this relation 'can lead to that extreme form of *amor fati*, love of the dominant and of his domination'. Boys in sport, from their first entry into the field, are political bodies, socialized, to varying degrees, through this twin narrative. In their apprenticeship (or servitude) they are taught to desire domination and so to desire the dominant (the sporting 'hero'). Through persistent training they come to embody this libidinal relation. By these terms then, correct boyhood-sport practice demands that they exalt those who are dominant in the field. Unsurprisingly, then, boys desire both the gifts these men can offer, and the men themselves, and they labour – and suffer – in their gratitude.

For such children, who encounter an adult 'willing' to exploit them sexually, the possibilities for resistance are already severely limited. Indeed, for the abused child-athlete, enchanted yet indebted by the game, their only way of acting (of retaining their sense of self) may be to make a *virtue* out of the (perceived) necessity to engage in sex with their coach. So whilst striving for the fullness of the sports gift, seduced by its potential, they pay their debt – they *play* the game. Tragically, this action only further compounds their debt. Nevertheless, despite their situation, they are far from inert and will also attempt to impose their own creative logic on this abusive relation. Gradually, their enchantment may fade and the possibilities for more radical resistance may emerge.

Conclusion

Sport makes many claims about what it offers children, what it *gives* them. But this is clearly a corruption of the truth. It is children that give to sport, generously and in good faith. Conversely, sport commonly renders them, almost instantly, in debt and extracts from them their most vital and essential gifts – imagination, creativity, irreverence, humour, etc. – demanding that they run 'within the lines' and adhere to rules that are not of their own invention. For some children, it is not just their physical labour they must give, but also their sexual labour.

One issue that occurs repeatedly within victim testimonies is the complicity that children and young people felt in the sexual acts they were subjected to. It is this complicity that secures their silence. Legal responses regarding the inability of a child to consent, albeit necessary, do little to acknowledge or explain this and obscure a child's agency and resistance. Victims, especially those with feelings of guilt and shame, want and deserve explanations that recognise their 'complicity' (their *action*) rather than ones which make them feel as though it has been swept under the carpet like a dirty secret. In formulating the relation between *coach*, *athlete* and *sport*, our conceptions of power and action will shape the explanations we can offer.

Whilst there are many more facets and features required of a comprehensive theory of CSAS, it is hoped that the above offers some ideas that may help make up some ground towards addressing these issues. In particular, this account should emphasize the crucial importance of the children's rights agenda and efforts to provide a physical culture *of* children, rather than *for* children; one which nurtures and encourages their questioning and creative physicality rather than rendering them indebted and vulnerable to exploitation, sexual or otherwise.

Note

1 Clearly, how these are expressed depends on perspective, but in fact this matters little as it is the *unity* between the *habitus* and *field* that matters, not whether these values are 'good' or 'bad'.

References

Anderson E (2010) *Sport, theory and social problems: A critical introduction.* London: Routledge.

Benedict J (1997) *Public heroes, private felons: Athletes and crimes against women.* Boston: Northwestern University Press.

Bourdieu P (1993) *Sociology in question.* Translated by R Nice. London: Sage.

Bourdieu P (1998) *Practical reason: On the theory of action.* Translated by R. Johnson et al. Cambridge: Polity Press.

Bourdieu P (2001) *Masculine domination.* Translated by R Nice. Cambridge: Polity Press.

Brackenridge CH (1992) Sexual abuse of children in sport: A comparative exploration of research methodologies and professional practice. In: *Pre-Olympic Scientific Congress*, Malaga, Spain, 14–19 July 1992.

Brackenridge CH (2001) *Spoilsports: Understanding and preventing sexual exploitation in sport.* London: Routledge.

Brackenridge CH and Kirby S (1997) 'Playing Safe?' Assessing the risk of sexual abuse to young elite athletes. *International Review for the Sociology of Sport* 32(4): 407–418.

Brackenridge CH and Fasting K (2005) The grooming process in sport: Narratives of sexual harassment and abuse. *Auto/Biography* 13: 33–52.

Cowburn M and Dominelli L (2001) Masking hegemonic masculinity: Reconstructing the paedophile as the dangerous stranger. *British Journal of Social Work* 31: 399–415.

David P (2005) *Human rights in youth sport: A critical review of children's rights in competitive sports.* London: Routledge.

Doan C (2005) Subversive stories and hegemonic tales of child sexual abuse: From expert legal testimony to television talk shows. *International Journal of Law in Context* 1(3): 295–309.

Gilbert R, Spatz Widom C, Browne K, Fergusson D, Webb E and Janson S (2009) Child maltreatment 1: Burden and consequences of child maltreatment in high-income countries. *The Lancet* Jan 3–Jan 9, 373: 68–81.

Hargreaves JA (1986) Where's the virtue? Where's the grace?: A discussion of the social production of gender relations in and through sport. *Theory, Culture & Society* 3(1): 109–121.

Hartill M (2011) *The sexual subjection of boys in organised male sport.* PhD Thesis, Edge Hill University, UK.

Herman JL (1990) Sex offenders: A feminist perspective. In: Marshall WL, Laws, DR and Barbaree HE (eds) *Handbook of sexual assault: Issues, theories and treatment of the offender.* New York: Plenum Press, pp.177–193.

Hyde L (1983/2007) *The gift: How the creative spirit transforms the world.* Edinburgh: Canongate.

IOC (International Olympic Committee) (2007) *Consensus statement on sexual harassment and abuse in sport.* http://www.olympic.org/documents/the%20ioc/official%20sha%20statement.pdf/

James A, Jenks C and Prout A (1998) *Theorizing childhood.* Cambridge: Polity.

Liddle AM (1993) Gender, desire and child sexual abuse: Accounting for the male majority. *Theory, Culture, and Society* 10: 103–126.

McNay L (2000) *Gender and agency: Reconfiguring the subject in feminist and social theory.* Cambridge: Polity.

Messner MA and Sabo D (1994) *Sex, violence and power in sports: Rethinking masculinity.* Berkeley, CA: The Crossing Press.

Pronger B (1999) 'Outta my endzone': Sport and the territorial anus. *Journal of Sport & Social Issues* 23(4): 373–389.

Rush F (1980) *The best kept secret: Sexual abuse of children.* New York: McGraw-Hill.

Seymour A (1998) Aetiology of the sexual abuse of children: An extended feminist perspective. *Women's Studies International Forum* 21(4): 415–427.

Shilling C (2004) Physical capital and situated action: A new direction for corporeal sociology. *British Journal of Sociology of Education* 25(4): 473–487.

United Nations (1989) *Convention on the rights of the child.* Geneva.

Ward T, Polaschek DLL and Beech AR (2006) *Theories of sexual offending.* Chichester: John Wiley and Sons Ltd.

Webb J, Schirato T and Danaher G (2002) *Understanding Bourdieu.* London: Sage.

Wykes M and Welsh K (2009) *Violence, gender and justice.* London: Sage.

46

TRANSCENDING THE (WHITE) STRAIGHT MIND IN SPORT

Caroline Fusco

Introduction

In 1997, Graham James, a former junior ice hockey coach was sentenced to three and a half years in prison after he pleaded guilty to sexually assaulting a teenage player (Sheldon Kennedy) hundreds of times. James was paroled in 2000. Then, in 2010, the Canadian press learned that James had been granted a federal pardon in 2007 (National Post, 2010; The Globe & Mail, 2010; The Toronto Star, 2010).

Following this revelation, there was much outrage about the criminal pardon system from both the Canadian federal government and the players who were abused by James. Federal Public Safety Minister Vic Toews stated that 'certain types of criminals cannot be rehabilitated' (The Toronto Star, 2010: A1), while one of the former National Hockey League (NHL) players said that James has 'never apologized' or 'shown any remorse' (National Post, 2010: A6) and called his pardon 'a slap in the face' (Toronto Sun, 2010: A4). More recently, in March 2012, James was arrested on new allegations of abuse and was subsequently sentenced to two years in prison for hundreds of sexual assaults on two of his former teenage players – ex-NHLer, Theoren Fleury, and Fleury's younger cousin, Todd Holt – while coaching them in the junior ice hockey ranks during the 1980s and early 1990s (CBC News Manitoba, 2012).

The sexual abuse of Sheldon Kennedy (victim, who was 14 years old when the abuse began) by Graham James (the perpetrator) was well known in ice hockey circles in Canada and the United States. Kennedy was coached by James, who was a highly respected and nationally-regarded coach, during the 1980s and early 1990s, both as a junior level ice hockey player in Winnipeg (Canada) and when he played for the Swift Current Broncos of Canada's junior ice hockey league. When the original story of James' sexual abuse was released in 1997, it garnered much media attention, especially when the public learned that Kennedy was sexually abused by James twice weekly, between the ages of 14 and 19. The story also mobilized Canadian sports organizations, particularly the Canadian Hockey Association, to develop policies on sexual harassment and abuse in sport (see Donnelly, 1999; Kirby et al., 2000). Although sexual abuse had taken place in other cultural institutions in Canada (e.g., the Catholic Church, Residential Schools for Aboriginal children), the existence of same-sex abuse in the hyper-masculine world of Canada's (so-called) national sport (ice hockey) came as a shock to the sports world (Fusco and Kirby, 2000; Shogan 2007).

Over the last decade, several scholars have examined media and sports organizations' responses to the Kennedy/James case, and to other sexual abuse cases that came to light around the same time. Many concluded that abuses of power in a sport like ice hockey are always a possibility as long as the pressures to perform, excel, and conform to team norms remain, and as long as the dream of playing professional sport remains a goal for young boys and men (Donnelly, 1999; Donnelly and Sparks, 1997). There was also an interrogation of: 1) the media's failure to quell the homophobia and moral panic that was generated about the 'case', particularly through the conflation of same-sex abuse, homosexuality and paedophilia (Fusco and Kirby, 2000); and 2) the lack of complexity given to the stories and experiences of sexual abuse (Shogan, 2007). Moreover, authors also documented that such abuse should not have been unexpected given the centrality of cultures of hazing in ice hockey, which often consisted of sexist and homoerotic rituals during team initiations (Kirby and Wintrup, 2002; Robinson, 1998).

In this chapter, I re-examine some of the discourses surrounding the Kennedy/James case with respect to, first, examining the framing of sexuality, and later, the framing of 'race' in sport. In all the media coverage, there was certainly an attempt to re-claim the hyper-masculine and heterosexual world of ice hockey; this was obvious in the many instances where James' homosexuality was foregrounded, whereas Kennedy was only ever described and represented as heterosexual. Within the context of ice hockey, various sports organizations' and media responses to the sexual abuse were not surprising given that there is:

> shame associated with homosexual abuse – in the world of macho sports it is easy to feel that one's peers would believe that one should have been able to prevent it, and that if one did not, it must have been consensual.
>
> *(Donnelly and Sparks, 1997: 202)*

A proliferation of research has critically interrogated sexual abuse and sexual harassment in sports (see Brackenridge, 1994, 1997, 2001; Brackenridge and Kirby, 1997; Fasting et al., 2002; 2004; Hartill, 2005). I do not wish to question the work that has been done to expose sexual abuse and sexual harassment in sport – these abuses of power must be eradicated – nor do I wish to dismiss the impact of sexual abuse on those players who were violated. My aim, rather, is to re-read the media discourses of abuse, paying attention to the blatant heterosexualizing of Kennedy, and to re-read this 'heterosexualizing' with respect to its implicit racialization through the work of several post-structuralist and post-colonial scholars. Using the Kennedy/James case as an illustrative example, I will show how the straight mind (Wittig, 1992) required the juxtaposition of heterosexuality with whiteness, which was set against the 'dark' threat of homosexuality and perversion in order to reclaim an idealized (white) and (heterosexual) hyper-masculine ice hockey world.

Sexual binaries and the straight mind in sport

In her essay 'The Straight Mind', Monique Wittig (1992) argues that discourse and practices of power are organized through the language of heterosexuality. Sex is naturalized as 'the straight mind' (Wittig, 1992: 34). Taken for granted and pervasively unsaid, heterosexuality is a 'core of nature: in all the texts of culture, structuring the categories of gender and sex and stubbornly resisting examination' (p. 34). Butler (1990) would later label this the 'heterosexualization of power' (p. 17). Wittig's (1992) interrogation of the straight mind has its historical strengths. Like Foucault (1978), she positions the creation of the heterosexual/homosexual binary firmly in the end of the nineteenth century with the rise of the sciences, particularly the biomedical sciences and psychoanalysis. She particularly critiques the power of psychoanalysis (and its experts) that fixed a heterosexual/homosexual binary in society's psyche, hence producing 'the straight mind'. Like Wittig, Foucault (1978), and later Sedgwick (1990), argue that science, medicine and psychoanalysis have contributed to the production of the homosexual 'personage', which was necessary to produce a 'society of normalization' (Foucault, 1978). These scholars have argued that the establishment of the homosexual subject allowed an emerging Victorian, male, bourgeoisie and (heterosexual) subject to know himself through a new 'abnormal' homosexual subject. The subsequent naturalization of heterosexuality led to what Wittig (1992) describes as a cultural predisposition to the discourses of 'you-will-be-straight-or-you-will-not-*be*' (p. 54, emphasis added). In such a world, heterosexuality comes to structure and dominate human relationships. To be outside this heterosexual norm means that one's gender and sexual identity are often marginalized, made invisible and rendered 'unintelligible' (Butler, 1990). Wittig argues that the straight mind requires the continual construction of marginalized identities in the form of binary opposites to maintain its centrality. She states:

> Yes, straight society is based on the necessity of the different/other level. It cannot work economically, symbolically, linguistically, or politically without this concept. This necessity of the different/other is an ontological one for the whole conglomerate of sciences and disciplines I call the straight mind.
>
> *(Wittig, 1992, p. 55)*

In western societies, a culturally dominant 'straight mind' has been responsible for naturalizing heterosexuality and vilifying homosexuality, which, since the late nineteenth century, has been historically categorized as a disease and a disorder (Foucault, 1978). Consequently, Wittig (1992) argues that the proliferation of the straight mind in 'scientific discourses as well as by the discourses of the mass media' (p. 53) have had real material consequences for sexual minoritized subjects.

Given the dominant position of 'the straight mind', it is not unexpected that a heterosexual/homosexual binary is called upon when same-sex sexual abuse occurs in sport. For example, in the Kennedy/James case, the straight mind was apparent in the media's framing of the two men. James was represented as the (homo)sexual predator who '. . . never believed that Kennedy shared his sexual tendencies' (Mofina, 1997: C2). Indeed, in various newspaper articles, James revealed that he knew Kennedy was not gay and only tolerated the abuse because of promises made to him by James concerning a future career in the NHL. Time and time again, James, the perpetrator, was reported as saying that Kennedy did not care about the sex and definitely did not enjoy his (James') sexual advances. Meanwhile, the media played up Kennedy's heterosexuality by reporting that he was not a willing participant in the sexual acts. The media constantly fore-grounded Kennedy's statements: 'there was no willingness on my part' (Lapointe, 1997: 3) and 'I (Kennedy) have nothing against gay guys . . . but this is wrong' (Christie, 1997: A1). First, this is troubling because despite the trauma of being a victim of a sexually abusive coach for many years, Kennedy was put in the position of having to justify and defend his (hetero)sexuality. Whether Kennedy was or was not heterosexual should not have been an issue in any circumstance. However, in the hyper-masculine world of ice hockey, where young men would be expected to defend themselves against such abuse, his sexuality had to be proved (Fusco and Kirby, 2000; Robinson, 1998). Moreover, Adams et al. (2010) suggest that inquiries that challenge one's masculinity and sporting prowess 'are inextricably tied with issues of gender, sexuality, courage, and sport in this context' (Adams et al., 2010, p. 293). Kennedy (the victim) was portrayed as a once troubled NHL player who was now a happily married (heterosexual) family man, while James was represented as the lonely, (homo)sexual and per-verted other. Many images in the newspapers showed Kennedy with his wife and daughter, whereas James was always pictured either alone or in images depicting him towering over the boys that he coached (Fusco and Kirby, 2000). The constant framing of the heterosexual/homo-sexual binary by all those involved – James, Kennedy and the media – served to confirm the straight mind's hegemony.

This analysis of course is not new. A proliferation of work in sexuality studies within sport sociology has explored how 'the straight mind' has shored up heterosexuality and has oppressed and caused violence to lesbians, gays, as well as transgendered and queer bodies in cultures of sport (see Caudwell, 2006). Indeed, many scholars in the field of sports sociology have examined the sexed, gendered and heteronormative world of sports. Pronger's (1990, 1999, 2000a, 2000b) groundbreaking work on homosexuality and homoerotic desire in sport has been particularly influential in the field and his work paved the way for the development of queer studies in sports sociology (see Sykes, 2006 for an overview).

It is beyond the scope of this chapter to document all the work on sexuality and sexual identity in sport. I will focus first on the 1990s and early 2000s, when studies of sexuality dem-onstrated that homosexuality and lesbianism were still vilified in mainstream sports environ-ments through sports team songs (Wheatley, 1994), drag performances (Shogan, 1999), ritual-ized (homo)erotic hazings (Kirby and Wintrup, 2002), and homophobic behaviour (Caudwell, 2006; Eng, 2006; Griffin, 1998). We know that homophobia and transphobia have also been pervasive in the micro-spaces of sport (Fusco, 1998), in interpersonal or inter-team relationships, and that the institutionalization of heteronormativity has caused systemic heterosexist responses to homosexual, queer, transgendered, and transsexual bodies at both national and international levels (Cavanagh and Sykes, 2006; Symons & Hemphill, 2006). Sport has had a long history of creating gender and sexual binaries, disavowing so-called deviant and/or non-normative bodies and rendering them other, thus securing the hegemony of 'the straight mind' (see Birrell and Cole, 1994; Cavanagh and Sykes, 2006; Pronger, 1990).

More recent work (Adams, 2011; Adams and Anderson, 2012; Anderson, 2011; Campbell et al., 2011; Cavalier, 2011) suggests that homophobia and heteronormativity may be decreasing in team sports and that shifting understandings of masculinity (in sports) may be helping to change conditions for sexual minoritized men in sport. Certainly, Adams et al. (2010) report that as homophobia reduces, language and its meanings can change in sport. However, whether these findings are relevant to the discourses and practices that emerge, particularly in hyper-masculine sports like ice hockey, after incidences of same-sex-abuse, remains to be seen. Evidently, there is also evidence that homophobia remains uncontested in some fan internet blog sites (Kian et al., 2011). Future research might investigate these internet sites and other media sources follow-ing revelations of same-sex sexual abuse to investigate whether 'the straight mind' and its sexual binaries and discourses are called on in order to maintain the 'deadly elasticity of heterosexist presumption' (Sedgwick, 1990: 68) in sports spaces. Additionally, MacDonald (2006) argues that scholars must pay attention to the racialized discursive practices and power relations that have sustained the heterosexual subject as white and middle class. As such, any interrogation of the role of 'the straight mind' in the production of sexual and gendered identifications in sport must pay attention to how such reproductions might also be racialized.

Racialization and the white straight mind in sport

Examining the production of sexuality in sport through an analysis of the heterosexual/homo-sexual binaries sometimes forecloses some crucial questions about the reproduction of 'race'. An analysis of sexuality in the Kennedy/James case may also require paying attention to the 'ways in which race operates discursively in the production of sexuality' (Storr, 1996, p. 77). Race, according to Storr, has played a constitutive role in 'sexology's understanding of both "normal" and "inverted" sexuality' (p. 79). This is important in the Kennedy/James case because Canadian ice hockey has a predominant image of whiteness (see Goss, 2012), as well as heterosexuality, although the NHL is working to eliminate homophobia (see Harrison, 2012). James, the (homo)sexual pervert, sullied the whiteness of hockey and the virtues of manliness, muscularity and morality, which have been taught through sport throughout its history as an antidote to homosexuality, immoral sexual practices and to 'dreaded effeminacy' (Kirk, 1998; Mangan, 1981; 1992).

Many studies of the history of sports have concluded that sexualization and racialization often worked together to secure an imperialist, white, heterosexual masculinity through sports (Budd, 1997; Mangan, 1992). But, what happens to the hyper-masculine and whitened space of a sport like ice hockey when issues of heterosexuality, homosexuality and sexual predation are jettisoned into public's arena? Unfortunately, the media representations in the Kennedy/James case that foregrounded the deviant (homo)sexual predator, while valorizing heterosexuality, were also juxtaposed with metaphors of light and darkness, which somehow served to confirm the (myth of the) innocence of hockey before the depravity of James' acts. Most probably, these representations were used to direct our attention towards what is understood as the immorality of sexual abuse. Contrasting light and dark metaphors does call forth another binary: one that positions an idealized clean and white(ned) image of ice hockey against the (sexualized) dirtiness of abuse. In ice hockey, where heterosexuality, masculinity and whiteness have been normalized and naturalized, such media narratives signal that the pure, white and heterosexually wholesome world of Canadian ice hockey was under assault from 'a dark side'. For example, the media reported that Kennedy's revelations 'opened the curtains on the darkest corners of his past', which 'dimmed the nostalgia of hockey' thus jettisoning 'the public's eye into some of society's darker and dirtier corners' (DePalma, 1997: A10). Newspapers also reported that the abuse occurred in pitch black and darkened rooms (Kennedy and Grainger, 2011). With such metaphors – of blackness and dirt etc. – the connection between sexual abuse and representations of darkness are solidified. Kennedy's status as a white, upper middle-class family man, with his (white) wife and daughter at his side is valorized as the ideal in hockey. Whereas James' (homo)sexual perversions are constituted as 'dark perversions'. Critical sport sociologist, Rick Gruneau, cited in the *New York Times* at the time of the abuse revelations, suggested that '[hockey's] current state of crisis is mostly felt by people who take a parochial view and who nostalgically yearn for a mostly white, mostly rural country it was in the 1950s' (see DePalma, 1997: A10). Gruneau's critique, and the media representations of darkness, harken back to Storr's (1996) reminder that scholars need to 'pay close attention to the (racial) imperatives and slippages at the heart of (sexuality) texts' (p. 86) and to closely interrogate the constitutive role that race might play in the formation of contemporary sexual and gendered identifications. Interestingly, these kinds of metaphors and representations are rarely, if ever, made about the sexual violence that many women have endured at the hands of ice hockey players or the sustained culture of women's sexual objectification in ice hockey (see Robinson, 1998; 2002). This absence confirms the imagined link among men's ice hockey: whiteness and heterosexuality. Thus, the juxtaposition of Kennedy's heterosexual, whiteness with the darkness and depravity of James' crimes might be said to have served to reproduce the dominance of the white straight mind.

Transcending the white straight mind

All cultures have light and shadows. We've always looked at the culture of hockey and other games in the light, and only now are considering their dark secrets. In this arena, we've looked at the idyllic and now we must cast our attention to the real.

(Christie, 1997: A22)

Presumably, the 'real' here is referring to a world of ice hockey that is, in reality, less than ideal – a sordid underbelly, so to speak – which is one that sports organizations, players, and spectators (purposely) ignore. They ignore it because it would expose many of the injustices that are already carried out on young boys' bodies (e.g., excessive training, removal from families at a very young age to live and train with junior teams, and, hence, putting them in the hands of potential predators, trading them for money etc.) to make their dreams of playing in the NHL a reality. The emphasis on the 'real' also turns my attention towards 'the (straight) mind' again. In the Kennedy/James case, the 'darkness' in sports – its 'sordid underbelly', homosexuality, (same-sex) sexual predation – disrupted the idealized constructs (i.e., hyper-heterosexual masculinity) that dominates the white (hetero)normative world of ice hockey.

While sexual abuse must be eradicated in sport, the framing of the Kennedy/James case and others abuse stories, particularly those that involve same-sex sexual abuse, draws our attention to how (hetero)normative binaries may be called upon to explain such predation. Unfortunately, such binaries appeared to be sensationalized in the media and subsequently may have come to be believed by those 'people who take a parochial view' (Gruneau cited in DePalma, 1997). These binaries direct our attention away from the multitude of other abuses of power that can also occur with children and young people in sport (Brackenridge, 2001; David, 2005), which are often implicated in creating the conditions for sexual abuses to occur in the first place (Shogan, 2007). Wittig (1992) argues that deconstructing the straight mind requires moving beyond the categories of sex and gender and destroying the discourses and practices of heterosexuality. Recently, queer theorists in sport studies have been engaging in this important work – questioning the production of difference, dis-identifying with the language of the oppressor, and challenging the constitution of categories such as the homosexual and other (see Caudwell, 2006). Scholars might continue to extend these studies in future applied research by asking: how might the sports world take on the task of eradicating sexual abuse (same-sex or otherwise) without reproducing the straight mind or without reproducing the language and practices of (hetero)normativity and whiteness?

References

Adams A (2011) 'Josh wears pink cleats': Inclusive masculinity on the soccer field. *Journal of Homosexuality* 58(5): 579–596.

Adams A and Anderson E (2012) Exploring the relationship between homosexuality and sport among the teammates of a small, Midwestern Catholic college soccer team. *Sport, Education and Society* 17(3): 347–363.

Adams A, Anderson E and McCormack M (2010) Gendered discourses in organized sport. *Journal of Language and Social Psychology* 29(3): 278–300.

Anderson E (2011) Masculinities and sexualities in sport and physical cultures: Three decades of evolving research. *Journal of Homosexuality* 58(5): 1–14.

Birrell S and Cole C (1994) Double fault: Renee Richards and the construction and naturalization of difference. In: Birrell S and Cole C (eds) *Women, Sport, and Culture*. Champaign, IL: Human Kinetics, pp. 373–397.

Brackenridge C (1994) Fair play or fair game: Child sexual abuse in sport organizations. *International Review for the Sociology of Sport* 29(3): 287–299.

Brackenridge C (1997) 'He owned me basically': Women's experience of sexual abuse in sport. *International Review for the Sociology of Sport* 32(2): 115–130.

Brackenridge C (2001) *Spoilsports: Understanding and Preventing Sexual Exploitation in Sport*. New York: Routledge.

Brackenridge C and Kirby S (1997) Playing safe: Assessing the risk of sexual abuse to elite child athletes. *International Review for the Sociology of Sport* 32(4): 407–418.

Budd M (1997) *The Sculpture Machine: Physical Culture and Body Politics in the Age of Empire*. New York: NYU Press.

Butler J (1990) *Gender Trouble: Feminism and the Subversion of Identity*. New York: Routledge.

Campbell J, Cothren D, Rogers R, Kistler L, Osowski A, Nathan Greenauer N and End C (2011) Sport fans' impressions of gay male athletes. *Journal of Homosexuality* 58(5): 597–607.

Caudwell J (ed) (2006) *Sport, Sexualities and Queer/Theory*. London: Routledge.

Cavalier E (2011) Men at sport: Gay men's experiences in the sport workplace. *Journal of Homosexuality* 58(5): 626–646.

Cavanagh S and Sykes H (2006) Transsexual bodies at the Olympics: The International Olympic Committee's policy on transsexual athletes at the 2004 Athens Summer Games. *Body & Society* 12(3): 75–102.

CBC News Manitoba (2012) Sex offender Graham James gets 2 years in prison. Available at: http://www.cbc.ca/news/canada/manitoba/story/2012/03/19/graham-james-sentence.html (accessed 3 October 2012).

Christie J (1997) Parental vigilance essential in junior hockey. *The Globe & Mail*, 11 January, A1 and A22.

David P (2005) *Human Rights in Youth Sport*. London: Routledge.

DePalma, A. (1997). Sex abuse jolts Canada's revered pastime: Hockey. *The New York Times*, 16 January, A10.

Donnelly P (1999) Who's fair game? Sport, sexual harassment and abuse. In: White P and Young K (eds) *Sport and Gender in Canada*. Toronto: Oxford University Press, pp. 107–128.

Donnelly P and Sparks R (1997) Moral panic: Child sexual abuse in sport. In: Donnelly P (ed) *Taking Sports Seriously: Social Issues in Canadian Sport*. Toronto: Thompson, pp. 200–205.

Eng H (2006) Queer athletes and queering sport. In: Caudwell J (ed) *Sport, Sexualities and Queer/Theory*. London: Routledge, pp. 49–61.

Fasting K, Brackenridge C and Walseth K (2002) Consequences of sexual harassment in sport for female athletes. *Journal of Sexual Aggression* 8(2): 37–48.

Fasting K, Brackenridge C, and Sundgot-Borgen J (2004) Prevalence of sexual harassment among Norwegian female athletes in relation to sport type. *International Review of the Sociology of Sport* 39(4): 373–386.

Foucault M (1978) *The History of Sexuality, Volume I: An Introduction*. New York: Vintage Books.

Fusco C (1998) Lesbians and locker rooms: The subjective experiences of lesbians in sport. In: Rail G (ed) *Sport and postmodern times*. Albany, NY: State University of New York Press, pp. 87–116.

Fusco C and Kirby K (2000) Are your kids safe? Media representations of sexual abuse in sport. In: Scraton S and Watson B (eds) *Sport, Leisure Identities and Gendered Spaces*. London: Leisure Studies Association, pp. 45–73.

Goss N (2012) NHL Playoffs 2012: Boston Bruins fans unleash racial slurs in response to loss. Available at: http://bleacherreport.com/articles/1161561-nhl-playoffs-2012-bruins-fans-unleash-racial-slurs-in-response-to-loss (accessed 26 April 2012).

Griffin P (1998) *Strong Women, Deep Closets: Lesbians and Homophobia in Sport*. Champaign, IL: Human Kinetics.

Harrison D (2012) Leafs' Burke in campaign to end homophobia in sports. Available at: http://www.cbc.ca/sports/hockey/nhl/story/2012/03/04/sp-nhl-brian-burke-youcanplay-campaign.html (accessed 4 March 2012).

Hartill M (2005) Sport and the sexually abused male child. *Sport, Education and Society* 10(3): 287–304.

Kennedy S and Grainger J (2011) *Why I Didn't Say Anything: The Sheldon Kennedy Story*. Toronto: Insomniac Press.

Kian E, Clavio G, Vincent J and Shaw S (2011) Homophobic and sexist yet uncontested: Examining football fan postings on internet message boards. *Journal of Homosexuality* 58(5): 680–699.

Kirby S, Greaves L and Hankivsky O (2000) *The Dome of Silence: Sexual Harassment and Abuse in Sport*. Halifax, Nova Scotia: Fenwood.

Kirby S and Wintrup G (2002) Running the gauntlet: An examination of initiation/hazing and sexual abuse in sport. *Journal of Sexual Aggression* 8(2), 49–68.

Kirk D (1998) *Schooling Bodies: School Practice and Public Discourse, 1880–1950*. London: Leicester University Press.

Lapointe J (1997) In Canada, troubling times for the national sport and the nation. *The New York Times*, 23 February, 3.

MacDonald M (2006) Beyond the pale: The whiteness of sports studies and queer scholarship. In: Caudwell J (ed) *Sport, Sexualities and Queer/Theory*. London: Routledge, pp. 33–46.

Mangan J (1981) *Athleticism in the Victorian and Edwardian Public School: The Emergence and Consolidation of an Ideal*. Cambridge: Cambridge University Press.

Mangan J (1992) *Britain's Chief Spiritual Export: Imperial Sport as Moral Metaphor, Political Symbol and Cultural Bond*. New York: Viking.

Mofina R (1997) James jailed: Former hockey coach pleads guilty, sentenced to three and a half years. *The Calgary Herald*, 3 January, C2.

National Post (2010) Fleury 'extremely disappointed' by report convicted coach pardoned. Available at: http://sports.nationalpost.com/2010/04/04/fleury-'extremely-disappointed'-by-report-convicted-coach-pardone (accessed 3 May 2012).

Pronger B (1990) *The Arena of Masculinity. Sports, Homosexuality and the Meaning of Sex*. New York: St. Martin's Press.

Pronger B (1999) Outta my endzone: Sport and the territorial anus. *Journal of Sport and Social Issues* 23(4): 373–389.

Pronger B (2000a) Homosexuality in sport – who's winning? In: McKay J, Messner M and Sabo D (eds) *Masculinities, Gender Relations and Sport*. London: Sage, pp. 222–244.

Pronger B (2000b) Queering sport? Theoretical reflections on the improbable. In: *North American Society for the Sociology of Sport Conference*, Colorado Springs, USA, 8–11 November 2000.

Robinson L (1998) *Crossing the Line: Sexual Harassment and Abuse in Canada's National Sport*. Toronto: McClelland and Stewart Inc.

Robinson L (2002) *Black Tights: Women Sport and Sexuality*. Toronto: Harper Collins Canada Ltd.

Robinson, L. (2012) *John Furlong biography omits secret past in Burns Lake*. [Online]. Available from: http://www.straight.com/news/john-furlong-biography-omits-secret-past-burns-lake [Accessed 1st November 2013].

Sedgwick E (1990) *Epistemology of the Closet*. Berkeley, CA: University of California Press.

Shogan D (1999) *The Making of High Performance Athletes: Discipline, Diversity, and Ethics*. Toronto: University of Toronto Press.

Shogan D (2007) *Sport Ethics in Context*. Toronto: Canadian Scholars' Press Inc.

Storr M (1996) The sexual reproduction of 'race': Bisexuality, history and racialization. In: Seidman S (ed) *Queer Theory/Sociology*. Malden, MA: Blackwell, pp. 73–88.

Sykes H (2006) Queer theories of sexuality in sports studies. In: Caudwell J (ed) *Sport, Sexualities and Queer/Theory*. London: Routledge, pp. 13–32.

Symons C and Hemphill D (2006) Transgendering sex and sport in the Gay Games. In: Caudwell J (ed) *Sport, Sexualities and Queer/Theory*. London: Routledge, pp. 109–128.

The Globe & Mail (2010) Former junior hockey coach Graham James will get bail. Available at: http://www.theglobeandmail.com/sports/hockey/former-junior-hockey-coach-graham-james-will-get-bail/article4180480/ (accessed 1 May 2012).

The Toronto Star (2010) Hockey coach in sex abuse case pardoned. Available at: http://www.thestar.com/news/canada/article/790202--hockey-coach-in-sex-abuse-case-pardoned (accessed 1 May 2012)

Toronto Sun (2010) Toews: rules that allowed James' pardon will be changed. Available at: http://www.torontosun.com/news/canada/2010/04/05/13468261-qmi.html (accessed 18 May 18 2012).

Wheatley E (1994) Subcultural subversions: Comparing discourses on sexuality in men's and women's rugby songs. In: Birrell S and Cole C (eds) *Women, Sport, and Culture*. Champaign, IL: Human Kinetics, pp. 193–220.

Wittig M (1992) *The Straight Mind and Other Essays*. Boston, MA: Beacon Press.

PART VIII

Gender and sexuality in the mediation of sport

47

SPORTING FICTIONS

In praise of masculinity?

Jeffrey Hill

I

There is a well-established convention in the British literary world that holds sport and serious literature to be incompatible. [1] '[T]he most durable and popular stories aspire to universality' the critic Mark Lawson (2008, p.2) has observed, '[but] sport is socially and internationally divisive'. One manifest feature of its divisiveness is sport's preoccupation with men and masculinity.

Perhaps because of this, few British novelists have given prominent attention to sport. In popular literature, however, it has provided a recurring subject of great commercial and ideological importance, much of it aimed at younger readers. JA Mangan's work, for example, has brought out the centrality of sport and male athleticism in the verse and song of late-nineteenth and early-twentieth century private school culture (Mangan, 2000). Sir Henry Newbolt's *Vitai Lampada* is a celebrated example, with its famous exhortation to 'play up, and play the game' (Newbolt, n d.: 131–133). Games were seen as character-building exercises that taught boys selfless leadership, and counteracted any leanings towards excessive intellectualism.

Jeffrey Richards has noted the importance of sport in the immensely popular stories of PG Wodehouse where, Richards says, proficiency in sport is 'the measure of a boy' (Richards, 1988: 136). This ideological imperative was not confined to middle-class, upper-class and aristocratic readers. School stories, usually set in private schools, were a staple ingredient of the weeklies aimed at boys whose schooling probably ended by the age of fourteen. The paradigmatic Billy Bunter of Greyfriars was a national figure of fun for readers of all social classes (Orwell, 1984). Dave Russell has commented that much of the soccer fiction written for the popular adolescent market in the 1920s drew upon themes from private school morality, such as 'fair play' and the virtues of amateurism (Russell, 1997: 110–111). Ideas such as these are not entirely absent in boys' literature of the later part of the century. The character-forming qualities of sport feature strongly in the stories of much-loved author Michael Hardcastle (Hardcastle, 1992). Moreover, sport literature was not confined to boys. There was a lucrative market in school stories for girls. Its leading exponent was Angela Brazil, at her height in the interwar years. Her fictional settings of the expensive school and its equally expensive sporting activities, usually involving horses, became a model for tales in mass readership weeklies for girls such as *School Friend*.[2] In the late-twentieth century similar locations and the moral codes they expressed remained evident in the work of popular authors Elinor M Brent Dyer and Bonnie Bryant (Brent Dyer, 1985; Bryant, 1993; Cadogan and Craig, 1976: ch. xiii).

It is all too easy to conclude of such literature, as George Orwell did, that it was little more than a means of reproducing conservative notions of class and gender among the nation's youth (Orwell, 1984: 104–105). There is undoubtedly a tendency in these texts to assign conventional gender roles, but at the same time not all cultural production of this kind has harmonised with the status quo. Alethea Melling's research on sporting tales for females in the 1920s has unearthed a wealth of literature dealing with soccer-playing heroines whose battles on the field are matched by a broader struggle for workers' rights, profit sharing and co-operatives. Stories such as 'Roy of the Rovers' and 'Football Island' appear to challenge conventional gender roles and morality (Melling, 1998). Challenge was also the keynote of Alf Tupper, 'The Tough of the Track', who appeared in the British boys' comic *Rover* (and later *Victor*) from the late 1940s until the early 1990s.[3] As the fictional athlete hero of the great age of British middle-distance running, his appeal to teenage readers derived not only from his immense sporting prowess, achieved through masculine traits of iron discipline and determination, but also from his social circumstances. At a time when successful athletes were often able to draw upon private or institutional resources for support, Tupper was an ordinary working man whose job permitted him little spare time for running. A major theme in the stories is Tupper's contest, both on and off the running track, against wealthy opponents from privileged backgrounds who are dismissive of Tupper's proletarian circumstances. To put it bluntly, there is, over and above Tupper's obvious 'manliness', a strong sense of class hostility and snobbery in the narrative which readers, even younger ones, could scarcely have failed to register. Tupper was not a symbol of the rightness of the social order so much as a reminder of its shortcomings (Hill, 2006; 2010).

II

In the USA the links between sport and the creative arts have on the whole been stronger than in Britain in both the elite and the mass market. Perhaps more than in Britain the popular forms of sport stories have tended towards a conservative influence in the representations of subjects such as family, social class, nation and gender. The genre, which owes much to the influence in the USA of *Tom Brown's Schooldays*, began in earnest with Gilbert Patten's tales of Frank Merriwell (Standish, 1902) in the late-nineteenth century, and continued through John R Tunis's small-town fables of *The Kid from Tompkinsville* (Tunis, 1987), to Clair Bee's stories of Chip Hilton of Valley Falls (Bee, 1998), at their peak of popularity in the 1950s and 1960s.[4] Michael Oriard's extensive study of sporting fictions reveals a persistent emphasis in texts aimed at juvenile readers on masculinity and idealised versions of manhood embodied in sporting heroes. As Oriard notes: 'the athlete hero is the dominant image in the mind of every father who encourages his son to play baseball or football' (Oriard, 1982: 36, 47).

It is in a more serious stratum of American literature, aimed at adult readers, where we find conventional masculinity questioned, and worked into a critique of sport itself. In the work of Bernard Malamud, Philip Roth, John Updike and Richard Ford sport is a notable presence, though with the possible exception of Roth's *The Great American Novel* (Roth, 1973) none of their works could aptly be described as a 'sport novel'. But without the recurring memories of his days as a neighbourhood basketball star would the life of Updike's Rabbit Angstrom (Updike, 2006), or Philip Roth's Swede Levov (Roth, 1998), make much sense? The sporting prowess of their early life, never to be recaptured, defined the best of them. In Malamud's *The Natural* (Malamud, 2003), a re-working of the Arthurian legend into a tale of baseball in the 1930s, the principal character's hubristic obsession to be 'the best there has ever been' leads to his eventual fall, in part through the agency of dangerous women.

In *The Sportswriter* (Ford, 1986) Richard Ford introduces his character Frank Bascombe, a version of the contemporary American 'crisis of masculinity'.[5] The chosen occupation in *The Sportswriter* is not accidental. It is the story of a man isolated, without bearings, and looking to sport – or to *writing* about sport – to provide him with the compass by which to re-direct his life. As an American male, born in the South, grown up in the post-Second World War years, college educated, and briefly drafted into the marines, it is more than likely that one of the plausible aspects of Bascombe's psychology will be sport. It is what men are expected to do if they are 'real' American men with a proper sense of tradition. 'If you're a man in this country', his editor tells him at one point, 'you probably already know enough to be a good sportswriter' (Ford, 1986: 41). The novel is not 'about' sport in the sense that its plot depends on a sports setting for its force, in the manner, for example, of Brian Glanville's soccer novel *The Rise of Gerry Logan* (Glanville, 1963). We learn nothing about sport as a lived practice from Ford's writing. But sport is a constant theme in the book, operating in various ways to illustrate Bascombe's predicament. His ex-wife ('X') is a golfer, who teaches the game at a local country club and who, after the divorce, plays 'the best golf of her life' on the mid-east club pro tour, 'challenging other groups of women in Pennsylvania and Delaware' (Ford, 1986: 373). Thus is expressed X's resourcefulness and energy, her ability to cope, even prosper, independently. For his part Bascombe possesses few aims, has few illusions about what life might offer or amount to. Sports writing, he is told by a colleague, teaches you that there are 'no transcendent themes in life' (Ford, 1986: 16). Bascombe's philosophy, if such it can be called, is a stoical one–damned-thing-after-another perspective on life. Even his writing on sport contributes to a process of illusion making, of what he calls 'false dramas'.

III

In Britain sport novels have rarely attained the canonical literary status enjoyed by their American counterparts. Cricket, one of the most popular games, provides a barometer of the country's sports writing. The game's literature is vast, but in both its fictional and factual forms has rarely achieved serious critical acclaim. It served, however, an important political function. Until the second half of the twentieth century much of it articulated the peculiar *aesthetic* of the game that blossomed in the period from the 1890s until the Great War – cricket's so-called 'Golden Age' – and which continued with some slight modifications through the interwar years. It was an aesthetic that lauded amateurism, proclaimed social leadership by an upper-middle and aristocratic elite, was hostile to the commercialism of mass culture, found grace and beauty in athletic performance, and sought intellectual reward in a slow and often complex unfolding of cricket's patterns of play. The game was more than the sum of its parts: it was a moral code, a form of gentlemanly, civilised behaviour. A century later one of the New York cricketers in Joseph O'Neill's novel *Netherland* could still claim that 'people, all people, Americans, whoever, are at their most civilised when they're playing cricket' (O'Neill, 2008: 204).

Cricket literature, then, was a conservative force: a *texte de plaisir* offering both a comforting reading experience and a supportive vision of the status quo. Anthony Bateman (Bateman, 2009) has noted how texts are invariably backward looking, evoking a nostalgia for the past, displaying a preoccupation with a rural England of settled social hierarchies, and located largely in the south of the country: the kind of place memorialised in Mary Russell Mitford's early-nineteenth century *Our Village* (Mitford, 1912). In many ways this literary construction of cricket reached its pinnacle in the interwar years, when the trauma of the Great War gave cricket's myth of a 'lost past' a renewed relevance and desirability. It evoked the pre-1914 era as one of 'normality', as in Siegfried Sassoon's 1928 work *Memoirs of a Foxhunting Man*, a thinly veiled autobiographical account of the author's early life (Sassoon, 1928). The centrepiece of the book is an account of the annual 'Flower Show Match' in which Sassoon offers an almost painfully nostalgic portrait of the pre-war world, with the cricket club as a hub of village life. The weather is 'blazing hot' and all sections of local society mingle to watch the cricket and stroll through the floral displays. It is a day of 'unclouded jollity' (Sassoon, 1928: 83).

A more acerbic view of cricket, marking a departure from Sassoon, is found in Hugh De Selincourt's *The Cricket Match* (De Selincourt, 1924).[6] The novel's story is compressed into the time between dawn and dusk on another shimmering hot summer day. All the markers of the conventional cricket novel are there: the team, led by the 'right sort' of person, is a microcosm of village (and national) society; the cricket ground is the focus of local summer activity; and in the friendly rivalry of the match against a nearby village the home team, after some uncertainty, eventually wins through with the evening given over to celebrations in the local pub. The village then returns to the blissful sleep from which, at the story's beginning, it is just awakening. *The Cricket Match*, a novel not without a wry humour, has rightly claimed a revered place in the literary history of the game, and few have seen it as anything other than a classic example of mainstream cricket writing. But as an incisive anthropological enquiry into the men and the relationships that make up the grassroots of cricket it also casts a critical gaze on the game, and of the English themselves. In the rural dwellers who frequently populate cricket literature, there is much to admire, but in their petty rivalries and false sense of esteem, also much to admonish. In this sense De Selincourt's novel has an ironic quality, an antidote to much of the celebratory cricket prose of this era.[7] A similar contrast to some of the more romantic representations of the game comes in Dudley Carew's tale of professional cricketer Alan Peveril, *The Son of Grief* (Carew, 1936).

Perhaps the most poignant example of this variant of the genre is Bruce Hamilton's *Pro: An English Tragedy* (Hamilton, 1946), a story framed by the familiar morbidity of the Great War generation. Entirely set in the world of cricket, *Pro* is the story of a professional player whose career begins just before the 1914–1918 war, reaches its peak in the mid-twenties, and comes to a halt some ten years later. His cricket career is beset by various forms of ill-luck, together with class prejudice and the inevitable sportsman's problems of ageing, and his life enters into an inexorable downward spiral. The final chapters of the novel describe a man by turns alone, demoralised, destitute and humiliated, who finally takes his own life.

Each of these novels subverts in different ways the linguistic conventions from which writers such as Sassoon had drawn. While they unquestioningly place men at the centre of the narrative, and retain an implicit belief in heterosexual norms, there is a clear intention to move away from the romantic sport hero, as well as to question the idea of a 'golden age'.

IV

The initiative that finally wrenched creative sport writing in Britain from its conservative conventions came with David Storey's *This Sporting Life* (Storey, 1960).[8] As with many of his fellow writers of this period Storey brought to his work a sharp awareness of working-class life, but was able to augment his discussion of class with a sensitive treatment of gender relations. His main male character is Arthur Machin, a rugby league player renowned for his strength, but in the character of Mrs Hammond, Machin's landlady, Storey brings into the centre of his narrative a finely drawn female character, as he had also done in *Flight Into Camden*, published in the same year. Storey places Machin in the world of sport – after work, the main site of 'maleness' – where, increasingly through the novel, he comes to understand the shallowness of received wisdoms of gender.

It is in his relationship with Mrs Hammond that Machin's masculinity is put to the test and found wanting. This has little to do with sex, success in which is the conventional social measure of masculine prowess. It has, however, everything to do with understanding women and being able to bridge a divide between the sexes that is created and re-created daily through countless forms of separation in work and play, driving men and women apart. The sporting life is, of course, the quintessential instrument of female exclusion, for women have no part in the football. Machin has an affair with Mrs Hammond, a withdrawn, desiccated, self-pitying woman. She is seeking to expunge the shame of a failed marriage, ended not in divorce but in the suicide of her husband. The event leaves her guilt-stricken and suspicious of any relationship with a man. At the same time, she is caged in a confining domesticity, caring for her two young children, taking in a lodger to make ends meet, and keeping alive the memory of her dead husband through the ritual daily cleaning of his boots. Nobody could be farther removed than Mrs Hammond from the glamorized, sexually submissive image of a woman conventionally associated with the masculine gaze, which is the image reproduced in the cheap novelettes that Machin reads. Yet this is what provides the fascination for Machin. He wants to arouse in her some spark of emotion for him. But all his efforts to establish a real relationship, shorn of the customary expectations of a society in which gender roles are rigidly performed, come to nothing. The novel is a bitter critique of contemporary British attitudes and establishes a theme that only fully came into public view with the rise of the women's movement in the later 1960s.

Though Storey has continued to produce some fine novels he has arguably never since attained the heights achieved in *This Sporting Life*. He certainly never returned to the subject of sport, although his influence might be traced in a number of later writers. Brian Glanville, for example, created a problematical male in his football novel (Glanville, 1963), which cleverly places issues of gender relations in a context of the changing nature of the game. JL Carr's *A Season in Sinji* (Carr, 1967) achieves a darker tone than almost all cricket novels before it by rejecting the genre's tired conventions: there are no idyllic settings, few noble deeds on the field, and the humour is deeply ironic. The cricket, as with other situations in the story, is the scene for intense psychological rivalries and conflicts between two men. Thomas Keneally (Keneally, 1986) returned to Storey's sport of rugby league, this time in an Australian setting, to examine the male sporting hero in a milieu where social class, immigration, religion and gender conspired to produce an unsettling and ultimately tragic life experience. While dealing directly with sport – there are some fine descriptions of rugby matches and dressing room relationships – Keneally also succeeds in placing it at an intersection of problems that shape modern Australian life. It is an outstanding novel, perhaps somewhat neglected in the light of the author's worldwide success with *Schindler's Ark* (Keneally, 1982), subsequently adapted for the cinema by Spielberg (Spielberg, 1993).

Keneally's is an exceptional novel in a sport fiction context for its global sensibility – varied European heritages (Irish, Italian, Belorussian) converge and conflict around the leading character's Australian identity. Likewise, in Joseph O'Neill's highly regarded *Netherland* (O'Neill, 2008) Hans van den Broek, a New York-based oil futures dealer, experiences similar confusions. The novel is set in the immediate aftermath of 9/11 and explores some of the uncertainties and concerns felt by people at that time. Indeed, the novelist Zadie Smith (Smith, 2009) sees *Netherland* as a story about 'anxiety'. Like his illustrious predecessors – Updike, Roth, Ford, even Scott Fitzgerald – O'Neill writes about the American condition. Strangely, therefore, the focus of Netherland's narrative is a game that has limited influence on the American imagination: cricket. But, as with Carr, it contains scarcely any of the devices traditionally associated with the genre. Indeed its story is one in which the principal character is forced steadily to shed illusions about many of the governing features of life: about America, marriage, family and cricket itself. In the leagues of New York Hans, as his name suggests a native of Holland but who has also lived in England, joins with other cricket-playing immigrants who are from a very different social and racial background. His fellow players are Afro-Caribbean or South Asian, and Hans is usually the sole white man in the match. He is thus made to understand life lived from the lower, non-privileged stratum of society – from, in fact, a 'netherland'. The novel's subject and its shifting chronology further challenge the sport story's traditional architecture, with its beginning, middle and end.

Resort to narrative irregularity is taken further in a novel published almost at the same time as O'Neill's. Jennie Walker's *24 for 3* (Walker, 2008) is slighter in both themes and length (it is, in fact, a novella) though, arguably, the sport fulfils a yet more central idea in the story.[9] It does so, however, in an enigmatic way. The narrative and plot of *24 for 3* are bounded in time by a cricket match – a five-day test between England and India. As befits the contemporary setting the match is experienced not at first hand but through the medium of television. The narrator is unusually a woman, for whom the game is an unfathomable masculine pastime – a 'foreign film without sub-titles' (Walker, 2008: 44). During the five days of the match her behaviour is as inexplicable to the reader as the rules and patterns of cricket are to the character herself; she moves uncertainly between husband and lover, a liaison recounted as a matter-of-fact arrangement without any suggestion of morality or guilt, or indeed any deep affection for either of the males in the triangle. At the same time she attempts, with rather more feeling, to restore a loving relationship with her missing teenage stepson. All the while cricket is happening, but it is not *described*. It is something the characters are aware of and interested in to a greater or lesser extent. It is a ritual against which they might be judged, according to their reactions to this seemingly arcane ludic form. The game also symbolises the element of unpredictability in their lives. Sport, and cricket more than most, has the capacity to upset expectations: 'even when one team is much better than the other, you never know for sure what's going to happen next, and nor do the players. By five o'clock all the probabilities could be overturned' (Walker, 2008: 53). For the serious cricket follower, expecting a traditional 'realist' treatment of the game, this whimsical novel will seem merely to offer a playful teasing of something sacred. Far from being a game we know, understand, and admire cricket becomes, like the world we inhabit, a site of unpredictability. Just as a cricket match can finish without a result, life's loose ends remain untied. Like *Netherland,* this is a study of anxiety.

Other recent novels have taken a similar, if less ambitious, direction. Malcolm Knox's *Adult Book* (Knox, 2004) deals with questions of social class and Australian identity, and makes one of his major characters a professional cricketer – a test playing 'ledge' (legend) no less. The cricket, a symbol of Australian national pride and masculinity, contains a perfect description of a long, career-saving test innings, with the obligatory follow-up television interview presented as wonderful irony. Knox also succeeds in weaving a theme of age and sexuality into the story. In a similar sense Romesh Gunesekera (Gunesekera, 2008) frames his story of a Sri Lankan man's quest for personal fulfilment between two contrasting cricket matches at the beginning and end of the novel, to show the game's capacity for affirming identity in a sometimes rootless and anonymous world. Sri Lanka is also the setting for Shehan Karunatilaka's *Chinaman: The Legend of Pradeep Mathew* (Karunatilaka, 2011), which revives the picaresque tradition of novel writing. It is an extraordinary, rambling, postmodern literary construction, at heart a story about a man's attempts to chronicle the exploits of a unique cricketer, Pradeep Mathew, whose bowling repertoire was based around his skill with the 'chinaman'.[10] *Chinaman* is, then, a quest story which refuses to confine itself to cricket. But, when all is said and done, it concerns one man's endeavours (with the help of his male friend) to create a legend out of another man's exploits.

V

In its popular forms fictional sport literature has generally placed men in the forefront of the action. Sport has been the testing ground for the proving of their 'manliness'. Women, while not entirely absent, have usually been found either in a secondary position or situated firmly within recognisably 'women's' sports. The gravitational pull of these conventions has exerted less influence over serious novelists, who have attempted to avoid some of the literary pitfalls noted by Lawson, though even here heterosexuality has tended to be the dominant gender theme. A few exceptions aside, gay relationships and the influence of queer theory await serious fictional exploration (Anderson, 2005; Cohen, 1997; Simmonds, 1998; Warren, 1974). In recent years many sport novels have at least moved away from 'his'-story, rendering *him* as a problematic and not always sympathetic partner in a relationship. Accompanying this has been a movement away from the conservatism of form that for a long time characterised sport fiction, in favour of a more playful and less reverential representation of what it is we mean by 'sport'.

Notes

1 See, for example, the views of novelist and sport journalist Brian Glanville (1967) *People in Sport*. London: Secker and Warburg: 15–28.
2 A long-running popular comic for younger female readers, established in 1919 (renamed *The Schoolgirl* from 1929–1940), revived as *School Friend* in 1950, merged with *June* in 1965 and then became *Tammy* in 1974.
3 The comics were published by the Scottish firm D C Thomson. In the mid 1950s *Rover's* circulation was approximately 300,000 but falling sales prompted its replacement in the early 1960s by the comic-strip *Victor*, which initially sold some half a million copies throughout Britain, chiefly in London, Lancashire and Yorkshire. (Figures kindly supplied by Mr Bill McLoughlin of D C Thomson.)
4 All were prolific writers. Patten (1866–1945), who wrote under the name of Burt L Standish, produced his Frank Merriwell stories over a period of twenty years from 1896, with spin-offs on radio in later years. Tunis (1889–1975) introduced Roy Tucker, the Kid, in 1940 and went on to publish many more sport stories, mainly about baseball. Bee (1896–1983), a leading basketball coach, wrote twenty-four novels in the Chip Hilton series from 1948 onwards.
5 Bascombe's life is followed up in (1996) *Independence Day*.London: Harvill Press [first published 1995] and (2006) *The Lay of the Land*. London: Bloomsbury Publishing.
6 Similar themes are present in AG MacDonnell (1964) *England, Their England*, London: Macmillan [first published 1933], mainly remembered for its chapter on cricket.
7 Leading examples are the poet and critic Edmund Blunden (1944) *Cricket Country*.London: Collins. And, from the 1920s to the 1970s, the journalist and critic Neville Cardus (see Bateman, 2009, ch.3).
8 See also the film adaptation, Lindsay Anderson dir. (1963) *This Sporting Life*. London: Independent Artists. Hill J (2005) Sport Stripped Bare: Deconstructing Working-Class Masculinity, *This Sporting Life*. *Men and Masculinities* 7(4): 405–432.
9 The name suggests a female author, but the novel is in fact by a man (Charles Boyle).
10 The left-armer's googly, known as the 'bosie' in Australia.

References

Anderson E (2005) *In the Game: Gay Athletes and the Cult of Masculinity*. Albany: SUNY Press.
Bateman A (2009) *Cricket, Literature and Culture: Symbolising the Nation, Destabilising Empire*. Farnham: Ashgate.
Bee C (1998) *Touchdown Pass*. Nashville, TN: Broadman and Holman [first published 1948].
Brent Dyer E M (1985) *The Chalet School Wins the Trick*. London: Armada.
Bryant B (1993) *Show Horse*. London: Bantam Books.
Cadogan, M and Craig P (1976) *You're a Brick Angela!: A New Look for Girls' Fiction 1839–1975*. London: Victor Gollancz.
Carew D (1936) *The Son of Grief*. London: Arthur Barker Ltd.

Carr JL (1967) *A Season in Sinji: A Novel*. London: Alan Ross.

Cohen C (1997) *Courted*. Tallahassee: Naiad Press.

De Selincourt H (1924) *The Cricket Match*. London: Jonathan Cape.

Ford R (1986) *The Sportswriter*. London: Vintage [first published 1985].

Glanville B (1963) *The Rise of Gerry Logan*. London: Martin Secker and Warburg.

Gunesekera R (2008) *The Match*. London: Bloomsbury.

Hamilton B (1946) *Pro: An English Tragedy*. London: The Cressett Press.

Hardcastle M (1992) *Soccer Special*. London: Dean.

Hill J (2006) I'll Run Him: Alf Tupper, Social Class and British Amateurism. *Sport in History* 26 (3): 502–519.

Hill J (2010) I Like to Have a Go at the Swanks: Alf Tupper and English Society, 1945–90. In: Dine P and Crosson S (eds) *Sport, Representation and Evolving Identities in Europe*. Bern: Peter Lang, pp.79–100.

Karunatilaka S (2011) *Chinaman: The Legend of Pradeep Mathew*. London: Jonathan Cape.

Keneally T (1986) *A Family Madness*. London: Sceptre [first published 1985].

Keneally T (1982) *Schindler's Ark*. London: Hodder and Stoughton.

Knox M (2004) *Adult Book*. London: Bloomsbury.

Lawson M (2008) The write track. *Guardian Review*, 2 August 2008.

Malamud B (2003) *The Natural*. New York: Farrar, Straus and Giroux [first published 1952].

Mangan JA (2000) *Athleticism in the Victorian and Edwardian Public School: The Emergence of an Educational Ideology*. London: Frank Cass.

Melling A (1998) Ray of the Rovers: The Working-Class Heroine in Popular Football Fiction, 1915–25. *International Journal of the History of Sport* 15 (1): 97–122.

Mitford MR (1912) *Our Village*. London: George Harrap and Co. [first published 1824–32].

Newbolt H (n.d.) Vitai Lampada. In: *Collected Poems 1897–1907*. London: Thomas Nelson.

O'Neill J (2008) *Netherland*. London: Fourth Estate.

Oriard M (1982) *Dreaming of Heroes: American Sport Fiction, 1868–1980*. Chicago: Nelson-Hall.

Orwell G (1984) Boys' Weeklies. In: Orwell G *The Penguin Essays of George Orwell*. Harmondsworth: Penguin, pp. 84–106.

Richards J (1988) *Happiest Days: The Public Schools in English Fiction*. Manchester: Manchester University Press.

Roth P (1973) *The Great American Novel*. New York: Holt, Rinehart and Winston.

Roth P (1998) *American Pastoral*. London: Vintage [first published 1997].

Russell D (1997) *Football and the English: A Social History of Association Football in England 1863–1995*. Preston: Carnegie Publishing.

Sassoon, Siegfried (1928) *Memoirs of a Fox-Hunting Man*. London: Faber and Faber. Available at www. books.google.co.uk (accessed 6 July 2010).

Simmonds D (1998) *Forty Love*. London: Silver Moon.

Smith Z (2009) Two Paths for the Novel. *London Review of Books*, 20 November, 89.

Spielberg S (1993) *Schindler's List*. US: Amblin/Universal.

Standish BL [Gilbert Patten] (1902) *Frank Merriwell's Chums*. London: Shurmer and Sibthorpe.

Storey D (1960) *This Sporting Life*. London: Longmans.

Tunis JR (1987) *The Kid From Tompkinsville*. New York: Harcourt, Brace, Jovanovich [first published 1940].

Updike J (2006) *Rabbit, Run*. London: Penguin Classics [first published 1960].

Walker J (2008) *24 for 3*. London: Bloomsbury.

Warren P N (1974) *The Front Runner*. New York: Morrow.

48

TRANSMITTING SOFTER MASCULINITY

Sports talk radio and masculinity

David Nylund

Introduction

Sports talk radio, which broadcasts sporting discussions, is a popular sport-media format with an almost exclusively male demographic. In addition to play-by-play coverage of local sports teams, most shows offer discussion and analysis of sport as part of their regular programming. These shows are generally characterized by an often-boisterous on-air style personality, and all-encompassing debate by both hosts and callers. Sports talk is available in both local and syndicated forms, and is carried in some form on both major North American satellite radio networks. In the United States, for example, most sports talk formatted radio stations air mostly syndicated programming, with ESPN and Radio Fox Sports Radio being the most popular.[1]

Sports talk radio then

Sports radio stations, similar to political talk radio, mushroomed in the 1980s with the rise of late capitalism, the deregulation of the radio industry, corporate media consolidation, and niche marketing (Douglas, 2002). Ceding the radio airwaves to niche marketing and late capitalism has predictably generated sports radio programming that mirrors the content, style and success of talk radio hosts, such as Rush Limbaugh in the United States, who champion right wing policies (Smith, 2002).[2] According to Goldberg (1998), Haag (1996), Mariscal (1999), and Nylund (2007), sports talk radio is just as hostile to feminists and gays as right wing political talk radio. These scholars suggest that sports radio has reproduced hegemonic masculinity, a dominant form of manhood predicated on competiveness, toughness, and the marginalization of women and gay men (Connell, 2000). In fact, according to Kevin Cook (1993: 20), sports talk radio, even more than political talk radio, feeds hegemonic masculinity as it is the only arena left for white men who have been 'wounded by the indignities of feminism, affirmative action, and other groups' quest for social equality'. In line with Cook's argument, Haag (1996) states:

> Sports talk show is a venue for the embattled White male seeking recreational repose;
> that it caters to this audience as surely as Rush Limbaugh articulates its discontents.

Some sports talk stations define their listening audience explicitly as the Atlanta sports station [The FAN] manager states, 'we make no pretensions about what we're doing here. The FAN is a guy's radio station. We're aiming at the men's bracket which is the hardest to reach.'

(p. 459)

Goldberg (1998) and Mariscal (1999) suggest that sports radio reinforces cultural hegemony. For instance, Mariscal believes that while the interchange between hosts and callers can be impassioned and dialogical, it is in reality a pseudo-civic participation due to corporatization of radio and the consequences of national syndication which undermines any semblance of local public discourse. Similarly, Goldberg (1998) argues that sports talk, rather than promoting free expression, promotes uniformity and threatens democracy in insidious ways:

Sports talk radio provides a covert political stage for those who think of themselves as nonpolitical or as politically disenfranchised. Like Limbaugh, though more discreetly, sports talk radio enables White men to express themselves as White and male.

(p. 217)

There is ample evidence that sports talk radio is an anti-democratic, sexist medium that reinforces homophobia and male hegemony. However, my listening and analysis of sports radio programmes over the past ten years reveals some contradictions and fissures to hegemony; this includes the nationally syndicated *Jim Rome Show*. The host of the show, Jim Rome, historically known for his 'macho' posturing and feminizing of athletes, has had many rich discussions on his show focusing on the discrimination against gay athletes. The following examples of the programme exemplify times when the show partially subverts hegemonic masculinity and homophobia. The first example relates to an editorial letter in the May 2003 issue of *Out* Magazine. In that issue, editor in chief, Brendan Lemon, stated that his boyfriend was a Major League baseball player. Lemon did not give names but hinted that the player was from an East Coast franchise. Rome and other conventional media programmes reacted quickly to the editorial. A media firestorm resulted in a rumour mill: players, fans, owners, and sports talk radio hosts swapped guesses and anxieties over the athlete's identity.

On May 18, 2003, Rome's monologue pondered these questions: What would happen if that person's identity became public? What would it mean for baseball, gays, and lesbians in sports in general, and for the man himself? Given that Lemon's boyfriend would be the first athlete in one of the 'big four' major-league team sports (baseball, football, basketball, and hockey) to come out *during* his career, what effect would this have on the institution of sport? Rome decided to pose this question to one of his interview subjects, well-respected baseball veteran, Eric Davis.

> Rome: What would happen if a teammate of yours, or any baseball player, would come out of the closet and say, 'I am gay'? What would the reaction be like? How badly would that go?
>
> Eric: I think it would go real bad. I think people would jump to form an opinion because everybody has an opinion about gays already. But I think it would be a very difficult situation because with us showering with each other . . . being around each other as men. Now, you're in the shower with a guy who's gay . . . looking at you . . . maybe making a pass. That's an uncomfortable situation. In society, they have never really accepted it. They want to come

out. And if that's the cause fine but in sports, it would definitely raise some eyebrows . . . I don't think it should be thrown at 25 guys saying, 'Yeah I am gay.'

[Rome changes the subject . . . no follow-up]

Rome asks a pointed question to Davis whose predictable homophobic response warrants more follow-up questions. Yet, Rome shifts the subject to something less problematic, letting Davis off the hook. After Rome ends the interview, he addresses Davis's comments in another monologue:

That's [Eric Davis] a 17 year respected major league ballplayer. And I think that's a representative comment of a lot of these guys. . . . He is a very highly regarded guy. This is why I asked him the question. And he answered it very honestly. He would be concerned about having a gay teammate . . . . For instance, when he's showering. Personally, I don't agree with the take. It's my personal opinion. However, I posed the question to see what the reaction would be. And this is what I have been saying since this story broke. This is why it would not be a good thing. This is why the editor of that magazine clearly was wrong and has never been in a locker-room or clubhouse. That's why it hasn't happened. Eric Davis' reaction is what you would expect. Not everybody would feel that way, but a large majority would. It would make it nearly impossible for a gay player to come out.

Here, Rome is aware of the potential difficulties that would occur for an openly gay ballplayer. However, he articulates his opinion in the safety of his 'expert' monologue, not in the presence of Eric Davis. He does not risk compromising his relationship with Davis by endorsing an unusually progressive stance in the presence of a famous ballplayer like Davis. But, when a listener calls immediately after the Davis interview, Rome responds differently:

Joe: I never imagined my first take would be on gays but I had to call. Being gay, it matters to no one but gays themselves. Why don't you guys, girls or gays . . . whatever you guys are. Just do us a favor, do yourselves a favor and keep it to yourselves. I mean . . . [Rome hangs up on the caller]

Rome: I think that's a very convenient response – 'It's an issue only because you make it an issue.' I don't agree with that frankly. It's an issue because they are often persecuted against, harassed, assaulted, or killed in some cases. That's why it is an issue. They are fired from jobs, ostracized. It's not only an issue because they are making it an issue. What you are saying is keep your mouth shut, keep it in the closet; you are not accepting them for whom they are and what they are. It's not an issue because they are making it an issue. It's an issue because of people saying things like, 'keep your mouth shut . . . we don't want you around . . . we don't want to know you people exist'. That's why it's an issue because of that treatment.

Rome's stance against homophobia demonstrates an appreciation of the injustices of homophobia and heterosexism, and positions him as avant-garde for the time. This position is worth mentioning, particularly in the context of a programme with an audience of mostly men steeped in traditional masculinity and for whom heterosexuality is the unquestioned norm. Rome's anti-homophobic stance represents the beginning of a fissure in hegemonic masculinity the way

Anderson (2005) describes in his research on gay athletes of the time. It potentially fostered a new awareness in Rome's listeners and invited new voices into this important conversation about masculinity and sexuality, potentially spurring a rethinking of masculinity and sports. Cutting off the first time caller due to his homophobic comment could be viewed as a productive accountable manoeuvre, which is notable since straight men do not have a rich history of holding other straight men responsible for homophobic slurs.

Jim Rome's anti-homophobic stances became widely known earning him praise by many gay and lesbian activist organizations. Several openly gay ex-athletes were interviewed by Rome, including American football players Esera Tuaolo and David Kopay, and baseball player Billy Bean, all who 'came out' once they retired from professional sports. These interviews were substantive and enlightening; it was clear that gay athletes felt supported and safe on Rome's show.

Sports talk radio today

The forward-thinking views of Jim Rome have continued over the past decade, and have inspired other sports radio hosts to oppose homophobia. Several sports radio programmes, including the Rome show and ESPN's *Mike and Mike Show*, applauded the courage of Chief Operating Officer and president of the National Basketball Association (NBA) franchise, Phoenix Suns Rick Welts, for his recent revelation that he is gay. In response to homophobic insults by NBA stars Kobe Bryant and Joakim Noah (both athletes were fined by the NBA for their comments), Jim Rome said on his May 23, 2011 show:

> Speaking of rattled, never thought I'd see the Bulls [Chicago NBA franchise] come unglued the way they did. Miami's defensive pressure certainly had something to do with it but that doesn't explain all the offensive fouls, shot clock violations and their getting hooked by Heat players and in Joakim Noah's case, a fan. Noah was caught on tape yelling a gay slur at a fan in the first quarter. How does that guy not know better than that?! Joakim, did you not see the league ding Kobe Bryant $100 grand for a similar incident? Or that Sun's president Rick Welts come out of the closet recently? Or even more importantly those Public Service Announcements the NBA is running where Grant Hill and today's guest Jared Dudley drop manual buzzers on people for letting that type of ignorance fly. The league has made it pretty clear you and everyone else better keep that ignorance out of your mouth.

Homophobia is swiftly losing hegemonic status both in high school and university sports (Anderson, 2011) and in mainstream professional sports. Remarks that were once dismissed as just a kind of acceptable trash-talk ('you're gay') in sports are now being challenged by a growing number of professional athletes, including basketball player Grant Hill, who was part of a campaign by the NBA to take a stance against homophobia. On NPR, Hill (interviewed by NPR host Scott Simon) on the subject, said:

> Simon: And why did you think this was so important to lend your voice to this issue [homophobia]?
> Hill: It's about words. You know, the most important thing is these words have meaning. And gay is not a bad word, but if you use it, you know, in a way that promotes negativity, then it is. Using gay to mean dumb or stupid: not cool. Not cool. Not in my house, not anywhere. It's not creative. It's offensive to gay people. And you're better than that.

Simon:	Did you get any flak for it?
Hill:	Yeah, I think so. You know, I'd say you have a – you probably have three sort of groups of people, you know. You know, you have those that get it and understand it and appreciate it. You probably have a group of folks who took it to heart, you know. You know what? That makes a lot of sense, you know. Maybe I wasn't quite aware. I'll be more careful in the language and the words that I use. And then you have sort of, you know, I guess for lack of a better word, folks that are just going to be ignorant.
Simon:	Charles Barkley – great player, for that matter, I think a very entertaining commentator, who's not known for pulling his punches – said that he had plenty of gay teammates in the NBA, and it was no big deal. Is that the case?
Hill:	I thought I heard, you know, that Charles had said, look, he probably had played with plenty of gay teammates. And, you know, I think the culture of male-dominated professional sports, that whole topic, you know, can be considered taboo. Our president, as you mentioned, Rick Welts, announced and came out last Sunday, the same day that our PSA aired for the first time. And for him, you know, I guess the pressure was such that he's been, you know, he's been hiding this for his entire life.
Simon:	Has sports reached – is sports beginning to approach a tipping point on this subject? I mean, as you note, you have what Rick Welts said, Sean Avery, the hockey player, says he's in favour of gay marriage, and Will Sheridan, who played for Villanova, says, well, I was gay when I played. I'm gay, and everyone knew it.
Hill:	I don't know if it's reaching a tipping point, but I certainly think there's more discussion, there's more conversation about this subject matter than at any other time. And I think more and more, people are more comfortable with coming out and expressing themselves. But, you know, do I anticipate athletes coming out of the closet now left and right? I don't know. But I think it certainly is – you know, it's just a good start to be able to talk about it and have these discussions.

Further anti-heterosexist advancement occurred in 2011, when Jared Max, one of the best-known voices in New York sports radio and current ESPN New York 1050 morning host of 'Maxed Out in the Morning', came out of the closet after talking about the other sports figures who have come out of the closet. On his July 2011 show he said:

Are we ready to have our sports information delivered by someone who is gay? Well we are gonna find out. Because for the last 16 years, I've been living a free life among my close friends and family, and I've hidden behind what is a gargantuan sized secret here in the sports world. I am gay. Yeah. Jared Max. The sports guy who is one of the most familiar faces in New York sports isn't quite like the majority. And while you already knew I was a little different, this might help make sense of it. But more so, I'm taking this courageous jump into the unknown having no idea how I will be perceived.

Max received overwhelming support from his listeners, other sports radio hosts, athletes and ESPN.[3]

There is sufficient evidence to argue that homophobia is being confronted head-on in the traditionally masculinist world of sports talk radio and in the larger sports media world. For example, recent research is showing that the sports media is considerably less homophobic and less interested in reproducing orthodox (hegemonic) masculine discourse than before. One illustration of contemporary research is Kian and Anderson's (2009) content analysis of newsprint after professional basketball player John Amaechi came out. Kian and Anderson concluded that print media writers revealed little homophobia and recurrently called for more acceptance of gays athletes. Similarly, Anderson and Kian (2012) show that attitudes toward concussions and risk in the National Football League (the American professional football league referred to as the NFL) are also transforming; players are increasing valuing the elimination of head trauma, instead of playing at all costs. Not only is this change occurring among players, but it is also evident in sport media. These counter-hegemonic moments in sports radio are indicative of, and situated within, some of the recent advancements in gay rights in the larger American political context: same-sex marriage, don't ask don't tell, the passing of hate crimes legislation, and Barrack Obama's recent support of marriage equality.

Sports talk radio and transphobia

Now, a word of caution: while there is much to acknowledge about the progress made in the sports media, it is equally important to ask which athletes are allowed to become visible. What is their social location? How is their sexuality represented? Who continues to be marginalized and not benefiting from this recent headway? Virtually all the gay athletes who have been highlighted in sports talk radio are white gay men who define homosexuality as an essentialist identity and mimic some aspects of traditional masculinity. Scholar Lisa Duggan (2003) claims that much of the recent visibility of gays and lesbians is framed within a post-Stonewall, homonormative, identitarian private discourse. According to Duggan, homonormativity is an apolitical gay male identity anchored in domesticity and consumption. Gay homonormative representations, in sports radio or shows such as *Glee* (popular with youth and with several openly gay and lesbian characters on the show), are increasingly tolerated within the dominant culture, while transgender persons are invisible or pathologised.

Some examples of the marginalization of athletes who transgress traditional gender norms included Jim Rome's ridiculing of former tennis star Martina Navratilova, referring to her as 'Martin' due to her 'mannishness'.[4] Navratilova, who has been public about her lesbian identity, has been overtly political about her stances on gender and sexuality. In the past, Martina has been loudly criticized for supporting and coaching Renee Richards, a transgender female who competed professionally on the women's circuit. ESPN sports radio host, Colin Cowhered, has made several transphobic insults including criticizing NBC for hiring broadcaster Keith Olbermann on their NFL programme show by saying on his programme that 'Olbermann is bright and talented and a really good broadcaster, but he's about as Middle-America as a transgender film festival.' Hence, sports talk radio both reflects and constitutes a homonormative, sexist, and transphobic discourse that benefits some, but not all sexual and gender minorities, particularly persons who resist assimilation into mainstream gay communities. This discourse is persuasively articulated by queer activist and writer Mattilda Bernstein Sycamore (2008):

> Even when the gay rights agenda does include real issues, it does it in a way that consistently prioritizes the most privileged while marginalizing everyone else. I'm using the term gay rights instead of the more popular term of the moment, GLBT rights, because GLBT usually means gay, with lesbian in parentheses, throw out the bisexuals,

and put transgender on for a little window-dressing. A gay rights agenda fights for an end to discrimination in housing and employment, but not for the provision of housing or jobs; domestic partner health coverage but not universal health coverage. The gay rights agenda fights for tougher hate crimes legislation, instead of fighting racism, classism, and transphobia in the criminal justice system.

(p. 2)

Conclusion

While there is a great deal of support that sports talk radio, similar to conservative talk radio reproduces sexism and homophobia, critical analysis indicates that this medium takes some surprising positions on gender and sexuality that contrast sharply with the prevailing discourse of conservative talk radio programmes. In particular, sports talk radio offers countervailing messages about gender and sexuality that intermittently disrupt hegemonic masculinity and homophobia. This reflects the changing culture of masculinity more broadly (Anderson, 2009, 2011, 2012).

Lastly, while these fractures of traditional masculinity offer hope and reflect (and may even shape on some small level) the advancement of gay rights, sports radio discourses are framed within the constraints of homonormativity. The real effects of homonormativity remind us as scholars and activists to problematize the gay rights movement by asking who is most benefiting from some of the recent progress (albeit limited and a long way to go) and who is disregarded. Sports talk radio discourse gives us an analytical prism to analyze and fight for the rights of gender non-conforming and transgender persons along with supporting the ongoing struggle for gay and lesbian rights.

Notes

1 Entertainment and Sports Programming Network, commonly known as ESPN, is an American global television and radio network focusing on sports-related programming including live and pre-taped event telecasts, sports talk shows, and other original programming.

2 Rush Limbaugh is an American radio talk show host and political commentator. His programme is the highest-rated talk show programme in the United States. Limbaugh is known for his championing of extreme right wing politics through a bombastic performance style. His popularity with a wide-ranging audience has allowed him to have a platform with conservative Republican politics influencing elected officials and public policy. Limbaugh is particularly known for his misogyny and critique of feminism popularizing the term 'feminazi' referring to about two dozen feminists 'to whom the most important thing in life is ensuring that as many abortions as possible occur.'

3 I listen to the show on an almost daily basis. There is overwhelming support and I have never heard a homophobic comment from the callers.

4 Rome's comments about Martina Navratilova on June 2, 2005 (I was listening to the programme while driving in my car that day).

References

Anderson E 2012 Shifting masculinities in Anglo-American countries. *Masculinities and Social Change*, 1(1): 60–79.

Anderson E 2011 Updating the outcome: Gay athletes, straight teams, and coming out at the end of the decade. *Gender & Society*, 25(2): 250–268.

Anderson E 2009 Inclusive masculinity: The changing nature of masculinities. New York, NY: Routledge.

Anderson E 2005 *In the game: Gay athletes and the cult of masculinity*. Albany, NY: State University of New York Press.

Anderson E and Kian T 2012 Contesting violence, masculinity, and head trauma in the National Football League. *Men and Masculinities*, 15(2): 152–173.

Connell RW 2000 *The men and the boys*. Berkeley, CA: University of California Press.

Cook K 1993 Media. *Playboy*, April Issue, pp. 20–21.

Douglas SJ 2002 Letting the boys be boys: Talk radio, male hysteria, and political discourse in the 1980s. In: Hilmes M and Loviglio J (eds) *Radio reader: Essays in the cultural history of radio*. New York: Routledge, pp. 485–504

Duggan L 2003 *The twilight of equality: Neoliberalism, cultural politics, and the attack on democracy*. Boston, MA: Beacon Press.

Goldberg DT 1998 Call and response: Sports, talk radio, and the death of democracy. *Journal of Sport & Social Issues*, 22(2): 212–223.

Haag P 1996 The 50,000 watt sports bar: Talk radio and the ethic of the fan. *The South Atlantic Quarterly*, 95(2): 453–470.

Kian EM and Anderson E 2009 John Amaechi: Changing the way sport reporters examine gay athletes. *Journal of Homosexuality*, 56(7): 799–818.

Mariscal J 1999 Chicanos and Latinos in the jungle of sports talk radio. *Journal of Sport & Social Issues*, 23(1): 111–117.

Nylund D 2007 *Beer, babes, and balls: Sports talk radio and masculinity*. Albany, NY: SUNY Press.

Smith M 2002 The Jim Rome Show and negotiations of manhood: Surviving in 'The Jungle'. In: North American Society for the Sociology of Sport, Indianapolis, IN, May 2002.

Sycamore MB 2008 *That's revolting: Queer strategies to resist assimilation*. Berkeley: Soft Skull Press.

49

SEXUALITY IN THE MEDIATION OF SPORT

Edward M. Kian

Introduction

Cultural attitudes have evolved rapidly toward greater tolerance and support for gays and lesbians throughout most first-world countries. Views toward gays and lesbians in the U.S. have also changed dramatically in recent years, with younger generations far more accepting than older generations. Highlighting the speed of this change in the U.S., the vast majority of reputable polls in 2011–2012 showed that a majority of American adults favoured gay marriage. This contrasted with the findings of all major polls before 2009 (Silver, 2011). In fact, former U.S. President George W. Bush's successful 2004 re-election campaign hinged largely upon his opposition of gay rights, an astute short-term strategy based on a 2004 Gallup poll that showed U.S. adults opposed gay marriage, 61:32% (MSNBC.com, 2004). In contrast, Barack Obama became the first sitting president to publicly express support for gay marriage before overwhelmingly winning re-election in a 2012 U.S. election that also saw gay marriage initiatives approved by voters in all four states where that issue was on the ballot.

Americans are also increasingly more open to having gay sexual relationships, or at least are now more honest when queried about those experiences. A recent study of sexual identity and behavior found 8% of U.S. adult males self-identified as gay and 15% of adult U.S. men acknowledged having at least one gay oral sexual experience before the age of 50 (Indiana University – Bloomington, Center for Sexual Health Promotion, 2011).

However, the increasing acceptance of gays and lesbians has been slow to transfer to professional sport, or at least through sport media coverage of gays and lesbians in sport. For example, no male athlete has ever publicly revealed his homosexuality or bisexuality while actively playing in any of the four major U.S. professional men's team sport leagues: Major League Baseball (MLB), National Basketball Association (NBA), National Football League (NFL), and National Hockey League (NHL).

A few male team sport professional athletes have come out during their careers, highlighted by Justin Fashanu, who was also Great Britain's first million-pound Black soccer player (King, 2004). Other prominent male team sport athletes to come out publicly while active included former English cricket star Steven Davies and Welsh rugby standout Gareth Thomas. Figure skater Rudy Galindo and diver Greg Louganis both publicly declared their homosexuality when ranked among the world's premier athletes, although media have framed both sports as feminine, meaning their revelations did not generate much surprise (Butterworth, 2006). Puerto Rican Orlando Cruz, however, became the first active athlete from the rugged sport of professional boxing to come out as gay in 2012.

Most prominent and open lesbian athletes competed in individual sports, such as tennis grand-slam champions Billie Jean King, Amelie Mauresmo, and Martina Navratilova (Forman and Plymire, 2005). Compared to men's sports, a few more prominent female team sport athletes came out during their careers, highlighted by bisexual basketball superstar Sherryl Swoopes (Chawansky and Francombe, 2011).

However, the dearth of openly gay athletes – particularly at the highest levels of men's team sports – leads to the question of whether gay athletes are almost non-existent in popular professional team sports, or rather, whether they have they simply not come out through mainstream media? FoxSports national sports columnist Jason Whitlock clearly believes the latter, theorizing that roughly 15% of athletes in the NFL – long viewed as the most popular and masculine sport in U.S. society – are gay men (Whitlock, 2013). However, since the answers to those questions are not yet known, this chapter will (1) briefly discuss the history and significance of masculinity in sport; (2) explain how media frame issues; (3) briefly examine the relation between hegemonic masculinity and sport media in terms of male–female ratios within sport media organizations, a masculine culture that permeates the sport media profession, and the plethora of research on how sport media frame men's and women's sport; (4) analyze attitudes toward gays and lesbians by sport media members; (5) provide a detailed look at the few research articles that examined sport media coverage of gay and lesbian athletes; and (6) delve into the possibilities for future research on sport media and homosexuality.

Masculinity in sport

From early childhood through adulthood, nearly all boys are socialized into sport (Messner, 2002). During much of history and throughout the world, women have mostly been discouraged from participating in athletics due to underlying fears that many sporting women are lesbians and that heterosexual females may possibly turn gay due to sport participation (Griffin, 1998). However, attitudes toward women in sport have become increasingly more accepting in most Western societies, especially over the past 30–40 years, evident by every participating country sending at least one female athlete to the London 2012 Summer Olympics (Bernstein, 2002; Kian et al., 2013).

Sport, however, has always been associated with boys and men, and still plays a primary role in defining the most desirable forms of masculinities (Connell, 1990). A common theme in sport-based scholarly research is that a version of masculinity, which Connell (1990) calls 'hegemonic', permeates all types of sport, at all levels, particularly professional men's team sports. Connell (2005) defined hegemonic masculinity as the configuration of gender practices that strengthen the positional dominance of men and subordination of women. Hegemonic masculinity reinforces androcentrism as a key tenet in Western society, hierarchically placing men and women who do not meet heterosexual gendered ideals in positions below men with masculine capital (Connell, 2005). The two most ostracized groups from hegemonic masculinity are women, and especially gay men (Anderson, 2005). Hegemonic social structures are frequently challenged, but are rarely changed without consent from the ruling group (Connell and Messerschmidt, 2005).

However, multiple studies in recent years have shown that attitudes of athletes, sport administrators, and even sporting fans are increasingly becoming more accepting of gays and non-traditional forms of masculinity (e.g., Adams et al., 2010; Anderson and McGuire, 2010;

Campbell et al., 2011; Cunningham, 2010; Fink et al., 2012; Melton et al., 2013). Anderson's (2009a) theorization of "inclusive masculinities" suggests that both homosexuality and fluid masculine identities are becoming more accepted throughout most modern societies, including within the most traditional hegemonic masculine structures such as organized men's team sports, military units, and increasingly more religious groups. Nevertheless, media continue to frame narratives that lead to assumptions that male athletes are heterosexual, especially in sports construed as essentially masculine. Meanwhile, media emphasize the femininity of female athletes, thus implicitly assuring consumers that most sporting women are heterosexual (Billings et al., 2002; Harris and Clayton, 2002).

Media framing

In modern, democratic-based societies with a free press, much of our knowledge and attitudes about key issues have been largely shaped by mass media (Tuchman, 1978). Framing is a term used to describe how media professionals decipher news by selecting specific points and then embedding that information (e.g., words, photographs, names, quotes, etc.) into content produced for external consumption (Scheufele, 1999). Accordingly, these frames help media consumers interpret and apply meanings toward these news events (Kuypers, 2002). However, once media consumers define content, it is difficult to change those definitions, most of which were likely impacted by media framing (Kian et al., 2011; Lind and Salo, 2002).

Hegemonic masculinity and sport media

Scholars have theorized that sport and mass media are two of the main institutions assisting in the preservation of hegemonic masculinity (e.g., Connell, 1990; Wenner, 2010). Many researchers who studied coverage of women and men's sport by media over the past three decades echoed the sentiments of Hilliard (1984), who asserted, "Sports and the media form a symbiotic relationship. Each depends on the other and economic interests govern both. In this view, neither the media nor the athletes are willing to challenge the assumptions upon which their economic success depends" (p. 252).

The primary means through which sport media assist in the maintenance of hegemonic masculinity is by focusing the vast majority of their coverage on men's sports regardless of the sport, level of competition, type of medium, or host country of the media outlet (e.g., Duncan and Messner, 2000; Kian et al., 2009; Sagas et al., 2000). The men's sports that receive the most media attention are framed as masculine, with content emphasizing attributes like aggressiveness, strength, and violence. However, men's participation in sports that have historically been portrayed as more feminine in nature (e.g., diving, gymnastics) receives minimal mainstream media coverage (Vincent et al., 2002). Further, media use code words and innuendo to frame men competing in sports seen as attractive to gays or abnormal for males, which may be why many fathers would cringe upon being told that their son could be a champion at figure skating or synchronized swimming (Bernstein and Kian, 2013).

In contrast, women who participate in sports that are socially construed as more feminine receive far more media coverage (especially visual images) than female athletes in what are commonly viewed as more masculine sports, such as rugby and basketball (Bruce et al., 2010; Lenskyj, 2013). Moreover, media frequently delve into the personal lives of female athletes, compare sporting women to men but almost never do the opposite, and are far more likely to point out perceived psychological frailties of female athletes (Eastman and Billings, 2000). Further, media regularly promote sex-appeal through visual coverage of attractive athletes from both sexes, but especially images of women deemed appealing to heterosexual men (Clavio and Eagleman, 2011).

Some scholars have correlated gender differences in media content as partly due to a lack of women employed at all levels and in all types of sport media (Creedon, 1998; Schell and Rodriguez, 2000). Men significantly outnumber women within all types of media and at all levels of sport journalism in every country where gender representation has been examined, including Australia, Canada, Great Britain, New Zealand, Spain, the Netherlands, and the U.S. (e.g., Capranica and Aversa, 2002; Claringbould et al., 2004; Strong and Hannis, 2007). For example, a detailed survey of North American sport journalists employed at newspapers and prominent Internet sites showed that men comprised 94% of sports editors, 90% of assistant sports editors, 90% of columnists, 89% of reporters, and 84% of copy editors (Lapchick et al., 2011). Women are rarely found among the media "gatekeepers" or editors who are largely responsible for determining which sports and athletes are worthy of coverage, as well as how much emphasis (e.g., time/space, prominence) should be placed on events (Hardin and Whiteside, 2009).

Several studies documented the prevalence of hegemonic masculinity within the overall culture and daily work routines of the male-dominated sport media industry (e.g., Kian, 2007; Pedersen et al., 2003). Beats and assignments covering the most popular, men's sports are highly coveted by reporters due to the prominence of the events, along with opportunities they provide for potential career advancement and networking (Cramer, 1994; Hardin and Shain, 2005).

Homosexuality and sport media

No known research has surveyed the statistical representation of gay sport media professionals, although one study did examine attitudes of sport media members towards gays and lesbians in the U.S. That survey found that the majority of newspaper sports reporters agreed that homophobia "is a problem" in both men's and women's sports (Hardin and Whiteside, 2009). In response to the statement, "I think that a professional male athlete would be accepted if he came out as gay while playing his sport," 78% either disagreed or strongly disagreed, with only 1% of respondents strongly agreeing. Moreover, 74% either agreed or strongly agreed with the statement, "I do not think it is appropriate to ever ask an athlete about his or her sexual orientation." Again a mere 1% strongly disagreed. From these results, Hardin and Whiteside (2009) concluded that ". . . reporters are likely to help athletes stay in the closet" (p. 67).

It should be noted that same survey showed that younger reporters (30 years old and under) were far more likely to ask athletes about their sexual orientation when compared to veteran counterparts, which correlates with the far higher levels of acceptances and support for gay and lesbian lifestyles amongst American youths (Silver, 2011). Likewise, younger reporters were more likely than older journalists to believe that an active professional male athlete would be accepted if he or she came out publicly.

Ironically, sport fans and even pro athletes are seemingly more accepting of homosexuality than the reporters who cover those sports. A *Sports Illustrated* poll showed 60% of NBA and 80% of NHL players said they would be comfortable with an openly gay teammate, and 86% of sports fans surveyed in a 2005 *Sports Illustrated* poll said they were fine with openly gay athletes in professional sports (Wertheim, 2005). Moreover, 93% of English soccer fans said they did not care if their favourite athletes were gay (Cashmore and Cleland, 2011). Based on these survey results, it appears that the "don't ask, don't tell" attitude toward homosexuality in sport exhibited by the "liberal media" contrasts with the increasingly more inclusive attitudes of sport fans and professional male athletes competing in the most rugged team sports.

Along with a lack of openly gay athletes, this "don't ask, don't tell" attitude toward gay and lesbian athletes by sport media may be one reason why there has been minimal media coverage related to gays in sport (Plymire and Forman, 2000; Staurowsky, 2012). Through its regular coverage about athletes' heterosexual partners – which contrasts with the omission of content on gay athletes' private lives – sport media strengthen heteronormativity, which affirms hetero-sexuality as natural and reinforces a culture where gays and lesbians are not respected as equals (Calhoun et al., 2011).

Research on coverage of gay and lesbian athletes by sport media

Whereas gender-based sport media research has delved into the implicit framing of lesbianism in sport (Duncan, 2006), a majority of the few studies on homosexuality and sport media have focused on media framing of openly gay athletes. Early research showed gay athletes of either sex – usually lesbians – were generally framed in negative ways (e.g., Burroughs et al., 1995; Crosset, 1995).

During the 1980s, the advent of acquired immune deficiency syndrome (AIDS) generated few U.S. sport-media stories or public sympathy, because it was "identified as a disease that, for the most part, affected only gay men" (Colby and Cook, 1991, p. 221). However, that errone-ous perception of this deadly disease and its lack of media coverage changed quickly in 1991 following the announcement that basketball superstar, Ervin "Magic" Johnson, had contracted the AIDS virus. Dworkin and Wachs (1998) studied mainstream media coverage of Johnson, boxer Tommy Morison, and openly gay diver, Greg Louganis, after each revealed that he had contracted AIDS. Most of the articles on Johnson and Morrison expressed shock that these two had been stricken with AIDS, while clearly noting that both athletes were heterosexual. How-ever, no article on Louganis described or speculated how he had contracted the virus. Dworkin and Wachs (1998) concluded, "media polices sexuality by presenting the causes of and solution to the HIV/AIDS epidemic by framing marriage, heterosexuality, and monogamy as 'safe' and by condemning homosexuality as 'dangerous'" (p. 13).

In contrast, more recent studies have shown sport media are now providing more positive narratives of openly gay and lesbian athletes, while also lambasting homophobia as antiquated bigotry (e.g., Chawansky and Francombe, 2011; Hardin and Whiteside, 2010). However, in nearly every examination of coverage of gay athletes, media still frame heterosexuality as normal and the standard basis for comparison of all other types of orientations even as they state their acceptance of gays and lesbians, and gay lifestyles (Hardin et al., 2009; Nylund, 2004).

A pair of scholarly articles on basketball player John Amaechi, a British native who is the latest of the six former U.S. major pro team sport athletes to come out as gay after retirement, showed that both international and U.S. sport media were supportive of Amaechi's declaration; although many narratives framed male team sport locker rooms as not ready for an openly gay, active athlete (Hardin et al., 2009; Kian and Anderson, 2009). Likewise, media positively framed Sherryl Swoopes' outing while she competed in the Women's National Basketball Association (Chawansky and Francombe, 2011).

Future of sport media research on gays and lesbians

It is inevitable that sport media members in much of the Western world will become more accepting of gay athletes, in part because acceptance is the majority view held by media consum-ers, who may simply turn to other outlets if dis-satisfied (Nemenov, 2011). Evidence of a shift in attitudes toward gay athletes' participation in sport is already evident among younger reporters (Hardin and Whiteside, 2009), and some of the most prominent male journalists in the sport media industry have been outspoken in their advocacy for gay rights and tolerance toward such athletes (Kian and Anderson, 2009; Nylund, 2007). Such changes are also transpiring within the pro athlete community. In his study on media coverage of rumours about a gay MLB standout, Butterworth (2006) noted that Mike Piazza countered the passivity and condemnation sport media have historically directed at anything they perceived as gay or effeminate by mocking the newsworthiness of any media inquiries on an athlete's sexual orientation, which he deemed unimportant.

These trends support Anderson's (2009b) use of the term "inclusive masculinity" which suggests that fluid masculine identities are becoming more accepted both within sport and culture as a whole, particularly within the younger generation. The existence of more inclusive forms of masculinity has made the public expressions of homophobia and misogyny unacceptable to many people, including those in male-dominated vocations that have historically been masculine domains, such as the locker room, Internet sport fan message boards, and the sport media profession (Anderson, 2009b; Cleland 2013).

Butterworth (2006) theorized that news of the first openly gay player actively competing for a prominent U.S. professional men's team sport will likely be framed by sport media as a symbol of a sports culture that "does not discriminate" (p. 153). That trend-setting athlete will also likely earn a fortune via endorsements from companies eager to target the highly affluent and well-educated gay and lesbian community (Anderson, 2005). A flood of current athletes at all levels may follow suit by publicly revealing their homosexuality in ensuing years, which, in turn, would lead to more scholarly examinations of media coverage of gay athletes.

References

Adams A, Anderson E and McCormack M (2010) Establishing and challenging masculinity: The influence of gendered discourses in football. *Journal of Language and Social Psychology* 29(3): 278–300.

Anderson E (2005) *In the Game: Gay Athletes and the Cult of Masculinity.* New York: State University of New York Press.

Anderson E (2009a) *Inclusive Masculinity: The Changing Nature of Masculinities.* New York: Routledge.

Anderson E (2009b) The maintenance of masculinity among the stakeholders of sport. *Sport Management Review* 12(1): 3–14.

Anderson E and McGuire R (2010) Inclusive masculinity and the gendered politics of men's rugby. *The Journal of Gender Studies* 19(3): 249–261.

Bernstein A (2002) Is it time for a victory lap? Changes in the media coverage of women in sport. *International Review for the Sociology of Sport* 37(3–4): 415–428.

Bernstein A and Kian EM (2013) Gender and sexualities in sport media. In PM Pedersen (ed) *Handbook of Sport Communication.* London: Routledge, pp.319–327.

Billings AC, Halone KK and Denham BE (2002) "Man, that was a pretty shot": An analysis of gendered broadcast commentary surrounding the 2000 men's and women's NCAA Final Four basketball championships. *Mass Communication & Society* 5(3): 295–315.

Bruce T, Hovden J and Markula P (2010) *Sportswomen at the Olympics: A global content analysis of newspaper coverage.* Rotterdam: Sense Publishers.

Burroughs A, Ashburn L and Seebohm L (1995) "Add sex and stir": Homophobic coverage of women's cricket in Australia. *Journal of Sport & Social issues* 19(3): 266–284.

Butterworth ML (2006) Pitchers and catchers: Mike Piazza and the discourse of gay identity in the national pastime. *Journal of Sport & Social Issues* 30(2): 138–157.

Calhoun AS, LaVoi NM and Johnson A (2011) Framing with family: Examining online coaches' biographies for heteronormative and heterosexist narratives. *International Journal of Sport Communication* 4(3): 300–316.

Campbell J, Cothren D, Rogers R, Kistler L, Osowski A, Greenauer N and End C (2011). Sports fans' impressions of gay male athletes. *Journal of Homosexuality* 58(5): 597–607.

Capranica L and Aversa F (2002) Italian television sport coverage during the 2000 Sydney Olympic Games. *International Review for the Sociology of Sport* 37(3–4): 337–349.

Cashmore E and Cleland J (2011) Grasswing butterflies: Gay professional football players and their culture. *Journal of Sport & Social Issues* 35(4): 420–436.

Chawansky M and Francombe JM (2011) Cruising for Olivia: Lesbian celebrity and the cultural politics of coming out in sport. *Sociology of Sport Journal* 28(4): 461–477.

Claringbould I, Knoppers A and Elling A (2004) Exclusionary practices in sport journalism. *Sex Roles* 51(11/12): 709–718.

Clavio G and Eagleman AN (2011) Gender and sexually suggestive images in sports blogs. *Journal of Sport Management* 25(4): 295–304.

Cleland J (2013) Discussing homosexuality on association football fan message boards: A changing cultural context. *International Review for the Sociology of Sport*. Epub ahead of print 13 March 2013. DOI: 10.1177/1012690213475437

Colby DC and Cook TE (1991) Epidemics and agendas: The politics of nightly news coverage of AIDS. *Journal of Health Politics, Policy and Law* 16(2): 215–250.

Connell RW (1990) An iron man: The body and some contradictions of hegemonicmasculinity. In MA Messner & DF Sabo (eds) *Sport, Men, and the Gender Order: Critical Feminist Perspectives*. Champaign, IL: Human Kinetics, pp.83–114.

Connell RW (2005) *Masculinities* (2nd ed). Berkeley, CA: University of California.

Connell RW and Messerschmidt J (2005) Hegemonic masculinity: Rethinking the concept. *Gender & Society* 19(6): 829–859.

Cramer JA (1994) Conversations with women sports journalists. In PJ Creedon (ed) *Women, Media and Sport: Challenging Gender Values*. Thousand Oaks, CA: Sage, pp.159–179.

Creedon PJ (1998) Women, sport, and media institutions: Issues in sports journalism and marketing. In LA Wenner (ed) *MediaSport*. London: Routledge, pp.88–99.

Crosset T (1995) *Outsiders in the Clubhouse: The World of Professional Women's Golf*. Albany, NY: State University of New York Press.

Cunningham GB (2010) Predictors of sexual orientation diversity in intercollegiate athletics departments. *Journal of Intercollegiate Sport* 3(2), 256–269.

Duncan MC (2006) Gender warriors in sport: Women and the media. In AA Raney and J Bryant (eds) *Handbook of Sports and Media*. Mahwah, NJ: Lawrence Erlbaum Associates, pp.231–252.

Duncan MC and Messner MA (2000) *Gender in Televised Sports: 1989, 1993 and 1999*. Los Angeles, CA: Amateur Athletic Foundation of Los Angeles.

Dworkin SL and Wachs FL (1998) "Disciplining the body": HIV-positive male athletes, media surveillance, and the policing of sexuality. *Sociology of Sport Journal* 15(1): 1–20.

Eastman ST and Billings AC (2000) Sportscasting and sports reporting. *Journal of Sport &Social Issues* 24(2): 192–213.

Fink JS, Burton LJ, Farrell AO and Parker HM (2012) Playing it out: Femaleintercollegiate athletes' experiences in revealing their sexual identities. *Journal for the Study of Sports and Athletes in Education* 6(1), 83–106.

Forman PJ and Plymire DC (2005) Amelie Mauresmo's muscles: The lesbian heroic in women's professional tennis. *Women's Studies Quarterly* 33(1/2): 120–133.

Griffin P (1998) *Strong Women, Deep Closets: Lesbians and Homophobia in Sport*. Champaign, IL: Human Kinetics.

Hardin M and Shain S (2005) Strength in numbers? The experiences and attitudes of women in sports media careers. *Journalism & Mass Communication Quarterly*, 82(4): 804–819.

Hardin M and Whiteside E (2009) Sports reporters divided over concerns about Title IX. *Newspaper Research Journal*, 30(1): 58–80.

Hardin M and Whiteside E (2010) The Rene Portland case: New homophobia and heterosexism in women's sports coverage. In HL Hundley and AC Billings (eds) *Examining Identity in Sports Media*. Thousand Oaks, CA: Sage, pp.17–36.

Hardin M, Kuehn KM, Jones H, Genovese J and Balaji M (2009) "Have you got game?" Hegemonic masculinity and neo-homophobia in U.S. newspaper sports columns. *Communication, Culture, & Critique* 2(2): 182–200.

Harris J and Clayton B (2002) Femininity, masculinity, physicality and the English tabloid press: The case of Anna Kournikova. *International Review for the Sociology of Sport* 37(3–4): 397–413.

Hilliard D (1984) Media images and female professional athletes: An interpretive analysis of magazine articles *Sociology of Sport Journal* 1(3): 251–262.

Indiana University – Bloomington, Center for Sexual Health Promotion (2011) *2010 National Survey of Sexual Health and Behavior*. Retrieved September 23, 2011, from the Center for Sexual Health Promotion Web site: http://www.nationalsexstudy.indiana.edu

Kian EM (2007) Gender in sports writing by the print media: An exploratory examination of writers' experiences and attitudes. *SMART* 4(1): 5–26.

Kian EM and Anderson E (2009) John Amaechi: Changing the way reporters examine gay athletes. *Journal of Homosexuality* 56(7): 799–818.

Kian EM, Bernstein A and McGuire JS (2013) A major boost for gender equality or more of the same? The television coverage of female athletes at the 2012 London Olympic Games. *Journal of Popular Television* 1(1): 143–149.

Kian EM, Fink JS and Hardin M (2011) Examining the impact of journalists' gender in online and newspaper tennis articles. *Women in Sport and Physical Activity Journal*, 20(1): 3–21.

Kian EM, Mondello M and Vincent J (2009) ESPN – The women's sports network? A content analysis of Internet coverage of March Madness. *Journal of Broadcasting & Electronic Media* 53(3): 477–495.

King C (2004) Race and cultural identity: Playing the race game inside football. *Leisure Studies* 23(1): 19–30.

Kuypers JA (2002) *Press Bias and Politics: How the Media Frame Controversial Issues*. Westport, CT: Praeger.

Lapchick R, Moss II A, Russell C and Scearce R (2011) The 2010–11 Associated Press Sports Editors racial and gender report card. Available at: http://www.tidesport.org/RGRC/2011/2011_APSE_RGRC_FINAL.pdf?page=lapchick/110517 (accessed 19 February 2012 from University of Central Florida, Institute for Diversity and Ethics in Sport web site).

Lenskyj HJ (2013) Reflections on communication and sport: On heteronormativity and gender identities. *Communication & Sport* 1(1/2): 138–150.

Lind RA and Salo C (2002) The framing of feminists and feminism in news and public affairs programs in U.S. electronic media. *Journal of Communication* 52(1): 211–228.

Melton EN, Cunningham GB and Shilbury D (2013) Examining the workplace experiences of sport employees who are LGBT: A social categorization theory perspective. *Journal of Sport Management*. Epub ahead of print 13 March 2013.

Messner MA (2002) *Taking the Field: Women, Men, and Sports*. Minneapolis: University of Minnesota Press.

MSNBC.com (2004) Civil unions for gays favored, polls show: Same-sex marriage debate increases support for such recognition. Available at: http://www.msnbc.msn.com/id/4496265/ns/us_news-same-sex_marriage/ (accessed 12 February 2012).

Nemenov A (2011) More countries accepting homosexuality: study. Available at: http://ph.news.yahoo.com/more-countries-accepting-gay-lifestyle-study-031409308.html (accessed 19 January 2012 from *Yahoo! News*).

Nylund D (2004) When in Rome: Heterosexism, homophobia, and sports talk radio. *Journal of Sport & Social Issues* 28(2): 136–168.

Nylund D (2007) *Beer, Babes, and Balls*. Albany, NY: State University of New York Press.

Pedersen PM, Whisenant WA and Schneider RG (2003) Using a content analysis to examine the gendering of sports newspaper personnel and their coverage. *Journal of Sport Management* 17(4): 376–393.

Plymire DC and Forman PJ (2000) Breaking the silence: Lesbian fans, the Internet, and the sexual politics of women's sport. *International Journal of Sexuality and Gender Studies* 5(2): 141–153.

Sagas M, Cunningham GB, Wigley BJ and Ashley FB (2000) Internet coverage of university softball and baseball web sites: The inequity continues. *Sociology of Sport Journal* 17(2): 198–205.

Schell LS and Rodriguez S (2000) Our sporting sisters: How male hegemony stratifies women in sport. *Women in Sport and Physical Activity Journal* 9(1), 15–35.

Scheufele DA (1999) Framing as a theory of media effects. *Journal of Communication* 49(1): 103–122.

Silver M (2011) Gay marriage opponents now in minority. Available at http://fivethirtyeight.blogs.nytimes.com/2011/04/20/gay-marriage-opponents-now-in-minority/# (accessed 10 March 2012 from *The New York Times* online).

Staurowsky EJ (2012) Sexual prejudice and sport media coverage: Exploring an ethical framework for college sports journalists. *Journal of the Study of Sports and Athletes in Education* 6(2): 121–140.

Strong C and Hannis J (2007) The visibility of female journalists at Australian and New Zealand newspapers: The good news and the bad news. *Australian Journalism Review* 29(1): 115–125.

Tuchman G (1978) *Making News: A Study in the Construction of Reality.* New York: Free Press.

Vincent J, Imwold C, Masemann V and Johnson JT (2002) A comparison of selected "serious" and "popular" British, Canadian, and United States newspaper coverage of female and male athletes competing in the Centennial Olympic games. *International Review for the Sociology of Sport* 37(3–4): 319–335.

Wenner L (2010) Sport, communication, and the culture of consumption: On language and identity. *American Behavioral Scientist* 53(11): 1571–1573.

Wertheim J (2005) Gays in sports: A poll. *Sports Illustrated* 102 April, 18.

Whitlock J (2013) Goodell can bring gay tolerance to NFL. Available at: http://msn.foxsports.com/nfl/story/manti-teo-gay-rumors-sexuality-questions-roger-goodell-can-push-nfl-acceptance-notre-dame-022613 (accessed 3 March 2013 from FoxSports.com).

50

GENDER, MEDIA AND THE SPORT SCANDAL

David Rowe

Introduction: sport as terrain of celebrity scandal[1]

Whenever a sport scandal erupts into public consciousness, melancholic statements inevitably follow in the media sphere that it has precipitated a 'loss of innocence'. For example, baseball's infamous Black Sox Scandal, in which the 1917 World Series was 'fixed' in a gambling conspiracy, has been described as 'Baseball's loss of innocence' (Goetsch, 2011). In the following century, revelations concerning the use of performance-enhancing drugs by athletes in baseball and in other sports resulted in reactions in the media such as 'Steroid scandal: a diehard fan mourns sports' loss of innocence' (Vongs, 2004). Sometimes, a hierarchy of scandal is constructed, meaning that what was once scandalous has become relatively routine, and new frontiers of lost innocence are found. Thus, after allegations in 2011 of child sex abuse (with all its additional connotations of innocence lost beyond those associated with sport fan disillusionment) by American football coaches at Pennsylvania State and Syracuse Universities, passages in the media such as the following were common:

> "The academic cheating, the recruitment violations, the gambling, taking steroids, that stuff has been a part of sports forever", Sailes [a Professor of sport sociology at Indiana University] said. "But the veracity, the seriousness (of the sex–abuse scandals) — this is the last bastion of American innocence, our kids. So yeah, this is the worst."
>
> *(quoted in Armour, 2011)*

Although generally treated as interruptions to the sports order, scandals are, in fact, inevitable products of it. They are integral components of globally-mediated sport, generating vivid news stories that intermittently pass through the 'media sports cultural complex' (Rowe, 2004, 2011) and often emerge as matters of broader news interest. Although sport and media are global institutions, they are still largely Western- and Anglophone-dominated. For this reason, the main scandal cases cited in this chapter are Western, especially emanating from the US, UK and Australasia. Without massive media coverage, which in the twenty-first century means an interactive combination of corporate and independent media organisations, citizen journalists, bloggers and 'social media' exchanges (Hutchins and Rowe, 2012), sport scandals cannot 'take flight', irrespective of their intrinsic seriousness. Indeed, the most significant sport scandals migrate quickly from the sports pages to the general news, first because contemporary sport stars have a cultural presence well beyond the world of sport followers, and can be counted among the most globally prominent and recognisable individual humans. Second, major sport scandals incorporate concerns that have wider socio-cultural ramifications than ethical conduct within sport and, indeed, often have little directly to do with sport per se. In this chapter the main focus is on the media sport scandal 'genre' of celebrity sportsman infidelity that is both sustained by, and illuminates, relations of gendered power within sport and the wider social formation.

There is a growing body of academic work devoted to celebrity and stardom in general (for example, Marshall, 1997; Rojek, 2001; Turner, 2004) and, specifically, within sport (Andrews and Jackson, 2001; Cashmore, 2002; Smart, 2005; Whannel, 2002). In such works the concepts of the celebrity and the star tend to be used interchangeably or are distinguished in a range of ways, including through assessments of level of achievement or lack of it, and via the industrial processes that 'produce' forms of celebrity. In many cases the terms celebrity and star are both deployed interchangeably and distinguished in the same work. This is not the appropriate context to explore this conceptual issue in detail, but the heuristic distinction is germane to the overall analysis. Sport stars are classified as those sportspeople (predominantly men) who have achieved high status within elite professional sport but whose level of recognition and esteem is limited beyond the cohort of dedicated sport fandom and is restricted in transnational terms. By contrast, sport celebrities constitute a small subset of sport stars (even more predominantly male) accorded common recognition (though not necessarily celebration) among people who do not pay close attention to their sporting careers or to the domain of sport, and whose mediated image registers within what can loosely be called the global cultural sphere (Rowe, 2011). Thus, celebrity status requires widescale awareness of, and substantial knowledge about, an individual's extra-sporting activities through intensive coverage across not only sport media, but entertainment, current affairs, general and specialist news (such as business), and so on.

This conceptual distinction is inexact and mutable. Ironically, a conspicuous media sport scandal may help turn a sport star into a celebrity, albeit an 'infamous' one, while the machinery of sporting celebrity can also generate greater interest among the previously uncommitted (Gilmour and Rowe, 2010). However, the chances of becoming a sport celebrity – and so of being implicated in a high-profile media scandal – are not evenly distributed. This inequality of opportunity, outcome and reward is, as argued next, clearly related to the gender order.

Gender, power and sport celebrity

While by no means all sport celebrities are male, their ranks are dominated by those who are relatively young, Western-born or domiciled men, and, particularly, by those who are, at least in terms of publicly projected identity, heterosexual. For example, *Forbes* magazine's 2010–2011 'rich list' of the world's 50 highest-paid athletes earned a combined US$ 1.4 billion but contained only one woman, the Russian tennis player Maria Sharapova (number 29), who had also been the only woman in the previous year's list. Table 51.1, which has been compiled from the list and augmented, gives a clear picture of sport's celebrity and gender order, as well as of the high level of representation of US sportsmen in a small number of individual and team sports. This pattern is replicated throughout the sport industry (broadly defined), with *Sports Business Journal's* (2011) list of the '50 most influential people in sports business' containing only three women, Melinda Witmer (Time Warner Cable, number 22), Alison Lewis (Coca-Cola, number 43) and Jeanie Buss (20), who co-owns the LA Lakers with her husband (meaning that the list is actually of 51 people!). The auto-reinforcing nature of sport's vertical and horizontal structure of gender power simultaneously produces celebrity as an effect of economic power

Table 51.1 World's highest-paid athletes May 2010–May 2011

Rank	Name	Income US$ in millions	Sports	Country
1	Tiger Woods	75	Golf	USA
2	Kobe Bryant	53	Basketball	USA
3	LeBron James	48	Basketball	USA
4	Roger Federer	47	Tennis	Switzerland
5	Phil Mickelson	46.5	Golf	USA
6	David Beckham	40	Soccer	UK
7	Cristiano Ronaldo	38	Soccer	Portugal
8	Alex Rodriguez	35	Baseball	USA
9	Michael Schumacher	34	Racing	Germany
10	Lionel Messi	32.3	Soccer	Argentina
11	Fernando Alonso	32	Racing	Spain
12	Rafael Nadal	31.5	Tennis	Spain
13 (tie)	Tom Brady	31	American football	USA
13 (tie)	Valentino Rossi	31	Racing	Italy
15	Lewis Hamilton	30	Racing	UK
16	Derek Jeter	29	Baseball	USA
17	Dale Earnhardt Jr.	28.5	Racing	USA
18	Yao Ming	27.7	Basketball	China
19	Dwight Howard	27.6	Basketball	USA
20	Dwyane Wade	26.2	Basketball	USA
21	Peyton Manning	26.1	American football	USA
22	Ichiro Suzuki	26	Baseball	Japan
23	Carmelo Anthony	25.1	Basketball	USA
24 (tie)	Kaka	25	Soccer	Brazil
24 (tie)	Manny Pacquaio	25	Boxing	Philippines
26	Jeff Gordon	24.9	Racing	USA
27	Ronaldinho	24.7	Soccer	Brazil
28	Amar'e Stoudemire	24.5	Basketball	USA
29	Maria Sharapova	24.2	Tennis	Russia
30	Wayne Rooney	24.1	Soccer	UK
31	Jimmie Johnson	24	Racing	USA
32	Kevin Garnett	23.8	Basketball	USA
33	CC Sabathia	23.6	Baseball	USA
34	Jim Furyk	23	Golf	USA
35	Vince Carter	21.8	Basketball	USA
36	Johan Santana	21.5	Baseball	Venezuela
37	Tim Duncan	21.2	Basketball	USA
38	Chris Paul	20.9	Basketball	USA
39 (tie)	Mark Teixeira	20.8	Baseball	USA
39 (tie)	Ryan Howard	20.8	Baseball	USA
41	Miguel Cabrera	20.3	Baseball	Venezuela
42	Rashard Lewis	20.1	Basketball	USA
43 (tie)	Todd Helton	19.6	Baseball	USA
43 (tie)	Ernie Els	19.6	Golf	South Africa
45 (tie)	Joe Mauer	19.3	Baseball	USA
46 (tie)	Dirk Nowitzki	19.3	Basketball	Germany
47	Barry Zito	19.2	Baseball	USA
48	Jahri Evans	19.1	American football	USA
49	Pau Gasol	18.9	Basketball	Spain
50	Michael Redd	18.8	Basketball	USA

Source: Compiled on the basis of *Forbes* (2011), which calculated athlete earnings from salaries, bonuses, prize monies, appearance fees, licensing and endorsements, excluding deduction of taxes or agents' fees.

and mediated visibility, alongside the conditions of its erosion. A reduction in athlete earnings caused by, for example, a decline in sporting performance and/or the withdrawal of corporate endorsement after a major scandal, may attract a blizzard of publicity but a decline in 'bank-ability'. Consequently, a respected sporting figure can be turned into an anti-hero or, worse, a figure of fun generating lists of jokes, as occurred in the recent dramatic case of the golfer Tiger Woods (McTague, 2009)

Although remaining the world's highest-paid athlete in late 2009 (as shown in Table 51.1), two years after a car crash near his home apparently precipitated by a domestic dispute, Woods saw his carefully crafted image as a 'conventional family man' exploded by media revelations of compulsive philandering (Starn, 2011). The ensuing scandal (combined with the problems of the US economy at the time) had direct financial implications for Woods in the sport business world; his earnings dropped by 40 per cent in only two years:

> The business of Tiger Woods has been taking on water the past two years. Sponsors like Accenture, AT&T, Gillette and PepsiCo have jumped ship since his November 2009 car crash and the resulting scandal. His golf course design business has been ham-mered by the economic downturn. His winless streak on the course is at 20 months and counting, and the former No. 1 golfer in the world is now ranked 13th. Woods' annual earnings have plummeted [US]$50 million over the past two years.
>
> *(Badenhausen, 2011: 1)*

It is an unremarkable observation that it was Woods's very newsworthiness that both fostered his celebrity status and initiated its post-scandal decline, but nonetheless important to note that it is the gender-skewed nature of the sport celebrity system that makes it much more likely that its most spectacular scandals involve sportsmen (Rowe, 2010).

It is for this reason that Garry Whannel's (2002: 1) influential book *Media Sport Stars* is sub-titled *Masculinities and Moralities*, arguing in its introduction that 'The image of sport stars, ques-tions of morality, of youth and of masculinity are all bound up together – to consider one is to consider the others.' Whannel (2002: 1) argues that sport becomes the pretext for anxieties and debates surrounding contemporary masculinity, occurring both within formal social institutions and across the mediated public sphere, 'As the intensity of media coverage of sport has increased, and as the sporting star system has become central to the media sport industry, the images of sport stars become the point of convergence of social anxieties over morality and masculinity'.

This 'male trouble' (Tomsen and Donaldson, 2003) is brought into sharp focus during a media scandal, which is usefully defined by James Lull and Stephen Hinerman (1997: 3) as 'a breach in moral conduct and authority' that: 'occurs when private acts that disgrace or offend the idealised, dominant morality of a social community are made public and narrativised by the media, producing a range of effects from ideological and cultural retrenchment to disruption and social change'.

Because the sphere of sport is so deeply infused with 'idealized, dominant morality' (per-haps most conspicuously encapsulated in the philosophy of Olympism – Guttmann, 2002) and, given its formative role in the shaping of hegemonic forms of masculinity and so of femininity (Aitchison, 2007; McKay, Messner and Sabo, 2001), it is especially fertile ground for the pro-duction of deeply gendered scandals with wider socio-cultural ramifications.

Thus, to return to the striking case of Tiger Woods, an explanation is required as to why an essentially private matter garnered massive news and current affairs coverage, often as the lead or main item, with even an august public service media organisation like the British Broadcasting Corporation (BBC) leading its main television news bulletin on 19 February 2010 with Woods's scripted apology in a 'news conference' at which no questions were permitted. In response to many viewer protests, the BBC responded:

> 'As the first sports personality to become a billionaire, Tiger Woods is a colossal figure in the sporting world and therefore of huge interest to many people.
>
> His highly unusual apology after his very public fall from grace is therefore, in our opinion, a big news story that warrants a prominent place in our bulletins.
>
> On that particular day we did not feel there was another story with bigger news impact.'
>
> *(quoted in Thomas, 2010)*

There is a circular de-historicised, de-politicised logic to this justification of news decision-making. The imputed 'news impact' could not be said to derive from the unpredictability or urgency of a tightly-controlled news event. That this should be deemed the biggest story of the day was clearly not just a matter of Woods's fame, but also because it activated discourses of gender, sex, fidelity, family, money, masculine power and the ideological positioning of women in intimate relationships with elite sportsmen (Rowe, 2010). The media do not invent such concerns *ex nihilo*, but work with existing socio-cultural value questions, amplifying and directing them in crucial ways here by means of the symbolically rich vehicle of the celebrity sport scandal. Therefore, the media are crucial agents of sport scandal production, selecting, interpreting and disseminating them in ways that render their details difficult for even non-sports fans to avoid. This is, then, a two-way process: as they unfold, media sport scandals signify a range of socially resonant meanings that inevitably articulate with pre-existing structures and processes of power. In turn, they offer possibilities of ideological reproduction and contestation of these manifestations of power. Because the body is a pivotal focus within the field of sport, its scandals routinely revolve around corporeality and, in the scandal genre addressed here, around sex, gender and celebrity image.

The celebrity sportsman infidelity scandal

Just as the BBC believed that there was no other 'story with bigger news impact' on the day of Tiger Woods's televised apology, eight years earlier and on the other side of the world, the first edition of the biggest selling newspaper in Melbourne had more pages of coverage of a sexual scandal, involving the leading Australian rules football player Wayne Carey and his vice captain's wife, than of the 9/11 demolition of the World Trade Centre (Robinson, 2002). Although not all have quite this level of 'news impact', there are many other sport celebrity scandals which, despite various contextual variations, have key ingredients in common. The stories within this scandal genre are comparatively banal – they do not involve, for example, the sexual violence of the case of boxer Mike Tyson (Sloop, 1997) or murder as in the trial of former American footballer OJ Simpson (McKay and Smith, 1995). They do not figure, either, within major moral panics, as occurred in the case of basketballer Earvin 'Magic' Johnson in the context of political reactions to HIV/AIDS in the late twentieth century (King, 1993; Rowe, 1994). Each of these instances, it should be noted, involves matters of 'race' as well as of sex and gender, given the African-American identities of the sportsmen involved. It is not possible in this chapter to do justice to this intermeshing of racialised, sexual and gender relations (see, for example, Carrington, 2010), but such complexity should clearly be recognised when analysing the 'messy realities' of structured social relations.

Tiger Woods's own connection to African-American identity is clearly pivotal to a comprehensive analysis of his case but, as the anthropologist Orin Starn (2011: xvi) observes, 'In its simplest form, this was a dismally prosaic domestic drama of marital infidelity', a 'drama' in which the:

> protocol is now every bit as ritualised as any village initiation ceremony. There's the breathless reporting of transgression; the blogosphere and tabloids digging for more evidence; the celebrity's attempt to evade, stonewall, or make excuses; and, of course, the solemn, sometimes teary public apology with an eye toward rehabilitation.
>
> *(p. xvii)*

While not all these elements are present in every case (for example, denial may be maintained and/or no public apology given), there is a discernible pattern in which allegations/revelations of infidelity by a leading sportsman attract intense media coverage with a pronounced tone of moral condemnation. This familiar narrative is accompanied by strong elements of *voyeurism* and prurience involving, in particular, highly sexualised representations of the 'mistress' and attempts to elicit from them (frequently via financial inducement to 'tell all') details of sexual encounters with celebrity sportsmen. The nature of the sport and media environment is crucial to the intensity and scope of such scandals. Thus, the English Premier League's rise as the richest in the world in the first decade of the twenty-first century occurred in the context of vigorous competition within the British media, especially the tabloid press and commercial current affairs television, that helped precipitate practices of celebrity scrutiny ranging from close but legal surveillance to illegal phone 'hacking' (*The Guardian*, 2011).

Several figures associated with British football were caught up in the latter, including Chelsea player Ashley Cole (who, like David Beckham, another subject of public allegations of infidelity, was married to a well-known singer, thereby doubling the story's newsworthiness). Cole, along with other high-profile players including John Terry, Wayne Rooney and Ryan Giggs, has been the subject of 'the breathless reporting of transgression' described above. In the case of Giggs, for example, affairs with his sister-in-law Natasha Giggs (later, as a result of the publicity, to appear on *Celebrity Big Brother*) and also a *Big Brother* contestant Imogen Thomas garnered enormous media coverage, with both women discussing their relationships with Giggs in the media. Attempts by both Giggs and Terry (who'd allegedly had an affair with a teammate's former girlfriend) to prevent media reporting of the matters through the so-called 'super injunctions' available under UK law provided further spice to the stories. In Giggs's case, the injunction was over-ridden by a Member of Parliament naming him under privilege after he'd already been identified via 75,000 Twitter posts (BBC, 2011). The intertwining of the sport and 'gossip' industries in such instances, as encapsulated in the notion of 'sportainment' (Andrews 2006: 41), starkly exposes how far sport, via media and celebrity culture, now travels from the field of play and any real concern with athletic performance.

The British tabloid media environment is notorious for the pursuit of such stories (the most notorious tabloid newspaper of all, the News Corporation-owned and Murdoch family-controlled *The News of the World*, was closed in 2011 after the extent of its illegal phone hacking was revealed). The pattern is also evident in other countries such as the USA, as in its media's coverage of leading basketballer Kobe Bryant's marital infidelities (although, it should be noted, a 2003 sexual assault civil suit was settled on undisclosed terms). In Lull and Hinerman's (1997: 21) tripartite typology of media scandals, these would be designated as the 'star' type, to be distinguished from the 'institutional' type involving organisational regimes and the 'psychodrama' concerning 'ordinary people' rather than celebrities. Here, narratives with celebrities at their core are:

Fleshed out dramatically with real-world characters, motivations, and plots, which appear chapter by chapter in news programs, on talk shows, and in the tabloid and mainstream press. The media narratives become widely-circulated conversational touchstones at home, at work, at school, and on the street. In the process, the star scandal not only raises questions about the integrity of individual celebrities, but reinforces the idea that even famous people finally must be held responsible to society's moral expectations.

In the specific instance of the male sport celebrity scandal, there is a particular conflict between the romantic conceptions of sporting nobility and the exposure of prosaic ethical failures. As Graeme Turner (2004: 106) argues, 'Unlike their counterparts in the entertainment industries, the sports star (particularly the male sports star) is asked to personify what signifies as the heroic in this society at this time.' The historically inherited male domination of both heroic sporting ideals and the institution of sport, predominantly constructs women as both outside and subordinate. Thus, in the infidelity scandal narrative that so preoccupies news and entertainment editors, the 'wronged' wife/partner is positioned as inevitably in competition over the male sport celebrity with the 'predatory' mistress/'groupie'. In some instances, the sportsman's wife may be blamed for her husband's confirmed or alleged infidelity, as in the case of Victoria Beckham (Rowe, 2010), while in others, her anchoring domestic role is emphasised. Although not strictly a celebrity sportsman infidelity case, the construction of such female 'archetypes' was conspicuously evident in media coverage of 'Magic' Johnson's announcement of his HIV positive status in 1991. It was at a time of intense (especially homophobic) stigmatisation of the condition in the US which first induced widespread shock and incomprehension within the media. This reaction was swiftly followed by a symbolic removal of Johnson's agency and shift of blame onto the 'buckle bunnies' who 'infected' vulnerable sportsmen (with little conception of, or concern for, reciprocal responsibility), and a contrasting emphasis on the nuclear family via Johnson's marriage to Earlitha 'Cookie' Johnson and their infant son Earvin III (King, 1993; Rowe, 1994).

This kind of diversion and exculpation of the male sport celebrity, though, may not always occur. When routinely described in the media as Tiger Woods' 'model girlfriend', Elin Nordegren was accused by some male golf journalists and, indeed, by his own late father Earl, of distracting him from his golf (Rowe, 2010). Later, though, as his wife she was overshadowed by media interest in the various women with whom he'd been involved (including models, waitresses and adult film actors), and details of their sexual encounters and his physical attributes, including his sexual stamina and penis size (Starn, 2011: 85ff.). Here the focus on, and identification with, the athletic body and its capacities that is central to orthodox sport spectatorship (Miller, 2001) is transferred to the 'field' of sex. Thus, a tabloid story reporting a young British barber's claim to have had a holiday sexual relationship in Cyprus with Natasha Giggs described her association with the footballer as a 'turn on': 'She didn't really take control in bed but she didn't have to. I couldn't help myself. She's got a stunning figure – and thinking she'd been with Ryan as well was quite a turn-on' (quoted in Coles, 2012). The 'news' ingredients of this story are revealing: a celebrity sportsman infidelity scandal involving his sister-in-law had led to her appearance on a reality television show for celebrities, and to her alleged sexual behaviour being reported in a national newspaper via a fan of the footballer. Here is a clear manifestation of Whannel's (2002) concept of 'vortextuality', the accelerated drawing of diverse media into a single story, with Woods's press conference leading the day's news agenda constituting its classic exemplar. At such a point, the scandal and its salacious details become part of the general cultural stock of knowledge even for those who barely know Ryan Giggs, Tiger Woods or their sporting prowess, thereby revealing both the power of the media sport scandal and the gendered relations of power within the media sports cultural complex.

Conclusion: reading the scandal

This chapter has addressed the phenomenon of the media sport scandal, especially the staple narrative of celebrity sportsman infidelity. This is only one such scandal genre in which gender and sex are deeply implicated. The emphasis on heterosexual men here reflects sport's gender/sexuality order, but it is just as analytically productive to interrogate scandals involving sportswomen or non-heterosexual men, which commonly involve either biological sexual classification, sexual orientation or gender identity (Anderson, 2005; Caudwell, 2006; Coad, 2008; Cole, 2000; Stevenson, 2002). It is extraordinary that, in the twenty-first century, to be a gay or lesbian sport professional can still sometimes be regarded as (in any way) 'scandalous', so highlighting the deep strain of heterosexism that remains within sport and elements of the socio-cultural world in which it is embedded. Persistent homophobia is a powerful explanation for the very small number of athletes to have 'come out', especially at the peak of their careers (other contributions to this *Handbook* deal with these questions in much greater depth).

This analysis of the celebrity media sport scandal seeks to focus critical attention on what, ironically, can be regarded as routine eruptions in which 'innocence' is repeatedly lost in outbreaks of 'vortextuality'. In this case, the loss is of carefully constructed images of nuclear family normalcy among the extraordinary ranks of male sporting celebrity. The resultant 'passion plays' rely heavily on confected, prurient outrage; clichéd reportage and 'insider' accounts; stock characters tending towards caricature, and ideologically-loaded assumptions of male promiscuity and female dependency. Considered analytical interrogation of this noisy phenomenon can usefully trace its gender dynamics, productively displacing the emphasis on 'news impact' with an understanding of the ways in which sport and media institutions construct male sporting celebrity in foregrounding one type of *faux* scandal while seeking to disguise another of much greater substance – the deeply gendered inequality of the media sports cultural complex itself.

Note

1   I thank Dr Vibha Bhattarai Upadhyay for her research assistance in the preparation of this chapter.

References

Aitchison CC (ed.) (2007) *Sport and Gender Identities: Masculinities, Femininities and Sexualities*. London and New York: Routledge.

Anderson E (2005) *In the Game: Gay Athletes and the Cult of Masculinity*. Albany, NY: SUNY Press.

Andrews DL (2006) *Sport-Commerce-Culture: Essays on Sport in Late Capitalist America*. New York: Peter Lang.

Andrews DL and Jackson SJ (eds) (2001) *Sport Stars: The Cultural Politics of Sporting Celebrity*. London and New York: Routledge.

Armour N (2011) Scandal, labor woes make 2011 one of sports' worst. *The Columbus Dispatch* [online], 30 December. Available at: http://www.dispatch.com/content/stories/sports/2011/12/30/sports-year-end.html (accessed 2 January 2012).

Badenhausen K (2011) The world's highest paid athletes. *Forbes* [online], 31 May. Available at: http://www.forbes.com/sites/kurtbadenhausen/2011/05/31/the-worlds-highest-paid-athletes/ (accessed 18 January 2012).

BBC (2011) Ryan Giggs named by MP as injunction footballer. [online] 23 May. Available at: http://www.bbc.co.uk/news/uk-13503847 (accessed 24 January 2012).

Carrington B (2010) *Race, Sport and Politics: The Sporting Black Diaspora*. London: Sage.

Cashmore E (2002) *Beckham*. Cambridge: Polity.

Caudwell J (ed.) (2006) *Sport, Sexualities and Queer/Theory*. London: Routledge.

Coad D (2008) *The Metrosexual: Gender, Sexuality, and Sport*. Albany, NY: State University of New York Press.

Cole CL (2000) One chromosome too many? In: Schaffer K and Smith S (eds) *The Olympics at the Millennium: Power, Politics and the Games*. New Brunswick: Rutgers University Press, pp. 128–146.

Coles J (2012) Rhodri Giggs' sex-mad Natasha wore me out. *The Sun* [online], 19 January. Available at: http://www.thesun.co.uk/sol/homepage/news/4070972/Ryan-Giggs-news-Rhodris-sex-mad-Natasha-wore-me-out-says-holiday-romeo-Graham-Griffiths.html (accessed 24 January 2012).

Forbes (2011) Full list: the world's highest-paid athletes. Available at: http://www.forbes.com/2011/05/31/highest-paid-athletes_slide.html (accessed 18 January 2012).

Gilmour C and Rowe D (2010) When Becks came to Sydney: multiple readings of a sport celebrity. *Soccer & Society* 11(3): 229–241.

Goetsch D (2011) Baseball's loss of innocence. *The American Scholar* [online], Spring. Available at: http://theamericanscholar.org/baseballs-loss-of-innocence/ (accessed 2 January 2012).

Guttmann A (2002) *The Olympics: A History of the Modern Games*. 2nd edition. Urbana and Chicago, IL: University of Illinois Press [first published in 1994].

Hutchins B and Rowe D (2012) *Sport Beyond Television: The Internet, Digital Media and the Rise of Networked Media Sport*. New York: Routledge.

King S (1993) The politics of the body and the body politic: Magic Johnson and the ideology of AIDS. *Sociology of Sport Journal* 10(3): 270–285.

Lull J and Hinerman S (eds) (1997) *Media Scandals: Morality and Desire in the Popular Culture Marketplace*. Cambridge, UK: Polity Press and New York: Columbia University Press.

McKay J and Smith P (1995) Exonerating the hero: Frames and narratives in media coverage of the O J Simpson story. *Media Information Australia* 75: 57–66.

McKay J, Messner M and Sabo D (eds) (2001) *Masculinities, Gender Relations, and Sport*. Thousand Oaks, CA: Sage.

McTague T (2009) Top 10 Tiger Woods jokes. *Mirror.co.uk*, 9 December. Available at: http://www.mirror.co.uk/news/top-10s/2009/12/09/top-10-tiger-woods-jokes-115875-21884388/ (accessed 22 January 2012).

Marshall PD (1997) *Celebrity and Power: Fame in Contemporary Culture*. Minnesota, MN: University of Minnesota Press.

Miller T (2001) *Sportsex*. Philadelphia, PA: Temple University Press.

Robinson S (2002) *Salacious Allegations: Culture, Public Relations and the Sports Scandal*. Unpublished Honours Thesis, The University of Newcastle, Australia.

Rojek C (2001) *Celebrity*. London: Reaktion.

Rowe D (1994) Accommodating bodies: Celebrity, sexuality and 'tragic magic'. *Journal of Sport & Social Issues* 18(1): 6–26.

Rowe D (2004) *Sport, Culture and the Media: The Unruly Trinity*. 2nd ed. Maidenhead: Open University Press.

Rowe D (2010) Attention la femme! Intimate relationships and male sports performance. In: Fuller LK (ed.) *Sexual Sports Rhetoric: Global and Universal Contexts*. New York: Peter Lang, pp. 69–81.

Rowe D (2011) *Global Media Sport: Flows, Forms and Futures*. London: Bloomsbury Academic.

Sloop JM (1997) Mike Tyson and the perils of discursive constraints: Boxing, race, and the assumption of guilt. In Baker A and Boyd T (eds) *Out of Bounds*. Bloomington, IN: Indiana University Press, pp. 102–122.

Smart B (2005) *The Sport Star: Modern Sport and the Cultural Economy of Sporting Celebrity*. London: Sage.

Sports Business Journal (2011) 50 most influential people in sports business. [online] 12 December. Available at: http://www.sportsbusinessdaily.com/Journal/Issues/2011/12/12/Most-Influential/1.aspx (accessed 31 January 2012).

Starn O (2011) *The Passion of Tiger Woods: An Anthropologist Reports on Golf, Race, and Celebrity Scandal*. Durham, NC: Duke University Press.

Stevenson D (2002) Women, sport and globalization: Competing discourses of sexuality and nation. *Journal of Sport & Social Issues* 26(2): 209–225.

The Guardian (2011) *Phone Hacking: How the Guardian Broke the Story*. London: Guardian Books.

Thomas L (2010) BBC's news coverage of Tiger Woods' apology sparks 'dumbing down' backlash. *Mail*

Online [online], 25 February. Available at: http://www.dailymail.co.uk/news/article-1253598/BBCs-news-coverage-Tiger-Woods-apology-sparks-dumbing-backlash.html#ixzz0jRxYpheR (accessed 2 January 2012).

Tomsen S and Donaldson M (eds) (2003) *Male Trouble: Looking at Australian Masculinities*. Melbourne: Pluto.

Turner G (2004) *Understanding Celebrity*. London: Sage.

Vongs P (2004) Steroid scandal: a diehard fan mourns sports' loss of innocence. *NewAmerica Media* [online], 7 December. Available at: http://news.newamericamedia.org/news/view_article.html?article_id=515 d8a9844622d2706e4435c8b000723 (accessed 2 January 2012).

Whannel G (2002) *Media Sport Stars: Masculinities and Moralities*. London: Routledge.

51

PORTRAYING SPORTING MASCULINITY THROUGH FILM

Reflections on Jorgen Leth's
A Sunday in Hell

Ian McDonald

Introduction

There is a very powerful and telling scene in *A Sunday in Hell,* Jorgen Leth's 1976 documentary about the Paris–Roubaix cycling race. It is the final sequence, and is perhaps the most visually arresting scene of a visually striking film. The race has finished and the exhausted looking cyclists, mired in dirt, are shown showering and washing themselves in the 'open-plan' bathhouse. Amidst their number are journalists, coaches and officials: all are male. Some of the cyclists, naked, conduct interviews while showering, others are chatting to each other across the shower booth divide, while some seem to be in a world of their own. The camera follows one of the undoubted superstars of cycling, Eddy Merckx, who wears a weary and resigned look, before settling on his rival, an angry and agitated Roger de Vlaeminck. With the peeling paint and plaster on the walls as the backdrop to the rows of showering booths, the rival sportsmen enjoy their moment of camaraderie. The scene evokes a distinctly working-class male setting. The mood is manly without aggression, tender without eroticism, encapsulating an ambivalent sporting masculinity.

A Sunday in Hell is not about a hyper-masculinity, a subordinate masculinity or a deviant masculinity. Rather *A Sunday in Hell* is about a cycling race, no more, no less! But as a film about a race, it is phenomenologically rich and aesthetically expressive (Christiansen, 2009). And in presenting a truly cinematic vision of the race, the film (inadvertently) portrays the cultural and historically-specific nature of what hegemonic masculinity looks like in the world of cycling. The expressive visual aesthetic, of which the final shower scene is but one example, sets *A Sunday in Hell* apart from documentaries that foreground the effects of hegemonic masculinity. Notable examples of these other films include George Butler's take on male and female bodybuilding in *Pumping Iron* (1977) and *Pumping Iron II: The Women* (1985), respectively. More recent examples are *Murderball* (2005), which deals with issues of masculinity and disability, and *100% Woman* (2006) that features transexuality and sport. In my own documentary practice, I have examined gay identity and football in *Brighton Bandits* (2007) and the politics of homophobia in *Justin* (2011). These films are addressing the issue and effects issues of hegemonic masculinity, whereas in *A Sunday in Hell*, masculinity is already and always present, accepted and embedded. The implication of this for critical analysis will be expanded upon below. But I begin this chapter with some reflections on the epistemological status of documentary films for a critical analysis of sport and society.

Epistemological concerns: a brief excursus

In their insightful critique of the sport historians' reliance on written texts, Phillips, O'Neil and Osmond (2007) argue that there has been a marked reluctance among historians to engage with visual and material culture (films, photographs and monuments) in their studies. They assert that historians tend to treat visual culture such as films as illustrative 'extras', and keep them on the periphery of the range of legitimate historical sources. Films can 'threaten the analytical and empirical connection central to written history, and the potential epistemological deviation promoted by film may corrupt the professional practices of written historians' (Phillips et al., 2007: 274). They cite the criticisms levelled by professional sport historians at the epic documentary series on the history of baseball (1994) by well known documentarian Ken Burns: 'The demands of this medium often means that the past is presented as uncomplicated, linear, and consensual with a strong sense of progress that plays on emotional states, usually through the lives of individuals, and focuses on the surface level of events, not analysis or debate.' Sports historians disdain the lack of scholarly rigour in most films, criticising them for their lack of comprehensiveness and their omission of key details.

Philips et al. argue that this privileging of the historical document, or what E.H Carr referred to as the 'fetishism of the document' (1987: 16) pushes mainstream historians to assess film as 'books on the screen' (Philips et al., 2007: 276). But, it is argued, films have a different relationship to the past, and 'deserve to be critiqued on criteria that matter to that relationship' (ibid.: 277). Films in general including documentaries 'encourage a more reflective approach to written history that highlights that written history, like filmic history, is a constructed artefact' (ibid.: 277). Furthermore, they assert that, 'film with a very large palette of creative options has the ability to engage an audience at a deep emotional and imaginative level that facilitates a unique connection with the past' (ibid.: 278).

The antipathy of historians to sport films can be linked up to an argument developed within documentary studies by the well-known theorist Bill Nichols (1991). Nichols discusses the problematic position occupied by documentaries within what he calls the 'discourse of sobriety'. Documentaries, he laments, as having limited utility as sources of authoritative knowledge, because of the inherent ambiguity in images as a form of communication. Images lack the analytical precision of the spoken word, and as a result are on the periphery of 'the discourse of sobriety'. The emblematic products of this discourse are the written essay, book, and the scientific report that contribute to and engage in communicative exchanges and influence policy in such areas as science, economics, politics, foreign policy, education, religion and warfare. Nichols notes the subordinate status of documentaries within the discourse because of their reliance on images rather than words. In the context of the cinema, images are illustrative 'mimetic distractions and counterfeitings', and although they may be framed in documentaries by the spoken or written word, 'they fall under attack due to the imagistic company it keeps' (ibid.: 4). Thus, 'instead of directly confronting an issue or problem, the discourse must ricochet off this image-based, illusionistic medium of entertainment' (ibid.: 4).

Nichols has argued that this attitude to documentaries is misplaced and that the documentary film *should* be seen as kin to the written essay or the scientific report. In so far as documentaries engage with real life, with issues of power and social change, in terms of a direct relation to 'the real as direct, immediate, transparent' (ibid.: 4) they too can have an 'air of sobriety'. This conception of documentaries opens up possibilities for them to be used as texts for serious critique. And as films that are seeking a direct relation to the real, Jorgen Leth's sport documentaries ought to be situated within the discourse of sobriety and understood as texts that convey complex and critical ideas on masculinity.

Jorgen Leth against 'lousy sport journalism'

Jorgen Leth is an internationally-renowned filmmaker with over forty films to his credit. Born in Denmark in1937, Leth made his first film in 1963, an experimental short on a Jazz pianist (*Stop for Bud*), while his latest film, a controversial and problematic take on male erotic desire, was completed in 2010 (*Erotic Man*). In between, Leth made a number of important and distinctive sport documentaries: some feature length, some short and some experimental. His most significant, and arguably best known, sport documentary is *A Sunday in Hell* (1976), a cinematically beautiful account of the notorious Paris–Roubaix cycling race of 1976: an annual one-day race that starts at Chantilly, some 50 km north of Paris, and finishes around 220 km further north in Roubaix on the border with Belgium. Leth had previously made two other films on cycling, the gritty *Stars and Water Carriers* (1974) on the 1973 Giro d'Italia and *The Impossible Hour* (1975) on Ole Ritter's attempt to set a world record for distance covered in an hour. *A Sunday in Hell* then, was the culmination of a productive engagement with the culture of elite cycle racing, reflecting a lifelong passion for cycling and a deep admiration for cycling stars. In addition to making films on competitive cycling, Leth has also made films on other sports, including experimental shorts on tennis and table tennis (respectively *Motion Picture*, 1970 and *Chinese Ping Pong*, 1972), and a feature documentary on football (*Michael Laudrup – A Football Player*, 1993). He has also made an anthropological film on a traditional sport from the Basque region, the eponymous *Pelota* (1983).

A Sunday in Hell is undoubtedly a beautifully constructed and visually arresting take on the Paris–Roubaix race. Leth is clearly a masterful filmmaker with a poetic eye who manages, through his film, to elicit deep social truths about the inner dynamics of the race and by extension of elite male competitive cycling. *A Sunday in Hell* is not a documentary designed to 'educate' nor is it primarily 'informational' (as is often erroneously assumed to be the functions of 'proper' documentaries). Neither is it a film intended to champion sporting ideologies, or expose dubious practices. In this sense *A Sunday in Hell* is the antithesis of the didactic documentary designed to inform, educate and entertain. Rather, it is a rhythmic and poetic work that interweaves an idiosyncratic narration with well-crafted images, sound-scaping and music to produce a suggestive and highly-ambivalent portrayal of a particular sporting tradition and of sporting heroism. As Leth (2003) himself has commented:

> I always thought that sport deserved better than lousy sport journalism. It should have other ways of describing it, talking about it. I am simply telling stories that I see in the sport, and I know that I am projecting values in to the sport, but I think they are there. Its epic material, for me it's the material of novels. I want to sing about the riders, the glories and the triumph, and the falls and the tragedies. It's all big epic material.

In his sport films, Leth's concern is to grasp the meanings produced by the race; to understand it in its own terms reveals a 'phenomenological inquisitiveness and analysis of aesthetic detail to the whole' (Skotte, 2007). *A Sunday in Hell* is not a sociological treatise or provocation about gender and sexuality in sport. But the rationale for using this film for a chapter on gender and sexuality is precisely because it does not explicitly address gender and sexuality. The film highlights a fundamental truth about all hegemonic social relations: they are already and always fully integrated into specific cultures. Social relations that get established as hegemonic tend by definition to be relatively uncontested. They are so taken for granted, and so embedded in culture that they become 'naturalised' and even eulogised. But by not announcing themselves as problematic does not mean that they are not problematic. And so it is the case with *A Sunday in Hell*, a film that is, actually, all about a particular type of sporting masculinity.

Leth's cinematic skill and his knowledge of cycling enable him to inadvertently present a nuanced insight into sporting masculinity. This sets it apart from films where didactic or programmatic impulses result in a crude foregrounding of gender relations. This is important as, like all good works of art, it leaves interpretive space for alternative and deeper readings not intended by the filmmaker. Leth's film is intended, and indeed succeeds, in capturing this ritualistic and epic race on its own terms. While the star riders and the actual race are central, they are integrated as part of an organic whole (the event) that includes, for example, the officials, the spectators, the media and the protesters.

Hegemonic masculinity in *A Sunday in Hell*

A Sunday in Hell opens with an un-named mechanic preparing a cycle for a race. The mechanic displays a dedication to his task, or rather craft. The patient camera work and Morricone's melancholic musical score elevate this otherwise mundane if necessary activity into a poetic artisanal act. Without a word being uttered, either by the narrator or the mechanic, the scene is set for 'a different way of describing and a different way of talking' about sport. The first quarter of this 111-minute film sets up the main protagonists in the film: the star riders and their intense rivalry. The two main characters are the superstars of cycling: the race-favourite Roger de Vlaeminck and his main challenger, Eddy Merckx, both from Belgium. In a telling early sequence these two star riders are preparing for the race ahead. De Vlaemink is having his legs shaved, his body massaged, and his blood pressure measured. Merckx is engrossed in examining his bike, measuring the height of the seat from the frame, tweaking the handlebars. De Vlaeminck's body and Merckx's bike – the muscular body and the performance machine mediated by the two heroes of cycling – point to the specificities of hegemonic masculinity appropriate to cycling.

Though dominance, aggression, intimidation, strength, power and heterosexuality are characteristics typically associated with hegemonic masculinity (Anderson 2009), it is important to note that hegemonic characteristics are not constant for all contexts. The exact form that hegemonic masculinity takes and the particular combinations of traits vary according to social context. Therefore the characteristics that attain hegemonic status in rugby union will not necessarily be dominant characteristics in cycling. Cycling, and the Paris–Roubaix in particular, is clearly a tough race to complete, let alone win. It certainly requires the staple set of qualities associated with hegemonic masculinity, such as strength, stamina, determination, courage as well as good strategic thinking and a bit of luck. However, the requirements of the sport also bring forth aspects that might be considered distinctly un-masculine, feminine even. Thus, the nature of the muscular body is lithe rather than bulked. The legs are smooth from being closely shaved. The bike is sleek rather than 'suped'. Cycling is a non-contact sport, but with an ever-present threat of contact that can result in disastrous consequences for the riders involved, the threat of a violent end is ever present. Indeed, as can be seen in the film, when a crash occurs it can be devastating to the bodies of the riders and to their bikes. The sight of cuts and gashes on bloodied bodies and twisted mettle of the bikes do not take on a heroic hue, especially given the pained grimaces of the cyclist. It hurts and there is no concealing the pain behind a stoic mask.

In short, there are specificities to the form that masculinity takes in competitive cycling. Each sport has to be understood on its own terms.

The Paris–Roubaix race is notorious because much of the latter parts of the race are on cobblestones, known as the 'impassable paves' and as the 'hell of the north'. Leth's narration builds up the sense of foreboding as the riders approach 'hell', described as 'Dantanesque' and where 'only the strong survive'. Images, music and narration combine to present a picture of 'man versus nature', where the race is less between cyclists, than a battle within the rider not to succumb to the tough terrain. The use of a stirring musical score and panoramic views of the peloton from the sky add a feeling of religious awe to the race. All of the cyclists, not just the stars or those in the leading pack, become heroic. This is where Leth looks for drama and finds something 'to sing about'. His respect for the riders is total: 'It is drama because of the sacrifices that the riders must make and the accidents that can happen, and all the courage it takes to do these races' (Leth 2003). Those that do succumb are not judged as failures, rather they are akin to the war-wounded, forced to withdraw because the forces of nature were just too strong for them. Their masculinity remains intact.

As the drama of the race intensifies, the narration focuses on those riders jockeying for best position in the leading packs. Here we become familiar with the supporting cast of characters: more Belgians in Freddy Maertens and Marc Demeyer, the German Ollie Ritter, and the Italian Francesco Moser. Yet, even as the race intensifies, Leth maintains an interest in the events that usually get edited out of mainstream media coverage. The most significant example of this is the coverage of a protest: something 'unexpected and irregular is happening to delay the start of the race . . . a provocation!' The film cuts from riders approaching the start line, straining to see what is happening in the distance, to close-ups of the faces of male protesters chanting against the owners of the Parisian Libre newspaper for redundancies being made amongst the printers. Rather than condemn or edit out this 'provocation', Leth embraces it as part of the unfolding drama. Leth comments wryly, 'A professional cyclist is a living bill board.' Then as the cyclists are forced to make their way in single file, running the gauntlet of protesters, he comments, 'why not borrow some space for a call for solidarity' as the protesters slap stickers onto the backs of the cyclists. The cyclists 'get ticked off about the capitalist organiser of the race. A political lesson for the road, but if they let the race go on, which they do, then the protesters have their own favourites.' A slap that is both political, but also encouraging. The intention of the protesters is not to stop the race, but simply to make their point.

Leth chooses to spend time with the male worker who is painting the name of the sponsor on the racetrack at the stadium where the race will end. This nod to the role of labouring men behind the scenes is reinforced at regular intervals through the film. So Leth lingers with workers putting up banners in towns ahead of the race passing through, or preparing the outside live broadcasting unit. When a car stops by to sell race souvenirs, it is boys and young men who rush to buy a commemorative cap or programme. Women are presented in supporting or servicing roles, reflecting the patriarchal culture of sport: they are seen either within shots of the cheering crowds lining the streets, or as adoring fans declaring that they are drawn to the race to look at the men's bodies, or they are seen serving drinks in roadside cafes and bars.

The unfolding epic drama is finally realised in the unexpected result of the race. Rivalry is a key narrative in the film, especially the personal enmity between de Vlaeminck and Freddy Maertens. The menacing and daunting figure of Merckx is never forgotten, but this is not to be his race. When Maertens is forced to withdraw after a serious crash, it is expected that de Vlaeminck will secure a historic 4th Paris–Roubaix victory. But in the final straight, the leading rider de Vlaeminck commits a tactical error and allows the underdog Marc Demeyer to overtake him and take victory in a time of 6 hours, 52 minutes and 4 seconds. Demeyer's role in the race is to support the challenge by his teammate Maertens to de Vlaeminck. And had Maertens not crashed out of the race, then Demeyer would not have been in such a position to launch his own attack to take the race. But as Leth declares, this was 'a beautiful win to the helper who got free reins, victory all the more sweet because it was snatched from de Vlaeminck'. Leth feels a sense of sporting joy and indeed political solidarity with the victory of Demeyer. This is a triumph of the downtrodden labourer over the royalty of cycling, a testimony to the creative potential of the working man once freed of obligation and subservience. Demeyer's victory makes us feel affinity with the workers putting up the banners and painting lines and solidarity with the protesting printers.

Conclusion

Drawing on the pioneering and evolving work of Connell on hegemonic masculinity (Connell and Messerschmidt 2005) scholars have insisted on the ineluctably gendered nature of sporting practice and culture. One of the most insightful critiques remains Holmlund's (1989) account of the construction of gender and sexuality (and indeed race) in the aforementioned *Pumping Iron* films, while more recent critiques have focussed on the intersections between gender and other forms of identity, such as Ghosh's (2013) account of hegemonic masculinity and disability in the aforementioned *Murderball*. In this chapter, my concern has been with the more understated and banal form of masculinity evident in *A Sunday in Hell*: one that is not evidently contested or problematised within its own cultural terms or within its representational form in the film.

A Sunday in Hell demonstrates that sporting masculinity is best grasped in its concrete expressions: that is in specific sports and at particular moments in time. The nature of cycling demands a particular kind of masculinity based on courage, determination, a hard body and a strong competitive spirit. Yet as a non-contact sport, requiring slim and shaven bodies riding sleek cycles, cycling masculinity looks very different from expressions of masculinity in contact sports such as rugby. This suggests that each sport offers different possibilities for opening up the contradictions and complexities in masculinity. In *A Sunday in Hell*, there is an unstated politics of masculinity that is homologous with working–class masculinity in industrial societies. Leth exalts the homosocial and collective ethos of this culture. The interdependence of the cyclists in the peloton is a function of the need to survive the race. Such interdependence produces moments of intimacy. Glimpses of this are shown in the film, when the riders help each other out in times of distress and where helpers of opposing teams support each other.

Portraying the delicate balance between masculinity and intimacy is rarely achieved in sport documentaries. It is managed in Leth's other celebrated film, *Pelota* (1983), on the cultural significance of this epynonymous traditional Basque sport. Like his cycling trilogy, Leth reveals himself to be at home in the homosocial world of sport with this sensitive portrayal of masculine bonds: between father and son in sustaining the craft of making the ball; between trainer and player to produce the next generation of champions; and in upholding a culture of respect for former champions. Only obliquely is the social and political context of Pelota revealed, through pointed but unexplained images of blacked-out bullet-marked road signs, or pro-ETA graffiti on training walls. Leth leaves plenty of interpretive space for the viewer to enter and pursue their particular analysis of the cultural politics of Pelota. Ron Peck's *Fighters* (1991) about a boxing gym in the East End of London is one other notable film that captures the paradoxes of masculinity. It is a complex, beautiful and touching portrayal of boxers, and prompts the viewer to think about the contradictions of sporting masculinity in arguably the most brutal contact sport.

The same dialectic of competition and cooperation, of dominance and subservience, of determination and sacrifice underpins the expressivist aesthetic of *A Sunday in Hell*. Leth gives us a penetrating and poetic insight into the ways in which sport provides a terrain for the ritualistic process of social male bonding. Hegemonic masculinity is maintained. Yet there is no discernible programmatic intent to *A Sunday in Hell* and it is all the better for it. *A Sunday in Hell* is a cinematic confirmation of 'sport as a male preserve' and as such is a valuable text for understanding the nuanced complexities of hegemonic sporting masculinity. Reflections on masculinity are not made by the narrator of the film, but are expressed visually. As a viewer, we have to interpret the significance of what is unstated, taken for granted, hegemonic. And in so doing, we are taking the first step in developing a critical awareness of how to name and mark masculine dominance in other spheres of sport.

The scene that best illustrates this is the final scene in the showers. This is where we began the chapter, and it is where we will end it. The shower scene is not only evocative of a working masculinity, but points towards a comradeship borne out of a common experience of hardship. And here, in the showers, conditions are shared, as the star riders like Merckx and de Vlaeminck are returned to the community of cyclists. Now all the cyclists are equal. Without the knowledge that these were the elite of professional cycling, and take away the cameras and the journalists, and we may be forgiven for thinking they are all coal miners at the end of a long shift. These are neither Reifenstahlian Olympian 'supermen' or unattainable celebrated 'superstars'. They are men who have trained hard and have just finished a hard day's work 'in hell'.

References

Anderson, E. (2009) *Inclusive Masculinity: The Changing Nature of Masculinities*. New York: Routledge.

Carr, E.H. (1987) *What is History?* (2nd edition). London: Penguin.

Christiansen, A.V. (2009) The Re-enchantment of the World: The Relationship Between Sport and Aesthetics Illustrated by Two Classic Cycling Films, *Sport in History*, Vol 29, No 1, pp 49–68

Connell, R.W. and Messerschmidt, J.W. (2005) Hegemonic Masculinity: Rethinking the Concept, *Gender and Society*, Vol 19, No 6, pp 829–859

Ghosh, S. (2013) Murderball: Hyper-capitalism and the Ethics of Narrative Forms in Life Writing, in *Gender and Genre in Sports Documentaries: Critical Essays*. Edited by Ingle, Z. and Sutera, D.M. Plymouth: Scarecrow Press, pp 35–50.

Holmlund, C.A. (1989) Visible Difference and Flex Appeal: The Body, Sex, Sexuality, and Race in the 'Pumping Iron' Films. *Cinema Journal*, Vol 28, No 4, Summer, pp 38–51

Nichols, B. (1991) *Representing Reality: Issues and Concepts in Documentary*. Bloomington: Indian Press.

Phillips, M.G., O'Neill, M.E., and Osmond, G. (2007) Broadening Horizons in Sport History: Films, Photographs, and Monuments', *Journal of Sport History* Vol 34, No 2, pp 271–293.

Skotte, K. (2007) *Adding Form to Top Form*, The Jorgen Leth Collection. Denmark: Danish Film Institute.

Filmography

Burns, K. (1994 / 18.5 hours) (a 9 episode series) *Baseball*. USA: PBS.

Butler, G. (1977 / 85mins) *Pumping Iron*. USA: Cinegate.

Butler, G. (1985 / 107 mins) *Pumping Iron II: The Women*. USA: Cinegate.

Duthie, K. (2006) *100% Woman*. USA: Artemis Dreams.

Leth, J. (1963 / 12 mins) *Stop for Bud*. Denmark: Danish Film Institute.

Leth, J. (1970 / 20 mins) *Motion Picture*. Denmark: Danish Film Institute.

Leth, J. (1972 / 14 mins) *Chinese Ping Pong*. Denmark: Danish Film Institute.

Leth, J. (1974 / 93 mins) *Stars and Water Carriers*. Denmark: Danish Film Institute.

Leth, J. (1975 / 45 mins) *The Impossible Hour*. Denmark: Danish Film Institute.

Leth, J. (1976 / 111mins) *A Sunday in Hell*. Denmark: Danish Film Institute.

Leth, J. (1983 / 47 mins) *Pelota*. Denmark: Danish Film Institute.

Leth, J. (1993 / 74 mins) *Michael Laudrup: A Football Player*. Denmark: Danish Film Institute.

Leth, J. (2003 / 9 mins) *A Conversation with Jorgen Leth*. Denmark: Danish Film Institute.
Leth, J. (2010 / 85 mins) *The Erotic Man*. Denmark: A Zentropa Entertainment/Nordisk Film production.
McDonald, I. (2007 / 40 mins) *Brighton Bandits*. UK: interventions.
McDonald, I. (2011 / 30 mins) *Justin*. UK: interventions.
Peck, R. (1991 / 101 mins) *Fighters*. UK: Second Run.
Rubin, H.A. and Shapiro, D.A. (2005 / 88 mins) *Murderball*.USA: ThinkFilm.

52

GENDER TROUBLE IN FEMALE SPORTS FILMS

Katharina Lindner

Introduction

This chapter is concerned with questions of sport, gender and sexuality in relation to cinema, with a specific focus on depictions of female athleticism. It brings into dialogue feminist critiques of women and/in sport as well as women and/in cinema, in an attempt to explore the ways in which gender and sexual identities are re-constituted in contemporary female sports films, including *Bring it On* (Reed, 2000), *Ice Princess* (Fywell, 2005), *The Cutting Edge* (Glaser, 1992), *Stick it* (Bendinger, 2006), *Wimbledon* (Loncraine, 2004), *Bend it Like Beckham* (Chadha, 2003), *Blue Crush* (Stockwell, 2002), *Love and Basketball* (Prince-Bythewood, 2000), *Girlfight* (Kusama, 2000) and *Million Dollar Baby* (Eastwood, 2004).

Much of the existing research concerned with representations of female athletes has focused on broadcast media and other non-fictional contexts, leading to a wealth of often useful insights. The representation of female athletes in fiction film, however, has not received much critical attention – and the literature that does exist is often problematic, as the specificity of either *cinematic* representation or of *athletic* performance tends not to be sufficiently acknowledged.

Research in this area, when undertaken by academics with an interest in sport and gender and with backgrounds in media/communication studies or sociology, often neglects to consider the distinctions between different media forms, leading to accounts of 'stereotypes' of female athletes in film (as either hypersexualised or masculinised/lesbianised) and of the 'inaccuracy' of filmic representations when contrasted with the situation of female athletes in 'reality'.

Within film studies, the longstanding and reciprocal relationship between sport and cinema, particularly its gendered dimension, is equally under-researched and has only recently received more sustained critical attention (Lindner, 2011a; Pearson, 2001). This is surprising considering the historical pervasiveness of athletic themes, sports-centred narratives and athletic bodies in (Hollywood) cinema, ranging from the frequent depiction of fictional and non-fictional boxing fights in early newsreel to Robert De Niro's and Hillary Swank's Oscar-winning performances as boxers in *Raging Bull* (Scorsese, 1980) and *Million Dollar Baby*.

Interestingly, a critical interest in female athleticism and physicality can be identified within those film studies debates that are more generally concerned with representations of gender and the female body in cinema. Specifically, this includes critical engagements with the action cinema that focus on the troubling significance of the active and muscular female body (see

Holmlund, 2001; Tasker, 1993). In fact, the female boxing film *Girlfight* is included in Beltrán's (2004) discussion of the 'New Latina hero' within the action genre, whereas the 'boxing film' (typically assumed to be about a male boxer) tends to be considered a sub-genre in its own right (Grindon, 1996; 2007).

While debates around the action genre usefully contextualise the significance of female athleticism, it is equally important to acknowledge the specifically *athletic* character of bodily 'action' in the female sports film as well as the implications of an engagement in sports as a very specific *socially-situated* and *gendered* bodily practice that differs considerably from the often 'fantastic' bodily action of the action genre.

The aim of this chapter is to acknowledge both the specificity of *athletic* performance as well as the specificity of *cinematic* representation. This means going beyond an account of the stereo-types/images of female athletes in cinema by considering questions of genre, narrative, specta-torship and viewing pleasures. This will allow for a consideration of how sports and cinema (as institutions that 'discipline' bodies in particular ways) contribute to our understandings of the athletic female body and its (potentially troubling) capabilities.

Pirouettes and knock-out punches: genre, narrative, spectacle, pleasure

The depiction of female athletes in central roles has increased dramatically in previous decades (Lindner, 2011a; Pearson, 2001) and there are some useful observations to be made as to the kinds of films athletic female protagonists feature in as well as to the types of sport depicted.

It is, firstly, worth noting that sporting activities themselves are gendered, with certain kinds of sports, such as figure skating, gymnastics or cheerleading, carrying feminine connotations. It is therefore no surprise that there are a number of films that depict female protagonists pursuing female-appropriate sports, including *Ice Princess* (figure skating), *The Cutting Edge* (figure skat-ing), *Stick it* (gymnastics) and *Bring it On* (cheerleading). Within the context of traditional gender relations, the depictions of athletic performances by female characters tend to be relatively 'safe' and non-threatening. The bodily shapes, movements and clothing fit neatly into established and heteronormative gender binaries, as the performance of (heterosexual) femininity is arguably written into the rules of the sports themselves (Feder, 1994).

These are some of the reasons why depictions of female gymnasts, cheerleaders and figure skaters are easily integrated into the established visual and narrative conventions of mainstream cinema. In fact, the (staged) performances by athletic female characters in these films resemble closely the kinds of performances identified by Mulvey (1975) as providing narrative oppor-tunities/excuses for the display of the female body as a sexualised and *to-be-looked-at* object for the actively desiring gaze of both the (male) characters within the films and the viewers of the film.

In her polemic about the patriarchal psychic structures of (mainstream) cinema, Mulvey points to the ways in which narrative and visual agency is associated with masculinity, while femininity, as it is inscribed on the female body on screen, tends to be associated with passivity and a lack of agency – and this binary constellation is, according to Mulvey (1975), linked to the specifically gendered viewing pleasures provided.[1] The fact that figure skating, gymnastics and cheerleading are sports in which winning and losing is determined by the decisions of (often male) judges who evaluate, among other things, the visually and aesthetically pleasing nature of the performance, adds to the significance of the controlling and objectifying gaze directed at the female body. The *to-be-looked-at* performances of athletic female characters in films such as *Ice Princess, The Cutting Edge* and *Bring it On* are therefore easily integrated into mainstream cinema's heteronormative narrative and looking constellations. Figure skating and cheerleading are suitable activities to be pursued by female characters within this representational context and its obsession with heterosexual romance and traditional gender binaries.

A central characteristic of female-appropriate sports is the disavowal of the powerful and assertive physicality of the female body. 'Good' and 'successful' performances demand the bodily strength and exertion, which are, of course, absolutely *necessary* for the execution of complex and demanding movements, to be denied. Although gymnasts, figure skaters and cheerleaders are required to develop strong, powerful and potentially troubling bodies in order to succeed in their sport, they are also required to ensure that the physicality of their bodies remains invisible and/or within the boundaries of acceptable femininity, which undermines the 'empowering' potential of girls' and women's engagement in these sports. While (some) athletic activities provide opportunities for the development of a sense of body ownership, confidence, and a sense of being 'in tune' with one's body, female-appropriate sports such as figure skating and gymnastics demand a continual awareness of what the performance, and as such the body, 'look like'. This means that athletes are involved in a process of perpetual self-surveillance and alienation. This internalisation of what Bartky (1988, p.72) calls the gaze of the 'anonymous patriarchal Other' constitutes an effective policing of appropriately and intelligibly feminine bodily forms and movements and reassuringly repositions the female body as an object *to-be-looked-at.*

That said, the active physicality of the characters, although denied, is potentially 'troubling' as it threatens to undermine traditional gender binaries that equate femininity with passivity and objecthood. There are, for instance, a number of sequences in *Ice Princess, The Cutting Edge* and *Bring it On* that hint at the characters' bodily strength. *Bring it On* shows the cheerleaders in the weightlifting gym. However, the characters do not actually lift weights, but merely use the gym as the setting for a conversation. The film thus points to the significance of bodily strength, but an athletic physicality is *not* inscribed at the level of the body itself. The bodies of the characters/actresses are rather unathletic, not overly muscular, and as such not overly 'troubling'.

The Cutting Edge contains a similar weightlifting sequence and we actually see the female protagonist, Kate (Moira Kelly) lift a dumbbell. The actual figure skating performances, however, tend to be devoid of references to Kate's corporeality, in favour of an emphasis on ethereality and weightlessness. The power and strength of Doug (D.B. Sweeney), the male skater and former ice hockey player, on the other hand, are certainly emphasised when he picks up Kate, throwing her up in the air as part of the performance. The potentially troubling implications of the female characters' athletic activities are thus disavowed through the negation of their physicality, which is necessary, it seems, for their integration into the films' heteronormative trajectories that ultimately lead to the climactic formation of the heterosexual couple.

The transgressive potential of female athleticism is additionally undermined by the 'unbeliev-ability' of the portrayal of bodily skill. Variously, actresses (rather than athletes) such as Kirsten Dunst in *Bring it on*, Michelle Trachtenberg in *Ice Princess* and Moira Kelly in *The Cutting Edge,* do not visibly *embody* particular athletic capabilities. Even careful editing cannot entirely conceal the fact that the actresses' bodies are, in fact, rather unathletic bodies and their movements, when framed in 'real time', seem clumsy and disjointed. When framed via complex editing techniques, they become unbelievably spectacular. The characters' athletic movements seem removed from the physicality of the 'real' bodies supposedly executing these movements.

The gymnastics film *Stick it* provides an interesting exception by featuring a visibly muscular female protagonist, Haley (Missy Peregrym), and by explicitly grounding her gymnastic perform-ances in the physicality of her body. Generally, however, there is a tendency for the most spectacu-lar performances to be framed in a way that imbues them with a flattened, abstract, and depthless quality and to take place in what Dyer (1992) might call a disembodied and 'utopian' realm.

A similar argument around a lack of authenticity can be made about Dunst's performance as professional tennis player, Lizzie, in *Wimbledon*. Dunst's athletic actions (tennis, running) seem awkward, inhibited and disjointed. She runs and plays tennis 'like a girl', and exhibits the typically feminine movement and comportment that Young (1980) discusses in her essay 'Throwing like a girl'.

Young suggests that women's bodily existence tends to be characterised by an 'inhibited intentionality' and by an essentially alienated relationship of women to their own bodies. This is particularly noticeable within the athletic context where women tend not to make use of their bodies' 'spatial and lateral potentialities' (Young, 1980: 143). These gendered differences in movement and comportment are acquired and learned, rather than 'natural', and they are indicative of larger socio-cultural pressures that inscribe binary differences on male and female bodies and their relation to space. The professional male tennis player, Peter, played by Paul Bettany, has a more naturally athletic physique and moves around the court much more comfortably. His performances are given additional 'substance' through the internal monologues, in which he comments on his actions during most tennis sequences.

Wimbledon follows, in straightforward fashion, the conventions of the romantic comedy, with the initially antagonistic and competitive relationship between the characters developing fairly predictably into a relationship of romantic and sexual attraction. The romance narrative is squarely situated within the athletic context, which arguably serves to assuage fears about the lesbian associations of female athleticism. These associations are particularly 'visible' in relation to tennis, with 'out' female tennis players such as Martina Navratilova and Amélie Mauresmo having considerable public/media profiles. *Wimbledon* therefore diverges from the established generic conventions of the (male) sports film, where sporting sequences tend to chart the ups and downs of the athletic character's way, ultimately to *sporting* success.

While heterosexual romance plays a role in most (male) sports films, these tend to be marginal narrative strands and the formation of the heterosexual couple follows on from, and is an 'incidental' side-effect of, sporting success. In *Wimbledon*, however, the priorities are reversed, with an initial narrative and visual emphasis on tennis gradually making way for narrative and visual concerns with heterosexual romance – at least in relation to Lizzie whose obsession with tennis turns into an obsession with Peter, and whose ultimate aim is not athletic success (anymore) but the successful integration into social, narrative and generic norms. The narratives of potential empowerment and independence that feminist critics (e.g., Choi, 2000; Heywood and Dworkin, 2003) tend to construct around girls' and women's engagement in sports are very much marginalised and undermined by the film.

The soccer film *Bend it Like Beckham* is more ambiguous in its portrayal of athletic skills. The authenticity of Jules's (Keira Knightley) and Jess's (Parminder Nagra) athletic performances are undermined by the actresses' lack of athletic skills, which is noticeable, for instance, in their run up to the ball at awkward angles. However, the film's transgressive potential lies, as I have suggested elsewhere (Lindner, 2011b), in Keira Knightley's tomboyish appearance and androgynous physique: the film's comically self-conscious acknowledgement of the lesbian associations of female athleticism as well as the narrative and visual ambiguities surrounding the female characters' relationship to each other. As in *Wimbledon*, the protagonists' relationship develops primarily *within* the sports context and it is the development of a (*physically*) close bond between the female characters that arguably opens the film up for a 'lesbian' reading.

Similar arguments can be made about the female surfing film *Blue Crush*, where the relationship between the central surfing characters Anne-Marie (Kate Bothworth) and Eden (Michelle Rodriguez) is overlaid with considerable visual and narrative ambiguity. Rodriguez's muscular physique and her role as Anne-Marie's best friend and training partner, who becomes explicitly jealous when Anne-Marie enters into a relationship with American footballer Matt (Matthew Davis), is central to the film's troubling of heteronormative conventions and constellations. In terms of narrative development and closure, Anne-Marie eventually chooses her surfing career (and Eden?) over Matt and the climactic moment towards the end of the film is in fact a sporting moment, with the heterosexual romance being at least temporarily sidelined. Here, Anne-Marie's athletic achievements are given narrative importance in their own right. In a way, this is similar to the final sequence in *Bend it Like Beckham*, which sees Jess and Jules walk onto an airplane that will take them to the United States where they will join a college team on a soccer scholarship. Their athletic achievements ultimately strengthen their relationship and the film's ending points to their continuing engagement in sport.

Overall, *Blue Crush, Bend it Like Beckham*, as well as films such as *Love and Basketball* and *Girlfight*, are explicitly critical about the social-cultural, interpersonal and material barriers and prejudices often faced by girls and women when pursuing gender-inappropriate sports. The acquisition of a powerful physicality and the engagement in antagonistic bodily contact is often perceived as a form of gender transgression. While films such as *Wimbledon* deal with the resulting tensions by situating female athleticism in a reassuringly heterosexualised genre (the romantic comedy) and thus re-establish binary frameworks of sex, gender and sexuality, films such as *Stick it* and *Million Dollar Baby* disavow these tensions by attempting to avoid questions of sexuality altogether. Questions about Hayley's and Maggie's (Hillary Swank) gender and sexual identities are always clearly 'there' – female sports films are always already 'about' gender and sexuality (Caudwell, 2009) – but never explicitly dealt with. Disavowal always leaves a trace of absence, however, and this is where possibilities for negotiation, fluidity and subversive viewing pleasures lie.

What imbues *Love and Basketball* and particularly *Girlfight* with potentially troubling qualities is that the films deal with the 'troubling' implications of female athleticism head on. Both films feature heterosexual romance narratives involving male and female athletic characters. In *Love and Basketball*, Monica (Sanaa Lathan) and Quincy (Omar Epps) are childhood friends and the film traces the ups and downs of their relationship alongside both characters' high school, college and professional basketball careers. The final images of the film see Monica play in a professional basketball game while Quincy is in the audience, together with their young daughter. While the film's ending celebrates heterosexual union and procreation alongside athletic success, it also deals quite explicitly with notions of female masculinity in the context of heterosexual romance. Monica is not necessarily feminised in order to fit into heteronormative binaries of gender and sexuality; rather, the film seems to reassure us that muscular women can quite easily fulfil traditionally feminine roles as mother and wife. *Love and Basketball* thus has transgressive potential but its overall significance is reassuring rather than challenging of the heteronormative status quo.

In *Love and Basketball*, Monica and Quincy compete directly against each other twice, with neither encounter taking place in an official sporting context. Instead, the characters go head to head on a private basketball court in the middle of the night, when Monica wants to play for Quincy's 'heart'. The second encounter is in their college dorm room when they play with a toy basketball 'for clothes' (a clearly sexualised game of striptease, rather than basketball). Following the film's title, heterosexual love and basketball are intimately intertwined in the film. This contrasts heavily with the relationship between Diana (Michelle Rodriguez) and Adrian (Santiago Douglas) in *Girlfight*, where the boxers meet in the ring on several occasions.

The boxing ring is a clearly marked space in which encounters between individuals are by definition violent and antagonistic, and much of the film deals very explicitly with the incompatibility of Diana's gender identity (her female masculinity) and her sexual identity as Adrian's girlfriend. It is, in fact, Adrian who seems to struggle with this tension the most as, within a heteronormative framework, his romantic involvement with Diana appears to raise questions about his own gender and sexual identity.

Their relationship is at its most fragile when she does, in fact, beat him in the ring in the film's climactic fight, with Rodriguez's muscular physique and powerful movements lending considerable authenticity and believability to this crucial narrative event. There are moments when the fighters' faces are not directly visible, making it impossible to distinguish physiques of the male and female boxers – sexual difference becomes invisible. The tensions between female masculinity and heterosexuality grappled with by the film are never reassuringly resolved. The film's ending is ambiguous and no (utopian) solution to the 'problem' of female masculinity is provided. This is arguably where the subversive implications of *Girlfight* lie.

The boxing film in particular has a long tradition within mainstream cinema and has established itself as a 'genre' with certain narrative structures and visual conventions since the very early days of cinema. Before concluding this chapter, I want to turn to this particular genre and consider the ways in which the female boxing protagonist 'troubles' its conventions.

Writing about the functional nature of genres, Altman (1999) points to their significance in isolating and providing symbolic solutions for socio-cultural problems and conflicts. Variously, the boxing film genre has been identified as being centrally concerned with notions of a 'troubled masculinity' (Woodward, 2007). In one of the most detailed discussions of the genre, Grindon (1996; 2007) argues that the boxing film evolves around the fundamental conflicts of body versus soul, opportunity versus difference, market values versus family values, anger versus justice, as well as the tension between the violence in the ring and the (heterosexual) romance surrounding the boxing action. These generic conflicts are played out over the body of the boxer, who is assumed to be male. As Woodward (2007, p.122) puts it, 'the archetypal boxer in film has traditionally been portrayed as a singular heroic figure of troubled masculinity'.

With regard to the narrative conventions, Grindon (1996: 57–59) suggests that the boxing film typically consists of (a variation of) the following structure:

Move 1: The Discovery. The protagonist is found to have a remarkable talent for fistfights [. . .]

Move 2: The Crisis. The values embodied in the protagonist's family and his sanctioned ambition are placed in crisis which drives the reluctant hero into the ring. Masculine pride provoked by poverty [can evoke such a crisis].

Move 3: The Promise. The boxer confirms his potential with his first victory in the ring [. . .]

Move 4: The Rise. In the gym the manager develops the boxer's craft [. . .]

Move 5: The Deal. The boxer, blocked by the brokers of the fight game, signs with a gangster promoter, against the advice of his manager, fiancée, brother, or other trusted confidant [. . .]

Move 6: Debauchery. The boxer abandons his previous regimen of training for parties and the fast life. The girlfriend from the old neighbourhood, disturbed by the transformation, is pushed aside by the vamp [. . .]

Move 7: Big Fight 1. The protagonist gains the title or wins the fight that assures him big status [. . .]

Move 8: The Dive. Rendered vulnerable by high living, isolated from his true friends, and in need of cash, the boxer yields to pressure from the gangster promoter and agrees to take a dive for some dubious reward [. . .]

Move 9: Big Fight 2. In an extended bout, the boxer suffers terrible punishment, but in a late round he regains his will and defeats his opponent; nevertheless, his career is over [. . .]

Move 10: Resolution/Epilogue. The end of the boxing career signifies the decline of the body [. . .]

Clearly, the socio-cultural conflicts and the narrative conventions identified here assert an understanding of the boxing film as a masculine genre and render the *female* boxing film problematic – I refer to this is as 'genre trouble'.

The genre's gendered conventions are based on the inherently masculine associations of the sport itself. As Oates (2006: 72) suggests: 'Boxing is for men and is about men, and *is* men.' Woodward (2007: 3) notes that Oates' comment 'is not only an empirical observation about the people who take part, but an expression of the powerfully gendered metaphors of the sport'. This highlights the troubling implications of the female boxer's embodiment of masculinity already identified in relation to *Girlfight*. The figure of the female boxer raises important questions 'about how and why women might "do" masculinity [. . .] and whether there are alternative reconfigurations of gender identities' (Woodward, 2007: 5–6).

Woodward usefully points to the problems surrounding the 'draw' and 'appeal' of the spectacular display of violence in boxing. It is the *spectatorship* of the spectacle of 'broken and damaged as well as fit and beautiful' (Woodward, 2007: 134) male bodies in violent physical contact that is full of tensions. These tensions are amplified when the broken and damaged but fit and beautiful bodies are the masculinised bodies of female boxers, such as Maggie's/Hillary Swank's in *Million Dollar Baby* or Diana's/Michelle Rodriguez's in *Girlfight*, raising important questions about the re-configuration of gender and sexual identities, the psychic investments made possible and the unconscious fears and desires thus addressed. If 'boxing heroes offer the fantasy of a stable masculinity' (Woodward, 2007: 128) in response to uncertainty and change, particularly in relation to gender roles, the female boxer's performance of masculinity certainly is deeply troubling. This manifests itself in the ways in which *Girlfight* does not manage, or refuses to even attempt, to resolve the generic problems 'caused' by its protagonist's embodiment of female masculinity.

With regard to *Million Dollar Baby*, the gender/genre trouble manifests itself in the film's generic code switching from boxing film to melodrama. Swank's performance as the female boxer, Maggie, has won widespread critical appraisal, as well as an Academy Award for Best Actress in a Lead Role in 2004. Much attention was drawn to the strict training regime the actress had undergone in preparation for the role, which saw her develop a visibly muscular and powerful body – the body of a boxer. The film highlights the physical strain of the boxer's training, and there is a visceral emphasis both on the power of her punches as well as on the severity of injuries sustained. There are two particularly visceral moments:

1) we hear the sounds of bones crunching and grinding when Maggie's coach Frank (Clint Eastwood) forcefully pushes her bloodied and broken nose back into place (upon Maggie's stubborn request, as she wants to continue fighting), and 2) we also hear her spine cracking in a slow-motion sequence that sees her fall onto the wooden frame of a stool when she is unexpectedly hit in between rounds by her devious opponent. This second incident is a key moment in

the narrative, as it results in Maggie being paralysed from the neck down, unable to move and perform even the most basic bodily functions without the help of others. It is as if the film hits the end of the 'generic road' at this point in the narrative, not knowing what to 'do' with its female boxing protagonist.

In the case of *Million Dollar Baby*, the solution to the 'problem' of female masculinity is to deny the character all bodily agency and to turn the film into a melodrama about precisely this lack of agency and the unjustness of Maggie's 'fate'. After a series of unsuccessful attempts, Maggie eventually manages to assert a final act of agency and commits suicide. While *Million Dollar Baby* has the potential to provide a serious challenge to established notions of gender and sexual difference, the film does not follow through and instead kills off the boundary-crossing female protagonist (similar, in a way, to the established cinematic treatment of the femme fatale).

Conclusion

This brief overview of eleven female sports films suggests that within the context of cinematic representation, female athleticism, particularly when 'believably' rooted in the physicality of bodies depicted, has the potential to challenge our understanding of gender and sexual binaries. Most of the films mentioned here provide a degree of visibility for muscular and athletic female bodies that are imbued with a sense of bodily and narrative agency. This agency tends to be variously undermined, however, by re-positioning the transgressive female characters in relation to heteronormative generic, narrative and visual contexts. The majority of athletic heroines can be found in comedic and/or romantic genres where sport provides a mere backdrop for the development of heterosexual romance.

The complete absence of filmic biographies (biopics) about female athletes (particularly considering the abundance of biopics about male athletes) is also worth noting. Nonetheless, *Girlfight* in particular, but also films such as *Million Dollar Baby*, *Stick it* and *Love and Basketball* place powerful and visibly athletic characters at the centre of their narratives. While the characters' bodily agency is various undermined, their troubling potential is never fully contained. These films and their commercial and critical success therefore ensure that certain narrative fragments and images of ambiguously gendered and powerful girls and women enter the popular imagination.

If, as Altman (1999) argues, the function of cinematic genres is to provide symbolic and often utopian solutions for contemporary socio-cultural problems, the relatively recent proliferation of female sports films and the often troubling entrance of female protagonists into traditionally male-centred genres, point to the wider, and potentially subversive, socio-cultural significance of female athleticism. The fact that reassuring 'solutions' to the 'problem' of female athleticism are provided, but often not convincingly so, also points to the significance of sport as a context that constitutes an important battleground where our commonsense understandings of sex, gender and sexuality continue to be challenged.

Note

1 The arguments provided by Mulvey in her seminal essay 'Visual pleasure and narrative cinema' (1975) have been criticised, challenged and developed in a number of different ways, but continue to be a central reference point in contemporary debates concerned with the representation of women in mainstream cinema.

References

Altman R (1999) *Film/genre*. London: BFI.

Bartky SL (1988) Foucault, femininity, and the modernisation of patriarchal power. In: Diamond I and Quinby L (eds) *Feminism and Foucault: Reflections on Resistance*. Boston: North-Eastern University Press, pp.61–86.

Beltrán M (2004) Más mácha: The new Latina action hero. In: Tasker Y (ed) *Action and Adventure Cinema*. London: Routledge, pp. 186–200.

Caudwell J (2009) *Girlfight* and *Bend it Like Beckham*: screening women, sport, and sexuality. *Journal of Lesbian Studies* 13(3): 255–271.

Choi PYL (2000) *Femininity and the Physically Active Woman*. London: Routledge.

Dyer R (1992) Entertainment and utopia. In: Cohen S (ed) *Hollywood Musicals: The Film Reader*. New York: Routledge, pp. 19–30.

Feder MA (1994) 'A radiant smile from the lovely lady': Overdetermined femininity in 'ladies' figure skating. *The Drama Review* 38(1): 62–78.

Grindon L (1996) Body and soul: The structure of meaning in the boxing film genre. *Cinema Journal* 35(4): 54–69.

Grindon L (2007) The boxing film and genre theory. *Quarterly Review of Film and Video* 24(5): 403–410.

Heywood L and Dworkin SL (2003) *Built to Win: The Female Athlete as Cultural Icon*. Minneapolis: University of Minnesota Press.

Holmlund C (2001) *Impossible Bodies: Femininity and Masculinity at the Movies*. London: Routledge.

Lindner K (2011a) Bodies 'in action': Female athleticism on the cinema screen. *Feminist Media Studies* 11(3): 321–345.

Lindner K (2011b) 'There is a reason why Sporty Spice is the only one of them without a fella . . .': The 'lesbian' potential of *Bend it Like Beckham*. *New Review of Film & Television Studies* 9(2): 204–223.

Mulvey L (1975) Visual pleasure and narrative cinema. *Screen* 16(3): 6–18.

Oates JC (2006) *On Boxing*. London: Harper Perennial.

Pearson DW (2001) The depiction and characterisation of women in sport film. *Women in Sport and Physical Activity Journal* 10(1): 103–124.

Tasker Y (1993) *Spectacular Bodies: Gender, Genre and the Action Cinema*. London: Routledge.

Woodward K (2007) *Boxing, Masculinity and Identity: The 'I' of the Tiger*. London: Routledge.

Young I (1980) Throwing like a girl: A phenomenology of feminine body comportment, motility and spatiality. *Human Studies* 3(1): 137–156.

Filmography

Bend it Like Beckham. 2003. Gurinder Chadha. UK.

Blue Crush. 2002. John Stockwell. USA.

Bring it On. 2000. Peyton Reed. USA.

Girlfight. 2000. Karyn Kusama. USA.

Ice Princess. 2005. Tim Fywell. USA.

Love and Basketball. 2000.Gina Prince-Bythewood. USA.

Million Dollar Baby. 2004 Clint Eastwood. USA.

Raging Bull. 1980. Martin Scorsese. USA.

Stick it. 2006. Jessica Bendinger. USA.

The Cutting Edge. 1992. Paul Michael Glaser. USA.

Wimbledon. 2004. Richard Loncraine. UK.

INDEX